CASES AND MATERIALS ON
WORKERS' COMPENSATION
Fourth Edition

By

Joseph W. Little
Professor of Law
University of Florida

Thomas A. Eaton
Professor of Law
University of Georgia

Gary R. Smith
Professor of Law
Emory University

AMERICAN CASEBOOK SERIES®

WEST
GROUP

ST. PAUL, MINN., 1999

 TEXT IS PRINTED ON 10% POST
CONSUMER RECYCLED PAPER

Dedication

This book is dedicated to the memories of Wex S. Malone and Marcus L. Plant whose original works provide the foundation for it.

As to personal dedications, Joseph W. Little recognizes Lucille and Caroline, Thomas A. Eaton recognizes Joanna, Amanda, and Andy.

Gary R. Smith makes his dedication to the memory of his mother, Louise Grant Smith.

*

Preface

This book originates in the workers' compensation portion of Workers' Compensation and Employment Rights book by the late Wex S. Malone, the late Marcus L. Plant, and Joseph W. Little. That book itself sprang from an earlier workers' compensation text authored by Malone and Plant. Hence, this book returns full circle to an exclusive and concentrated focus on workers' compensation instead of the more generalized employment rights approach employed for the preceding fifteen or so years.

Two major factors explain the workers' compensation focus. Foremost is that the topic is important and rich enough to receive the full attention of an entire course and an entire book. The place of compensation for industrial injuries in our culture and law is not waning and neither is the need for lawyers who are educated to cope with the legal issues. Many, if not most, law schools offer courses in the subject. Workers' compensation also remains this country's longest standing, most comprehensive and most successful "tort reform." Moreover, a study of the workers' compensation system may yield valuable insights into contemporary tort reform proposals pertaining to other fields.

The second major reason for exclusive attention to workers' compensation is almost the mirror image of the first. Developments in other employment areas, e.g., OSHA, anti-discrimination, and social security, continue to produce new volumes of materials that collectively justify separate treatment independent of workers' compensation. Indeed, it has almost become too much of a task to press workers' compensation and the other employment rights topics into a single two or three hour course. Hence, we have opted for separation.

The basic structure of this book is generally modelled after the workers' compensation portion of its predecessor. Nevertheless, some changes in chapter organization have been made and each chapter has been thoroughly revised, adding large amounts of new case and text materials and eliminating those portions that are superseded or outdated.

We know that we are bound to have made some mistakes in editing, in case selection, and in textual materials and urge the readers of the book to contact any of us with corrections, comments, and suggestions.

JOSEPH W. LITTLE
THOMAS A. EATON
GARY R. SMITH

*

Summary of Contents

ÖAppendices

*

Table of Contents

Table of Cases

The principal cases are in bold type. Cases cited or discussed in the text
are roman type. References are to pages. Cases cited in principal
cases and within other quoted materials are not included.

*

CASES AND MATERIALS ON
WORKERS' COMPENSATION
Fourth Edition

*

Chapter 1

EMPLOYEES' REMEDIES PRIOR TO AND APART FROM WORKERS' COMPENSATION

SECTION 1. THE NEED FOR A WORKERS' COMPENSATION SYSTEM

A beginning student of workers' compensation might sensibly inquire, "What is the need for a special compensation system for work injuries?" Although a full answer requires a detailed examination of the history and interrelationship among the rate of production of injuries and death suffered by workers in industry, the law of torts as applied to work injuries, and the social structure for treating otherwise uncompensated injuries suffered by individuals, essential facts as they existed at the time the initial British workers' compensation act was enacted in 1906 can be succinctly put.

    1.   Industrial injuries were a virtual scourge of working people in the nineteenth and early twentieth centuries. This point is amplified below.

    2.   The law of torts was not a compensation system, but instead, was a means of making wrongdoers accountable for wrongful acts that caused harm. Hence, injuries that did not fit within the confines of tort law went uncompensated under it.

    3.   The notion of the welfare state was ill developed. Hence, unfortunate victims of injuries of any sort often had recourse only to uncertain and parsimonious charity.

This section elaborates the first point and the next the second. The third will be left to stand on its own, save as it is supported inferentially by the examination of the other two.

In modern times we know a lot about how many work injuries occur, why they occur, and what they cost. The data in Table 1 lend an inference that industry at large remains a dangerous and costly enterprise for the workers that make it go. These are consequences of an economy employing upwards of 100 million workers to produce a gross national product exceeding $1 trillion.

Table 1

Work Injury Data *—1997

Numbers of Workers, Injuries, and Deaths**

Total No. Workers	130,810,000
Total unintentional-injury-related deaths ***	5,100
Disabling Injuries ****	3,800,000

Time Lost

Time Lost in 1997 from 1997 injuries	80 million days
Time Lost in 1997 from pre–1997 injuries	45 million days
Estimated future time loss from 1997 injuries	60 million days

Financial Costs

Total Costs 1997 work injuries *****	$ 127.7 billion
Wage and Productivity Losses 1997 work injuries	$ 63.4 billion
Medical Costs 1997 work injuries	$ 20.7 billion
Administrative Expenses 1997 work injuries	$ 26.5 billion
Employer Costs 1997 work injuries	$ 11.9 billion
Other Costs ******	$ 5.2 billion
Cost per worker	$ 980
Cost per death	$ 890,000
Cost per disabling injury	$ 28,000

Workers' Compensation Payments
(estimated) 1995 *******

Total payments	$ 43.5 billion
Medical and hospital	$ 16.7 billion
Wages	$ 26.8 billion

* Source: *Accident Facts*, 1998 Edition, National Safety Council, pages 48, 51, and 58.

** The data in this table were extracted from *Accident Facts* 1998 Edition, National Safety Council, pp. 48, 51, and 58.

*** Bureau of Labor Statistics data from the Census of Fatal Occupational Injuries indicates an additional 1,100 to 1,300 deaths each year due to intentional injuries (homicide and suicide).

**** A disabling injury is one that causes work loss beyond the day of the injury. Bureau of Labor Statistics data indicate about 4 million additional nondisabling injuries occur each year.

***** This includes $3.1 billion as direct property loss in fires. No other property damage is included.

****** Includes $2.0 billion in motor-vehicle damage and $3.2 billion in fire losses. No other property damage is included.

******* Source: National Academy of Social Insurance.

These modern data, grim as the picture they depict may be, do not convey the danger inherent in nineteenth century industry in which machinery was more primitive and dangerous and the institutional concern for safety was much lower. Whereas empirical accounts of those days are imperfect, current observers captured them in dramatically descriptive accounts. One of the most telling is summed up in this 1893 statement of the first Secretary of the Interstate Commerce Commission:

> There is something appalling in the statement that more hardworking and faithful railway employees in the United States went down in sudden death last year than the entire number of Union men who died at the Battle of the Wilderness; nearly as many as those who died the bitter death at Spotsylvania; more than three times the number of the Union dead at Lookout Mountain, Missionary Ridge and Orchard Knob combined, and that more of the grand army of railway men of this country were cut and bruised and maimed and mangled last year than all the Union wounded and missing on the bloody field of Gettysburg; (and) nearly equal in number to the wounded and missing in the reign of death and devastation of Shiloh, first and second Bull Run and Antietam combined ...[1]

The probability of death or injury in certain occupations, particularly railroading, was fearful. For example, one commentator assessed "a brakeman's chances of dying a natural death in 1888 [as] 1 to 47" and the "average life expectancy of a switchman in 1893 [as] seven years."[2] Worse, many of the victims were children, especially in textile industries in which many women and children were employed. An 1888 account of the situation in England reported:

> Formerly accidents were a frequent source of mischief to the children employed in Cotton Mills, owing to the machinery not being sufficiently guarded; their fingers and hands were often crushed and lacerated, the skin and muscles being in some instances stripped off to the bone; and I have reason to believe ... that this great evil still exists to a considerable extent.[3]

The same reporter made a "survey of a Manchester Sunday School that revealed that 45 per cent of the boys present 'were found to have been ... injured in a greater or lesser degree,'" which was thought to understate the true injury rate among working children "since only the best conditioned part of them [factory children] attend Sunday Schools."[4]

These data and accounts of the physical risks are only a part of the story so far as injured workers are concerned. The other part, and often the larger part, was the consequences of industrial injuries and death to

---

1. Melvin L. Griffith, "The Vindication of a National Public Policy Under the Federal Employers' Liability Act," 18 Law and Contemp. Prob. 160, 163 (1953), quoting Edward A. Moseley.

2. Id., at 162, 163.

3. P. Bartrip's, Workmen's Compensation in Twentieth Century Britain (1987), 3, quoting N. Gould.

4. Id.

the economic and emotional well being of the victims. Again adverting to the nineteenth century, one observer concluded:

> Probably the most important requirement for a Victorian workman, in a largely full-employment but still relatively low-welfare society, was for a fit and healthy body. Only with such could he undertake the full-time work necessary to keep himself and his family in food, clothing and shelter without recourse to the dreaded Poor Law, private charity, or other forms of non-wage financial support. One of the greatest threats to bodily and material sufficiency, particularly for miners, railwaymen, merchant seamen and others in dangerous occupations, was provided by industrial injury without compensation.[5]

The remainder of this book deals primarily with the plan that is intended to minimize the threat of "industrial injury without compensation."

The modern reader will have concluded by now that society ought to spend at least as much energy in preventing injuries as in compensating them. Many people believe, quite wrongly, that nineteenth century tort law was deliberately shaped to remove the costs of industrial injuries from industry.[6] The truer view is that the industrial revolution imposed a hierarchy of remote institutional activity upon a common law legal system that was premised upon individual human accountability and that was incapable of accommodating, through established common law processes, to the peculiar demands of institutionalized risks.[7] Whatever the cause, however, the consequences were the same: nineteenth century industry did largely externalize the cost of injuries upon workers and their families by failing to create an industrial ethic to promote safety and to provide benefits when injuries did occur. A major factor in this was, no doubt, that the status of the law pertaining to liability for industrial injuries created no incentive for the captains of industry to prefer safety over injuries. Nevertheless, some judges were aware that

---

5. Id., at 1.

6. There is an orthodox view of the negligence concept to which I believe most legal scholars and historians would subscribe that runs as follows: Until the nineteenth century a man was liable for harm caused by his accidents whether or not he was at fault; he acted at his peril. The no-fault standard of liability was relaxed in the nineteenth century under the pressure of industrial expansion and an individualistic philosophy that could conceive of no justification for shifting losses from the victim of an accident unless the injurer was blameworthy (negligent) and the victim blameless (not contributorily negligent). The result, however, was that accident costs were "externalized" from the enterprises that caused them to workers and other individuals injured as a byproduct of their activities.

R. Posner, "A Theory of Negligence," 1 J.Legal Studies 29 (1972).

7. After extensive examination of late nineteenth century and early twentieth century appellate decisions, Posner concluded, "I discern no systematic bias in the law of negligence as it was applied between 1875 and 1905 in favor of industrial growth and expansion ..." Id., at 73. This conclusion, while probably correct, neglects the historic fact that the law of negligence had been mainly fixed in its primary features before 1875. Better proof of the point that the makers of the law were not in some sort of sub silentio conspiracy with the captains of industry is obtained by textual examination of the facts of the precedential decisions almost all of which arose in pre-industrial revolution contexts.

their application of tort law had, through its broad economic consequences, the power to induce safer workplaces. This was adverted to in Justice O'Neall's dissenting opinion in Murray v. South Carolina Railroad Company [see Section 2] wherein he said:

> But, it is said, it would be impolitic to make the defendants liable for any injury accruing to a fireman, from the neglect of the engineer. This would be worth inquiring into with great care in the Legislature; but, in a Court, I think we have nothing to do with the policy of a case; the law of it is our guide. But if we are to look to the policy, then I should argue that the more liability imposed on the railroad company, the more care and prudence would be thereby elicited. This result is what the community desires. For it secures life and property, committed to their care.

The remainder of this chapter provides a brief overview of various strategies that have been employed in an effort to alleviate the hardships created by workplace injury and diseases. Any comprehensive approach to this goal must strive both to prevent injuries and to compensate those that occur. In the United States, positive regulation of workplace safety was left primarily to the individual states until Congress enacted the Occupational Safety and Health Act (OSHA) in 1970. That Act and its state counterparts constitute the current central regulatory mechanism to avoid workplace injuries. Section 4 describes the basic structure, operation, and limitations of OSHA.

The compensation objective is to alleviate the economic consequences of injury to the individual worker.[8] While workers' compensation laws constitute the current central legally mandated mechanism to provide economic assistance to disabled workers, it is but one of many possible approaches. Section 2 of this chapter examines the application of tort law to workplace injuries with particular emphasis on the doctrinal limitations on liability that existed at the time most workers' compensation laws were initially adopted. Section 3 briefly explores statutory schemes other than workers' compensation, with special emphasis on the Federal Employers' Liability Act (FELA) and social security.

SECTION 2. THE COMMON LAW AS APPLIED TO EMPLOYEES' WORKPLACE INJURIES

The story of industrial accidents and the law is filled with striking incongruities. Nearly everywhere today, two radically different methods exist side by side for determining the claims of injured employees against their employers. These methods stand in sharp opposition to each other both in theory and in practical effect; yet the choice between them may be determined by seemingly trivial considerations. Even today, in em-

---

8. Of course, the goals of injury prevention and compensation are not entirely separate. The central insight of the law and economics movement is that liability for payment of compensation may create an incentive to reduce risk. See G. Calabresi, The Cost of Accidents (1970). One critical factor in evaluating various compensation systems is their impact on safety incentives. See R. Victor, Workers' Compensation and Workplace Safety: The Nature of Employer Financial Incentives (1982).

ployments not covered by workers' compensation statutes, injured employees will be obliged to prove that their employers were negligent, and may be required to prove that they, the employees, were not aware of the danger created by that negligence. Furthermore, in some jurisdictions employees may not be permitted to recover if the injuries suffered were caused by the negligence of a fellow employee. Like other plaintiffs in negligence suits these employees may see their recoveries diminished (or even barred in a few jurisdictions) as a result of their own contributory negligence. By contrast, other injured employees, whose situations are indistinguishable except for their being employed in employments covered by workers' compensation statutes, will succeed in establishing claims for compensation. They will recover by merely showing that, while working, they were hurt by a cause that arose out of work. Neither their own negligence nor that of their employers or fellow employees will bar or diminish their entitlement to benefits. But, although their chances of recovery are thus immeasurably enhanced, they will often recover benefits in amounts less commensurate with the losses suffered at least as measured by principles of tort damages. Rather than recover an amount that covers all economic and non-economic losses, they will be granted a sum fixed by statute that represents only a part of lost wages. This award is called compensation. They will also receive reimbursement for some or all of the medical and rehabilitation costs of curing the injuries and coping with their effects. In making comparisons between these two systems, the reader should bear in mind that the vast majority of American workers are now covered by workers' compensation laws. Hence, as to most work injuries, the discussion of antecedent tort doctrines provides historical setting rather than the current legal basis for recovering against employers for work place injuries and deaths.

The first procedure referred to above is the familiar common law of negligence. The second procedure is the legislative compensation scheme prescribed to provide remedies for all injured employees and their families irrespective of fault, a job the law of torts was never intended or able to do. How tort law failed to satisfy the need for a general work injury compensation scheme is briefly summarized in succeeding paragraphs.

THE FELLOW SERVANT DEFENSE

Negligence law was in its earliest stages when the English courts were first called upon to fix the rights of an injured employee against his employer in Priestley v. Fowler (1837) 3 M & W 1, 150 Eng.Rep. 1030. The plaintiff was injured when a van, negligently overloaded by a fellow servant, broke down and threw him violently to the ground. The plaintiff sued his employer, claiming that the employer was vicariously liable to him for the negligent acts of his co-worker. Lord Abinger, C.B., in denying recovery dwelt at length upon the consequences (regarded by him as absurd) which could follow if a master were made responsible to one servant for harm inflicted through the negligence of his fellow servants. Abinger's attention was focused upon simple accidents occurring within a typical master-servant relationship as it existed prior to the physical separation of employers and employees in large scale industrial employments. At that time servants, even those in commercial rather than purely domestic pursuits, were often members of the master's household. Consequently, they were thought to be entitled to no more care than were the master himself and members of his household. The appreciation of how advanced industrial and transportation employments institutionalized risks and separated employees physically from employers still lay ahead at the time of the decision. Nevertheless, Priestley v. Fowler fixed common law precedents that later were applied in the new and different contexts. That decision is regarded as the fountainhead of two distinct, but related, propositions: first, the principle of respondeat superior subjecting the master to liability for the torts of the servant does not apply where the suit is by one servant against the master for the negligence of a fellow servant; and, second, a worker, by accepting employment, assumes the risk that he may be injured or killed by reason of dangerous working conditions that he could discover for himself if he were alert. For these the master is therefore not responsible.

The introduction at this particular time in history of the fellow-servant rule and the doctrine of implied assumption of risk was disastrous for worker safety. It came immediately on the threshold of revolutionary developments in transportation which were initiated by the then novel steam propelled railroad and the emergence of the dangers of the factory age. The coming of the industrial revolution brought a profound change in the relationship of employers to employees. Enterprise came to be conducted through the agency of corporations which were incapable of any personal fault and which could act only through agents or employees. The owners of capital and even the factory bosses no longer worked side by side with the general employees, as in the pre-industrial era, but became physically separated. The idea that employers and employees were equally exposed to all the risks of the employment was no longer true. But cases like Priestley v. Fowler, coupled with a rigid view of *stare decisis,* disabled the courts from taking a fresh look at what care the general principles of the evolving law of negligence should demand from employers to protect employees in the drastically different industrial setting. For this reason the fellow-servant rule as applied in cases such as the one that follows, threatened to extinguish any prospect of employers' liability for negligence to transportation and industrial workers.

JAMES MURRAY v. SOUTH CAROLINA RAILROAD COMPANY

26 S.C.L. 385, 36 Am.Dec. 268.
(Charleston. Feb., 1841).

Before O'NEALL J., Barnwell, July Extra Term, 1838.

This was an action on the case, against the defendants, for an injury sustained in their service.

The plaintiff is a tailor by trade. He resided at Aiken, and applied to Capt. Robertson, the agent of the company, for employment. He declined employing him, on account of his intemperate habits and consequent rashness. He, however, went on to Charleston, and was employed as a second fireman, on the 18th of May. He selected the engine and engineer to which he was to be attached and under whom he was to serve. William E. Perry was the engineer. About the 27th of May, 1837, the plaintiff's second or third trip, as the engine was ascending the road from Charleston, near the Four Hole Swamp, just before entering an excavation, and within about three hundred yards of it, one of the witnesses (Johnson, the first fireman,) said he saw a horse standing near the commencement of the excavation, within ten steps of the road, feeding slowly towards it: he touched the engineer on the back, and asked him if he saw the horse; he made no reply: the engine ran on: the plaintiff said to the engineer, "stop we are in danger:" the engine still proceeded, until within fifty or sixty yards of the horse: this witness said he then put his hand on the "escape steam valve," and told the engineer again to stop, for there was danger of running over the horse, and pointed towards him: he, the engineer, then shut off the steam: by this time the horse stepped upon the road, and there stood: the engine with the steam shut off, ran within six or eight feet of the horse: the engineer gave her all the steam she could carry, to carry her as quick as possible, and with the least danger, over the horse. At this moment, this witness took hold of the awning post, and swung himself outside the engine, for the purpose of jumping off on the left hand side of it: in this position he could see under the engine which struck and ran over the horse: as it left the road on the right hand side, the witness jumped off on the left. His post was on the left, and the plaintiff's on the right, of the engine: the brake to stop the engine was on the right, and nearer the plaintiff than the witness: when the engineer shut off the steam, the brake was not let down: (he said he was too much agitated by fear to think of the brake:) had it been let down, the engine might have been stopped. As the engine left the road, the plaintiff's leg dropped between the foot board of the engine and tender, and as these two came violently together, when the engine stopped, his leg was crushed, and his thigh was afterwards amputated midway. This witness gave it as his opinion, very distinctly, that the accident might have been avoided, and resulted from the carelessness of the engineer, in not stopping the engine as soon as cautioned: he thought that as the engine was running only at the rate of ten or twelve miles per hour, it might have been stopped before they reached the horse. He said it was not the fireman's duty to let down the brake, unless ordered by the engineer. Meredith, the conductor of the train, said, just as they emerged from an excavation, he saw the horse about fifteen yards from the road, moving from behind some bushes, and running in an oblique direction towards the road, and in the direction the engine was pursuing; he ran thus about twenty yards, when he leaped upon the road between the rails, just at the entrance of another excavation: as he did so, the engine struck him, and passed over him, and was thrown off the track. The engine was running from sixteen to twenty miles an hour. From the time this witness saw the horse, he said that he thought the only way to avoid him was to outrun him. He said, that to stop the engine, it is the duty of the engineer to shut off the steam, and the firemen to let down the "brake;" it is, however, the engineer's duty to order the fireman to let down the brake. Perry was proved to be a skillful professional engineer. The witnesses, Robertson and Ross, concurred in saying, that it was the duty of the engineer to shut off the steam, and the fireman to let down the brake, (and that was the particular duty of the second fireman) whether ordered by the engineer or not to stop the engine and prevent any accident. About three hundred feet is as short a space as within which the engine can be stopped, when running at the average rate of fifteen miles an hour.

The jury were instructed that the plaintiff's service subjected him to _Jury Instruction_ all the ordinary risks and perils of the employment. Each officer of the company, as to strangers and inferiors, was to be considered as the company; and every command or act given or done by him, must be regarded as given or done by the company themselves. If a superior officer had given an order to an inferior, to do an act not necessary to be done, and not within the duty of the inferior, and in doing it, injury resulted to the inferior, then the company would be responsible. If, in running the road, a superior officer (the engineer) did his duty so carelessly as to subject a servant of the company to unnecessary danger, and which the servant could not avoid, then the company would be liable. But if the peril, from which the injury resulted, was unavoidable, or if the engineer did every thing ordinary prudence suggested, to avoid it—and, notwithstanding, a servant sustained injury, it would be one of the risks to which his contract of service subjected him, and he could not recover. So, too, if the servant, (the second fireman,) did not do his duty, and to its neglect (as not letting down the brake) the injury might be fairly ascribed, then, in that case, his injury would be attributable to himself and he could have no redress against the company.

The facts under these instructions, were submitted to the jury. I thought, and still think, there was very little proof to justify a verdict, but still that little may sustain the verdict, $1500, found by the jury for the plaintiff.

The defendants appeal, on the annexed grounds.

GROUNDS OF APPEAL

1. Because the plaintiff, being a fireman actually employed on the car to which the accident occurred, cannot recover against the company in whose service he was.

2. Because the ordinary risks of the occupation of the plaintiff are to be sustained by himself, and the accident was the result of such risks.

3. Because the plaintiff himself was partly in charge of the car to which the accident occurred, and might have prevented it himself, by the timely discharge of his own duty.

4. Because the plaintiff, being a tailor by trade, imposed himself upon the company as fireman, and the accident is attributable to his own negligence and want of skill.

5. Because it was clearly proved, that there was no want of skill or diligence on the part of the engineer, or other servants of the company.

6. Because the accident itself was unavoidable, and the verdict is contrary to the evidence in all these particulars.

Curia, per EVANS, J. In the consideration of the question involved in this case, I shall assume that the verdict establishes the fact that the plaintiff's injury was the effect of the negligence of the engineer, and then the question arises whether the railroad company is liable to one servant for an injury arising from the negligence of another servant. The business of the company is the transportation of goods and passengers. Its liability in these respects, is, in general, well defined and understood by the profession; and if the plaintiff's case came within any of the principles applicable to these cases, we should have no difficulty in deciding it. The application of steam power to transportation on railroads, is of recent origin, but the principle by which the liability of a carrier is fixed and ascertained, is as old as the law itself. There is nothing in the fact, that the defendant is a corporation, except that of necessity it must act altogether by agents. The liability is precisely the same as if the defendant was an individual acting by the agency of others. The principle is the same, whether you apply it to a railroad, a steamboat, a wagon, a stage coach, or a ship. If this plaintiff is entitled to recover, I can see no reason why the owner of any of the above modes of conveyance, should not be liable under the same circumstances. If the owner of a wagon should employ two men, one to drive and the other to load, and either of them should so negligently perform his work as to injure the other, the owner of the wagon would be liable. The principle will extend to all the vocations of life wherein more than one person is employed to effect a single object; and a new class of liabilities would arise, which I do not think has ever heretofore been supposed to exist. It is admitted, no case like the present has been found, nor is there any precedent suited to the plaintiff's case, unless he stands in the relation of a passenger to the company. In this point of view, his counsel has chosen to regard him, for I understand the declaration alleges he was a passenger. Now, a passenger is every where spoken of as one who pays for transportation. In all the operations necessary for this, he is passive. The moment he becomes an operator, for then his character is changed, he becomes the servant of the company, and not its passenger. It would be a confusion of terms so to regard him. He is no more a passenger than a sailor or a stage driver. There is nothing in the definition of bailment, or the classification of the different kinds of liability growing out of that relation, which applies to the plaintiff's case, and if he is entitled to recover, it must be on principles which apply equally to all operations of life in which agents are employed. There is no question that, in general, the principal is liable for the acts of the agent, performed in the execution of his agency, or in and about the business of his principal. Thus, the owners of a railroad would be liable to passengers for an injury sustained by the negligence of any of its servants, superior or subordinate, because it is implied in the undertaking to carry, not only that the road and cars are good, but that the servants employed are competent and will perform their duty. For the loss of goods, the law annexes a still greater responsibility. So, also, if one employ an agent to execute any work whereby an injury may result to a stranger, the law requires it to be done with care, and if a stranger sustain an injury, his principal is liable, as was decided in O'Connell v. Strong, (Dud.Rep. 265.) But the plaintiff is neither a passenger nor a stranger, and if he can recover, it must be in his hermaphrodite character as a passenger fireman. In the cases above enumerated, the principal is represented by the agent, and unless he is liable, the great operations of life cannot be carried on—no man would have adequate security for his person or his property. The owner of goods would not trust them on a railroad, or a steamboat, if his only security was the liability of the mere servants employed. No passenger would commit his safety to a railroad, steamboat, or stage coach, if, in case of injury, he could look to none but the agents usually employed about these modes of transportation. So, also, no man would have any guarantee for the security of his property, if his only remedy for negligence was the irresponsible or insolvent agents which another might employ. In all these, and similar cases, the reasons of the liability of the principal are clear, and the law books are full of cases or precedents which apply to them; but it is not so with the plaintiff's case; there is neither authority nor precedent for it.

It was said, in the argument, that if the engineer had been the owner of the road, he would have been liable. Of this I apprehend there would have been no doubt, but then his liability would have arisen, not from his being the owner, but because the injury arose from his own act. That he is now liable, seems to me to admit of no doubt. But it by no means follows as a consequence, that because he is liable, those who employ him are liable also. One acting as agent may subject himself to liability in a variety of cases, for which his principal would not be liable; and this may be as well in cases of contract as in cases of tort. The extent of the liability of the principal, for the acts of the agent, can, in general, be readily ascertained from the object of the contract, and the relative position of the parties. A passenger desires to be transported from one place to another; the carrier undertakes to do this, and is liable if he fails. It is wholly immaterial by whose default the injury resulted. There has been a breach of the contract, and he has a right to look to him with whom his contract was made. With the plaintiff, the defendants contracted to pay hire for his services. Is it incident to this contract that the company should guarantee him against the negligence of his co-servants? It is admitted he takes upon himself the ordinary risks of his vocation; why not the extraordinary ones? Neither are within his contract—and I can see no reason for adding this to the already known and acknowledged liability of a carrier, without a single case or precedent to sustain it. The engineer no more represents the company than the plaintiff. Each in his several department represents his principal. The regular movement of the train of cars to its destination, is the result of the ordinary performance, by each, of his several duties. If the fireman neglects his part, the engine stands still for want of steam; if the engineer neglects his, everything runs to riot and disaster. It seems to me, it is, on the part of the several agents, a joint undertaking, where each one stipulates for the performance of his several part. They are not liable to the company for the conduct of each other, nor is the company liable to one for the misconduct of another; and, as a general rule, I would say, that where there was no fault in the owner, he would be liable only for wages to his servants; and so far has this doctrine been carried, that in the case of seamen, even wages are forfeited if the vessel be lost, and no freight earned.

In the above observations, I have endeavored to confine myself strictly to the case before the Court. It is not intended to prejudge other questions, which may arise between the company and its servants; nor do I mean to say, that a case may not occur where the owner, whether an individual or company, will be liable for the acts of one agent to another; but then it must be in such cases as where the owner employs unfit and improper persons as agents, by whose ignorance or folly another is injured. Upon such a case it will be time enough to express an opinion when it arises. The present is not such a case. The engineer, according to the evidence, was competent, though he may have been rash in the particular instance in which the plaintiff's injury was sustained. He was known to the plaintiff as well as to the company, for it appears by the report that he selected the engineer under whom he was willing or prepared to serve. It seems to me the plaintiff is not, therefore, entitled to retain his verdict, and a motion for a new trial is granted.

RICHARDSON, EARLE, BUTLER, HARPER, DUNKIN, JJ. and CC., concurred.

JOHNSON, CHANCELLOR. I concur in this opinion, and will only add a word in illustration of my own views of the question.

The foundation of all legal liability, is the omission to do some act which the law commands, the commission of some act which the law prohibits, or the violation of some contract by which the party is injured. There is no law regulating the relative duties of the owners of a steam car, and the persons employed by them to conduct it. The liability, if any attaches, must therefore arise out of contract. What was the contract between these parties? The plaintiff, in consideration that the defendants would pay him so much money, undertook to perform the service of fireman on the train. This is all that is expressed. Is there anything more implied? Assuming that the injury done, was in consequence of the negligence of the engineer, the defendants would not be liable, unless they undertook to answer for his diligence and skill. Is that implied? I think not. The law never implies an obligation in relation to a matter about which the parties are or may, with proper diligence, be equally informed. No one will ever be presumed to undertake for that which a common observer would at once know was not true. The common case of the warranty of the soundness of a horse, notoriously blind, may be put in illustration. The warranty does not extend to the goodness of the eyes, because the purchaser knew or might have known, with proper care, that they were defective.

Now the plaintiff knew that he was not to conduct the train alone. He knew that he was to be placed under the control of the engineer. He knew that the employment in which he was engaged was perilous, and that its success was dependent on the common efforts of all the hands; and, with proper diligence and prudence, he might have been as well, and it does not follow that he might not have been better informed than the defendants, about the fitness and security of all the appointments connected with the train. If he was not, is it was his own want of prudence, for which defendants are not responsible. If he was, he will be presumed to have undertaken to meet all the perils incident to the employment.

There is not the least analogy between this case and that of common carriers of goods or transporters of persons. They are liable in respect to the price paid. Not so here. The plaintiff paid nothing for his transportation; on the contrary, he was to be paid for his labor, and for the perils to which he was exposed, as incident to his employment. No prudent man would engage in any perilous employment, unless seduced by greater wages than he could earn in a pursuit unattended by any unusual danger.

O'NEALL, J., dissenting. This case was tried by myself, and although, had I been on the jury, I should have found for the defendants, yet there were certainly facts in the evidence, which might have led another to a different conclusion; and, therefore, I am not disposed to disturb the verdict. This makes it necessary to consider the legal doctrine which I laid down to the jury.

In substance, I held, that if the injury to the plaintiff resulted from the negligence of the engineer, then the plaintiff was entitled to recover. This doctrine, a large majority of my brethren think erroneous, and however much deference is due to their opinions, yet, as I consider them to be wrong, I think it my duty to state my own views.

This case is one of the first arising out of the conveyance of human beings by locomotives on railroads. It goes beyond the ordinary case of a passenger, and presents a claim on the part of a hired servant, against his employers, for an injury sustained in their service. If it arose out of any of the old-fashioned modes of conveyance, managed by the defendants themselves, could there be a doubt that they would be liable, if the injury resulted from negligence? Take the case of a stage coach, driven by the owner, and let it be supposed that the plaintiff was hired as a guard, and that he was injured in that employment, by the careless driving of the defendant, who would hesitate to say that he was entitled to recover? No one who had a proper regard to legal principles.

Is there any distinction in law as to the effect which the employment of the plaintiff is to have, in the different kinds of service in which he may engage? I think there is none. If Mr. Tupper, the able and efficient officer of the company, had, in person, managed the engine, and the plaintiff had been injured by his carelessness, I would most respectfully ask, how could it be pretended that the company was not liable?

I admit here, once and for all, that the plaintiff, like any other servant, took, as consequence of his contract, the usual and ordinary risks of his employment. What is meant by this? No more than that he could not claim for an injury, against which the ordinary prudence of his employers, their agents or himself, could provide. Whenever negligence is made out as the cause of injury, it does not result from the ordinary risks of employment.

How far are the defendants liable for the acts of the engineer? In the language used in Bacon's Abridgment, Tit. Master and Servant, letter R., "it is highly reasonable that they should answer for such substitute, at least civiliter; and that his acts, being pursuant to the authority given him, should be deemed the acts of the master." Now, to this authority, it will not do to say the defendants did not authorize the engineer to run his engine so carelessly as to injure the plaintiff. They put him in command of it, and authorized him with it to run the road. If, in the doing of this act, which is according to their authority, he acts negligently, then they are liable for the consequences, for they result from the doing of their business, by one then employed by them. The cases of Drayton ads. Moore, and Parker & Co. v. Gordon, (Dudley's Rep. 268 [270].) and of O'Connell v. Strong, (Ib. 265.) are full to this point. In ordinary cases, this would not be questioned. But it is supposed that this case is not governed by the ordinary rules applicable to cases of liability, arising out of the relation of master and servant. I am at a loss to conceive any just reason for this motion. The law, it seems to me, is to be regarded as a general science, applicable to every case coming within the letter or the reason of the rule. Where it is within neither, it becomes an exception to it. It is only necessary to state this case, to see that it is within both the letter and reason of the rule; for the defendants employ the plaintiff to act under the command of another of their servants. In such a case, the servant in command is in the place of the employers. When they hire another to engage in a service, where neither his own care nor prudence can shield him from injury, which may arise from the act of another of their agents, having the control of him, the question of their liability depends upon the care used by such superior agent. The ordinary rule in cases of hiring goods, is, that the hirer should use that degree of care which a prudent man would take of his own goods. If this degree of care is shown, then the hirer is not liable for any injury which may result to the goods hired. This rule, it seems to me, must, necessarily, be that which applies to this case. Is more favor to be bestowed on a man's goods than on his person? It would be strange that this should be so.

* * *

But, it is said, it would be impolitic to make the defendants liable for any injury accruing to a fireman, from the neglect of the engineer. This would be worth inquiring into with great care in the Legislature; but, in a Court, I think we have nothing to do with the policy of a case; the law of it is our guide. But if we are to look to the policy, then I should argue that the more liability imposed on the railroad company, the more care and prudence would be thereby elicited. This result is what the community desires. For it secures life and property, committed to their care.

I think the motion ought to be dismissed.

GANTT, J., concurred.

J. JOHNSTON, CH., also dissenting. It may not diminish the force of the observations made by MR. JUSTICE O'NEALL, if I state very briefly the reasons which induce me to concur in his dissent.

It is admitted that the duties and liabilities between masters and hired servants result only from the nature and terms of the contract which forms the relation; and that neither party is allowed to extend or abridge the contract. That the master cannot exact other services than those stipulated for; nor, by any indirection, subject the servant to any other than the ordinary perils incident to the employment; and that if he does, by any agency whatever, or by any means, whether of design or negligence, accumulate upon the servant, while in the performance of his duty, any dangers beyond these inherent in the service itself, they fall upon the latter, not as a servant, (for his contract does not bind him to endure them,) but as a man, and the law entitles him to redress.

* * *

The elements of the contract between him and the defendants are these: On their part, so far as they were to contribute to the propelling of the cars, that they would carry him safely; and, on his part, that on the trip he would perform certain offices. With respect to the last, he was their servant; with regard to the first, he was their passenger; and as their passenger they have crippled him. The distinction is plain, and the propriety of applying it would be as plain, if instead of being stationed where he was, he had only been a clerk, hired by the company to travel up and down in the cars, and take a minute of their operations. Yet, on principle, no discrimination can be drawn against him on account of his being a fireman, and not travelling clerk; because he had as little connection with, or control over, the department from which his injury sprang, or the agent to whom it was exclusively committed by the defendants, as if he had been assigned any imaginable duty in the remotest part of the train.

Notes

1. Underlying the fellow-servant immunity were the notions of assumption of risk and mutuality of risk. In the formative era, the servant was as likely to expose the master to danger as vice versa and was equally able to look out for his own safety as was the master. Hence, servants and masters were under mutual obligations and had more or less equal capacities to look out for themselves and each other. That being so, the courts thought it natural to conclude that a servant had bargained away any claim to hold the employer responsible for any of the dangers normally incident to his employment. At first this even included dangers created by the master's direct negligence. An employee, recognizing that there was danger involved, by remaining at work was deemed to have accepted the situation. The fact that few servants had any prospect of alternative employment and thus had no real option to staying on the job except to surrender their livelihoods was never considered to be a compelling factor in the development of this body of law. The prospect of the carelessness of a fellow worker was merely one of the risks assumed. Bartonshill Coal Co. v. Reid (1858) 3 Macq. 266 (H.L.).

2. The unfairness to injured workers of the unbridled fellow servant rule as applied in the industrial setting was not without its critics even at the very beginning, as evidenced by the two powerful dissents to the South Carolina decision. Moreover, nineteenth century doctrine evolved devices to soften the rigors of the rule. One was to acknowledge limitations as to who was a fellow servant for whose carelessness the employer was not responsible, and another was to treat certain activities as nondelegable duties of the master, whose breach, even by the direct negligence of a fellow servant, was chargeable to the master even as to an injured co-worker.

3. Because most work injuries to employees are now compensated under workers' compensation laws, the fellow servant defense is now rarely litigated. These facts lead one court to abolish the rule as serving no useful purpose. Buckley v. City of New York, 56 N.Y.2d 300, 452 N.Y.S.2d 331, 437 N.E.2d 1088 (1982). Nevertheless, the defense could arise in employments not covered by a workers' compensation statute.

ASSUMPTION OF RISK

The idea that employees impliedly assume the known risks of employment was initially coupled with the idea that employers owed employees no duty of care as to the recognized risks of employment. In fact, as the courts began to hold masters accountable for "nondelegable" duties, the scope of assumption of risk gradually was limited to "ordinary risks"—a term of art that embraces all dangers not arising out of a breach of any nondelegable duty of the employer. As a corollary, courts observed that the doctrine of implied assumption of risk has no application whenever the master has been guilty of negligence in the discharge of a nondelegable duty. In that context, the term, implied assumption of risk, is mere tautology.

All the above presupposes, however, that the employee is not actually aware of the danger of the encountered risk and has impliedly "assumed" the risk merely by entering the employer's service. But what effect is to be given the fact that—"implied" assumption aside—the worker actually knew of the danger at the time it was encountered? Should the employee be denied a recovery under these circumstances even though the dangerous condition resulted from a breach of some recognized duty owed by the master? Should the employee be allowed to recover for harm done by a fully known and understood danger? Because liability is for negligence, the master's duties can be fully discharged even with respect to nondelegable duties, either by remedying the condition or by warning employees of the dangers that the master should realize the employee may not discover. Restatement, Second, Agency § 492, particularly comment f. In short, the employer's obligation is to use reasonable care to protect employees who are not in a position to protect themselves. But an employee who knows of the danger—however created—assumes the risks of the danger it poses. Restatement, Second, Agency § 521. Nevertheless, assumption of risk will not bar (or diminish) recovery unless the worker was both familiar with and conscious of the encountered peril. Inexcusable ignorance of the danger might subject the employee to the defense of contributory negligence (to be determined usually by the jury), but it does not amount to an assumption of risk. Moreover, because assumption of risk in employment amounts to a negativing of any duty resting on the employer, the defense does not apply to duties that are independent of common law, except as it may also amount to contributory negligence. Pittsburg, C., C. & St. Louis Ry. Co. v. Moore, 152 Ind. 345, 53 N.E. 290 (1899); Restatement, Second, Agency § 524.

The assumption of risk defense has been greatly constrained by the movement that saw to the widespread adoption of comparative negligence doctrine. See, e.g., Meistrich v. Casino Arena Attractions, 31 N.J. 44, 155 A.2d 90 (1959). Under this view, which has come to prevail, implied assumptions of risk are treated as forms of contributory negligence that may diminish but not bar tort recoveries.

CONTRIBUTORY NEGLIGENCE

Contributory negligence was perhaps the least formidable of the employer defenses and remains so in the relatively few cases now involving tort liability. In application to employment injuries the common law defense that an injured party who was contributorily negligent cannot recover from a negligent defendant is subject to the exceptions that a negligent employee may recover if the employer had the last clear chance, or was guilty of gross, wilful, or wanton negligence. Nevertheless, because industrial workers are regularly exposed to risks of injury through momentary forgetfulness or lack of caution, the defense often imposes a genuine obstacle to recovery.

Where the alleged negligence of the employer is failure to provide a reasonably safe place to work or to furnish suitable tools or equipment, an employee who should have been aware of the danger and failed to take reasonable precautions to avoid it may be barred from recourse (or have recovery diminished under a modern comparative negligence rule). Nevertheless, the worker is not obliged to inquire as to latent defects, and may assume that the employer has made a reasonable inspection of the premises or equipment and has provided all necessary protection. Furthermore, an employee's knowledge of the existence of a defect does not necessarily compel a finding of contributory negligence if it appears that the worker was unaware of the threat to safety, and some courts refuse to apply contributory negligence to known and understood risks unless the apparent risk was imminent. Forgetfulness of a specific danger is not necessarily contributory negligence, particularly where the scene of the employee's operations is shifting constantly or where duties demand undivided attention. Some decisions hold that an employee who is ordered by a superior to encounter a known and understood risk or is assured that there is no danger, is not contributory negligence.

Employers' duties to correct dangerous conditions must normally be performed by the employees. Ordinarily, if the workers assigned to do these tasks are properly instructed and equipped for that work, they cannot recover if by chance they are injured by the defective conditions they are repairing. Similarly, if they neglect to do the job assigned them and the danger remains, they cannot recover if injured thereby.

The common law bar of recovery to a contributorily negligent plaintiff has now been supplemented by diminished recovery under some variant of the comparative negligence doctrine in almost all common law jurisdictions. See, e.g., Hoffman v. Jones, 280 So.2d 431 (Fla.1973).

SECTION 3. LEGISLATIVE REFORMS APART FROM WORKERS' COMPENSATION

Judicial decisions that liberalized the common law duties of employers were only a reflection of the growing public concern for the financial insecurity of the working classes. This concern found an expression in the legislative halls as well. The chief target for action was the fellow-servant rule. In 1877 a committee of the House of Commons urged that the rule be substantially modified by statute. In response, the Parliament enacted the English Employer's Liability Act of 1880. Stats. 43 & 44. Vict.C. 42. This act, however, left contributory negligence and assumption of risk defenses unaffected. Its chief advantage for workers was to establish for England the vice principal doctrine, which was already in effect by virtue of judicial decisions in many United States jurisdictions. Finally, Parliament abolished the fellow-servant defense in 1948. Personal Injuries Act, 1948, 11 & 12, Geo. VI.C. 41, § 1. In addition, the multiplication of statutory duties (chiefly the Factories Acts of 1937, 1948, 1959, and 1961) served to enhance substantially injured workers' prospects for recovery. Samuels, Factory Law (8th Ed.1969).

Although a few American states had enacted statutes for the benefit of workers prior to the enactment of the English Employers Liability Act, these related mainly to employees of railroad companies. The great tide of legislative reform did not swell until after 1880. The statutes varied considerably both in scope of coverage and in scope of the substantive changes brought about. See 5 Labatt, Master and Servant (2d Ed.1913). Colorado was the first state to abolish the fellow-servant rule for all employments. Colo.Stat.Ann. (1911) § 2060. Most states were content to follow the English model and most confined even this reform to railway employees. Often, the acts amounted to no more than statutory recognition of earlier judicial modifications of the fellow-servant rule. See, e.g., Shohoney v. Quincy, O. & K.C.R. Co., 231 Mo. 131, 132 S.W. 1059 (1910).

VIOLATION OF STATUTE

Under general negligence doctrine a court may treat a penal statute or regulation pertaining to safety of employees as particularizing the standard of care employers owe employees, thereby making a violation negligence per se. Bayne v. Todd Shipyards Corp., 88 Wash.2d 917, 568 P.2d 771 (1977). The statute or regulation must be intended to protect employees of the claimant's class against the particular risk encountered. Restatement, Second, Torts § 288. In addition, courts are inclined to treat violations of statutes with more general purposes as evidence of negligence rather than as negligence per se. Restatement, Second, Torts § 288(B)2.

The Federal Occupational Safety and Health Act of 1970, (OSHA), examined in more detail hereafter, was designed to avoid injuries to workers by imposing positive obligations upon employers to satisfy safety standards and regulations in the workplace. Nevertheless, OSHA, by its own terms, creates no new basis for compensation for injuries but is wholly regulatory in approach. The measure contains the following provision to minimize its effect in civil proceedings for damages:

> Nothing in this Chapter shall be construed to supersede or in any manner affect workmen's compensation law or to enlarge or diminish or affect in any other manner the common law statutory rights, duties, or liabilities of employers and employees under any law with respect to injuries, diseases, or death of employees arising out of, or in the course of employment. 29 U.S.C.A. § 653(B)(4).

Accordingly, the courts have generally held that a violation of OSHA or of regulations promulgated thereunder cannot serve as the independent basis for a civil suit for damages. See, e.g., Pedraza v, Shell Oil Co., 942 F.2d 48, 52 (1st Cir.1991). Nevertheless, this restriction against a new basis of liability does not prevent a court from instructing a jury in a proper case that an employer's violation of OSHA can be considered as evidence of negligence or even, as negligence per se. Id. at 264. A state-by-state summary of the evidentiary impact of OSHA standards can be found in M. Rothstein, Occupational Safety and Health Law § 513 (3d Ed.1990).

FEDERAL RAILROAD SAFETY ACTS

The Safety Appliance Act of 1893, 27 Stat. 531 (1893), which related to braking systems and car couplers for rail carriers in interstate commerce, was the first federal legislative pertaining to the field of employee safety. The Act prescribed penalties for violations, but provided no express right of action by injured persons. It did, however, limit the operation of common law defenses as follows:

> Any employee of any such common carrier who may be injured by any locomotive, car, or train in use contrary to the provision of this act shall not be deemed thereby to have assumed the risk thereby occasioned, although continuing in the employment of such carrier after the unlawful use of such locomotive, car, or train has been brought to his knowledge.

A companion statute, the Boiler Inspection Act, Act of February 11, 1911, was enacted in 1911.

Although neither of these statutes created a new basis of liability, both had the effect of extending the reach of negligence liability under the theories discussed above. See, e.g., San Antonio & Arkansas Pass Ry. Co. v. Wagner, 241 U.S. 476, 36 S.Ct. 626, 60 L.Ed. 1110 (1916) (liability for violation constitutes "negligence" under FELA) and Brady v. Terminal R.R. Ass'n, 303 U.S. 10, 58 S.Ct. 426, 82 L.Ed. 614 (1938) (liability is established in a claim similar to a common law suit for negligence.) Recovery under the safety statutes is not restricted to employees of the offending carrier. Brady permitted an employee of one railroad to recovery against a connecting carrier that delivered a defective car to plaintiff's employer. Because the claimant was a railroad employee, the safety statute's abolition of assumption of risk applied.

FEDERAL EMPLOYERS' LIABILITY ACT

In the early twentieth century, the railroad industry was both the largest and most dangerous source of employment. In 1907, 11,839 of an estimated one million railroad workers were killed in occupationally-related incidents. Elkind, Should the Federal Employers' Liability Act Be Abolished?, 17 The Forum 415, 418 (1981). It is not surprising, then, that the railroad industry became the focal point of reform. The Federal Employers' Liability Act (FELA) was the first comprehensive federal statute to displace state tort law in application to a discrete category of workplace injuries. FELA was initially enacted in 1906, but was declared unconstitutional under the interstate commerce jurisprudence of the day because the Supreme Court construed it to be an invalid attempt to regulate *intrastate* commerce. Employers' Liability Cases, 207 U.S. 463, 28 S.Ct. 141, 52 L.Ed. 297 (1908). It was reenacted in 1908 in a constitutional form that regulated only interstate railroad activities.

Organized labor did not support the passage of the FELA, but favored the creation of a federal no-fault compensation system for injured railroad workers. Elkind, Should the Federal Employers' Liability Act Be Abolished?, 17 The Forum 415 (1981). FELA is not a no-fault compensation system and retains many of the basic characteristics of tort litigation. Under it, the obligation to compensate an injured worker is conditioned upon proof of employer fault, and the measure of recovery is full compensatory damages. Nevertheless, FELA modifies common law tort doctrine in several important respects. The 1908 Act adopted a pure comparative negligence standard, except that the employee's negligence would not reduce recovery where the injury was caused by the employer's violation of a federal safety statute or regulation. Moreover, the defense of assumption of risk was eliminated in cases involving violations of safety statutes.

In 1939, Congress substantially amended FELA to enlarge its scope to include "any employee ... whose duties ... shall be the furtherance of interstate or foreign commerce ... or shall, in any way directly or closely and substantially, affect such commerce ..." This language brought clerical employees and others not directly involved in the more dangerous aspects of railroading under the protection of the FELA. This aspect of the 1939 amendments played a major role in the Supreme Court's post-New Deal expansion of the reach of the commerce clause. See, Reed v. Pennsylvania Railroad Co., 351 U.S. 502, 76 S.Ct. 958, 100 L.Ed. 1366 (1956). The 1939 amendments also abolished the assumption of risk defense in all cases. See, Tiller v. Atlantic Coast Line R.R. Co., 318 U.S. 54, 63 S.Ct. 444, 87 L.Ed. 610 (1943).

FELA doctrine has continued to evolve primarily through judicial interpretation. In reading the following case, the student should consider the similarities and differences between a claim brought under FELA and one pursued under traditional principles of state tort law.

ARMSTRONG v. KANSAS CITY SOUTHERN RAILWAY COMPANY

United States Court of Appeals, Fifth Circuit, 1985.
752 F.2d 1110.

Before WILLIAMS, JOLLY, and HILL, CIRCUIT JUDGES.

ROBERT MADDEN HILL, CIRCUIT JUDGE:

The Louisiana & Arkansas Railway Co. (L & A) appeals from a jury verdict holding it liable under § 1 of the Federal Employers' Liability Act (the Act or FELA)[1] for injuries incurred by one of its brakemen in an automobile accident. L & A challenges the sufficiency of the evidence to support the jury verdict. In addition, L & A appeals from the district

---

1. This FELA suit is grounded solely upon the negligence provisions of § 1 of the Act, 45 U.S.C. § 51, which provide in pertinent part that a common carrier by railroad shall be liable for

"injury or death resulting in whole or in part from the negligence of any of the

officers, agents, or employees of such carrier, or by reason of any defect or insufficiency, due to its negligence, in its cars, engines, appliances, machinery, track roadbed ... or other equipment."

court's dismissal of its third party indemnity action against Miller Cab Company (Miller).[2] L & A contends that the jury's implicit finding of negligence on the part of Miller in the FELA action entitled L & A to indemnity under Louisiana law. For the reasons that follow, we affirm the judgment of the district court.

I. CASE HISTORY

Armstrong brought this action against Kansas City Southern Railway Company (KCS) and L & A, under the Act, for injuries he sustained in an automobile accident during the course of his employment with L & A as a brakeman.[3] KCS and L & A filed a third-party complaint against Miller and its insurer, New Hampshire Insurance Company, seeking indemnity should judgment in Armstrong's action be rendered against them. After the jury rendered a verdict in favor of Armstrong and against KCS and L & A, the third-party indemnity claim, which was tried concomitantly by the district court, was dismissed.

The testimony and exhibits established the following facts. On the evening of September 22, 1978, Armstrong was travelling as a brakeman on a freight run from New Orleans to Alexandria, Louisiana. The freight train approached Alexandria during the early hours of September 23, in the vicinity of Willow Glen River Road. Armstrong, pursuant to orders from L & A, disembarked from the train to assist in placing a cut of cars on a side track and to allow another crew to board and complete the train's journey to Shreveport. In accordance with its custom, L & A summoned a taxicab, owned and operated by Miller, to the railroad crossing at Willow Glen River Road to transport Armstrong and his co-worker Murphy Batiste to the railroad's yard office. . . .

[Armstrong was injured when] an eastbound motorist struck the cab from the rear. The cab then rolled forward approximately thirty yards. As a result of this collision Armstrong suffered neck injuries.

Upon the district court's entry of judgment in favor of Armstrong, the railroads moved for judgment notwithstanding the verdict or alternatively for a new trial. The railroads also filed a motion to delete KCS from the judgment as the parties had agreed that L & A was the proper party. After a hearing, the district court denied the motion for judgment notwithstanding the verdict and/or new trial and granted the motion to delete KCS from the judgment. L & A then duly perfected this appeal.

II. SUFFICIENCY OF EVIDENCE

The jury found that the driver of the cab owned by Miller was negligent and that such negligence was a legal cause of damage to Armstrong. L & A contends, however, that the evidence was insufficient to justify a jury verdict of negligence in Armstrong's favor. More specifi-

---

2. The parties do not dispute that Miller, the third party defendant that was transporting Armstrong at the time of the accident, was L & A's agent for the purposes of the Act.

3. KCS is the parent corporation of L & A.

cally, L & A asserts that the driver of the cab could not have reasonably foreseen that another motorist would strike the cab from the rear. As we believe sufficient evidence supports the jury verdict, we decline to hold that the district court's denial of L & A's motion for judgment notwithstanding the verdict constitutes reversible error.

The Act allows recovery of damages for personal injuries to an employee of a railroad if the injuries resulted "in whole or in part from the negligence of any of the officers, agents, or employees of such carrier." 45 U.S.C. § 51. Under the Act, a railroad will be liable if its negligence or its agent's negligence played any part, even the slightest, in producing the employee's injury. *Richardson v. Missouri Pacific Railroad Co.*, 677 F.2d 663, 665 (8th Cir.1982) (citing *Rogers v. Missouri Pacific R.R.*, 352 U.S. 500, 506, 77 S.Ct. 443, 448, 1 L.Ed.2d 493 (1957)). "Since the act explicitly makes an employer liable if an injury results only in part from his negligence, the common-law proximate cause standard is modified, and the employee has a less demanding burden of proving causal relationship." *Nivens v. St. Louis Southwestern Railway Co.*, 425 F.2d 114, 118 (5th Cir.1970). Nevertheless, we note that L & A is correct in asserting that Armstrong's prima facie case under the Act must include all the same elements as are found in a common law negligence action. Specifically, he still has the burden of proving that the "employer, with the exercise of due care, could have reasonably foreseen that a particular condition could cause injury; foreseeability is 'an essential ingredient' of negligence under the Act." *Id.* (quoting *Gallick v. Baltimore & Ohio Railroad Co.*, 372 U.S. 108, 117, 83 S.Ct. 659, 665, 9 L.Ed.2d 618 (1963)).

Addressing the function of this Court in reviewing a jury finding of negligence under the Act, the Supreme Court has stated:

> Only when there is a complete absence of probative facts to support the conclusion reached does a reversible error appear. But where, as here, there is an evidentiary basis for the jury's verdict, the jury is free to discard or disbelieve whatever facts are inconsistent with its conclusion. And the appellate court's function is exhausted when the evidentiary basis becomes apparent, it being immaterial that the court might draw a contrary inference or feel that another conclusion is more reasonable.

Lavender v. Kurn, 327 U.S. 645, 653, 66 S.Ct. 740, 744, 90 L.Ed. 916 (1946), *quoted in Lang v. Texas & Pacific Railway Co.,* 624 F.2d 1275, 1278 (5th Cir.1980).

In the instant case, there exists a sufficient evidentiary basis for the jury to infer negligence on the part of the cab driver. It was dark; nevertheless, the cab driver stopped on Willow Glen River Road in the eastbound lane approximately four or five feet from the elevated railroad crossing and failed to turn on his emergency flashing lights. Further, the cab driver could have parked on the adjacent shoulder of the road or in a nearby parking lot. From this evidence, it was reasonable for the jury to infer negligence; more specifically, this evidence sufficiently supports the inference that the cab driver, with the exercise of due care, could have reasonably foreseen that parking his cab in such a position and manner at that time in the morning could result in a rear-end accident.

The testimony of Murphy Batiste, the passenger in the cab, does cast some doubt on the evidence supporting the jury's conclusion. Batiste testified that the shoulder of the road was too narrow for the cab to safely pull off the road; he also testified that the crossing was not elevated thus establishing uninhibited vision on the part of oncoming motorists. The jury was free, however, to give more credence to Armstrong's testimony than to Batiste's and to infer that the cab driver was negligent in stopping the cab at that time and location and in that manner. Similarly, evidence tending to establish the negligence of the motorist who ran into the rear of the cab does not preclude the jury's finding that the cab driver's negligence played at least *some part* in Armstrong's injuries. Because there is not a complete absence of probative facts to support the finding of negligence, we reject [the] contention that there was insufficient evidence to support the jury verdict.

III. INDEMNITY

L & A next contends that the district court erred in finding that L & A is not entitled to indemnity under Louisiana law in its third-party action against Miller and its insurer. In considering L & A's indemnity action against Miller and its insurer, the district court stated it was not bound by the fact finding of the jury as to the negligence of the cab driver. The court, after making credibility choices, found that the cab driver was not negligent. The court went on to state that even if he had been found negligent, the cab driver's negligence must have been a "substantial producing cause to the accident" under Louisiana law in order for L & A to prevail on its third-party indemnity claim. The district court then found that the cab driver's assumed negligence was not a substantial producing cause of the accident and that the sole cause of the accident was the negligence of the motorist who ran into the rear of Miller's taxi cab.

While L & A's negligence under the Act is determined as a matter of federal law interpreting and implementing the Act, L & A's right to indemnity is determined by state law. To succeed in his FELA action against L & A, Armstrong was required to show that Miller's cab driver was negligent in the manner and place in which he stopped his cab and that such negligence played *some part, however slight,* in producing Armstrong's injury. *See Rogers,* 352 U.S. at 506, 77 S.Ct. at 448. To succeed in its third party indemnity action against Miller, however, L & A was required to show under Louisiana law that Miller's fault or negligence was the *proximate cause* of Armstrong's injury. *See Dupree v. Pechinay Saint Gobain Co.,* 369 So.2d 1075, 1081–82 (La.App.), *cert. denied,* 371 So.2d 1341 (La.1979) (citing *Appalachian Corp. v. Brooklyn Cooperage Co.,* 151 La. 41, 91 So. 539, 541 (1922)). . . .

L & A asserts that even though it is without fault, it is nevertheless statutorily required under FELA to pay for the acts or omissions of

Miller. It argues that because the jury found Miller negligent in Armstrong's FELA action, L & A is entitled to indemnification for the damages it was required to pay as the result of Miller's negligence. This argument ignores the different causation standards of these two actions: the FELA action is governed by federal law while the indemnity action is governed by state law. In *Nivens v. St. Louis Southwestern Railway Co.,* 425 F.2d 114 (5th Cir.1970), we stated:

> The standards of liability for negligence under § 1 of the Act are significantly broader than in ordinary common-law negligence actions. The Supreme Court has succinctly stated the now settled principle that in these cases,
>
> > "the test of a jury case is simply whether the proofs justify with reason the conclusion that employer negligence played any part, even the slightest, in producing the injury * * *. It does not matter that, from the evidence, the jury may also with reason, on grounds of probability, attribute the result to other causes * * *. The employer is stripped of his common-law defenses and for practical purposes the inquiry in these cases today rarely presents more than the single question whether negligence of the employer played any part, however small, in the injury or death which is the subject of the suit." *Rogers v. Missouri Pac. Ry.,* 352 U.S. 500, 506–508, 77 S.Ct. 443, 449, 1 L.Ed.2d 493 (1957).
>
> Since the Act explicitly makes an employer liable if an injury results only in part from his negligence, the common-law proximate cause standard is modified, and the employee has a less demanding burden of proving causal relationship.

Id. at 118.

The district court found that even if the cab driver was negligent, his negligence was not the proximate cause of Armstrong's injuries; rather, the court determined the sole cause of the accident was the negligence of the motorist who rear-ended the taxi cab. The district court's finding is reviewed on appeal under the clearly erroneous standard. * * *

The record adequately supports the district court's finding. Batiste, Armstrong's co-worker, testified that there was insufficient room on the shoulder of the road to allow the taxi cab to completely pull off the road and that the railroad crossing was not elevated. He also testified that there were no cars in the area and no cars in the lane opposite to the taxi cab, that the night was clear and that an oncoming motorist would have been able to see the flashing lights on the track as well as the parking lights of the stopped taxi cab. While the testimony of Armstrong to a certain extent contradicts Batiste's testimony, an appellate court is in a particularly poor position to second guess the district court's credibility choices among differing pieces of testimony. *Ayers v. United States,* 750 F.2d 449 at 456 (5th Cir.1985). Because we believe that there was sufficient evidence to support the district court's finding that the cab driver's negligence did not proximately cause Armstrong's injury, we decline to hold that the district court erred in dismissing L & A's indemnity action against Miller. The district court's denial of L & A's motion for judgment notwithstanding the verdict was proper.

Accordingly, the judgment of the district court is AFFIRMED.

Notes

1. Are Armstrong's injuries fairly considered to be costs of running a railroad?

2. *Armstrong* illustrates several of the tort-like qualities of FELA litigation. The claim is filed in a state or federal court with a jury serving as the fact finder in many instances. Liability hinges on a finding that the railroad or its agent was negligent. Moreover, compensation in both a traditional tort or FELA case is measured in terms of the actual loss to the particular claimant. The individualized damage remedy means that two workers suffering what seem to be similar injuries may recover vastly different sums of money. Compare Kelly v. Illinois Cen. Gulf R.R., 552 F.Supp. 399 (W.D.Mo.1982) (employee who lost a leg awarded $2,000,000) with Flanigan v. Burlington N. Inc., 632 F.2d 880 (8th Cir.1980) (employee who lost a leg awarded $500,000). Although not an issue in *Armstrong*, FELA retains conduct-based defenses applied through the principles of pure comparative negligence. See, e.g., Gish v. CSX Transp. Inc., 890 F.2d 989 (7th Cir.1989) (damage award reduced by percentage of employee's negligence in attempting to lift a 175 lb. manhole cover without assistance); and Plambeck v. Union Pacific R.R. Co., 232 Neb. 590, 441 N.W.2d 614 (1989) (damage award reduced by percentage of employee negligence in failing to obey workplace safety rules).

3. While *Armstrong* highlights similarities between FELA and tort law, it also illustrates some important differences. Evidence sufficient to support Armstrong's claim against the railroad under FELA does not support the railroad's claim for indemnity under traditional tort principles. The differences between a FELA action and a conventional tort action were described by the Supreme Court as follows:

> Under this statute the test of a jury case is simply whether the proofs justify with reason the conclusion that employer negligence played *any part, even the slightest,* in producing the injury or death for which damages are sought ... The employer is stripped of his common-law defenses and for practical purposes the inquiry in these cases today rarely presents more than the single question whether negligence of the employer played *any part, however small,* in the injury or death. ... [T]he special features of this statutory negligence action [FELA] make it significantly different from the ordinary common-law negligence action.
> ...

Rogers v. Missouri Pacific R.R. Co., 352 U.S. 500, 506–510, 77 S.Ct. 443, 1 L.Ed.2d 493 (1957) (emphasis added and footnotes omitted).

It seems fair to say that courts require less proof of negligence in FELA cases than in ordinary tort actions. See, e.g., Ringhiser v. Chesapeake & Ohio Ry. Co., 354 U.S. 901, 77 S.Ct. 1093, 1 L.Ed.2d 1268 (1957) (engineer answering call of nature while hidden inside gondola car, injured when cars were switched without knowledge of his presence); Gallick v. Baltimore & Ohio Railroad Co., 372 U.S. 108, 83 S.Ct. 659, 9 L.Ed.2d 618 (1963) (insect bite possibly attributable to stagnant pond near right of way); Pehowic v. Erie Lackawanna R.R. Co., 430 F.2d 697 (3d Cir.1970) (employee stung by bee in undergrowth accumulated near right of way); and, Ybarra v. Burlington Northern, Inc., 689 F.2d 147 (8th Cir.1982) (employee was injured while lifting a 40–50 lb. bucket of oil in violation of employer safety rule; jury could award damages based on employer's negligence in failing to enforce the safety rule). Moreover, courts appear to apply less stringent standards of causation in FELA actions. See, e.g., Kernan v. American Dredging Co., 355 U.S. 426, 78 S.Ct. 394, 2 L.Ed.2d 382 (1958) (lamp on boat carried at lower than eight feet above water level in violation of Coast Guard visibility regulation, ignited oil on surface of water, resulting in injury from burn); and, Mitchell v. Missouri–Kansas–Texas Railroad Co., 786 S.W.2d 659 (Tex. 1990) (error to instruct jury in terms of common law proximate cause; the proper standard under FELA was whether the employer's negligence played "any part, even the slightest" in producing the injury or death).

4. A wide variety of injuries and forms of misconduct come within the coverage of the FELA. "Negligence" under the statute embraces assault by one worker upon another in the course of employment, Jamison v. Encarnacion, 281 U.S. 635, 50 S.Ct. 440, 74 L.Ed. 1082 (1930); false imprisonment and detention over night, no physical consequences alleged, Slaughter v. Atlantic Coast Line R.R., 302 F.2d 912 (D.C.Cir.1962), declined to follow, Teague v. National R.R. Passenger Corp., 708 F.Supp. 1344 (D.Mass.1989); and, failure to provide medical attention for ill worker in emergency, Rival v. Atchison, Topeka & Santa Fe Ry., 62 N.M. 159, 306 P.2d 648 (1957). The Act has been interpreted to cover an occupational disease (silicosis) arising from employment, Urie v. Thompson, 337 U.S. 163, 69 S.Ct. 1018, 93 L.Ed. 1282 (1949), and nervous breakdown caused by unreasonably heavy work, McMillan v. Western Pacific R.R. Co., 54 Cal.2d 841, 9 Cal.Rptr. 361, 357 P.2d 449 (1960).

5. A railroad employer may be liable on principles of imputed negligence. For example, a railroad that procured a public taxi for an employee who was injured while being transported in the cab that lacked seat belts was held liable under FELA for its "negligent" selection of the vehicle even though the taxicab proprietors were exonerated of liability. Benson v. Penn Central Transportation Co., 463 Pa. 37, 342 A.2d 393 (1975). Similarly, in Sinkler v. Missouri Pacific R.R. Co., 356 U.S. 326, 78 S.Ct. 758, 2 L.Ed.2d 799 (1958), the Supreme Court held a railway employer liable for injury caused to its employee by the negligence of an independent contractor hired by the railway. The court observed:

> In interpreting the FELA, we need not depend upon common law principles of liability. This statute, an avowed departure from the rules of the common law * * * was a response to the special needs of railroad workers who are daily exposed to the risks inherent in railroad work and are helpless to provide adequately for their own safety * * * The

cost of human injury, an inescapable expense of railroading, must be borne by someone, and the FELA seeks to adjust that expense equitably between the worker and the carrier. 356 U.S. 326, 329, 78 S.Ct. 758, 762, 2 L.Ed.2d 799.

6. Critics of FELA maintain that it has become, in effect, a "no-fault" system of compensation without any corresponding reduction in administrative costs. Relaxed standards of negligence and causation coupled with tort damage rules is said to be unfair and to subject railroads to a competitive disadvantage with other modes of transportation. Schwartz and Mahshigian, The Federal Employers' Liability Act, A Bane for Workers, A Bust for Railroads, A Boon for Lawyers, 23 San Diego L.Rev. 1 (1986); Haynes and Anderson, The Federal Employers' Liability Act: A Compensation System in Urgent Need of Reform, 34 Fed.Bar News & J. 310 (1987). Defenders of FELA assert that it serves as a real and valuable incentive to promote workplace safety and that it operates at a cost comparable with that incurred by workers' compensation systems. See, Phillips, An Evaluation of the Federal Employers' Liability Act, 25 San Diego L.Rev. 49 (1988).

7. The Jones Act, 41 Stat. 1007, 46 U.S.C.A. § 688, extended FELA principles to employment of seamen. See, O'Donnell v. Great Lakes Dredge & Dock Co., 318 U.S. 36, 63 S.Ct. 488, 87 L.Ed. 596 (1943); Yehia v. Rouge Steel Corp., 898 F.2d 1178 (6th Cir.1990).

SOCIAL SECURITY DISABILITY BENEFITS

The federal social security acts provide benefits to disabled workers under a plan that is at the same time broader in scope and more limited in specific application than the typical workers' compensation plan as described in succeeding portions of this text. Federal disability benefits are broader in scope in that they are payable without regard to what caused the disability; that is, the act imposes no requirement that the disability have any connection to the disabled worker's employment. By contrast, the disability plan is more limited in specific application in that it provides only earnings loss benefits—no medical benefits—and only to workers who are totally injured for extended periods of time.

The disability benefits plan is one element of the federal Old Age Survivors and Disability Insurance scheme (OASDI) that was part of President Franklin D. Roosevelt's new deal legislative package of the mid–1930s. This part of the social security plan is referred to as an insurance system because it is funded by employment and excise taxes imposed upon both employees and employers and creates benefit entitlements as a matter of right. These taxes are paid in respect of wages paid and self-employment income earned, and are generally known as social security taxes. They are collected from employees by withholding them from the wages paid by employers. The employers periodically submit the withheld income taxes paid by employees and an equal amount payable by them as excise taxes to the United States Treasury where the funds are ultimately deposited to the exclusive credit of social security trust funds from which benefits are paid.

The original social security act did not include the disability benefits element. The history of that element has been described as follows:

"The original American OASI program, adopted in the depression days of 1935, provided for the two groups most obviously and urgently in need of protection, the unemployed and the aged. Widows and dependent children were soon added to the beneficiaries.

"World War II interrupted the progress of social security legislation, but in 1948 the Advisory Council on Social Security recommended that benefits be provided also for the disabled. A series of bitter debates followed, reminiscent of [later] battles over Medicare, with sharply divided camps warning of the dire consequences of passage or failure of the legislation. Protection for disabled workers came only in 1956 after a long and bitter struggle, and then only for the permanently and totally disabled. The legislation provided that insured persons who were so disabled could retire at 50 or older and receive the OASI benefits to which they would have been entitled at normal retirement age. There were no benefits for dependents. In contrast to the pattern in other countries, the adopted definition of disability was unusually strict; and there was no provision for higher benefits where constant attendance was needed. * * * Benefits for the wives and children of the disabled were added in 1958, and the age 50 requirement was dropped in 1960. Work requirements for eligibility were also liberalized."[9]

Both the scope and the limits of the disability benefits plan are revealed by the structure of the statutory plan as follows:

Disability insurance benefits are payable to a worker who:

(A) is insured for disability insurance benefits * * *,

(B) has not attained the retirement age [historically 65, but now variable],

(C) has filed an application for disability insurance benefits, and

(D) is under a disability * * *.[10]

Unless the worker has had prior qualifying disabilities under specified conditions, monthly disability payments begin the month after the expiration of a waiting period of five consecutive calendar months of disability.[11] (What is the purpose for imposing such a requirement? Does it tell anything about the philosophy of the disability benefits?)

In order to be "insured for disability insurance benefits" in any month, a person must have had a history of employment that satisfies the criteria prescribed by the statute. Although the requirements are detailed, a simplified test is whether the worker had 10 full years of

9. Cheit, "Workmen's Compensation, OASDI: The Overlap," 3 Industrial Relations 63, 65 (1964).

10. 42 U.S.C.A. § 423(a).

11. 42 U.S.C.A. § 423(c); prior to 1972 amendments (Pub.L. 92–603) the waiting period was six months.

employment in insured work.[12] Satisfying that test always satisfies the "insured" criterion and meeting lesser periods of coverage sometimes qualifies young workers and others in special circumstances.

In addition to satisfying the foregoing requirements, a worker must also be "disabled." The statutory definition of that term bears stating in full:

(d)(1) The term "disability" means—

(A) inability to engage in any substantial gainful activity by reason of any medically determinable physical or mental impairment which can be expected to result in death or which has lasted or can be expected to last for a continuous period of not less than 12 months; or

(B) in the case of an individual who has attained the age of 55 and is blind * * * inability by reason of such blindness to engage in substantial gainful activity requiring skills or abilities comparable to those of any gainful activity in which he has previously engaged with some regularity and over a substantial period of time.

(2) For purposes of paragraph (1)(A)—

(A) an individual * * * shall be determined to be under a disability only if his physical or mental impairment or impairments are of such severity that he is not only unable to do his previous work but cannot, considering his age, education, and work experience, engage in any other kind of substantial gainful work which exists in the national economy, regardless of whether such work exists in the immediate area in which he lives, or whether a specific job vacancy exists for him, or whether he would be hired if he applied for work. * * * "[w]ork which exists in the national economy" means work which exists in significant numbers either in the region where such individual lives or in several regions of the country.

* * *

(3) For purposes of this subsection, a "physical or mental impairment" is an impairment that results from anatomical, physiological, or psychological abnormalities which are demonstrable by medically acceptable clinical and laboratory diagnostic techniques.[13]

A student might refer back to this provision after examining the requirements of a compensable injury under workers' compensation laws to re-emphasize how limited the application of the federal disability benefits plan truly is.

A qualified disabled worker is entitled to a "primary insurance amount" determined by formula on the basis of the amount of time employed in insured employment and the rate of earnings during that time.[14] In addition, spouses and children of qualified disabled workers are

---

12. 42 U.S.C.A. § 423(c).

13. 42 U.S.C.A. § 423(d).

14. 42 U.S.C.A. § 423(a)(2).

entitled to a benefit equal to one-half the primary insurance amount, if the conditions of the statute are satisfied.[15]

Although the criteria for what is a disability are set by the Social Security Act, the Secretary of Health and Human Services may enter into an agreement with designated state agencies to have the actual medical determinations made by them.[16]

Because the federal disability program imposes no causal nexus between the claimant's employment and the disability, many disabled workers receive social security disability benefits but no workers' compensation benefits. Nevertheless, a worker who is disabled by a work injury might be entitled to benefits from both sources, thus permitting some disabled workers to receive combined benefits in amounts that exceed pre-injury earnings. The initial federal disability benefits law made no deduction to prevent this, which proved to be a source of discontent among employers. In 1972 the National Commission on State Workmen's Compensation Laws recommended that social security benefits be reduced in the presence of workers' compensation benefits (R. 3.18).

Thereafter, Congress enacted the following provision:

If for any month prior to the month in which an individual attains the age of 65—

    (1) such individual is entitled to [disability benefits] . . . and

    (2) such individual is entitled for such month to—

        (A) periodic benefits on account of his or her total or partial disability (whether or not permanent) under a workmen's compensation law or plan of the United States or a State, the total of his [disability] benefits shall be reduced (but not below zero) by the amount by which the sum of

    (3) such total of [disability] benefits for such month, and

    (4) such periodic benefits payable (and actually paid) for such month to such individual under such laws or plans, exceeds the higher of—

    (5) 80 per centum of his "average current earnings." * * *

Does this "overlap" deduction provide a systematic cost savings to the combined workers' compensation and social security disability benefits system? Does it make any difference as to how the savings is allocated?

[handwritten margin note: Set-off provision]

DEPARTMENT OF PUBLIC HEALTH, DIVISION OF RISK MANAGEMENT v. WILCOX
Supreme Court of Florida, 1989.
543 So.2d 1253.

PER CURIAM.

* * *

In a worker's compensation proceeding, the respondent, Muriel Wilcox, was awarded temporary total and permanent total disability

---

15. 42 U.S.C.A. § 402(b), (c), (d).   **16.** 20 C.F.R. § 404.1520.

benefits, costs, interests, and medical expenses. Her employer, the State of Florida, Department of Public Health, Division of Risk Management, subsequently determined that Wilcox was also receiving federal social security benefits, and reduced the amount of her workers' compensation award pursuant to the offset provision in section 440.15(9), Florida Statutes (1985).

Wilcox contends that the setoff provision in section 440.15(9) cannot be taken by her employer on its own accord, but rather must be authorized by the deputy commissioner. The Third District Court of Appeal agreed with Wilcox and held that her employer could not take the setoff unilaterally. The court held that the compensation award could only be reduced by the deputy commissioner in a modification proceeding. *Wilcox,* 504 So.2d at 444 (Fla.1987).

The state, as the employer, argues that the offset provision is self-executing and can be taken unilaterally. Thus, the issue presented is whether Wilcox's employer (the state) may unilaterally take the setoff authorized by section 440.15(9). We hold that it may.

Section 440.15(9)(a), Florida Statutes (1985), requires that weekly workers' compensation benefits be reduced by the amount that they and social security benefits, in the aggregate, exceed eighty percent of the injured worker's average weekly wage.[1] The language is unequivocal. The offset is mandatory if the combined benefits exceed eighty percent of the worker's salary. Correspondingly, at the federal level, 42 United States Code section 424a (1935), requires that the Social Security Administration take the setoff if it is not taken under a state workers' compensation program.

We note at the outset that section 424a was enacted to prevent injured workers from receiving "windfall" benefits from the combination of social security disability benefits and workers' compensation benefits.[2] Congress feared that the duplication of benefits would reduce a worker's

---

1. Section 440.15(9)(a), Florida Statutes (1985), states:

> Weekly compensation benefits payable under this chapter for disability resulting from injuries to an employee who becomes eligible for benefits under 42 U.S.C. § 423 shall be reduced to an amount whereby the sum of such compensation benefits payable under this chapter and such total benefits otherwise payable for such period to the employee and his dependents, had such employee not been entitled to benefits under this chapter, under 42 U.S.C. §§ 423 and 402, does not exceed 80 percent of the employ-

ee's average weekly wage. However, this provision shall not operate to reduce an injured worker's benefits under this chapter to a greater extent than such benefits would have otherwise been reduced under 42 U.S.C. § 424(a) [sic]. This reduction of compensation benefits is not applicable to any compensation benefits payable for any week subsequent to the week in which the injured worker reaches the age of 62 years.

2. Kristal, *Social security disability benefits: Benefit or burden to the severely injured workers' compensation claimant?*, 61 Fla.B.J. 65 (July/Aug. 1987).

incentive to return to work impeding rehabilitative efforts.[3] Several states, including Florida, enacted similar statutes requiring state employers to take the setoffs first, thereby saving money. Although section 440.15(9) does not expressly address whether an employer may take the setoff unilaterally, section 424a clearly allows the Social Security Administration to do so.[4]

The rationale underlying the federal statutory scheme is sound. The Social Security Administration has knowledge of the amount of social security benefits an employee receives. It must then obtain information regarding the amount of workers' compensation benefits from the state that is administering the plan.[5] When the Social Security Administration has this information, the amount of the setoff can be quickly and easily determined by using a simple mathematical calculation. The federal statute recognizes this and thus allows the setoff to be taken administratively. We find the federal scheme persuasive.[6]

Similarly, section 440.15(9)(c) imposes no obligation on the employee to inform his employer that he has begun receiving social security disability benefits, nor does it require the employee to calculate the requisite eighty percent limit and remit the excess. Rather, the employer must take the initiative in determining the applicability of the reduction. No deduction can be taken until the employer receives the worker's social security disability information from the Social Security Administration. Then, the setoff only can be taken prospectively. *Department of Transportation v. Lindsey,* 383 So.2d 956 (Fla. 1st DCA 1980).

Thus, section 440.15(9) requires a Florida employer to obtain the same reliable information that the federal statute demands. Since both the Florida employer and the Social Security Administration rely upon the same information in determining the applicability of the setoff, we see no reason why the state setoff should not also be self-executing. Therefore, we hold that the setoff provision in section 440.15(9) may be taken administratively by an employer/carrier.

We reject the respondent's contention that the setoff can be made only by the deputy commissioner in a modification proceeding. This

---

3. *Id.*

4. 42 U.S.C. § 424a(h)(2) states:

The Secretary [of the Department of Health and Human Services] is authorized to enter into agreements with States, political subdivisions, and other organizations that administer a law or plan subject to the provisions of this section, in order to obtain such information as he may require *to carry out the provisions of this section.*

Thus, the Social Security Administration is authorized to obtain the necessary information in order to take the setoff administratively.

5. *Id.*

6. Our statutes recognize the persuasiveness of federal laws in the workers' compensation area. Section 440.44(1), Florida Statutes (1985), states:

(1) INTERPRETATION OF LAW.—As a guide to the interpretation of this chapter, the Legislature takes due notice of federal social and labor acts and hereby creates an agency to administer such acts passed for the benefit of employees and employers in Florida industry, and desires to meet the requirements of such federal acts wherever not inconsistent with the Constitution and laws of Florida.

proceeding would insure against an employer miscalculating the amount of the setoff. We fail to see how this possible benefit to the employee outweighs the additional expense and delay it imposes on the employer. The employer has little incentive to miscalculate the amount of the setoff because review by the deputy commissioner is always available to the employee. The First District Court of Appeal has consistently held that the offset provision in section 440.15(9) is self-executing. *See Colonel's Table v. Malena,* 412 So.2d 64 (Fla. 1st DCA 1982); *Florida Power & Light Co. v. Adkins,* 377 So.2d 57 (Fla. 1st DCA 1979); *Borden, Inc. v. Butler,* 377 So.2d 795 (Fla. 1st DCA 1979); *Sherrod Dry Wall v. Reeves,* 378 So.2d 301 (Fla. 1st DCA 1979).

Accordingly, we hold that the setoff provision in section 440.15(9) is self-executing in nature and therefore, can be taken unilaterally by the employer. We quash the decision of the Third District Court of Appeal and remand the case for further proceedings consistent with this opinion.

It is so ordered.

SECTION 4. PREVENTING WORK INJURIES: THE OCCUPATIONAL SAFETY AND HEALTH ACT

Prior to 1970 Congress left the regulation of industrial safety standards, practices and procedures primarily to the states. In that year, responding to an annual toll of approximately 14,000 industrial deaths and millions of injuries, Congress assumed a new role of preventing industrial accidents through the enactment of the Occupational Safety and Health Act of 1970 (OSHA). Although OSHA requirements can be expensive for many employers to meet and their violation can result in substantial penalties, it does not set up the potential adversarial relationship between a claiming employee and a defending employer (or benefits agency) as do tort law and various compensation programs. No court has ruled that OSHA creates private compensatory rights for employees. Because of that, the conflicts under OSHA arise primarily between employers and the agencies charged with administering the law; namely, the Secretary of Labor and the Occupational Safety and Health Review Commission. Accordingly, legal disputes under OSHA usually arise in the processes for setting and enforcing safety standards. The following is a brief overview of the Act, highlighting those processes.

OSHA applies to employers "engaged in a business affecting commerce."[17] As written, its application apparently extends to the furtherest reaches of Congress' commerce clause power without being foreshortened by any limits on the size of covered employers such as is seen in the Fair Labor Standards Act of 1938 and in Title VII of the Civil Rights Act of 1964. For example, OSHA has been applied to cover workers who were

---

17. Occupational Safety and Health Act § 651 et seq.
of 1970, Pub.L. 91–596, § 3(5), 29 U.S.C.A.

clearing land that would later grow grapes to be used to make wine for sale in commerce. Godwin v. OSAHRC, 540 F.2d 1013 (9th Cir.1976).

OSHA imposes a basic duty on employers under the so-called general duty clause:

> [Each employer] shall furnish to each of his employees employment and a place of employment which are free from recognized hazards that are causing or are likely to cause death or serious physical harm to employees; [and] shall comply with occupational safety and health standards promulgated under [OSHA].[18]

The correlative duties of employees are to "comply with occupational safety and health standards and all rules, regulations, and orders * * * which are applicable to their own actions and conduct."[19] In addition to the basic duties, employers are obliged to comply with specific occupational safety and health standards that are promulgated by the Secretary of Labor.[20] The Secretary may have the assistance of a National Advisory Committee on Occupational Safety and Health, composed of representatives of management, labor, occupational safety and occupational health professions, and the public;[21] an advisory standard setting committee;[22] the Secretary of Health and Human Services;[23] and the specially created National Institute for Occupational Safety and Health.[24]

The stringency tone of OSHA standards is set by the criterion that standards dealing with "toxic materials or harmful physical agents" are to assure that "to the extent feasible * * * no employees will suffer material impairment of health or functional capacity even if such employee has regular exposure to the hazard * * * for the period of his working life."[25]

OSHA standards are promulgated by rule[26] under rulemaking procedures prescribed by the Act.[27] The process includes publishing the proposed rule in the Federal Register and affording an opportunity for comment.[28] If requested, the Secretary must hold a public hearing.[29] Any person adversely affected by an OSHA standard may seek judicial review of the promulgating process in a United States Court of Appeals at any time before the expiration of 60 days from the date the Secretary promulgates it.[30] The Secretary's administrative determination of the factual predicate for any standard will be conclusively upheld in the courts if supported by "substantial evidence considered in the record as

18. Id., § 5(a).

19. Id., § 5(b).

20. Id., § 6(a).

21. Id., § 7(a). The Committee is charged to "advise, consult with and make recommendations * * * on matters relating to the administration of the Act."

22. Id., § 7(b).

23. Id., § 20(a)(2). Formerly, Health, Education and Welfare.

24. Id., § 22(c).

25. Id., § 6(b)(5).

26. Id., § 6(a).

27. Id., § 6(b)(1).

28. Id., § 6(b)(2).

29. Id., § 6(b)(3).

30. Id., § 6(f).

a whole,"[31] but the reviewing courts exercise plenary review of questions of law.

Employers may seek temporary variances[32] while they are attempting to comply with standards, or permanent variances issued where the employer has demonstrated by a preponderance of evidence that the variant conditions would be "as safe and healthful as those which would prevail if he complied with the standard."[33]

The Secretary's primary enforcement tools are the authority to enter work places, inspect working conditions, question employees and employers, and inspect records kept by employers concerning occupational deaths and injuries as required by regulations issued under the Act.[34] The Secretary, upon presenting "appropriate credentials", may enter a work place "without delay and at reasonable times"[35] * * * "to inspect and investigate during regular working hours and at other reasonable times, and within reasonable limits and in a reasonable manner"[36] working conditions, machinery and so forth. Initially, the Secretary took the position that the law authorized inspectors to make warrantless searches without notice over the objection of employers. Rejecting that argument, the Supreme Court held in Marshall v. Barlow's Inc., 436 U.S. 307, 98 S.Ct. 1816, 56 L.Ed.2d 305 (1978), that a search warrant is required. Nevertheless, the criterion for the Secretary's getting a warrant is less stringent than probable cause. It will be enough for the Secretary to present the judicial officer with "an administrative plan containing specific neutral criteria." Then the warrant will issue.

Once within a work place, the OSHA investigator has the authority to make a walk-around inspection while accompanied by a representative of the employer and one designated by the employees.[37] Acknowledging that the Secretary will not be able to inspect all work places within a reasonable period of time, the Act provides for employees or their representatives to make written requests that the Secretary make inspections under circumstances where a violation of a standard "threatens physical harm or * * * an imminent danger exists."[38] The Secretary must have procedures of informal review, including written explanation, of refusals to issue citations in situations where employees or their representatives have given written notice of an alleged violation and no citation is issued thereafter.[39]

Obviously, the foregoing investigatory scheme will generate disputes between employers and the Secretary and also between employees and the Secretary. In some instances, the process becomes entangled in general labor-management disputes, but more often, it leads to enforcement actions under the Act.

31. Id., § 6(f).
32. Id., § 6(b)(6).
33. Id., § 6(d).
34. Id., § 8.
35. Id., § 8(a)(1).

36. Id., § 8(a)(2).
37. Id., § 8(e).
38. Id., § 8(f)(1).
39. Id., § 8(f)(2).

Upon finding a violation of the Act, the Secretary must issue a written citation to the employer, fixing a reasonable time for abatement.[40] Thereafter, the Secretary may propose a penalty[41] in an amount that varies according to whether the violation is "wilful and repeated,"[42] "serious"[43] or only "nonserious,"[44] or is a failure to correct a violation within the period permitted.[45] Within 15 working days from receipt of notice of the proposed penalty, the employer must notify the Secretary of the intention to contest either the citation or the proposed penalty. If this is not done, the citation and proposed penalty become final and *"not subject to review by any court or agency."*[46] If the employer contests the citation or proposed penalty, or if an employee or employee's representative contests the time period fixed for abatement, the Occupational and Safety Health Review Commission must review the matter and give an opportunity for a hearing.[47] The Commission may modify, affirm or vacate the Secretary's citation or proposed penalty or give other appropriate relief.[48]

Despite the fact that the Commission's order can impose a civil fine, the employer is not entitled to a trial by jury in a court on the question of whether or not the Act was violated. According to Atlas Roofing Co., Inc. v. Occupational Safety, Etc., 430 U.S. 442, 97 S.Ct. 1261, 51 L.Ed.2d 464 (1977), new statutory rights created by Congress, such as those in OSHA, do not fall under the injunction of the Seventh Amendment. Although the Commission's order becomes final 30 days after issuance, any person *"adversely affected or aggrieved"* may obtain appellate review in an appropriate United States court of appeals by filing a petition seeking to have the order modified or set aside within 60 days of its issuance.[49] Although fact findings of the Commission are binding if supported by "substantial evidence on the record considered as a whole," the appellate court may order the Commission to hear additional evidence in appropriate situations.[50] United States courts of appeal also enforce Commission orders through the contempt powers.[51]

In addition to civil penalties, the Act imposes criminal penalties for wilful violations of standards and orders that cause the death of an employee;[52] provides remedies in Federal district courts for employees who are discharged or discriminated against by employers because of activities authorized by the Act;[53] outlaws the giving of an employer

40. Id., § 9(a).

41. Id., § 10(a).

42. Id., § 17(a). Civil penalty not more than $10,000 per violation.

43. Id., § 17(b). Civil penalty of up to $1,000 per violation.

44. Id., § 17(c). Civil penalty of up to $1,000 per violation.

45. Id., § 17(d). Civil penalty of up to $1,000 per day of delay.

46. Id., § 10(a).

47. Id., § 10(c).

48. Id., § 10(c).

49. Id., § 11(a).

50. Id., § 11(a).

51. Id., § 11(b).

52. Id., § 17(e). Fine not more than $10,000; or 6 months imprisonment; or both for first conviction.

53. Id., § 11(c). Federal district courts may issue restraining orders and order appropriate relief, including rehiring and back pay.

advance notice of an inspection;[54] outlaws the making of false statements[55] by any person; and, outlaws the assaulting or killing of enforcement personnel.[56]

OSHA relates to accident prevention and has no effect on the reparation functions of state workers' compensation laws.[57] Moreover, courts are apparently unanimous in holding that OSHA creates no private cause of action for injured workers, either against an employer, see, e.g., Knight v. Burns, Kirkley & Williams Constr. Co., Inc., 331 So.2d 651 (Ala.1976), or the federal government for failure to enforce OSHA rigorously. See e.g., Davis v. United States, 536 F.2d 758 (8th Cir.1976). Nevertheless, state courts may admit an OSHA standard as evidence to particularize an employer's standard of care in a negligence action. DiSabatino Brothers, Inc. v. Baio, 366 A.2d 508 (Del.1976).

To the extent that OSHA standards do not relate to a given "occupational health or safety issue" the states may assert regulatory jurisdiction.[58] Moreover, states may assume responsibility for developing and enforcing standards in areas preempted by OSHA standards upon approval of a state plan by the Secretary of Labor.[59] Although neither federal nor state governments or agencies are under the jurisdiction of OSHA enforcement procedures,[60] heads of federal departments are directed to establish programs for federal employments consistent with OSHA standards.[61] Moreover, one of the criteria for approval of a state enforcement plan, is that adequate protection of state employees be assured "to the extent permitted by its law."[62]

COMMENTARY

Not all theorists believe that direct regulation is a better way to internalize the costs of work injuries than tort litigation is. The following extract (footnotes omitted) from Pierce, "Encouraging Safety: The Limits of Tort Law and Government Regulation," 33 Vanderbilt Law Rev. 1281, 1308–1319 (1980) discusses some of the limitations.

"IV. DIRECT REGULATION AS A SUBSTITUTE FOR, OR A
SUPPLEMENT TO, THE MARKET AND TORT LAW

"A. *Advantages of Direct Regulation*

"Direct regulation is usually justified on the theory that, in some areas at least, the combination of the market and tort law has proven ineffective as a mechanism for encouraging safety. Thus, it is the failure of other parts of the legal system to internalize accident costs that forces reliance upon direct safety regulation. Once the inadequacies of the operation of the market and tort law are

54. Id., § 17(f). Fine not more than $1,000; or 6 months imprisonment; or both.

55. Id., § 17(g). Fine not more than $1,000; or 6 months imprisonment; or both.

56. Id., § 17(h).

57. Id., § 4(b)(4).

58. Id., § 18(a).

59. Id., § 18(b).

60. Id., § 3(5).

61. Id., § 19.

62. Id., § 18(c)(6).

recognized in a particular context, direct regulation appears to be the only available option for reducing accident costs. As demonstrated in the prior parts of this Article, the market and tort law are increasingly less effective (and more costly). Hence, the growth of direct regulation and its rapid spread to new areas is both understandable and seemingly justified.

"The theory underlying direct regulation is relatively simple; if an activity is producing too many accident costs, prohibit the activity or require that it be carried on in a different manner. There is no reason in theory why direct regulation cannot produce an optimal level and pattern of spending on safety. As with the market and tort law, however, direct regulation in practice falls well short of its theoretically attainable goals.

"B. Limits of Direct Regulation

"1. Setting Appropriate Standards

"A major problem inherent in direct regulation is the difficulty of determining which safety standards or rules will produce the optimum level of spending on safety. The current debate focuses on the extent to which explicit quantification and comparison of the costs and benefits of various standards should be relied upon in lieu of purely subjective balancing of safety against costs. If cost-benefit analysis (CBA) can be applied to the process of establishing safety standards with acceptable results, direct regulation provides a promising alternative means of encouraging safety. Thus, to evaluate the efficacy of safety regulation, it is first necessary to explore the major impediments to the use of CBA as a means of determining optimal safety standards.

"Determining causal relationships is, of course, indispensable to calculating the benefits of a proposed safety standard. Yet, this determination is often difficult, and the result is invariably imprecise. Carcinogenicity determinations provide a particularly apt illustration of the problem. With respect to most suspected carcinogens, it is impossible even to be certain that the agent causes cancer in humans, though animal test results provide reasonably reliable indications. Determining with a high degree of confidence the number of cases of cancer that the particular agent will cause at particular exposure levels is beyond the state of the art. ... In determining carcinogenicity, as in many other areas of accident causation, the state of the art and data availability limit regulators to a crude approximation of causal relationships.

"It must be recognized, however, that regulatory agencies are probably institutionally better suited to determine causation than are courts. The regulatory agency can deal with statistical and probabilistic causation with all the data gathering and calculational advantages of a centralized decisionmaker. By contrast, courts have great difficulty dealing with probabilistic and joint causation, have limited access to relevant data, and have virtually no ability to make sophisticated calculations. Moreover, curing these deficiencies would be prohibitively expensive because of the large number of courts and the institutional characteristics of courts as decisionmakers.

"A second advantage enjoyed by a centralized regulatory decisionmaker is the ability to determine the "cause" of accidents by identification of the entity that can avoid accident costs most effectively and at least cost. As Professor Calabresi has demonstrated, the party causally responsible for a particular type of accident in this sense often is not even before the court in a tort action. [G. Calabresi, The Costs of Accidents (1970), at 256.] Again, trying to cure this defect in the tort system would vastly increase its already staggering administrative costs by transforming every tort case into a polycentric dispute of the type the judicial system simply has not been able to accommodate. Thus, while causation remains a major problem in the centralized decisionmaking of regulatory agencies, those agencies are better able to deal with the problem than courts.

"Determining causal relationships, however, is only one of many problems with the use of CBA. After causal relationships have been approximated, it is necessary to calculate the magnitude of costs and benefits using a common denominator, usually dollars. CBA has been subject to considerable criticism on the basis that it is much easier to calculate costs of regulation than to calculate benefits. In fact, calculating either side of the equation is very difficult, and significant costs of regulation often are omitted.

[Discussion of difficulties of putting a price on a human life is omitted.]

"There are other costs that flow from the use of CBA as well. Use of CBA to set safety standards necessarily produces high transaction costs in the regulatory process. A thorough CBA for a proposed safety standard requires hundreds of highly skilled manhours. Even assuming that efficient decisionmaking procedures are used, the regulatory system permits (and often, as a practical matter, demands) that several CBAs be conducted for any proposed standard which is subject to dispute. The regulatory transaction costs become staggering when the quite rational requirement of incremental CBAs and CBAs for proposed alternatives are added.

"The final major difficulty in establishing safety standards based on CBA is the tremendous potential for manipulation of the numerical ratio. As Amory Lovins has persuasively demonstrated, result-oriented technicians can use a variety of techniques in calculating the CBA to mask what otherwise would be recognized as blatant biases and analytical errors. The often symbiotic relationship between regulators and a narrow constituency causes this potential abuse of CBA to take on considerable importance.

"Throughout the foregoing discussion, I have assumed that a quantitative decisionmaking aid should be employed to determine appropriate safety standards for use in direct regulation. There is, of course, the alternative, supported by many, of relying entirely upon a combination of subjective decisionmaking and absolute pursuit of safety. Congress often eschews use of CBA in favor of subjective absolutism in determining safety standards. Four significant problems with this approach are apparent. First, if the agency actually follows the absolute safety mandate, the result is likely to be overspending on some aspects of safety and underspending on others, with a significant net reduction in accident costs avoided per dollar spent on safety. Second, subjective decisionmaking is as likely to mask biases, errors, and result-oriented regulation as is decisionmaking aided by CBA. Third, regulators confronted with a mandate to obtain absolute safety still use some form of *sub rosa* quantified balancing. Fourth, when agencies use a combination of official subjective absolutism and *sub rosa* quantified balancing, irrational patterns of spending on safety inevitably evolve.

"Actual adherence to an absolute standard of safety in a particular area necessarily produces badly skewed safety spending patterns. It is impossible for society to pursue an absolutist philosophy in all contexts or even to do so with respect to a broad category of risks, such as involuntary exposure risks. Given this basic premise, it necessarily follows that total accident costs always can be reduced by shifting safety spending from an activity in which absolutism has prevailed to virtually any other activity. This proposition is very simple to prove using the marginal analysis that is central to microeconomics.

"Subjective decisionmaking has been used effectively for years as a means of disguising biases and analytical flaws in order to reach a predetermined result dictated by factors never alluded to in the decision itself. Just as the good numbers mechanic can engage in mathematical subterfuge, the good verbal mechanic can use semantic tricks to hide political favoritism, vindictiveness, and incomplete analysis. Indeed, because there is more precision and uniform terminology in the language of mathematics, it is easier to demonstrate the flaws in a decision reached with the aid of a quantification tool such as CBA than to pierce the artful prose of a poorly reasoned but cleverly written subjective decision. Thus, the manipulation of decisionmaking tools by result-oriented regulators and technicians must be attacked through more basic changes in institutional decisionmaking.

"It is highly unlikely that any agency with an absolutist mandate actually follows that mandate consistently and eschews all efforts to balance the costs and benefits of safety standards. Rather, agencies make at least rough calculations covertly and disguise the quantitative basis for their decision through the use of ambiguous subjective terminology. As a result, the actual basis for the decision is never publicly revealed, the decisionmaking pattern is grossly distorted by *sub rosa* calculations in which implicit values are irrationally determined, and the potential for politically motivated, result-oriented decisions is even greater than in a system relying explicitly on quantification aids.

"OSHA's approach to determining safety standards for toxic chemicals provides a good example of how the process can work. OSHA disavows all reliance upon CBA in establishing safety standards. Based upon a reasonably well-supported interpretation of its organic act, OSHA takes the position that safety standards for workers are required to provide as much safety as is "feasible," and that the concept of feasibility negates any inference that costs should be balanced against benefits. Of course, OSHA is still required to apply the term "feasible" in determining standards. With some assistance from the courts, OSHA has defined "feasible" as any standard that will not place a substantial number of affected employers out of business. In other words, what began as an absolutist basis for standards was transformed into a basis dependent upon determinations of the financial viability of each affected industry and the major firms within that industry. As a result, OSHA's interpretation still requires use of mathematical aids in decisionmaking. Only the nature of the calculations and the values inherent in the results differ from a traditional CBA calculation.

* * *

"2. Other Costs and Limits of Direct Regulation

"There are problems associated with direct safety regulation in addition to those encountered in determining safety standards. In a dynamic economy, significant technological and economic changes occur rapidly. Yet recalculating CBAs for every conceivable alternative standard in response to changes in economic or technologic factors is prohibitively expensive. As a result, safety standards rapidly become obsolete.

"Enforcement too is a major problem of direct regulation. Some studies have shown that safety standards in the occupational safety area have no effect whatsoever on the actual level of accident costs. There undoubtedly are circumstances in which some safety standards have some beneficial effect, but the empirical data on the relationship between safety standards and accident costs are not encouraging.

"There is also considerable evidence that direct safety regulation increases the concentration of market power in an industry. Some of this effect probably is attributable to economies of scale in providing safety and, to that extent, it must be accepted as a consequence of any method of inducing greater safety. Much of the concentration effect of safety regulation, however, is attributable to economies of scale in conducting tests, filing reports, and otherwise complying with the administrative burdens attendant to direct regulation.

"Perhaps the most important disadvantage of direct safety regulation is its effect upon individual freedom. Substitution of direct safety regulation for market-determined levels of safety has significant implications for freedom and the ability of individuals to choose the mixture of comfort, pleasure, and risk they prefer. Safety decisions made in the context of direct regulation necessarily are based upon some measure of average or median tastes and preferences. The individual with a strong aversion to risk or a strong taste for risk must simply accept that level of risk determined collectively to be acceptable to society. The Pareto optimality and accommodation of individual tastes theoretically attainable through the market (were it not for externalities and transaction costs) is impossible to achieve through direct regulation. Some degree of constraint upon individual tastes and freedom is absolutely essential in any society, but complete abandonment of the market and internalization of accident costs in all areas of safety would force reliance upon direct regulation so pervasive as to undermine totally the individual freedom so highly prized in our society. . . . "

See also, Shavell, "Liability for Harm Versus Regulation for Safety," 13 J. of Legal Studies 357 (1984).

A more pragmatic limitation on a regulatory strategy for improving workplace safety is the availability of resources to enforce standards. Consider the following assessment of OSHA's performance:

Enforcement of the statutory duties through workplace inspections by compliance officers and issuance of citations has been glaringly inadequate "to assure so far as possible every working man and women in the Nation safe and healthful working conditions." The reasons are not difficult to discern.

First, the resources devoted to the effort are not equal to the task. The statute covers some 5 million workplaces with 85 million employees. At its peak, OSHA had less than 3,000 inspectors, and in 1987 had less than 1200 federal inspectors. Even with scheduled inspections limited to more hazardous industries, establishments cannot be inspected once in five years.

The inadequacy of inspections is indicated by the fact that Sweden, with a working population of 4 million makes as many health and safety inspections each year as the United States with a working population of more than 100 million.

* * *

The second source of enforcement inadequacy has been the puniness of penalties. With the remote likelihood of being inspected, recalcitrant employers will be induced to comply only by penalties sufficient to make violations unprofitable. The statutory schedule of penalties is plainly inadequate, with the maximum for a serious violation being $1,000, and the maximum for a repeated or willful violation of $10,000. OSHA, however, seldom imposes these meager maximums, as the cases studied have shown, with serious violations typically resulting in penalties of a few hundred dollars. Penalties in 1985 averaged only $77.68 per violation. (85 Colum.L.Rev. at 138, n. 138). As the Second Circuit said in Olin Construction Co. v. OSHRC, 525 F.2d 464, 467 (2d Cir.1975), "As for the penalties, we are amazed at their paucity, reflecting more of a license than a penalty."

The real puniness of the penalty is frequently somewhat disguised by settlements for substantially less than those proposed in the citation. To obtain a settlement, monetary penalties may be completely eliminated, even where serious violations have been cited. See, Donovan v. OCAW, 718 F.2d 1341, 1343 n. 5 (5th Cir.1983); and "serious" violations may be recharacterized as "nonserious," see Donovan v. International Union, Allied Industrial Workers, 722 F.2d 1415, 1416 (8th Cir.1983).

* * *

M. Franklin, A. Goldman and C. Summers, Legal Protection For the Individual Employee 461–463 (1989). See also, Office of Technology Assessment, U.S. Congress, Preventing Illness and Injury in the Workplace (1985) ("OSHA and the State programs have been able to inspect * * * at most, 4 percent of all establishments and less than 20 percent of manufacturing establishments each year. In addition, the penalties for violations are, on average, very low, and in most cases, much smaller than the potential costs of controls.").

Despite criticisms of OSHA, the death rate in all industries in the United States fell from 18 deaths per 100,000 workers in 1969, the year preceding OSHA's enactment, to 10 deaths per 100,000 workers in 1987 (Accident Facts 1988, p. 35). This correlation supports the value of OSHA. The difficulty in attributing cause and effect, however, is shown by the fact that, without OSHA, the death rate fell from 38 deaths per 100,000 workers in 1938 to 18 deaths per 100,000 workers in 1969. Perhaps this suggests that as industry becomes safer, ever more costly new measures will be required to make additional gains. Whether new money spent in the work safety field could be allocated to other fields (i.e. highway and home safety) with greater overall savings in lives, suffering and dollars is a legitimate economic and political question, but not a legal question as such.

Chapter 2

THE COMPENSATION PRINCIPLE

SECTION 1. HISTORICAL AND CONSTITUTIONAL BACKGROUND

The reader can only conjecture as to what the law of employment injuries would be like if state legislatures had taken the course of FELA to enlarge the common law duties of employers and emasculate the fellow servant, assumption of risk and contributory negligence defenses. Perhaps the outcomes would have varied immensely from state to state, depending upon differing political pressures, but the answer will never be known because of the pervasive emergence of workers' compensation, which substituted a different method of compensating employment injuries and deaths.

The compensation movement originated on the European continent and was first adopted in the German Compensation Act of 1884 after two years of legislative consideration in that country. Under the German Act, the first thirteen weeks of a worker's disability caused by either sickness or accident was compensated from a Sickness Fund supported by the compulsory contributions of both employers and employees. Payments for more extended disabilities were made from an Accident Fund which employers alone financed. The German Act was initially restricted to hazardous occupations, such as mining, manufacturing, and transportation, but was extended several times until, finally, in 1911 it embraced all employments. For a full account of the history and development of the German Act see Twenty-fourth Annual Report of the Commissioner of Labor, 1909, Vol. 1, pp. 975–1493.

In Great Britain, following several unsuccessful legislative attempts to rectify the shortcomings of the common law, Parliament adopted the Workmen's Compensation Act of 1897. The initial British bill was also confined to hazardous employments. It differed from the German Act, however, by placing the funding responsibility exclusively on the shoulders of employers, who were permitted to secure the benefits by purchasing insurance from private companies. Various amendments broadened the scope of the Act, until in 1906 it applied to almost all employments. During this same period the compensation scheme spread throughout

45

continental Europe, and by 1908 workers' compensation laws existed in almost all countries except the United States. The Compendium on Workmen's Compensation of the National Commission on State Workmen's Compensation Laws (1973), pp. 61–98, provides a study of comparative approaches to work injury compensation in international perspective.

Shortly after the turn of the twentieth century sporadic attempts were made in Maryland and Montana to adopt the compensation principle for limited groups of industries. Both statutes were declared unconstitutional. See, e.g., Cunningham v. Northwestern Improvement Co., 44 Mont. 180, 119 P. 554 (1911). (The Maryland statute was held unconstitutional by a lower court, and no appeal was taken.) In many other states commissions were appointed to investigate the need to compensate industrial injuries and to recommend specific measures. The report of the influential New York commission concluded: that the existing common law system provided woefully insufficient compensation by way of damages for injured workers and their families; that common law litigation imposed substantial court costs and attorneys' fees upon employers and produced little corresponding benefit for workers; and that the extended amount of time required to take a case to trial forced many needy employees into a Hobson's choice—either to forego money needed immediately for support and cure, or to accept a disadvantageous settlement in order to secure ready cash. New York Employers' Liability Commission, First Report (1910) Vol. 1. The report is summarized in Dodd, Administration of Workmen's Compensation (1936) pp. 19–26. This report was a primary impetus in the enactment of the New York workers' compensation statute, which was closely modelled after the 1906 British Act. Students may compare the description of that act as contained in the next case with any modern workers' constitution statute to adjudge how influential it has been down to the present.

NEW YORK CENTRAL R.R. CO. v. WHITE

Supreme Court of United States, 1917.
243 U.S. 188, 37 S.Ct. 247, 61 L.Ed. 667.

MR. JUSTICE PITNEY delivered the opinion of the court:

A proceeding was commenced by defendant in error before the Workmen's Compensation Commission of the State of New York, established by the Workmen's Compensation Law of that state, to recover compensation from the New York Central & Hudson River Railroad Company for the death of her husband, Jacob White, who lost his life September 2, 1914, through an accidental injury arising out of and in the course of his employment under that company. The Commission awarded compensation in accordance with the terms of the law; its award was affirmed, without opinion, by the appellate division of the supreme court for the third judicial department, whose order was affirmed by the court of appeals, without opinion. 169 App.Div. 903, 152 N.Y.S. 1149, 216 N.Y. 653, 110 N.E. 1051. Federal questions having been saved, the present writ of error was sued out by the New York Central Railroad Company, successor, through a consolidation of corporations, to the rights and liabilities of the employing company. * * *

The errors specified are based upon these contentions: (1) that the liability, if any, of the railroad company for the death of Jacob White, is defined and limited exclusively by the provisions of the Federal Employers' Liability Act of April 22, 1908, chap. 149, 35 Stat. at L. 65, Comp.Stat.1913, § 8657, and (2) that to award compensation to defendant in error under the provisions of the Workmen's Compensation Law would deprive plaintiff in error of its property without due process of law, and deny to it the equal protection of the laws, in contravention of the 14th Amendment.

* * * [The court disposed of the contention that the controversy was controlled by FELA by pointing out that decedent's work bore no direct relation to interstate commerce. The conclusion on this point, though no longer valid under later constructions of the commerce clause, permitted the Court to reach the critical workers' compensation issues.]

We turn to the constitutional question. The Workmen's Compensation Law of New York establishes forty-two groups of hazardous employments, defines "employee" as a person engaged in one of these employments upon the premises, or at the plant, or in the course of his employment away from the plant of his employer, but excluding farm laborers and domestic servants; defines "employment" as including employment only in a trade, business, or occupation carried on by the employer for pecuniary gain, "injury" and "personal injury" as meaning only accidental injuries arising out of and in the course of employment, and such disease or infection as naturally and unavoidably may result therefrom; and requires every employer subject to its provisions to pay or provide compensation according to a prescribed schedule for the disability or death of his employee resulting from an accidental personal injury arising out of and in the course of the employment, without regard to fault as a cause, except where the injury is occasioned by the wilful intention of the injured employee to bring about the injury or death of himself or of another, or where it results solely from the intoxication of the injured employee while on duty, in which cases neither the injured employee nor any dependent shall receive compensation. By § 11 the prescribed liability is made exclusive, except that, if an employer fail to secure the payment of compensation as provided in § 50, an injured employee, or his legal representative, in case death results from the injury, may, at his option, elect to claim compensation under the act, or to maintain an action in the courts for damages, and in such an action it shall not be necessary to plead or prove freedom from contributory negligence, nor may the defendant plead as a defense that the injury was caused by the negligence of a fellow servant, that the employee assumed the risk of his employment, or that the injury was due to contributory negligence. Compensation under the act is not regulated by the measure of damages applied in negligence suits, but in addition to providing medical, surgical, or other like treatment, it is based solely on loss of earning power, being graduated according to the average weekly wages of the injured employee and the character and duration of the disability, whether partial or total, temporary or permanent; while in case the injury causes death, the compensation is known as a death benefit, and includes funeral expenses, not exceeding $100, payments to the surviving wife (or dependent husband) during widowhood (or dependent widowerhood) of a percentage of the average wages of the deceased, and if there be a surviving child or children under the age of eighteen years an additional percentage of such wages for each child until that age is reached. There are provisions invalidating agreements by employees to waive the right to compensation, prohibiting any assignment, release, or commutation of claims for compensation or benefits except as provided by the act, exempting them from the claims of creditors, and requiring that the compensation and benefits shall be paid only to employees or their dependents. Provision is made for the establishment of a Workmen's Compensation Commission with administrative and judicial functions, including authority to pass upon claims to compensation on notice to the parties interested. The award or decision of the Commission is made subject to an appeal, on questions of law only, to the appellate division of the supreme court for the third department, with an ultimate appeal to the court of appeals in cases where such an appeal would lie in civil actions. A fund is created, known as "the state insurance fund," for the purpose of insuring employers against liability under the law, and assuring to the persons entitled the compensation thereby provided. The fund is made up primarily of premiums received from employers, at rates fixed by the Commission in view of the hazards of the different classes of employment, and the premiums are to be based upon the total pay roll and number of employees in each class at the lowest rate consistent with the maintenance of a solvent state insurance fund and the creation of a reasonable surplus and reserve. Elaborate provisions are laid down for the administration of this fund. By § 50, each employer is required to secure compensation to his employees in one of the following ways: (1) By insuring and keeping insured the payment of such compensation in the state fund; or (2) through any stock corporation or mutual association authorized to transact the business of workmen's compensation insurance in the state; or (3) "by furnishing satisfactory proof to the Commission of his financial ability to pay such compensation for himself, in which case the Commission may, in its discretion, require the deposit with the Commission of securities of the kind prescribed in § 13 of the Insurance Law, in an amount to be determined by the Commission, to secure his liability to pay the compensation provided in this chapter." If an employer fails to comply with this section, he is made liable to a penalty in an amount equal to the pro rata premium that would have been payable for insurance in the state fund during the period of noncompliance; besides which, his injured employees or their dependents are at liberty to maintain an action for damages in the courts, as prescribed by § 11. * * *

The scheme of the act is so wide a departure from common-law standards respecting the responsibility of employer to employee that doubts naturally have been raised respecting its constitutional validity. The adverse considerations urged or suggested in this case and in kindred cases submitted at the same time are: (a) That the employer's property is taken without due process of law, because he is subjected to a liability for compensation without regard to any neglect or default on his part or on the part of any other person for whom he is responsible, and in spite of the fact that the injury may be solely attributable to the fault of the employee; (b) that the employee's rights are interfered with, in that he is prevented from having compensation for injuries arising from the employer's fault commensurate with the damages actually sustained, and is limited to the measure of compensation prescribed by the act; and (c) that both employer and employee are deprived of their liberty to acquire property by being prevented from making such agreement as they choose respecting the terms of the employment.

In support of the legislation, it is said that the whole common-law doctrine of employer's liability for negligence, with its defenses of contributory negligence, fellow servant's negligence, and assumption of risk, is based upon fictions, and is inapplicable to modern conditions of employment; that in the highly organized and hazardous industries of the present day the causes of accident are often so obscure and complex that in a material proportion of cases it is impossible by any method correctly to ascertain the facts necessary to form an accurate judgment, and in a still larger proportion the expense and delay required for such ascertainment amount in effect to a defeat of justice; that, under the present system, the injured workman is left to bear the greater part of industrial accident loss, which, because of his limited income, he is unable to sustain, so that he and those dependent upon him are overcome by poverty and frequently become a burden upon public or private charity; and that litigation is unduly costly and tedious, encouraging corrupt practices and arousing antagonisms between employers and employees.

In considering the constitutional question, it is necessary to view the matter from the standpoint of the employee as well as from that of the employer. For, while plaintiff in error is an employer, and cannot succeed without showing that its rights as such are infringed * * *, yet, as pointed out by the court of appeals in the Jensen Case (215 N.Y. 526), the exemption from further liability is an essential part of the scheme, so that the statute, if invalid as against the employee, is invalid as against the employer.

The close relation of the rules governing responsibility as between employer and employee to the fundamental rights of liberty and property is, of course, recognized. But those rules, as guides of conduct, are not beyond alteration by legislation in the public interest. No person has a vested interest in any rule of law, entitling him to insist that it shall remain unchanged for his benefit. * * * The common law bases the employer's liability for injuries to the employee upon the ground of negligence; but negligence is merely the disregard of some duty imposed by law; and the nature and extent of the duty may be modified by legislation, with corresponding change in the test of negligence. Indeed, liability may be imposed for the consequences of a failure to comply with a statutory duty, irrespective of negligence in the ordinary sense; safety appliance acts being a familiar instance. * * *

The fault may be that of the employer himself, or—most frequently—that of another for whose conduct he is made responsible according to the maxim respondeat superior. In the latter case the employer may be entirely blameless, may have exercised the utmost human foresight to safeguard the employee; yet, if the alter ego, while acting within the scope of his duties, be negligent,—in disobedience, it may be, of the employer's positive and specific command,—the employer is answerable for the consequences. It cannot be that the rule embodied in the maxim is unalterable by legislation.

The immunity of the employer from responsibility to an employee for the negligence of a fellow employee is of comparatively recent origin, it being the product of the judicial conception that the probability of a fellow workman's negligence is one of the natural and ordinary risks of the occupation, assumed by the employee and presumably taken into account in the fixing of his wages. * * * The doctrine has prevailed generally throughout the United States, but with material differences in different jurisdictions respecting who should be deemed a fellow servant and who a vice principal or alter ego of the master, turning sometimes upon refined distinctions as to grades and departments in the employment. * * * It needs no argument to show that such a rule is subject to modification or abrogation by a state upon proper occasion.

The same may be said with respect to the general doctrine of assumption of risk. By the common law the employee assumes the risks normally incident to the occupation in which he voluntarily engages; other and extraordinary risks and those due to the employer's negligence he does not assume until made aware of them, or until they become so obvious that an ordinarily prudent man would observe and appreciate them; in either of which cases he does assume them, if he continues in the employment without obtaining from the employer an assurance that the matter will be remedied; but if he receive such an assurance, then, pending performance of the promise, the employee does not, in ordinary cases, assume the special risk. * * * Plainly, these rules, as guides of conduct and tests of liability, are subject to change in the exercise of the sovereign authority of the state.

So, also, with respect to contributory negligence. Aside from injuries intentionally self-inflicted, for which the statute under consideration affords no compensation, it is plain that the rules of law upon the subject, in their bearing upon the employer's responsibility, are subject to legislative change; for contributory negligence, again, involves a default in some duty resting on the employee, and his duties are subject to modification.

It may be added, by way of reminder, that the entire matter of liability for death caused by wrongful act, both within and without the relation of employer and employee, is a modern statutory innovation, in which the states differ as to who may sue, for whose benefit, and the measure of damages.

But it is not necessary to extend the discussion. This court repeatedly has upheld the authority of the states to establish by legislation departures from the fellow-servant rule and other common-law rules affecting the employer's liability for personal injuries to the employee. * * *

It is true that in the case of the statutes thus sustained there were reasons rendering the particular departures appropriate. Nor is it necessary, for the purposes of the present case, to say that a state might, without violence to the constitutional guaranty of "due process of law," suddenly set aside all common-law rules respecting liability as between employer and employee, without providing a reasonably just substitute. Considering the vast industrial organization of the state of New York, for instance, with hundreds of thousands of plants and millions of wage earners, each employer, on the one hand, having embarked his capital, and each employee, on the other, having taken up his particular mode of earning a livelihood, in reliance upon the probable permanence of an established body of law governing the relation, it perhaps may be doubted whether the state could abolish all rights of action, on the one hand, or all defenses, on the other, without setting up something adequate in their stead. No such question is here presented, and we intimate no opinion upon it. The statute under consideration sets aside one body of rules only to establish another system in its place. If the employee is no longer able to recover as much as before in case of being injured through the employer's negligence, he is entitled to moderate compensation in all cases of injury, and has a certain and speedy remedy without the difficulty and expense of establishing negligence or proving the amount of the damages. Instead of assuming the entire consequences of all ordinary risks of the occupation, he assumes the consequences, in excess of the scheduled compensation, of risks ordinary and extraordinary. On the other hand, if the employer is left without defense respecting the question of fault, he at the same time is assured that the recovery is limited, and that it goes directly to the relief of the designated beneficiary. And just as the employee's assumption of ordinary risks at common law presumably was taken into account in fixing the rate of wages, so the fixed responsibility of the employer, and the modified assumption of risk by the employee under the new system, presumably will be reflected in the wage scale. The act evidently is intended as a just settlement of a difficult problem, affecting one of the most important of social relations, and it is to be judged in its entirety. We have said enough to demonstrate that, in such an adjustment, the particular rules of the common law affecting the subject matter are not placed by the 14th Amendment beyond the reach of the lawmaking power of the state; and thus we are brought to the question whether the method of compensation that is established as a substitute transcends the limits of permissible state action.

We will consider, first, the scheme of compensation, deferring for the present the question of the manner in which the employer is required to secure payment.

Briefly, the statute imposes liability upon the employer to make compensation for disability or death of the employee resulting from accidental personal injury arising out of and in the course of the employment, without regard to fault as a cause except where the injury or death is occasioned by the employee's wilful intention to produce it, or where the injury results solely from his intoxication while on duty; it graduates the compensation for disability according to a prescribed scale based upon the loss of earning power, having regard to the previous wage and the character and duration of the disability; and measures the death benefits according to the dependency of the surviving wife, husband, or infant children. Perhaps we should add that it has no retrospective effect, and applies only to cases arising some months after its passage.

Of course, we cannot ignore the question whether the new arrangement is arbitrary and unreasonable, from the standpoint of natural justice. Respecting this, it is important to be observed that the act applies only to disabling or fatal personal injuries received in the course of hazardous employment in gainful occupation. Reduced to its elements, the situation to be dealt with is this: Employer and employee, by mutual consent, engage in a common operation intended to be advantageous to both; the employee is to contribute his personal services, and for these is to receive wages, and, ordinarily, nothing more; the employer is to furnish plant facilities, organization, capital, credit, is to control and manage the operation, paying the wages and other expenses, disposing of the product at such prices as he can obtain, taking all the profits, if any there be, and, of necessity, bearing the entire losses. In the nature of things, there is more or less of a probability that the employee may lose his life through some accidental injury arising out of the employment, leaving his widow or children deprived of their natural support; or that he may sustain an injury not mortal, but resulting in his total or partial disablement, temporary or permanent, with corresponding impairment of earning capacity. The physical suffering must be borne by the employee alone; the laws of nature prevent this from being evaded or shifted to another, and the statute makes no attempt to afford an equivalent in compensation. But, besides, there is the loss of earning power,—a loss of that which stands to the employee as his capital in trade. This is a loss arising out of the business, and, however it may be charged up, is an expense of the operation, as truly as the cost of repairing broken machinery or any other expense that ordinarily is paid by the employer. Who is to bear the charge? It is plain that, on grounds of natural justice, it is not unreasonable for the state, while relieving the employer from responsibility for damages measured by common-law standards and payable in cases where he or those for whose conduct he is answerable are found to be at fault, to require him to contribute a reasonable amount, and according to a reasonable and definite scale, by way of compensation for the loss of earning power incurred in the common enterprise, irrespective of the question of negligence, instead of leaving the entire loss to rest where it may chance to fall,—that is, upon the injured employee or his dependents. Nor can it be deemed arbitrary and unreasonable, from the standpoint of the employee's interest, to supplant a system under which he assumed the entire risk of injury in ordinary cases, and in others had a right to recover an amount more or less speculative upon proving facts of negligence that often were difficult to prove, and substitute a system under which, in all ordinary cases of accidental injury, he is sure of a definite and easily ascertained compensation, not being obliged to assume the entire loss in any case, but in all cases assuming any loss beyond the prescribed scale.

Much emphasis is laid upon the criticism that the act creates liability without fault. This is sufficiently answered by what has been said, but we may add that liability without fault is not a novelty in the law. The common-law liability of the carrier, of the innkeeper, or him who employed fire or other dangerous agency or harbored a mischievous animal, was not dependent altogether upon questions of fault or negligence. Statutes imposing liability without fault have been sustained. St. Louis & S.F.R. Co. v. Mathews, 165 U.S. 1, 22, 41 L.Ed. 611, 619, 17 Sup.Ct.Rep. 243. . . .

We have referred to the maxim, respondeat superior. In a well-known English case, Hall v. Smith, 2 Bing. 156, 160, 130 Eng.Reprint, 265, 9 J.B. Moore, 226, 2 L.J.C.P. 113, this maxim was said by Best, Ch. J., to be "bottomed on this principle, that he who expects to derive advantage from an act which is done by another for him, must answer for any injury which a third person may sustain from it." And this view has been adopted in New York. Cardot v. Barney, 63 N.Y. 281, 287, 20 Am.Rep. 533. The provision for compulsory compensation, in the act under consideration, cannot be deemed to be an arbitrary and unreasonable application of the principle, so as to amount to a deprivation of the employer's property without due process of law. The pecuniary loss resulting from the employee's death or disablement must fall somewhere. It results from something done in the course of an operation from which the employer expects to derive a profit. In excluding the question of fault as a cause of the injury, the act in effect disregards the proximate cause and looks to one more remote,—the primary cause, as it may be deemed,—and that is, the employment itself. For this, both parties are responsible, since they voluntarily engage in it as coadventurers, with personal injury to the employee as a probable and foreseen result. In ignoring any possible negligence of the employee producing or contributing to the injury, the lawmaker reasonably may have been influenced by the belief that, in modern industry, the utmost diligence in the employer's service is in some degree inconsistent with adequate care on the part of the employee for his own safety; that the more intently he devotes himself to the work, the less he can take precautions for his own security. And it is evident that the consequences of a disabling or fatal injury are precisely the same to the parties immediately affected, and to the community, whether the proximate cause be culpable or innocent. Viewing the entire matter, it cannot be pronounced arbitrary and unreasonable for the state to impose upon the employer the absolute duty of making a moderate and definite compensation in money to every disabled employee, or, in case of his death, to those who were entitled to look to him for support, in lieu of the common-law liability confined to cases of negligence.

This, of course, is not to say that any scale of compensation, however insignificant, on the one hand, or onerous, on the other, would be supportable. In this case, no criticism is made on the ground that the compensation prescribed by the statute in question is unreasonable in amount, either in general or in the particular case. Any question of that kind may be met when it arises. * * * We recognize that the legislation under review does measurably limit the freedom of employer and employee to agree respecting the terms of employment, and that it cannot be supported except on the ground that it is a reasonable exercise of the police power of the state. In our opinion it is fairly supportable upon that ground. And for this reason: The subject matter in respect of which freedom of contract is restricted is the matter of compensation for human life or limb lost or disability incurred in the course of hazardous employment, and the public has a direct interest in this as affecting the common welfare. * * *

We conclude that the prescribed scheme of compulsory compensation is not repugnant to the provisions of the 14th Amendment, and are brought to consider, next, the manner in which the employer is required to secure payment of the compensation. By § 50, this may be done in one of three ways: (a) State insurance; (b) insurance with an authorized insurance corporation or association; or (c) by a deposit of securities. * * *

The system of compulsory compensation having been found to be within the power of the state, it is within the limits of permissible regulation, in aid of the system, to require the employer to furnish satisfactory proof of his financial ability to pay the compensation, and to deposit a reasonable amount of securities for that purpose. * * *

Judgment affirmed.

Notes

1. Six years before *White* was decided, the New York Court of Errors and Appeals had invalidated the New York compulsory compensation statute of 1910 on the ground that it denied due process of law to both employers and employees by imposing liability without fault upon employers and by arbitrarily restricting the amount to be recovered by employees. Ives v. South Buffalo Ry. Co., 201 N.Y. 271, 94 N.E. 431 (1911). During the period between the *Ives* and *White* decisions most states adopted initial compensation statutes. Of thirty-three states, only *eight* imposed compulsory compen-

sation laws, and of these eight, *four* did so only after the state constitutions were amended. Consequently, under these early statutes, a choice was made available to employers and employees as to whether the compensation principle or the common law should apply.

2.   Because of initial concerns about the constitutionality of the workers' compensation principle, see e.g., Ives v. South Buffalo R. Co., 201 N.Y. 271, 94 N.E. 431 (1911), the legislatures of many states (e.g., California, Illinois, Kansas, Massachusetts, New Hampshire, New Jersey, and Wisconsin) applied the statutes only to those employers and employees who elected to accept their provisions. In time, the threat of unconstitutionality largely disappeared and most statutes now prescribe compulsory coverage (perhaps excepting New Jersey, South Carolina and Texas.) Even the remaining "elective" statutes strongly encourage employers to elect coverage by amending the common law to exclude or modify the three common law defenses in actions brought by employees against employers as to work injuries. The Report of the National Commission on State Workmen's Compensation Laws (1972) recommends (R.2.1) that workers' compensation be made compulsory in all respects. What choices, if any, does your state's current statute afford?

3.   *White* allayed fears of fundamental constitutional impediments and the compensation scheme thereafter proliferated rapidly. See also Mountain Timber Co. v. State of Washington, 243 U.S. 219, 37 S.Ct. 260, 61 L.Ed. 685 (1917) upholding the constitutionality of the Washington exclusive state fund type law (i.e., benefits are secured by a state fund financed by employers rather than by private insurance.) Nevertheless, specific provisions of statutes that arbitrarily excluded certain activities or workers from general schemes were thereafter occasionally declared unconstitutional as violative of equal protection or due process. Gallegos v. Glaser Crandell Co., 388 Mich. 654, 202 N.W.2d 786 (1972) (exclusion of agricultural workers paid on a piecework basis and agricultural workers who do not work 35 or more hours per week, held invalid), partially overruled by Eastway v. Eisenga, 420 Mich. 410, 362 N.W.2d 684 (1984); De Monaco by Giacobe v. Renton, 18 N.J. 352, 113 A.2d 782 (1955) (exclusion of newsboys; similar); and De Ayala v. Florida Farm Bureau Cas. Ins., 543 So.2d 204 (Fla.1989)(statute providing lesser death benefit for alien workers than non aliens denies equal protection). Cf., Price v. All American Engineering Co., 320 A.2d 336 (Del.1974) (statute retroactively increasing compensation benefits held constitutional). By 1920 all but eight states had adopted workers' compensation statutes, and the system became universal when Mississippi adopted a statute in 1949. As indicated in the next chapter, however, this does not mean that all employees are covered by compensation. For example, most statutes do not apply to employments with a small number of employees. As to those employments, the common law of torts, as amended if at all, continues to apply. For a summary of the historical development of Workers' Compensation, see Compendium on Workmen's Compensation, National Commission on State Workmen's Compensation Laws (1973), pp. 11–19.

4.   *White* upheld the constitutionality of the most extensive "tort reform" legislation that had ever been enacted. Does the quid pro quo analysis employed therein suggest that the legislature must, as a matter of due process, provide some alternative remedy or commensurate benefit before

taking away a person's common law tort remedy? In a 1978 decision that upheld the constitutionality of a statutory limitation on damages for nuclear accidents, the Supreme Court expressed doubt that a quid pro quo is always required. Duke Power Co. v. Carolina Environmental Study Group, Inc., 438 U.S. 59, 98 S.Ct. 2620, 57 L.Ed.2d 595 (1978). Therein, the Court stated: "Initially, it is not at all clear that the Due Process Clause in fact requires that a legislative enacted compensation scheme either duplicate the recovery at common law or provide a reasonable substitute remedy. However, we need not resolve this question here since the Price–Anderson Act does, in our view, provide a reasonably just substitute for the common-law or state tort law remedies it replaces." Id. at 88, 98 S.Ct. at 2638.

5. Despite *Duke Power*, the constitutional dimension of *White's* quid pro quo analysis resurfaced as a central feature of late twentieth century challenges to tort reform legislation. Compare Fein v. Permanente Medical Group, 38 Cal.3d 137, 211 Cal.Rptr. 368, 385 n. 18, 695 P.2d 665, 681 n. 18 (1985), appeal dism'd for want of a substantial federal question, 474 U.S. 892, 106 S.Ct. 214, 88 L.Ed.2d 215 (1985) (upholding the constitutionality of a $250,000 cap on noneconomic damages for medical malpractice and noting that "even if due process principles required some 'quid pro quo' to support [the cap] ... the preservation of a viable medical malpractice insurance industry in this state ... [is] an adequate benefit ...") and Smith v. Department of Insurance, 507 So.2d 1080, 1088 (Fla.1987) (striking down under the Florida constitution a $450,000 cap on noneconomic damages, in part, because the legislation did not provide "an alternative remedy and commensurate benefit" to individuals suffering greater injury). See also Samsel v. Wheeler Transport Services, Inc., 246 Kan. 336, 789 P.2d 541 (1990) (collecting cases), and Bair v. Peck, 248 Kan. 824, 811 P.2d 1176 (Kan. 1991), examining the limits of how far a legislature may go in limiting the rights of employees in an amendment to an existing remedial statute before the initial quid pro quo is invalidated.

6. Most states require employers to secure the payment of workers' compensation benefits in one of two ways: either to purchase insurance from a private insurance company or to qualify as self-insurers. Various methods have been adopted to compel the securing of insurance, including criminal penalties and enhancing the amount of compensation the employer must pay (e.g. California, Colorado, and Georgia). See § 54, Workmens' Compensation and Rehabilitation Law, App. B. A few states (e.g. Nevada, North Dakota, Oregon, Puerto Rico, and Wyoming) have established state insurance funds as the exclusive source for the payment of compensation claims. The funds are supported by assessments against employers and exclude the participation of private insurance companies. In a few other states employers are permitted either to participate in the state fund, to secure protection from a private insurer, or to establish themselves as self-insurers. See §§ 46–56, Workmens' Compensation and Rehabilitation Law, App. B. What choices have been made in the statute of your state?

7. At one time private insurers were commonly thought to have enjoyed a 40 percent profit factor on rates charged employers. More recent studies, however, suggest that when all relevant factors are taken into account, the true loading factor is probably less than 25 percent. It is also true that insurance rates tend to fluctuate in inverse relationship to prevail-

ing interest rates in the economy. Although private insurers incur costs of sales and taxes that are avoided by compulsory state funds, this approach is often opposed as an inappropriate governmental usurpation of a function that should be performed in the private sector. The Report of the National Commission on State Workmen's Compensation Laws (R.6.20) recommends leaving the choice of insuring method to each state.

SECTION 2. THE THEORY OF WORKERS' COMPENSATION

Workers' compensation rests upon the principle that employers and entrepreneurs who enjoy the economic benefits of businesses should ultimately bear the cost of the injuries and deaths that are incident to the manufacture, preparation and distribution of goods and services. This principle always applied to the accidental destruction of capital structures, machinery and equipment used to produce and distribute industrial goods and services. Fixing up and replacing these losses has always been treated as a cost of doing business without consideration of whether the losses resulted from someone's fault or from an unavoidable source. Workers' compensation applies the same principle, irrespective of fault, to injuries and deaths of the employees. The projected cost of these injuries and deaths can be secured in advance through the medium of insurance.

Under workers' compensation the element of personal fault loses all significance except in extreme cases. In theory, the employer initially absorbs the cost of work injuries, and ultimately passes it down the stream of commerce in the prices of products until it is spread in dilution among the consuming public. So long as all competing employment units in a given industry are uniformly affected, no producer gains any substantial competitive advantage or suffers any appreciable loss by reason of the uniform application of the compensation principle. On a more specific level, however, some employers are less able to pass on the costs than others. For example, an American producer of a good may not be able to raise the price to pay for added workers' compensation expenses if the good is in direct competition with similar goods manufactured in jurisdictions with lower workers' compensation costs. Nevertheless, these micro-economic imperfections have not defeated the universal adoption of workers' compensation laws and their economic consequences are outside the scope of this book's treatment of the legal aspects of the law in application.

If the compensation principle is to operate effectively, the costs of industrial injuries and deaths must be predictable and fixable in an amount that will not disrupt the exchange of goods and services. Thus, reasonable predictability and moderate cost are necessary from the broad economic viewpoint. They are also desirable from the personal point of view of employers and, apart from specific injuries, from the point of view of workers at large. Frequently, an injured employee's greatest need is for immediate cash to ameliorate the initial shock of the injury. If the amount of a compensation claim is so high as to encourage disputation, the delays of the old system and disputes about the validity of the compensation law compromise will be resurrected, perhaps undermining the humane purposes of compensation plan. Hence, the plan must compensate most injuries without dispute. From a general societal standpoint, it is also desirable to establish a moderate compensation rate that does not invite malingering and even feigned injury. Also, from a general economic point of view, if the overall cost of compensation constitutes a relatively small part of the total cost of production, more room is left for free play of competition among producers.

On the other hand, compensation levels must be high enough to provide adequate income to replace lost earnings of injured workers and to create an incentive for employers to adopt injury prevention measures. Otherwise employers would be tempted to take the risk of paying workers' compensation claims on the cheap instead of making more costly expenditures to avoid injuries.

Compensation differs from the conventional damage liability in two important respects: fault on the part of either employers or employees is made irrelevant; and compensation is made payable according to a prescribed and limited scheme. All modern workers' compensation statutes accept these two foundational premises, no matter how markedly they may differ in other particulars.

As noted in *White,* workers' compensation represents a compromise in which both employers and employees surrender certain advantages in order to gain others deemed to be more important. Employers give up the immunity that would otherwise apply in cases where they were not at fault, and employees surrender their former right to full damages in the few instances when they could recover under tort law and accept more modest assured benefits for all injuries and deaths. The importance of the *compromise* cannot be overemphasized, and the various statutes vary greatly with reference to the proper point of balance. Variables include: the amount of weekly compensation payments; the duration of the period in which compensation is to be paid; the amount of the death benefits; and, the amount of payable medical costs. The constitutionality of any compensation statute will be influenced by a court's evaluation of the basic point of compromise established in it. If a court believes that the statutory compromise unduly favors employers, it is tempted to restrike the balance by adopting an interpretation that favors workers. This ameliorating power is embodied in the oft-repeated maxim that remedial statutes are to be liberally construed to accomplish their intended purposes. Using it, a sympathetic court may transform a compensation act drawn in a spirit of extreme conservatism into a fairly liberal instrument. Conversely, courts may narrowly interpret an act that greatly favors workers, leaving employers little reason to complain. Much of the apparent unevenness and conflict in compensation decisions among the various jurisdictions may be attributed to the different point of balance established in different statutes. See, 1973 Compendium on Workmen's Compensation, pp. 21–26.

SECTION 3. COMPENSATION AS SOCIAL INSURANCE

Workers' compensation bears the imprint of social legislation in many important respects. The scheme contemplates that compensation is to be measured in terms of basic support rather than in terms of the true value of all aspects of a worker's personal loss. To this end, workers' compensation benefits are usually paid weekly in amounts proportioned to the amount of lost wages, rather than in a single lump sum. These payments are usually exempt from the claims of creditors. Nevertheless, some compensation statutes and cases tend to treat workers' compensation as merely a modified form of tort liability. As later chapters reveal, many statutes exclude (or limit) the payment of benefits to employees who at the time of accident are engaged in unlawful conduct, or who violate safety statutes, or who are intoxicated, or who intend to injure themselves or another worker. Moreover, courts sometimes avoid compensating an "undeserving" worker by administering the requirement that the accident "arise out of" the employment in a manner that excludes a particular injury. On the other hand, some statutes enhance the amount of compensation paid in respect of injuries caused by serious and willful misconduct of employers. All these adjustments based upon the content of behavior are plainly derogatory of the pure compensation principle, which would ignore the element of blameworthiness and allocate all costs of industrial injuries and deaths to employers and, ultimately, the consumers of goods and services. Nevertheless, they reflect the fact that compensation statutes, like all others, must be applied by human decision makers who are apt to take into account extremely aberrant behavior in construing the balances and compromises embodied within them.

Some courts manifest an almost irresistible urge to assimilate the compensation statutes into tort law. This is partially explained by the fact that employees in many jurisdictions obtain compensation by making a claim against the employer or the latter's insurer. In some jurisdictions (e.g., Alabama, Louisiana, Tennessee, Wyoming) compensation claims are asserted in court just like any other litigated matter, and nearly all the laws permit compromises between employers and employees. Furthermore, the scheme is somewhat adversarial in nature even though fault is immaterial; that is, the injured worker attempts to extract money directly from the employer. This adversarial context can be highlighted by contrasting it to a general social welfare system in which the injured worker's claim is made against a benefits agency and does not directly involve the employer. This mode is epitomized in the New Zealand plan, which completely assimilates workers' compensation into a national comprehensive social security scheme that is financed by general taxation rather than by private insurance. Similarly, the British worker's compensation system is now administered within the social security system of Great Britain. Social Security Act of 1975 (c. 14); Chapter IV. An English worker who is hurt on the job is eligible for more compensation benefits than if hurt while unemployed or injured outside employment, but the benefits are obtained from the national insurance fund. The additional money is provided through a separate Industrial Injuries Fund financed by contributions from employers, employees, and the general treasury. It is also true, however, that the current British plan apparently poses no bar to tort suits against employers who are negligent in causing work injuries. Does your state's statute permit this? A comparison among objectives and methods in American, British and New Zealand plans is found in 1 A. Larson, The Law of Workmen's Compensation (1990) §§ 3.10–3.40.

Although, as noted above, some statutes employ courts as the administering agencies, workers' compensation claims are more generally administered initially by an administrative tribunal. The goal is to provide a more expert forum for the resolution of compensation disputes than is afforded by courts of general trial jurisdiction. This specialization permits the proof of facts without resort to technical rules of evidence, and the evaluation of specialized and recurring fact situations, particularly on medical questions, by an expert fact-finder (the hearing officer) who possesses more training and experience in dealing with them than lay juries would. Moreover, unlike court adjudication, administrative determination of compensation awards provides a mechanism to oversee the payment of continuing awards, and provides an administrative system for reporting accidents, rehabilitating injured workers, administering the insurance features of the act, studying the overall performance of the plan, and issuing periodic reports and recommendations for legislative attention.

In the United States the interrelationship between workers' compensation systems, which are largely privately financed, and the ever-expanding social security system has become complex. The difficulty was enhanced in 1958 by the enactment of the federal social security disability benefits plan referred to in Chapter 1. The same National Commission on State Workmen's Compensation Laws that in 1972 recommended that social security disability benefits be reduced in the presence of workers' compensation benefits also recommended that workers' compensation death benefits be reduced by the amount of social security benefits paid to the deceased worker's family (R.3.27). The Commission rejected a proposal to disassemble workers' compensation and to assign the components to other programs, and also rejected proposals to assign permanent total disability claims exclusively to the federal social security system, to assign temporary disability cases exclusively to state temporary disability insurance programs, to administer the medical component under an expanded Medicare program, and to assign rehabilitation programs to state departments of vocational rehabilitation. This package was deemed to be too complex for resolving current conflicts. Report of the National Commission on State Workmen's Compensation Laws (1972), page 120. Although a variety of public and private programs offer income and medical protection to disabled workers, the extent of overlap between workers' compensation and other benefits programs, such as federal disability and old-age insurance benefits, unemployment compensation insurance benefits, veterans' benefits, FELA, Jones Act, and no-fault automobile compensation plans, is not believed to be large. 1973 Compendium on Workmen's Compensation, page 58.

Despite the economic and administrative advantages of workers' compensation, the scheme has its limitations and is far from uniform in detail among the states. The Report of the National Commission summarizes five objectives against which specific programs should be evaluated: broad coverage; protection against interruption of income; sufficient medical care and rehabilitative services; encouragement of safety; and prompt and efficient administration of an effective delivery system. (Report, at 117.) The Commission deemed many state plans to be inadequate by these measures and the general failure of state legislatures to rectify shortcomings led to the introduction of federal legislation (Senate Bill 420, 96th Congress, 1st Session) to prescribe minimum standards for state workers' compensation plans. If this had been enacted, it would have constituted a partial federal take-over of a traditionally state-controlled area of the state system. Opinions differ as to the desirability and propriety of federal intervention. See Workmen's Compensation: National Commission on State Workmen's Compensation Laws: Import for Oklahoma (1973) 26 Okla.L.R. 453; Potential Federalization of State Workmen's Compensation Laws—The Kansas Response (1976) 15 Washburn L.J. 251. So far, Congress has not adopted legislation of this sort.

SECTION 4. THE ACCEPTANCE OF WORKERS' COMPENSATION

Workers' compensation is now a stable part of the legal and economic employment enterprise throughout the United States. Although the details of the laws are being constantly adjusted, no proposal to repeal them or to replace them with drastically different plans is likely to receive generous attention anywhere. Hence, workers' compensation is a given, and the basic compromise, discussed above, is accepted. For these reasons, little writing is to be found about what would be a better way for dealing with industrial injuries and death.

Curiously enough, the current level of acceptance does not reflect the initial lack of enthusiasm for the plan upon its emergence as law. The following excerpt describes the reaction in England, which was not unlike the reaction in the United States. Particularly noteworthy is the lukewarm reception given workers' compensation by organized labor:

"THE SIGNIFICANCE OF WORKMEN'S COMPENSATION[1]

"The Workmen's Compensation Act was greeted in emotional terms by its supporters and opponents. The latter anticipated rising unemployment, deteriorating industrial relations, destruction of self-reliance and ruination for the friendly societies. Some felt it would cripple the

---

1. P. Bartrip, Workmen's Compensation   and Social Policy (1987), pp. 11–12.
in Twentieth Century Britain; Law, History

international competitiveness of British industry, despite the fact that other countries, notably Germany, already had similar or more comprehensive legislation. On the other hand, its champions considered it to be 'a great boon' to workers and 'one of the leading enactments of the century'. One historian, echoing a [union] president, terms the Act 'revolutionary' and has even gone so far as to claim: 'There can be no doubt that the Workmen's Compensation Act was one of the most important ever passed by Parliament'. In 1897 the significance of the Act was only imperfectly understood. * * * It may be noted here however that in terms of achievements on the factory floor, as opposed to the principles it enshrined, the word 'revolutionary' is an inappropriate description of the 1897 Act. At first it applied to only a minority of workers; except for coal miners after 1934 it provided no guarantee of compensation. The coming of workmen's compensation certainly did not place accident victims in the 'circumstances of independence and luxury' anticipated by some. Nevertheless, it was a great step forward. In comparison with the position in the 1830s the injured worker, relieved of the necessity to prove fault, enjoyed an immeasurably improved position.

"According to William Beveridge, workmen's compensation was 'the pioneer system of social security'. In one sense this was an accurate characterisation, for the Act established a working class entitlement or right, that is, to a measure of financial security in the event of work injury, which corresponded to other rights won in the course of the nineteenth century such as the vote, freedom to form trade unions and to work in reasonable conditions. Moreover, by recognising that there should be public solutions to social problems the Act furthered the idea that the beneficiaries of a worker's labour owed him support in such circumstances as illness and old-age. As a speaker at the 1898 [union] conference put it: 'if ... the national prosperity depends on the well-being of the worker, the necessary corollary is that the state should care for him in times of sickness ... [and] old age'. Thus, although passed by a Conservative Government, the Workmen's Compensation Act can, in some ways, be viewed as a forerunner of the Liberal Welfare Reforms (which included the Workmen's Compensation Act, 1906) of the Edwardian era. In other respects, however, the Act was decidedly different, particularly in that it provided no public funds and a very limited administrative function for government. Furthermore, the terms of the 1897 Act, whereby claims were to be against individual employers who would be entitled to oppose claimants in the courts, meant that the workmen's compensation system would, in many respects, be similar to the tort system.

"Finally, it is worth asking why a Workmen's Compensation Act became law in 1897. The question is particularly intriguing in that the groups one might expect to have pressed for it, the [coalition of union] and the individual unions, were, * * * no more than lukewarm towards the reform. They claimed to be uninterested in compensation as opposed to industrial safety. But if trades unionists were not behind the Act, who was? In general terms the Act reflected, as some later welfare legislation did, the growing influence of the enfranchised working classes and the competition among the political parties for their support. More specifically, emphasis needs to be given to the role of individuals such as Ashley, Chadwick and Chamberlain. But their views gained legislative acceptance only because they found support elsewhere. In fact, paradoxically, Chamberlain's compensation ideas were received with enthusiasm by few parties. They were influential because they represented an acceptable compromise to an intractable problem. Lawyers, who first raised the insurance solution, liked it because it did not interfere with the sanctity of the common law as employers' liability reform threatened to do. Business interests came to accept workmen's compensation as a necessary evil, better at least than the alternative of a tough liability law. The Conservative Party saw it as a means of outmanoeuvring the Liberals and attracting working class support. Labour leaders grudgingly supported it as a benefit which was on offer whereas their favoured outcome was not practical politics. Workmen's compensation was, therefore, the solution which least divided the various interest groups.

"That it came about in 1897 can only be explained by reference to the reform process over more than two decades, to the example set by other nations, especially Germany, and to a growing realisation that if Britain were to compete with its international rivals more would have to be done to promote national efficiency. Part of the answer to this was greater investment in welfare."

SECTION 5. THEORY, POLICY, AND POLITICS

There is relatively little dispute about general theory and objectives of a workers' compensation system. The theory is one of cost internalization—the cost of workplace injuries and diseases should be internalized by the enterprise and reflected in the price of goods and services. As stated by the National Commission in 1972, a workers' compensation system should: (1) provide broad coverage of employees and work-related injuries and diseases; (2) provide substantial protection against interruption of income; (3) provide sufficient medical care and rehabilitation services; (4) encourage workplace safety; and (5) deliver benefits in an efficient and effective manner. (Report at 117–18).

Can all of these goals be achieved at the same time? For example, what is the appropriate level of benefits that provides both employer and employee with sufficient incentives to avoid workplace injuries and at the same time provides for sufficient medical care and substantial protection against income loss? If benefit levels are increased to provide for greater protection against income loss, will employers and their insurers contest a greater percentage of claims and thereby reduce the efficiency of the system? These questions are difficult to answer as a matter of economic theory. In the real world of workers' compensation, the answers are provided by legislators, administrators, and judges in decisions wherein theoretical niceties often give way to political realities.

The initial prevailing view was that workers' compensation statutes are remedial in character and, accordingly, are to be liberally construed in favor of providing benefits to injured workers. See, e.g., Alvarez v. Liberty House, Inc., 85 Hawai'i 275, 942 P.2d 539, 542 (Haw.1997). The politics in much social legislation in the late twentieth century turned away from remedies and toward cost cutting. In some states this movement resulted in statutory abrogation of pro-compensation liberality in favor of a statement of neutrality. This excerpt from the New Mexico statute is illustrative:

> It is the intent of the legislature in creating the workers' compensation administration that the laws administered by it to provide a workers' benefit system be interpreted to assure the quick and efficient delivery of indemnity and medical benefits to injured and disabled workers at a reasonable cost to the employers who are subject to the provisions of the Workers' Compensation Act … and the New Mexico Occupational Disease Disablement Law. It is the specific intent of the legislature that benefit claims cases be decided on their merits and that the common law rule of "liberal construction" based on the supposed "remedial" basis of workers' benefits legislation shall not apply in these cases. The workers' benefit system in New Mexico is based on a mutual renunciation of common law rights and defenses by employers and employees alike. Accordingly, the legislature declares that the Workers' Compensation Act and the New Mexico Occupational Disease Disablement Law are not remedial in any sense and are not to be given a broad liberal construction in favor of the claimant or employee on the one hand, nor are the rights and interests of the employer to be favored over those of the employee on the other hand.

N.M.S.A. § 52–5–1 (1998). Florida adopted a similar provision, § 440.015 Fla. Stat. (1997), as did Colorado, but the Colorado measure was quickly repealed. See, Co. St. 8–40–102 (1994) (Historical and Statutory Notes).

The remainder of this book focuses on doctrinal aspects of workers' compensation law, which is the area of greatest concern for most attorneys. The student, however, should evaluate the cases and the statutes by reference to compensation theory and the underlying social policies.

Chapter 3

THE EMPLOYER–EMPLOYEE RELATIONSHIP

SECTION 1. INTRODUCTION

Because workers' compensation is designed to provide benefits only to employees and their survivors, the student must understand what employment means as contemplated under the statutes. Because employment is a particular kind of contractual relationship, whether or not one person is an employee of another ultimately depends upon whether a contract of employment was entered into by them. In most instances, the employment relation is not disputed. Often a written application and acceptance will memorialize it. Nevertheless, many injuries occur under circumstances in which one person appears to be working for another in some capacity but no contract has ever been overtly executed or even discussed by the parties. Under these circumstances the courts are left to interpret the factual context of what transpired and whether it satisfies the legal criteria of an employment contract as opposed to some other relationship.

In the days before the industrial revolution, employment was referred to as the master-servant relationship, reflecting the close personal relationship and propinquity between the employer and employee. The elements of that relationship were well known to judges and lawyers before the inception of the compensation movement and were inevitably imported into it. A leading factor has always been whether the purported master had the legal right to control the details of how the purported servant did assigned work. If so, the master-servant relationship existed; if not, some other relationship existed, such as principal-independent contractor. The outcome of this test often determined whether the master was legally liable to some third person for harm done by the negligent act of someone else in performing the master's work. If the actor was a servant, then the master was vicariously liable under the *respondeat superior* doctrine. If an independent contractor, then the independent contractor, but not the master, was liable.

As would be expected, rules applicable to contract formation, torts and agency were transplanted into compensation law without much debate as to the appropriateness of application in the new scheme. This was particularly true of the "control" test of *respondeat superior*, whose use in compensation cases produced much confusion in early decisions. The courts were slow to accept the truth that the relatively narrow scope of the common law master-servant relationship did not conform to the broad workers' compensation goal of distributing the cost of employment injuries through the economic system. In more recent years, the ramifications of the employment relationship have been expanded by the emergence of other pieces of social legislation, such as unemployment compensation, wage and hour legislation, social security, and anti-discrimination legislation, all of which tend to broaden to some extent the meaning of the employment relationship. The social welfare goals of these statutes lead many courts to reach beyond the strict tests of the master-servant relationship in determining who is an employee. One court, for example, applied a "totality of the circumstances" test, including especially "the extent of the economic dependence of the worker upon the business he serves and the relationship of his work to the operation of that business," to award workers' compensation benefits to a claimant who would hardly have been a servant under the common law. Biger v. Erwin, 108 N.J.Super. 293, 261 A.2d 151, 154 (1970) (jockey for only one race held to be employee of owner who was in the business of racing horses.) This broadening of the reach of the employment relationship, even under statutes that purport to apply common law tests, is common.

The social welfare character of workers' compensation becomes more understandable as the student tackles questions pertaining to which employments are included within the coverage of the statutes. Some employments readily lend themselves to transmitting the cost of employment injuries and deaths down the channels of commerce to the consuming public; while other employments, such as domestic service, hirings by charitable and religious undertakings, and perhaps some agricultural employments, do not fit the theory. Furthermore, because workers' compensation requires employers to secure compensation benefits in advance by purchasing insurance, many employments are too small, too transitory, or otherwise find it too difficult to administer workers' compensation, to be brought within the schemes. Legislatures do not want the imposition of workers' compensation to be an engine for destroying employments of these kinds and have often exempted them by classification schemes. These exemptions create many specific disputes as to whether coverage applies to a particular injury.

In addition, considerable legislative and judicial ingenuity has been expended in fixing the boundary between employment and other similar relationships that fall outside the coverage of the statutes. These include principal and independent contractor, buyer and seller, lessor and lessee, and even debtor and creditor. Furthermore, mixed relationships sometimes present themselves. For example, an employee may participate in the profits (and possibly losses) of the employing enterprise either as a stockholder, a corporate officer, or a partner. Should these special relationships affect whether or not worker's compensation is payable to the worker? Should the worker's personal capacity to purchase personal health and accident insurance have a bearing on whether workers' compensation should apply?

SECTION 2. THE CONTRACT OF EMPLOYMENT

JOHNSON v. CITY OF ALBIA
Supreme Court of Iowa, 1927.
203 Iowa 1171, 212 N.W. 419.

FAVILLE, J. On November 15, 1923, the plaintiff was in the employ of the defendant, as the engineer in charge of its pumping plant. He had been engaged in such employment for the seven years preceding. On the morning of November 15, he notified the chairman of the waterworks committee that he would terminate his services that evening. Pursuant to such notice, the committee immediately made arrangements with one Seibert to take the job thus to be vacated by the plaintiff. The plaintiff operated the engine and pumps until 7:15 p.m., at which time he had the tanks filled. At that hour he left the plant for home. On the way home he met Seibert and advised him where he would find the key. Under plaintiff's contract of employment, he was furnished with a residence near the plant and with a place to keep his cow and his portable garage. He had vacated the residence on November 15, and had moved his family into another house down town. This latter was the residence to which he came after leaving the plant at 7:15 p.m. There still remained upon his employer's premises his cow, his portable garage and a car therein, and his tools, consisting of a sledge, a screwdriver, and three wrenches. * * *

Upon the testimony of the plaintiff himself, the defendant predicates its contention that the relation of employer and employe between plaintiff and defendant was fully terminated on the evening of November 15. The accident under consideration occurred on the morning of November 16. The plaintiff returned to the plant at 8 o'clock that morning, solely for the purpose of getting his tools. He found Seibert there, and found him in trouble with the machinery. He was unable to start one of the pumps. This pump had a defective valve, which required a peculiar manipulation in order to start it. This defect was explained by the plaintiff to Seibert. Seibert requesting the assistance of the plaintiff to start the pump, he went into the pumphouse and into the pit where the pumps were located for the purpose of rendering such assistance. While engaged in such attempt, he was accidently caught in some gearing and lost his left arm as a result. The tools which plaintiff left at the pumphouse on the evening of November 15 were his personal property and the necessary tools which he used in the operation of the plant. He testified that he left them there on that evening that they might be used in case of necessity. So far as appears, they were the only tools at the plant which were available for use at the time the accident occurred on the morning of November 16. The purpose of the plaintiff in going to the plant on the morning of November 16, was solely to get his tools and to make preparations for removing the rest of his property, and incidentally to milk his cow.

The trial court decided the case solely on the ground that a fact question was involved, and that the order of the Industrial Commissioner was conclusive on the court. If there is a disputed question of fact, the decision of the commissioner is binding on the court. The conclusions of law of the commissioner on undisputed facts are, however, proper questions for the determination of the court. Three questions appear to be involved: (1) Was the employe still within the scope of his employment at the time of the injury when he returned to get his tools? (2) Did an emergency arise at the time which called for assistance to the new engineer and clothed him with sufficient authority to bind the city in employing the workman at that time? (3) Is there evidence of such a custom among engineers that the outgoing engineer shall assist the incoming one as made the workman an employe at the time?

I.   Was appellee still an employe under his original employment?

At the time the injury occurred, Code Supplement of 1913 was in force, and section 2477m16, par. (b) is as follows:

> " 'Workman' is used synonymously with 'employe' and means any person who has entered into the employment of or works under contract of service express or implied or apprenticeship for an employer."

In Knudson v. Jackson, 191 Iowa 947, 183 N.W. 391, we considered this paragraph of the statute in considering the meaning of the word "employe," and in said case reviewed the authorities at length, and held that we cannot enlarge the provisions of the statute and that an employe within the meaning of this act, "in order to come under this statute, must have a contract of service, express or implied, with the employer who is sought to be charged with liability." The question at once, then, in the case, is whether or not the appellee at the time of the injury, to wit, on November 16, had a contract of employment, express or implied, with the appellant. According to his own testimony he had quit on the 15th of November. He had notified the waterworks committee of the city council in the forenoon of that day that he would quit, and he turned in his key. There is no claim that he was ever employed by the city council thereafter. He came to the place of his employment for a purely personal reason, namely, to secure his tools that were located on the premises. He did not come there to assist the new engineer or to do any work. At the request of the new employe, he attempted to assist him in the operation of the machinery on the place. This was purely voluntary on his part. There is no intimation in the record that any person authorized to engage employes for the city even so much as knew that the appellee was on the premises, and there is no suggestion that any one in behalf of the appellant requested, or in any manner authorized, the appellee to assist the regular employe of the appellant who was then in charge of the work.[1]

The appellee places great reliance upon the following quotation from 1 Honnold on Workmen's Compensation, p. 353, where the rule is stated as follows:

> "An employe is under the protection of the Compensation Act even after his *discharge,* providing he be injured upon the premises of the employer while remaining there for reasons connected with his former employment."

This quotation from Honnold is supported by a single case in the footnote, to wit, Goering v. Brooklyn Mining Company, 2 Cal.I.A.C.Dec. 124. In that case an employe a few minutes after being discharged, was cleaning up his work preparing to leave the premises. He was injured by an accident, and it was held that such accident occurred in the course of his employment, and that he was entitled to compensation.[2] Neither the text nor the authority sustaining it are broad enough to support the appellee's contention in the instant case. It is obvious that a different situation is presented where, without the knowledge of the former employer, a discharged employe, the next day or later, after he has left the premises and terminated his contract of employment, re-enters the premises for purposes of his own, and voluntarily assists the new employe in performing his work. * * *

III. The appellee claims that at the time of his employment and service there was a general custom in that locality between engineers and their employers that upon the termination of the service of the employed engineer it was his duty to impart reasonable instruction and extend reasonable aid to his successor in the operation of the plant. The Industrial Commissioner made no finding that there was such a rule and custom prevailing in that locality. His decision does not rest upon any proof of custom. In fact he does not refer to the question in his award, so we have no decision whatever upon this question, and hence nothing to review. In any event, he could not have found that such was established under the record in this case. Furthermore, there is no contention that, if a custom existed as claimed, it was known to the appellant, or that it was so general that appellant was bound to know of it. In the Mitchell case the discharged workman had certain duties to perform in direct connection with finishing or cleaning up his work, under specific orders. His employment and orders included this very work and while engaged

---

1. [**Editor's Note.**] Generally an ordinary workman has no authority to hire. Roach v. J.S. Bryan & Sons Corp. (1938) 184 Okl. 211, 86 P.2d 304; Board of Com'rs of Wells County v. Merritt (1924) 81 Ind. App. 488, 143 N.E. 711 (workman injured several hours after undertaking his indisposed brother's job, but before any representative of the employer had knowledge of the substitution). Conversely, an employee cannot be transferred to the employ of another without his consent. Holloway v. G.O. Cooley & Sons (1946) 208 S.C. 234, 37 S.E.2d 666 (employer sold his business without knowledge of his employee).

2. [**Editor's Note.**] Accord, Peterson v. Moran (1952) 111 Cal.App.2d 766, 245 P.2d 540. Cf. Nash v. Longville Lbr. Co. (1921) 148 La. 943, 88 So. 226 (suit in tort by employee who quit job due to reckless action of foreman and subsequently was attacked by him with an axe).

in it he was injured. It was also shown to be the custom that he should do this work. Not so in the case at bar. The appellee had quit the employment the day before the injury. He had surrendered his key to the premises. He was not there to complete any unfinished work. He did not go there at all for the purpose of aiding the new engineer. He went there *solely* for his own private purpose—to get his tools. While there the new engineer asked him to assist him in starting the pump. This he tried to do and was injured.

However deplorable the accident, the claimant cannot recover unless he comes within the class provided for by the statute.

There is no disputed fact question in the case. Upon the facts as found by the Industrial Commissioner the claimant was not within the coverage of the statute.

The judgment must be reversed.

EVANS, C. J. (dissenting). I am not able to concur in the majority opinion. In my judgment it presents a too restricted view of the operation of the Workmen's Compensation Act, and emphasizes the letter in violation of the spirit thereof. * * *

The plaintiff pleaded, and the evidence tended to prove, that at the time of plaintiff's employment and service there prevailed a general custom or rule in that locality as between engineers and their employers, that upon the termination of the services of the employed engineer, it was his duty to impart reasonable instruction and extend reasonable aid to his successor in the operation of the plant. It is the contention of the plaintiff that he was fulfilling his obligation in obedience to this rule at the time of his injury, and that, for the purpose of such service and within its scope, he was still an employe of the defendant within the meaning of the Compensation Act, notwithstanding that he had already quit the general service of the employer. Here is the pivot of the case. If the contract of employment had been in writing, and if such writing had imposed such obligation upon the employe, it would hardly be claimed but that the obligation to perform such duty rested upon him, notwithstanding he had terminated his general service. The contract, however, was oral. Even an oral agreement to such effect would have been equally binding upon him. But no such express agreement was made. Nor is there any evidence of *any* express agreement in the oral contract of employment. It appears to have been informal and to rest upon legal implication. If there was a general custom, as contended by the plaintiff, and as found by the Industrial Commissioner, it would become a part of the contract of employment by legal implication. If the rule established by the prevailing custom became a part of the contract of employment, then it has an important bearing upon the question whether the relation of employer and employe was terminated on the evening of November 15.

The termination of the relation of employer and employe, within the meaning of the Compensation Act, is often, if not usually, a mixed question of law and fact. It is not necessarily accomplished by mere words, however direct and positive they may be. A discharge may be peremptory and a resignation may be immediate and abrupt, and yet for certain purposes that are incidental to the termination of the employment, and for a reasonable time the relation may continue; that is to say, there may be duties owing by one to the other, or privileges due to one or the other, which are incidental to the termination of the employment. The law allows a reasonable time for the performance of such duties, or the exercise of such privileges. In the performance of such duties or the exercise of such privileges within such reasonable time, the relation of employer and employe is deemed to continue within the meaning of the Compensation Act. For instance it is quite universally held that a discharged employe has a right, after his discharge, to enter upon the premises of his employer for the purpose of removing his tools. While so engaged within a reasonable time, he is deemed an employe and not a trespasser, nor a licensee, and is under the protection of the Compensation Act. Not only so, but he is bound by the limitations of the Compensation Act, and may not resort to a common-law remedy for injuries, which he may suffer at such time. * * *

* * * When he got to the pumphouse, he found Seibert in trouble and apparently helpless to furnish the necessary amount of water to supply the town. Seibert, as a witness for the defendant, described his own state of mind as follows: "When Johnson came up and inquired how everything was, I swore." It is clear that Johnson at this juncture found Seibert in need of instruction and help, even though he had not expected to find him in such state. It was his clear duty under the implications of his contract of employment to render such reasonable assistance as he could. In responding in good faith to that duty, he was to that extent an employe and within the protection of the Compensation Act. Such was our holding in the Mitchell case. In that case the duties, which the employe was performing were not imposed by any express provisions of his contract, but were imposed by a general custom, which prevailed in that locality, and which became a part of his contract by legal implication only. Such is the situation in the case at bar. So far as the facts of this case are concerned, I have taken no account of conflicting evidence. The facts which I have assumed, all have the support of evidence and I would give effect to the finding of the Commissioner accordingly.

I would affirm.

Notes

1. See also, Roush v. Town of Esmond, 73 S.D. 406, 43 N.W.2d 547 (failure to follow the statutory procedure for executing a municipal contract of hire resulted in a denial of compensation to person informally employed by officials to remove abandoned electric poles and wires; dissent); State v. Industrial Com'n, 250 Wis. 140, 26 N.W.2d 273 (1947) (student nurse who failed to comply with civil service regulations was not an employee of state, even though working in state hospital). Can these situations be distinguished from illegal employments, discussed infra?

2. Courts sometimes rely on other aspects of the law of contracts to resolve workers' compensation disputes. Compensation may be denied, for example, when a contract of hire exists but is voidable because of the employee's fraudulent misrepresentations in the employment application. See, e.g., Georgia Electric Co. v. Rycroft, 259 Ga. 155, 378 S.E.2d 111 (1989) (misrepresented prior injuries). Compensation will be allowed, however, if the fraudulent misrepresentations are unconnected with the injury. See, e.g., Byrd's Electric & Plumbing, Inc. v. Johnson, 199 Ga.App. 621, 405 S.E.2d 548 (1991).

3. At one time, many states closely restricted or prohibited contracts between spouses. Bendler v. Bendler, 3 N.J. 161, 69 A.2d 302 (1949), overruled by Romeo v. Romeo, 84 N.J. 289, 418 A.2d 258 (1980), examined the effect of these restrictions upon compensation rights. These restrictions are now largely or wholly repudiated. See, e.g., Flynn v. State Compensation Com'r, 141 W.Va. 445, 91 S.E.2d 156 (1956).

ASPEN HIGHLANDS SKIING CORPORATION
v. APOSTOLOU

Supreme Court of Colorado, En Banc, 1994.
866 P.2d 1384.

JUSTICE LOHR delivered the Opinion of the Court.

We granted certiorari to review the decision of the Colorado Court of Appeals in Aspen Highlands Skiing Corporation v. Apostolou, 854 P.2d 1357 (Colo.App.1992), which sustained an award of workers' compensation benefits to John J. Apostolou. The issue on appeal was whether under the facts of this case, Apostolou was an "employee" of Aspen Highlands Skiing Corporation (Highlands), and therefore entitled to such benefits, when he was injured while working for Highlands on the ski patrol. We affirm the judgment of the court of appeals.

I. John J. Apostolou was employed by Highlands as a part-time ski instructor during the 1989–1990 ski season. As part of his compensation for this work, he was given a photographic identification card (photo ID) that enabled him to ski free at any time at Aspen Highlands.

In January 1990, Highlands told its ski instructors that it needed persons with CPR qualifications [Ed., "cardiopulmonary resuscitation"] and first aid training to work on ski patrol. The ski patrol consisted of two categories of workers: professionals, who worked full-time and were paid a salary, and other workers, who worked part-time, received no monetary compensation, but were given photo IDs that enabled them to ski free at any time at Aspen Highlands.

Apostolou mentioned that he had the requisite qualifications and was referred to the ski patrol director. Because he already had a photo ID, Apostolou negotiated an agreement with the ski patrol director to receive daily ski passes for his girlfriend in exchange for his ski patrol work. The agreement entitled the girlfriend to as many daily ski passes as she was able to use during the period that Apostolou performed ski patrol duties. Each pass had a retail value of $36.00, and Apostolou would not have agreed to work on the ski patrol if the arrangement had not been made.

On February 20, 1990, Apostolou fell while on ski patrol duty, injuring his knees. A week later he underwent surgery on his right knee. As a result of his injuries, Apostolou was unable to continue working as either a ski instructor or a ski patrol person. Apostolou filed a workers' compensation claim. Highlands and its workers' compensation insurer, Colorado Compensation Insurance Authority (CCIA), contested the claim, asserting that Apostolou was not an employee at the time of his injuries, but was a volunteer, and as such, not entitled to workers' compensation benefits. After a hearing, an administrative law judge (ALJ) concluded that Apostolou was working as an employee of Highlands at the time he was injured and ordered Highlands and CCIA to provide compensation. The Industrial Claim Appeals Panel affirmed the ALJ's order, and the Colorado Court of Appeals, with one judge dissenting, in turn affirmed the order of the Panel. See Aspen Highlands Skiing Corp. v. Apostolou, 854 P.2d 1357 (Colo.App.1992). We granted certiorari to determine whether the ALJ erred in determining that Apostolou was an employee of Highlands at the time he was injured and therefore was entitled to workers' compensation benefits.

II.   In Colorado, workers' compensation legislation "provides exclusive remedies for compensation of an employee by an employer for work-related injury." Triad Painting Co. v. Blair, 812 P.2d 638, 641 (Colo. 1991). Under the Workmen's Compensation Act of Colorado (the Act), an employee is entitled to receive compensation for an injury incurred while "performing service arising out of and in the course of his employment," s 8–52–102(1)(b), 3B C.R.S. (1986), and "proximately caused by an injury ... arising out of and in the course of his employment ...," ... An employee, as relevant here, is defined as "[e]very person in the service of any ... private corporation ... under any contract of hire, express or implied ... but not including any persons who are expressly excluded from [the Act]...." s 8–41–106(1)(b), 3B C.R.S. (1986) (now appearing at s 8–40–202(1)(b), 3B C.R.S. (1993 Supp.)). In 1989, the Colorado legislature amended the Act to exclude a class of persons from the definition of "employee" by adding the following provision: " '[E]mployee' excludes any person who volunteers his time or services as a ski patrol person, a ski instructor, ..." ...

We first consider whether Apostolou was an "employee" of Highlands under the basic definition of that term. We then address Highlands' argument that Apostolou was not an employee because he was not paid "wages" as that term is defined in the Act. Finally, we address Highlands' contention that Apostolou volunteered his services and therefore was among the persons specifically excluded from the definition of "employee" by the 1989 amendment.

A.   The initial question is whether Apostolou satisfied the basic definition of "employee" as a person "in the service of" Highlands "under any contract of hire, express or implied." See s 8–41–106(1)(b).

In Denver Truck Exchange v. Perryman, 134 Colo. 586, 307 P.2d 805 (1957), we noted that "[a] contract of hire is subject to the same rules as other contracts even though workmen's compensation laws are liberally construed in our state." Id. at 593, 307 P.2d at 810. We also stated: " 'A contract is an agreement which creates an obligation. Its essentials are competent parties, subject matter, a legal consideration, mutuality of agreement, and mutuality of obligation.' " Id. at 592, 307 P.2d at 810 (quoting 17 C.J.S. 310, s 1a). A contract of hire may be formed even though not every formality attending commercial contractual arrangements is observed as long as the fundamental elements of contract formation are present. . . .

In Hall v. State Compensation Ins. Fund, 154 Colo. 47, 387 P.2d 899 (1963), a hospital provided free lunches to a person working with a volunteer service unit at the hospital. In holding that the person was not working under a contract of hire, we noted: "She was not under contract—at no time did she expressly or by implication obligate herself to the hospital, nor did the hospital at any time obligate itself to her." Id. at 50, 387 P.2d at 901.

Under the facts as found by the ALJ, a contract of hire existed between Aspen and Apostolou. Apostolou negotiated with his employer and agreed to work only in exchange for the benefit of daily passes for his girlfriend. He worked under Highlands' direction, with the expectation of compensation in the form of the daily passes. The ALJ determined that "[i]n essence, [Apostolou] obligated himself to perform ski patrol services for [Highlands] and in return, [Highlands] obligated itself to provide free daily ski passes to [Apostolou] or his designee." Under those circumstances, we conclude that Apostolou worked under a contract of hire and fell within the basic definition of "employee" for the purposes of the Act.

B. Highlands, however, urges us to construe the term "employee" as defined in section 8–41–106(1)(b) to include the requirement that a "contract of hire," which is an essential part of the definition, must provide for the payment of "wages," and that for this purpose we should employ the definition of "wages" found [in the Colorado statute]. Highlands asserts that such a construction would provide a desirable measure of clarity in distinguishing between employees and persons who volunteer time and services as ski patrol persons and thus are excluded from the definition of employee under . . . the Act. . . . A ski pass is not included in the definition of "wages," so the adoption of Highlands' proposed statutory construction would result in the conclusion that Apostolou was not an employee of Highlands. [Ed., the statutory definition of "wages" included: "reportable tips, the amount of the employee's cost of continuing the employer's group health insurance plan and, upon termination of the continuation, the employee's cost of conversion to a similar or lesser insurance plan, and the reasonable value of board, rent, housing, and lodging received from the employer, the reasonable value of which shall be fixed and determined from the facts * * * in each particular case, but shall not include any similar advantage or fringe benefit not specifically enumerated above."].

Highlands' proposed construction finds no support in the statutes. Section 8–47–101(2) appears in a section of the Act providing rules for determining the average weekly wage of an injured employee for the purpose of computing compensation payments. See s 8–47–101(1), 3B C.R.S. (1986). There is no suggestion that it was intended to have any application to the determination of employee status. Moreover, the term "wages" is not used in the definition of "employee" applicable here. See s 8–41–106(1)(b), 3B C.R.S. (1986) (an "employee" is "[e]very person in the service of any ... private corporation ... under any contract of hire, express or implied"). Therefore, there is no basis to utilize the definition of "wages" in determining the meaning of the term "employee."

In deciding whether a person is an employee for purposes of workers' compensation laws, other jurisdictions have not found the form of compensation determinative of the existence of an employer-employee relationship. ... Betts v. Ann Arbor Public Schools, 403 Mich. 507, 271 N.W.2d 498 (1978) (claimant paid in form of training, college credits, and the meeting of prerequisites for the state teaching requirements was an "employee"). Accordingly, we reject the argument that an employment contract must provide for the payment of "wages" in order that one employed under such a contract may qualify as an "employee" under the Act.

C. We now turn to Highlands' principal argument for reversal: that Apostolou was expressly excluded from the definition of "employee" by legislative amendment in 1989 as a "person who volunteers his time or services as a ski patrol person ... for a passenger tramway operator...." See ch. 67, sec. 2, s 8–41–106(5), 1989 Colo.Sess.Laws 409, 410. As the ALJ noted, it is undisputed that Highlands is a passenger tramway operator. The crucial question is whether Apostolou volunteered his time or services within the meaning of the statutory exclusion.

Familiar principles guide us in construing a statute. Foremost among them is that our task is to determine and give effect to the intent of the legislature. ... This intention is to be determined primarily from the statutory language, giving effect to the statutory terms in accordance with their commonly accepted and understood meanings. ... Words or phrases that have acquired a technical or particular meaning, however, whether by legislative definition or otherwise, must be construed in accordance with the acquired meaning. ... Statutes susceptible to more than one interpretation are ambiguous and must be construed in light of the legislative intent and purpose. ... If statutory language is ambiguous, a court may consider the legislative history in determining the intent of the legislature. ...

The common definition of "volunteer" is "[a] person who gives his services without any express or implied promise of remuneration." Black's Law Dictionary 1576 (6th ed. rev. 1990). Highlands contends, however, that the legislature intended "any person who volunteers his time or services as a ski patrol person," within the context of section 8–41–106(5), to include all those persons who work on ski patrol duty without monetary compensation but who receive ski passes entitling them to ski free at any time. It asserts that a ski pass is not remuneration, but a fringe benefit regularly given to "volunteers" within the ski industry, that this practice was recognized by the legislature when it adopted section 8–41–106(5), and that the legislature did not intend the receipt of a ski pass to preclude application of the exclusion.

We find it unnecessary to determine whether ski patrol workers who receive ski passes for personal use as a gratuity consistent with an allegedly standard practice of a passenger tramway operator are excluded from the definition of employee by section 8–41–106(5), for the facts do not correspond to any such practice. Apostolou did not receive a ski pass for himself as a standard fringe benefit provided to persons whose services are otherwise uncompensated. Instead, he specifically bargained for daily passes to be issued to his girlfriend, would not have worked on the Highlands ski patrol absent an agreement by Highlands to issue such passes, and entered into an agreement with Highlands involving mutual obligations. Apostolou obligated himself to perform ski patrol services, and Highlands obligated itself to provide the ski passes. The ALJ specifically addressed the issue of whether Apostolou volunteered his time and services and made the following findings and conclusions: The respondent-employer [Highlands] approached its workers, including the claimant [Apostolou], seeking persons with CPR and first aid knowledge. The claimant, possessing such a background, was sent to interview with Mr. Smith, the director of the ski patrol. During the interview, the claimant expressed his reluctance to perform ski patrol duties if he was to receive only another photo ID ski pass since he already possessed one. As Mr. Smith was unwilling or unable to issue a photo ID ski pass to the claimant's girlfriend, it was agreed between the claimant and Mr. Smith that the claimant would receive unlimited free daily ski passes in return for performing duties as a ski patrolman. In essence, the claimant obligated himself to perform ski patrol services for the respondent-employer and in return, the respondent-employer obligated itself to provide free daily ski passes to the claimant or his designee. If such an arrangement had not been made available to the claimant, he would not have performed duties as a ski patrolman. The daily ski pass is valued at $36.00. If the claimant worked eight hours per day and obtained a ski pass for each day that he worked, the financial return for his performance of ski patrol duties would be $4.50 per hour. Under these circumstances, it cannot be concluded that the claimant volunteered his services to the respondent-employer. Rather, it is concluded that the claimant was an employee of the respondent-employer when he injured his knees on February 20, 1990, while performing duties as a ski patrolman. The factual findings in the ALJ's order are fully supported by substantial evidence in the record and are therefore binding on this court. See Fulton v. King Soopers, 823 P.2d 709, 712–13 (Colo.1992). Based on these facts, we conclude that Apostolou did not volunteer his services within the common meaning of that phrase and that the special meaning urged by Highlands even if accepted is not applicable. Accordingly, we agree with the conclusion of the ALJ, as did the court of appeals, that under the facts as found in the ALJ's ruling, it cannot be concluded that Apostolou volunteered his services to Highlands within the meaning of section 8–41–106(5).

III. We hold that the ALJ correctly concluded that Apostolou was an employee of Highlands at the time he was injured based on the facts as he found them. We find it unnecessary and inappropriate to go beyond the facts of this case in delineating the scope of the exclusion in section 8–41–106(5).

We affirm the judgment of the Colorado Court of Appeals.

JUSTICE VOLLACK, dissenting:

The majority holds that, because the claimant, John Apostolou, bargained for his position as a member of the ski patrol in exchange for ski passes for his girlfriend, he is not a "volunteer" under section 8–40–301(4), 3B C.R.S. (1993 Supp.), and is thus not excluded from receiving workers' compensation benefits. The majority affirms the decision of the administrative law judge that Apostolou was an employee of Aspen Highlands for purposes of receiving benefits under the Workers' Compensation Act, and was not a volunteer under the statute. Because I believe that, by the language of the statute, the legislature clearly intended to exclude someone in Apostolou's position from benefits, and because I do not believe an employment relationship was created between the parties, I dissent.

* * *

Apostolou is a sympathetic claimant. His injury prevented him from working for eight months. At the time of the hearing he had accumulated over $15,000 in medical bills, and it was possible that he needed additional surgery. The majority, however, should not create a legal fiction that Apostolou was an employee of Aspen Highlands so that he may collect workers' compensation benefits. The statutory language is clear: volunteer ski patrol members are not "employees" under the Workers' Compensation Act. The majority circumvents section 8–40–301(4) and, through judicial fiat, creates a new class of employees to receive workers' compensation benefits: those who have "bargained" for some condition of their volunteer position. In my opinion, the legislature clearly intended, by the language of the statute, that someone in Apostolou's circumstances was not entitled to workers' compensation benefits. I dissent.

I am authorized to say that Chief Justice ROVIRA and Justice SCOTT join in this dissent.

Notes

1. Grant v. Blazer Coordinating Council of Youth Development, 111 N.J.Super. 125, 267 A.2d 568 (N.J.Co. 1970) found that an unpaid welfare-

recipient trainee in a public work training program was an employee for the purposes of the New Jersey workers' compensation law. The court acknowledged that payment of wages is *a* factor to be considered in making an employment determination but explicitly concluded that "it is not a controlling factor." The court also held that the fact that the so-called employer was a nonprofit organization was not determinative. Upon appeal the appellate court affirmed, stating: "the County Court's determination of the existence of an employer-employee relationship and the modification of the award was reasonably reached on sufficient credible evidence present in the record considering the proofs as a whole, with due regard to the expertise of the Judge of Compensation and his opportunity to appraise the credibility of witnesses." Grant v. Blazer Coordinating Council of Youth Development, 116 N.J.Super. 460, 282 A.2d 769, 770 (1971). Accord, Tommy Nobis Center v. Barfield, 187 Ga.App. 394, 370 S.E.2d 517 (1988) (trainee in federally funded job training program is an "employee", trainee received $100 per week), and Wright v. Wilson Memorial Hospital, Inc., 30 N.C.App. 91, 226 S.E.2d 225 (1976) (student in laboratory assistantship program received room and board). See also Scissons v. City of Rapid City, 251 N.W.2d 681 (S.D.1977) (poor "relief worker" who was compensated with voucher coupons redeemable at area stores was held to be an employee of the county).

2. Are "student teachers" employees? If so, are they employees of the school districts where they train or the colleges where they receive academic credit? Compare, Betts v. Ann Arbor Public Schools, 403 Mich. 507, 271 N.W.2d 498 (1978) (student teacher is an employee of the school district; course credit and experience are "value received"), cited in the principal case, with School Dist. No. 60, Pueblo County v. Industrial Commission, 43 Colo.App. 38, 601 P.2d 651 (1979) (student teacher is an employee of the university that paid the school district to accept its students). See also Ryles v. Durham County Hospital Corporation, Inc., 107 N.C.App. 455, 420 S.E.2d 487 (N.C.App.1992)(technical institute respiratory therapy student became an "apprentice" under the workers' compensation statute while delivering respiratory therapy treatments in a hospital; as a consequence, workers' compensation immunity barred a tort suit against the hospital).

3. The defendant's truck, transporting lethal gases in an area remote from its headquarters, wrecked and imperiled the surrounding countryside. The chief of police called on plaintiff, an off-duty worker of an unrelated employer, an expert in toxic gases, for help and plaintiff was injured. Is he entitled to compensation? If so, who is the employer, the police agency or the trucking company? See Tipper v. Great Lakes Chemical Co., 281 So.2d 10 (Fla.1973).

4. Citizens called on by officials to perform a public service are sometimes not regarded as employees under workers' compensation laws. Compare Metropolitan Dade County v. Glassman, 341 So.2d 995 (Fla.1976) (claimant ordered to report for jury duty injured at the courthouse, not employee of county) with Yount v. Boundary County, 118 Idaho 307, 796 P.2d 516 (1990) (opposite result). Where the public service is performed in emergencies, the cases often turn on customary practices and the legal authority of the requesting officer to enlist assistance. Compare, Conley v. Industrial Commission, 43 Colo.App. 10, 601 P.2d 648 (1979) (compensation awarded dependents of an "off duty" but "on call" police officer who was

killed while directing traffic during a flood in a neighboring county; informal practice of law enforcement agencies to assist others in emergencies) and Moore v. State, 200 N.C. 300, 156 S.E. 806 (1931) (claimant deputized by forest warden to assist in putting out a fire was entitled to compensation), with Morley v. Workmen's Compensation Appeal Bd., 49 Pa.Cmwlth. 98, 410 A.2d 110 (1980) (former mayor injured while assisting chief of police in directing traffic at scene of an accident was not an "auxiliary policeman"; compensation denied) and Leon County v. Sauls, 151 Fla. 171, 9 So.2d 461 (1942) (constable requested that Sauls assist him in making an arrest; compensation denied).

5.   Questions of employment status also arise in cases involving mutual assistance arrangements. In Gant v. Industrial Com'n, 263 Wis. 64, 56 N.W.2d 525 (1953), a claimant farmer was denied recovery for an injury received while returning work on a neighbor's farm in accordance with local custom, and in Alexander v. J.E. Hixson & Sons Funeral Home, 44 So.2d 487 (La.App.1950) a florist injured while lifting a casket lid pursuant to a mutual assistance agreement between him and an undertaker in their respective endeavors was not an employee of the undertaker. But compare, Debold v. H.P. Martell & Sons, 300 Minn. 296, 219 N.W.2d 623 (1974) (claimant who often exchanged equipment and services with subcontractor held to be employee of the latter).

6.   If money is paid an apparent employee, must it be paid in return for work performed? In Smith v. Valentine Estates, Inc., 45 A.D.2d 789, 357 N.Y.S.2d 150 (1974), a youngster was given an odd job on a construction site to keep him busy and deter him from damaging the property. The court found that no employer-employee relationship existed. Similarly, no employment was found where a father, in order to stop his minor son's excessive demands for money, ordered his company to pay the son a weekly salary of $35.00. The court regarded this an "allowance", despite the fact that the son, who lived with the father, did some work in the father's plant. Caldwell v. Caldwell, 55 So.2d 258 (La.App.1950). A contrary result was reached under similar facts in Denius v. North Dakota Workmen's Compensation Bureau, 68 N.D. 506, 281 N.W. 361 (1938). The Idaho statute excludes from the definition of "employee" members of the employer's family "dwelling in his house." Idaho Code § 72–213.

7.   One person may be held to be the employer of another, even though an independent third person actually pays the employee for the service rendered. Claremont Country Club v. Industrial Accident Com'n, 174 Cal. 395, 163 P. 209 (1917) (caddy was employee of country club although paid by individual players); Board of Educ. of the City of Chicago v. Industrial Com'n, 57 Ill.2d 339, 312 N.E.2d 244 (1974) (claimant held to be an employee of the Board of Education despite the fact that P.T.A. paid salary); and Workmen's Comp. Appeal Bd. v. American Mut. Liability Ins. Co., 19 Pa.Cmwlth. 502, 339 A.2d 183 (1975) (paper company salesman with bad eyesight hired a driver; driver held to be employee of paper company).

8.   People who volunteer services temporarily or in emergencies have been variously treated: Edwards v. Hollywood Canteen, 27 Cal.2d 802, 167 P.2d 729 (1946) (volunteer hostess "jitterbugged" with over-zealous Marine; not an employment relationship); Armitage v. Trustees of Mt. Fern Method-

ist Episcopal Church, 33 N.J.Super. 367, 110 A.2d 154 (1954) (church member injured while doing work on church building to discharge his pledge at stipulated hourly rate, not an employment relationship); Glamm v. City of Amsterdam Fire Dept., 54 A.D.2d 996, 388 N.Y.S.2d 55 (1976) (volunteer assisting fireman held not to be employee, arrangement ambiguous); Charlottesville Music Center, Inc. v. McCray, 215 Va. 31, 205 S.E.2d 674 (1974) (fifteen-year-old boy did not expect compensation for helping his friend erect shelves, not an employee). Should it make a difference in actions such as these whether the injured person is claiming benefits which the employer denies, or whether the claimant is suing the employer in tort and the employer is claiming that workers' compensation applies?

SECTION 3. EMPLOYMENTS DISTINGUISHED FROM OTHER RELATIONS

MARCUM v. STATE ACCIDENT INS. FUND
Court of Appeals of Oregon, 1977.
29 Or.App. 843, 565 P.2d 399.

PER CURIAM.

The issue in this worker's compensation appeal is whether the claimant was an employee or an independent contractor. The hearings officer ordered compensation, the Workmen's Compensation Board reversed and the circuit court affirmed the Board's determination that claimant was not an employee of the La Grande Country Club, Inc., when he sustained his injury. We agree with the analysis by the trial court and adopt it as our own:

"Claimant is fifty-three years of age and is regularly employed as a logger. By reason of the nature of his work as a logger, the claimant is laid off from his regular employment in the spring of each year. In April, 1975, he was laid off from logging and was seeking other work. Claimant had pruned trees in prior years and had the necessary equipment to engage in such activity, so he submitted a bid to the La Grande Country Club to prune dead wood from some of the trees on the golf course. Claimant had the low bid of $25.00 per tree, and this was accepted by the club. The number of trees involved was not clear from the evidence, but it appears that from 20 to 30 trees were to be pruned. Claimant was to supply his own tools and equipment. He hired an assistant to help him and agreed to pay the assistant $12.50 per tree. After five or six days on the job, claimant was injured. The Referee concluded that the claimant was an employee of the club, rather than an independent contractor. The Board, on de novo review, reversed the Referee's order and found claimant to be an independent contractor.

"The basic facts are not in dispute. Thus, the question of employee or independent contractor status is one of law. Woody vs. Waibel, 276 OR. 189 [554 P.2d 492] (1976). ORS 656.005 provides that control is the essential ingredient in the test for determining who is a servant. It is right of control, rather than actual exercise of control, that is determinative. Bowser v. SIAC, 182 OR. 42 [185 P.2d 891] (1947). The principal factors showing right of control are (1) direct evidence of right or exercise of control; (2) method of payment; (3) the furnishing of equipment; and (4) the right to fire. 1A Larson's Workmen's Compensation Law, Section 44.00.

"EVIDENCE OF RIGHT OR EXERCISE OF CONTROL

"Harry Karns was the member of the Board of Directors of the La Grande Country Club responsible for seeing that the trees were pruned and the golf course otherwise maintained. He accepted claimant's bid and showed him what needed to be done. He did not tell him how to do the work or what hours the claimant was required to maintain. Claimant was permitted to hire his own helper and determine the rate of compensation for the helper. The Referee concluded that an employer-employee relationship existed because Mr. Karns felt he could exercise control and because the club paid the hired helper directly, rather than through the claimant. However, the testimony by Mr. Karns indicates that the only control he felt he had was to direct the claimant to do a good job and to terminate the claimant if he failed to do so. Larson states that an owner, without becoming an employer, is entitled to as much control of the details of the work as is necessary to insure that he gets the end results from the contractor that he bargained for in the contract. 1A Larson's Workmen's Compensation Law, Section 44.20. The evidence indicates that Mr. Karns was only interested in exercising enough control that he received the result bargained for.[1]

"There was insufficient evidence to establish control.

"METHOD OF PAYMENT

"Claimant, as noted, was paid at the rate of $25 per tree. In paying the claimant and his help, the club did not withhold anything for taxes or insurance. Larson indicates that payment on a piece-work basis gives no strong indication either way of the status of employment. 1A Larson's Workmen's Compensation Law, Section 44.33(b).[2]

---

1. **[Editor's Note.]** Accord: Coastal Timberlands, Inc. v. Brown, 141 Ga.App. 800, 234 S.E.2d 373 (1977); Laub v. Meyer, Inc., 70 Idaho 224, 214 P.2d 884 (1950). Cf. Bowser v. State Industrial Acc. Comm., 182 Or. 42, 185 P.2d 891 (1947) (Hauler who supplied his own truck required to coordinate his work with that of other haulers, treated as employee, although the numerous details controlled by employer seemed to be no more elaborate than were necessary in order to accomplish the end result).

2. **[Editor's Note.]** Payment of hourly or daily wage strongly suggests an employer-employee relation: Nochta v. Industrial Comm., 7 Ariz.App. 166, 436 P.2d 944 (1968); Schneider v. Village of Shickley, 156 Neb. 683, 57 N.W.2d 527 (1953); Worth v. C.T. Hubbell Lumber Corp., 29 A.D.2d 1025, 289 N.Y.S.2d 519 (1968).

Will the wage earner normally be subjected to more control than the worker who is paid by the job? Farnam v. Linden Hills Cong. Church, 276 Minn. 84, 149 N.W.2d 689 (1967). Does the wage earner normally secure an entire undertaking upon which he can compute profits and accident cost?

Conversely, payment for the whole of a designated piece of work strongly indicates a principal-contractor relationship. Haller v. Department of Labor & Industries, 13 Wash.2d 164, 124 P.2d 559 (1942) (contract to clean out a well for $100).

"With respect to the payment from the club to the hired helper, the evidence is that the hired helper first went to the claimant and requested payment and the claimant in turn requested the club to pay the hired helper directly. This accommodation on the part of the club does not indicate employment status.[3]

"Furnishing of Equipment

"Claimant furnished all the necessary equipment to do the job. The equipment included saws and a pickup. This factor indicates a relationship of independent contractor. 1A Larson's Workmen's Compensation Law, Section 44.34.[4]

"Right to Fire

"The right to fire, it is often said, is the power to control. 1A Larson's Workmen's Compensation Law, Section 44.35. In this case, Mr. Karns indicated only that he felt he had the right to terminate the contract if the claimant was not properly doing his job. It is noted by Larson, 'The unqualified right to fire must be distinguished from the right to terminate the contract of an independent contractor for bona fide reasons of dissatisfaction * * *. The exercise of such a right is still consistent with the idea that a satisfactory end result is all that is aimed at by the contract.' 1A Larson's Workmen's Compensation Law, Section 44.35.[5]

"This Court agrees with the Board that in the application of the control test the evidence indicates that the claimant is an independent contractor. The claimant on appeal, however, now contends that the

3. [Editor's Note.] Cf. Karcher Candy Co. v. Hester, 204 Ark. 574, 163 S.W.2d 168 (1942) (truck drivers for candy company paid on commission and were authorized to pick up helpers; helper regarded as direct employee of company). Characteristically, the enterpriser will combine the labor of others in performing his contractual service. To this he adds his organizational and managerial prowess and exacts a profit.

4. [Editor's Note.] Procopio v. Foss & Voigt, Inc., 10 N.J.Super. 504, 77 A.2d 293 (1950) (distributor of linoleum secured services of driver who operated two trucks of his own, payment by the ton; held principal-contractor relation despite fact that arrangement appeared to be regular and continuous); Anno. (1939) Teamster or Truckman as Independent Contractor or Employee under Workmen's Compensation Acts, 120 A.L.R. 1031. Compare the situation where the alleged employee furnishes elaborate specialized equipment with the situation of the ditch digger who uses his own shovel. Swain v. Monona County, 163 N.W.2d 918 (Iowa 1969).

5. [Editor's Note.] "We cannot conceive of an independent contractor subject to being summarily, or within a period of twenty four hours, dismissed without liability as the contract states, and yet not be under the order and control of another party." Industrial Comm. v. Meddock, 65 Ariz. 324, 330, 180 P.2d 580, 585 (1947) (contract employing quarrymen carefully drawn so as to designate workers as independent contractors, with absence of control specified; workers nevertheless regarded as employees); Barker v. Curtis, 199 Tenn. 413, 287 S.W.2d 43 (1956) (right to terminate services and control of details made mine operator an employee, despite fact that he supplied all labor and part of equipment). Noted, 24 Tenn.L.Rev. 917 (1957); Golosh v. Cherokee Cab Co., 226 Ga. 636, 176 S.E.2d 925 (1970) (right to terminate sufficient to support employee status); Fanning v. Apawana Golf Club, 169 Pa.Super. 180, 82 A.2d 584 (1951) (caddy held employee of golf club because it retained power to dismiss him by depriving him of access to club property; unimportant that individual golfers paid all fees for services). But compare Wendlandt v. Industrial Comm., 256 Wis. 62, 39 N.W.2d 854 (1949), noted 35 Cornell L.Q. 912 (1950) (statute designating caddies as employees held unconstitutional).

Court should consider 'the relative nature of the work' test. Claimant cites as his authority Woody vs. Waibel, supra. In this case, the Supreme Court quoted Larson and set forth the essential ingredients of this test to be as follows:

' * * * [T]he character of the claimant's work or business—how skilled it is, how much of a separate calling or enterprise it is, to what extent it may be expected to carry its own accident burden and so on—and its relation to the employer's business, that is, how much it is a regular part of the employer's regular work, whether it is continuous or intermittent, and whether the duration is sufficient to amount to the hiring of continuing services as distinguished from contracting for the completion of a particular job.' Woody vs. Waibel, supra [276 Or.], at page 195 [554 P.2d 492].

"Larson has indicated that the most difficult and controversial cases on status are those involving services, such as we have in this case. He goes on to note as follows:

'The two poles between which the area of controversy lies are these: First, it must be conceded that, in an ordinary industrial operation, the maintenance and repair of the plant are an integral part of the business. It is just as relevant to the production process to wash the windows as it is to clean the machinery. The repair of equipment is as relevant as its operation. At the opposite extreme, it must also be conceded that every businessman cannot be held to be the direct employer of every plumber, electrician or painter that he might call in to do necessary work on the premises.' 1A Larson's Workmen's Compensation Law, Section 45.31.

"This case can be distinguished from Woody vs. Waibel, supra. In the *Woody* case, the employee transported timber which formed an essential and regular part of the marketing enterprise of the employer. In this case, Mr. Karns testified that pruning trees was essential to the club, but it should be noted that Mr. Karns also testified that the pruning of trees had not been done for about 15 years. In the *Woody* case, the employee's job required close cooperation with the other employees of the employer. In this case, claimant had no working relationship with the other employees of the club. Most importantly, in the *Woody* case the employee was hired on a continuing basis. In this case, the claimant had never before worked for the club.

"Testimony from Mr. Blackman, a person who also bid on this same job, indicated that pruning trees does require some expertise. Although the claimant was a logger by profession, he testified that he regularly did odd jobs during the off season and had pruned trees for other people in the past. The claimant testified that he was expected to do the job quickly and the evidence indicates that not too much time was involved in performing the contract. The evidence, as noted, was that 20 to 30 trees were to be pruned and that claimant was to receive $25.00 per tree. He was injured after five or six days and the club paid a total of $300.00 to the claimant and his hired helper. Claimant indicated that he was entitled to an additional $50.00 from the club. If this is so, claimant must have performed about one-half to two-thirds of the entire contract in the five or six days he was working. As noted by Larson:

> 'Ordinarily, when the job to be done is one that becomes necessary at unpredictable intervals, and when it is not a protracted one, a specialist called in to handle the particular repair or installation is an independent contractor. ...' 1A Larson's Workmen's Compensation Law, Section 45.31(b).

"As stated by Larson, every business cannot be held to be the direct employer of every repairman on their premises. Mr. Blackman's testimony indicates that a person engaged in pruning trees, such as he, can be expected to carry his own workmen's compensation insurance. Under all the circumstances, this Court concludes that in applying the relative nature of the work test, the claimant is an independent contractor."

Affirmed.

KIRKWOOD v. INDUSTRIAL COMMISSION
Supreme Court of Illinois (1981).
416 N.E.2d 1078, 84 Ill.2d 14, 48 Ill.Dec. 556.

RYAN, JUSTICE:

The issue in this appeal is whether the Industrial Commission's finding that the claimant was not an employee, but an independent contractor, when he was injured, was against the manifest weight of the evidence. The claimant, Herman J. Kirkwood, had been applying siding to a home pursuant to an agreement with Security Roofing and Siding Co., Inc. (Security). He was injured after falling from a scaffold. He filed an application for adjustment of claim under the Workmen's Compensation Act (Ill.Rev.Stat.1977, ch. 48, par. 138.1 et seq.). The arbitrator and Industrial Commission denied compensation. The circuit court of Coles County confirmed the decision of the Industrial Commission. The claimant appeals directly to this court under our Rule 302(a) (73 Ill.2d R. 302(a)). We hold that the decision of the Industrial Commission was not against the manifest weight of the evidence.

The claimant had been applying siding to homes since 1970. He had worked for Kool Vent Company for about a year when he and his brother formed Kirkwood Brothers Construction Company. They were in business under that name for approximately seven years. In October 1977, the company ceased doing business and claimant joined a partnership called Woolen Home Improvement, which also was engaged in applying siding. On August 1, 1978, the claimant withdrew as a member of that partnership. On that same date, the claimant, his son and two friends, Bob Green and Bob Craft, began to do the same work on projects supplied by Security. Project negotiations were discussed solely between Security and the customer. After negotiations were complete, Security would add that project to the work list posted at its office. The siding crews with which Security dealt could then pick a project from the list. The claimant, his son and his friends comprised one of these crews.

Job specifications and materials for projects on which the claimant's crew worked were provided by Security. The crew did not pay for materials. The crew provided its own tools, equipment, trucks, and scaffolding. It likewise set its own hours and applied the siding without supervision. A representative of Security would, from time to time, visit the job site to be sure the work was satisfactory. The crew made no warranties to the customer beyond those made by Security.

The crew was paid on a piecework basis, that is, by the amount of material applied to a building, receiving a lump sum check at the end of each job. The checks were made out to either Kirkwood Home Improvements or Kirkwood Applicating. No taxes or social security were withheld by Security. Expenses were deducted by the claimant, who then divided the remainder among the crew members. Security's checks to Kirkwood were paid from Security's general account, not its payroll account.

On August 21, 1978, claimant was injured while working at a project site. The scaffolding which was owned and erected by the claimant collapsed, causing him to fall approximately 20 feet. After the claimant's injury, the crew discontinued further work on the project. Security paid Kirkwood Applicating for work already done on the project and arranged to have another applicating service complete the job.

The arbitrator, in denying compensation, found that the claimant was operating as an independent contractor on August 21, 1978, and that the relationship of employee and employer did not exist between Kirkwood and Security on that date. The Industrial Commission affirmed, and the circuit court of Coles County confirmed the decision of the Commission. In appealing to this court, the claimant argues that he was an employee and not an independent contractor and that the Industrial Commission's decision to the contrary is against the manifest weight of the evidence and must be reversed. * * *

Determining whether one is an independent contractor or an employee is often a vexing problem. (*O'Brien v. Industrial Com.* (1971), 48 Ill.2d 304, 307, 269 N.E.2d 471.) Since many jobs contain elements of each, there is no clear line of demarcation between the status of employee and independent contractor. ... For this reason, when the facts of a particular case are susceptible to either interpretation, it is within the Industrial Commission's province to draw inferences and evaluate the credibility of the witnesses in arriving at a decision. ... On review, that decision will only be reversed if it is against the manifest weight of the evidence. ...

This court has considered various factors in resolving the question of whether a workman is an employee or an independent contractor; *i.e.,* amount of supervision and control, the method of making payment, the right to discharge, the skills required, the source of materials and tools, and the work schedule. Most frequently emphasized is the right to control the workman and the details of his work. (See *O'Brien v. Industrial Com.* (1971), 48 Ill.2d 304, 269 N.E.2d 471.) The pronouncements of this court in this area are necessarily binding on the Commission and are followed by it in making its determinations. The approach this court has followed could conceivably lead to inconsistent results in identical factual situations, as the claimant argues has happened in this case as compared to *Mastercraft* and *Kirkwood*. Such results are irksome, particularly to Herman Kirkwood, the claimant in this case since in *Kirkwood v. Industrial Com.* he was found to be an employer, whereas in this case, under very similar arrangements, when he is the claimant, he is found to be an independent contractor.

Professor Larson suggests that the traditional elements considered by courts in determining whether a workman is an employee or an independent contractor were adopted from the common-law master-servant concept and are not particularly appropriate in determining whether a workman is an employee for purposes of workmen's compensation acts. For instance, the degree of control that can be exercised over a workman and the performance of his work is a significant factor in determining whether the master is to be held liable vicariously for the acts of his servant. However, workmen's compensation law is concerned not with injuries *by* the employee, but injuries *to* the employee, and the right to control his activities does not have the same significance as it has in determining whether the employer should be responsible for the acts of his servant. Professor Larson suggests that the right to control the workman should not be the most relevant factor in determining if a workman is an employee in a compensation case. More important to consider is the nature of the claimant's work in relation to the regular business of the employer. (1C A. Larson, Workmen's Compensation secs. 43.42, 43.50 (1980).) This approach can be best explained by quoting from Professor Larson's treatise:

> "The theory of compensation legislation is that the cost of all industrial accidents should be borne by the consumer as a part of the cost of the product. It follows that any worker whose services form a regular and continuing part of the cost of that product, and whose method of operation is not such an independent business that it forms in itself a separate route through which his own costs of industrial accident can be channelled, is within the presumptive area of intended protection." 1C A. Larson, Workmen's Compensation sec. 43.51, at 8–17 to 8–18 (1980).

In section 43.52, under the heading of "Relativity as essential part of test," Professor Larson states:

> "Note that the factor here stressed is in two parts: the nature of the claimant's work, and its relation to the employer's work. The nature of the claimant's work, in the abstract, is seldom a safe guide in itself, and for this reason it is dangerous to rely on precedents classified solely by the character of the worker's job—for example, to say that window-washers are usually held to be employees while

lawyers are usually held to be independent contractors. If I, as a private householder, call upon a window-washing company and engage it to do what amounts to one day's work on my house, I am probably not an employer. But an industrial plant which at regular intervals keeps this same company busy doing what otherwise would be done through its own employees could be held an employer. Similarly, when I seek the services of a lawyer, on the occasion of one of my rare encounters with the legal process, the lawyer is obviously not my employee. But the same lawyer, engaged continuously by a law firm or insurance company, can be an employee.

This test, then, which for brevity will be called the 'relative nature of the work' test, contains these ingredients: the character of the claimant's work or business—how skilled it is, how much of a separate calling or enterprise it is, to what extent it may be expected to carry its own accident burden and so on—and its relation to the employer's business, that is, how much it is a regular part of the employer's regular work, whether it is continuous or intermittent, and whether the duration is sufficient to amount to the hiring of continuing services as distinguished from contracting for the completion of a particular job." 1C A. Larson, Workmen's Compensation sec. 43.52, at 8–19 to 8–20 (1980).

This court, while adhering to the belief that the right to control the details of a worker's performance is the essential element in determining whether a worker is an employee has, nonetheless, on several occasions acknowledged the significance of the nature of the work performed in relation to the general business of the employer. . . .

We believe that the approach suggested by Professor Larson would lead to more consistent and more logical results than emphasizing the common-law master-servant elements of tort liability. Indeed, the latter approach may well have led to a contrary conclusion in the case now before us. The tests presently applied in determining whether a worker is an employee or an independent contractor are the results of court pronouncements and could no doubt be abandoned by judicial decision. . . . The tests now applied are long-standing, business relationships have been structured in consideration of them, and insurance protection against compensation claims has been tailored with these tests in mind. It could be unnecessarily disruptive, and expose employers to risks against which they have had no opportunity to insure, for this court to abruptly abandon its previous approach and follow the suggestions of Professor Larson. In any event, it would be inappropriate for this court in this case to abandon consideration of the elements heretofore deemed significant in favor of Professor Larson's suggestions, since the suggestions were neither briefed nor argued.

For the reasons heretofore stated in this opinion, the judgment of the circuit court of Coles County is affirmed.

Judgment affirmed.

Simon, J., took no part in the consideration or decision of this case.

Notes

1. Do the circumstances incident to entering the pruning contract suggest that Marcum had sufficient bargaining power to negotiate in advance that compensation be provided for injuries suffered by himself and his helper? Is the answer relevant in determining whether Marcum should be regarded as a contractor or an employee? Does the workers' compensation statute express an intention that those risks be absorbed by the club?

2. Many courts rely primarily, if not exclusively, on the "right to control" test to determine whether a worker is an "employee" for purposes of workers' compensation. See, e.g., RBF Holding Co. v. Williamson, 260 Ga. 526, 397 S.E.2d 440 (1990); Wangen v. City of Fountain, 255 N.W.2d 813 (Minn.1977); and Walling v. Hardy Construction, 247 Mont. 441, 807 P.2d 1335 (1991). Other courts consider the "right to control" test in conjunction with "the relative nature of the work" test. *Marcum* and *Kirkwood* are examples of this. See also, Schaefer v. North Dakota Workers Compensation Bureau, 462 N.W.2d 179 (N.D.1990). By contrast, a few courts suggest that the "relative nature of the work" test is *the* appropriate test to resolve the employment-independent contractor dispute. See, e.g., Haynie v. Tideland Welding Service, 631 F.2d 1242 (5th Cir.1980) (under the Longshoremen's and Harbor Workers' Compensation Act).

Do you agree with the proposition that the "right to control" test may be used to determine whether an employer is to be held vicariously liable for harm caused to a third person by a particular worker's act while simultaneously the "relative nature of the work" test is applied to determine whether the same employer would be liable to provide workers' compensation benefits to the same worker for injuries arising out of the same accident? It is possible that a worker could be an employee of a particular employer as to a particular act for one purpose and not the other?

3. Numerous courts have awarded compensation to insurance sales agents despite the absence of control over the details of the work and despite overt attempts to exclude the employment status by the terms of the contract. See, e.g., Gordon v. New York Life Ins. Co., 300 N.Y. 652, 90 N.E.2d 898 (1950), and Davis v. Home Ins. Co., 291 So.2d 455 (La.App.1974). Compare Burton v. Crawford & Co., 89 N.M. 436, 553 P.2d 716 (1976) (claims adjuster regarded as independent contractor); Hackler v. Swisher Mower & Machine Co., 284 S.W.2d 55 (Mo.App.1955) (part time salesman of lawn mowers regarded as independent contractor), and Huebner v. Industrial Com'n, 234 Wis. 239, 290 N.W. 145 (1940) (soliciting agent for newspaper was assigned a territory and required to check in at end of each day's work, but was free to work or not as he saw fit; held independent contractor).

4. In determining employment status, many decisions look to the economic and social objectives that underlie the workers' compensation legislation. Laurel Daily Leader, Inc. v. James, 224 Miss. 654, 80 So.2d 770 (1955) (newsboy held to be an employee for purposes of compensation although court conceded he would not be a servant for the purposes of *respondeat superior* liability); N.L.R.B. v. Hearst Publications, 322 U.S. 111, 64 S.Ct. 851, 88 L.Ed. 1170 (1944) (newsboys treated as employees under National Labor Relations Act). These decisions fit with the general view that remedial statutes should be liberally construed to satisfy their purposes. Do

they also fit with the economic assumptions about how best to distribute the costs of work injuries?

In the latter decades of the twentieth century some legislatures retreated from judicial decisions that had applied statutes liberally to protect the interests of employees. See, e.g., N.L.R.B. v. Town & Country Electric, Inc., 516 U.S. 85, 91, 116 S.Ct. 450, 454, 133 L.Ed.2d 371 (1995), noting that the holding in N.L.R.B. v. Hearst, which had held newsboys to employees rather than independent contractors, had been statutorily overruled. Running somewhat counter to that trend is this modification to the Colorado workers' compensation statute:

(2)(a) Notwithstanding any other provision of this section, any individual who performs services for pay for another shall be deemed to be an employee, irrespective of whether the common-law relationship of master and servant exists, unless such individual is free from control and direction in the performance of the service, both under the contract for performance of service and in fact and such individual is customarily engaged in an independent trade, occupation, profession, or business related to the service performed. * * *

(b)(I) * * *

(II) To prove independence it must be shown that the person for whom services are performed does not:

(A) Require the individual to work exclusively for the person for whom services are performed; except that the individual may choose to work exclusively for such person for a finite period of time specified in the document;

(B) Establish a quality standard for the individual; except that the person may provide plans and specifications regarding the work but cannot oversee the actual work or instruct the individual as to how the work will be performed;

(C) Pay a salary or at an hourly rate instead of at a fixed or contract rate;

(D) Terminate the work of the service provider during the contract period unless such service provider violates the terms of the contract or fails to produce a result that meets the specifications of the contract;

(E) Provide more than minimal training for the individual;

(F) Provide tools or benefits to the individual; except that materials and equipment may be supplied;

(G) Dictate the time of performance; except that a completion schedule and a range of negotiated and mutually agreeable work hours may be established;

(H) Pay the service provider personally instead of making checks payable to the trade or business name of such service provider; and

(I) Combine the business operations of the person for whom service is provided in any way with the business operations of the service provider instead of maintaining all such operations separately and distinctly. * * *

Co. St. § 8–40–202 (1998). Is a provision such as this better or worse for workers as a whole?

5. In a few states some independent contractors may be entitled to compensation from the entity for whom the contracted work is being done. See, e.g., Wisconsin Statutes § 102.07(8)(a): "[With omitted exceptions] every independent contractor is, for the purpose of this chapter an employe of any employer under this chapter for whom he or she is performing service in the course of the trade, business, profession or occupation of such employer at the time of the injury." See also La.R.S. 23:1021 (as amended by La.Acts 1948, No. 179, § 1) which extends compensation to all contractors who do a substantial amount of manual labor. The broadest provision is in the Colorado statute which authorizes an award to any contractor doing work which is part of the business of the principal or employer. Colo.Rev. Stats. section 8–48–401. Do these provisions unnecessarily go beyond what is needed to satisfy the remedial and economic premises of the workers' compensation scheme?

6. Nurses and interne physicians in regular employment of hospitals are usually regarded as employees. Matter of Bernstein v. Beth Israel Hospital, 236 N.Y. 268, 140 N.E. 694 (1923) (compensation awarded even though under New York vicarious liability rule hospital would *not* be liable to third persons for interne's negligence); Nordland v. Poor Sisters of St. Francis, 4 Ill.App.2d 48, 123 N.E.2d 121 (1954) (interne was employee of hospital, not of surgeon whom he was assisting at time of injury); State Compensation Ins. Fund v. Industrial Accident Comm., 124 Cal.App.2d 1, 268 P.2d 40 (1954) (special registered nurse for charity patient paid by polio fund, held to be employee of hospital); Industrial Com'n v. Navajo County, 64 Ariz. 172, 167 P.2d 113 (1946) (county physician treated as employee although he performed duties in his office and apparently carried on private practice); West Virginia Coal & Coke Corp. v. State Comp. Com'r, 116 W.Va. 701, 182 S.E. 826 (1935) (physician devoting full time to single industrial concern is covered, but a physician employed only for specific instances is not).

7. Attorneys employed on retainers for extensive services over an indefinite period have occasionally been held to be employees. Industrial Comm. v. Moynihan, 94 Colo. 438, 32 P.2d 802 (1934). Contra, Associated Indem. Corp. v. Industrial Acc. Comm., 56 Cal.App.2d 804, 133 P.2d 698 (1943). Cf. Egan v. N.Y. State Joint Legislative Committee, 2 A.D.2d 418, 158 N.Y.S.2d 47 (1956) (attorney for legislative committee held to be employee). New Independent Tobacco Warehouse, No. 3 v. Latham, 282 S.W.2d 846 (Ky.1955) (architect hired for single project; gave full time and paid on hourly basis; held to be contractor and not employee). Ministers have been regarded as employees of their churches despite the personal and religious character of the services. Meyers v. Southwest Region Conference Ass'n of Seventh Day Adventists, 230 La. 310, 88 So.2d 381 (1956); Potash v. Bonaccurso, 179 Pa.Super. 582, 117 A.2d 803 (1955) (ritual slaughterer of cattle, held employee of packer). Cf. New York Workmen's Compensation Law Ann. (McKinney 1990) § 3 (18) (ministers excluded from coverage of act). Other persons performing highly skilled services who have been regarded as employees include: a licensed pilot, Murray v. Industrial Acc. Commission, 216 Cal. 340, 14 P.2d 301 (1932); a singer in a nightclub who was

designated as an "artist" or "principal" in the contract of hire, Russell v. Torch Club, 26 N.J.Super. 75, 97 A.2d 196 (1953); and a professional model, Reyes v. Cowles Magazine, Inc., 5 A.D.2d 708, 168 N.Y.S.2d 660 (1957). But cf. Fisher v. J.F.G. Coffee Co., 221 Tenn. 333, 426 S.W.2d 502 (1967) (decedent devoted part of time to piloting aircraft for several firms, held to be contractor despite payment on per hour basis).

8. Buyers and sellers sometimes exercise such a high degree of control over the other's activities that one may be deemed the employee of the other at a particular point in time. A buyer, for example, may direct the seller to process goods before passing title and exercise considerable control over the seller's conduct in so doing. Myers v. Newport Co., 17 La.App. 227, 135 So. 767 (1931) (complainant injured while cutting timber he had contracted to sell to defendant; held to be employee). Conversely, a vendor may sometimes take such a direct interest in a purchaser's conduct in reselling the commodity, that the vendee for resale may hardly be distinguishable from the ordinary commission salesman. This issue arises most frequently in connection with newspaper sellers. Balinski v. Press Pub. Co., 118 Pa.Super. 89, 179 A. 897 (1935) (newsboy regarded as non-employee independent purchaser for resale); Laurel Daily Leader, Inc. v. James, 224 Miss. 654, 80 So.2d 770 (1955) (newsboy regarded as employee even though he did not have privilege of returning unsold papers; court was not impressed by defendant's contention that newsboy was "little merchant".) Similarly, milk deliverers and cart peddlers of commodities such as ice cream who work on defined routes and maintain a perpetual inventory of products purchased for resale are frequently regarded as employees. Glielmi v. Netherland Dairy Co., 254 N.Y. 60, 171 N.E. 906 (1930) (milkman).

SECTION 4. STATUTORY TREATMENT OF PARTICULAR EMPLOYMENTS

SANDBURN v. HALL
Appellate Court of Indiana, in Banc, 1951.
121 Ind.App. 428, 96 N.E.2d 912.

WILTROUT, CHIEF JUDGE. Appellant filed his application for workmen's compensation. The Industrial Board entered an award that he take nothing thereby, and he seeks a review of that award.

The board, with one member not concurring, found: "That on the 25th day of July 1949, plaintiff was performing services both casual and not in the course of employers' regular business for the defendant herein. That on said date plaintiff sustained accidental injuries while performing such services when a piece of plaster fell into plaintiff's left eye resulting in the loss of the industrial vision thereof."

Appellant points out that the burden of establishing that appellant's employment was casual was upon the employer, Meek v. Julian, 1941, 219 Ind. 83, 36 N.E.2d 854, and argues that the evidence, which was substantially uncontradicted, does not sustain the finding that the employment was casual. We must therefore consider the evidence most favorable to appellees. Scott v. Rhoads, 1943, 114 Ind.App. 150, 51 N.E.2d 89.

Appellee John Hall operates the Hall Sales Company, characterized in the evidence as a hardware and machinery business and also as a farm equipment and sales service. The business is owned by Hall and his wife. Appellant never performed any service for this business.

Hall purchased a lot upon which was located a dwelling house and a barn or garage. The house was purchased for his own residence and for no other purpose. He decided to make the house more modern. It did not have a bathroom or a modern kitchen, and needed repairs. To install the bathroom upstairs some changes were required in the general outline of the building.

Appellant and his father were carpenters. Hall engaged appellant and his father to do the work except the electrical wiring and plumbing. They started the work three or four days after the hiring. Neither party contends that the appellant was an independent contractor. They worked steadily, going to work each morning at about the same time and quitting at about the same time, unless lack of material caused them to quit earlier. The plumbing work caused some interruption. Appellant had no other employment while working on this job.

Appellant started working on the house during the first part of July, 1949, and was injured on July 25, 1949. On that date he was plastering a ceiling when plaster fell in his eye.

The work was completed by others after appellant's injury, it being completed somewhere between six and eight weeks after the work was begun.

The questions of whether appellant's employment was casual and whether it was in the usual course of the trade, business, occupation or profession of the employer are questions of fact for the determination of the Industrial Board. If there is any evidence of probative value to sustain the finding of the board, including legitimate inferences which may be drawn from the evidence, such finding is conclusive, and we may not disturb it. J.P.O. Sandwich Shop, Inc. v. Papadopoulos, 1938, 105 Ind.App. 165, 13 N.E.2d 869.

The compensation acts of most American jurisdictions contain provisions regarding casual employments. The statutes of a few states have provided a specific and arbitrary definition of casual employment. In the states, including Indiana, where no statutory definition has been adopted, the usual and ordinary definitions of the word "casual" as given by the lexicographers find acceptance. Mason v. Wampler, 1929, 89 Ind.App. 483, 166 N.E. 885; Coffin v. Hook, 1942, 112 Ind.App. 549, 45 N.E.2d 369; Lasch v. Corns, Ind.App.1950, 89 N.E.2d 553, 555. While these definitions are helpful, as we said in the last above-cited case: "There is no hard and fast rule by which it can clearly and unfailingly be determined where to draw the line between employments which are casual and those which are not. Each case must rest, in the final analysis, upon its own facts and circumstances."

Here the employment was for a single job which would last for a considerable period of time, and the work to be done was substantial in its nature.

Appellant's employment cannot be said to have been fortuitous, uncertain, occasional, haphazard, unsystematic, irregular, happening by chance or accident or without design. Neither was it casual.

It is stated in 58 Am.Jur., Workmen's Compensation, § 94, p. 645: "Whether an employment for a single job or piece of work is or is not to be regarded as causal depends upon the circumstances. The determination of the question may be governed by the length of time contemplated, or by the nature of the contract of employment. While the mere fact that an employment is for a single job does not necessarily make it casual, an employment for one job which occurs by chance or with the intention and understanding on the part of both the employer or employee that it shall not be continuous, cannot be characterized as permanent or periodically regular, and the great majority of the cases hold that such an employment, which is to last but a short time, not more than three or four days or a week, and is for a limited and temporary purpose, is casual. But an employment, though for a single piece or job of work, which lasts for several weeks or months, or for an indefinite period, is usually regarded as regular and not casual employment."

Again it is stated by 2 Schneider, Workmen's Compensation Law 108, § 279(i) (Perm. ed. 1942): "If there is a single employment which lasts for several weeks or months, or for an indefinite period, it is not considered as casual."

It is said in 71 C.J., Workmen's Compensation Acts, § 179, p. 436: "An employment on a building or in repairing a structure will not be regarded as casual where the work for which claimant was engaged will extend for an indefinite period, or will require a considerable length of time for its completion." * * *

Award reversed, with instructions for further proceedings not inconsistent with this opinion.

Casual Employments

Few compensation schemes contemplate that every employer is always obliged to pay compensation to every employee who is injured at work. Some statutes restrict coverage to workers of employers that are engaged in a business enterprise of some kind and many require additionally that the worker be employed in furtherance of the employer's business. See, e.g., Lackey v. Industrial Commission of Colorado, 80 Colo. 112, 249 P. 662 (1926).

Many statutes also exclude coverage of "casual workers" whose employment is fortuitous and those who are hired for an isolated job of a temporary nature. Despite the fact that these two restrictions on coverage are different and do not rest upon the same policy considerations, most statutes entangle the two. The provisions fall into five general types:

(A) Statutes that exclude all "casual" employments (e.g. Idaho, Maryland, New Jersey, and Tennessee);

(B) Statutes that exclude all employments not in the course of the employer's trade, business or occupation, but that make no distinction between the "casual" and noncasual nature of the employment (e.g. Georgia, Illinois, Kansas, Louisiana, Maine, Massachusetts, South Dakota, Texas and Wisconsin);

(C) Statutes (probably representing the majority) that exclude employments only if they are both "casual" and not in the course of the employer's trade, business or occupation (e.g. Alabama, Arizona, Arkansas, California, Colorado, Connecticut, Delaware, Florida, Indiana, Iowa, Minnesota, Montana, Nebraska, Nevada, New Mexico, North Carolina, North Dakota, Oregon, Ohio, Pennsylvania, Rhode Island, South Carolina, South Dakota, Utah, Vermont, Virginia, Wyoming);

(D) Statutes that exclude employment if they are either "casual" or are not in the course of the employer's trade, business or occupation (e.g., Missouri);

(E) Statutes that cover all employees (not otherwise excluded) without reference to casualness or business character of the employment (e.g., Mississippi). Donald v. Whatley, 346 So.2d 898 (Miss. 1977).

This diversity is further complicated by inconsistent court interpretations of the various provisions. Some states treat the term "casual" as referring exclusively to the unstable duration of the employment in point of time as defined by the contract of hire. See, e.g., Moore v. Clarke, 171 Md. 39, 187 A. 887 (1936) (Jockey hired by professional race horse owner to ride in a single race denied compensation). Other courts have found that the term "casual" relates, not to the contract of hire, but to the nature of the work to be done and the relationship of this work to the business of the employer. Courts employ several different interpretive treatments. See, e.g., Dillard v. Jones, 58 Idaho 273, 72 P.2d 705 (1937), Privette v. South Carolina State Forestry Comm., 265 S.C. 117, 217 S.E.2d 25 (1975), Stephens v. Industrial Comm., 26 Ariz.App. 192, 547 P.2d 44 (1976), and McFall v. Barton–Mansfield Co., 333 Mo. 110, 61 S.W.2d 911 (1933).

Even where the term "casual" refers to the irregular or temporary character of the employment, statutes seldom provide guidelines as to when work is sufficiently transitory or temporary to deny coverage. Moreover, statutes that require a connection of some sort between the work done by the employee and the business of the employer seldom define the connection with precision. Sometimes the statute excludes activities "not for pecuniary gain," as in New York and Maryland; others exclude casual employment where the worker is employed "otherwise than for the purpose of the employer's trade;" and, still others exclude casual employments that are "not in the usual course" of the employer's trade or business. Under the Indiana statute in Sandburn, no inquiry into the "casual" character of the employment is pertinent if the work being done is part of the business or trade of the employer, but even this is not always easy to determine. See, e.g., Nelson v. Stukey, 89 Mont. 277, 300 P. 287 (1931) (dentist, who was also owner of an apartment house with fifteen dwelling units, hired claimant to erect an addition thereto; claimant entitled to compensation under statute similar to one in principal case).

Most jurisdictions include essential maintenance and repair work as being within the course of the business even where the work is not routine and requires the services of an expert. See, e.g., Tuscaloosa Compress Co. v. Hagood, 229 Ala. 284, 156 So. 633 (1934). The same is usually true of remodeling and even new construction work in connection with an established business. See, e.g., Mashburn v. Ne–Hi Bottling Co., 191 Tenn. 135, 229 S.W.2d 520 (1950) (construction of new driveway to bottling plant).

Employment of only a few hours, or even days, is often regarded as casual. Nevertheless, employments that are only periodic in occurrence and in duration are usually covered if they recur regularly. The decisions tend to treat one-time employments necessitated by an unexpected emergency as casual. Compare Ludwig v. Kirby, 13 N.J.Super. 116, 80 A.2d 239 (1951), with Tipper v. Great Lakes Chemical Company, 281 So.2d 10 (Fla.1973). Employments that result from an advance plan of the employer are usually treated as non-casual. See, e.g., Graham v. Green, 31 N.J. 207, 156 A.2d 241 (1959).

Minimum Number of Employees

Workers' compensation statutes commonly exclude employers having fewer than a designated number of employees. This reflects a balance between assuring coverage for every employee and relieving small employments from the fixed costs of injuries suffered by workers without any fault on the part of the employer. This is particularly important to many new business ventures as they start up, often on financial shoe strings. Not wishing to make it too difficult for people to start new economic enterprises, legislatures strike a public policy balance by exempting small employments from the expense of workers' compensation until they reach a level of success signified by the minimum number of employees required for coverage. Is this justified? What is the potential tort liability of the exempted employers?

Provisions of this kind appear in about one-third of the states. The most commonly designated minimum employment sizes are three, four, or five. Most numerical minimum provisions, like the one in the principal case, refer to "regular" employment, but the terms "regular" and "continuous" are not synonymous, as demonstrated by employments that vary by season or demand. Mobile Liners v. McConnell, 220 Ala.

562, 126 So. 626 (1930) (employer hired minimum number of employees only when vessels were in port; held injured stevedore employee was covered). Nevertheless, the minimum number must be regularly employed *together* for some reasonable duration at a point in time not too much in advance of the time of the accident. When this occurs, the courts interpret the numerical minimum liberally in favor of coverage. Typically, only covered employees are included in determining compliance with the minimum provisions. See, e.g. Bettman v. Christen, 128 Ohio St. 56, 190 N.E. 233 (1934). Thus independent contractors, partners, casual workers and other excluded employees are not counted in satisfying the minimum number. Brook's, Inc. v. Claywell, 215 Ark. 913, 224 S.W.2d 37 (1949).

Statutes differ in the treatment accorded employees of employers who conduct several different businesses. In counting the minimum number of employees, most courts include only the employees in the particular business in which the injured employee was engaged. Nevertheless, multiple for-profit operations that are conducted simultaneously are sometimes deemed to constitute a single business and all employees are added together for the purposes of the statute. Chaney v. Industrial Comm., 120 Colo. 111, 207 P.2d 816 (1949) (poultry raising operation and retail outlet for cooked chicken combined for purpose of determining conformity with numerical minimum). Contra., Cohenour v. Papet, 72 So.2d 915 (Fla.1954) (sandwich shop and rental residential property on same lot of land did not constitute a single business).

The Report of the National Commission on State Workmen's Compensation Laws (1972) recommends (R2.2) that all employments be covered without regard to the number of employees. Do you agree? What is the rule in your state?

Illegal Employments

In most states minors employed in violation of child labor statutes are provided compensation by workers' compensation statutes either by express statutory provision or, where silent, by judicial interpretation. See, e.g., Fanion v. McNeal, 577 A.2d 2 (Me.1990). In nearly half of these states illegally employed minors are entitled to additional compensation, frequently double the standard amount (e.g., Alabama, Florida, Indiana, Massachusetts, New York, and Wisconsin). See, Robles v. Mossgood Theatre–Saunders Realty, 53 A.D.2d 972, 385 N.Y.S.2d 822 (1976) (a minor's misrepresentation of his age did not preclude recovery of double compensation). In a few states (e.g., Illinois, and New Jersey) an illegally employed minor has the option to claim compensation or to sue for tort damages, and in some jurisdictions illegally employed minors who suffer work injuries may recover damages in tort litigation solely because of having been unlawfully employed. These decisions exclude from the minor's tort cause of action the requirement that the minor prove that the employer was actually negligent and that the injury was caused by the employer's negligence. Restatement, Second, Torts § 286, comment (e) (1966); Whitney–Fidalgo Seafoods, Inc. v. Beukers, 554 P.2d 250

(Alaska 1976) (illegally employed child may proceed in tort against an employer who has knowingly entered into an illegal contract with him); and, Sloan v. Coit International, Inc., 292 So.2d 15 (Fla.1974) (employing a minor without obtaining the statutory permits was negligence per se without regard to whether the factors that required obtaining the permits caused the injury.)

As to other varieties of illegal employments, a number of jurisdictions distinguish between employments in prohibited businesses, Snyder v. Morgan, 9 N.J.Misc. 293, 154 A. 525 (1931) (employee hired as bartender during prohibition denied compensation), and employments under contracts that are illegal for other reasons, Massachusetts Bonding & Ins. Co. v. Industrial Acc. Comm., 19 Cal.App.2d 583, 65 P.2d 1349 (1937) (night club hostess compensated for injuries received during employment of a type prohibited by California statute) and Commonwealth ex rel. Carter v. Myers, 205 Pa.Super. 478, 211 A.2d 46 (1965) (councilman unlawfully employed by city as street supervisor, held to be an employee although law prohibited his being paid by the city.)

AGRICULTURAL AND FARM EMPLOYMENTS

Most compensation statutes expressly exclude some or all agricultural and farm laborers from coverage, but a few extend coverage to agricultural or dairy laborers while engaged in the operation of designated farm machinery (See, e.g., South Dakota).

What is and what is not a farming or agricultural pursuit is often disputed. Manning v. Win Her Stables, Inc., 91 Idaho 549, 428 P.2d 55 (1967) (training race horses not agricultural), overruled by Tuma v. Kosterman, 106 Idaho 728, 682 P.2d 1275 (1984). Coverage is usually determined by the nature of the employee's work, rather than the type of business conducted by the employer. Dost v. Pevely Dairy Co., 273 S.W.2d 242 (Mo.1954) (janitor maintaining heat for greenhouses awarded compensation; describes distinction between agricultural pursuit and farm labor). Cf. Fidelity Union Cas. Co. v. Carey, 55 S.W.2d 795 (Tex.Com.App.1932) (employee in covered non-agricultural pursuit of an employer, who also raised hogs, was injured while in a pursuit that benefitted both the covered and exempted aspects of the operation; compensation awarded.) Similarly, where the employer is engaged in two coordinated businesses, e.g. one cultivates farm products and the other processes them for market, the worker's right to compensation is determined by the work being done at the time of accident. Pestlin v. Haxton Canning Co., 299 N.Y. 477, 87 N.E.2d 522 (1949) (employee injured while topping beets in the field using topping machinery and crates provided by the cannery; held to be engaged in excluded farming operation.) Quaere, suppose topping operation had been conducted in the cannery building? See Goodson v. L.W. Hult Produce Co., 97 Idaho 264, 543 P.2d 167 (1975) (employer engaged in both raising and marketing potatoes; employer hurt while washing seed potatoes for sale was employed in covered non-agricultural business.)

Agricultural workers are covered on the same basis as other workers in only a few states (e.g., California and Ohio). Noting this, the Report of the National Commission on State Workmen's Compensation Laws (1972) observed:

The plight of the injured farm worker is no less serious than that of a worker in a manufacturing plant or a retail store. Indeed, the farm worker is the least likely to have personal insurance or savings. Administrative problems, however, make universal coverage for farm workers more difficult to achieve than coverage for most other employees. The predominance of part-time help on farms, their geographical dispersion, and the fact that migrant farm workers may work for many different employers during the course of the year present difficulties in reporting, rating, medical care, rehabilitation, and auditing * * *.

The Commission recommended that agricultural workers be treated as any other workers after a transitional period of some sort. Do you agree? What does your state's statute provide in this respect?

Does excluding agricultural employees from coverage violate equal protection or due process clauses of state or federal constitutions? See Gallegos v. Glaser Crandell Co., 388 Mich. 654, 202 N.W.2d 786 (1972) (exclusion of agricultural workers paid on a piecework basis and agricultural workers who do not work 35 or more hours per week held to be invalid), overruled by Eastway v. Eisenga, 420 Mich. 410, 362 N.W.2d 684 (1984).

Domestic Employments

Although most workers' compensation statutes entirely exclude coverage of domestic employees in private homes, a few do cover regularly employed domestics and those employed under prescribed circumstances. For example, Iowa and Kansas provide coverage if the payroll exceeds a specified amount; Kentucky provides coverage if more than one employee is engaged in the household; and Massachusetts, South Dakota and Utah determine coverage by reference to the number of hours the domestic servant works each week.

Some states exclude domestic service and all other non-business employments by exempting coverage of activities that are "not for pecuniary gain," and others do so by excluding employments that are not in the course of the employer's trade, business or occupation (e.g. Georgia, Illinois, Louisiana, Maine, South Dakota, Texas and Wisconsin). Aetna Cas. & Sur. Co. v. Estate of Thomas, 547 S.W.2d 694 (Tex.Civ. App.1977) (claimant worked part time as household employee and part time as business employee; accident while he was household employee, compensation denied).

Most statutes do not exclude coverage of employees who work in the employers' home in some capacity other than domestic service. Nevertheless, coverage of these workers is hindered by two considerations. First, some provisions exempt all employments having fewer than a designated number of employees, and, second, most exempt "casual" employments as referred to above.

The Report of the National Commission on State Workmen's Compensation Laws (1972), recommends (R2.5) that household workers and all casual workers be covered under workers' compensation at least to the extent that they are covered by the federal social security insurance laws. Do you agree?

CHARITABLE AND NON-PROFIT EMPLOYMENTS

Organizations that conduct non-profit pursuits, such as charities, churches and many hospitals, present a workers' compensation quandary. These organizations usually produce no profitable goods and services whose prices would serve to distribute the costs of injuries. Still, work injuries occur in charitable endeavors and their employees are as needful of assistance as any others. Some statutes expressly exclude charitable employers (e.g., Arkansas, North Dakota, and Mississippi), and others exclude employments not carried on "for pecuniary gain" (e.g., Idaho). Compensation is usually denied under statutes of the latter category unless the business has a profit element. See, e.g., Dillon v. St. Patrick's Cathedral, 234 N.Y. 225, 137 N.E. 311 (1922). Where statutes are silent except for the usual requirement that the employment must be in the trade or business of the employer, the decisions are divided: most cover employees of charitable and non-profit institutions, e.g., Meyers v. Southwest Region Conference Ass'n of Seventh Day Adventists, 230 La. 310, 88 So.2d 381 (1956) (minister of church); Smith v. Lincoln Memorial University, 202 Tenn. 238, 304 S.W.2d 70 (1957) (legislative silence on non-profit employers indicates intention to cover), but a few do not, e.g., Caughman v. Columbia Y.M.C.A., 212 S.C. 337, 47 S.E.2d 788 (1948) (advances the doubtful argument that tort immunity of charities prevents the application of the compensation statute). Compare Spokane Methodist Homes, Inc. v. Department of Labor, 4 Wash.App. 598, 483 P.2d 168 (1971) (exclusion of charitable institution from coverage affected by subsequent abolition of tort immunity).

The Report of the National Commission on State Workmen's Compensation Laws (1972) recommends (R2.7) that employees of charitable employments be covered.

PUBLIC EMPLOYMENTS AND OFFICERS

Although employees of a state, its political subdivisions and other public bodies are afforded at least limited coverage by most acts, the statutory variations are no less than bewildering. In some states coverage of public employees is compulsory and as comprehensive as in other employments (e.g., Arizona, California, Florida, Idaho, Montana, Nevada, North Dakota, Utah and Wisconsin), and in others compensation is compulsory for public employees although it is only elective in private employments (e.g., New Jersey). In some states employees of towns and certain other designated units are not covered unless coverage is voted by the community (e.g. Alabama, North Carolina, Vermont, and West

Virginia). In Massachusetts compensation is compulsory for state employments, but is merely elective as to city and county employments, and in Delaware compensation is elective as to state and some other governmental employments.

Many statutes distinguish between covered "employees" and excluded "officers" or "officials." An increasing number of states expressly include public officials within compensation coverage, sometimes subject to limitations (e.g., Arizona, Colorado, Indiana, Iowa, Maine, Montana, New Jersey and Wisconsin). Nevertheless, many acts still either expressly exclude public officers or have been so interpreted by the courts, commonly on the ground that a public officer is not a person "in the service of another under a contract of hire or apprenticeship." Anno. (1949) 5 A.L.R.2d 415, 418. No reasons based upon compensation policy have ever been stated for excluding all officials or for making what seem to be arbitrary distinctions between those that are elected and those appointed.

Whether police officers are covered has proved to be particularly disputatious. Several decisions exclude them on the ground that, as officers, they do not serve under a contract of hire. Mitchell v. James, 182 So.2d 144 (La.App.1966). The same conclusion has also been applied to firefighters. Jackson v. Wilde, 52 Cal.App. 259, 198 P. 822 (1921). Nevertheless, many decisions hold that even in the absence of an express provision police officers and firefighters are covered employees, Fahler v. City of Minot, 49 N.D. 960, 194 N.W. 695 (1923) (police officer); City of Huntington v. Fisher, 220 Ind. 83, 40 N.E.2d 699 (1942) (firefighters). Many statutes expressly cover them. What does your statute provide on this score?

Is a juror hurt while serving on jury duty covered by workers' compensation? Conceding that the number of jurisdictions that denies coverage exceeds the number that grants coverage by a factor of nine-to-one, the Idaho Supreme Court held that the Idaho statute that applies to "all public employments" does cover jurors. Yount v. Boundary County, 118 Idaho 307, 796 P.2d 516 (1990).

HAZARDOUS BUSINESSES AND EMPLOYMENTS

Early fears that workers' compensation statutes would violate constitutional due process clauses prompted many legislatures to restrict coverage to hazardous or ultra-hazardous employments. This apprehension proved to be unfounded as did a once-popular contention that statutes could not mandate employers to provide insurance to secure benefits for employees who were not regularly exposed to risk of serious injury. Presently, few states (e.g. Wyoming and North Dakota) restrict compulsory coverage to "hazardous" businesses. The restricted statutes pose a range of issues not existing under the more common statutes of universal coverage. For example, are all workers of a hazardous business covered, or only those who face the characteristic danger of the employment? Is coverage controlled by the nature of the business, or by the nature of the injured employee's duties? The Report of the Commission on State Workmen's Compensation Laws (1972) recommends (R2.3) that coverage be extended without regard to hazardousness of business. Do you agree?

SECTION 5. STATUTORY EMPLOYMENTS

OAKWOOD HEBREW CEMETERY ASSOCIATION v. SPURLOCK

Court of Appeals of Virginia, 1992.
1992 WL 441851 (Va.App.).

COLEMAN, JUDGE.

Oakwood Hebrew Cemetery Association (Association) appeals the Workers' Compensation Commission award of temporary total and permanent partial disability benefits to Massie Charles Spurlock. The Association contends that the commission erred in making an award of compensation because (1) the Association does not have the requisite number of employees to come within the jurisdiction of the Act, Code s 65.1–28 (now Code s 65.2–101); (2) Spurlock was an independent contractor, not an employee of the Association, and, thus, the Association is not liable to him under the Workers' Compensation Act; and (3) mowing and maintenance that the Association contracted to be performed by Charles Lineberry, Spurlock's immediate employer, is not part of the "trade, business or occupation" of operating a cemetery and, thus, Spurlock was not a statutory employee of the Association within the meaning of Code s 65.1–29 (now Code s 65.2–302).

We hold that because the Association has four executive corporate officers who are deemed employees by Code s 65.1–4 (now Code s 65.2–101), the Association did not come within the purview of the Act. Thus, the commission had jurisdiction to hear Spurlock's claim. We also hold that the Association did not raise the defense before the commission that Spurlock was an independent contractor. Thus, the Association is procedurally barred from raising that claim as a defense for the first time on appeal. Finally, because mowing and grounds-maintenance is part of the "trade, business or occupation" of operating a cemetery, we uphold the commission's decision that the Association was the statutory employer of Spurlock when he was injured.

The Association is incorporated. It has four executive officers. It is engaged in the business of operating a cemetery. Jerome Meyer is president and chief operating officer of the Association. He handles the routine business of running the cemetery, which includes selling cemetery lots. The Association has no other regular employees. Instead, it contracts with others to perform the services it offers. It contracts with Burruss's Vault Company for the opening of graves. It contracts with Chester W. Lineberry for the maintenance work on the cemetery grounds. Additionally, the financial aspects of the Association's business are handled by the Trust Department of Southern Bank and Trust Company.

Massie Charles Spurlock was employed by Chester Lineberry. Lineberry regularly sent Spurlock to do the maintenance work at the Association's Oakwood Cemetery. Spurlock's job entailed maintenance of headstones, keeping flowers in place on the graves, and mowing the grass. He worked each Friday, after completing his shift at his regular job as a maintenance worker for Forest Lawn Cemetery. He was paid $20 per week for the services he performed on Friday for Oakwood Cemetery.

On Friday, October 20, 1989, while starting his lawn mower, Spurlock's right foot slipped under the mower, and he suffered the traumatic amputation of four toes. Spurlock filed a Workers' Compensation claim against Chester Lineberry and the Association, seeking temporary total and permanent partial disability benefits.

After a hearing, the deputy commissioner dismissed Spurlock's claim, concluding that neither Lineberry nor the Association had the number of employees required by Code s 65.1–28 (now Code s 65.2–101) to come within the purview of the Act. On review, the commission affirmed the deputy commissioner's decision as to Lineberry, but reversed with regard to the Association. The commission concluded that the Association came within the Act because it has four executive officers who are deemed employees by Code s 65.1–4 (now Code s 65.2–101) and, thus, the Association did not fall within the exemption of Code s 65.1–28 (now Code s 65.2–101) for a business with "less than three employees." Additionally, the commission ruled that the Association was the statutory employer of Spurlock because it contracted with Lineberry, Spurlock's immediate employer, to perform work that is part of the "trade, business or occupation" of the Association. Thus, the commission held that the Association was liable to Spurlock for workers' compensation benefits. The Association appealed from this decision.

We hold that the commission had jurisdiction over Spurlock's claim against the Association. Code s 65.1–28 (now Code s 65.2–101) exempted certain employers from the coverage of the Workers' Compensation Act. Code s 65.1–28 provided: "This Act shall not apply to ... any person, firm or private corporation, including any public service corporation, that has regularly in service less than three employees in the same business within the Commonwealth." (emphasis added). The Association contends that it had no "employees" and, thus, by virtue of Code s 65.1–28, the commission had no jurisdiction to hear Spurlock's claim. The Association acknowledges that because the corporation has four officers, the commission concluded that it had three or more employees. Code s 65.1–4 includes "[e]very executive officer" within the definition of an "employee." [Ed. Code s 65.2–101 provides: " 'Executive officer' means the president, vice president, secretary, treasurer or other officer, elected or appointed in accordance with the charter and bylaws of a corporation."] The Association argues, however, that the Association was composed of "trustees," rather than "officers" and that "trustees" are not deemed employees by Code s 65.1–4. The uncontradicted evidence proves that the corporation had four executive officers who are deemed "employees" within the meaning of Code s 65.1–4. Thus, we reject the Association's argument.

Code s 65.1–4 defines "employee." It provides: "Every executive officer elected or appointed and empowered in accordance with the charter and bylaws of a corporation, municipal or otherwise, shall be an employee of such corporation under this Act." The plain language of the statute, by which we are bound, ..., provides that executive officers of a corporation are deemed to be employees within the Act. Moreover, the commission has consistently held that corporate officers are employees of the corporation, even when they are not compensated for their services. See Polozzi v. Custom Travel & Designs, Inc., 68 O.I.C. 100, 102 (1989). . . . ."[T]he construction accorded a statute by public officials charged with its administration . . . is entitled to be given weight by the court." Baskerville v. Saunders Oil Co., 1 Va.App. 188, 193, 336 S.E.2d 512, 514 (1985) (citation omitted). Where an agency's construction of a statute has been consistent and long continued, it is entitled to great deference because in such a case, the "legislature will be presumed to have acquiesced therein." Id.

Jerome Meyer, president of the Association, testified that the Association is incorporated and has four corporate officers. Code s 65.1–4 clearly states that the corporate officers are "employees" of the corporation. Consequently, because the Association does not have less than three employees regularly in service, it does not come within the exemption provided by Code s 65.1–28. Thus, the commission had jurisdiction over Spurlock's claim against the Association.

The Association next argues that Spurlock was an independent contractor, rather than an employee and, thus, the Association is not liable to pay workers' compensation benefits to him. Spurlock contends that the Association did not raise this issue before the commission, and, therefore, it is procedurally barred from raising it for the first time on appeal. We agree with Spurlock. An issue that is not disputed before the commission will not be considered on appeal. Green v. Warwick Plumbing & Heating Corp., 5 Va.App. 409, 412–13, 364 S.E.2d 4, 6 (1988) . . . . . The record shows that the Association never contended before the commission that Spurlock was an independent contractor. Consequently, the Association is procedurally barred from interposing the defense for the first time on appeal.

Finally, the Association contends that the commission erred in concluding that mowing and maintenance was part of its "trade, business or occupation" of operating a cemetery. Thus, the Association argues that the commission erred in holding that the Association was the statutory employer of Spurlock. In response, Spurlock argues that we should not reach the merits of this issue because the Association also did not raise this issue before the commission. The issue was raised before the deputy commissioner by the Assistant Attorney General representing the Uninsured Employers' Fund. The issue was raised by a party adverse to Spurlock and was considered and decided by the deputy commissioner and by the commission. Consequently, we reject Spurlock's contention that the issue is procedurally barred.

Code s 65.1–29 provides: s 65.1–29. Liability of owner to workmen of subcontractors.—When any person (in this section and ss 65.1–31 and 65.1–32 referred to as "owner") undertakes to perform or execute any work which is a part of his trade, business or occupation and contracts with any other person (in this section and ss 65.1–31 to 65.1–34 referred to as "subcontractor") for the execution or performance by or under such subcontractor of the whole or any part of the work undertaken by such owner, the owner shall be liable to pay to any workman employed in the work any compensation under this Act which he would have been liable to pay if the workman had been immediately employed by him. (Code 1950, s 65–26; 1968, c. 660.) The primary purpose of this statute "is to 'protect the employees of subcontractors who are not financially responsible and to prevent employers from relieving themselves of liability (for compensation) by doing through independent contractors what they would otherwise do through direct employees.' " Bassett Furniture Indust., Inc. v. McReynolds, 216 Va. 897, 902, 224 S.E.2d 323, 326 (1976). If mowing and maintenance, which the Association contracted to be performed by Chester Lineberry, Spurlock's immediate employer, is part of its "trade, business or occupation" of operating a cemetery, then, pursuant to Code s 65.1–29 (now Code s 65.2–302), it is liable to pay compensation benefits to Spurlock as his statutory employer, just as if Spurlock had been directly employed by the Association.

Deciding what is the "trade, business or occupation" of an entity is a "mixed question of law and fact." Henderson v. Central Telephone Co., 233 Va. 377, 382, 355 S.E.2d 596, 599 (1987). The test for determining whether the activity engaged in by a subcontractor is part of the "trade, business or occupation" of the "owner" varies depending on whether the "owner" is engaged in private business or is a public utility or governmental entity. Id. at 382–83, 355 S.E.2d at 599–600. If the "owner" is a public utility or governmental entity, a court must consider "the laws under which they were created and under which they functioned in determining their trade, business, or occupation." Ford v. City of Richmond, 239 Va. 664, 667, 391 S.E.2d 270, 272 (1990). . . . If the entity is private in nature, however, the test is not one of whether the subcontractor's activity is useful, necessary, or even absolutely indispensable to the statutory employer's business, since, after all, this could be said of practically any repair, construction, or transportation service. The test . . . is whether this indispensable activity is, in the business, normally carried on through employees rather than independent contractors. Henderson, 233 Va. at 382–83, 355 S.E.2d at 599 (quoting Shell Oil Co. v. Leftwich, 212 Va. 715, 722, 187 S.E.2d 162, 167 (1972) (citation omitted) (emphasis in original)).

The Association is engaged in the private enterprise of operating a cemetery. The dispositive issue is whether mowing and maintenance of a cemetery, the activity which Lineberry contracted to perform, is "normally" performed by employees of those in the business of operating a cemetery, rather than independent contractors. Jerome Meyer testified that maintenance is a normal part of the business of running a cemetery. Spurlock, himself, was a regular, full-time employee of Forest Lawn Cemetery, another cemetery enterprise, where he mowed and maintained the cemetery as the regular duties of his employment. In fact, Chester Lineberry, who performed the contracted services for the Association on a part-time basis, was also a regular, full-time employee of Forest Lawn Cemetery. Additionally, Lineberry testified that his two brothers were employees of Mount Calvary Cemetery, doing maintenance work, and the work which he did is typical of what is done in mowing and maintaining cemeteries. Lineberry testified that people in his position could generally be found in any cemetery. The evidence established that mowing and maintenance of cemeteries are activities normally performed by employees of those in the business of operating a cemetery, rather than by independent contractors. Moreover, while the commission may have erroneously alluded to Code s 57–24 defining the powers and duties of trustees who have been appointed by the court as the basis for its holding that mowing and maintenance were part of the Association's "trade, business, or occupation," even though the trustees of the Association were not appointed pursuant to Code s 57–23, the statute recognizes and incorporates the customary and generally recognized duties of operating and maintaining a cemetery. It is apparent that mowing and maintenance are part of the "trade, business, or occupation" of operating a cemetery, and the evidence establishes that cemeteries usually have employees who perform that function. The Association may not escape liability for workers' compensation benefits by contracting for the performance of the mowing and maintenance services it provides, rather than by hiring regular employees. Consequently, we hold that the mowing and maintenance activity that Lineberry contracted to perform for the Association is part of the Association's "trade, business or occupation" within the meaning of Code s 65.1–29, and, thus, the Association was Spurlock's statutory employer when he was injured.

For the foregoing reasons, we affirm the commission's decision awarding workers' compensation benefits to Spurlock. Affirmed.

Notes

1.   All states (except perhaps California, Delaware, Iowa, Maine, Rhode Island and West Virginia) include a "Statutory Employment" or "Contracting Under" provision of some sort. See § 1(b), Workmen's Compensation and Rehabilitation Law, Appendix B. The purpose is to assure that workers on large projects and enterprises are not excluded from workers' compensation coverage by virtue of a fractionation of the employment activities among a number of independent employers, some of which may be too small to be covered under the statutes or financially irresponsible in securing benefits. The statutes specify a statutory employer who must assume workers' compensation liability for all employees within the statutory employment. Under these provisions, the statutory employer is liable to pay workers' compensa-

tion benefits to statutory employees who are the actual employees of some other employer. Usually statutory employment liability is not restricted to a technical "contractor" who has subcontracted some part of a major project to subcontracting employers, but extends to any person who seeks to perform business through a contractor.

Statutory employment provisions do not necessarily apply to all contractual arrangements that result in leaving some employees without adequate workers' compensation coverage. The business arrangements between large buyers of raw materials from small sellers, which is fairly common in the lumbering industry, may have this effect. Hart v. Richardson, 272 So.2d 316 (La.1973) (employee of independent buyer of timber for corporation held to be covered under corporation's workers' compensation policy that covered independent contractors). Similarly, a so-called lessor may enter a leasing arrangement in order to avoid workers' compensation liability to the so-called lessee's employees. See, e.g., Washel v. Tankar Gas, Inc., 211 Minn. 403, 2 N.W.2d 43 (1941) (employee of filling station leased from distributor held entitled to compensation from latter).

2. As in *Spurlock*, a frequently disputed matter under statutory employment provisions is whether the work of the injured employee is as part of the regular business of the statutory employer. A single job of erecting, demolishing or repairing a capital structure of the principal will usually be regarded as outside the statutory employer's regular business, unless the principal is in the business of construction for others or for its own business purposes, as is often true of power companies and oil producing concerns. See, e.g., Ray v. Monsanto Co., 420 F.2d 915 (9th Cir.1970) (installation of furnace for phosphate producer was not regular business of producer; producer not liable for benefits for employee of installing contractor); Burroughs v. Walmont, Inc., 210 Va. 98, 168 S.E.2d 107 (1969) (employee of supplier held not to be the employee of a general contractor to whom claimant was delivering supplies when injured); Cinnamon v. International Business Machines Corp., 238 Va. 471, 384 S.E.2d 618 (Va. 1989)(injured employee of subcontractor of building contractor possessed no tort cause of action against the contracting property owner who was not in the contracting business). Cf. Weaver v. Mutual Building & Homestead Ass'n, 195 So. 384 (La.App.1940) (mortgage loan company liable to employees of contractor who repaired dwellings on which company held mortgages); and, MacMullen v. South Carolina Electric & Gas Co., 312 F.2d 662 (4th Cir.1963) (construction of power generator part of the business of power company; power company liable to employees of contractor.)

Recurrent minor repairs, redecorating, window washing and similar ancillary operations are usually regarded as part of the business of the principal. Bailey v. Mosby Hotel Co., 160 Kan. 258, 160 P.2d 701 (1945) (floor waxing in hotel). Cf. American Radiator Co. v. Franzen, 81 Colo. 161, 254 P. 160 (1927) (window washing in industrial establishment not part of business). Factors commonly considered are: the past and present practices in the principal's and similar businesses; whether the activity is customarily carried out by the principal's own workers; the regularity or irregularity of the occurrence of the work; and, the specialized or non-specialized character of the work. In making this determination, Finlay v. Storage Technology Corporation, 764 P.2d 62, 67 (Colo. En Banc 1998) ruled that "courts should consider the elements of routineness, regularity, and the importance of the contracted service to the regular business of the employer."

3. In some states the statutory employer is "primarily" liable to pay the compensation benefits to the injured statutory employee (e.g., La.R.S. (1989) § 23:1061; Wash.Rev.Stat. (1990) § 51.12.07). This means the employee can claim benefits first from the statutory employer and the statutory employer can seek indemnity from the true employer. In other states (e.g., Arkansas, Illinois, Massachusetts, Minnesota, Missouri, New Jersey, New York, North Carolina) the statutory employer is secondarily liable and pays the compensation only if the actual employee of the injured worker is uninsured, insolvent, or not covered under the law. Under either view, a statutory employer who is compelled to pay benefits to a statutory employee is entitled to seek indemnity over from an actual employer that is covered by the law (e.g., New York Workmen's Compensation Law (McKinney 1990) § 56.) Under some statutes, however, a statutory employer that expressly undertakes to assume direct responsibility for compensating statutory employees may forego the indemnity right. Andrews v. Spearsville Timber Co., Inc., 343 So.2d 1008 (La.1977). The distinction between primary and secondary liability of the statutory employer may be important in determining whether the latter is exempt from a tort claim by the statutory employee. See Eger v. E. I. Du Pont DeNemours Company, 110 N.J. 133, 539 A.2d 1213 (1988)(contrasting the laws of New Jersey under which statutory employers are immune to tort suits from employees of subcontractors and the laws of South Carolina under which they are not immune).

4. In the absence of a provision such as that referred to in the principal case, decisions differ on whether employees of intermediate contractors should be added in computing the numerical minimum of employees required for statutory employment coverage. Several states have held that a statutory employer is liable to pay compensation to statutory employees if the sum of all statutory employees and those of the statutory employer satisfies the minimum. Compare Withers v. Black, 230 N.C. 428, 53 S.E.2d 668 (1949) (principal contractor hired fewer direct employees than the required minimum but employees of subcontractors were added to reach the minimum), Bradshaw v. Glass, 252 Ga. 429, 314 S.E.2d 233 (1984) (general contractor who did not employ the minimum number of employees is not responsible for payment of workers' compensation benefits under a statutory employer provision), and Jackson v. Fly, 215 Miss. 303, 60 So.2d 782 (Miss. 1952)(statutory employer liable for workers' compensation payments to employees of a subcontractor only if the subcontractor has the minimum number of employees required for coverage). Does the *Spurlock* opinion of itself permit a determination of what would have been the outcome of the case under Virginia law if the court had deemed the corporate offices *not* to have been employees?

SECTION 6. MULTIPLE EMPLOYERS

WEDECK v. UNOCAL CORPORATION

California Court of Appeal, First District, 1997.
59 Cal.App.4th 848, 69 Cal.Rptr.2d 501.

KLINE, PRESIDING JUSTICE.

Rowena Wedeck appeals the trial court's grant of summary judgment in favor of respondent Unocal Corporation. On appeal, she challenges the trial court's determination that Unocal was her special employer as a matter of law and that she was, therefore, statutorily barred from bringing a tort action against Unocal for personal injuries received while she was working at Unocal. We shall affirm the judgment.

FACTUAL AND PROCEDURAL BACKGROUND

In May 1992 Wedeck began working for Lab Support, an agency which is in the business of placing technical employees with other companies on a temporary basis. In August 1992, Wedeck, who has a Bachelor of Science degree in Chemistry, accepted an assignment through Lab Support to work at the Unocal refinery in Rodeo as a full-time chemist. Amy Conner * * * , who was the account manager for Lab Support, arranged for Wedeck's work assignment at Unocal. That assignment was confirmed by a letter agreement from Lab Support to Unocal dated August 20, 1992, which set forth the terms and conditions of Wedeck's assignment at Unocal. Paragraph 6 of the terms and conditions stated: "Customer and Lab Support agree that all personnel provided by Lab Support in connection with this Agreement are employees and/or contractors of Lab Support, but that such personnel shall receive all technical direction from the designated manager of Customer. Customer shall otherwise contact such personnel through Lab Support."

Wedeck worked at Unocal for nearly a year, from August 24, 1992 until August 13, 1993. Unocal paid Lab Support an hourly rate for Wedeck's work and Wedeck was paid by submitting weekly time cards, supplied by Lab Support and signed by both Wedeck and Unocal, to Lab Support. The time cards included a "Client Agreement" which stated, in part: "We [the client] understand that the supervision of the assigned LSI [Lab Support, Inc.] employee for the agreed upon duties is our (the client's) responsibility. [P] We further agree to provide any general or specific safety training necessary to perform the assignment * * * "

At Unocal, Wedeck worked in the Chemical Laboratory performing analytical tests on various materials and product samples generated by Unocal's refinery. She received training and instruction from Unocal chemists at the start of and, as necessary, during the time she worked at Unocal concerning the work she was performing. Wedeck was required to follow Unocal's procedures as set forth in its Chemical Laboratory Chemical Procedures Manuals, and she periodically referred to these manuals, which were placed at the locations where she worked within the laboratory, for guidance.

Unocal notified Wedeck of her work assignments in a regular schedule which identified the specific chemical testing and analyses she was to perform during that period. Unocal provided Wedeck with the equipment and tools she needed to perform her job, including safety equipment which was supplied to all temporary chemists working in the laboratory. [Ed., "Wedeck used her own safety glasses, which she had received from Lab Support, although she understood that she could use a pair of Unocal's safety glasses if she forgot to bring her own."] Wedeck was required to perform weekly quality assurance tests on her work. A Unocal employee in charge of quality assurance would periodically check the log book in which Wedeck had recorded results of her quality assurance tests. Unocal's Chemical Laboratory Supervisor, Dale Iverson, was Wedeck's site supervisor during her time at Unocal.

Other than several phone conversations regarding safety, Lab Support provided no training or instruction to Wedeck regarding her work at Unocal; provided her with none of the tools or equipment necessary to perform her job (other than safety glasses and pamphlets on safety issues); and had no involvement in assigning the work she performed there.

In July 1993, Dale Iverson submitted a service contract requisition which requested that a purchase order be generated to "provide temporary laboratory staffing in accordance with the attached agreement." The August 20, 1992 letter, with its accompanying terms and conditions, was attached to the requisition form. On the reverse side of the purchase order, which was generated by Unocal on July 28, 1993 in response to Iverson's request, was a printed list of terms and conditions; paragraph 16 of those terms and conditions stated that if work is performed on company property, "[s]ervice work is to be entirely under Supplier's supervision, direction and control. Company retains no control over the operative details of Supplier's work. Supplier shall take special precautions to eliminate or minimize risks 'peculiar' to supplier's work."

Neither Unocal nor Lab Support intended the terms on the reverse side of the purchase order to modify or supersede the prior agreement between the two companies. Conner did not read the terms and conditions on the reverse side of the purchase order before signing it, and understood it to be only a written acknowledgment by Unocal of Wedeck's work assignment. Conner had no authority to modify the standard terms and conditions contained in all of Lab Support's agreements with outside companies, including the August 20, 1992 agreement regarding Wedeck.

On July 27, 1994, Wedeck filed a complaint alleging that she suffered personal injuries from exposure to chemicals while working at Unocal's laboratory. Unocal raised an affirmative defense, asserting that it was Wedeck's special employer at the time she allegedly sustained the injuries and that, consequently, the complaint was barred under the Workers' Compensation Exclusive Remedy Rule pursuant to Labor Code section 3602. Unocal thereafter filed a motion for summary judgment based on this defense, which the trial court denied, having found that the purchase order (Fact No. 42) raised a triable issue of fact as to whether Unocal was in fact Wedeck's special employer.

Unocal then filed a motion for reconsideration of its summary judgment motion. The trial court considered additional evidence submitted by Unocal concerning Fact No. 42 and granted both the motion for reconsideration and the motion for summary judgment, concluding that Wedeck had raised no triable issue of material fact disputing Unocal' s status as her special employer. This timely appeal followed.

DISCUSSION

* * *

II.

Wedeck contends the trial court erred in finding that Unocal was Wedeck's special employer and on that basis granting Unocal's motion for summary judgment.

In Riley v. Southwest Marine, Inc. (1988) 203 Cal.App.3d 1242, 1247–1248, 250 Cal.Rptr. 718, the Court of Appeal explained the concept of special employment: "A 'special employment' relationship arises when an employer lends an employee to another employer and relinquishes to the borrowing employer all right of control over the employee's activities. [Citation.] The borrowed employee is ' "held to have two employers—his original or 'general' employer and a second, the 'special' employer." ' [Citations.] In this dual employer situation, the employee is generally limited to a statutory workers' compensation remedy for injuries he receives in the course of his employment with the special employer; he may not bring a separate tort action against either employer."

The question whether a special employment relationship exists is generally a question of fact reserved for the jury. (Kowalski v. Shell Oil Co. (1979) 23 Cal.3d 168, 175, 151 Cal.Rptr. 671, 588 P.2d 811.) "However, if neither the evidence nor inferences are in conflict, then the question of whether an employment relationship exists becomes a question of law which may be resolved by summary judgment." (Riley v. Southwest Marine, Inc., supra, 203 Cal.App.3d at p. 1248, 250 Cal.Rptr. 718 * * *

"Factors relevant to determining whether an employee is the borrowed employee of another include: (1) whether the borrowing employer's control over the employee and the work he is performing extends beyond mere suggestion of details or cooperation; (2) whether the employee is performing the special employer's work; (3) whether there was an agreement, understanding, or meeting of the minds between the original and special employer; (4) whether the employee acquiesced in the new work situation; (5) whether the original employer terminated his relationship with the employee; (6) whether the special employer furnished the tools and place for performance; (7) whether the new employment was over a considerable length of time; (8) whether the borrowing employer had the right to fire the employee and (9) whether the borrowing employer had the obligation to pay the employee." (Riley v. Southwest Marine, Inc., supra, 203 Cal.App.3d at p. 1250, 250 Cal. Rptr. 718.) Of these considerations, the primary one in determining whether a special employment relationship exists is whether the special employer has "[t]he right to control and direct the activities of the alleged employee or the manner and method in which the work is performed, whether exercised or not...." (Kowalski v. Shell Oil Co., supra, 23 Cal.3d at p. 175, 151 Cal.Rptr. 671, 588 P.2d 811, internal quotation marks omitted * * *

"Circumstances which tend to negate the existence of a special employment relationship include the following factors: the worker is skilled and has substantial control over operational details, the worker is not engaged in the borrower's usual business, the worker works only for a brief period of time, does not use the tools or equipment of the borrowing employer but uses his own tools or the tools of the lending employer and the borrower employer neither pays the worker nor has the right to discharge him." (Riley v. Southwest Marine, Inc., supra, 203 Cal.App.3d at p. 1250, 250 Cal.Rptr. 718.)

In Riley, * * * the following facts, from Riley's own deposition testimony, unequivocally established that a special employment relationship existed between Riley and Southwest Marine: He agreed to the Southwest Marine work assignment; he was an unskilled general laborer working exclusively at Southwest Marine's job site; Southwest Marine personnel trained him, provided his daily job instructions, and supervised his work; Southwest Marine provided all safety equipment and work tools; Riley had worked for Southwest Marine more than briefly, i.e., for over seven months at the time of his injury; and Riley believed Southwest Marine had the power to discharge him. ..."In sum, Southwest Marine had the right to control and direct Riley's activities and the manner in which he performed the work; Southwest Marine did not merely make suggestions of details or cooperation." (Ibid.) Furthermore, Riley's evidence showing he was Manpower's employee did not raise a material factual dispute because Riley was in a dual employment situation. * * *

The court then rejected Riley's argument that the general rule barring separate tort actions against special employers should not be extended to the labor brokerage situation. "Extensive nationwide case law * * * hold[s] the 'special employment' or 'borrowed servant' doctrine applies to the labor brokerage situation and bars an employee who is injured while on assignment from a labor broker, such as Manpower, from bringing a tort suit against the assigned employer. [Citations.]" (Riley v. Southwest Marine, Inc., supra, 203 Cal.App.3d at pp. 1251–1252, 250 Cal.Rptr. 718; ...

In the present case, the undisputed facts show that the primary consideration—whether Unocal had the right to control and direct Wedeck's activities and the manner in which her work was performed—

must be decided in favor of Unocal. Wedeck received ongoing training and instruction from Unocal chemists concerning the work she was to perform in the Chemical Laboratory; she referred to Unocal procedures manuals and followed Unocal's procedures and instructions in performing her work; Unocal provided Wedeck with all of her work assignments in the laboratory; and her quality assurance tests were monitored by Unocal supervisors for completeness. * * *

Wedeck's argument that triable issues remain regarding her factual allegations of self-supervision and technical skill is without merit. First, with respect to the former allegation, Wedeck asserts that the minimal time Unocal chemists spent training her to perform Unocal's work as well as Dale Iverson's inability to recall the specific chemists who trained her or the exact dates he reviewed her work show that a triable issue remains as to her self-supervision. However, neither the brevity of the training she received nor Iverson's inability to remember the day-to-day details regarding supervision changes the undisputed facts that Wedeck understood she would not be supervised by Lab Support and that she was expected to carry out her job duties as she was trained to do by Unocal supervisors, do the work assigned by Unocal supervisors, and perform regular quality assurance tests which were subject to supervisory review. That she performed her job without constant intervention by supervisors does not negate the undisputed fact that she was subject to Unocal's control and direction. "As indicated, the control need not be exercised. It is sufficient if the right to direct the details of the work is present." ... Kowalski v. Shell Oil Co., supra, 23 Cal.3d at p. 175, 151 Cal.Rptr. 671, 588 P.2d 811.)

Similarly, with respect to the technical skill as a chemist Wedeck brought to the job, although most of the relevant cases involve unskilled workers, the record again shows that, regardless of the experience and knowledge she brought with her, Wedeck was trained by Unocal and was subject to Unocal's ongoing direction and control in performing her job. Despite Wedeck's assertion that she had "substantial control over operational details" * * * , the record demonstrates that she was expected to exercise her technical skill in the way dictated by Unocal's systems and procedures. (See 3 Larson, Workers' Compensation Law, supra, s 44.32(c), pp. 8–104–8–105 ["It should be stressed * * * that the absence of exercise of control has seldom been given any weight in showing absence of right of control, since the non exercise can often be explained by lack of occasion for supervision of the particular employee, because of his competence or experience."].)

Wedeck also attempts to refute the evidence of Unocal's supervision of her work by characterizing the direction she received at Unocal as merely informational, arguing that Unocal simply did not exercise the kind of control that would give rise to a special employment relationship. "The fact that instructions are given as to the result to be achieved does not require the conclusion that a special employment relationship exists." (McFarland v. Voorheis–Trindle Co., supra, 52 Cal.2d at p. 704, 343 P.2d 923.)

In McFarland, the plaintiff, a master mechanic and experienced equipment operator, was employed by a tractor company and was operating a bulldozer at the defendant's job site when he was injured. (Id. at p. 701, 343 P.2d 923.) "No control was exercised by the defendant over the plaintiff in the performance of his duties as mechanic and repairman. Nor does it appear that the defendant instructed the plaintiff or other operators in the running of their equipment. The defendant's superintendent, in assigning work, designated the job to be done, such as a road to be cut or brush to be cleared within surveyed lines, and the details of that work were left to the judgment of the individual equipment operators. It appears that the plaintiff was operating under such instructions when the accident occurred." (Id. at p. 705, 343 P.2d 923.) * * * The present case does not resemble those relied on by Wedeck. Wedeck was not sent in briefly to Unocal to perform a task, with unlimited discretion in how she achieved the result. She was given specific training by Unocal, was expected to and did follow Unocal's particularized procedures, and was given regular assignments by Unocal supervisors during the nearly one year she worked at the chemical laboratory. The undisputed facts show that the direction given to Wedeck at Unocal was not merely informational.

Application of the great majority of the secondary factors to the undisputed facts also leads to the conclusion that Wedeck was Unocal's employee. Wedeck performed Unocal's work at Unocal's job site using, with only minimal exceptions, Unocal's tools and equipment; Lab Support and Unocal agreed that Wedeck would be wholly trained and supervised by Unocal; Wedeck accepted the assignment with Unocal and acquiesced in all of the conditions of work in Unocal's Chemical Laboratory; Unocal paid Lab Support an hourly rate for Wedeck's work, and Lab Support paid her; and she worked at the laboratory for nearly one year. * * *

With respect to the factor concerning the right to fire the employee, Wedeck's supervisor at Unocal, Dale Iverson, understood he had the authority to terminate Wedeck's employment. Wedeck, on the other hand, understood that if Unocal no longer wanted her services, it would so inform Lab Support, which would in turn inform her. Wedeck argues that her testimony created a triable issue of fact because the factor regarding the right to discharge the employee would require that Unocal had the right to fire Wedeck from her job with Lab Support, not just to remove her from her position with Unocal.

In Kowalski v. Shell Oil Co., supra, 23 Cal.3d at page 177, 151 Cal.Rptr. 671, 588 P.2d 811, the Supreme Court stated: "Evidence that the alleged special employer has the power to discharge a worker 'is strong evidence of the existence of a special employment relationship * * * .' [Citation.]" However, the court concluded that the ability to terminate the special employment or have the employee removed from the premises of the special employer is not necessarily probative of the existence of a special employment relationship. "[T]hat an alleged special employer can have an employee removed from the job site does not necessarily indicate the existence of a special employment relationship. Anyone who has the employees of an independent contractor working on his premises could, if dissatisfied with an employee, have the employee removed. Yet, the ability to do so would not make the employees of the independent contractor the special employees of the party receiving the services." (Id. at p. 177, fn. 9, 151 Cal.Rptr. 671, 588 P.2d 811.)

Kowalski was not concerned with the right of a special employer to terminate an employee from his or her general employment. Rather, the court was merely cautioning that "the power of the alleged special employer to terminate the special employment relationship is not determinative, since that power will always be present." (Santa Cruz Poultry, Inc. v. Superior Court, supra, 194 Cal.App.3d at p. 581, fn. 1, 239 Cal.Rptr. 578.) Thus, we disagree with Wedeck to the extent she contends, relying on Kowalski, that a triable issue of fact arises from an evidentiary conflict as to Unocal's ability to discharge her from employment at Lab Support. Despite retaining the right to terminate the special employment relationship, the ability of a special employer to discharge the employee from his or her general employment would be unusual indeed, particularly in the labor broker context.

Moreover, even if the power to actually discharge the employee is a proper factor for consideration in the present situation, the factual dispute about Unocal's ability to terminate Wedeck from her employment does not raise a triable issue of material fact, given the strength of the other factors—particularly with respect to Unocal's right to control and direct Wedeck's activities—in demonstrating that Wedeck was the special employee of Unocal. . . . . .

DISPOSITION

The judgment is affirmed.

Notes

1. Numerous statutes expressly treat the lent employee issue. See Ill.Rev.Stats. (1988) c. 48 § 138.1(a)(4); Conn.Gen.Stat.Ann. § 31–292; and Mass.G.L.A. c. 152 § 18 (as amended 1969). These measures usually retain the compensation liability of the lending employer in addition to that of the borrower and provide for the adjustment of the two employers' liabilities as between themselves. Chicago's Finest Workers Co. v. Industrial Comm., 61 Ill.2d 340, 335 N.E.2d 434 (1975) (lending employer liable only if borrowing employer does not pay benefits; lender is entitled to indemnity). Liability of both lender and borrower is recognized by judicial decision in several states. See Leggette v. J.D. McCotter, Inc., 265 N.C. 617, 144 S.E.2d 849 (1965) (citing other supporting jurisdictions).

2. Disputes about who is liable to pay compensation to a borrowed employee frequently involve employees who assist each other in carrying out common work, as for example employees of two subcontractors or of one subcontractor and the principal contractor. See Dupre v. Sterling Plate Glass & Paint Co., Inc., 344 So.2d 1060 (La.App.1977) (employee of subcontractor

stopped on way back from coffee break to help employee of another subcontractor, held not borrowed).

3. Labor broker cases, such as *Wedeck*, frequently raise the question, "In workers' compensation cases, who is the employer, the labor broker or the customer company?" Should worker injuries be considered a cost of the business of supplying labor or a cost of the business of the customer company? The prevailing view treats the labor broker as the "general employer" and the customer company as a "special employer". See, e.g., Lindsey v. Bucyrus–Erie, 161 Ariz. 457, 778 P.2d 1353 (1989); Santa Cruz Poultry, Inc. v. Superior Court, 194 Cal.App.3d 575, 239 Cal.Rptr. 578 (1987); Sheets v. J.H. Heath Tree Service Inc., 193 Ga.App. 278, 387 S.E.2d 155 (1989); and Goodman v. Sioux Steel Co., 475 N.W.2d 563 (S.D.1991) (collecting cases). United States Fidelity & Guaranty Company v. Technical Minerals, Inc., 934 S.W.2d 266 (Ky.1996), applied the Kentucky statute to treat the employer who hired temporary workers to be a contractor and the company supplying the temporary workers to be a subcontractor. Under this analysis, the "contractor" hiring employer was both immune to tort suits by a temporary worker and liable to pay workers' compensation benefits for injuries sustained, subject to indemnification from the "subcontractor" who had supplied the temporary worker. In some instances whether the employee consented to having been "lent" to the customer company is disputed. See, e.g., Pato v. Sweeney Steel Service Corp., 117 A.D.2d 984, 499 N.Y.S.2d 286 (1986).

4. As in *Kowalski*, which was cited extensively in the principal case, the actual determination of what employment status exits is typically deemed to be a factual question for determination by a jury in tort cases. According to *Wedeck's* quotations from *Kowalski*, what are the important factors? Should the same analysis apply to cases in which the worker is attempting to avoid being found to be an "employee," as in *Wedeck*, and those in which the worker is claiming workers' compensation benefits against an "employer's" denial of responsibility? See, e.g., Appeal of Longchamps Electric, Inc., 137 N.H. 731, 634 A.2d 994 (N.H. 1993)(factual determination of compensation appeal board sustained).

5. Should the "employer" that is not liable for payment of workers' compensation be immune from tort suit? See section 3, Chapter 11.

NATIONAL AUTOMOBILE & CAS. INS. CO. v. INDUSTRIAL ACC. COMM.

District Court of Appeal, California, 1947.
80 Cal.App.2d 769, 182 P.2d 634.

SHINN, ACTING PRESIDING JUSTICE. Petitioner, the insurance carrier of Glenn Growers Cooperative, Inc., hereinafter called Cooperative, seeks annulment of an award made against it by respondent commission on the two grounds that (1) the claimant, Frank Pitt, was not at the time of his injury acting within the course of his employment by the Cooperative, and (2) was not covered by petitioner's policy of compensation insurance. In support of the first ground petitioner contends that Pitt at the time of his injury was either working solely in the course of his employment by Eibe and Huffman Warehouse Company, Inc., hereinafter called Warehouse Company, in which event petitioner should wholly escape liability, or working in the course of a joint employment by the Cooperative and the Warehouse Company, in which event petitioner's liability should be reduced proportionately. Respondent commission found, in effect, that Pitt was injured solely in the course of his employment by the Cooperative. The initial issue therefore is whether Pitt was solely employed by the Cooperative or employed both by the Cooperative and the Warehouse Company. The facts of the employment relationship between Pitt, the Cooperative, and the Warehouse Company existing at the time of the injury are not in dispute. * * *

The Cooperative operated a rice drier which adjoined the buildings of the Warehouse Company. Pitt served as the manager of both concerns, but his salary and the compensation insurance premiums thereon were paid entirely by the Cooperative, pursuant to an oral arrangement it had with the Warehouse Company during the entire period of Pitt's dual employment. The arrangement was that solely in return for Pitt's services as manager of the Warehouse Company, it made available its scales and a portion of its premises, including part of its warehouse, to the Cooperative. Pitt's injury occurred in the part of the warehouse used by the Warehouse Company, and at that time he was engaged in the supervision of a shipment of rice by the Warehouse Company. However, Pitt divided his working time between the two concerns and when engaged in the work of the one, he was always on call by the other. * * *

* * * The only inference that may properly be drawn from the facts of the instant case is the one of dual employment of Pitt by the Cooperative and the Warehouse Company. Petitioner is therefore entitled to object to the erroneous discharge by the commission of the insurance carrier of the Warehouse Company. Hartford Accident & Indemnity Co. v. Industrial Accident Comm., 8 Cal.2d 589, 591, 67 P.2d 105.

The commission's legal conclusion of sole employment by the Cooperative cannot be sustained. As will be developed more fully, its referee's holding to that effect involved a patent misconstruction of the purpose and effect of the arrangement between the Cooperative and the Warehouse Company as to Pitt's employment. Moreover, the holding was based upon the erroneous conception that the employers could by agreement between themselves control the matter of their liability. This conception runs counter to the now well-established principle in workmen's compensation cases in this state that no apportionment of liability between employers or their insurance carriers can affect a claimant's rights against them. National Automobile Ins. Co. v. Industrial Accident Comm., 23 Cal.2d 215, 221, 143 P.2d 481; American Motorists Ins. Co. v. Industrial Accident Comm., 8 Cal.2d 585, 588, 67 P.2d 103. Finally, as will be amplified, the facts of the employment relationship before us, when analyzed, point clearly to the conclusion of dual employment rather than single employment. The fact that Pitt received his entire salary from the Cooperative does not establish that concern to be his sole employer. Guarantee Ins. Co. v. Industrial Accident Comm., 22 Cal.2d 516, 520, 139 P.2d 905; Independence Indemnity Co. v. Industrial Accident Comm., 203 Cal. 51, 58, 262 P. 757. The fact that the Cooperative alone paid the compensation insurance premiums upon Pitt's salary is likewise inconclusive. American Motorists Ins. Co. v. Industrial Accident Comm., supra. Similarly, the fact that no part of Pitt's salary was paid to him directly by the Warehouse Company does not prevent the existence of an employment relationship between them. * * * The terms of the arrangement between the Cooperative and the Warehouse Company as to Pitt's employment show that no part of the services rendered by him to either concern was gratuitous and that the Warehouse Company in reality bore its share of the cost of his services by furnishing to the Cooperative, in return for Pitt's services to the Warehouse Company, the use of certain of its property rent free. The right to control and direct Pitt's work in detail, whether exercised or not, was possessed by both concerns and gave rise to an employment relationship between Pitt and both of them. Industrial Indemnity Exchange v. Industrial Accident Comm., 26 Cal.2d 130, 135, 156 P.2d 926. The commission's finding to the effect that the Cooperative was Pitt's sole employer is contrary to and unsupported by the evidence.

The dual employment of Pitt being established, there remains the question whether as a matter of law such employment was concurrent or joint. The Cooperative claims that Pitt's dual employment was concurrent and therefore that at the time of his injury he was acting only within the course of his employment by the Warehouse Company. It is true that at the time of his injury Pitt was in the portion of the warehouse used by the Warehouse Company rather than the Cooperative and was engaged in supervising a shipment of rice by the Warehouse Company in which the Cooperative had no interest. Consequently his work at the moment of injury was directly for and under the immediate control of the Warehouse Company.[1] Moreover, the more usual bases for the holding of joint employment do not exist here. So far as the record shows there was no joint hiring. Cf. Page Engineering Co. v. Industrial Comm., 322 Ill. 60, 152 N.E. 483, 485. These two employers were not engaged in some species of joint enterprise for their mutual benefit.[2]

---

1. [Editor's Note.] Wood v. Market– Arlington Co., 15 N.J.Misc. 272, 190 A. 785 (1937) (Claimant worked indiscriminately under mutual arrangement for service station operator and car repairman who occupied same premises; injured while changing tire for service station; only latter liable for compensation); Murphy Supply Co. v. Fredrickson, 206 Wis. 210, 239 N.W. 420 (1931) (Watchman hired to watch two buildings; owner of one paid wage and was partially reimbursed by other; injury while watchman was in one building; owner of other building was not liable for compensation). * * * Two different problems may be involved in cases of this type: (1) Are all employers subject to compensation liability?; (2) if only one is liable, should compensation be computed on the basis of the amount contributed by the employer so liable, or on the total wage received from all? Cases collected in Annotation (1924) 30 A.L.R. 1000, supplemented at 58 A.L.R. 1395.

2. [Editor's Note.] Ragos v. Industrial Accident Comm., 83 Cal.App. 313, 256 P. 487 (1927) (Lessor and lessee of apartment house undertook cooperatively to clean it and make minor repairs with lessor assuming responsibility for repairs, and lessee for cleaning; plaintiff hired by lessee, injured while cleaning; both parties jointly and sev-

* * * Pitt was not engaged at the moment of his injury in the common work of both.[3] * * * [citations of authorities omitted]. On the other hand, the elements of concurrent employment do not exist here. Pitt's employers did not act independently of each other in their employment of him. Cf. Western Metal Supply Co. v. Pillsbury, 172 Cal. 407, 418, 156 P. 491, Ann.Cas.1917E, 390. There was not a separate and individual employment of him by each. Cf. Becker v. Industrial Accident Comm., 212 Cal. 526, 533, 298 P. 979; Kinsman v. Hartford Courant Co., 94 Conn. 156, 108 A. 562. His duty to serve the one was not independent of his corresponding duty to serve the other. Cf. Bamberger Elec. R. Co. v. Industrial Comm., 59 Utah 257, 203 P. 345, 346; Kirkpatrick v. Yeamans Motor Co., 143 Kan. 510, 54 P.2d 960, 964.

The answer to the legal question whether the dual employment of Pitt was concurrent or joint turns upon the correct construction of the purpose and effect of the arrangement between Pitt's two employers concerning his employment. The fact that Pitt, under the arrangement, was carried only on the payroll of the Cooperative does not militate against the conclusion of joint employment. San Francisco–Oakland Terminal Rys. v. Industrial Accident Comm., supra, 180 Cal. at pages 125, 126, 179 P. 386. As previously indicated, under the arrangement the Warehouse Company in reality bore the cost of Pitt's services to it. It is true that Pitt's services to his two employers was several in the sense that he did not do the particular work of both simultaneously. But just as the burden of his salary was shared between them, so were his services likewise shared between them. He did not give a specific portion of his working time to each but all of it to both. Cf. Sargent v. A.B. Knowlson Co., 224 Mich. 686, 195 N.W. 810, 811, 30 A.L.R. 993. This is shown by Pitt's testimony that when working for the one, he was always on call by the other. McGowan, the common president of the two employers and apparently Pitt's immediate superior, also understood the purpose and effect of the arrangement to be one of joint employment of Pitt. That is the plain purport of his testimony to the effect that when injured Pitt was performing not only his duties as manager of the Warehouse Company but also his duties as manager of the Cooperative, pursuant to the arrangement between the two concerns. That arrange-

erally liable for compensation); * * * United States Fidelity & Guaranty Co. v. R.H. Macy & Co., 156 F.2d 204 (2d Cir.1946) (manufacturer's demonstrator held jointly employed by store), noted (1947) 47 Col. L.Rev. 316.

3. [Editor's Note.] Even though one of two employers has no interest in the work to be done for the other, he may be jointly liable for compensation if his work and the work for the other is being discharged simultaneously at the time of accident: Perry Canning Co. v. Industrial Comm., 75 Utah 1, 281 P. 467 (1929) (Salesman authorized to purchase fruit by two competing packing companies injured while on trip to visit prospective seller, even though chances fa-

vored that prospect would deal with one of the companies to the exclusion of the other); Vance v. Hut Neckwear Co., 281 App. Div. 151, 118 N.Y.S.2d 327 (1952) (Similarly, salesman travelling for two concerns injured during off season for sale of goods of one of them); Standard Accident Ins. Co. v. Industrial Accident Comm., 123 Cal.App. 443, 11 P.2d 401 (1932) (Salesman representing two manufacturers injured on trip to serve both; joint and several liability despite fact that monthly salary from one employer was four times the salary from other; liability not apportioned in terms of respective wages paid). Note (1938) 51 Harv.L.Rev. 941.

ment was such that his employment for each corporation required him also to work for the other. It is a reasonable inference from the testimony of these two men regarding Pitt's employment relationship to the two concerns that had his services to the one been unsatisfactory, the other would have terminated its end of the dual employment as well—in short, that his employment by them was joint. . . . [t]he service Pitt was performing at the time of his injury was in furtherance of the arrangement made for the mutual benefit of his joint employers and was incidental thereto. The service being joint, the employment was joint. Where employment is joint, it is not the rule in this state to impose liability solely on the employer whose particular work was being done at the moment of injury.

* * *

The award is annulled and the case is returned to the commission for such further proceedings as may be necessary for a proper apportionment of liability between these employers and their insurance carriers.

SECTION 7. EMPLOYEE PARTICIPATION IN EMPLOYER'S ENTERPRISE

HIRSCH v. HIRSCH BROS.

Supreme Court of New Hampshire, 1952.
97 N.H. 480, 92 A.2d 402.

Petitions, for compensation brought under the Workmen's Compensation Law, Laws 1947, c. 266, as amended, by Albert Hirsch, an officer, director and stockholder of the defendant Hirsch Brothers, Inc., and by the dependent wife and son of Carl Hirsch, a deceased officer, director and stockholder, against the company and its insurer. Trial by the Court (Wescott, J.). Decree awarding compensation to all plaintiffs.

The defendants excepted in each case to a finding and a ruling that the plaintiff Albert and the decedent Carl Hirsch were employees of the company at the time of the accident on June 30, 1951. The defendants also excepted to the denial of certain requests for findings and rulings, and to the denial of their motion to set aside the decree. * * *

The findings and rulings of the Trial Court follow:

"Findings of Fact

"On the date of the accident, June 30, 1951, Albert E. Hirsch and his brother, Carl Hirsch, were the owners of Hirsch Brothers, Inc., a corporation formed in 1947 and engaged in general earth excavation and road building work. The stock of the corporation consisted of 162 shares, of which Albert owned 32 shares and Carl owned 130 shares. Albert was President, Assistant Treasurer, Working Foreman and Superintendent; and Carl was Vice–President and Treasurer. Carl supervised many of the jobs and both men engaged in operating trucks and bulldozers and performed any other work which would be required of any workman or employee of the company. The brothers received $1.75 an hour while working for the corporation, and the Workmen's Compensation premiums were based not only on the wages of the other workmen, but were also based on the earnings of Carl and Albert Hirsch. They received no compensation for their work as officers of the company. The employees put in eight hour days, which usually included every weekday. Matters of policy concerning the operation of the Corporation were decided by the two brothers after working hours, usually during the evenings. Prior to the accident, the corporation had been awarded a contract by the State of New Hampshire to build a piece of road in East Lempster, New Hampshire. The brothers decided to buy another shovel and needed a new low-bed trailer for the transportation of the shovel. A man by the name of Kibby, having a place of business at White River Junction, Vermont, advertised heavy equipment for sale. On Saturday, June 30, 1951, both men were working; Albert in the shop preparing equipment for the new job, and Carl supervising an excavation job in Lawrence, Massachusetts. Carl returned about 11 A.M. and they decided to fly in a private plane, partly owned by Albert, to the West Lebanon airport to inspect a low-bed trailer owned by Kibby. With Albert at the controls they flew to West Lebanon, saw the Kibby equipment and decided not to buy it. They left West Lebanon airport between three and three-thirty P.M., with Albert at the controls. On the way home they ran into bad weather and the plane crashed. Both men were injured, but Carl never regained consciousness and died on July 6, 1951. Both men were receiving $1.75 per hour during the time required for the airplane trip. Carl left a wife and son, aged 16 years, both wholly dependent upon him for support. * * * "

DUNCAN, JUSTICE. The defendants' exceptions present the question of whether at the time of the accident on June 30, 1951, Carl and Albert Hirsch could be found to have been acting as "employees" of the insured corporation within the meaning of the Workmen's Compensation Law. The statutory definition of "employee," so far as pertinent, is as follows: "Employee, shall mean any person in the service of an employer subject to the provisions of this chapter under any contract of hire, express or implied, oral or written * * *." Laws 1947, c. 266, § 2, subd. II.

The defendants contend that the evidence required a finding that Carl was acting in an executive capacity when he suffered the injury which resulted in his death; and that Albert was acting in a like capacity at the time of his injury, or if not, was "merely performing an accommodation"; and that neither was an "employee" of the corporation for purposes of compensation. The plaintiffs take the position that both could properly be found to have been acting in non-executive capacities, and further that corporate executives are within the statutory definition of employees.

The finding that Carl and Albert Hirsch were employees of Hirsch Brothers, Inc., when the accident occurred was warranted by the evidence. The fact that each of them was a stockholder, director, and officer of the employer clearly did not preclude recovery by them as employees, if their injuries arose out of and in the course of the exercise of the functions of employees rather than executives. See White v. Arnold Wood Heel Company, 90 N.H. 315, 319, 8 A.2d 737; Higgins v. Bates Street Shirt Company, 129 Me. 6, 149 A. 147; Emery's Case, 271 Mass. 46, 170 N.E. 839.

According to the evidence, both brothers were regularly employed at work of a nonexecutive nature, for compensation at an hourly rate for an eight hour day. On the day of the accident, prior to the trip to West Lebanon, Albert was working in the company shop in Pelham preparing equipment for a new job, and Carl was supervising excavation work in Lawrence, Massachusetts. They interrupted their work for the purpose of the trip, and probably would have resumed it upon return, had the accident not occurred. They were paid at their regular hourly rate for the time required for the trip.

Under the by-laws of the corporation, the management of the corporation was vested in a board of three directors. The brothers were the surviving directors, the third director, their father, having deceased a month previously without replacement. As a matter of practice, questions of policy were decided by the brothers outside of regular working hours, and they received no pay for services or for the performance of official duties beyond the wages paid to them on an hourly basis. According to the by-laws, Carl, as treasurer, had "charge of all the financial affairs of the corporation," with power to sign checks, and with the president to execute contracts binding upon the corporation. The duties prescribed for the office of president, held by Albert, were to preside at meetings, sign checks, and execute contracts. In practice, Albert ordinarily purchased supplies, small tools, and automotive parts when needed, but major purchases including those of heavy equipment, were made by Carl.

The trip during which the accident occurred was made for the purpose of inspecting a low-bed trailer, with a view to purchase. The decision to inspect the trailer had been reached by the brothers after regular working hours, on a previous evening. The question of actual purchase was left to Carl. In ordinary course he would have traveled by automobile, but to save time, he arranged on the day of the accident for Albert to fly him to West Lebanon in a plane in which the latter had an interest. If upon these facts the Hirsch brothers were employees of the corporation within the meaning of the act, it is not questioned that their injuries and the resulting death of Carl arose out of and in the course of their employment. Laws 1947, c. 266, § 2, subd. III.

Under the Workmen's Compensation Act as it stood before the comprehensive amendment of 1947, workmen not engaged in manual or mechanical labor had been brought within the scope of the act, Cf. Brown v. Conway Electric Light and Power Company, 82 N.H. 78, 129 A. 633; Davis v. W.T. Grant Company, 88 N.H. 204, 185 A. 889 but legislative retention of the word "workmen" was thought to exclude from benefits employees whose functions were executive. * * *

* * * It is sufficient that the Hirsch brothers were injured under circumstances warranting a finding that they were not then acting in executive capacities. If it might have been found that Carl so acted in deciding whether to purchase the trailer, such a finding was not compelled. The finding that he was an employee was one that he was acting "in the service of" the company "under a contract of hire." It could be found that in inspecting the trailer he was called upon to exercise no discretion conferred upon him in any official capacity. The corporate policy that a suitable trailer should be purchased had already been decided. The determination of whether the particular trailer was suitable was a matter capable of delegation to a qualified servant. The finding and ruling that Carl was an employee was warranted by the evidence and will not be disturbed. Cf. Rowe v. Rowe–Coward Co., 208 N.C. 484, 181 S.E. 254; Claude H. Wolfe, Inc. v. Wolfe, 154 Fla. 633, 18 So.2d 535.

The evidence also warranting the finding and ruling that Albert was an employee of the company was even plainer. He was present for the purpose of transporting Carl, for which he received an hourly wage. He was "rendering an act of service in driving." Donovan v. Abbott Worsted Mills, Inc., 90 N.H. 450, 452, 10 A.2d 456, 457. The language of the Donovan case is equally applicable to both Albert and Carl: "In his journey * * * he was an employee in the performance of an errand for his employer, whatever his means of locomotion * * *." * * * The exceptions to the finding and ruling are overruled. * * *

Notes

1. Most statutes draw no distinction between the coverage of highly salaried administrative employees and the ordinary manual wage earners. Most commonly, coverage is universal but some states explicitly exclude corporate officers, e.g. Iowa and Oregon, while others explicitly include them, e.g., Minnesota, New Jersey, New York, and California. In some states corporate officers may elect coverage, e.g., Wash.Rev.Stat. (1990) section 51.12.020(8), and in others they may reject it, e.g., Miss.Code Ann. (1990) section 71–3–79. Does your statute provide any election to corporate officers?

2. In the absence of a special statutory provision the dual capacity doctrine enunciated in the principal case is widely recognized, and the claimant will generally be regarded as engaged in a non-executive activity. Meca Magnetics, Inc. v. Industrial Comm., 40 Ill.2d 103, 237 N.E.2d 707 (1968) (president of corporation injured in auto accident while driving with papers to a consultant held to be employee under the circumstances). Cf. Mine Service Co. v. Green, 265 S.W.2d 944 (Ky.App.1954) (president killed while attending executive's meeting; dual capacity doctrine repudiated and compensation allowed).

Despite the dual capacity doctrine, some decisions treat corporate executives with extensive stock holdings as employers and deny compensation irrespective of the nature of the work being done. Martines v. Terminal Methods, Inc., 101 R.I. 599, 225 A.2d 790 (1967) (claimant was sole employee and also sole stockholder); Ben–Jay Food Distributors v. Warshaw, 70 So.2d 564 (Fla.1954) (all stock owned by claimant and wife). Cf. Claude H. Wolfe, Inc. v. Wolfe, 154 Fla. 633, 18 So.2d 535 (1944) (president held 92 out of 100 shares, held to be an employee); and Industrial Comm. v. Lavach, 165 Colo. 433, 439 P.2d 359 (1968) (president of one man corporation entitled to compensation).

3. An employee whose pay is contingent upon the profits of the employer but who does not share losses is a covered employee. Brewer v. Central Constr. Co., 241 Iowa 799, 43 N.W.2d 131 (1950) (engineer to receive twenty percent of profits of construction firm). In the absence of a specific statutory basis for coverage, however, a partner is generally denied compensation even though a contract wage is paid in addition to a share in profits. Metro Constr., Inc. v. Industrial Comm., 39 Ill.2d 424, 235 N.E.2d 817 (1968). Contra, Trappey v. Lumbermen's Mut. Cas. Co., 229 La. 632, 86 So.2d 515 (1956); and Ohio Drilling Co. v. State Industrial Comm., 86 Okl. 139, 207 P. 314, 25 A.L.R. 367 (1922). Nevertheless, many statutes permit elective coverage for partners in a partnership and many also permit sole proprietors to elect coverage. What does your statute provide in this regard?

SECTION 8. RETALIATORY DISCHARGE EXCEPTION TO EMPLOYMENT AT WILL

Freedom of contract is one of the strongest tenets of the common law. Moreover, the concept has been given constitutional status in the United States as is indicated by the reasoning of New York Central R.R. v. White, supra, chapter 2, and many other decisions. See, e.g., Pierce v. Ortho Pharmaceutical Corp., 84 N.J. 58, 417 A.2d 505, 509 (1980). The common law applied this doctrine to employment contracts in a specific and concrete manner: contracts of employment-at-will—that is, those that are indefinite in duration of the period of service and those that reserve the discretion in either party to terminate at any time for any reason—may be terminated by any party for any reason or for no reason at all without constituting a breach of contract. See, Smith v. Piezo Technology and Prof. Adm'rs, 427 So.2d 182 (Fla.1983). In application to workers' compensation, the employment-at-will doctrine raises the question of whether an employer may discharge an at-will employee in retaliation for the employee's having made a claim for workers' compensation benefits. The common law at-will doctrine holds that the employer may do so with impunity beyond paying the underlying workers' compensation claim.

FRAMPTON v. CENTRAL INDIANA GAS COMPANY
Supreme Court of Indiana, 1973.
260 Ind. 249, 297 N.E.2d 425.

HUNTER, JUSTICE.

Plaintiff-employee brought an action against her former employer seeking actual and punitive damages for retaliatory discharge. The Henry Circuit Court dismissed the complaint pursuant to TR. 12(B)(6) IC 1971, 34–5–1–1 (failure to state a claim upon which relief can be granted). The plaintiff appealed. The First District Court of Appeals, in an opinion by Presiding Judge Robertson, affirmed the trial court's dismissal.

The complaint sets out the following facts:

Plaintiff, an employee of defendant injured her arm while working. Defendant and their insurer paid her hospital and medical expenses, as well as her full salary, during the four months she was unable to work. However, they did not inform her of further benefits that might have been available. When she did return to the job she performed capably. Approximately 19 months after the injury, defendant and its insured were notified of a 30 per cent loss in the use of her arm. Although hesitant to file a claim for fear of losing her job she did so, and received a settlement for her injury. About one month later she was discharged from her employment without reason being given.

Plaintiff prayed for $45,000 in actual damages, and:

" ... punitive or exemplary damages in the amount of $135,000.00 which is triple the amount of her actual damages because of the Defendant's intentional acts in defiance of the legislative intent of the Workmen's Compensation Laws which if allowed to persist would effectively thwart the public policy of the State of Indiana."

Workmen's compensation acts are designed to afford injured workers "an expeditious remedy both adequate and certain, and independent of any negligence on their part or on the part of the employer." Prior to workmen's compensation, workers were faced with the harshness of the common law. The employee's only remedy was an action in tort against the employer—actions which were rarely successful. This lack of success is attributed to the common law defenses of assumption of risk, contributory negligence and the fellow servant rule which were accorded inordinate deference.

Workmen's compensation statutes are in derogation of the common law and provide, for those covered, an exclusive remedy for injuries sustained "in the course of" and "arising out of" one's employment. The basic policy behind such legislation is to shift the economic burden for employment connected injuries from the employee to the employer.

"One of the purposes of the Workmen's Compensation Act is to transfer from the worker to the industry in which he is employed and ultimately to the consuming public a greater portion of economic loss due to industrial accidents and injuries." (authorities omitted)

Mann et al. v. Schnarr (1950), 228 Ind. 654, 667, 95 N.E.2d 138, 143.
* * *

Workmen's compensation is for the benefit of the employee. Hoffman v. Brooks Const. Co. (1942), 220 Ind. 150, 41 N.E.2d 613. Accordingly, it is well-established that the Act be liberally construed in favor of the employee so as to not negate the Act's humane purposes. Goldstone

v. Kozma (1971), Ind.App., 274 N.E.2d 304; Prater v. Indiana Briquetting Corp. (1969), 253 Ind. 83, 251 N.E.2d 810.

The Act creates a *duty* in the employer to compensate employees for work-related injuries (through insurance) and a *right* in the employee to receive such compensation. But in order for the goals of the Act to be realized and for public policy to be effectuated, the employee must be able to exercise his right in an unfettered fashion without being subject to reprisal. If employers are permitted to penalize employees for filing workmen's compensation claims, a most important public policy will be undermined. The fear of being discharged would have a deleterious effect on the exercise of a statutory right. Employees will not file claims for justly deserved compensation—opting, instead, to continue their employment without incident. The end result, of course, is that the employer is effectively relieved of his obligation.

Since the Act embraces such a fundamental, well-defined and well-established policy, strict employer adherence is required. IC 1971, 22–3–2–15 (Ind.Ann.Stat. § 40–1215 [1965 Repl.]) states:

> "No contract or agreement, written or implied, no rule, regulation or *other device* shall, in any manner, operate to relieve any employer in whole or in part of any obligation created by this act." (our emphasis)

We believe the threat of discharge to be a "device" within the framework of 22–3–2–15, and hence, in clear contravention of public policy. By denying transfer and allowing the trial court's dismissal to stand we would be arming unethical employers with common law authority. Once an employee knows he is remediless if retaliatorily discharged, he is unlikely to file a claim. What then is to prevent an employer from coercing an employee? Upholding retaliatory discharge opens the door to coercion and other duress-provoking acts.

Retaliatory discharge for filing a workmen's compensation claim is a wrongful, unconscionable act and should be actionable in a court of law. Although, we know of no other cases in this or in any other jurisdiction holding that such a discharge is actionable, there has been a parallel development in landlord and tenant law. Courts in several jurisdictions have held that "retaliatory evictions" offend public policy.[4] "Retaliatory evictions" usually result from a tenant's reporting health or safety code violations to an appropriate administrative body. The tenant, quite often unable to motivate the landlord to make necessary repairs and improvements, reports the violations. The landlord, angered by the tenant's temerity, either gives the tenant notice to quit or effectively evicts the tenant by raising the rent to an unreasonable level. The cases hold that retaliatory eviction may be raised as an affirmative defense in an action

---

4. Edwards v. Habib (1968), 130 U.S.App.D.C. 126, 397 F.2d 687; Schweiger v. Superior Court (1970), 3 Cal.3d 507, 90 Cal.Rptr. 729, 476 P.2d 97; Portnoy v. Hill (1968), 57 Misc.2d 1097, 294 N.Y.S.2d 278; Dickhut v. Norton (1970), 45 Wis.2d 389, 173 N.W.2d 297; Wilkins v. Tebbetts (Fla. App.1968), 216 So.2d 477 are just a few examples. *Edwards* is considered to be the landmark case in the area.

by the landlord for possession. Going one step further, a recent California decision holds that a landlord's retaliation is the basis of an affirmative cause of action.[5] It should be noted that the California Court of Appeal based its holding on a public policy embodied in a particular section of the Civil Code and not upon any statutorily created cause of action.

Retaliatory discharge and retaliatory eviction are clearly analogous. Housing codes are promulgated to improve the quality of housing. The fear of retaliation for reporting violations inhibits reporting and like the fear of retaliation for filing a claim, ultimately undermines a critically important public policy.

In summary, we hold that an employee who alleges he or she was retaliatorily discharged for filing a claim pursuant to the Indiana Workmen's Compensation Act (IC 1971, 22–3–2–1 et seq. (Ind.Ann.Stat. § 40–1201 et seq. [1965 Repl.])) or the Indiana Workmen's Occupational Diseases Act (IC 1971, 22–3–7–1 et seq. (Ind.Ann.Stat. § 10–2201 et seq. [1965 Repl.])) has stated a claim upon which relief can be granted. We further hold that such a discharge would constitute an intentional, wrongful act on the part of the employer for which the injured employee is entitled to be fully compensated in damages. Of course, the issue of retaliation should be a question for the trier of fact.

We agree with the Court of Appeals that, under ordinary circumstances, an employee at will may be discharged without cause. However, when an employee is discharged solely for exercising a statutorily conferred right an exception to the general rule must be recognized.

For all the foregoing reasons, the petition for transfer is hereby granted and the order of dismissal by the trial court pursuant to TR. 12(B)(6) is hereby reversed. This cause is remanded to the Henry Circuit Court for further proceedings not inconsistent with our opinion.

PRENTICE, J., dissents.

Notes

1. How important in the Frampton decision is the statutory language outlawing the use of "devices" by employers to relieve themselves of workers' compensation obligations? The Florida supreme court applied the following provision to reach the same conclusion:

> No employer shall discharge, threaten to discharge, intimidate or coerce any employee by reason of such employee's valid claim for compensation or attempt to claim compensation under the Workers' Compensation Law.

Smith v. Piezo Technology and Prof. Adm'rs, 427 So.2d 182 (Fla.1983). A Texas statute that prohibits an employer from firing an employee "because an employee has in good faith" filed a workers' compensation claim has been applied in like manner, Azar Nut Company v. Caille, 734 S.W.2d 667 (Tex.1987). Similarly Wiley v. Missouri Pacific Railroad Company, 430 So.2d

1016 (La.App.1982), held that the retaliatory discharge of a workers' compensation claimant violates this statute:

> Art. 2749. If, without any serious ground of complaint, a man should send away a laborer whose services he has hired for a certain time, before that time has expired, he shall be bound to pay to such laborer the whole of the salaries which he would have been entitled to receive, had the full term of his services arrived.

2. Several decisions hold the exceptions to the employment-at-will doctrine in tight rein. See, e.g., Clifford v. Cactus Drilling Corporation, 419 Mich. 356, 353 N.W.2d 469 (1984) (retaliatory discharge exception does not apply to discharge based upon absences from work caused by work related injury as opposed to discharge for making a claim); Daniel v. Magma Copper Company, 127 Ariz. 320, 620 P.2d 699 (1980) (retaliatory discharge exception does not apply to discharge based upon employee's threat to sue employer for nonjob related injury); Burrow v. Westinghouse Electric Corp., 88 N.C.App. 347, 363 S.E.2d 215 (1988) (retaliatory discharge exception does not apply to discharge based upon employee's refusal to drive under dangerous conditions); Rozier v. St. Mary's Hospital, 88 Ill.App.3d 994, 44 Ill.Dec. 144, 411 N.E.2d 50 (1980) (retaliatory discharge exception does not apply to discharge of employee who had lied to employer about job-related matters); and, Rowland v. Val–Agri, Inc., 13 Kan.App.2d 149, 766 P.2d 819 (1988) (retaliatory discharge exception does not apply to discharge based upon employee's having taken six months' consecutive leave.)

3. Can an employer be restrained from firing an employee-at-will claimant in the absence of specific statutory authority? See, e.g., Kelsay v. Motorola, Inc., 74 Ill.2d 172, 23 Ill.Dec. 559, 384 N.E.2d 353, 357 (1978), where the court stated:

> The Workmen's Compensation Act, in light of its beneficent purpose, is a humane law of a remedial nature. .... It provides for efficient remedies for and protection of employees and, as such, promotes the general welfare of this State. Consequently, its enactment by the legislature was in furtherance of sound public policy.... We are convinced that to uphold and implement this public policy a cause of action should exist for retaliatory discharge.

* * *

> We are not convinced that an employer's otherwise absolute power to terminate an employee at will should prevail when that power is exercised to prevent the employee from asserting his statutory rights under the Workmen's Compensation Act. As we have noted, the legislature enacted the workmen's compensation law as a comprehensive scheme to provide for efficient and expeditious remedies for injured employees. This scheme would be seriously undermined if employers were permitted to abuse their power to terminate by threatening to discharge employees for seeking compensation under the Act. We cannot ignore the fact that when faced with such a dilemma many employees, whose common law rights have been supplanted by the Act, would choose to retain their jobs, and thus, in effect, would be left without a remedy either common law or statutory. This result, which effectively

relieves the employer of the responsibility expressly placed upon him by the legislature, is untenable and is contrary to the public policy as expressed in the Workmen's Compensation Act. We cannot believe that the legislature, even in the absence of an explicit proscription against retaliatory discharge, intended such a result.

See also Sventko v. The Kroger Company, 69 Mich.App. 644, 245 N.W.2d 151 (1976), and Rowland v. Val–Agri, Inc., 13 Kan.App.2d 149, 766 P.2d 819 (1988).

4. The public policy exception to the employment at will doctrine originated in non-workers' compensation cases. For example, the plaintiff in Monge v. Beebe Rubber Company, 114 N.H. 130, 316 A.2d 549 (1974), had been fired from her at-will job for refusing to submit to unwanted sexual advances. In the course of a decision that awarded the former employee breach of contract damages, the court stated:

> In all employment contracts, whether at will or for a definite term, the employer's interest in running his business as he sees fit must be balanced against the interest of the employee in maintaining his employment, and the public's interest in maintaining a proper balance between the two. *See* Note, California's Controls On Employer Abuse of Employee Rights, 22 Stanford L.Rev. 1015 (1970). We hold that a termination by the employer of a contract of employment at will which is motivated by bad faith or malice or based on retaliation is not the best interest of the economic system or the public good and constitutes a breach of the employment contract.

316 A.2d at 551. See also, Cerracchio v. Alden Leeds, Inc., 223 N.J.Super. 435, 538 A.2d 1292 (1988) (retaliatory discharge of employee who reported OSHA violation gives rise to private tort action). Cf. Pierce v. Ortho Pharmaceutical Corporation, 84 N.J. 58, 417 A.2d 505 (1980) (although retaliatory discharge is wrongful if contrary to a public policy, claimant failed to establish that Hippocratic oath contained a clear mandate to justify fired employee's refusal to work.)

In an extremely limited exception to the employment at will doctrine, Haddle v. Garrison, ___ U.S. ___, 119 S.Ct. 489, 142 L.Ed.2d 502 (1998), held that an employer's conspiracy to fire an employee for having answered a federal grand jury subpoena to testify against the employer's interests created a cause of action for injury to "person or property" under 42 U.S.C. Sec.1985(2).

5. May the discharged employee seek a tort remedy for the underlying work injury in a retaliatory claim? Cornejo v. Polycon Industries, Inc., 109 Wis.2d 649, 327 N.W.2d 183 (App.1982), held that worker's compensation is the exclusive remedy.

Chapter 4

INJURIES OCCURRING WITHIN THE COURSE OF EMPLOYMENT

SECTION 1. INTRODUCTION—THE CLASSIFICATION OF RISKS COVERED BY THE COMPENSATION ACT

Determining whether the workers' compensation statute applies to a particular issue is frequently disputed in compensation claims. In each case an employee has been exposed to some risk that has resulted in injury or death, and the court must determine whether this risk falls within the protection of the statute. If it does, the employer must pay benefits and is immune to tort liability. If it does not, the worker receives no compensation benefits but is not statutorily barred from bringing a tort action.

Employment risks can be classified in several different ways, but any system of classification is useful only to the extent that it enables the decision maker to fix attention on some particular facet of the issue. Risks are frequently classified as to *character* or *source*. What *kind* of risk brought about the accident? Is it a type of risk covered by the statute? From this viewpoint the easiest risks to deal with are those that arise from a hazard that is peculiar to the employer's dangerous business—as where an electrician is killed by a lethal charge or a mechanic catches a hand in dangerous machinery. The coverage of injuries that are inherently incident to dangerous jobs was uppermost in the minds of the legislatures when the compensation statutes were enacted.

Nevertheless, under most modern compensation statutes, recovery is not confined to the peculiar risks of the employer's business or to risks posed by inherently dangerous endeavors. The acts protect against all risks of employment, even if they are not of the special type that caused the legislature to include the employer's business within the compensation statute. Hence, an employee who is hired to operate dangerous machinery can claim compensation not only if injured by the machinery, but also if burned in a campfire built to provide warmth to the workers. Modern statutes do not require that the worker be doing hazardous work at the time of the injury. If the injury or death was caused by a risk that is normal or usual in the type of work being done by the employee, recovery is routinely obtained.

Courts must often probe deeper. Even if it is admitted that employees are protected against all the normal risks of employment, what is and what is not such a normal risk must still be determined. The compensation acts invented a new term, i.e., did the injury *arise out of the employment?* This test concentrates upon the character and source of the harmful risk to determine whether the injuries it causes are properly charged to the employment. For example, although the operator of dangerous machinery is plainly entitled to compensation if he slips on the oily floor of the factory where he works, the same employee may be denied recovery if he was struck by lightening while at work. Whether the risk of death by lightening *arose out of* the employment would be a prominent feature of the dispute.

Even though a risk is of such a character and source as to clearly fall within the protection of the compensation act, questions may still arise as to *when* and *where* the risk was encountered. What was this employee doing at the time of the injury? And where was it being done? For example, compensation acts protect truck drivers against risk of collision. But when? Suppose the collision occurred while the driver was riding in a private vehicle on the way home after work? Is the relationship of time and place between accident and employment sufficiently close to bring the situation within the statute? Does the compensation principle justify requiring the employer to be burdened with the costs of the employee's injury or death? In short, did the accident occur while the employee was *within the course of employment?*

Often both the "arising out of" and "within the course of" employment issues arise in a single case. For example, suppose an employee is struck by lightning or injured by a tornado during lunch hour, or while resting, or while going home at the close of the day's work? For coverage to apply, the decision must be that both limbs of the test are satisfied. Nevertheless, the fact that one limb is plainly satisfied may influence a court's decision on the other. For example, the fact that the accident was a type closely associated with the nature of the employment may persuade a court to favor the employee where the time-place relation between accident and job is fairly in doubt; and, also, an employee who was injured while directly engaged in the employer's work may be compensated for risks that would be excluded from coverage if they had been encountered while the worker was loitering or temporarily attending to personal affairs. The close affinity of the two inquiries is demonstrated throughout the pages that follow.

The materials in this chapter deal principally with questions of what effect to give to the time that the injury occurred and the place where it happened. These inquiries naturally include a consideration of the activity the employee was engaged in when injured or killed—was it working, or eating lunch, or standing by, or attending to personal affairs, or what?

SECTION 2. INJURIES SUFFERED DURING SOCIAL, RECRE-ATIONAL AND SIMILAR ACTIVITIES

JOCQUELYN H. SHUNK v. GULF AMERICAN LAND CORP.

Supreme Court of Florida, 1969.
224 So.2d 269.

ERVIN, CHIEF JUSTICE. We review an order of the Florida Industrial Commission reversing an order of the Judge of Industrial Claims in this case.

In order to reflect the factual situation involved herein, it is necessary to set forth the same at some length, as follows:

Claimant, Mrs. Jocquelyn H. Shunk, testified she has a real estate license; that her employment with Gulf American Land Corporation was to find prospective lot purchasers and to solicit them to travel in a plane provided by employer from the points where the prospects were assembled and emplaned to her employer's real estate development near Naples, Florida.

In Daytona Beach, Florida, claimant solicited one Luther Carrol Tanly, with the knowledge of her immediate supervisor, Howard Keller, to make the plane trip. In the course of persuading Tanly to make the trip, Mrs. Shunk had dinner with Tanly and Keller, and a Mrs. Catherine W. Morris, her fellow employee. After a late dinner (completed about 12:30 A.M.) the night of the claimant's accident, according to claimant's version of the affair, she accompanied Tanly to the Ritz Apartments in Daytona Beach where he was stopping. She said she went to his apartment for the purpose of ascertaining where he stayed so that she could awaken him in time the next morning to see that he got on board the plane along with other prospective customers for the trip to Naples.

It is uncontradicted that it was her duty to assist in seeing that sufficient prospective customers, necessary to fill the required quota for a plane load, were on board in time for scheduled flights to Naples. In this instance, the plane was scheduled to depart from the airport at Daytona Beach at 7:00 A.M., with Tanly included in the quota leaving on the plane that morning.

Claimant testified that upon arriving at the Ritz Apartments she had an altercation with Tanly; that he made improper advances toward her; that in attempting to elude him, she fell 25 feet from a window of the apartment building, injuring herself. The injury occurred at about 2:30 A.M.

Mrs. Shunk testified she had only had two cocktails, one before dinner and one afterwards; that she became nauseated after eating shrimp at the dinner, and that upon arriving at Tanly's apartment she asked him if she could use his bathroom to relieve her nausea. She testified that upon leaving the bathroom and attempting to leave the apartment Tanly's advances and the altercation ensued.

Her unusual hours of employment, sometimes lasting into the early morning hours, and the method of soliciting prospects for plane trips and land sales, were corroborated by the testimony of Mrs. Morris. * * * (other testimony corroborating or contradicting claimant's version omitted).

Mr. Howard Keller, the immediate supervisor of the claimant, testified by deposition that the duties of the solicitors employed by Gulf American Land Corporation included the following: Finding prospects anywhere, any time, any place they could do so (including restaurants, beaches, motels); obtaining from the prospects their hotel or motel room numbers, telephone numbers, and the responsibility for getting the prospects up early in the mornings to catch the 7:00 A.M. plane for the real estate development located near Naples. Mr. Keller stated in this case it was definitely Mrs. Shunk's responsibility and a part of her job to get Mr. Tanly on the plane the morning following the dinner. He testified that to the best of his knowledge all of them, including Mrs. Shunk, were sober when they returned to the San Marina Motel (headquarters of the prospect solicitors) from the late dinner, conversation, cocktails, etc. Mr. Keller testified in his deposition that almost anything Mrs. Shunk or any of the other lady solicitors did in securing prospective customers was part of their jobs, for which they were paid. He stated they had no regular working hours, but worked all the time getting people to go on the plane trips, and then seeing that they woke up and got on the planes.

In his compensation order, the Judge of Industrial Claims found on the "evidence presented * * * as well as the candor and demeanor of the witnesses who testified * * * ", that in the course and scope of her employment Mrs. Shunk accompanied Mr. Tanly to his apartment to ascertain his room number. The Judge of Industrial Claims accepted the testimony of the claimant as corroborated by Mr. Keller and other witnesses for the claimant, including Mrs. Catherine Morris, and found that the accident and injury arose out of and in the course of her employment and are compensable.

However, the Full Commission reversed, holding:

"We believe that the judge of industrial claims has erred in finding this claim compensable. We feel that the facts clearly show that the claimant had deviated from her employment prior to the accident. Surely it cannot be said that merely because the claimant was working in an area other than her home area, that she must be considered to be in her employment during an evening involving a late dinner and visits to cocktail lounges. Whatever motivation the claimant may have had for jumping from the window, we feel that the injury cannot be considered to have arisen out of and in the course of her employment."

It is quite true that the particular circumstances related above present a suspicious inference that claimant was not acting in the course of her employment at the time of her injury; that there may have been a deviation by claimant from her employment, and that her presence in the apartment at the late hour may have been a social engagement of her own, rather than one required for the discharge of her employment duties. However, a suspicious inference in these particular circumstances is not necessarily conclusive. The nature of claimant's employment, according to the testimony, involved solicitation, salesmanship and persuasion, and follow-up action to see that prospective customers were on scheduled flights to the development site, not dischargeable only during working hours normal to most employees. Consequently, it seems fairly well established that promotion of real estate sales to prospective customers of the kind here considered involves techniques and methods in a special class that have been found to be necessary in persuading prospective customers to agree to make the related plane trips.

In a debatable situation, such as this one, we conclude we should rest our judgment with the trier of the facts and lay aside our skepticism and natural inclination to be cynically suspicious. * * *

The writ is granted; the Commission's order of reversal is quashed with direction that the order of the Judge of Industrial Claims be reinstated.

It is so ordered.

DREW, THORNAL and BOYD, JJ., concur.

ROBERTS and ADKINS, JJ., and SPECTOR, DISTRICT COURT JUDGE, dissent.

Notes

1. Injuries that occur while employees are actively performing assigned work when and where they are supposed to do it are always within the course of employment. Nevertheless, whether the employee is "at work" is often disputed, especially when social relations and business get mixed as in Shunk. The question of whether social activities are "part of the job" arises often in sales work and compensation is frequently granted. See, e.g., Green v. Heard Motor Co., 224 La. 1078, 71 So.2d 849 (1954) (car salesman took airplane ride with intoxicated pilot; no immediate prospect of sale). Moreover, recovery is not restricted to salesmen. In Harrison v. Stanton, 26 N.J.Super. 194, 97 A.2d 687 (1953), an undertaker persuaded his assistant to join the Optimists' Club. In preparing to attend the Optimists' Annual Party, the assistant suffered a traffic injury in driving his car to procure a baby sitter. The injury was held to be in the course of employment with undertaker. Cf. University of Denver v. Nemeth, 127 Colo. 385, 257 P.2d 423 (1953) (student employed by university to clean up grounds, injured while playing football; evidence indicated that continuance of his job depended on his participation in organized athletics; held to be compensable). But compare State Comp. Ins. Fund v. Industrial Comm., 135 Colo. 570, 314 P.2d 288 (1957) (no recovery under almost identical facts).

2. Whether or not injuries suffered by employees who participate on company sponsored athletic teams outside regular work hours are within the course of employment engenders much dispute. If the athletic contest takes place on the working premises during the lunch hour or a regular rest or

recreation period, recovery is usually allowed. If, however, the contest is held at some place of the employees' own choosing and takes place after working hours, compensation is less frequently granted. Compare Burnett v. INA, 810 S.W.2d 833 (Tex.App.1991) (compensation denied to employee injured in softball game at company-sponsored picnic; employer received no benefit apart from general improvement of health and morale of employees) with Maycheck v. Tibbets Water & Waste, Inc., 61 A.D.2d 862, 401 N.Y.S.2d 916 (1978) (compensation awarded to employee injured in city-league softball game; team was organized by supervisory personnel). The following factors, inter alia, seem to affect the outcome: the extent of advertising of and public relations benefit from the event enjoyed by the employer; the employer's power to control the activity; the extent to which the event is part of an organized recreational scheme; and, the extent the employer supports the activity—such as allowance of paid time for participation, provision of uniforms, payment of fees, and rent. The greater the benefit to the employer, the more likely these injuries are to be compensable. On the other hand, if the employer seems merely to be accommodating the desires of the employees, compensation is less likely. Wisconsin has supplied a statutory rule on this point: "An employe is not performing service growing out of and incidental to employment while engaging in a program designed to improve the physical well-being of the employe, whether or not the program is located on the employer's premises, if participation in the program is voluntary and the employe receives no compensation for participation." Wis.Stat.Ann. § 102.03(3) (1990).

3. Similarly, courts differ sharply in the compensability of injuries suffered at employer-sponsored outings, dinners and other social events. Considerations similar to those above influence the outcomes. Compare Hanks v. Grey Wolf Drilling Company, 574 So.2d 531 (La.App.1991) (compensation awarded to worker hurt at company awards dinner; encouragement of company loyalty provides mutual benefit to employer) with Brown v. W.C.A.B., 138 Pa.Cmwlth. 560, 588 A.2d 1014 (1991) (compensation denied to employee who suffered accident while crossing public road after leaving employer sponsored, voluntary, after hours Christmas party for all employees); and Chorley v. Koerner Ford, Inc., 19 N.Y.2d 242, 279 N.Y.S.2d 4, 225 N.E.2d 737 (1967) (similar; compensation awarded employee who suffered heart attack while attempting to follow up strenuous jitterbug with intercourse; dissent observed this was not an industrial accident from the "common sense viewpoint of the average man.")

4. The treatment to be accorded to injuries sustained by employees conducting patriotic or civic acts outside regular work hours at the employer's request has not been uniform. Compare Burton v. Board of Educ. of Verona, 21 N.J.Misc. 108, 31 A.2d 337 (Dept. of Labor, 1943) (school teacher assisting in issuance of war ration books at the school house, compensation denied) with Casson v. Industrial Comm., 24 Ariz.App. 385, 539 P.2d 189 (1975) (employer requested that employee serve as member of volunteer fire department, compensation granted). See also Egan's Case, 331 Mass. 11, 116 N.E.2d 844 (1954) (compensation awarded to taxi driver injured while responding to police officer's call; held that answering police officer's call is a compensable street risk). Are these injuries properly chargeable to the employment under the compensation principle?

5. Frequently employers request or encourage employees to engage in non-work activities that are intended to improve the employees' health, education or general well being. Injuries suffered in the course of these activities are usually compensable. See, e.g., Lampkin v. Harzfeld's, 407 S.W.2d 894 (Mo.1966) (saleswoman suffered allergic reaction to flu shots encouraged by employer; compensation allowed. List of authorities in accord); McDaniel v. Sage, 174 Ind.App. 71, 366 N.E.2d 202 (1977) (harm from injection administered for relief of headache unrelated to employment; compensable); Jones v. Hartford Acc. & Indem. Co., 811 S.W.2d 516 (Tenn. 1991) (compensation awarded employee injured while acting as union agent on union's time; because employee was taking a message to union president at the direction of the employer, the activity met the "mutual benefit" test); Mikkelsen v. N.L. Industries, 72 N.J. 209, 370 A.2d 5 (1977) (compensation awarded worker injured off duty while returning from union hall where he had attended collective bargaining meeting); Dallas County Pulpwood Co. v. Strange, 257 Ark. 799, 520 S.W.2d 247 (1975) (compensation awarded claimant injured while transporting equipment just purchased as his own property to work site); Sandmeyer v. City of Bemidji, 281 Minn. 217, 161 N.W.2d 318 (1968) (compensation awarded police officer shot while engaged in target practice off-duty); Evans v. Valley Diesel, 111 N.M. 556, 807 P.2d 740 (1991) (compensation awarded to employee hurt while locking up employer's premises after completing work there on his personal car on his own time); Watson v. Nassau Inn, 74 N.J. 155, 376 A.2d 1215 (1977) (employee injured during off hours while taking work clothes from his room off premises to his home for cleaning; compensation awarded).

Nevertheless, when the relationship to employment grows remote, compensation is often denied. See, e.g., Dunavin v. Monarch Recreation Corporation, 812 P.2d 719 (Colo.App.1991) (compensation denied ski instructor hurt while skiing on free time; hearing officer found no benefit to employer); Costa v. New York State Workmen's Compensation Bd., 34 A.D.2d 585, 308 N.Y.S.2d 93 (1970) (employee injured while en route to take promotional examination suggested by employer in view of new opening; compensation denied); Fantasia v. Hess Oil & Chemical Corp., 110 N.J.Super. 360, 265 A.2d 565 (1970) (picketing employee run over in traffic during lockout; compensation denied); and, Miller v. Greene County, 171 Pa.Super. 494, 90 A.2d 262 (1952) (employee dissatisfied with tools provided by his employer, furnished his own; injured while sharpening them at home after hours; compensation denied); and Nichols v. Jay Truck Driver Training Center, 815 S.W.2d 450 (Mo.App.1991) (compensation denied survivors of employee killed when crushed by falling car when jacks collapsed while decedent was repairing his personal vehicle on employer's premises after working hours; no mutual benefit).

TAYLOR v. EWING
Superior Court of Pennsylvania, 1950.
166 Pa.Super. 21, 70 A.2d 456.

RHODES, PRESIDENT JUDGE. This is a workmen's compensation case in which the compensation authorities made an award to claimant. The court of common pleas affirmed the award and entered judgment for claimant. Defendant's insurance carrier has appealed.

The facts are not in dispute. The question is whether claimant sustained his injury as a result of an accident within or outside the course of his employment with defendant.

Defendant was an automobile dealer in Beaver, Pennsylvania, and in his business he maintained a garage, showroom, and used car lot. Claimant had been employed by defendant for some time as a general utility man at a weekly wage of $35. Claimant's customary duties consisted of cleaning the offices, showroom, and garage, and servicing cars. On the morning of July 10, 1947, claimant having no other duties to perform at that time at the garage or showroom, defendant directed him to proceed to defendant's home and cut some grass with a power lawn mower which defendant owned. While attempting to adjust the belt on the power mower, to which defendant called claimant's attention, claimant accidentally sustained an injury to the index finger of his right hand, which necessitated amputation of a portion of the finger.

Appellant at the time the accident occurred had issued to defendant a "Standard Workmen's Compensation and Employers' Liability Policy." The premises of defendant were described as located at Wayne and Fourth Streets, and Third and Sassafras Lane, Beaver, Pennsylvania. The policy described the business of the insured as follows: "Garages and Automobile Dealers, including accessories, service stations—all employees except office" * * *

In Krchmar v. Oakland Beach Company, 155 Pa.Super. 430, at page 433, 38 A.2d 710, at page 712, we said: "In general, where the accident occurs off the premises of the employer, the proofs must establish that the employee was actually engaged in furthering the business of the employer at the time of the injury. Palko v. Taylor–McCoy Coal & Coke Co. et al., 289 Pa. 401, 137 A. 625. Otherwise, if the act in which the employee was engaged when injured off the premises, was not connected with the employer's business, it must appear that the employer ordered or directed the act. Merely permitting the employee to do the act without directing or ordering its performance will not support an award. Gibson v. Blowers Paint Service et al., 140 Pa.Super. 216, 14 A.2d 154."

Defendant is in no position to say that the services performed for his benefit and at his direction by claimant were not in the course of claimant's employment. Matis v. Schaeffer, 270 Pa. 141, 113 A. 64; Geary v. Martin, 101 Pa.Super. 311. If it had not been for claimant's employment in defendant's business, he would not have been in the place where he was injured, at which time he was working under the direction and control of defendant and in consequence of the relationship of employer and employe.

The Workmen's Compensation Act, 77 P.S. § 1 et seq., was passed for the purpose of protecting employes. An employe does not step in and out of his regular employment with every changing task ordered to be done by his employer. His general employment, not such particular act, ordinarily controls. See Zapos v. Demas, 106 Pa.Super. 183, 161 A. 753 * * * [further citations omitted].

If claimant had been engaged in regular work of a dual nature, appellant's argument would be applicable. But claimant did not become a domestic employe or servant by performing the incidental task which defendant directed him to do when injured, and there was no contract of hiring for domestic service. This work did not terminate the existing status of claimant as an employe in the regular course of defendant's business; he was still working in the sphere of activity in which he was employed and paid. There was no severance of the relationship covered by the insurance policy of appellant, and it is immaterial that defendant and his wife had a liability policy relating to domestic employes. Claimant was engaged in executing a positive command of his employer merely incidental to the business in which claimant was employed by defendant, and the act did not take him out of the course of that employment. "We may well surmise what would have happened to his job had he refused to do this work without any other excuse than that he was not hired for that purpose." Nugent Sand Co. v. Hargesheimer, 254 Ky. 358, 71 S.W.2d 647, 649. See 172 A.L.R. 387. * * *

Judgment is affirmed.

Notes

1. Accord: Echo Enterprises Inc. v. Aspinwall, 194 Ga.App. 444, 390 S.E.2d 867 (1990), and Harry Fleming Washer Service v. Industrial Comm., 36 Ill.2d 272, 222 N.E.2d 490 (1966).

How closely is the issue in the principal case related to the issue of the borrowed employee and dual employment? See Chapter 3. See, also, Keasey v. Mitzel Bros., 135 Pa.Super. 460, 5 A.2d 631 (1939) (compensation awarded worker employed by partnership engaged in supply business who was directed by a partner to paint his house). Most of the decisions hold that employees are to be compensated while carrying out an order that has nothing to do with the business of the employer only if the order was expressly given by the employer. See, e.g., Sellers v. Reice Constr. Co., 124 Kan. 550, 262 P. 19 (1927). Should it be important that the employee knows that the person giving non-job related orders has no authority to do so? See, e.g., Liberty Mut. Ins. Co. v. Neal, 55 Ga.App. 790, 191 S.E. 393 (1937) (compensation awarded cotton mill worker who was directed by overseer to cut wood which the overseer then sold to the employer at a profit; the overseer was deemed to be a vice principal).

2. An employee who renders personal assistance to a third person at the employer's request is in the course of his employment while so doing. Even in the absence of specific orders, the employee who is injured while performing an act of courtesy for a patron or customer is usually regarded as acting within the course of employment because of the good will garnered to the employer. See, e.g., Olsen v. State Acc. Ins. Fund, 29 Or.App. 235, 562 P.2d 1234 (1977) (compensation awarded worker injured during lunch break while repairing bicycle for coworker; superior observed and did not object). See also Riley v. Perkins, 282 Ala. 629, 213 So.2d 796 (1968). Nevertheless, some courts reject the general good will benefit argument and deny recovery where the assisted person is a stranger to the business. Contrast Rowley v. Industrial Comm., 15 Utah 2d 330, 392 P.2d 1016 (1964) (denying recovery)

and Ace Pest Control, Inc. v. Industrial Comm., 32 Ill.2d 386, 205 N.E.2d 453 (1965) (awarding recovery).

3.   An employee who without orders by the employer renders assistance for the personal benefit of a co-worker may act outside the course of his employment in so doing. Compare Olson Rug Co. v. Industrial Comm., 215 Wis. 344, 254 N.W. 519 (1934) (compensation denied employee injured while driving ill co-worker home in another town; employer had no duty to transport the ill worker home) with Continental Casualty Co. v. Industrial Comm., 28 Wis.2d 89, 135 N.W.2d 803 (1965) (compensation awarded in respect to employee accidentally killed on the work premises during working hours while helping a superior with a purely personal task; *Olson* distinguished on the basis of time and place of occurrence). Situations where an employee undertakes a job assigned to another laborer are more difficult. If the undertaking is merely for the personal convenience of the claimant or the person assisted, or if the task is undertaken to satisfy the claimant's curiosity or desire to experiment, compensation is sometimes denied. See, e.g., Utah Copper Co. v. Industrial Comm., 62 Utah 33, 217 P. 1105 (1923) (fireman and brakeman on train exchanged jobs on successive runs of train in order to equalize their respective exposures to inclement weather; compensation denied). Where, however, the claimant is acting primarily to further the employer's interests by assisting another worker, compensation may be allowed. In these cases the courts will seek to discover a custom or practice to give mutual assistance, or will rely upon knowledge and ratification of the practice by employers and other representatives. See, e.g., Groves v. Marvel, 59 Del. 73, 213 A.2d 853 (1965) (compensation awarded to off duty employee who was hurt while helping co-employee with his work; activity created good will for customers).

SECTION 3. INJURIES SUFFERED BY EMPLOYEES MINISTERING TO PERSONAL NEEDS OR PLEASURE

LECKIE v. H.D. FOOTE LUMBER CO.

Court of Appeals of Louisiana, Second Circuit, 1948.
40 So.2d 249.

KENNON, JUDGE. This is a suit for 400 weeks compensation, less 70 weeks previously paid. The petition alleges that plaintiff was employed as a saw filer and scaler; that, while in the course of his employment, and, while attempting to trim a piece of lumber by the use of a power driven cut off saw, he received an injury which resulted in the loss of a substantial portion of his left hand, * * *

The District Court found for plaintiff and the case is before us on appeal from that judgment.

Plaintiff was second in charge to a Mr. Baum in the operation of defendant's sawmill. His specific tasks were to scale such logs as were received at the mill and to file crosscut saws. In addition, he performed general tasks around the mill and was free to do whatever seemed necessary in facilitating the mill's operation.

The injury occurred on a Saturday afternoon while only plaintiff and defendant's manager, Mr. Baum, were present at the mill. They were performing the customary Saturday task of preparing the small mill for its weekend shutdown. Part of this weekly shutdown work consisted of burning out the slab pile so as to reduce the fire hazard. Mr. Baum went to the burning pit, leaving plaintiff to attend to the operation of the two engines, which operated the mill machinery, including a blower which accelerated the burning of the slabs and waste. Plaintiff was being paid for this Saturday afternoon work. In addition to being on duty with the engines, he was available—and used when occasion required—to scale any logs that might arrive on Saturday afternoon.

The mechanical set-up of the mill was such that when it was desired to operate the blower which accelerated the burning of waste, all the other machinery connected to the engines was also automatically put in operation. Included in the machinery which was necessarily—though idly—operating on the Saturday afternoon in question, was a circular cut off saw situated about ten feet from the motors which plaintiff was attending. Plaintiff's injury occurred when he picked up a short piece of scrap lumber and proceeded to run it through the cut off saw. Plaintiff's petition alleged that his purpose in using the saw at the time was "to trim a piece of lumber." Defendants introduced evidence at the trial that the material was only a piece of slab, less than 30 inches long, incapable of being used for lumber and that plaintiff's purpose was to cut it in two pieces for his own use as stove wood. The District Court found—and the record amply sustains this finding—that the board being trimmed by plaintiff at the time of his injury was not fit for sale and was usable only as fire wood.

After 70 weeks, defendants discontinued paying compensation and the defense in the present suit is that plaintiff at the time of his injury had turned aside from his employment and was engaged in a task which served his own interest exclusively and had not sufficient relationship to his employment to entitle him to benefits under the compensation law.

Plaintiff's contention is that he was simply taking advantage of the fact that the nature of the duty he was performing—namely, that of watching the engines and being available for the scaling of such logs as might be brought to the mill—permitted him to cut some stove wood for himself; that, when he was injured, he had not left the place of his employment or ceased to perform the duties required of him at the time.

The record discloses that the defendant lumber company permitted its employees to carry away for fuel slabs which otherwise would have been burned as waste and had permitted employees at convenient times while on duty to cut such slabs into convenient lengths for wood. The alternative method of disposing of waste slabs was to place them in the conveyer trough (situated some four feet from the cut off saw) to be carried to the burning pit.

The case turns upon a question of law. Is compensation due an employee who is injured, while at his place of duty, while watching machinery as required by his employer, while available on the premises for his other duty of scaling any logs that might arrive, but whose injury occurs when the employee is also performing some other act for his own benefit? * * *

In an earlier Supreme Court case, Kern v. Southport Mill, Ltd., 174 La. 432, 141 So. 19, the Court laid down the rule that in determining whether an accident arises out of the employment, it is necessary to consider only two questions. First, was the employee then engaged about his employer's business *and not merely* pursuing his own business or pleasure and second, did the necessity of the employer's business reasonably require that the employee be at the place of the accident at the time the accident occurred.

In the case before us, plaintiff's injury "arose out of his employment" according to the test set forth in the *Kern* case. Certainly the necessities of the employer's business reasonably required him to be at the place of the accident at the time the accident occurred and, while he was incidentally pursuing his own business in that he was trimming stove wood for himself, he was also satisfactorily performing the required duty of attending to the operation of the motors. He was also about his employer's business to the extent that he was available at the mill site in the event logs should arrive for scaling. The fact that he was at the time, and without ceasing to attend to his employer's business, using the cut off saw, which otherwise would have been idle, for his own benefit did not alter the inescapable fact that he was also at the time performing the duties required of him by his employment. * * *

To sum up, we find as a matter of fact that at the time plaintiff Leckie was injured, he was not engaged in trimming lumber for the benefit of his employer, nor was he engaged in the picking up of boards as a part of any clean-up duty which might have benefited his employer. We find that Mr. Leckie's duty at the time of his injury, as assigned to him by defendant's foreman, was to attend to the running of the engines and machinery, including the blower, and to keep himself available to scale any logs that might arrive at the mill. We find that his injury resulted when he, taking advantage of the fact that his duties did not require the use of his hands for any purpose at the minute, picked up a small board and proceeded to cut some stove wood for his own personal use.

We think that under the Louisiana authorities plaintiff is entitled to compensation. * * *

The judgment is affirmed, with costs.

(Dissenting opinion of HARDY, J. omitted.)

ON REHEARING

TALIAFERRO, JUDGE. The facts of this case are clearly set out in our former opinion. They will not be at length iterated herein. The members of this Court are unanimous in the opinion that plaintiff when injured had turned aside from his over-hour duties to his employer and was engaged in the performance of an act purely for his own interest and benefit; that is, to convert a discarded and non-commercial piece of timber into stovewood for his own use; that in so doing he unnecessarily exposed himself to the dangerous instrumentality that caused the injury but for which the accident would not have happened.

The accident happened in the course of plaintiff's employment, but to entitle him to recover compensation, of course, it must be found and held that it arose out of and/or was incidental to such employment. In other words, did the turning aside to engage in a purely personal, dangerous act, several feet from where he was required to be to perform his duties, for the moment, deprive plaintiff of the benefits of the Workmen's Compensation Law, as regards an accident that occurred while he was so engaged? On this question a majority of this court takes the affirmative. The question is one of law arising from the factual findings of the Court's entire membership.

In cases of this character the courts of this state have frequently held that whether or not an injury arises out of the employment depends necessarily upon the facts and circumstances of each case. No hard and fast rule in such cases is possible of intelligent adoption. If it should be held that the facts of this case warrant recovery by plaintiff, it is difficult to perceive to what extent the rule might be carried. Can it logically be said that had the accident occurred fifty feet farther from the exact locus of his duties, it would not be compensable, whereas since it happened only ten feet therefrom, it is compensable? We believe the factor of distance is not entirely controlling. To the nature of the act of deviation or turning aside should be accredited controlling influence.

The testimony shows that about the immediate locus of the accident plaintiff had assembled a goodly quantity of discarded pieces of lumber he evidently intended to carry home for stovewood. And, it is shown that plaintiff's superiors did not offer objection to this being done, nor to the use of the saws, when not otherwise engaged, to cut the pieces into appropriate lengths, but in so doing in each instance, the employee acted for himself and not for his employer. He was subserving his own personal interest. * * *

For the reasons herein assigned, the judgment from which appeal was taken is reversed, and plaintiff's suit is hereby dismissed at his cost.

KENNON, J., dissents for the reasons assigned in the original opinion, contained herein.

Notes

1. Decisions differ as to whether injuries suffered on work premises by employees while performing non-prohibited acts for their personal benefit during spare time are compensable. Compare Bell v. Dewey Bros., Inc., 236 N.C. 280, 72 S.E.2d 680 (1952) (watchman washing his own car; practice not prohibited and was known to employer; compensation denied) and Ranger Ins. Co. v. Valerio, 553 S.W.2d 682 (Tex.Civ.App.1977) (during idle moment deliveryman attempted to dislodge a rabbit from a culvert; compensation

denied) with Chrisman v. Farmers Cooperative Ass'n, 179 Neb. 891, 140 N.W.2d 809 (1966) (service station operator repairing his own car; compensable) and Lee v. Middleton Logging Co., 198 Ga.App. 585, 402 S.E.2d 536 (1991) (compensation denied to off-duty employee who came to work site on day off and was hurt after his offer of help to on site subcontractor was rejected). The outcome may be influenced by the time at which the accident occurred. An injury suffered during a stand-by period of enforced idleness caused by the nature of the employer's work is often compensable, and the fact that the employee devotes free time to personal purposes does not arbitrarily serve to deny compensation. See, e.g., Parker v. Travelers Ins. Co., 142 Ga.App. 711, 236 S.E.2d 915 (1977) (compensation awarded mechanic working on his own car in garage during slack period with knowledge of employer); and Spencer v. Chesapeake Paperboard Co., 186 Md. 522, 47 A.2d 385 (1946) (compensation awarded worker hired to fill beater in papermill; suffered burns when pants caught on fire while taking a nap beside operating machine). But, if the employee converts a stand-by period to personal purposes by abandoning the job or engaging in prohibited conduct or in conduct that is inconsistent with the satisfactory performance of assigned duties, compensation is often denied. See, e.g., Como v. Union Sulphur Co., 182 So. 155 (La.App.1938) (foreman of construction crew left his post to dynamite fish downstream); and Hills v. Servicemaster of Conn. River Valley, Inc., 155 Conn. 214, 230 A.2d 604 (1967) (floor cleaner injured tampering with elevator contrary to orders).

2. Compensability of injuries suffered by employees while standing by for possible call to work may be influenced by the imminence of an expected call to return to duty. The messenger who is merely told to remain on the premises for the afternoon and the employee who is subject to occasional call while at home will be less likely to be awarded compensation than a worker who faces a temporary lull in his work while waiting for a tool. Compare Blackley v. City of Niagara Falls, 284 App.Div. 51, 130 N.Y.S.2d 77 (1954) (policeman subject to call at all times; not within course of employment when going home) and Johnson v. Employee Benefits Ins. Co., 25 Or.App. 215, 548 P.2d 519 (1976) (compensation denied range rider subject to call by two-way radio; injured while beyond range of radio on personal errand on day off) with Paige v. City of Rahway, 74 N.J. 177, 376 A.2d 1226 (1977) (compensation awarded water works supervisor on call, who was assaulted and robbed at home during period), and Meo v. Commercial Can Corp., 76 N.J.Super. 484, 184 A.2d 891 (1962) (compensation awarded management employee battered by striking employees while entering his car at home preparing to go to work.)

3. The argument for recovery in the stand-by or on-call cases is strengthened if the activity in which the employee was engaged at the time of injury, although personal to the employee, nevertheless can be related to the conditions of employment. Compare Clapham v. David, 232 App.Div. 458, 251 N.Y.S. 245 (1931) (compensation awarded nurse of obstreperous child, on twenty-four hours duty, injured while taking short bicycle ride at employer's suggestion to calm her nerves); Fidelity & Cas. Co. of New York v. Industrial Acc. Comm., 176 Cal.App.2d 541, 1 Cal.Rptr. 567 (1959) (compensation awarded survivors of employee subject to call in employment in Indonesia who drowned while swimming in order to get relief from humidi-

ty); Miller v. F.A. Bartlett Tree Expert Co., 3 N.Y.2d 654, 171 N.Y.S.2d 77, 148 N.E.2d 296 (1958) (compensation awarded worker injured at tree surgery conference while taking shower in preparation for indoor session after a day in the field), with Yates v. Naylor Industrial Services, Inc., 569 So.2d 616 (La.App.1990) (compensation denied on-call employee who received call to report to assignment in distant town while on personal hunting trip and was injured on way to his home to pick up clothing; claimant was "simply too far removed from employment").

4. Employees who suffer injuries while occupying housing the employer requires them to live in either expressly or by absence of any reasonable alternative are usually deemed to be within the course of employment and compensable. This result, sometimes referred to as the "bunkhouse rule," applies even though the employee is not engaged in actual work at the time and may even be sleeping or administering to personal needs. See, e.g., Wood v. Kings Park State Hospital, 266 App.Div. 804, 41 N.Y.S.2d 391 (1943) (compensation awarded to clerical hospital employee for injury sustained after working hours while dressing in own room; employee was subject to general on-call regulation to perform "usual or special tasks" on holidays and at other times). For the rule to apply, however, the injury must be occasioned by a "risk distinctly associated with the conditions under which the claimant lived." See, e.g., Littles v. Osceola Farms Co., 577 So.2d 657 (Fla.App.1991) (employee killed in "bunkhouse" by disgruntled fellow employee lover not within rule).

Even resident employees who are not subject to call are occasionally regarded as within the course of employment when injured on the premises. See, e.g., Feliciano v. Woodlea Nursery, 57 A.D.2d 979, 394 N.Y.S.2d 109 (1977) (compensation awarded migrant worker who fell downstairs in employer-provided housing on day off) and Kilcoyne's Case, 352 Mass. 572, 227 N.E.2d 324 (1967) (compensation awarded non-on-call employee because the employer was benefitted by the employee's presence). Decisions are often influenced by the character of the activity in which the employee was engaged at the time of the accident. Thus, in Gowan v. Harry Butler and Sons Funeral Home, 204 Kan. 210, 460 P.2d 606 (1969), compensation was awarded a resident domestic employee who broke a leg while changing her dress. Although she was not subject to call, care of her clothing was deemed to be sufficiently related to the discharge of her duties to assure coverage. Contrast Reed v. Loon Lake Hotel, 283 App.Div. 763, 128 N.Y.S.2d 112 (1954) (compensation denied non-on-call domestic employee injured from unknown cause while asleep on premises).

The compensability of an injury suffered by a resident employee who is not subject to call may also be influenced by the nature of the hazard that brought about the injury. Compare Finnegan v. Biehn, 276 N.Y. 50, 11 N.E.2d 348 (1937) (compensation awarded dependents of resident janitor who burned to death in a fire caused by overturning of oil heater in apartment without central heating system) and John H. Kaiser Lumber Co. v. Industrial Comm. of Wisconsin, 181 Wis. 513, 195 N.W. 329 (1923) (compensation awarded mill employee attacked by crazed fellow worker while sleeping in bunkhouse with sixty others) with Pisko v. Mintz, 262 N.Y. 176, 186 N.E. 434 (1933) (compensation denied janitor injured in apartment house fire caused by his smoking in bed) and Fireman's Fund Indem. Co. v.

Industrial Accident Comm., 39 Cal.2d 529, 247 P.2d 707 (1952) (compensation denied resident employee injured fifty feet from premises while taking a walk at end of work day).

PACHECO'S DEPENDENTS v. ORCHIDS OF HAWAII

Supreme Court of Hawaii, 1972.
54 Hawaii 66, 502 P.2d 1399.

RICHARDSON, CHIEF JUSTICE.

This appeal, pursuant to HRS § 386–88 (Supp.1971) arises out of a workmen's compensation claim by the dependents of Wilma P. Pacheco, deceased, against her employer, Orchids of Hawaii. The claim was denied by the Director of the Department of Labor and Industrial Relations. On appeal, the Labor and Industrial Relations Appeals Board made an award of compensation.

The facts are not in dispute having been stipulated by the parties.

Mrs. Pacheco was employed by Orchids of Hawaii (hereinafter "Employer") on and prior to July 7, 1967. She worked as a member of a production team in an "assembly line" operation.

It was employer's policy to allow a 15–minute coffee break each morning and afternoon during regular working hours. Employees customarily used refreshment facilities on the premises, however, they were free to leave the premises during coffee breaks.

On July 7, 1967 Mrs. Pacheco was given her paycheck after lunch and before the afternoon coffee break. Since it was anticipated that she would work late, the afternoon coffee break afforded Mrs. Pacheco the only opportunity to cash her check before the banks closed. Once previously during her coffee break, Mrs. Pacheco had gone to a bank to cash her paycheck.

At 2:48 P.M. on July 7th, Mrs. Pacheco punched out on her time card to take her afternoon break. With one of three other women employees driving, Mrs. Pacheco left employer's premises intending to cash her paycheck at the nearest bank. Mrs. Yamamoto, Mrs. Pacheco's supervisor, observed the departure and cautioned the group to hurry back.

While the ladies were on their way to the Waiakea branch of the Bank of Hawaii, some three blocks away, their automobile was struck broadside resulting in Mrs. Pacheco's death.

The major issue in this case is whether Mrs. Pacheco's death is compensable under section 386–3 of the Hawaii Revised Statutes. The relevant provision of that section reads "[i]f an employee suffers personal injury ... *by accident arising out of and in the course of the employment*" he or his dependents are entitled to recover under workmen's compensation. (Emphasis added.)

This court has not fully considered the extent of that critical phrase in our workmen's compensation plan, but we are not inclined to unduly restrict its scope.

The stipulated facts present a borderline case which is not adequately covered by existing law.[2] Professor Larson states:

> Now that the coffee break has become a fixture of many kinds of employment, close questions continue to arise on the compensability of injuries occurring off the premises during rest periods or coffee breaks of various durations. It is clear that one cannot announce an all-purpose "coffee break rule," since there are too many variables that could affect the result.[3]

Compensation for off-premises, rest period injuries is appropriate in Professor Larson's view when the employer "can be deemed to have retained authority over the employee."[4] Authority is said to be retained where, measured by the duration of the break and the distance from the employee's desk, the employment itself was not interrupted.[5]

Bodensky v. Royaltone, Inc., 5 A.D.2d 733, 168 N.Y.S.2d 908 (1957) relies on the reasoning in *Caporale* and is persuasive on the issue of whether off-premises, "coffee-break" injuries should be compensable. Royaltone permitted its employees a 15–minute coffee break each day. Claimant's practice of leaving the building during this time was known to her employer and allowed. On returning from a coffee shop about a block away, claimant injured herself. The court based its award of compensation on a finding that the employment was not interrupted because the break was an approved one of limited duration and restricted in scope.

We reject appellant's notion that Balsam v. New York State Division of Employment, 24 A.D.2d 802, 263 N.Y.S.2d 849 (1965) is controlling in the present case.

In *Balsam* claimant was injured when she went to a bank to cash a personal check prior to having coffee, but during her rest period. Since employees were free to leave the premises only for coffee at a designated shop, claimant's injury occurred during the course of a "purely personal mission."[6] This deviation from a "prescribed sphere of recreational endeavor"[7] resulted in the dismissal of the claim.

The case at hand does not involve an employee who strayed from an authorized activity, therefore, we find *Balsam* inapposite.

2. *See* Jordan v. Western Electric Co., Inc., 1 Or.App. 441, 463 P.2d 598, 600 (1970) n. 1 for a representative listing of those cases which allow and those which disallow recovery for injuries occasioned during break time.

3. 1 Larson, Workmen's Compensation Law 245, § 15.54 (1968).

4. *Id.*, p. 247.

5. Caporale v. Department of Taxation and Finance, 2 A.D.2d 91, 153 N.Y.S.2d 738 (1956), aff'd., 2 N.Y.2d 946, 162 N.Y.S.2d 40, 142 N.E.2d 213 (1957).

6. Balsam v. New York State Division of Employment, 24 A.D.2d 802, 263 N.Y.S.2d 849, 850 (1965).

7. *Id.*

We adopt as a general rule the proposition that an employee, who is allowed to venture off-premises during an authorized work break, and who is injured in the course of reasonable and necessary activity incidental to such break, should be compensated.

A scheduled coffee break serves the dual function of providing an employee a brief respite from his job as well as affording him an opportunity to tend to matters of a personal nature. The former objective has been viewed as a benefit to the employer, because a refreshed employee is often a more productive one. The latter type of activity may or may not directly benefit the employer, but is allowed as a convenience to the employee. An employer may derive substantial benefits from an employee who is allowed time away from the job to accomplish pressing personal business. Injuries occasioned by employees pursuing necessary personal matters off employer's premises are compensable in our view as work-connected, especially if the employer acquiesces in such practices.

Applying the above principles to the present case we find that there is substantial evidence to support a claim for compensation.

Deceased was observing her regular afternoon coffee break when the fatal accident occurred. It was her employer's policy to allow *ex premises* departures during the break for the convenience of the employees. Once previously, deceased had ventured out to cash her paycheck without censure. On the day of the accident, deceased was among a group of employees which was observed departing for the bank by a supervisor. Since late work beyond banking hours was anticipated, it was necessary for deceased to use her free time to cash her paycheck. A substantial benefit accrued to the employer because his production line closed down simultaneously rather than sporadically throughout the workday. The regularly scheduled break promoted a smooth-running, efficient operation.

Based on the foregoing, we affirm the award of the Labor and Industrial Relations Appeals Board, * * *.

LEVINSON, JUSTICE (dissenting).

This case is before us upon stipulated facts and presents a question of first impression under Hawaii's Workmen's Compensation Law.[1] The question is whether an employee who is injured off the employer's premises during an unpaid coffee break but while en route to a bank to cash a paycheck has suffered an injury "arising out of and in the course of the employment." A majority of this court is of the opinion that compensation should be awarded. It reasons that "an employee who is allowed to venture off-premises during an authorized work break, and who is injured in the course of reasonable and necessary activity inciden-

---

1. The relevant provision, HRS § 386–3, provides in pertinent part as follows:

Injuries covered. If an employee suffers personal injury either by accident arising out of and in the course of the employment or by disease proximately caused by or re-

sulting from the nature of the employment, his employer or the special compensation fund shall pay compensation to the employee or his dependents as hereinafter provided.

tal to such break, should be compensated." In my view, neither the result reached nor the reasoning adopted to support it can be justified under present authority or sound public policy. I dissent.

* * *

I.

In order to focus on the precise issue presented by this record, it is useful first to canvass those matters which this case does not involve.

At the time of the accident, Mrs. Pacheco was quite clearly neither on the premises nor under the control of her employer. She was, instead, on her own time in the company of three other employees, each having no managerial responsibilities, * * * in an automobile four-tenths of a mile away from her employer's premises, * * *. Nor was Mrs. Pacheco, in my view, under the constructive control of her employer. * * * When she left her employer's premises, the only restriction placed upon her was time. She could go wherever she pleased and do whatever she wanted as long as she returned to work in 15 minutes. If Mrs. Pacheco is deemed to have been under the constructive control of the employer merely because her time was restricted, then any activity in which she might have engaged while off premises during the period of the coffee break also must be deemed to have been under the employer's control. In none of the reported cases has the element of control ever been stretched so far.

There is nothing in the facts, all of which were stipulated, indicating that the employer had any knowledge, either actual or constructive, of Mrs. Pacheco's intent to cash her paycheck during the coffee break. Absent such knowledge, it cannot be said that the employer acquiesced in her activity, * * *. Under the stipulation, there is no indication that the employer was aware of the fact that Mrs. Pacheco left the premises for the purpose of cashing her paycheck or that she had ever done so previously. She did, in fact, do so on one previous occasion, but we cannot assume that her employer had knowledge of it. Mrs. Pacheco's supervisor may have guessed at the purpose of the off-premises jaunt, but that is mere speculation.

Although Mrs. Pacheco was required to work later than usual, her trip to the bank was at most convenient to her personally and had nothing to do with her ability to work late. Check cashing was certainly not one of her duties as an employee, ...

Nor can it be said that the employer derived a benefit from the activity. . . . The paycheck could have been cashed at some other time and place. Since Mrs. Pacheco anticipated working late, it may have been more convenient for her to cash it during her coffee break. But this was merely a matter of personal convenience unrelated to her work. At most it was intended to save her some inconvenience after work. Cf. Comment, "Workmen's Compensation: The Personal Comfort Doctrine," 1960 Wis.L.Rev. 91. Mrs. Pacheco, for example, did not attempt to go to the bank so that she could pay for a meal while at work, or purchase some article essential to her employment.

The answer to the argument that cashing a check for her personal convenience only is sufficient to render an employer responsible for compensation is that it then would follow that injuries arising out of any activity that might conceivably make employment more convenient for the employee also would be compensable. The connection between an employee's personal convenience and the employment is too tenuous to justify compensation. There is a logical distinction, I believe, between the circumstances under which an employee takes a breath of fresh air, smokes a cigarette, uses the bathroom or talks to another employee, see 1 Larson, The Law of Workmen's Compensation § 21 (1965), and those circumstances under which he goes to a bank to cash his paycheck, ... takes an airplane ride, ... or goes shopping at a grocery store for his family, ...

If Mrs. Pacheco had not engaged in the activity that led to her accident, she might have been anxious about having cash with which to purchase commodities or entertainment for her family. No doubt her anxiety would in some sense affect her while she was at work. But if the avoidance of such anxiety is considered, apart from mere personal convenience, to be of such benefit to the employer so as to render the latter responsible for injuries resulting from employee activities which relieve such anxiety, then with equal force practically any activity engaged in by an employee benefits the employer, whether engaged in during working or leisure hours. Compensation based on anxiety is even more tenuous than compensation based on personal convenience unrelated to work. It is unheard of in the reported cases.

Finally, the check cashing activity was not in accordance with custom, ... pursuant to any special arrangement between the employer and the bank, ... or engaged in by Mrs. Pacheco while she was subject to call, ... The stipulation is silent with respect to any custom or special arrangement and it would be improper to assume their existence. With respect to the possibility of Mrs. Pacheco's being subject to call, the stipulation is precisely to the contrary. Mrs. Pacheco was free to do as she pleased during her coffee break and upon leaving her employer's premises she was restricted only in the time in which she could achieve her check cashing purpose. In view of the fact that on the day of the accident delay in production was a matter of concern, it is significant that Mrs. Pacheco's supervisor merely admonished a hasty return. If Mrs. Pacheco was subject to call, her supervisor certainly would have ordered her to remain on the premises.

II.

Flushed against this background the issue is reduced to the question whether an injury is compensable merely because it occurred during an authorized coffee break. Apart from this time element, the check cashing activity had nothing to do with employment under present authority.

I would have thought that there would be little doubt that an injury occurring during a coffee break, without more, would not be compensable. The majority, however, indicates a contrary view. No authority is cited, and no authority exists, to support that conclusion.

* * *

Assuming that the majority is correct in its assertion that a coffee break is an incident of employment and that check cashing is a reasonable and necessary incident of a coffee break, still, the two activities are not merged into a single incident of employment, coffee breaks, or into employment itself merely by the stroke of a pen or a vote cast in favor of compensation. Coffee breaks are considered, if at all, incidents of employment not only because of the short interval between the time work is stopped and the time it is resumed but also because:

> The drinking of coffee and similar beverages, or the eating of a snack ... during recognized breaks in the daily work hours is now so generally accepted in the industrial life of our Nation as to constitute a work-related activity falling into a general class of activities closely related to personal ministrations so that engaging in such activity does not take an employee out of the course of his employment. In re Helen F. Gunderson, Docket No. 54–36, U.S. Dep't of Labor, Employees' Compensation Appeals Board, April 13, 1955, quoted in 1 Larson, *supra* at 245 n. 18 (1965).

Coffee breaks are not part of employment itself; they are incidents of employment. They are incidents of employment because the activity and not the time in which the activity engaged in is incidental to employment. The reason for the rule, that the drinking of coffee or relaxing is closely related to employment, defines and limits its reach. Drinking coffee or relaxing during a coffee break is itself one step removed from employment. A trip to a bank to cash a paycheck during a coffee break is still another step removed. In my view, a line must be drawn at this point.

There is, I believe, a clear distinction between injuries that arise out of activities that are directly related to the primary purpose of a coffee break and injuries that arise out of activities that are merely incidental to it. ... Check cashing is an activity falling in the latter and not the former category and is therefore without the coverage of workmen's compensation.

This distinction is supported by all the reported cases in which an injury occurred during a coffee break. In those cases in which compensation was awarded, the employee was injured while actually drinking coffee, ... in a place where he intended to drink coffee, ... or en route to or from such a place, ... But in those cases in which compensation was denied, the employee was injured while pursuing some other activity unrelated to the drinking of coffee or relaxation.

* * *

The distinction is also supported by sound public policy. The broad sweep of the reasoning adopted by the majority will lead, in my view, to the restriction of activities in which employees will be allowed to engage during coffee breaks. In order to avoid liability, or, more precisely, an increase in premiums, employers will restrict authorized activities. Employees are not machines to be limited to such a narrow gauge. As a matter of policy, employees should be free to do as they please during coffee breaks; provided, however, that the employer is responsible only for injuries that are directly related to the primary purpose of the coffee break. If this court is unwilling to draw the line at that point, the employer will draw the line himself, at the expense of the employee.

III.

In awarding compensation in this case, the court sets itself adrift in this area without chart or compass. I fail to see any logical distinction between check cashing and activities that are directly related either in purpose or reason to check cashing, such as shopping for groceries, ... or purchasing Christmas tree decorations,.... Each is equally incidental, reasonable and necessary, if at all, to a coffee break. Where would the majority draw the line? Would it include sky diving or drag racing under circumstances where it is lawful and does not exceed the time allowed for a coffee break? The risk of injury involved in all of these activities is clearly distinguishable from the risk incident to using a coffee break for the primary purpose for which it was intended, the drinking of coffee and relaxation. In pondering the various fact situations that will arise following this case, the majority would do well to consider the following oft-quoted passage from *The Voyages of Sinbad the Sailor:*

> And, lo, the master of the ship vociferated and called out, threw down his turban, slapped his face, plucked his beard, and fell down in the hold of the ship by reason of the violence of his grief and rage. So all the merchants and other passengers came together to him and said to him, "O master, what is the matter?" and he answered them: "Know, O Company, that we have wandered from our course, having passed forth from the sea in which we were, and entered a sea of which we know not the routes."

I would reverse the Decision and Order of the Labor and Industrial Relations Appeals Board and dismiss the claim.

Notes

1. Contrary to the principal case, most courts hold that employees who leave the employer's premises on short personal errands are outside the course of employment, even if the employer permits or acquiesces in the activity. Hinkle v. W.C.A.B., 175 Cal.App.3d 587, 221 Cal.Rptr. 40, 43 (1985) denied recovery in a similar check cashing incident, stating, "The essential rule is that an off-duty personal activity, transpiring in an area beyond the employer's dominion and control and yielding neither advantage nor benefit to the employer, is not within the course of employment." Although ac-

knowledging the validity of the "essential rule" of *Hinkle*, a Florida court permitted recovery in a similar case because of an extraordinary risk posed by hazards in the general locality in which the employment was located. Toyota of Pensacola v. Maines, 558 So.2d 1072 (Fla.App.1990). See also St. Anthony Hospital v. James, 889 P.2d 1279 (Okla. App. 1994)(off duty nurse who slipped and fell while entering the hospital where she worked to pick up her pay check on her day off held to be covered by workers' compensation). Hoffmann v. Workers' Compensation Appeal Board, 711 A.2d 567 (Pa. Cmwlth.Ct.1998), declined to follow *James* and noted that the decisions were divided in opinion on the issue." As to other decisions, compare Holditch v. Standard Accident Ins. Co., 208 F.2d 721 (5th Cir.1953) (compensation denied one of several employees taking lunch on premises who was injured while going next door to secure chewing gum for the group) with Prater v. Indiana Briquetting Corp., 253 Ind. 83, 251 N.E.2d 810 (1969) (similar; compensation awarded).

2. Most courts also deem employees who take meals off premises on unpaid lunch breaks to be outside the course of employment, both while eating and while proceeding to and from the eating place. The mealtime journey is usually treated like the trip to and from work generally, discussed hereafter. See, e.g., Wallace v. Copiah County Lumber Co., 223 Miss. 90, 77 So.2d 316 (1955). Similarly, if the employee injured off premises during lunch hour can claim one of the exceptions to the general going and coming rule, discussed infra, he will be entitled to compensation.

More generally, if the nature of the employee's duties require substantial adjustment of personal eating habits, as where only a hurried lunch can be taken at varied times and places, off premises injuries have been regarded as within the course of employment. See, e.g., Relkin v. National Transp. Co., 18 A.D.2d 137, 238 N.Y.S.2d 575 (1963) (taxi driver ate in cafeterias); Western Greyhound Lines v. Industrial Accident Comm., 225 Cal.App.2d 517, 37 Cal.Rptr. 580 (1964) (female bus driver assaulted in restaurant); and Pettit v. Keller, 9 Ohio App.2d 91, 223 N.E.2d 67 (1967) (claimant obliged to grab a snack whenever time permitted).

3. The courts are in virtual uniform agreement that an accident occurring on the premises during a lunch hour or recreation or rest period is compensable if it can be attributable to some recognizable hazard in the employment environment and if it happened near the authorized place for eating or recreation. See, e.g., Nicholson v. Industrial Comm., 76 Ariz. 105, 259 P.2d 547 (1953) (employee had been discharged for day, injured by collapsing platform while eating lunch); and Texas Employers' Ins. Ass'n v. Davidson, 295 S.W.2d 482 (Tex.Civ.App.1956) (compensation awarded employee who slipped on piece of material used in factory while going to garbage can in order to deposit lunch wrappings). It may be immaterial whether the worker is required to eat on the premises or does so by choice. See, e.g., Kennecott Corp., Kennecott Minerals Company Div. v. Industrial Comm., 675 P.2d 1187 (Utah 1983) (compensation awarded survivors of an employee killed while getting a drink of water on employer's premises out of his work area during lunch break; personal comfort doctrine permits recovery for incident that was not so unusual or unreasonable that it could not be considered an incident of employment).

4. The decisions as to lunchtime accidents resulting in part by the employee's desire to satisfy curiosity or for entertainment are also not harmonious. Compare Coates v. J.M. Bucheimer Co., 242 Md. 198, 218 A.2d 191 (1966) (compensation denied employee who explored premises during lunch hour) and McKim v. Commercial Standard Ins. Co., 179 S.W.2d 357 (Tex.Civ.App.1944) (compensation denied hatmaker who was injured when he went downstairs to sales department to purchase a hat) with Dyer v. Sears, Roebuck & Co., 350 Mich. 92, 85 N.W.2d 152 (1957) (compensation awarded employee injured while descending stairs on premises following lunch intending to go to nearby building to pay a bill) and Moore v. Superior Stone Co., 242 N.C. 647, 89 S.E.2d 253 (1955) (compensation awarded employee who experimented with blasting machine during lunch hour and set off three hundred dynamite caps). When compensation is awarded, courts are likely to stress that the employee's mission was in some way beneficial to the employer or that the risk of injury was enhanced by the employment environment. See, e.g., Flamholtz v. Byrde, Richards & Pound, Inc., 37 A.D.2d 645, 322 N.Y.S.2d 382 (1971) (compensation awarded employee injured on way to bank to cash paycheck; mode of payment preferred by employer); Scheffler Greenhouses, Inc. v. Industrial Comm., 66 Ill.2d 361, 5 Ill.Dec. 854, 362 N.E.2d 325 (1977) (compensation awarded employee who swam in pool on premises as relief from humidity); and Turner v. United States Fidelity & Guar. Co., 339 So.2d 917 (La.App.1976) (compensation awarded employee who shot himself playing with coworker's pistol while waiting on premises for lunch whistle; employer had not forbidden or disapproved practice of bringing pistols to premises).

5. Employees who are injured on the employer's premises before and after work while washing, changing clothes, warming themselves and otherwise preparing for beginning or leaving work, are often deemed to be within the course of employment. See, e.g., Montanaro v. Guild Metal Products, 108 R.I. 362, 275 A.2d 634 (1971) (compensation awarded employee who customarily arrived an hour early because of transportation difficulties) and Hill v. Terrazzo Mach. & Supply Co., 279 Minn. 428, 157 N.W.2d 374 (1968) (compensation awarded employee who arrived a few minutes early and fell on premises while leaving to mail letter).

Employees are also deemed to be within the course of employment for a reasonable amount of time needed to leave the premises even after quitting the job or being fired, and courts also generally hold that terminated employees are within the course of employment when returning to collect unpaid wages. Compare Carter v. Lanzetta, 249 La. 1098, 193 So.2d 259 (1966) (compensation awarded employee who was injured while leaving work premises twenty to thirty minutes after having been fully paid for one-day employment) and Parrott v. Industrial Comm., 145 Ohio St. 66, 60 N.E.2d 660 (1945) (compensation awarded to former employee who was injured on premises when he returned to pick up his final pay check two days after pay day) with Olson v. Hurlbert–Sherman Hotel Co., 210 App.Div. 537, 206 N.Y.S. 427 (1924) (compensation denied employee who returned for pay five days after quitting). Suppose the employee returns for clothes or tools after termination of the contract of hire? See, Johnson v. City of Albia, supra.

SECTION 4. INJURIES CAUSED BY HORSEPLAY AMONG CO-WORKERS

BURNS v. MERRITT ENGINEERING
Court of Appeals of New York, 1951.
302 N.Y. 131, 96 N.E.2d 739.

DYE, JUDGE. The sole question posed on this appeal is whether the claimant's disability for which he has been awarded workmen's compensation benefits arose out of his employment, there being no question that the incident giving rise to the injury occurred on the employer's premises during working hours.

The facts are these: At five minutes before quitting time on Saturday, October 13, 1947, and before he had checked out, the claimant, a machinist employed in the machine department of the employer's plywood factory, went to the electrical department for the purpose of getting an automobile ride to his home with one Fothergill, a friend and coemployee. This was a common practice known to the employer. During the conversation Fothergill offered claimant a drink from a bottle containing a clear liquid and labeled "Barclay's Gin". The claimant, after satisfying himself that the department's "straw boss" who was changing his clothes nearby was not watching, took the bottle, stepped behind a large noisy electrical machine designated as a "DC converter" where he would be concealed from view, unscrewed the cork and drank. The bottle contained not gin as he expected, but carbon tetrachloride, a fact known to Fothergill but deliberately withheld from claimant. Fothergill had obtained the liquid with the employer's permission from the company's supply room for his personal use. Later, while claimant was riding home with Fothergill, he became violently ill. The poisonous liquid did severe damage to his internal organs, resulting in the disability complained of.

Claimant at the time was a member of a labor union, the United States Steel Workers of America, which, in acting as bargaining agent, had negotiated a contract with the employer which read in part, viz.: "possession of or drinking liquor or any alcoholic beverage on company property at any time * * * is forbidden and shall constitute a just cause for immediate dismissal."

The testimony is conflicting as to whether the claimant knew about this rule prior to the accident—the employer adducing testimony that each employee had a copy of the contract and that it was accepted and obeyed by the employees, and that it knew of no violation—whereas the claimant would only admit that he learned about the rule at the hearing. Whether or not he knew about such rule prior to the accident is not determinative of the issue here, which is not whether his act, under the rule warranted dismissal, but whether he should be denied compensation because his injuries did not arise out of his employment. In other words, did his conduct under the circumstances amount to an abandonment of his employment as a matter of law?

It is well established that disregard of the precise terms of employment does not necessarily constitute an abandonment thereof, ... nor does violation of a rule not promulgated but which under the circumstances might reasonably be implied, bar compensation benefits, Matter of Lang v. Franklin Ry. Supply Co., 272 App.Div. 988, 73 N.Y.S.2d 1. * * * Viewed in the light of these authorities, a violation—if such there was—of the no-drinking rule under penalty of dismissal, may and should not be treated any differently for purposes of compensation than the violation of any other rule designed to improve plant efficiency and to safeguard employees. * * * [Citation of authorities omitted].

Here the board has found as a fact, from all the surrounding circumstances, that the injuries arose out of the claimant's employment. The contention of the employer and its insurance carrier that the employee by breaking the no-drinking rule forfeits compensation must be rejected, and he may not be penalized for an intention to do so because he drank from a bottle labeled gin in an expectation that it contained gin. When he unwittingly drank carbon tetrachloride knowingly handed to him by a coemployee—who had it with the employer's permission—he was not injured because he violated a rule of the plant, but, on the contrary, because he was the innocent victim of a cruel and senseless joke. When so viewed the employer is not to be exonerated from the consequences of such an act under a theory that it constituted an abandonment of employment but, rather, he may be held under the theory that the injurious act fell naturally into that category of conduct known to the law as "horseplay". To be victimized by a prank perpetrated by a coemployee has long been recognized as an incident of employment, as something reasonably to be expected, a peril of service; an indulgence in a moment's diversion from work to joke with or play a prank upon a fellow workman is a matter of common knowledge to everyone who employs labor, Matter of Leonbruno v. Champlain Silk Mills, 229 N.Y. 470, 128 N.E. 711, 13 A.L.R. 522; ... and an employee so injured will be allowed compensation benefits if the board is satisfied that the acts were incidental to the employment. * * * These general principles are equally available here, particularly as it is quite apparent from the evidence that the claimant, although collaborating or participating in the event, was not the instigator thereof but was its innocent victim.

Perhaps it would be well to say also that an award in horseplay cases should not depend on evidence of foreseeability. It is an important element, ... but not necessarily conclusive. To introduce such an arbitrary and anomalous rule hardly seems consonant with the liberal policy incident to the administration of the statute. The test is whether the injurious horseplay may reasonably be regarded as an incident of the employment, Matter of Leonbruno v. Champlain Silk Mills, supra,—rather than the foreseeability of a particular prank—that supports the finding of fact that it arose out of the employment.

Furthermore, the claimant here is in very much the same position as the victim of an unprovoked assault—malicious or friendly—and the principles pertaining thereto are equally pertinent here. * * * [citation of New York assault cases omitted].

The order appealed from should be affirmed, with costs.

FULD, JUDGE (dissenting).

A company rule forbade the drinking of intoxicating liquor and an agreement between the employer and the union, of which the employees were members, rendered a violation of that rule basis for "immediate dismissal." The rule was, as noted in the court's opinion 302 N.Y. 133, 96 N.E.2d 740, "accepted and obeyed by the employees," and there is not the slightest evidence either that any employee had ever before taken a drink while on the job, that the employer by word or conduct had ever relaxed the rule, or that it had ever indicated that it would permit drinking on the premises. Under such circumstances, it passes understanding to hold that an employee who furtively accepts a drink, *believing it to be gin,* is entitled to compensation because the fellow employee, who offered him the drink, endowed with a cruelly perverted sense of humor, had filled the proffered bottle with poisonous carbon tetrachloride.

Our inquiry here, as in all workmen's compensation cases, is whether the injury arose out of—as well as in the course of—the employment. In the case before us, there is no suggestion that the drinking was done, even in the remotest or most farfetched sense of the term, in the course of any assigned job, or that it was a *permitted* incidental diversion which the employer had knowledge of and had impliedly adopted through sufferance or acquiescence. Here, claimant's act—and it is important to bear in mind that he could never have become the victim of the prank in question until and unless he first performed that act—was just as far removed from the scope of his employment as it would have been had he become ill from drinking bad liquor from a bottle which he himself had brought into the factory, in violation of a company rule, to assuage his thirst with an occasional nip. Surely, no one could possibly claim that the employee was entitled to compensation in such a case merely because the drinking had occurred in the factory during working hours. See Elliott v. Industrial Accident Comm., 21 Cal.2d 281, 284, 131 P.2d 521, 144 A.L.R. 358. In the California case, Elliott, having become ill during working hours, took a drink—"as * * * medication"—from a bottle which he believed held wine, though in fact it contained carbon tetrachloride. Although the court upheld the ensuing award, it was at pains to caution that the result would have been different if the employee had taken a drink "of intoxicating liquor for the mere satisfaction of a desire therefor * * * rather than * * * for medicinal purposes," 21 Cal.2d supra, at page 284, 131 P.2d at page 522.

It does not end our task to declare that the employee was the victim of a prank or horseplay, for, if, when the injury occurred, he had stepped out of his working environment, had abandoned his employment, in order to indulge in an extra-employment caper or activity, it would necessarily follow that his injury neither arose out of his employment nor resulted from a risk of that employment. ... That being so, all relationship to the prank and horseplay cases is obliterated, any reliance upon them misplaced. In any event, though, whether the claimant's extra-employment activity is to be deemed an incident of employment depends in large measure upon whether it has been regularized by long indulgence, upon whether there has been "continuity of practice—conduct which has gained acceptance". ... Thus, in affirming an award for compensation in the McCarthy case, supra, 295 N.Y. 443, 68 N.E.2d 434, we stressed the "long-continuing custom and practice" of the conduct there involved and the "continued series of related and similar incidents participated in by all the employees," 295 N.Y. at page 447, 68 N.E.2d at page 436, and in the Remington Rand case, supra, 300 N.Y. 715, 92 N.E.2d 58, where the employee took a drink of carbon tetrachloride at a New Year's party held in the factory, under the belief, also induced by a practical joker, that it was whiskey, we upheld the award solely upon the ground that the evidence was ample to sustain the finding that the employer, knowing that the drinking of intoxicating liquor occurred at such parties, sanctioned the practice and, by that token, transformed such drinking and its attendant consequences into risks of the employment.

We have seen that here the case was entirely different. The record establishes that there never before had been any drinking in the factory—this being "*a single isolated incident* which originated solely and entirely in the injured employee's own act," Matter of Industrial Comr. [Siguin] v. McCarthy, supra, 295 N.Y. 443, 447, 68 N.E.2d 436—and the employer had never permitted, or even intimated that he would have permitted, such conduct. There is no escape from the conclusion that, when claimant was injured, he had deliberately abandoned his employment in order to indulge in an activity entirely unrelated to his work—and the employer's rule against drinking forcefully points up and accentuates the fact of such abandonment.

I am not suggesting that the violation of every company rule disqualifies an employee from compensation for resulting injuries. Some rules, such as those prescribing work routines or protective devices, are designed expressly for the individual employee's personal protection, and it would frustrate the very purpose and aim of the Workmen's Compensation Law, Consol.Laws, c. 67, to hold that a violation of that type of rule removed the employee from his employment. ... Not so, however, where the rule, such as the one before us, is obviously designed to protect not only the violator but his fellow employees whose safety is dependent upon his careful and sober operation of machinery or other equipment. It impresses me as principle turned topsy-turvy to sanction payment of compensation to an employee who performs—or believes that he is performing—an act that calls for summary dismissal.

The order appealed from should be reversed and the claim dismissed.

Loughran, C.J., and Conway and Froessel, JJ., concur with Dye, J.

FULD, J., dissents in opinion in which LEWIS and DESMOND, JJ., concur. Order affirmed.

Notes

1. Horseplay decisions fall into two categories: those in which the claimant was an innocent victim who did not participate in the prank; and those in which the victim instigated the horseplay or actively participated in it. Claimants in the first category are almost always compensated unless the employee is deemed to be outside the course of employment for some independent reason. See, e.g., Leonbruno v. Champlain Silk Mills, 229 N.Y. 470, 128 N.E. 711 (1920) and Sizemore v. State Workmen's Compensation Com'r, 160 W.Va. 407, 235 S.E.2d 473 (1977) (employee waiting to leave work premises sustained a playful wallop on the head). Some decisions seem to deny recovery for all horseplay injuries regardless of who instigated it. See, e.g., Kight v. Liberty Mut. Ins. Co., 141 Ga.App. 409, 233 S.E.2d 453 (1977) (compensation denied to worker hurt when co-worker pulled a chair from under him) and Walsh Construction Co. v. Hamilton, 185 Ga.App. 105, 363 S.E.2d 301 (1987) (compensation denied to worker hurt in fight with co-worker who had accused claimant of begging food).

2. Some courts brand instigating claimants as "aggressors," similar to fight situations, and deny them compensation unless one of several conflicting and ill-defined exceptions applies. Compare Jones v. Hampton Pontiac, 304 S.C. 440, 405 S.E.2d 395 (1991) (compensation denied to worker hurt while demonstrating a karate kick to a co-worker) with Industrial Com'r v. McCarthy, 295 N.Y. 443, 68 N.E.2d 434, 435 (1946), which announced an exception that permits a horseplay instigator or participant to recover if the practice has "long been part and parcel, an incident, of the employment." This was applied to award compensation in Montpetit v. Standard Shade Roller Corp., 277 App.Div. 1066, 100 N.Y.S.2d 640 (1950) (practice of throwing water was known to the employer, although workers had been warned not to engage therein; compensation allowed). This so-called "New York" exception merges into an even more liberal view many courts apply to relatively minor horseplay episodes. As one court said:

> For the purposes of the compensation act the concept of course of employment is more comprehensive than the assigned work at the lathe. It includes an employee's ministrations to his own human needs: he must eat; concessions to his own human frailties: he must rest, must now and then have a break, and he sometimes, even on the job, plays practical jokes on his fellows. Course of employment is not scope of employment. The former, as the cases so clearly reveal, is a way of life in a working environment. If the injury results from the work itself, or from the stresses, the tensions, the associations of the working environments, human as well as material, it is compensable. Why? Because those are the ingredients of the product itself. It carries to the market with it, on its price tag stained and scarred, its human as well as its material costs. So says the statute. It does not become us to ignore its plain commands. * * *

Crilly v. Ballou, 353 Mich. 303, 326, 91 N.W.2d 493, 505 (1958). Compare Carvalho v. Decorative Fabrics Co., 117 R.I. 231, 366 A.2d 157 (1976) (airhose playfully inserted in worker's rectum; compensation awarded; immaterial whether victim was or was not a participant) with City of Miami v. Granlund, 153 So.2d 830 (Fla.1963) (police officer pointed at his head a gun mistakenly believed to be unloaded; compensation denied; deviation from job too flagrant). As the doctrine has matured, courts are inclined to apply a four part test: (1) was the deviation from employment extensive or serious; (2) was it intermingled concurrently with the actual performance of duties; (3) is the practice customary in the employment; and (4) does the employment anticipate some horseplay? See, e.g., Petrie v. General Motors Corp., 187 Mich.App. 198, 466 N.W.2d 714 (1991) (compensation denied with regard to worker who left his work area, climbed onto overhead hoist where he had no business, and was electrocuted).

3. Should an injury be regarded as arising out of the employment if it resulted from a practice unknown to the employer but that might have been expected under the circumstance of the employment? See Johnson v. Loew's, Inc., 7 A.D.2d 795, 180 N.Y.S.2d 826 (1958), affirmed 8 N.Y.2d 757, 201 N.Y.S.2d 775, 168 N.E.2d 111 (1960) (employee injured while attempting to shoot paper clip with rubber band; employer charged with knowledge that messenger boys engaged in the practice; compensation awarded). Compare Hayes Freight Lines, Inc. v. Burns, 290 S.W.2d 836 (Ky.1956) (worker injured by horseplay with fire crackers; compensation to be awarded if employer knew of and acquiesced in the practice).

SECTION 5. INJURIES CAUSED BY EMPLOYEES' WILFUL MISCONDUCT AND VIOLATIONS OF RULES AND INSTRUCTIONS

CAREY v. BRYAN & ROLLINS

Superior Court of Delaware, Sussex, 1955.
49 Del. 387, 117 A.2d 240.

HERRMANN, JUDGE. The Industrial Accident Board awarded workmen's compensation to the claimant for injuries sustained by him when a pickup truck, which he was driving, ran off the road and struck a telephone pole. According to the uncontroverted testimony of the claimant, he was driving in a 50 mile per hour zone at a speed of "better than fifty-five; 55, 65, something like that". While driving at that speed, the claimant attempted to light a cigarette and, in so doing, the cigarette dropped to the seat or the floor of the truck. The claimant reached down to search for and recover the cigarette, lost control of the vehicle and ran off the road into the pole. At the hearing before the Board, the claimant stated that he was "driving too fast" and that he "lost control" of the truck.

This case has been before this Court upon a prior appeal. See Carey v. Bryan & Rollins, Del.Super., 105 A.2d 201. The award of the Industrial Accident Board was there reversed and the case was remanded for the purpose, *inter alia,* of determination by the Board of the following questions:

"1) Did Carey violate the speed Statute?

"2) Did Carey violate the Statute governing reckless driving?

"3) If he violated either or both of such Statutes, was the violation 'wilful'?

"4) If there was a wilful violation, was it the proximate cause of the accident?"

Upon the remand, the Board heard further evidence upon the intoxication issue involved in this case, but the Board permitted no further evidence on the four questions above mentioned. The Board made its determination as to those questions upon the basis of the record of the original hearing. It was decided by the Board that (1) the claimant violated the speed statute but (2) this violation was not "wilful" and (3) the claimant did not violate the statute prohibiting reckless driving.

The portion of the Workmen's Compensation Statute involved here, being 19 Del.C. § 2353(b) derived from 1935 Code ¶ 6106, provides as follows:

"(b) If any employee be injured as a result of his intoxication, or because of his deliberate and reckless indifference to danger, or because of his wilful intention to bring about the injury or death of himself, or of another, or because of his wilful failure or refusal to use a reasonable safety appliance provided for him, or to perform a duty required by statute, he shall not be entitled to recover damages in an action at law, or compensation or medical, dental, optometric or hospital service under the compensatory provisions of this chapter. The burden of proof under the provisions of this subsection shall be on the employer."

This appeal raises two principal questions for decision:

1) Was the claimant guilty of "wilful failure to perform a duty required by statute" such as to constitute a forfeiture of compensation rights under 19 Del.C. § 2353(b); or, as it might be otherwise stated, does the violation of a penal motor vehicle statute, *per se*, constitute a "wilful failure" and forfeiture under § 2353(b)?

2) Did the Board err in refusing to permit further evidence on the four questions to be decided on the remand?

In the prior opinion in this case, this Court stated, 105 A.2d at 204:

"In view of the clear prohibition of the Statute, it is held that the claimant is not entitled to compensation if he wilfully violated the Motor Vehicle Law governing speed or reckless driving and if such violation was the proximate cause of the accident...."

The word "wilful" is the key word in this case. That word, as used in the subsection of the Statute here involved, was considered by this Court in Lobdell Car Wheel Co. v. Subielski, 2 W.W.Harr. 462, 125 A. 462, 464. The Court there stated:

"The word 'willful' may be defined with a reasonable degree of satisfaction, although the definitions vary in some respects, depending somewhat upon the meaning intended to be conveyed by its use with other words. In the present statute we believe it was used to define an act done intentionally, knowingly, and purposely, without justifiable excuse, as distinguished from an act done carelessly, thoughtlessly, heedlessly or inadvertently."

There is no evidence in this case that the claimant intentionally and deliberately exceeded the speed limit or drove recklessly, knowingly and purposely, without justifiable excuse. The employer has the burden of proof under the forfeiture provisions of the Workmen's Compensation Statute. See 19 Del.C. § 2353(b). The employer has not been able to point to anything in the evidence which would compel the inference that the actions of the claimant were intentional, deliberate and "wilful". Most operators of motor vehicles have, at one time or another, found themselves driving at 60 or 65 miles per hour on the open highway carelessly, thoughtlessly and inadvertently, without conscious intention to exceed the speed limit. While an inference of wilfulness might be the only reasonable inference to be drawn from such speed within city or town limits, no such inference is created where, as here, the speed limit was 50 miles per hour.

Similarly, no inference of deliberation or intention, or conscious indifference to consequences, is compelled by the fact that, while driving along the open highway, the claimant reached down to recover the cigarette he had started to light. It is common knowledge that drivers often do this as a matter of reflex action and impulse, carelessly and thoughtlessly but without conscious intention, to prevent burns to the person, clothing or upholstery. This may be folly and negligence when driving at 60 miles per hour but, as a matter of law, it does not constitute "wilful" reckless driving in the absence of some evidence of deliberation.

The employer contends that a violation of a penal statute, such as the motor vehicle statute prohibiting speeding and reckless driving, in and of itself constitutes a "wilful failure to perform a duty required by statute" and a forfeiture of compensation rights under the provisions of § 2353(b). The employer places principal reliance upon Aetna Life Ins. Co. v. Carroll, 169 Ga. 333, 150 S.E. 208, 211. In that case, the Supreme Court of Georgia held that violation of a penal statute, such as the motor vehicle speed law, in and of itself constituted "willful misconduct" and "willful failure * * * to perform a duty required by statute" so as to bar rights under the Georgia Workmen's Compensation Statute.

The *ratio decidendi* of the case is that an employer should not be compelled to compensate an employee for his injury, or his dependents for his death, caused by the employee's violation of a criminal statute. I find the rule of the *Carroll* case to be unacceptable for the following reasons: (1) That case deals with the construction of the words "willful misconduct" which do not appear in the Delaware statute although, in other respects, the pertinent provision of the Georgia statute is almost identical with ours. (2) In Delaware, violation of a penal motor vehicle statute, without more, constitutes negligence *per se*. It is settled that negligence alone will not defeat recovery of workmen's compensation. (3) There is such conflict and confusion among the various statutes and decisions relating to this phase of the law of workmen's compensation, precedents from other jurisdictions are of little value. Compare King v. Empire Collieries Co., 148 Va. 585, 139 S.E. 478, 479, 58 A.L.R. 193. The only reasonable course, therefore, is to confine ourselves to the precise language of our Statute and an attempt to determine the intention of our Legislature. (4) I find the rule of the *Carroll* case to be unacceptably harsh when considered in the light of the humanitarian purposes of the Workmen's Compensation Law. It does not seem consonant with the spirit of such legislation to hold that a forfeiture of all rights of compensation may result from an inadvertent and unintentional violation of a traffic law. * * *

It is held that violation of a penal motor vehicle statute does not, *per se,* constitute a "wilful failure to perform a duty required by statute" and forfeiture under 19 Del.C. § 2353(b) and that, in order to invoke the forfeiture provisions of the Workmen's Compensation Law, the employer has the burden of proving by a preponderance of the evidence that the violation of the statute was "wilful", i.e., intentional and deliberate and not just careless and inadvertent. In the instant case, the employer was unable to make such a showing either by direct or circumstantial evidence. * * *

I find no reversible error in the proceedings of the Industrial Accident Board and, therefore, the award to the claimant will be affirmed.

Notes

1. A number of compensation statutes expressly deny compensation of injuries caused by the "willful misconduct" of an employee. These provisions usually create affirmative defenses, imposing the burden of proof on the employer, and, under the liberal construction of the statutes in favor of their remedial purposes, seldom defeat claims unless the employee violated an established safety rule. For example, courts frequently hold that even gross negligence does not amount to willful misconduct. Allen v. Columbus Mining Co., 207 Ky. 183, 268 S.W. 1073 (1925) (employee lay down for nap very near a fire on an operating forge; compensation awarded), and Lumbermens Mut. Cas. Co. v. Amerine, 139 Ga.App. 702, 229 S.E.2d 516 (1976) (worker injured while playfully riding on the rear wheel of bicycle; compensation awarded). Neither do courts treat inexcusable ignorance or bad judgment as willful misconduct. See, e.g., Tyree v. Commonwealth, 164 Va. 218, 179 S.E. 297 (1935) (willful misconduct "involves the idea of premeditation and determination to do the act, though known to be forbidden"). The Georgia Supreme Court summed up the requirements of this defense as follows:

> 1. (a) The general rule is that mere violations of instructions, orders, rules, ordinances, and statutes, and the doing of hazardous acts where the danger is obvious, do not, without more, as a matter of law, constitute wilful misconduct.

(b) Such violations or failures or refusals generally constitute mere negligence, and such negligence, however great, does not constitute wilful misconduct or wilful failure or refusal to perform a duty required by statute, and will not defeat recovery of compensation by the employee or his dependents.

(c) Wilful misconduct, or wilful failure or refusal to perform a duty required by statute, is more than negligence or even gross negligence; it involves conduct of a criminal or quasi-criminal nature, the intentional doing of something, either with the knowledge that it is likely to result in serious injury, or with the wanton and reckless disregard of its probable consequences.

(d) Wilful misconduct includes all conscious or intentional violations of definite law or rules of conduct, as distinguished from inadvertent, unconscious, or involuntary violations.

2. (a) Whether the employee was guilty of wilful misconduct, or was guilty of wilful failure or refusal to perform a duty imposed on him by statute, [are] questions of fact for the [Board of Worker's Compensation], and the findings of the [Board] upon these questions are final, and will not be disturbed where there is evidence to support them.

Roy v. Norman, 261 Ga. 303, 404 S.E.2d 117, 118 (1991) (worker burned while making up fire with gasoline in paper cup not disqualified for willful misconduct).

2. Nevertheless, a deliberate violation of a reasonable safety rule that causes an injury of the type the rule was designed to prevent is frequently held to be willful misconduct. Consequently, some decisions deny compensation to a disobedient employee even though the violation related to the method of doing assigned work and the employee was plainly within the course of employment at the time. See, e.g., Mills v. Virginia Electric Co., 197 Va. 547, 90 S.E.2d 124 (1955) (injury resulted from employee's failure to use rubber gloves when handling high tension wire; compensation denied). Do these decisions comport with the basic premises of the compensation laws?

3. A recurring fact pattern involves workers who misrepresent their physical condition in order to secure employment and later suffer an injury on the job. A typical case involves a worker who failed to disclose prior back injuries on the employment application and then re-injured the back while lifting a heavy object. Professor Larson advocates denying compensation if three factors exist: (1) the employee must have knowingly and wilfully made a false representation as to physical condition; (2) the employer must have relied upon the false representation and this reliance must have been a substantial factor in the hiring; and (3) there must have been a causal connection between the false representation and the injury. 1C A. Larson, Workmen's Compensation § 47.53 (1991). Some courts have incorporated this defense under the general "wilful misconduct" workers' compensation provisions. See, e.g., Shaw's Supermarkets, Inc. v. Delgiacco, 410 Mass. 840, 575 N.E.2d 1115 (1991) (collecting cases). Other courts treat the fraud as

rendering the "contract of hire" voidable. See, e.g., Georgia Electric Co. v. Rycroft, 259 Ga. 155, 378 S.E.2d 111 (1989). Still others refuse to recognize this defense in the absence of a more specific statutory provision. See, e.g., Kraus v. Artcraft Sign Co., 710 P.2d 480 (Colo.1985).

4.   Some statutes deny or limit compensation to employees who willfully refuse to obey a safety regulation or willfully fail to use a safety device furnished by the employer. Some of these provisions augment a willful misconduct provision (e.g., Alabama, Delaware, Georgia, South Dakota, Tennessee, Virginia, West Virginia), and others serve as a partial substitute for it (e.g., Florida, Indiana, Kansas, Louisiana, Oklahoma, South Carolina). Under some statutes, both safety rule violations and failures to use safety devices are employer defenses (e.g., Alabama, Florida, Georgia, Indiana, Louisiana, Virginia, and West Virginia), and under others only failure to use a safety device is a defense (e.g., Delaware, Kansas, Oklahoma, South Dakota, and Tennessee). Another group of statutes does not deny compensation because of employees' misconduct, but reduces the amount of compensation awarded (e.g., ten percent in North Carolina and South Carolina; fifteen percent in Kentucky, Missouri, Utah, and Wisconsin; fifty percent in Colorado). Failure of an employee to comply with or report violations of OSHA standards will not be deemed to be willful misconduct if the employer has not enforced the standard as a specific employment rule. See, e.g., Wyle v. Professional Services Industries, Inc., 12 Va.App. 684, 406 S.E.2d 410 (1991).

5.   Many statutes, such as the statute in the principal case, couple the willful misconduct disqualification with disqualifications based upon intoxication. Ordinarily, the employer's proof of mere intoxication at the time of the injury will not suffice to invoke this disqualification unless the employer also proves that the intoxication was a cause of the injury. See, e.g., Dobbs v. Liberty Mutual Insurance Company, 811 S.W.2d 75 (Tenn.1991) and Wyle v. Professional Services Industries, Inc., 12 Va.App. 684, 406 S.E.2d 410 (1991). The same requirement has been applied to proven drug use under general willful misconduct standard. See, e.g., Thomas v. Helen's Roofing Company, Inc., 199 Ga.App. 161, 404 S.E.2d 331 (1991) (presence of cocaine in worker's urine not of itself sufficient to prove fall from roof was caused by willful misconduct).

6.   Under statutes that have no "willful misconduct" provisions, courts rarely, if ever, deny compensation merely because an employee violated an employer's safety rule. 1 A. Larson, Workmen's Compensation Law (1990) § 33.10. Moreover, an employee's violation of a rule that is frequently disregarded and not diligently enforced by employers will not be deemed to be "willful." See, e.g., Sloss–Sheffield Steel & Iron Co. v. Nations, 236 Ala. 571, 183 So. 871 (1938). In short, the decisions that treat failure to use a safety device as disqualifying "willful misconduct" are rare. Often, even intentional avoidance of the use of such a device is not deemed to be "willful" in this sense. For example, courts will not regard the failure to use a defective device as willful, nor the non use of one the employee believes to be defective. See, e.g., Herring v. Hercules Powder Co., 222 La. 162, 62 So.2d 260 (1952) (the claimant disconnected airbrakes because they frequently

became loose over rough terrain). Nor will the employee's non use of a device under particular circumstances that would create new perils or interpose a serious obstacle to the effective discharge of duties be deemed to be disqualifying behaviour. See, e.g., American Steel Foundries v. Fisher, 106 Ind.App. 25, 17 N.E.2d 840 (1938). Courts also limit the reach of this defense by treating equipment such as a vehicle's horn, brakes or even its sides as something other than safety devices. See, e.g., Cole v. List and Weatherly Construction Co., 156 So. 88 (La.App.1934) (a ladder was a device for ascending and descending and not primarily for safety). The cases that do deny compensation under this defense require the employer to show that the failure to use the device bore a clear causal relation to the injury or death, e.g., Herring v. Hercules Powder Co., supra, and that the employer furnished the device and made its availability known to the employee. See, e.g., Armour & Co. v. Little, 83 Ga.App. 762, 64 S.E.2d 707 (1951) (failure to give express warning that a rake was a safety device defeated the defense) and Nashville, Chicago & St. Louis Ry. v. Wright, 147 Tenn. 619, 250 S.W. 903 (1923) (posting notice pertaining to use of goggles was not enough to deny compensation if the employee had not read it).

7. Under statutes that have no "willful disregard" and violation of safety act provisions, an employee's violation of a safety statute has no effect upon the compensability of an injury. Should it? Even if the statute contains an express provision as indicated in the principal case, the *willful* violation requirement often makes the defense unavailable. Accord with principal case: Philbrick Ambulance Service v. Buff, 73 So.2d 273 (Fla.1954) (driver of ambulance injured while running red light; compensation awarded). Nevertheless, an egregious violation may defeat compensation. See, e.g., Young v. American Ins. Co., 110 Ga.App. 269, 138 S.E.2d 385 (1964) (employee injured in collision while driving in excess of 100 m.p.h. in a 70 m.p.h. speed zone; compensation denied because of willful violation).

8. As a general matter none of the willful misconduct disqualifications deny recovery in the absence of proof that the specific misconduct was a specific cause of the injury. For example, under the New York disqualification for injuries suffered by an employee while "performing an illegal act," a claimant who was injured while illegally driving without a license was entitled to benefits in the absence of proof that the unlicensed status resulted from a lack of driving skill and the lack of skill caused the accident. Anderson v. William Cohen Iron Works, 38 N.Y.2d 511, 381 N.Y.S.2d 457, 344 N.E.2d 389 (1976). Similarly, the Massachusetts statute that disqualifies a worker injured by reason of "wilful misconduct" has no application unless the misconduct is a cause of the injury. See, e.g., Shaw's Supermarkets, Inc. v. Delgiacco, 410 Mass. 840, 575 N.E.2d 1115 (1991) (worker who misrepresented physical condition on job application will be disqualified under the provision only if the worker knowingly and wilfully made a false statement, the employer relied on the false statement in the hiring, and there is a causal connection between the false statement and the injury).

SECTION 6. INJURIES SUFFERED BY EMPLOYEES WHILE COMING TO AND GOING FROM WORK

HAMMOND v. GREAT ATLANTIC & PACIFIC TEA CO.

Supreme Court, New Jersey, 1970.
56 N.J. 7, 264 A.2d 204.

PROCTOR, J. In this workmen's compensation case, the sole issue is whether petitioner is entitled to recover for injuries she received when she fell at a point near her employer's premises shortly after leaving work. Both the Division of Workmen's Compensation and the County Court held that petitioner's injuries were not compensable since the accident did not arise out of and in the course of her employment. N.J.S.A. 34:15–7. The Appellate Division affirmed in an unreported *per curiam* opinion. We granted certification. 55 N.J. 161, 259 A.2d 913 (1969).

The material facts are undisputed. Petitioner, Honora Hammond, was employed as an executive secretary by the respondent, The Great Atlantic & Pacific Tea Company. She had held the position for nineteen years. Respondent's building in which petitioner worked is on the corner of Sherman Avenue and East Peddie Street in Newark. The building's entrance is on Sherman Avenue which runs north and south. East Peddie Street runs east and west. The respondent maintains a parking lot for the use of its employees on the south side of East Peddie Street, about 300 feet to the east of the intersection of Sherman Avenue and East Peddie Street. After leaving work, employees using the lot would normally walk north on Sherman Avenue to the intersection and then east on East Peddie Street, across Sherman Avenue, past a diner and a rag factory, and continue on the same side of East Peddie Street until they reached the lot. Both East Peddie Street and its adjoining sidewalk were in "very bad condition" with "broken sidewalks" and "slabs of concrete missing." According to the respondent's superintendent, it was a typical run-down factory neighborhood.

Mrs. Hammond relied on her husband or public transportation to get to work. Transportation from work for four years preceding her accident was furnished by a woman co-employee who parked her car in the lot provided by the respondent. Mrs. Hammond rarely walked to the lot herself because of the poor condition of the sidewalk and because of a limp which gave her difficulty in walking. The limp was the result of a preexisting arthritic hip which had left one leg an inch and a half shorter than the other.[1] She generally left respondent's building, walked north

---

1. The judge of compensation found that petitioner waited for her ride home at the northeast corner of Sherman Avenue and East Peddie Street instead of walking to the parking lot "because apparently the sidewalk [to the parking lot] was not in good condition and the distance was greater." The county court found that petitioner waited at the corner "because of convenience to her and her driver, and not by reason of the neighborhood conditions or street conditions." We think the county

on the sidewalk of Sherman Avenue, crossed East Peddie Street and some adjoining railroad tracks, and finally crossed Sherman Avenue to a spot where she waited to be picked up by her co-employee. The distance from respondent's building to the point where she waited for her ride was substantially less than the distance from the building to the parking lot.

On December 12, 1966, Mrs. Hammond left work at the end of the day and proceeded toward the corner where she usually waited to be picked up. While en route she fell near the railroad tracks and incurred the injuries for which she now claims compensation.

The judge of compensation and the county court judge both reasoned that the "going and coming" rule, which denies compensation for injuries incurred while traveling to or from work, barred petitioner's recovery. The Appellate Division affirmed, reasoning that petitioner could only recover if she were injured while en route to the parking lot; it was conceded that she was not.

Under our Workmen's Compensation Act, the basic test for compensability is whether an injury arises out of and in the course of employment. An accident arises out of employment when it results from risks reasonably incidental to the employment. Geltman v. Reliable Linen & Supply Co., 128 N.J.L. 443, 446, 25 A.2d 894 (E. & A.1942). An accident arises in the course of employment when "it occurs while the employee is doing what a man so employed may reasonably do within a time during which he is employed, and at a place where he may reasonably be during that time." Bryant Adm'x. v. Fissell, 84 N.J.L. 72, 77, 86 A. 458 (Sup.Ct.1913). Out of the basic test for compensability a subordinate doctrine was developed by the courts known as the "going and coming" rule. See Gullo v. American Lead Pencil Co., 119 N.J.L. 484, 196 A. 438 (E. & A.1938). This rule, which denies compensation for accidents occurring while the employee is going to or coming from work, produced many harsh results which led courts to carve out numerous exceptions to it. These exceptions include situations where the employee is on a special mission for his employer. Bobertz v. Board of Education, 135 N.J.L. 555, 52 A.2d 827 (E. & A.1947), where the employer furnishes transportation to and from the place of employment, Rubeo v. Arthur McMullen Co., 117 N.J.L. 574, 579, 189 A. 662 (E. & A.1937), where the use of an automobile or other form of vehicle is required in the performance of the contract of service, Demerest v. Guild, 114 N.J.L. 472, 476, 176 A. 558 (E. & A.1935), and where the employer pays for the employee's transportation, Filson v. Bell Telephone Laboratories, Inc., 82 N.J.Super. 185, 197 A.2d 196 (App.Div.1964). Even these exceptions have been broadly construed to comport with the liberal philosophy behind the enactment of the Workmen's Compensation Act. See, e.g.,

court ignored the undisputed testimony that petitioner waited at the corner because of her disability and the poor condition of the sidewalk. The Appellate Division indicated that it doubted the validity of the county court's conclusion by expressly refusing to take a position on the point. In its view the point was immaterial to the decision.

Ricciardi v. Damar Products Co., 45 N.J. 54, 211 A.2d 347 (1965); Lehigh Navigation Coal Co. v. McGonnell, 120 N.J.L. 428, 199 A. 906 (Sup.Ct. 1938), aff'd o.b. 121 N.J.L. 583, 3 A.2d 581 (E. & A.1939). Thus, in *Ricciardi,* supra, an accident occurring on the way home from a company picnic was held to be compensable within the special mission exception. And in *Lehigh,* supra, compensation was allowed when an employee was killed after his employer had provided a commutation ticket for railroad commutation although the accident occurred 75 to 100 feet from the place where he would board the train.

The large number of exceptions and their application by the courts have led one commentator to remark that "the exceptions are so numerous that they have swallowed the rule." Horovitz, "Workmen's Compensation: Half Century of Judicial Developments," 41 Neb.L.Rev. 1, 51 (1961).[2] He and others have suggested that the rule be abandoned in its entirety. Id. at 52. See also Pound, "Comments on Recent Important Workmen's Compensation Cases," 15 NACCA L.J. 45, 86–87 (1955); Note, "Arising 'out of' and 'in the Course of' the Employment Under the New Jersey Workmen's Compensation Act," 20 Rutgers L.Rev. 599, 613–21 (1966). This criticism of the rule seems well founded. It can reasonably be argued that travel to and from work should be compensable as incidental to the employment. See dissenting opinion of Justice Jacobs in Moosebrugger v. Prospect Presbyterian Church, 12 N.J. 212, 96 A.2d 401 (1953). As Chief Justice Weintraub, writing for a majority of this Court, commented, "that rule [going and coming rule] is not free from dispute since travel to and from the place of work quite obviously is essential to the work itself." Ricciardi v. Damar Products Co., 45 N.J. supra at 61, 211 A.2d at 350. Not only is travel to and from work essential to the employment, but it is in many cases attendant with greater risks than the actual work itself. As the author of the Note in 20 Rutgers L.Rev., supra at 620, wrote:

> With an increasing number of automobiles on the highways adding to the hazards of driving to work along with the latest industrial safety precautions decreasing the likelihood of injury at work, the trip to and from the regular place of work is in many instances the most hazardous part of the working day. Conditions and necessary incidents of employment have subjected the worker to those hazards; therefore, the courts should consider whether the trip to and from work is not within the reasonable contemplation of the employer as constituting part of his relationship with the employee.

See also 41 Neb.L.Rev., supra at 52.

The present case is illustrative of this point. Assuredly, petitioner faced far less risk of injury seated at her desk than she did in transit to or from work when one considers the conditions in the vicinity of her place of employment. And it can hardly be said that these risks were not

---

2. Horovitz notes that there are at least 19 exceptions and that Larson adds many more which are supported by cases throughout the country. 41 Neb.L.Rev., supra at 51.

incurred in conduct incidental or indeed essential to her employment. But we need not consider here the question of whether the going and coming rule should be abandoned. Our comments are set forth merely to emphasize that the rule should be construed liberally within the spirit of the workmen's compensation legislation. As Justice Francis noted in O'Brien v. First Camden Nat. Bank & Trust Co., 37 N.J. 158, 163, 179 A.2d 740, 742 (1962): "Too easy reference to the subordinate going and coming precept manifestly pointed in the direction of injustice in particular fact complexes." Workmen's compensation legislation is designed to place the cost of accidental injuries which are work-related upon the employer who can make these funds available out of his operating expenses, and this legislative goal must always be kept in mind when considering factual patterns presented.

Viewing the present case in accordance with the philosophy of our Workmen's Compensation Act, we believe petitioner's injuries are compensable. Our courts have recognized that where an employee suffers accidental injuries in a parking lot provided by his employer, the employee is entitled to compensation. Rice v. Pharmaceuticals, Inc., 65 N.J.Super. 579, 168 A.2d 201 (App.Div.1961); Buerkle v. United Parcel Service, 26 N.J.Super. 404, 98 A.2d 327 (App.Div.1953). Cf. Konitch v. Hartung, 81 N.J.Super. 376, 195 A.2d 649 (App.Div.1963). The "great majority of jurisdictions" also consider parking lots owned or maintained by the employer part of the employer's premises, and accordingly allow compensation for injuries incurred thereon. 1 Larson, Workmen's Compensation Law § 15.41 (1968). It is also clear that injuries are compensable which occur while an employee is traveling between two portions of his employer's premises. Zabriskie v. Erie R.R. Co., 86 N.J.L. 266, 92 A. 385 (E. & A.1914); see generally 1 Larson, supra, § 15.14. As a result, most courts treat an injury occurring in a public street between the plant and the parking lot as compensable since it occurred on a necessary route between two portions of the employer's premises. 1 Larson, supra, § 15.14; Lewis v. Walter Scott & Co., Inc., 50 N.J.Super. 283, 141 A.2d 807 (App.Div.1958). In Lewis, petitioner was a member of a "car pool" which parked in a lot provided by the employer. Petitioner was injured when he slipped and fell on an icy sidewalk while walking from the employee parking lot to the entrance of the building in which he worked. The only means of reaching the building from the lot was along the public sidewalk where the accident occurred. The Appellate Division allowed compensation holding that the accident arose out of and in the course of employment.

Since we agree with the holding in Lewis, the question presented by this appeal becomes a narrow one. Petitioner's fall was accidental and accordingly she would have received compensation if she had fallen while en route to the parking lot; we need only decide whether her shorter walk to a nearby corner in order to wait for her driver-co-employee precludes compensation. Under the circumstances, we do not think that it does. There is no doubt that the parking lot was maintained for the benefit of the employer and its employees. Respondent's building is in the factory section of Newark and its interests are better served by providing means for employees to use their own transportation facilities. See McCrae v. Eastern Aircraft, 137 N.J.L. 244, 59 A.2d 376 (Sup.Ct. 1948). That benefit was not diminished because petitioner waited for her rider at a spot nearby the normal route to and from the parking lot. We cannot accept respondent's contention that petitioner should not recover because she was beyond its control when she left its premises. There are numerous instances of compensable accidents which occur when the employee is beyond his employer's control. See O'Brien v. First Camden Nat. Bank & Trust Co., supra; Ricciardi v. Damar Products Co., supra; Filson v. Bell Tel. Labs., Inc., supra. See also 20 Rutgers L.Rev., supra at 618.

We think petitioner's injuries unquestionably occurred in the course of her employment. She was in a place where she might "reasonably be" considering the condition of the public streets and sidewalks and her preexisting physical condition. Her injuries arose out of the employment since the risk of her accident was reasonably incidental thereto.

The judgment of the Appellate Division is reversed and the matter is remanded to the Division of Workmen's Compensation for a determination of the amount of compensation to which petitioner is entitled.

Notes

1. As indicated in the principal case, injuries suffered while the employee is going to or coming from work are generally regarded as outside the course of the employment. Within the course is commonly held to begin and end at the threshold of the employer's establishment. See, e.g., Wausau Underwriters Ins. Co. v. Potter, 807 S.W.2d 419 (Tex.App.1991) (injuries sustained on public streets when going to or coming from work are not compensable); Constantineau v. First Nat. Bank in Albuquerque, 112 N.M. 38, 810 P.2d 1258 (App.1991) (compensation denied to employee injured while walking to place of work from city public parking facility not provided especially for employer's workers); and Tate v. Bruno's Inc./Food Max, 200 Ga.App. 395, 408 S.E.2d 456 (1991) (compensation denied employee injured after leaving work from shopping mall store while driving out of shopping mall parking lot where both shoppers and store employees parked). With these compare Arrington v. Goldstein, 23 N.J.Super. 103, 92 A.2d 630 (1952) (compensation awarded employee who reached employer's premises and was blown back into street by eighty mile per hour gust of wind), Owens v. Southeast Arkansas Transportation Co., 216 Ark. 950, 228 S.W.2d 646 (1950) (compensation awarded employee struck while dashing across the street to catch bus), and Husted v. Seneca Steel Service, 50 A.D.2d 76, 375 N.Y.S.2d 911 (1975) (compensation awarded employee preparing to enter employer's parking lot, who was impelled into the lot and injured there by a collision in public way).

The principal case illustrates difficulties that often arise in defining exactly where the threshold lies. Many decisions extend the concept to permit recovery in situations far removed from the employee's work premises. See, e.g., Board of Trustees v. Novik, 87 Md.App. 308, 589 A.2d 976 (1991) (compensation awarded to employee injured while walking on public street toward work place from parking lot provided by her employer); Briggs v. Passaic Bd. of Educ., 23 N.J.Super. 79, 92 A.2d 513 (1952) (closed public street adjacent to school regarded as school premises); and Smith v. Industrial Accident Comm., 18 Cal.2d 843, 118 P.2d 6 (1941) (entire island road system under control of employer, regarded as premises for employee who worked at various places on roads). In line with extending the meaning of where the threshold is, some decisions hold that an employee who is on *private* premises near the place of employment at the time of injury is entitled to compensation. See, e.g., Cerria v. Union News Co., 31 N.J.Super. 369, 106 A.2d 745 (1954) (compensation awarded employee who was injured in railroad terminal building where his employer leased space and operated a concession).

2. The doctrine most commonly employed to permit recovery for coming and going injuries is to treat risks of travel as risks of the employment if the risk exposes the worker to a threat of danger greater than that to which the general travelling public is exposed. See, e.g., Cudahy Packing Co. of Nebraska v. Parramore, 263 U.S. 418, 44 S.Ct. 153, 68 L.Ed. 366 (1923); Jaynes v. Potlatch, 75 Idaho 297, 271 P.2d 1016 (1954), and Toyota of Pensacola v. Maines, 558 So.2d 1072 (Fla.App.1990). These decisions award compensation to employees injured by some abnormal risk in the public road or public transportation system that the employees of the particular employer must confront more frequently than most members of the general travelling public, usually because of location. Many decisions pinpoint some specific hazardous highway condition such as a railway crossing or an area of highly congested traffic. Moreover, when the exposure of the worker to some particular travel danger is dramatic and obvious, courts tend to ignore the fact that the place of accident was some distance removed from the premises. Compare Diffendaffer v. Clifton, 91 Idaho 751, 430 P.2d 497 (1967) (compensation awarded reforestation project worker injured while proceeding to work on isolated and dangerous narrow mountain road several miles from place of work) and Bechtel Corp. v. Winther, 262 Ark. 361, 556 S.W.2d 882 (1977) (compensation awarded employee drowned in lake while attempting to cross causeway one quarter mile from premises), with Quarant v. Industrial Comm., 38 Ill.2d 490, 231 N.E.2d 397 (1967) (compensation denied teacher injured in congested traffic on way to work) and Eisenberg v. Industrial Comm., 65 Ill.2d 232, 2 Ill.Dec. 366, 357 N.E.2d 533 (1976) (compensation denied welfare worker assaulted near entrance of work premises in dangerous neighborhood). Nevertheless, many courts insist that the place of injury or the source of danger, although not necessarily on the employer's premises proper, must be immediately adjacent to them, and many announce that workers' compensation does not protect coming-and-going workers on the entire journey merely because it is dangerous. See, e.g., Boone v. Industrial Comm., 12 Ariz.App. 521, 472 P.2d 490 (1970) (compensation denied elevator man obliged to pass through dangerous neighborhood on way to work; assaulted eleven blocks from building where employed).

Conversely, unless the predicament of the worker can in some way be carved out from the general hazards of travel, compensation will be denied even though the place of accident is immediately adjacent to the premises. See, e.g., Ocean Pavilion v. Betancourt, 578 So.2d 467 (Fla.App.1991) (compensation denied worker hurt at place of special danger by causative force having nothing to do with special danger); and Templet v. Intracoastal Truck Line, Inc., 255 La. 193, 230 So.2d 74 (1969) (compensation denied worker for injury suffered in collision on public street while making left turn into employer's premises where there was no special hazard). Contrast Greydanus v. Industrial Accident Comm., 63 Cal.2d 490, 47 Cal.Rptr. 384, 407 P.2d 296 (1965) (identical facts, compensation awarded). The decisions disagree as to whether the danger must lie on the only available route to the employer's premises, whether it must lie on the most conveniently and frequently used route, or whether it is sufficient that the employee uses the dangerous route with the tacit consent of the employer. Compare Collier v. B.F. Goodrich Co., 90 Ohio App. 181, 104 N.E.2d 600 (1950) (safe route provided by employer; employees, however, regularly used railroad right of way as approach; compensation denied), with Sokolowski v. Best Western, 813 P.2d 286 (Alaska 1991) (compensation awarded employee for injury suffered while jaywalking at dangerous place, but only because of the absence of any reasonably safe and convenient alternative route to work) and Doyle v. Penton Lumber Co., 56 So.2d 774 (La.App.1952) (compensation allowed employee who took seldom used short cut along railroad right of way).

3. A number of statutes embody one of several variations of "going and coming" rules. For example, the Wisconsin statute provides:

2. Any employe going to and from his or her employment in the ordinary and usual way, while on the premises of the employer, or while in the immediate vicinity thereof if the injury results from an occurrence on the premises, any employe going between an employer's designated parking lot and the employer's work premises while on a direct route and in the ordinary and usual way, or any fire fighter or municipal utility employe responding to a call for assistance outside the limits of his or her city or village, unless that response is in violation of law, is performing service growing out of and incidental to employment.

3. An employe is not performing service growing out of and incidental to his or her employment while going to or from employment in a private or group or employer-sponsored car pool, van pool, commuter bus service or other ride-sharing program in which the employe participates voluntarily and the sole purpose of which is the mass transportation of employes to and from employment.

Wis.Stat.Ann. 102.03 (1990). A provision added to the Kansas statute during the time legislatures were "tightening up" workers' compensation statutes in the final decade of twentieth century provides:

The words "arising out of and in the course of employment" as used in the workers compensation act shall not be construed to include injuries to the employee occurring while the employee is on the way to assume the duties of employment or after leaving such duties, the proximate cause of which injury is not the employer's negligence. An employee shall not be construed as being on the way to assume the duties of employment, if the employee is a provider of emergency services responding to an emergency.

K.S.A. 44–508(f) (1998). The final sentence of this provision was enacted as an amendment to the first. Despite the fact that the accident in Estate of

Soupene v. Lignitz, 265 Kan. 217, 960 P.2d 205 (1998) occurred after the first portion of the statute was enacted but before the final portion was, the Kansas supreme court held that the final sentence merely clarified but did not change underlying law and, thus, upheld a decision that the highway crash death of an unpaid voluntary firefighter who was on the way to a fire was compensable under the statute.

Does your statute have a provision such as these? Do the approaches of these statutes lessen the scope of dispute?

Commentary

The decisions have widely acknowledged four general exceptions to the coming and going rule.

1. *Going to and Coming from Work, Off Premises, Special Errand.* Once an employee enters employment at one site, subsequent trips between separated work sites during the work day are usually deemed to be within the course. See, e.g., Hinkle v. Lexington, 239 N.C. 105, 79 S.E.2d 220 (1953) (cemetery caretaker on way to funeral establishment to determine whether there were any graves to be dug); and Wilson v. Rowan Drilling Co., 55 N.M. 81, 227 P.2d 365 (1950) (head driller had duty to secure transportation for other drillers from nearby town to drill site; injured while going from town to drill site; no payment for transportation and no payment for travel time; compensation awarded).

Similarly, the trip from home to work or return may in some cases be regarded as a substantial part of the duties to be performed by the worker, especially when the worker has no fixed first work site. See, e.g., Guest v. Workmen's Comp. Appeals Bd., 2 Cal.3d 670, 87 Cal.Rptr. 193, 470 P.2d 1 (1970) (police officer injured on trip from home to place of special assignment rather than to usual duty station); Le Vasseur v. Allen Electric Co., 338 Mich. 121, 61 N.W.2d 93 (1953) (electrician temporarily laid off, received call from employer to do a special job at a school; injured en route from home); Bengston v. Greening, 230 Minn. 139, 41 N.W.2d 185 (1950) (bookkeeper with regular hours called by employer for emergency on Saturday, which was not ordinarily a work day; injured returning home after alighting from car in front of her home); and Briggs v. American Biltrite, 74 N.J. 185, 376 A.2d 1231 (1977) (employee injured en route to work pursuant to overtime call, where such calls were infrequent). Contrast Moosebrugger v. Prospect Presbyterian Church of Maplewood, 12 N.J. 212, 96 A.2d 401 (1953) (sexton injured on way to open church at night for group meeting; compensation denied); Phillips v. Fitzhugh Motor Co., 330 Mich. 183, 46 N.W.2d 922 (1951) (employee, with no regular hours, injured on way home from visit to office initiated because of pressing work; compensation denied); Lyons v. Ford Motor Co., 330 Mich. 684, 48 N.W.2d 154 (1951) (employee killed on way home after working overtime; compensation denied); and Foster v. Brown Transport Corp., 143 Ga.App. 371, 238 S.E.2d 738 (1977) (on-call employee injured while en route to answer a call to duty; compensation denied).

Employees who are regularly engaged in travelling or have no fixed place for the performance of their duties are sometimes regarded as within the course of their employment from the moment they leave home for work until the moment they return. Compare Bickley v. South Carolina Elec. & Gas Co., 259 S.C. 463, 192 S.E.2d 866 (1972) (lineman called out to make emergency repairs wherever needed; awarded compensation); and Sentara Leigh Hosp. v. Nichols, 12 Va.App. 841, 407 S.E.2d 334 (1991) (compensation denied to homecare nurse injured while en route to patient's home on ground that mere absence of regular workplace did not create exception to going and coming rule); and, Matter of Glickman v. Greater New York Taxpayers, 305 N.Y. 431, 113 N.E.2d 548 (1953) (compensation denied claims investigator, whose duties were performed in various neighboring areas, who was killed while returning to work area from vacation home to resume duties).

2. *Riding in Vehicle Supplied by Employer.* Where the employer undertakes to transport the employee to and from work the journey is usually deemed to be within the course of employment. See, e.g., Hansen v. Estate of Harvey, 119 Idaho 333, 806 P.2d 426 (1991) (compensation awarded when employee was killed when employer's truck taking him to work site ran off highway); Neyland v. Maryland Cas. Co., 28 So.2d 351 (La.App.1946) (employer provided bus and charged employees fare; could have discontinued at any time; compensation awarded for accident while riding in vehicle); and Katz v. Katz, 137 Conn. 134, 75 A.2d 57 (1950) (employer regularly transported employee home in company vehicle; employee was injured while attempting to ride public bus on one occasion company vehicle was not available; compensation awarded). Contrast, White v. State, 338 Mich. 282, 61 N.W.2d 31 (1953) (employer furnished employee car for duties and permitted employee to drive it to and from home; compensation denied for injury suffered on trip home); and Gwin v. Liberty Northwest Ins. Corp., 105 Or.App. 171, 803 P.2d 1228 (1991) (compensation denied to worker injured while travelling in company truck for a weekend at home from a distant worksite where the worker was on a six month assignment; worker was free to bring his own car on the assignment and used employer's truck with permission for personal convenience only).

Occasional casual transportation may not come within the exception to the coming and going rule. Compare Makal v. Industrial Comm., 262 Wis. 215, 54 N.W.2d 905 (1952) (employee injured while in his own car proceeding to secure employer's car which he was obliged to drive to work; compensation denied), and Thompson v. Bradford Motor Freight Line, 148 So. 79 (La.App.1933) (implied understanding that employee could ride home on any of employer's trucks that might happen to be going in his direction, but no undertaking to provide regular transportation; compensation awarded).

3. *Payment by Employer for Time of Travel or Travel Expense.* When the employer pays the employee for the time consumed by travel to and from work or pays the travel expenses, the journey is ordinarily regarded as within the course of employment. See, e.g., Provident Life & Accident Ins. Co. v. Barnard, 236 Va. 41, 372 S.E.2d 369 (1988) (compensation paid to worker in travelling to first work site when employer paid mileage expenses); Cardillo v. Liberty Mut. Ins. Co., 330 U.S. 469, 67 S.Ct. 801, 91 L.Ed. 1028 (1947) (car pool arrangement; fact that wages were not being paid the decedent at time of accident immaterial); In re Jensen, 63 Wyo. 88, 178 P.2d 897 (1947) (employer paid one employee a daily amount to bring fellow employees to work in his car; employee being so transported entitled to

compensation); O'Reilly v. Roberto Homes, 31 N.J.Super. 387, 107 A.2d 9 (1954) (employee paid six dollars for extra night job; actual work consumed only fifteen to thirty minutes, but travel time consumed an hour; no specific agreement as to payment for travel; compensation awarded); and Griffith Const. Co. v. Workmen's Compensation Appeals Bd., 9 Cal.App.3d 606, 88 Cal.Rptr. 346 (1970) (workers in remote desert area were allowed subsistence pay; justified conclusion that pay contemplated expense of travel to and from work even though accommodations were available at work site; compensation awarded).

The decisions vary on compensation for injuries suffered during deviations from paid travel to or from work. Compare Dooley v. Smith's Transfer Co., 26 N.J.Misc. 129, 57 A.2d 554 (1948) (employee injured on highway leading to home ten hours after leaving premises and after having engaged in many personal activities; compensation denied) with Reading & Bates, Inc. v. Whittington, 208 So.2d 437 (Miss.1968) (employee drinking while driving home; stopped, went behind car to relieve himself; stepped into hole; compensation awarded).

4. *Travelling Employees.* Employees, such as sales agents, who are paid to travel are within the course while actually travelling, and many decisions also compensate injuries suffered while these employees are eating, sleeping, or enjoying recreation. See, e.g., Ridgway v. Combined Ins. Companies of America, 98 Idaho 410, 565 P.2d 1367 (1977) (employee on two weeks training program injured while proceeding from hotel to restaurant; compensation awarded); David Wexler & Co. v. Industrial Comm., 52 Ill.2d 506, 288 N.E.2d 420 (1972) (salesman "on the road" on Memorial Day; went fishing and was killed while returning to motel; compensation awarded); and, McKay v. Republic Vanguard Ins. Co., 27 A.D.2d 607, 275 N.Y.S.2d 742 (1966) (traveller died of carbon monoxide poisoning while highly intoxicated and asleep in motel; compensation awarded).

KAPLAN v. ALPHA EPSILON PHI SORORITY

Supreme Court of Minnesota, 1950.
230 Minn. 547, 42 N.W.2d 342.

MATSON, JUSTICE. Certiorari to review an order of the industrial commission denying compensation on the ground that relator's injury did not arise out of and in the course of her employment.

Relator, Dora Kaplan, was employed as house mother for the respondent Alpha Epsilon Phi Sorority. She lived in the sorority house, which is located near the University of Minnesota campus in Minneapolis. Girls who come from homes outside the city live and regularly take their meals in the sorority house. Other members from the Twin Cities area eat occasional meals at the house. Relator, who was subject to call 24 hours a day, performed duties akin to those of a mother in looking after her home and family. She ordered the food, supervised the preparation of meals and household cleaning, acted as a chaperon, hostess, confidante and adviser for the girls, and was responsible for the observance of reasonable hours.

Relator sustained her injury on the evening of October 31, 1947, after she had left the sorority house, which is located on Tenth avenue southeast and Fifth street. She walked on the west side of Tenth avenue until she reached Fourth street, where she proceeded to cross to the east side of Tenth avenue. As she was about to step up on the opposite Tenth avenue curb, which had been greased by Halloween pranksters, she slipped, fell, and broke her hip. Relator testified that at the time she was on her way to Grays Drug Store located about four blocks to the east at the corner of Fourteenth avenue southeast and Fourth street to purchase bandages to replenish the supply which she maintained as part of the sorority house first-aid kit, and that she intended, after making such purchase, to take a streetcar to attend religious services at Temple Israel, where she had been a communicant for 20 years.

1.   Although the evidence will reasonably sustain a finding that relator's intended trip to Temple Israel was a personal mission and not a mission undertaken as part of her duties as spiritual supervisor for the girls or for the benefit of the sorority generally in cultivating favorable public relations with the parents of present and future sorority members, the decision of the industrial commission must be reversed and the matter remanded for a rehearing, in that the findings, taken as a whole, were made under an erroneous application of the law. Where an award or denial of compensation has been made through a misapprehension or misapplication of a controlling principle of law, the case may be remanded to the commission for rehearing. Hogan v. Twin City Amusement Trust Estate, 155 Minn. 199, 193 N.W. 122; Klika v. Independent School Dist. No. 79, 161 Minn. 461, 202 N.W. 30; 6 Dunnell, Dig. & Supp., § 10426.

The commission's majority opinion, in reversal of the referee's findings, after determining that relator's dominant purpose in leaving the sorority house was to go on a personal mission to Temple Israel, held that the accident did not arise out of and in the course of her employment, although at the time of her injury she may have been on her way to the drugstore to buy bandages for her employer. Apparently, the commission assumed that, if the trip to the drugstore was but an incidental part of her personal activities that evening, it necessarily followed that any injury sustained on that trip did not arise out of her employment. The application of the dominant-motive or dominant-purpose rule does not call for a construction which arbitrarily holds the entire journey of an employe to be wholly "fish or fowl" without regard to whether a deviation or detour is involved. An errand or movement of an employe, the purpose of which is dominantly personal, *may* involve a deviation or detour which is made *necessary* by the employer's business; and, if an injury occurs during such deviation or detour, it arises out of and in the course of the employment. In a number of cases we have so held. Confusion has apparently resulted from the application of the dominant-purpose test in Olson v. Trinity Lodge, 226 Minn. 141, 146, 32 N.W.2d 255, 258, wherein we said: "If a movement on the part of an employe is undertaken from a mixture of motives, the major motive or dominant purpose thereof, as a general rule, controls in determining whether an injury sustained in the course of such movement arises out of and in the course of his employment."

The authoritative scope of the dominant-purpose rule becomes clear if we keep in mind the controlling facts to which it was applied in the Olson decision. In that case, the employe had but a *single destination, namely, the lodge building,* to which he was en route for the two distinct or dual purposes of (1) personally enjoying the comforts of his private rent-free room, and (2) tending the employer's furnace. If either purpose had been eliminated, the trip to the lodge building would, nevertheless, have been made because of the remaining purpose. It therefore became pertinent to ascertain which purpose was dominant. Obviously, the dominant purpose was the employment, in that the cold January weather created an immediate and compelling necessity for tending the furnace, which had not been taken care of since morning. No deviation or detour was involved, and therefore the dominant-purpose test, without qualification, was both sufficient and decisive. Cf. Erickson v. Erickson & Co., 212 Minn. 119, 2 N.W.2d 824.

2–3. In keeping with our former decisions, where a principal movement or errand of an employe is accompanied by a deviation or detour therefrom, the dominant-purpose test should be used for the limited function of determining, when the principal movement or errand is undertaken from a mixture of motives, whether such principal movement or errand belongs to the employer or to the employe personally.

Of course, if the employment creates the necessity for the principal errand in the sense that it would not have been made in the absence of such necessity, the principal errand unquestionably belongs to the employer, although the employe is serving at the same time some purpose of his own. If, however, the personal business or activities of the employe create the necessity for the principal errand in the sense that it would not have been made if such employe's personal business or activities had been abandoned, the principal errand belongs to the employe, although he is serving at the same time some purpose of the employment. Where the necessity which gives birth to an errand may be ascribed exclusively to either the employment *or* to the employe's personal affairs—that is, the necessity of one to the exclusion of the other—there is no need to consider or give weight to the dominant purpose as a separate and distinct element. We may have a situation, however, such as in the Trinity Lodge case, where a dual-purpose errand would have been made even though one of the purposes, whether it was that of the employment or that of the employe personally, might have been absent, and in that event the element of dominant motive or purpose would become of primary importance in determining to whom the principal errand belonged. When the character of the principal movement has thus once been determined, accidental injuries sustained during a detour or deviation are to be ascribed to the employment or to the employe personally, as the case may be, in compliance with the following rule—which is in accord with our decisions—as stated in Barragar v. Industrial Comm.,

205 Wis. 550, 553, 238 N.W. 368, 369, 78 A.L.R. 679: "* * * it is essential * * * to determine whether, *at the outset,* the trip in question was that of the employer, or that of the employee. Having determined that it was the employer's trip, the employee is engaged in his employer's business and acting within the scope of his employment while going to and returning from the terminus of the trip. If it is the employee's trip, he is not within the scope of his employment while en route to, or returning from, the terminus of his trip. In case it is the employer's trip, and there are any detours for purely personal objectives, such detours must be separated from the main trip and the employee held to be outside the scope of his employment during such detour. *If it is his own trip, then such detours as are made for the purpose of dispatching business for his employer must be held to be within the scope of his employment.*" (Italics supplied.) * * *

The rule as above stated clarifies the controlling principles applicable to the instant case. Assuming that relator here left the sorority house for the dominant purpose of attending religious services at Temple Israel for her own personal reasons, her accidental injuries, nevertheless, arose out of and in the course of her employment *if at the time of the accident, as a deviation from her own personal mission, she was in the act of going to the drugstore to obtain bandages for her employer.* In the absence of a specific finding as to whether she was on her way to the drugstore for the purpose of her employment, it becomes necessary to remand the case to the commission for rehearing.

4. Although we have observed that the evidence sustains a finding that relator's intended trip to Temple Israel was for her own individual purpose and not for her employer, we do not say that a finding to the contrary might not possibly be sustained. Upon rehearing, new findings should also be made as to the purpose of her trip to the synagogue, in that the findings heretofore made *may* have been controlled by the erroneous assumption that her contemplated attendance at the synagogue could not be attributed to her employment unless such attendance would be of "material benefit" to the employer. If the employment creates the necessity for an employe's errand, it is wholly immaterial whether such errand is beneficial or detrimental to the employer. Although the term "benefit" may have been used in an entirely different sense, nevertheless, in view of the resulting uncertainty, new findings are necessary.

The matter is remanded to the commission for rehearing and decision in accordance with this opinion. Relator is allowed $250 attorney's fees upon this appeal.

Reversed and remanded with directions.

Notes

1. Marks' Dependents v. Gray, 251 N.Y. 90, 93, 167 N.E. 181 (1929) the lead dual-purpose decision, laid down this rule: "[i]f the work of the employee creates a necessity for travel, he is in the course of his employ-

ment, though he is serving at the same time some purpose of his own. * * * If, however, the work has had no part in creating the necessity for travel, if the journey would have gone forward though the business errand had been dropped, and would have been cancelled upon failure of the private purpose, though the business errand was undone, the travel is then personal, and personal the risk." Id., at 182–183. This is frequently termed the "dominant purpose" rule. In Marks' Dependents v. Gray a plumber's helper was injured on a trip to a neighboring city to meet his wife. His employer had requested him to do a minor repair job while there—a task which presumably would not have been undertaken otherwise. The court denied compensation saying, "[w]e hold that Marks was not placed upon the highway by force of any duty owing to his employer, and that the risk of travel was his own." Id., at 183. Similarly, in Miller v. Bill Miller's Riviera, Inc., 21 N.J.Super. 112, 90 A.2d 889 (1952), the steward of a New Jersey restaurant, while on an extended vacation motoring trip in Florida, purchased six boxes of grapefruit to be shipped home to his employer. Later he was killed on the return trip north. Compensation was denied. See also Clover v. Snowbird Ski Resort, 808 P.2d 1037 (Utah 1991), acknowledging that the employee is not within the course if the primary motivation is personal despite the performance of some incidental employment errand.

If the trip for personal purposes would not have been made if the business had not required a similar trip, compensation is almost always awarded. See, e.g., Matthews v. Naylor, 42 Cal.App.2d 729, 109 P.2d 978 (1941). The most difficult situations are those where the trip would have been made anyway and the employer's business would also have required the same or a similar trip irrespective of the personal motivation for the particular dual purpose journey. See, e.g., Rosencrantz v. Insurance Service Co., 2 Or.App. 225, 467 P.2d 664 (1970) (employee killed on trip to a single site for the dual purposes of paying personal debts and collecting on debts owed to employer; compensation awarded for "concurrent cause" injury); and Standard Oil Co. v. Smith, 56 Wyo. 537, 111 P.2d 132 (1941) (compensation awarded to employee returning from vacation trip who picked up two barrels of oil for employer at intermediate point on route home and was killed before reaching final destination; special trip would not have been made for two barrels alone, but a trip would be required eventually for a larger quantity of oil). If these cases are correct, does "dominant purpose" mean anything more than that the business required that the same or a similar mission be performed irrespective of the personal motive that also inspired the trip?

The Nebraska Supreme Court applies a rule that awards compensation if the employer's needs required the trip to be made at some time even though it need not have been coincidental with the employee's personal journey. Jacobs v. Consolidated Telephone, 237 Neb. 772, 467 N.W.2d 864 (1991). A few statutes apply the dual purpose rule to exclude only those trips that would have been made even though there were no business purposes. See, for example, Vernon's Ann.Tex.Rev.Civ.Stats.Ann., Art. 8308–1.03(12) (1991) which provides: "Course and scope of employment" ... does not include ...

(B) travel by the employee in the furtherance of the affairs or business of his employer if such travel is also in furtherance of personal or private affairs of the employee unless:

(i) the trip to the place of occurrence of the injury would have been made even had there been no personal or private affairs of the employee to be furthered by the trip; and

(ii) the trip would not have been made had there been no affairs or business of the employer to be furthered by the trip.

Texas courts have held that this statute must be applied to the entirety of a dual-purpose trip (i.e. an entire weekend) and not merely to the specific segment in which the accident occurred. See, e.g., Employers Casualty Company v. Hutchinson, 814 S.W.2d 539 (Tex.App.1991).

2.   Injuries suffered by employees who are directed by employers to perform errands while en route to home from work or vice versa are often compensated. Compare Knipe v. Texas Employer's Ins. Ass'n, 234 S.W.2d 274 (Tex.Civ.App.1950), affirmed 150 Tex. 313, 239 S.W.2d 1006 (1951) (compensation awarded oil driller injured while returning home from isolated area under instruction to report progress to central office when returning home); Hall v. Aetna Life Ins. Co., 158 So. 658 (La.App.1935) (compensation awarded employee assigned to deliver work cards to laborers on way home and who was killed at railroad crossing on way home with cards in his pocket) with Mims v. Nehi Bottling Co., 218 S.C. 513, 63 S.E.2d 305 (1951) (compensation denied employee who regularly dropped letters in mailbox on way home and who was injured while making a personal stop in a laundry before reaching the mailbox).

What constitutes an employment errand? Compare Blackman v. Great American First Sav. Bank, 233 Cal.App.3d 598, 284 Cal.Rptr. 491 (1991) (employee who had car crash after leaving work on way to attend college course provided as an employment fringe benefit not within the course) and Industrial Comm. v. Harkrader, 52 Ohio App. 76, 3 N.E.2d 61 (1935) (compensation denied teacher who required a kettle for a school pageant, retraced her steps home after having started to school, procured the kettle and was injured while leaving her home), with Gelbart v. New Jersey Federated Egg Producers Ass'n, 17 N.J.Misc. 185, 7 A.2d 636 (1939) (compensation awarded employee who was charged with duty of opening establishment, forgot key, retraced steps home and was thereafter injured).

3.   After the overall trip is determined to be personal or business, the issue of whether an injury suffered on a deviation from the principal purpose can still arise. Is a detour from a business trip for a personal mission covered? A detour from a personal trip for a business purpose?

(A) If the trip is essentially a business trip with a business destination and a separate personal destination ahead on the same route and an accident occurs before reaching either destination, the accident is within the course of employment. See, e.g., Brenneisen v. Leach's Standard Service Station, 806 S.W.2d 443 (Mo.App.1991) (compensation awarded for death of off-duty employee who was driving to place of employment on day off to drop off soiled work uniforms for laundering before continuing personal affairs) and Levy v. Levy's Bazaar, 257 App.Div. 885, 12 N.Y.S.2d 131 (1939) (compensation awarded employee injured while on an employment errand while also transporting his mother to a more distant site).

(B) If the trip is essentially a business trip and the employee reaches the employment destination first and then proceeds onward to personal destination, injuries suffered after leaving the business destination are not within the course. Compare State v. Russo, 155 Ohio St. 341, 98 N.E.2d 830 (1951) (compensation denied) with Avila v. Pleasuretime Soda, Inc., 90 N.M. 707, 568 P.2d 233 (1977) (compensation awarded employee who detoured from route home in order to perform a personal errand and was injured after leaving the errand destination but before reaching the route home).

(C) If the trip is essentially a business trip and the employee detours from the route for a personal errand, injuries suffered by the employee after completing the personal errand but before reaching the business route from which he had departed are not within the course. See, e.g., Public Service Co. v. Industrial Comm., 395 Ill. 238, 69 N.E.2d 875 (1946) (compensation denied employee who had reached business destination and proceeded farther for personal errand; injured on return toward business destination but prior to reaching it) and Warren v. Globe Indem. Co., 217 La. 142, 46 So.2d 66 (1950) (travelling employee who was killed on purely personal journey after completing work activities was not within the course of employment).

(D) If the trip is essentially a business trip and the employee detours from the shortest route for a personal errand, the decisions divide as to whether to compensate injuries suffered by employees while angling back from the errand site toward the ultimate business destination on a direct route, although longer than without the detour. Compare Federal Mut. Liability Ins. Co. v. Industrial Accident Comm., 94 Cal.App. 251, 270 P. 992 (1928) (compensation awarded), with Red Arrow Bonded Messenger Corp. v. Industrial Accident Comm., 39 Cal.App.2d 559, 103 P.2d 1004 (1940) (compensation denied).

(E) If the trip is essentially a personal trip or an extension beyond a personal destination for an employment purpose, an injury suffered while making the employment detour at any time before returning to the route selected for a continuation of the personal trip is within the course of employment. See, e.g., Sater v. Home Lumber & Coal Co., 63 Idaho 776, 126 P.2d 810 (1942).

4. In line with the tendency to expand the exceptions to the going-to-and-coming-from rule, some decisions compensate injuries that occur during deviations for entirely personal errands if the deviations are not "extensive." See, e.g., Thomas v. Certified Refrigeration, Inc., 392 Mich. 623, 221 N.W.2d 378 (1974), awarding compensation to a refrigeration serviceman who was injured while driving his child to school in a company truck kept at his home at night, even though the school was in the opposite direction from the work site and the injury occurred an hour before work was to begin. In describing the trip as for a "dual purpose," the court suggested that whenever an employee drives an employer's truck in public, bearing the employer's name and business address and with the employer's consent, any injury suffered will be considered within the course of employment. Do the underlying economic premises support this conclusion?

5. The "dual purpose" issue also arises when an employee takes work home to be done at night. Does the mere fact that the employee is taking papers home in a briefcase remove the trip from the coming and going rule? Ordinarily not. Compare Sylvan v. Sylvan Bros., 225 S.C. 429, 82 S.E.2d 794 (1954) (compensation denied with the observation, "[a] member of this court who takes a brief home with him to read is not in the course of his employment when on the way to or from his office") with Levi v. Interstate Photo Supply, 46 A.D.2d 951, 362 N.Y.S.2d 70 (1974) (compensation awarded employee who frequently worked at home but was not required to; assaulted while returning to home with work papers which he intended to use there). By contrast, compensation may be awarded if the home is made the work site because of some particular need, or if the home is a usual place of employment. See, e.g., Berry's Coffee Shop, Inc. v. Palomba, 161 Colo. 369, 423 P.2d 2 (1967) (delicacy of subject of conference made office an unsuitable place; employee and manager went to employee's home) and Kaycee Coal Co. v. Short, 450 S.W.2d 262 (Ky.1970) (equipment had been installed in the home to permit work there).

Injuries that employees suffer while actively working at an in-home business situs are compensable, but injuries caused by general premises risks are disputable. Compare Joe Ready's Shell Station and Cafe v. Ready, 218 Miss. 80, 65 So.2d 268 (1953) (employee who did bookkeeping work at home accidentally shot herself while removing husband's shotgun from couch in preparing to sit down to perform her duties, compensation awarded) and Glasser v. Youth Shop, 54 So.2d 686 (Fla.1951) (employee who took books home to prepare a report was injured after completing work in upstairs room while descending stairs with books in his hands to breakfast; compensation denied).

SECTION 7. SYNTHESIS: RELATIONSHIP OF "WITHIN THE COURSE" AND "ARISING OUT OF" TESTS

STROTHER v. MORRISON CAFETERIA

Supreme Court of Florida, 1980.
383 So.2d 623.

ALDERMAN, JUSTICE.

We have for review by petition for writ of certiorari an order of the Industrial Relations Commission reversing the order of the judge of industrial claims and denying claimant Blanche Strother workers' compensation on the basis that while her injuries did arise out of her employment, they were not sustained in the course of her employment. The commission rendered a contrary decision in *Sixty–Seven Liquors v. Gamel,* IRC No. 265–25–3664 (IRC Jan. 1979), *cert. denied,* 383 So.2d 628 (Fla.1980), and awarded compensation to a doorman-bouncer who had been injured away from the employer's premises and outside his working hours on the ground that his injury was clearly shown to have arisen out of his employment.

The sole issue in this case of first impression is whether Strother sustained a compensable accident when she was assaulted outside the time and space limits of her employment. We hold that Strother's injuries, which had their origin and cause entirely within the course of her employment and which arose out of her employment, are compensable.

Strother, a cashier at Morrison's Cafeteria, was charged with the responsibility of handling the payment of food bills from customers from mid-afternoon to closing at nine each night. Although not a part of her regular employment, on two occasions she drove the cafeteria's manager to the bank to deposit the day's receipts. On the two days preceding the incident which resulted in the injury for which she now seeks workers' compensation, Strother observed two men in the cafeteria who were not customers or employees. On the evening of the incident, she noticed the same two men enter the cafeteria in the same manner as they had entered on the two previous days. This evening, she left work and drove directly home (some fifteen or twenty minutes' drive from the cafeteria) where she was assaulted by and her purse was taken by one of the men whom she had observed in the cafeteria.

The judge of industrial claims determined that Strother was injured in a compensable accident since the circumstances of her employment exposed her to a greater risk than that of a regular cashier and that the assault arose out of and in the course of her employment. The judge accepted Strother's testimony that she was followed and attacked by the same men who were at the cafeteria, and he concluded that they thought she was carrying the cafeteria's money since they demanded "the money or deposits."

Relying on *Hill v. Gregg, Gibson & Gregg, Inc.*, 260 So.2d 193 (Fla.1972), Strother argues that her injuries are compensable because they "arose out of and in the course of employment" as this language is defined by *Hill*. She submits that her injuries arose out of and solely because of conditions connected with her employment.

Respondents, on the other hand, rely on *Bituminous Casualty Corp. v. Richardson*, 148 Fla. 323, 4 So.2d 378 (1941), and *Southern Bell Telephone and Telegraph Co. v. McCook*, 355 So.2d 1166 (Fla.1977), and recite that to be compensable, the assault must not only have arisen out of Strother's employment but also must have occurred within the time and space limits of her employment. Respondents further contend that this case does not fall within the special hazard exception to the going and coming rule.

Section 440.02(6), Florida Statutes (1977), defines injury, for purposes of the workers' compensation act, as "personal injury or death by accident arising out of and in the course of employment, and such diseases or infection as naturally or unavoidably result from such injury." Our early decision of *Bituminous Casualty Corp. v. Richardson* construed this language as requiring a showing that the injury both arose out of employment *and* occurred in the course of employment. "Arising out of" was defined to mean the origin or cause of the accident. "In the course of" employment was defined as the time, place, and circumstances under which the accident occurs. We stated as a general rule that the accident must occur while the employee is acting within the duties of his employment or in some act incidental thereto. *See also Foxworth v. Florida Industrial Commission,* 86 So.2d 147 (Fla.1955), wherein we stated that compensation coverage is confined to an injury arising out of and in the course and scope of employment and both circumstances must appear before compensation can be awarded; *Travelers Ins. Co. v. Taylor,* 147 Fla. 210, 3 So.2d 381 (1941), wherein we held that arising out of and in the course of employment are used conjunctively, and it is indispensable to recovery that both of them be established; *Fidelity & Casualty Co. of New York v. Moore,* 143 Fla. 103, 196 So. 495 (1940), wherein it was held that to arise out of and in the course of employment, an injury must occur within the period of employment at a place where the injured employee may reasonably be and while he is reasonably fulfilling duties of his employment or is engaged in something incidental thereto.

More recently, in *Southern Bell Telephone and Telegraph v. McCook,* we reaffirmed our decision of *Bituminous Casualty Corp. v. Richardson* and explained that "arising out of" and "in the course of" were separate elements which must be proved to establish a compensable accident. In *McCook,* we were concerned with the "arising out of" element rather than "in the course of." Relying on *Suniland Toys & Juvenile Furniture, Inc. v. Karns,* 148 So.2d 523 (Fla.1963), we defined "arising out of" to mean originating in some risk connected with employment or flowing as a natural consequence from the employment.

Although in several decisions, we have referred to the distinct and separate nature of the two elements of "arising out of" and "in the course of," we have also, in other decisions, tended to merge these two factors together into a test of work connectedness. In *Fidelity & Casualty Co. of New York v. Moore,* we said:

> The cases generally hold that for an injury to arise out of and in the course of one's employment, there must be some causal connection between the injury and the employment *or* it must have had its origin in some risk incident to or connected with the employment *or* that it flowed from it as a natural consequence. *Another definition* widely approved is that the injury must occur within the period of the employment, at a place where the employee may reasonably be, and while he is reasonably fulfilling the duties of his employment or engaged in doing something incidental to it.

196 So. at 496 (emphasis added).

Then in *Sweat v. Allen,* 145 Fla. 733, 200 So. 348 (1941), we allowed recovery to a deputy sheriff who, while on his way to work, was struck by a delivery truck and sustained injury to his leg which ultimately resulted in its amputation. We determined that by the nature of his employment, the deputy was continuously under a duty to protect the peace and safety of the community and to apprehend those guilty of its violation. In explanation of our result, we declared that an injury must both arise out of and be in the course of employment and proceeded to recite the alternative definitions for arising out of and in the course of one's employment which we had earlier enunciated in *Fidelity & Casualty Co. of New York v. Moore.*

Again, in *Suniland Toys & Juvenile Furniture, Inc. v. Karns,* we relied on the alternative definitions established by *Fidelity & Casualty Co. of New York v. Moore* to award compensation to an employee who had sustained an allergic reaction to a typhoid inoculation administered at a physician's office. We said: "[T]o be compensable, an injury must have originated in some risk connected with the employment or flowing as a natural consequence from the employment." 148 So.2d at 524.

In our 1972 decision of *Hill v. Gregg, Gibson & Gregg, Inc.,* we again emphasized the alternative nature of the definitions established in *Fidelity & Casualty Co. of New York v. Moore.* We quashed the commission's order which denied compensation and held that an assault which arose out of Hill's employment was compensable even though it did not occur on the employer's premises or during working hours, and we said:

> From their orders, it appears the Judge of Industrial Claims and the Industrial Relations Commission looked only to the last definition [*i.e.,* the injury must occur within the period of employment, at a place where the employee may reasonably be, and while he is reasonably fulfilling the duties of his employment or engaged in doing something incidental to it] and concluded Petitioner could not recover because he was not injured while at his job site working and benefiting his employer. While such a conclusion is proper under the fourth *Moore* definition, it is not determinative of the issue. It is necessary to also consider the first three definitions. All are alternatives. *Sweat v. Allen,* 1941, 145 Fla. 733, 200 So. 348.

260 So.2d at 195.

It is apparent that our prior decisions have developed inconsistent interpretations of the statutory language "arising out of and in the course of employment." One line of cases establishes a two-prong test of work connectedness where both prongs must be separately proven. The other line of cases effectually develops an arising out of and an originating in the course of employment test where either element may suffice. The present case has spotlighted the uncertainty created by the conflicting lines of cases. A resolution of this conflict must be made before we can determine whether Strother's injury is compensable.

Larson, in his treatise *Workmen's Compensation Law,* volume 1A, section 29.00, discusses this problem area of workers' compensation law and analyzes numerous decisions from other jurisdictions involving fact situations somewhat similar to the present case where indisputably the injury arose out of the employment and where the originating cause of the injury occurred entirely within the time and space limits of employment, but where the actual injury occurred while the employee was not acting within the duties of his employment. He asserts that grave injustice occurs when courts insist on the separateness of "arising out of'' and "in the course of" when the latter denotes occurrence within the period of employment at a place where the injured employee may reasonably be and while he is reasonably fulfilling duties of employment or is engaged in doing something incidental thereto. He suggests that the more reasoned approach, consistent with the goals of workers' compensation acts, is not to apply these concepts entirely independent of each other but rather to view them as parts of a single test of work connectedness where deficiencies in the strength of one factor may, in some cases, be made up by the strength in the other. He proposes that the term "arising" in the statutory phrase "arising out of and in the course of employment" be employed not only to modify "out of" but also to modify "in the course of" and then declares that arising connotes origin, not completion or manifestation. Summarizing his analysis, Larson concludes that in the cases allowing compensation for the type of injury with which we are presently concerned, the common element is the fact that the originating cause of injury arose out of and in the course of employment:

> The time bomb, so to speak, is constructed and started ticking during working hours; but it happens to go off at a time and place remote from the employment. The hazards of the employment, whether the animosity of a fired employee, a needle-like shaving in the eyebrow, or dynamite cap in the pocket, follow the claimant beyond the time and space limits of his work, and there injure him.

Larson, *Workmen's Compensation Law*, volume 1A, section 29.22 at 5–376–77.

The early case of *Matter of Field v. Charmette Knitted Fabric Co.*, 245 N.Y. 139, 156 N.E. 642 (1927), authored by Justice Cardozo laid the groundwork in these types of cases for utilizing the originating in the course of employment test. There recovery of workmen's compensation was allowed to a general manager and superintendent of a mill who was assaulted outside working hours and off employment premises by an employee he had discharged. On the work premises, the employee had moved threateningly toward the superintendent but had been pulled away. Justice Cardozo said: "[C]ontinuity of cause has been so combined with contiguity in time and space that the quarrel from origin to ending must be taken as one." 156 N.E. at 643. He explained that this assault was engendered on the work premises.

In cases analogous to the present one, other jurisdictions, whose workers' compensation acts speak in terms of an injury by accident "arising out of and in the course of employment," have seen fit to adopt Larson's originating rationale to avoid the inequity and illogic of denying compensation to one whose injuries indisputably arose out of employment and where the originating cause of the injury occurred during working hours and on the employment premises. For example, in *Thornton v. Chamberlain Manufacturing Corp.*, 62 N.J. 235, 300 A.2d 146 (1973), while on the job, Thornton, a production foreman, reprimanded an employee for repeated failure to wear safety glasses and several times reported these failures to the employer. One of these times, the employee threatened Thornton by saying he would take care of Thornton's eyes later. The employee was terminated from his employment and nine days thereafter attacked Thornton and said, "Remember me, remember me." As a result of this attack, Thornton sustained total loss of vision in his right eye. Thornton was denied compensation by the commission because his injuries did not occur in the course of employment, and the county court affirmed. The New Jersey Supreme Court reversed and found that, unquestionably, the attack had its genesis in Thornton's employment. He incurred his attacker's wrath and enmity because he had performed his assigned employment duty. Had he been at work when the attack occurred, there would have been no question as to the compensability of his injuries. The New Jersey court found Larson's construction of "arising out of and in the course of" reasonable and conducive to the advancement of the basic purpose of the workmen's compensation act and concluded:

> Here the injuries were caused in every realistic sense by petitioner's exposure at work. We can think of no reason why the Legislature would want to deny relief because the work-generated force overtook petitioner at one moment rather than another.

300 A.2d at 149. *See also Daniello v. Machise Express Co.,* 119 N.J.Super. 20, 289 A.2d 558 (1972), *aff'd,* 122 N.J.Super. 144, 299 A.2d 423 (App.Div.1973).

In *Graybeal v. Board of Supervisors of Montgomery County,* 216 Va. 77, 216 S.E.2d 52 (1975), claimant, a county prosecutor, was injured by a bomb explosion at his home. The bomb was placed by an individual whom he had successfully prosecuted for second-degree murder and who, after conviction, vowed revenge on everyone who had anything to do with his conviction. The Supreme Court of Virginia acknowledged its earlier rulings that an accident occurs in the course of employment when it takes place within the specified time, space, and circumstance of the employment but modified the rule for the particular facts of the case before it where the accident arose in the course of employment. The court explained that a modified rule is permitted by the statutory language "arising . . . in the course of the employment." It then proceeded to give arising its ordinary meaning of originating but further explained:

> Upon first examination, this rule might appear to constitute a blending into one single test of the dual "arising out of" and "in the course of" requirements. But *the "arising out of" requirement refers to causation,* only incidentally related to considerations of time and space, and must be satisfied by a showing of causal connection between work and injury. *The "course of" requirement, on the other hand, refers to continuity of time, space and circumstances,* only incidentally related to causation. *This requirement must be satisfied by a showing of an unbroken course beginning with work and ending*

with injury under such circumstances that the beginning and the end
are connected parts of a single work-related incident.

216 S.E.2d at 54 (emphasis added).

This originating in the course of employment test has been carefully
limited to those situations where the fact that originated the cause of
injury occurred entirely within the time and space limits of employment.
The Court of Appeals of New York, in *Malacarne v. City of Yonkers*
Parking Authority, 41 N.Y.2d 189, 391 N.Y.S.2d 402, 359 N.E.2d 992
(1976), denied compensation to a parking lot employee who was shot in
the back and killed while outside his sister's home by an assailant who
had demanded the money bag containing parking lot receipts which the
employee usually deposited in the bank across the street from his
employment. The court determined that there was no evidence to indicate that an event ultimately culminating in the employee's death
occurred within working hours and at the business premises and reasoned:

> Consequently, if, in the case before us, there had been substan-
> tial evidence rather than mere conjecture to support a finding that
> an attempted robbery had begun at the deceased's point of depar-
> ture from the parking lot itself, the board might have been entitled
> to consider whether that event and the subsequent shooting were
> but two parts of a whole. The reality, however, is that there was not
> a scintilla of evidence of any earlier event related to the shooting.
> The "money bag" statement attributed to the decedent during the
> testimony before the referee does not supply it. That bare statement
> did not include, for instance, anything to indicate that suspicious
> persons had been lurking in the vicinity of the parking lot, or that
> anyone had been seen to follow the decedent from there or, for that
> matter, that he had observed anyone following him at any time
> during his half hour's drive to his sister's house until he had already
> arrived on her street. Even assuming that the decedent had in fact
> made the "money bag" statement and, in doing so, had accurately
> quoted his assailant, on the record here we are left then with
> nothing but speculation on which to base a choice from among the
> countless number of possibilities of where, how or why the assailant
> came to the erroneous belief that Malacarne would have a money
> bag on him when he arrived at his sister's house.

391 N.Y.S.2d at 407–8, 359 N.E.2d at 995–996.

We find the construction of "arising out of and in the course of
employment," proposed by Larson and adopted by several jurisdictions
to be reasonable and conducive to the basic purposes of the workers'
compensation act. Essentially, the preliminary predicate for the two-
pronged work connectedness test was laid in *Fidelity & Casualty Co. of*
New York v. Moore and Hill v. Gregg, Gibson & Gregg, Inc.

We hold that to be compensable, an injury must arise out of
employment in the sense of causation and be in the course of employment in the sense of continuity of time, space, and circumstances. This

latter factor may be proved by showing that the causative factors occurred during the time and space limits of employment.

Thus, employing this test, we hold that Strother's injury is compensable. There is no issue that the injury sustained as a result of the assault arose out of employment. Furthermore, it had its genesis at the place of employment since the assailants were actually on the business premises, casing it so to speak, and, then when Strother left, they followed her home and there assaulted her and robbed her of her purse which they thought contained the cafeteria's cash-receipts. The time bomb began ticking while she was on the business premises and during working hours.

Accordingly, the order of the Industrial Relations Commission is quashed, and the order of the judge of industrial claims is reinstated.

It is so ordered.

Notes

1.   See Technical Tape Corp. v. Industrial Comm., 58 Ill.2d 226, 317 N.E.2d 515 (1974) for a similar holding. Can the Florida court's conclusion that Strother's injury is compensable be justified on the basis of any of the approaches noted heretofore? Was there any special errand? Did the accident occur on or near the work premises? Was the spot where the accident happened one of peculiar peril? Was the risk an ordinary incident of Strother's employment? Are you satisfied with the outcome? Why?

Does the mere fact that a risk arises out of employment satisfy the within the course of employment requirement? Can we surmise that an accident is compensable whenever it either arises out of the employment or occurs during the course of it, and that it need not satisfy *both* requirements? Or is it enough to note that the two requirements interact upon each other? That is, will a strong showing of "arise-out-of" serve to compensate for a weak showing of "during-course-of"?

2.   The next chapter permits consideration of the converse situation; that is, can a strong showing of "within the course of" compensate for a weak showing of "arising-out-of"? See, e.g., Mitchell v. Employers Mut. Liability Ins. Co., 341 So.2d 35 (La.App.1976).

Chapter 5

INJURIES ARISING OUT OF
THE EMPLOYMENT

SECTION 1. THE JOB AS THE SOURCE OF THE HARMFUL AGENCY

To effectuate the workers' compensation goals of carving out "employment risks" from the general body of perils that beset all mankind and making them a cost of doing business, compensation statutes prescribe standards to distinguish compensable employment injuries from those that are not compensable. The approach devised in the original British workers' compensation act has been adopted virtually universally: namely, an employment injury must "arise out of" and be suffered "within the course" of the employment. If the "within the course" criterion is satisfied, the "arising out of" criterion is undisputed in most actions; that is, if a boiler explodes, or a worker slips and falls while involved in strenuous employment effort, this issue is rarely contested. No one can sensibly argue that these injuries ought not be treated as a cost of doing business. By contrast some injuries are plainly not the responsibility of the employer, as for example, an injury caused entirely by a genetic deficiency.

Between the classes of indisputably compensable and indisputably non-compensable injuries there is a wide, gray area of dispute. Suppose, for example, a lightning bolt strikes a highway worker hard at work on the roadway. Does it comport with the underlying workers' compensation economic premises to burden the employer with the costs of the resulting injury any more so than to require the employer to pay for the same injuries had the lightning struck the same employee while walking at the same spot on the road on a day off? Or, suppose a worker suffers a heart attack at work caused by a combination of work stress and a congenitally weak heart. Can a principled argument be made to treat the so-called "neutral" source injuries (i.e., lightning strike) different from what might be called "mixed" sources injuries (i.e., a heart attack)? To what extent may this issue be resolved by attempting to isolate the "source" of the causative force of the injury?

189

In examining the following materials the student should consider whether isolating the source of the injury was important to the courts' resolutions of the "arising out of" issues.

DAVIS v. HOUSTON GENERAL INS. CO.
Court of Appeals of Georgia, 1977.
141 Ga.App. 385, 233 S.E.2d 479.

MARSHALL, JUDGE.

This appeal arises out of an award denying compensation to a claimant for workmen's compensation. Appellant Mrs. Davis, claimant below enumerates as error the denial of compensation as affirmed by the Georgia Board of Workmen's Compensation and the superior court.

As relevant to these proceedings, the facts show that Mrs. Davis was employed as a nurse's aide at the Shoreham Convalescent Center, Inc. She had been so employed for about four or five months. On December 18, 1974, after completing her normal day's work, Mrs. Davis was putting on her outer coat preparatory to going home. Apparently she had placed her right arm in the coat and reached behind to place her left arm into the coat sleeve. At that time she felt a "pop." She reported this incident to her supervisor, but experienced no immediate pain, discomfort or other physical limitation. Several weeks later Mrs. Davis experienced a second episode involving the lifting of a patient, but that episode is not a part of this litigation. Following the second episode, Mrs. Davis was required to undergo two back operations and apparently is unable to perform her duties as before. In her own testimony, Mrs. Davis admitted that she had never experienced any back pain or limitation nor had she ever experienced any back trouble of any kind prior to the "pop" which occurred on December 18, 1974. On the basis of this evidence, the administrative law judge concluded that Mrs. Davis was injured in the course of her employment but that the injury did not arise out of her employment. Mrs. Davis enumerates as error this conclusion. *Held:*

The appellees, insurer and employer, admit that the injury occurred in the course of employment but continue to deny that the injury arose out of employment. The terms "in the course of" and "out of" are not synonymous. Both must occur to render the case a compensable one. Maryland Cas. Co. v. Peek, 36 Ga.App. 557, 559, 137 S.E. 121. The words "arising out of" mean that there must be some causal connection between the conditions under which the employee worked and the injury which she received. The causative danger must be incidental to the character of the employment, and not independent of the relation of master and servant. The accident must be one resulting from a risk reasonably incident to the employment. Thornton v. Hartford Accident etc. Co., 198 Ga. 786, 792, 32 S.E.2d 816.

An accident "arises out of" employment when there is apparent to the rational mind, upon consideration of all the circumstances, a causal connection between the conditions under which the work is required to be performed and the resulting injury. Under this test, if the injury can be seen to have followed as a natural incident of the work, and to have been contemplated by a reasonable person familiar with the whole situation as a result of the exposure occasioned by the nature of the employment, then it arises "out of" the employment. But it excludes an injury which can not fairly be traced to the employment as a contributing proximate cause and which comes from a hazard to which the workman would have been equally exposed apart from the employment. The causative danger must be peculiar to the work. It must be incidental to the character of the business, and not independent of the relation of master and servant.

In this case the administrative law judge, acting as the "reasonable person" heard testimony that for four or five months Mrs. Davis had worked as a hospital aide without any difficulty. She had never had any back trouble. On the day of the alleged injury she was engaged in an effort (putting on her coat) which logically was a hazard to which she was equally exposed apart from her employment. There was absolutely no evidence that the "pop" which occurred while putting on her outer coat was related in any way to or caused by the peculiar nature of her duties. In the absence of any evidence showing a connection between the strain of reaching behind to pull on a coat and the duties of a nurse's aide or that the duties of a nurse's aide were incidental to or the probable causation of the "pop," it was not unreasonable for the "rational mind" of the administrative law judge, upon a consideration of all the evidence to fail to find a causal connection between the conditions under which the work was required to be performed and the resulting injury.

A finding of fact by an administrative law judge or the State Board of Workmen's Compensation, when supported by any evidence, is conclusive and binding upon both the superior court and this court. Speight v. Container Corp., 138 Ga.App. 45, 46–47, 225 S.E.2d 496. The finding of the administrative law judge in this case is fully supported by the evidence before him.

Judgment affirmed.

Note

Compare, Strategic Marketing Systems v. Soranno, 559 So.2d 353 (Fla. App. 1st DCA 1990) (claimant, a computer operator, "popped" his knee when arising to change position in his chair; no impact was suffered and claimant had no history of knee trouble; compensation denied on ground that "mere occurrence of an injury at work, without more, is not compensable").

SECTION 2. EMERGENCE OF THE POSITIONAL RISK DOCTRINE—STREET RISKS

In an effort to confer meaning on the spare "arising out of" phrase the courts in the earliest decisions adopted an approach which came to be known as the "increased risk" test; namely, "Was the risk of the particular injury greater for the worker than for someone not so employed?" Another way of expressing this was to ask whether the harmful agency was or not "peculiar" to the employment. Later experience, however, showed that this inquiry did not resolve all issues appropriately. For example, suppose the cause of harm was not a lightning flash, but merely an ordinary traffic crash that the general travelling public must confront? Is this a stronger or weaker case for imposing liability on the employer? The following case and those in succeeding sections demonstrate the evolution and varieties of theories the courts have developed to deal with them.

DONAHUE v. MARYLAND CAS. CO.

Supreme Judicial Court of Massachusetts, 1917.
226 Mass. 595, 116 N.E. 226.

Application by Patrick M. Donahue for compensation for injuries under the Workmen's Compensation Act, resisted by Thomas J. Flynn & Co., employer, and the Maryland Casualty Company, insurer. From the judgment on the decision of the Industrial Accident Board awarding compensation, the insurer appeals. Reversed, and decree entered for insurer.

CROSBY, J. The evidence presented to the committee of arbitration was in substance as follows: The claimant, who was employed by the insured in the sale of church goods, on February 21, 1916, left his employer's place of business in Boston, and proceeded by train to Lowell and thence by electric cars to the village of Collinsville in Lowell. Upon leaving the electric cars, he went to the house of a clergyman, which was distant about ten minutes' walk from the car line, and after completing his business there left and started to walk back. He had proceeded about thirty-five or forty feet when he slipped on the ice and fell, sustaining a broken ankle. When injured he was walking in the middle of the street, the sidewalk being impassable on account of ice. He was employed principally as a traveling salesman, but worked in the store during the Christmas and Easter seasons. More than half of the time he was outside his employer's store visiting different places throughout New England for the purpose of selling church goods. He traveled by steam railroads, electric cars, and on foot,—using cars when available. When he left the house of the clergyman he intended to take a car to Lexington to sell some goods there. The committee found that the employee received an injury in the course of and arising out of his employment.

At the hearing before the Industrial Accident Board in addition to the evidence before the committee above recited, the employee testified:

"I was going to get a car to Lexington when I fell. The street was a mass of ice. I never saw anything like it before or since."

The finding that the injury was received in the course of the employment was warranted. The question remains whether there was any evidence that the injury arose out of the employment. An injury arises out of the employment when there is a causal connection between the conditions under which the work is to be performed and the resulting injury. An injury cannot be found to have arisen out of the employment unless the employment was a contributing, proximate cause. If the risk of injury to the employee was one to which he would have been equally exposed apart from his employment, then the injury does not arise out of it. As was said by this court in McNicols' Case, 215 Mass. 497, at page 499, 102 N.E. 697, L.R.A.1916A, 306:

"The causative danger must be peculiar to the work and not common to the neighborhood. It must be incidental to the character of the business and not independent of the relation of master and servant."

The undisputed evidence shows that while the employee was walking along the street in the course of his employment on his way to the electric car line, he slipped upon the ice and received the injury for which he seeks compensation. Manifestly the injury so received did not result in any proper sense from a risk incidental to the employment. It seems plain that the danger of the employee's slipping upon the ice in a public street was not peculiar to his work, but was a hazard common to persons engaged in any employment who had occasion to travel along the streets. The risk of slipping upon the icy pavement was common to the public who had occasion to pass over it on foot. It was a danger due to climatic conditions to which persons in that locality, however employed or if not employed at all, were equally exposed. * * *

As the hazard of slipping on the ice in the street was not a causative danger peculiar to the claimant's employment, the injury received could not properly be found to have arisen out of the employment.

The decree of the superior court must be reversed, and a decree entered in favor of the insurer.

So ordered.

KATZ v. A. KADANS & CO.

Court of Appeals of New York, 1922.
232 N.Y. 420, 134 N.E. 330.

Pound, J. This is a workmen's compensation case. Louis Katz, the claimant, was a dairyman's chauffeur. On May 7, 1920, when he was driving his employer's car west on Canal street after delivering some cheese, an insane man stabbed him. A lot of people were running after the insane man and he stabbed any one near him. The question is whether claimant's injuries arose out of his employment.

If the work itself involves exposure to perils of the street, strange, unanticipated, and infrequent though they may be, the employee passes along the streets when on his master's occasions under the protection of the statute. This is the rule unequivocally laid down by the House of Lords in England:

"When a workman is sent into the street on his master's business, * * * his employment necessarily involves exposure to the risks of the streets and injury from such a cause [necessarily] arises out of his employment." Finlay, L.C., in Dennis v. White, [1917] L.R.App.Cas. 479.

So we have to concern ourselves only with the question whether claimant's accident arose out of a street risk.

Cases may arise where one is hurt in the street, but where the risk is of a general nature, not peculiar to the street. Lightning strikes fortuitously in the street; bombs dropped by enemy aircraft do not expose to special danger persons in a street as distinguished from those in houses.[1] Allcock v. Rogers, [1918] House of Lords, 11 B.W.C.C. 149. The danger must result from the place to make it a street risk, but that is enough if the workman is in the place by reason of his employment, and in the discharge of his duty to his employer. The street becomes a dangerous place when street brawlers, highwaymen, escaping criminals, or violent madmen are afoot therein as they sometimes are. The danger of being struck by them by accident is a street risk because it is incident to passing through or being on the street when dangerous characters are abroad.

Particularly on the crowded streets of a great city, not only do vehicles collide, pavements become out of repair, and crowds jostle, but mad or biting dogs may run wild, gunmen may discharge their weapons, police officers may shoot at fugitives fleeing from justice, or other things may happen from which accidental injuries result to people on the streets which are peculiar to the use of the streets and do not commonly happen indoors.

The risk of being stabbed by an insane man running amuck seems in a peculiar sense a risk incidental to the streets to which claimant was exposed by his employment. Matter of Heidemann v. Am. Dist. Tel. Co., 230 N.Y. 305, 130 N.E. 302, does not hold that where the street risk is one shared equally by all who pass or repass, whether in or out of employment, it should be shown that the employment involves some special exposure; that the night watchman is exposed by his employment to the risk of being shot by accident as he nears a sudden brawl which it is his duty to investigate, while the night clerk whose business brings him on the street, but whose duty is not to seek danger, is not so exposed. We decided the case before us and no other, dwelling naturally upon those features of the situation which emphasized the connection between the risk and the employment. But the fact that the risk is one to which every one on the street is exposed does not itself defeat compensation. Members of the public may face the same risk every day. The question is whether the employment exposed the workman to the risks by sending him on to the street, common though such risks were to all on the street. Moran's Case, 234 Mass. 566, 125 N.E. 591; Dennis v. White, supra.

---

1. [**Editor's Note.**] But cf. Roberts v. Newcomb & Co. (1922) 201 App.Div. 759, 195 N.Y.S. 405 (messenger injured by bomb in Wall Street intended for wealthy broker; compensation allowed).

The order should be affirmed, with costs.

HOGAN, CARDOZO, and CRANE, JJ., concur.

HISCOCK, C.J., and McLAUGHLIN and ANDREWS, JJ., dissent.

Order affirmed.

Notes

1. In addition to street risk injuries, courts have awarded compensation for injuries caused by numerous risks that are not inherent and peculiar to travel on highways. Examples include, Scandrett v. Industrial Comm., 235 Wis. 1, 291 N.W. 845 (1940) (portions of a building thrown into the street by a windstorm); Friel v. Industrial Comm., 398 Ill. 361, 75 N.E.2d 859 (1947) (a football kicked into the street shattered glass in the worker's vehicle); Everard v. Women's Home Companion Reading Club, 234 Mo.App. 760, 122 S.W.2d 51 (1938) (a worker jammed a splinter into his foot on the highway); and City of Chicago v. Industrial Comm., 389 Ill. 592, 60 N.E.2d 212 (1945) (a worker stubbed a toe on a curb). Decisions such as these eliminate any requirement that the agency that caused the harm be an ordinary risk of the highway, such as a negligently driven vehicle, blowout, or defective pavement. The proposition applied by these cases was expressed by United Service Ins. Co. v. Donaldson, 254 Ala. 204, 48 So.2d 3, 6, 7 (1950), as follows:

> As to 'street accidents,' or 'perils of the street or highway,' this Court has adopted the more liberal view that in case of workmen whose duties require them to be continually or frequently in or upon the street or highway and who are injured as a result thereof, the injury is one arising out of their employment.

2. All courts are not so generous in what is a street risk. See, e.g., Gooch v. Industrial Comm., 322 Ill. 586, 153 N.E. 624 (1926) (iceman injured in street by toy bomb discharged in Fourth of July celebration; compensation denied); and Morrow v. Orscheln Bros. Truck Lines, 235 Mo.App. 1166, 151 S.W.2d 138 (1941) (dust blown into claimant's eye while in the street; would have been a street risk if stirred up by traffic, but not because merely carried by wind), and Liebman v. Colonial Baking Co., 391 S.W.2d 948 (Mo.App. 1965) (employee was assaulted in street for no apparent reason, compensation denied).

SECTION 3. INJURIES CAUSED BY ACTS OF NATURE AND FORTUITOUS FORCES FROM OUTSIDE THE EMPLOYMENT

WHETRO v. AWKERMAN
Supreme Court of Michigan, 1970.
383 Mich. 235, 174 N.W.2d 783.

T.G. KAVANAGH, J. These cases were consolidated pursuant to our order. * * *

They turn on the same question, for the damages for which workmen's compensation was awarded in each case were caused by the Palm Sunday, 1965, tornadoes which devastated parts of southern Michigan.

Carl Whetro was injured when the tornado destroyed the residence wherein he was working for his employer and seeks reimbursement for his medical expenses. Henry E. Emery was killed when the motel in which he was staying while on a business trip for his employer was destroyed by the tornado, and his widow seeks compensation for his death.

In each case the hearing referee found that the employee's injury arose out of and in the course of his employment. The award was affirmed by the appeal board in each case and by the Court of Appeals in the Whetro case.

The defendant-appellants in both cases base their defense on the assertion that tornadoes are "acts of God" or acts of nature and injuries which are caused by them do not arise "out of" the employment and hence are not compensable under the workman's compensation act. * * * For this reason they maintain that the cases were erroneously decided as a matter of law and the awards should be set aside.

The appellants in each case maintain that the injury did not arise "out of" the employment because that phrase, as it is used in the act, refers to a causal connection between the event which put in motion the forces which caused the injury and the work itself or the conditions under which it is required to be performed.

Employment as a caretaker-gardener or salesman, they argue, does not include tornadoes as incidents or conditions of the work, and the path of injury is determined by the tornado, not the employment.

Appellants cite a series of Michigan decisions involving injury by lightning: Klawinski v. Lake Shore & M.S.R. Co. (1915), 185 Mich. 643, 152 N.W. 213; Thier v. Widdifield (1920), 210 Mich. 355, 178 N.W. 16; Nelson v. Country Club of Detroit (1951), 329 Mich. 479, 45 N.W.2d 362; Kroon v. Kalamazoo County Road Commission (1954) 339 Mich. 1, 62 N.W.2d 641, in which compensation was denied, and assert that a tornado is like lightning in that it acts capriciously, leaving its victims and the untouched side by side. The decisions in all of these "lightning cases" denied compensation on the ground that the injury did not arise "out of" the employment because the employment did not expose the workman to any increased risk or to a more hazardous situation than faced by others in the area.

The Court of Appeals was able to distinguish between a tornado and a bolt of lightning as a causative force of injury and base its decision affirming the award for Carl Whetro on the reasoning of the Massachusetts supreme court in *Caswell's* case (1940), 305 Mass. 500, 26 N.E.2d 328, wherein recovery was allowed for injuries received when a brick wall of the employer's factory was blown down on workmen during a hurricane. This "contact with the premises" met the requirement that the injury arise "out of" the employment in the mind of the Court of Appeals.

We are unable to accept the distinction drawn between a tornado and bolt of lightning when viewed as the cause of an injury. As we see it, a tornado, no less than a bolt of lightning or an earthquake or flood is an "act of God" and if the phrase "out of" the employment in the workmen's compensation act necessarily entails the notion of proximate causality, no injury received because of an "act of God" should be compensable.

But we are satisfied that it is no longer necessary to establish a relationship of proximate causality between employment and an injury in order to establish compensability. Accordingly we no longer regard an "act of God" whether it be a tornado, lightning, earthquake, or flood as a defense to a claim for a work-connected injury. Such a defense retains too much of the idea that an employer should not pay compensation unless he is somehow at fault. This concept from the law of tort is inconsistent with the law of workmen's compensation.

The purpose of the compensation act as set forth in its title is to promote the welfare of the people of Michigan relating to the liability of employers for injuries or death sustained by their employees. The legislative policy is to provide financial and medical benefits to the victims of work-connected injuries in an efficient, dignified, and certain form. The act allocates the burden of such payments to the most appropriate source of payment, the consumer of the product. * * *

Fault has nothing to do with whether or not compensation is payable. The economic impact on an injured workman and his family is the same whether the injury was caused by the employer's fault or otherwise.

We hold that the law in Michigan today no longer requires the establishment of a proximately causal connection between the employment and the injury to entitle a claimant to compensation. The cases which have allowed recovery for street risks, * * * increased risks, * * * and on-the-premises accidents * * * were made without consideration of the proximate causal connection between the nature of the employment and the injury. They have brought the law in Michigan to the point where it can be said today that if the employment is the occasion of the injury, even though not the proximate cause, compensation should be paid. * * *

Accordingly, we hold that the employment of Carl Whetro and Henry E. Emery in each case was the occasion of the injury which they suffered and therefore the injuries arose "out of" and in the course of their employment.

The award in each case is affirmed.

[Omitted is an appendix listing chronologically Michigan cases demonstrating the evolutionary trend in Michigan leading to this decision. Omitted also is the special concurring opinion of Black, J.]

T.E. BRENNAN, C.J. (dissenting). The function of the workmen's compensation act is to place the financial burden of industrial injuries upon the industries themselves, and spread that cost ultimately among the consumers.

This humane legislation was developed because the industrialization of our civilization had left in its wake a trail of broken bodies.

Employers were absolved from general liability for negligence, in exchange for the imposition of more certain liability under the act.

But it is a mistake to say that employers were absolved from fault. Liability is the basis of legal remedy. Fault is the basis of moral responsibility.

The workmen's compensation law is society's expression of the moral responsibility of employers and consumers to the workmen whose health and whose lives are sacrificed to industrial and commercial progress and production.

Fault is not the same thing as proximate cause. The compensation law does not use the word *cause*. Rather, it expresses the concept of employer and consumer responsibility in the phrase "arising out of and in the course of" the employment.

The terms "arising out of" and "in the course of" are not redundant. They mean two different things. An adulterous cobbler shot at his last by his jealous wife may be "in the course of" his employment. But the injury does not "arise out of" his job. On what basis of moral responsibility should his injuries be paid for by his employer? By what logic would society decree that his disability should add a farthing to the price of shoes?

The workmen's compensation law is not a utopian attempt to put a price tag on all human suffering and incorporate it into the cost of living.

Lightning, flood, tornadoes and estranged wives will always be with us, in this vale of tears. They were the occasion of human injury when our forebears were tilling the soil with sharp sticks. They are not a by-product of the industrial revolution, nor are they in any sense the moral responsibility of those who profit by, or enjoy the fruits of, our modern industrialized society.

I would reverse without apology for the precedents.

DETHMERS and KELLY, JJ., concurred with T.E. BRENNAN, C.J.

Notes

1. The decisions pertaining to injuries and deaths caused by lightning, windstorm, earthquake and other acts of nature can generally be placed in one of four categories as follows:

(a) The increase in risk caused by the employment must have been a cause in fact of the injury or death. See, e.g., Campbell 66 Express, Inc. v. Industrial Comm., 83 Ill.2d 353, 47 Ill.Dec. 730, 415 N.E.2d 1043 (1980) (travel requirement of truck driver's employment increased risk to injury from inclement weather). This approach formerly prevailed in

Michigan, but is now generally rejected. Kroon v. Kalamazoo County Road Comm., 339 Mich. 1, 62 N.W.2d 641 (1954).

(b) The working environment at the time must have exposed the worker to a greater risk of injury or death by an act of nature than "one not so employed" would have been exposed to. Hill v. St. Paul Fire & Marine Ins. Co., 512 S.W.2d 560 (Tenn.1974). The increase in risk may be created by a variety of factors. Parrish Esso Service Center v. Adams, 237 Ark. 560, 374 S.W.2d 468 (1964) (worker obliged to go out in storm to protect employer's property); State Highway Dept. v. Kloppenberg, 371 S.W.2d 793 (Tex.Civ.App.1963) (employee worked on high ground close to bridge; struck by lightning); and Arrington v. Goldstein, 23 N.J.Super. 103, 92 A.2d 630 (1952) (worker thrown into street by hurricane; proximity of ten story building contributed to erratic gusts of wind). Contrast J.I. Case Co. v. Industrial Comm., 36 Ill.2d 386, 223 N.E.2d 847 (1966) (employee paralyzed by lightning; compensation denied); and Crow v. Americana Crop Hail Pool, Inc., 176 Neb. 260, 125 N.W.2d 691 (1964) (worker struck by tornado while driving a truck on employment mission; compensation denied; employment did not cause increase of risk).

(c) Although not enhancing the likelihood of a natural disaster, the work environment makes the consequences more severe for the worker when it occurs. This approach is sometimes referred to as the "contact with the premises doctrine." See, e.g., Inland Steel Co. v. Industrial Comm., 41 Ill.2d 70, 241 N.E.2d 450 (1968) (worker on building injured by tornado; heavy tile roof tended to fall into building rather than be thrown out and away; compensation awarded) and Ingram v. Bradley, 183 Neb. 692, 163 N.W.2d 875 (1969) (unstable ticket booth blown down upon employee, compensation awarded).

(d) The work required the employee at the place where the injury occurred. This is positional risk test applied in the principal case. Other cases include Harvey v. Caddo De Soto Cotton Oil Co., 199 La. 720, 6 So.2d 747 (1942) (employee at work when tornado struck, compensation awarded) and Wiggins v. Knox Glass, Inc., 219 So.2d 154 (Miss.1969) (same). Would you draw a distinction between permitting recovery under the positional risk test in the many cases in which the injured worker was actively working at the spot where the natural disaster struck, and in cases where the employee was then doing no work, such as the employee Emery in the principal decision who was asleep in a motel when it was fortuitously struck by a tornado? Is it sufficient to say that if he had not been employed as he was, he would have been safely sleeping at a place of less actual risk? If so, does anything remain of the "arising out of" requirement? The positional risk test was rejected by Brady v. Louis Ruffolo & Sons Construction Company, 143 Ill.2d 542, 161 Ill.Dec. 275, 578 N.E.2d 921 (1991) (worker injured when truck slid off abutting icy public street and crashed through building where employee was working; compensation denied in absence of proof that construction of building increased risk of harm). See also Gayler v. North American Van Lines, 566 N.E.2d 84 (Ind.App.1991) (worker injured in car crash while en route to employer-authorized treatment for work related injuries; causal connection to work severed by aberrant driving of third person whose car caused the crash).

2. Many decisions permit recovery for injuries caused by fortuitous forces, having no connection with either the injured employee or the employer, that come onto the work site and injure or kill an employee. See, e.g., Industrial Indem. Co. v. Industrial Accident Comm., 95 Cal.App.2d 804, 214 P.2d 41 (1950) (while working in a bar, the employee was killed by a bullet fired at a customer by the customer's irate spouse; compensation awarded); Gargiulo v. Gargiulo, 24 N.J.Super. 129, 93 A.2d 598 (1952), affirmed 11 N.J. 611, 95 A.2d 646 (1953) (while at work, a butcher's helper was accidentally struck by an arrow shot by small boy next door: "But for the employment, the appellant would not have been in the back yard and in the path of the arrow," 24 N.J.Super. at 132, 93 A.2d at 600); and Powell v. Great Western Ry. Co. 1 [1940] All Eng.Rep. 87 (a locomotive fireman was hit by pellet from air gun: "The accident happened to the workman because the workman's duties required him to be on the engine. Thus, it seems to me to follow that the accident arose out of the employment." Id. at 90). Other decisions permitting recovery for harm done by random risks that are extraneous to the employment include: Baran's Case, 336 Mass. 342, 145 N.E.2d 726 (1957) (stray bullet); Kitchens v. Department of Labor & Employment, Division of Labor, 29 Colo.App. 374, 486 P.2d 474 (1971) (accidental shooting while waiting for employer's vehicle); and, Avis v. Electrolux Corp., 2 A.D.2d 717, 151 N.Y.S.2d 542 (1956) (salesman's eye injured by talon of roving owl).

3. New York decisions generally allow compensation without referring to the positional risk doctrine. Instead the courts stress the New York statutory presumption that the accident arose out of the employment. See e.g., DeAngelis v. Garfinkel Painting Co., 20 A.D.2d 162, 245 N.Y.S.2d 485 (1963).

4. Some courts have expressly refused to extend the positional risk doctrine to places other than streets unless the employment environment created an "increased risk" of harm. In addition to the decisions referred to in the principal case, see Lathrop v. Tobin–Hamilton Shoe Mfg. Co., 402 S.W.2d 16 (Mo.App.1966) (runaway automobile crashed through window of factory where claimant worked; compensation denied; positional risk doctrine rejected); and, Christiansen v. Hill Reproduction Co., 262 App.Div. 379, 29 N.Y.S.2d 24 (1941) (salesman killed while waiting for customer at a bar; compensation denied).

5. A few states reject positional risk in favor of an "actual risk" test. The Virginia Supreme Court explained this doctrine as follows:

> Under this test, if the injury can be seen to have followed as a natural incident of the work and to have been contemplated by a reasonable person familiar with the whole situation as a result of the exposure occasioned by the nature of the employment, then it arises "out of" the employment. *But it excludes an injury which cannot fairly be traced to the employment as a contributing proximate cause and which comes from a hazard to which the workman would have been equally exposed apart from the employment.* The causative danger must be peculiar to the work and not common to the neighborhood. It must be incidental to the character of the business and not independent of the relation of master

and servant. It need not have been foreseen or expected, but after the event it must appear to have had its origin in a risk connected with the employment, and to have flowed from that source as a rational consequence.

Baggett Transp. Co. v. Dillon, 219 Va. 633, 638, 248 S.E.2d 819, 822 (1978). Applied, Hill City Trucking, Inc. v. Christian, 238 Va. 735, 385 S.E.2d 377 (1989) (long distance truck driver shot after being stopped by robbers while on the road; compensation denied). See also In re McNichol, 215 Mass. 497, 102 N.E. 697 (1913), and Hughes v. St. Patrick's Cathedral, 245 N.Y. 201, 156 N.E. 665 (1927) ("actual risk" test adopted in heat exposure case).

6. Most of the decisions in which the positional risk theory is arguably applicable involve what are often referred to as "neutral" risks. That is, they are neither distinctly employment nor distinctly personal in character. Another modality is that the cause of an injury is simply unknown, making it impossible to attribute a cause and effect relationship between the harmful agency and either the employment or to an act or characteristic personal to the injured employee. Where an employee falls for no explainable reason, compensation is generally awarded if the activity in which the worker was engaged at the time was being done in the line of duty. See, e.g., Burroughs Adding Machine Co. v. Dehn, 110 Ind.App. 483, 39 N.E.2d 499 (1942); Ball v. Workmen's Compensation Appeal Bd., 19 Pa.Cmwlth. 157, 340 A.2d 610 (1975); and, Circle K Store No. 1131 v. Industrial Comm., 165 Ariz. 91, 796 P.2d 893 (1990) (claimant fell after depositing employer's trash bag in garbage dumpster while on her journey home. Compensation granted on basis that claimant would not have been at dumpster "but for" her assigned employment duty, thereby raising a presumption of "arising out of" that employer had not rebutted). The decisions, however, are not uniform. See, e.g., Finn v. Industrial Comm., 165 Colo. 106, 437 P.2d 542 (1968).

SECTION 4. INJURIES CAUSED BY IMPORTED AND PERSONAL RISKS

HILL–LUTHY CO. v. INDUSTRIAL COMM.
Supreme Court of Illinois, 1952.
411 Ill. 201, 103 N.E.2d 605.

CRAMPTON, JUSTICE. Arthur L. Rumple filed an application with the Industrial Commission for adjustment of compensation, charging that he lost the sight of an eye as the result of an accident arising out of, and in the course of, his employment. An arbitrator's award of compensation was sustained by the commission. Upon *certiorari* to the circuit court of Peoria County the decision of the commission was set aside. We have granted a petition for writ of error, and the record is submitted for further review.

The facts are not in dispute. Claimant was the only witness who testified. He was employed to drive a truck carrying soft water tanks, and to deliver the tanks to customers' homes, where he installed them. On the morning of July 31, 1947, after having delivered and installed one of the tanks, he entered the truck and started the motor. Before moving on to the next stop, however, he proceeded to light a cigarette. When he struck the match the head of it flew off, hitting him directly in the left eye and inflicting the injury in question. After receiving medical treatment and hospitalization he returned to work on November 17, 1947. It was stipulated herein that the loss of the left eye was the direct result of the burning by the match head on July 31, 1947.

Since the facts are uncontroverted the question whether claimant's injuries arose out of, and in the course of, his employment is one of law. Math Igler's Casino, Inc. v. Industrial Comm., 394 Ill. 330, 68 N.E.2d 773. The Workmen's Compensation Act requires that an accidental injury, to be compensable, must not only be sustained in the course of the employment but must also arise out of it. It is clear plaintiff in error's injury was received in the course of his employment, for the accident occurred within the period of the employment at a place where he reasonably may have been in the performance of his duties and while he was fulfilling those duties or engaged in something incidental thereto. But it is equally clear that the injury did not arise out of his employment. It arose from a cause having no relation to the nature of the employment. To entitle a claimant to obtain workmen's compensation benefits under the statute, his injury must be of such character that it may be seen to have had its origin in the nature of, or have been incidental to, the employment, or it must have been the result of a risk to which, by reason of the employment, the injured employee was exposed to a greater degree than if he had not been so employed. Loyola University v. Industrial Comm., 408 Ill. 139, 96 N.E.2d 509.

In the case at bar, the injury was caused by the defective match head, which flew off as plaintiff in error attempted to light a cigarette. The use of matches or the act of smoking was in no way incidental to the employment. The risk encountered was entirely divorced from it, and was one to which the general public is equally exposed while performing such acts in homes or elsewhere for personal enjoyment and comfort. The moving cause of the injury was not peculiar to the work but was common to the public. It was not incidental to the character of the employer's business but was entirely independent of the relationship of employment. In short, there was no causal connection between Rumple's employment and his injury.

Plaintiff in error has called our attention to a number of cases from foreign jurisdictions wherein injuries suffered while attempting to smoke or perform other acts of personal comfort were held to be compensable. No purpose would be served, however, by distinguishing each such case herein. Examination of their facts discloses direct connections between the injuries and conditions relating to the employment. Where clothing becomes oily, greasy, or otherwise inflammable from the nature of the work, the risk of igniting it in the act of smoking is obviously greater than it would be under ordinary conditions. Where an injury is incurred from a fall, or from breaking the glass in a door, or from being struck by an automobile or other object, or from an explosion of some substance on the employer's premises, any of which may occur while the employee has stopped for a smoke or is in the act of lighting a pipe or cigarette, its origin in the nature or conditions of the employment is not by virtue of the act of smoking but by virtue of the other factors involved.

Plaintiff in error contends that an employee may do those things which are necessary for his own health and comfort, such as smoking, warming himself, seeking shelter, or leaving work to answer a call of nature, procure a drink, food, or fresh air, and that such acts will be considered incidental to his employment. Several cases are cited upholding awards where the injuries were sustained in the course of such activities. But plaintiff in error fails to distinguish between the requirement that the injury arise out of the employment and the requirement that it be sustained in the course of the employment. Cases holding that no break in the employment is caused by the mere fact that the employee is engaging in the incidental activities referred to can be of no aid to him. The issue here concerns the origin or cause of the accident. The rule is well settled that an injury arises out of the employment when there is apparent to the rational mind a causal connection between the conditions under which the work is to be performed and the resulting injury. Under this test, if the injury can be seen to have followed as a natural incident to the work and as a result of the exposure occasioned by the nature of the employment, then it arises out of the employment. But the rule excludes an injury which cannot fairly be traced to the employment as a contributing proximate cause, and which comes from a hazard to which the workman would have been equally exposed apart from the employment. Risks of injury from defective matches used in the act of smoking are clearly those to which the general public is exposed. They are not within the contemplation of workmen's compensation acts, even though the injured person, at the time he suffered his injury, may have been performing duties incident to, and in the course of, his employment. See Ceisel v. Industrial Comm., 400 Ill. 574, 81 N.E.2d 506.

Given its logical effect, the contention of plaintiff in error would have the employer liable for any injury sustained by his employee, provided only that it occur while the latter is engaged in his employment. But the Workmen's Compensation Act does not make the employer an insurer of the safety of his employees while engaged in his service. Its intention is to protect the employee against the risks and hazards taken in order to perform the tasks assigned to him, and if no such risk or hazard caused, or contributed to cause the injury, the employee is not entitled to compensation.

We conclude that the judgment of the circuit court of Peoria County was correct, and it is affirmed, accordingly.

Judgment affirmed.

Notes

1. But apparently contra, Puffin v. General Electric Co., 132 Conn. 279, 43 A.2d 746 (1945) (employee smoking during rest period; cigarette ignited angora sweater; compensation awarded).

2. Even a personal risk, such as smoking, eating, or drinking, may be compensable if causally enhanced in some way by the duties of the employment or the work environment. Cases that have awarded compensation include Burton v. Broadcast Music Inc., 31 A.D.2d 557, 294 N.Y.S.2d 406 (1968) (corporation president on travel killed by fire started in hotel suite; asleep for several hours following business conference in which there was smoking and drinking); Snyder v. General Paper Corp., 277 Minn. 376, 152 N.W.2d 743 (1967) (travelling employee choked to death on large piece of steak at hotel dinner where he was entertaining a prospective customer); Steel Sales Corp. v. Industrial Comm., 293 Ill. 435, 127 N.E. 698 (1920) (employee burned when matches carried in his pocket for personal use were ignited through friction contact with a work locker); Boullier v. Samsan Co., 100 R.I. 676, 219 A.2d 133 (1966) (intense fumes in factory obliged worker to go to rest room to smoke; fumes ignited by flame); and Bletter v. Harcourt, Brace & World, Inc., 30 A.D.2d 601, 290 N.Y.S.2d 59 (1968) (young editor fell while attempting to execute a dance step in a self-operated elevator, because, as he testified, "I was in good spirits because I was enjoying the job. * * *;" compensation awarded). Perhaps the most lenient decision on this point is Wiseman v. Industrial Accident Comm., 46 Cal.2d 570, 297 P.2d 649 (1956) (corporation officer on trip spent leisure time with woman in hotel for romantic purposes; both burned to death in fire started by careless smoking in bed; compensation awarded). Contra, Kaplan v. Zodiac Watch Co., 20 N.Y.2d 537, 285 N.Y.S.2d 585, 232 N.E.2d 625 (1967) (travelling employee who had spent the night at a motel, entangled his leg in his trousers; fell and sustained a back injury; compensation denied because the risk was exclusively personal).

3. Injuries caused by risks imported into the employment for the employee's personal convenience and pleasure have been variously treated. Compare Hatfill v. Industrial Comm., 202 Ill.App.3d 547, 148 Ill.Dec. 67, 560 N.E.2d 369 (1990) (compensation denied employee injured while jumping over ditch in employer's parking lot as a short cut to his car; personal risk doctrine precludes recovery), and Ward v. Halliburton Co., 76 N.M. 463, 415 P.2d 847 (1966) (employee was killed when his hunting gun accidentally discharged while he was fetching his work uniform from his car; compensation denied); and Loveless v. Industrial Comm., 6 Ariz.App. 345, 432 P.2d 600 (1967) (claimant, an overseer whose job required him to carry a gun was shot as result of handing it to his son for examination; compensation denied), with Joe Ready's Shell Station and Cafe v. Ready, 218 Miss. 80, 65 So.2d 268 (1953) (employee of service station preparing to do bookkeeping work at home was shot while removing her husband's hunting gun from sofa; compensation allowed).

4. Suppose the employee is injured while attempting to start or maintain a private automobile on the employer's premises during work hours? The decisions vary. Fisher Body Division, General Motors Corp. v. Industrial Comm., 40 Ill.2d 514, 240 N.E.2d 694 (1968) (claimant was injured when his car battery blew up while he was trying to start his car in employer's lot on cold day; compensation denied). Compare Buerkle v. United Parcel Service, 26 N.J.Super. 404, 98 A.2d 327 (1953) (employee slipped on ice while taking a battery booster to his stalled vehicle on the employer's parking lot; compensation awarded); and California Cas. Indem. Exchange v. Industrial

Acc. Comm., 21 Cal.2d 751, 135 P.2d 158 (1943) (employee tripped on hem of her skirt while alighting from vehicle after a personal errand; compensation awarded).

5. Suppose the employee brings contaminated or otherwise harmful food to work and is injured while consuming it during a lunch break? Goodyear Aircraft Corp. v. Industrial Comm., 62 Ariz. 398, 158 P.2d 511 (1945) (employee injured when defective soft drink bottle that he had brought to work broke while he was opening it; compensation awarded). Contrast Williams v. Industrial Comm., 38 Ill.2d 593, 232 N.E.2d 744 (1967) (clerk choked on doughnut bought at employer's store and eaten on premises; risk was regarded as personal and compensation denied).

GEORGE v. GREAT EASTERN FOOD PRODUCTS, INC.

Supreme Court of New Jersey, 1965.
44 N.J. 44, 207 A.2d 161.

HALL, J.

In this workmen's compensation case, the employee died from a fractured skull sustained as the result of an idiopathic fall (used in the sense of a fall caused by a purely personal condition having no work connection whatever) "in the course of" his employment. An attack of dizziness, apparently induced by some cardiovascular condition, precipitated the occurrence. He did not strike anything until his head hit the level concrete floor upon which he was standing, bringing about the injury. The Division of Workmen's Compensation dismissed the petitions seeking compensation for the period between the injury and death some few weeks later and for dependency benefits. The Essex County Court reached the same result on appeal and the Appellate Division affirmed in an unreported opinion, holding the case was controlled by this court's 4–3 decision in Henderson v. Celanese Corp., 16 N.J. 208, 108 A.2d 267 (1954), where the pivotal facts were essentially the same. We granted certification. 43 N.J. 261, 203 A.2d 715 (1964). Petitioners urge reconsideration of the rule of Henderson.

In Henderson, a case of first impression in this jurisdiction, the majority, in deciding that the accident was noncompensable, conceded the existence of a division of authority in the precise situation among the other states, but determined that the rationale of some of our earlier cases dealing with the statutory language that a compensable injury must also derive from an accident "arising out of" the employment, R.S. 34:15–7, N.J.S.A., dictated the result reached. The underlying thesis was taken from Spindler v. Universal Chain Corp., 11 N.J. 34, 39, 93 A.2d 171, 173 (1952):

> "If it [the fall] was occasioned by or was the result of a disease or physical seizure and was not contributed to by 'what the workman had to do,' it is not compensable. On the other hand, if the fall 'would not have occurred but for the services rendered' in the employment, it is covered by the statute."

(The burden of proof to establish the idiopathic cause was placed on the employer. 11 N.J., at p. 38, 93 A.2d 171.) The seeming exclusionary breadth of this thesis was, however, qualified by saying that, even if the inception of the fall was occasioned by a personal condition and non-work connected, the resulting injury was compensable if that injury was caused or contributed to by some added hazard or special condition of the employment. Concrete floors were found not to fall in that category because they are "usual and common in industrial plants" and "[t]he same consequences would probably have been forthcoming had the appellant suffered his seizure in the street or in his home." 16 N.J., at p. 214, 108 A.2d, at p. 270.

The result of the rule is the drawing of an obviously indefinite and, to us, unsatisfactory line. . . . If the inception of the fall has the slightest connection with the employment, the resulting injury is compensable. Freedman v. Spicer Manufacturing Corp., 97 N.J.L. 325, 116 A. 427 (E & A 1922) (where an employee became dizzy as a result of an inoculation recommended by the employer and fell to the floor, fracturing his skull); Hall v. Doremus, 114 N.J.L. 47, 175 A. 369 (Sup.Ct.1934) (where an employee watching a cow in parturition was so overcome as to faint and fall to the concrete floor, fracturing his skull). If the employee is caused to fall idiopathically and is located in the course of his employment at even a slight height at the fall's inception or is standing at floor level and on the way down falls into a pit or strikes a table, chair, desk, stove, machinery or some other object situate on the employment premises, the resulting injury is compensable. . . . Seemingly also, he would be compensated if, through sheer awkwardness, he tripped over his own feet and fell to the floor or, by reason of a congenitally weak back, fell on his head when leaning over to pick up a pencil. But not so, according to Henderson and Stulb v. Foodcraft, Inc., 76 N.J.Super. 384, 184 A.2d 673 (Law Div.1962), if he suffered a spontaneous attack of vertigo and struck nothing but the floor during his descent from a standing posture. The distinctions are neither consistent nor meaningful. Either no consequence of an idiopathic fall should bring compensability or the nature of the result alone should be looked to as the determinant.

We think the latter principle ought to govern as expounded in the rationale so cogently advanced by Judge Clapp in his dissenting opinion in the Appellate Division in Henderson, 30 N.J.Super. 353, 360, 104 A.2d 720 (relied upon by the minority in this Court, 16 N.J., at p. 215, 108 A.2d 267). Even at the time Henderson was decided, it seemed evident that it was enough, in conjunction with the fundamental principle that "an employer takes an employee as he finds him," to constitute an occurrence an "accident" if either the circumstance causing the injury *or* the result on the employee's person was unlooked for, regardless of whether the inception or the underlying reason for the circumstance or result was personal or work connected. . . . There can be no question about the proposition at the present time. . . . Here, as Judge Clapp pointed out, "both the circumstance causing the injury (the striking of the floor) and the consequence upon the employee's person were unexpected." 30 N.J.Super., at p. 361, 104 A.2d, at p. 724. We also completely endorse the second necessary element of his thesis that such an unlooked-for mishap arises "out of" the employment when it is due to a condition of the employment—i.e., a risk of *this* employment, and that the impact with the concrete floor here clearly meets that test. Our conclusion therefore is that Henderson was incorrectly decided and should no longer be followed.

Of course, we do not mean to intimate that an employee is entitled to compensation for some idiopathic incident in and of itself, as, for example, where one suffers a non-work connected heart attack or convulsion at work and simply dies at his desk or machine or falls to the floor and suffers no injury from the impact. No such claim is made here.

The judgment of the Appellate Division is reversed and the matter remanded to the County Court for further proceedings consistent with this opinion.

Notes

1. Accord, Chapman, Dependents of v. Hanson Scale Co., 495 So.2d 1357, 1361 (Miss.1986) (claimant suffered idiopathic gran mal seizure, fell and hit head on concrete floor; death resulted but no evidence was presented that gran mal seizure was the sole cause; "We consider exposure to falls upon a concrete floor a sufficient risk attendant upon employment so that an injury caused in part thereby is compensable"). A true idiopathic fall injury is one that is caused by the fall itself rather than the personal physical condition or attribute that caused the fall. If the fall can be attributed to work conditions, or even if it is found to be the result of an unexplained "neutral" risk, compensation is usually awarded for injuries suffered when the falling body strikes the floor or some item in the work place. The decision in George, treating the idiopathic fall as an unexplained fall, and thus the injury a compensable injury, represents what is probably a minority position. But, see, Nowlin v. Industrial Commission, 167 Ariz. 291, 806 P.2d 880 (1990) (compensation awarded receptionist whose unexplained back injury occurred as she was sitting down in her receptionist's chair; the injury resulted from an actual risk of the job activity).

2. In most jurisdictions the victim of an idiopathic fall must show that the employment or its environment enhanced the risk of injury in some way, either in having accentuated the weakness of the personal condition, thereby contributing to the cause of the fall, or by having exposed the falling person to the risk of suffering a more dangerous collision than would be expected in a non-work setting. The latter situation is sometimes referred to as the "increased risk hazard." Contrast Leon County School Bd. v. Grimes, 548 So.2d 205 (Fla.1989) (an employee's leg brace, required because of weakness caused by polio, gave way causing him to fall to a *carpeted* floor; compensation denied), and Protectu Awning Shutter Co. v. Cline, 154 Fla. 30, 16 So.2d 342 (1944) (worker fainted from idiopathic cause and fractured skull on *concrete* floor; compensation awarded on basis of increased hazard). See, also, Ledbetter v. Michigan Carton Co., 74 Mich.App. 330, 253 N.W.2d 753 (1977).

SECTION 5. INJURIES CAUSED BY FIGHTS AND ASSAULTS AMONG CO-WORKERS

HARTFORD ACCIDENT & INDEM. CO. v. CARDILLO

United States Court of Appeals for the District of Columbia, 1940.
72 App.D.C. 52, 112 F.2d 11.

RUTLEDGE, ASSOCIATE JUSTICE. The appeal is from an order of the District Court dismissing the complaint of the Hartford Accident and Indemnity Company, employer's insurance carrier, against Frank A. Cardillo, deputy commissioner of the United States Employees' Compensation Commission, and Ray Bridges, to enjoin enforcement of a compensation order favoring Bridges. The findings of fact, insofar as they are pertinent to the appeal are as follows:

On October 10, 1938, the claimant Bridges, "while employed as a helper in the employer's [Sanitary Grocery Company, Inc.] produce warehouse and engaged in loading vegetables on the employer's truck, sustained personal injury resulting in his disability when a co-worker assaulted him suffering a laceration of the right eyebrow and a fracture of the right maxilla; * * * that the work performed by the claimant was supervised by a checker, Roy Downey; that in directing the claimant in the performance of his duties Downey addressed the claimant as 'Shorty'; that the claimant resented being called 'Shorty' and when Downey continued to so address the claimant, the latter called Downey a vile name; that Downey thereupon struck the claimant a blow on the right side of the face with his fist, inflicting the injuries above described; that the claimant did not strike or attempt to strike his superior, Downey; that Downey was the aggressor in the assault * * *." From these facts the deputy commissioner concluded "that the injury had its origin in the employment and that it arose out of and in the course of the said employment."

It is not contended that the injury did not occur "in the course of the employment," since it took place at the very time that Bridges was loading the truck for the employer. But the arguments of the plaintiff are directed against the finding that it "arose out of" the employment. Plaintiff asserts that the assault by Downey upon Bridges was caused by a purely personal quarrel, which had no relation to their work and, therefore, that the injury is not compensable. This is predicated on the facts as found and on other evidence not mentioned in the findings. That was to the effect that for about two months Downey and Bridges, while at work, had engaged in friendly banter concerning the respective merits of their watches, which was renewed on the morning of the injury. It is claimed that this led to the altercation and made it an entirely personal quarrel, unrelated to the work. * * *

[There follows an excellent but lengthy discussion of the shift by courts away from the increased risk notion whenever the employee was injured or killed at a time when and at a place where he was securely within the course of his employment. The court notes the emergence of the positional risk approach, which, the opinion observes, is in recognition of the fact that the work brings the employee within its peril and makes it, for purposes of compensation, "part of the work".] The opinion continues:

Recognition that this is so came more easily as to physical than as to human forces. As with street risks, the early disposition in cases of human action was to emphasize the particular act and its nature, except anomalously when it involved merely negligence of the claimant or fellow employees. The statutory abolition of common law defenses made easy recognition of the accidental character of negligent acts by the claimant and fellow servants. The extension to their accidental (i.e., nonculpable, but injurious) behavior was not difficult. So with that of strangers, including assault by deranged persons, and their negligence intruding into the working environment. But these extensions required a shift in the emphasis from the particular act and its tendency to forward the work to its part as a factor in the general working environment. The shift involved recognition that the environment includes associations as well as conditions, and that associations include the faults and derelictions of human beings as well as their virtues and obediences. Men do not discard their personal qualities when they go to work. Into the job they carry their intelligence, skill, habits of care and rectitude. Just as inevitably they take along also their tendencies to carelessness and camaraderie, as well as emotional make-up. In bringing men together work brings these qualities together, causes frictions between them, creates occasions for lapses into carelessness, and for fun making and emotional flare-up. Work could not go on if men became automatons repressed in every natural expression. "Old Man River" is a part of loading steamboats. These expressions of human nature are incidents inseparable from working together. They involve risks of injury and these risks are inherent in the working environment. * * * This view recognizes that work places men under strains and fatigue from human and mechanical impacts, creating frictions which explode in myriads of ways, only some of which are immediately relevant to their tasks. Personal animosities are created by working together on the assembly line or in traffic. Others initiated outside the job are magnified to the breaking point by its compelled contacts. No worker is immune to these pressures and impacts upon temperament. They accumulate and explode over incidents trivial and important, personal and official. But the explosion point is merely the culmination of the antecedent pressures. That it is not relevant to the immediate task, involves a lapse from duty, or contains an element of volition or illegality does not disconnect it from them nor nullify their causal effect in producing its injurious consequences. Any other view would reintroduce the conceptions of contributory fault, action in the line of duty, nonaccidental character of voluntary conduct, and independent, intervening cause as applied in tort law, which it was the purpose of the statute to discard. It would require the application of different basic tests of liability for injuries caused by volitional conduct of the claimant and those resulting from negligent action, mechanical causes and the volitional activities of others.

The limitation, of course, is that the accumulated pressures must be attributable in substantial part to the working environment. This implies that their causal effect shall not be overpowered and nullified by influences originating entirely outside the working relation and not substantially magnified by it. Whether such influences have annulling effect upon those of the environment ordinarily is the crucial issue. * * *

It follows that the judgment must be affirmed. Taking full account not only of the findings but of all the evidence, it is clear that the entire sequence of incidents occurred not only while the claimant and his assailant were at work, but as a natural and normal product of working together. The record shows no private or personal relations between them. The discussion about watches, if that were material as contended by appellant, was carried on in the normal intercourse of employee with employee. It was not relevant to any particular duty; neither was it an interruption or a departure from the work, much less an "independent, intervening agency." If "personal," it was one of those personal things which employees constantly do, not only while, but because they are working together. All this may be said also concerning the use of the respective appellations of "Shorty" and "Skinny," both in the banter and in the official acts of giving and receiving orders. The claimant may have been at fault in resenting his superior's ridicule, expressed perhaps as much in tone as in language, by repeated use of the diminutive nickname, both personally and officially. His remonstrance should have ended the practice. When it did not, the fighting word sprang to the lips, and the superior employee responded with his fist. Claimant may have been at fault, but he was the aggressor neither in the banter nor in the physical encounter. We do not put the case on the narrow ground that Downey was Bridges' superior and as such owed him the duty not to belittle him or ridicule his physical stature. Fault there was on both sides, the graver perhaps in Downey for the fact that he was the superior and knew not when to stop. But compensability in these circumstances is not a matter of comparative fault. The entire sequence of events arose out of the fact that the work of the participants brought them together and created the relations and conditions which resulted in the clash. Nothing in the record shows that Bridges was intoxicated or had any intention to injure himself or another. He was guilty at most of contributory fault. But it was not sufficient, within either the statutory language or the principle of our previous decisions, to constitute a departure from the work, a matter *purely* personal, or a disconnecting intervening agency. * * *

The judgment is affirmed.

Notes

1. Where an assault arises out of a dispute among co-workers concerning the performance of the employer's work, the working tools, the protection of the employer's property, the collection of money owed the employer,

or some other aspect of the employment, compensation is generally awarded. See, e.g., State v. Purmort, 143 Ga.App. 269, 238 S.E.2d 268 (1977) (fight arose out of a dispute as to method of doing work); and Alpine Roofing Co. v. Dalton, 36 Colo.App. 315, 539 P.2d 487 (1975) (following a dispute over his paycheck, claimant was dismissed immediately; while still on the premises he was assaulted following a heated exchange with his foreman; compensation awarded).

2. Many decisions also award compensation for injuries suffered by workers in fights among themselves arising from disputes over non-work matters. See, Mutual Implement & Hardware Ins. Co. v. Pittman, 214 Miss. 823, 59 So.2d 547 (1952) (assault resulted from horseplay between employees; compensation awarded), noted, 1953 Wash.U.L.Q. 113; (1953) 10 Wash. & Lee L.Rev. 133; Chanin v. Western Union Telegraph Co., 271 App.Div. 763, 64 N.Y.S.2d 670 (1946) (fight resulted from bragging of pugilistic ability), noted, 45 Mich.L.Rev. 1070; Townsend Paneling, Inc. v. Butler, 247 Ark. 818, 448 S.W.2d 347 (1969) (worker assaulted for refusal to make a bet with co-worker); De Nardis v. Stevens Const. Co., 72 N.J.Super. 395, 178 A.2d 354 (1962) (worker injured in fight in dispute over an umbrella); and Keyhea v. Woodard–Walker Lumber Co., 147 So. 830 (La.App.1933) (families of two workers resided in employer's mill quarters; one worker killed another over attentions the decedent had paid the assailant's wife; compensation awarded on the ground that the employees' being constantly thrown together in employment aggravated personal enmity).

3. Many courts deny compensation for injuries caused by a "personal" dispute even though the claimant's employment brought the disputatious parties into contact. See, e.g., , Malco, Inc. v. Industrial Comm., 65 Ill.2d 426, 3 Ill.Dec. 448, 358 N.E.2d 1133 (1976) (assault arose out of dispute over paycheck "pool" or "poker"; compensation denied although the plaintiff was actively at work when assaulted); Nash–Kelvinator Corp. v. Industrial Comm., 266 Wis. 81, 62 N.W.2d 567 (1954) (claimant who signed what was believed to be a communist inspired peace petition was battered by fellow workers; compensation denied); Birchett v. Tuf–Nut Garment Mfg. Co., 205 Ark. 483, 169 S.W.2d 574 (1943) (employee assaulted when she seized newspaper belonging to co-worker; court conceded plausibility of reasoning in *Cardillo,* but denied its application to the facts involved and denied compensation); Texas Indem. Ins. Co. v. Cheely, 232 S.W.2d 124 (Tex.Civ. App.1950) (false report on one worker of insults allegedly made by another worker led to assault; compensation denied on ground that attack was "personally" motivated), and, Scholtzhauer v. C. & L. Lunch Co., 233 N.Y. 12, 134 N.E. 701 (1922) (waitress shot when she sharply declined a co-worker's request for a date; compensation denied).

4. The statutes of several states (e.g. Alabama, Georgia, Oregon, Pennsylvania, Texas, and Wyoming) contain special assault provisions that commonly *exclude* "injuries caused by the act of a third person or fellow employee intended to injure the employee for reasons personal to him, and not directed against him as an employee or because of his employment." See, e.g., Kessen v. Boise Cascade Corp., 71 Or.App. 545, 693 P.2d 52 (1984) (applying Oregon statute). In other states (e.g. Arizona, Hawaii, Idaho, North Dakota, Utah, Vermont, and the Longshoremen's Harbor Workers Act), the statutes *include* "an injury caused by the willful act of a third

person directed against the employee because of his employment." See, e.g., Lippmann v. North Dakota Workmen's Comp. Bureau, 79 N.D. 248, 55 N.W.2d 453 (1952) (second type of statute above regarded as intended to enlarge coverage of Act).

5. Initially, most courts denied compensation to any claimant who was the "aggressor" in a fight among employees even in the absence of any special statutory provision. Horvath v. La Fond, 305 Mich. 69, 8 N.W.2d 915 (1943) (decedent attacked fellow worker in an altercation related solely to employer's business; aggression made the fight personal and severed any causal relation with employment; compensation denied); and Staten v. Long Turner Const. Co., 185 S.W.2d 375 (Mo.App.1945) (aggressive act regarded as conduct outside the course of employment; compensation denied). These decisions have been criticized as improperly re-injecting employee fault into compensation disputes and later decisions tend to reject the aggressor doctrine and permit compensation. See, e.g., State Compensation Ins. Fund v. Industrial Accident Comm., 38 Cal.2d 659, 242 P.2d 311 (1952), Southern Cotton Oil Division v. Childress, 377 S.W. 2d 167 (Ark. 1964)(compensation paid in regard to worker killed in horseplay accident when an air hose thrust into his mouth burst his lungs; who was instigator held to be irrelevant), and Jolly v. Jesco, Inc., 271 Minn. 333, 135 N.W.2d 746 (1965) (dispute over method of doing work; compensation awarded). See also Ringier America v. Combs, 41 Ark.App. 47, 849 S.W.2d 1, 2 (Ark.App.1993) (noting a trend toward abolishing the aggressor doctrine and also noting that "an injury to a non-participating victim of horseplay is compensable."). 1 A. Larson, Workmen's Compensation (1991) § 11.15(c), observes that the abolition of the aggressor doctrine is "one of the most rapid * * * reversals in the volatile history of compensation law." Nevertheless, a few jurisdictions continue to deny benefits to aggressors in work-related fights. See, e.g., Johnson v. Nanias (Bridal Originals), 738 S.W.2d 164 (Mo.App.1987) and Rorie v. Holly Farms Poultry Co., 306 N.C. 706, 295 S.E.2d 458 (1982).

6. The statutes of many states, the Longshoreman's Act, and the United States Employees Compensation Act exclude injuries resulting from "willful intention to injure another" or from "willful misconduct." As commonly applied, these provisions require more aggression than mere verbal abuse, an impulsive punch, simply "being to blame," and other forms of minor misconduct by the injured employee. One court justified awarding compensation, saying: "Arguments, altercations and assaults are as inevitable as they are undesirable. Where they arise out of the employment, they may properly be regarded as an employment hazard. Such actions are misconduct but are not serious misconduct unless of a grave and aggravated character. Such actions are not willful misconduct unless deliberate or premeditated." Newell v. Moreau, 94 N.H. 439, 445, 55 A.2d 476, 481 (1947). See also Youmans v. Coastal Petroleum Co., 333 S.C. 195, 508 S.E.2d 43 (S.C.App.1998)(a finding that claimant spontaneously struck a supervisor who addressed him angrily with a racial slur did not barred claimant's recovery for injuries suffered in ensuing fight); In re Tripp's Case, 355 Mass. 515, 246 N.E.2d 449 (1969) (victim struck first blow in fight related to employment; held not to be disqualifying "serious and willful misconduct"); and Velotta v. Liberty Mut. Ins. Co., 241 La. 814, 132 So.2d 51 (1961)

(claimant hurled a pair of trousers at co-worker; took a serious beating in return; "aggressor doctrine" repudiated).

IN RE QUESTION SUBMITTED BY THE UNITED STATES COURT OF APPEALS FOR THE TENTH CIRCUIT v. MARTIN MARIETTA CORPORATION

Supreme Court of Colorado, En Banc, 1988.
759 P.2d 17.

VOLLACK, JUSTICE.

* * *

I.

In March 1983 Deborah Tolbert was employed by Martin Marietta as an entry level professional. Arthur Martinez was a janitor, a coemployee at Martin Marietta. Tolbert was on her way to lunch in the company cafeteria on the Martin Marietta premises when she was attacked and raped by Martinez.

[The sole issue considered here is whether Tolbert's tort suit against her employer is barred by the workers' compensation statute.]

[T]he narrow issue of law presented here is whether the injury suffered by Tolbert "arose out of and in the course of" her employment, . . .

* * *

The phrases "arising out of" and "in the course of" found in section 8–52–102(1)(c) are not synonymous, and a claimant must prove both requirements. *Industrial Comm'n v. London & Lancashire Indem. Co.,* 135 Colo. 372, 376, 311 P.2d 705, 707 (1957). The parties do not dispute that this incident occurred "in the course of" Tolbert's employment with Martin Marietta, so "arising out of" is the phrase at issue here. . . .

An accident "arises out of" employment when there is a causal connection between the work conditions and the injury. . . . For an injury to be compensable under the Act, there must be a sufficient nexus between the employment and the injury. . . . The determination of whether an employee's injuries arose out of an employment relationship depends largely on the facts presented in a particular case. . . . "The totality of the circumstances must be examined in each case to see whether there is a sufficient nexus between the employment and the injury." *City & County of Denver School Dist. No. 1 v. Industrial Comm'n,* 196 Colo. 131, 133, 581 P.2d 1162, 1163 (1978); . . .

This nexus or causality requirement is subject to more than one definition. As the federal district court stated, the phrase "arising out of" has been interpreted "in a number of different ways" in various jurisdictions which "have developed different tests of causality." . . . The court also rested its analysis on the observation that "Colorado courts have not consistently applied any single test to determine whether an assault by a co-employee arises out of the employment relationship." . . . The issue becomes what test or standard to apply to this "arising out of" language of the Act.

This court has most frequently used the positional-risk or "but for" standard to define the "arising out of" language.[4]

> An important and growing number of courts are accepting the full implications of the positional-risk test: An injury *arises out of* the employment if it would not have occurred *but for* the fact that the conditions and obligations of the employment placed claimant in the position where he was injured. . . . This theory supports compensation, for example, in cases of stray bullets, roving lunatics, and other situations in which the only connection of the employment with the injury is that its obligations placed the employee in the particular place at the particular time when he was injured by some neutral force, meaning by "neutral" neither personal to the claimant nor distinctly associated with the employment.

1 Larson, *Workmen's Compensation Law* § 6.50, at 3–6 (1985) (emphasis in original) (hereinafter 1 Larson); *Aetna Life Ins. Co. v. Industrial Comm'n,* 81 Colo. 233, 254 P. 995 (1927) (first application of the positional-risk doctrine in Colorado); . . . In *Aetna,* we used this definition of the positional-risk test:

> [W]hen one in the course of his employment is reasonably required to be at a particular place at a particular time and there meets with *an accident,* although one *which any other person then and there present would have met with irrespective of his employment,* that accident is one "arising out of" the employment of the person so injured.

81 Colo. at 236, 254 P.2d at 996 (emphasis added).

* * *

"Cognizant of the Act's broad remedial objective, the Colorado courts have interpreted this standard of compensation to include injuries arising from the intentional acts of a co-employee, as long as the requisite degree of job relatedness is present." *Bennett v. Furr's Cafeterias, Inc.,* 549 F.Supp. 887, 890 (D.Colo.1982) (footnote omitted). The

---

4. Five different tests can be used in this analysis: peculiar-risk doctrine, increased-risk doctrine, actual-risk doctrine, positional-risk doctrine, and the proximate cause test. 1 Larson §§ 6.00, 6.20 to .60, at 3–1, 3–4 to–11. Prior to *Aetna,* Colorado courts have also applied the "increased-risk" test of causality, which calls for compensation *only if* the claimant's employment increased the claimant's risk of injury above the risk to which the general public is exposed. *See Industrial Comm'n v. Ernest Irvine, Inc.,* 72 Colo. 573, 212 P. 829 (1923). The hazard, out of which arose the injury which caused the death of Lewis, was not common to the general public; the injury would not have occurred but for his employment, and the act being performed by him was within the scope of his duties. He was doing the duty which he was employed to perform, hence received the injury "in the course of" the employment; a reasonable person familiar with the entire transaction on that evening would have contemplated the result as probable from the exposure occasioned by the nature of the employment, hence the injury "arose out of" the employment.

Id. at 580, 212 P. at 832.

positional-risk test, as applied by this court in the past, is the appropriate test in assessing the case before us now. The positional-risk test is formulated to assess whether there is a sufficient relationship between the employment and the injury to justify compensation under the Act. * * * By reviewing the totality of the circumstances using this test, the act's intentional or non-intentional character alone is not dispositive. Rather, the "neutral force" provides the necessary distinction between conflicts imported into the work place from outside work, as opposed to a neutral force which would have happened to the employee who happened to be in that particular place at that particular time.

* * *

[W]e must determine whether Tolbert's injuries "arose out of" her employment for purposes of the Workmen's Compensation Act, keeping in mind that there must be a causal connection between the work conditions and the injury. "The expression 'arising out of' refers to the *origin* or *cause* of the injury." *Deterts v. Times Pub. Co.,* 38 Colo.App. 48, 51, 552 P.2d 1033, 1036 (1976) (emphasis in original). To arise out of employment, however, an injury "need not always be a direct result of an employment-related cause." *Irwin v. Industrial Comm'n,* 695 P.2d 763, 765 (Colo.App.1984). This "but for" test supports compensation in cases in which "the only connection of the employment with the injury is that its obligations placed the employee in the particular place at the particular time when he was injured by some neutral force." 1 Larson § 6.50, at 3–6. A neutral force is one which is not personal to the victim, nor distinctly associated with the employment. *Id.*

Determination of the Act's coverage of assaults by co-workers requires the positional-risk analysis, as earlier adopted by this court in *Aetna.* This interpretation of the Act is supported by the rationale that "[i]nstead of being so placed by his duties as to receive the impact of a random bullet or a falling cornice, the claimant is so placed as to receive the impact of his co-worker's personality." 1 Larson § 11.16(a), at 3–239. Applying the positional-risk doctrine, the test is whether the employee, in the course of her employment, was reasonably required to be at a particular place at a particular time and there met with a "neutral force", meaning that any other person then and there present would have met with attack. *Aetna,* 81 Colo. at 235–36, 254 P.2d at 996. The "only connection" required between the employment and the injury is that the job "placed the employee in the particular *place* at the particular *time* when [s]he was injured by some *neutral force,* meaning by 'neutral' neither personal to the claimant nor distinctly associated with the employment." 1 Larson § 6.50, at 3–6 (emphasis added).

A.

Does the Workmen's Compensation Act of Colorado, . . . provide [a] remedy for an employee against her employer:

(1) for injuries resulting from a sexual assault by a co-worker which was motivated by considerations neither personal to the injured employee nor distinctly associated with the employment?

As to the time element, it is evident that Tolbert's work obligations caused her to be present on the grounds of Martin Marietta. The mere fact that an employee is on lunch hour does not prohibit worker's compensation coverage, as long as the incident occurred within a time during which the worker is employed. * * *

The employee need not necessarily be engaged in the actual performance of work at the moment of injury in order to receive compensation. *University of Denver v. Nemeth,* 127 Colo. 385, 257 P.2d 423 (1953). Tolbert was also at a place where she "may reasonably be," on the premises of Martin Marietta during her lunch hour. Finally, she was doing what she "may reasonably do": walking to the company cafeteria.

> It arises out of the employment if it is connected with the nature, *conditions, operations or incidents of the employment....* "[N]o break in the employment is caused by the mere fact that the workman is ministering to his personal comforts or necessities, as by warming himself, or seeking shelter, or by leaving his work to relieve nature, or to procure drink, refreshments, food, or fresh air, or to rest in the shade."

Golden Cycle Corp., 126 Colo. at 71–72, 246 P.2d at 904 (quoting 1 Honnold, Workmen's Compensation § 111, at 382) (emphasis added). An employee need not necessarily be engaged in the actual performance of work at the moment of the injury. *Packaging Corp. v. Roberts,* 169 Colo. 316, 455 P.2d 652 (1969). Clearly, this case meets the time requirement.

B.

The "place" element requires that the injury have occurred at a place where the worker may reasonably be. "Under even the broadest rule, the but-for test, it must be emphasized that the test is not 'but for the bare existence of the employment,' but rather 'but for the conditions and obligations of the employment.'" 1 Larson § 11.22, at 3–261. Tolbert's presence in the Martin Marietta building where the attack took place was a direct result of her employment. "But for" the conditions and obligations of her employment with Martin Marietta—being at work on the day in question and using the cafeteria provided by her employer—Tolbert would not have been present at this particular location, traveling to the company cafeteria, which caused her to be vulnerable to her attacker. An employee walking from a work station to the employer cafeteria is certainly in a place where a worker "may reasonably be at the time." The place requirement, therefore, is met.

C.

The third requirement is that the injury must have been caused by a neutral force.

Wilful assaults upon the claimant, like injuries generally, can be divided into *three categories:* those that have some *inherent connection with the employment,* those that are *inherently private,* and those that are neither, and may therefore be called *"neutral."*

1 Larson § 11.31, at 3–275 (emphasis added). The first category, assaults which have an inherent connection with employment, are those in which a dispute arises out of "enforced contacts" which result from the duties of the job. 1 Larson § 11.22, at 3–261. The second category, assaults which are inherently private, are those in which " 'the animosity or dispute that culminates in an assault is imported into the employment from claimant's domestic or private life, and is not exacerbated by the employment.' " *Velasquez v. Industrial Comm'n,* 41 Colo.App. 201, 203, 581 P.2d 748, 749 (1978) (quoting 1 Larson § 11.21). Such assaults do " 'not arise out of the employment under any test.' "[9]*Id.*

The third category of neutral assaults includes "assaults which are in essence equivalent to blind or irrational forces, such as attacks by lunatics, drunks, small children, and other irresponsibles; completely unexplained assaults; and assaults by mistake." 1 Larson § 11.31, at 3–275. The characteristic of a neutral or unexplained assault is that "[n]othing connects it with the victim privately; neither can it be shown to have had a specific employment origin." *Id.* at 3–287. If an employee is exposed to the unexplained assault "because he is discharging his duties at that time and place," then the injuries are generally compensable.[10] *Id.* * * *

The parties agree that there was no personal or private motivation for Martinez' attack and rape of Tolbert. . . . The rape was not directly associated with Tolbert's employment and there was no indication that Martinez had specifically selected Tolbert as a victim. Prior to the assault, Tolbert and Martinez "had only the slightest contacts, and those were only at Martin Marietta." . . . The federal district court held: "There is nothing to indicate that any other woman—whether or not a Martin employee—who happened to be in the same area at the time of the attack would not have become the victim." . . .

The parties agree that Tolbert was not on duty when attacked; she was on her lunch hour. She was not at her assigned work place, nor was

9. Inherently private assaults typically involve disputes over spouses. Compensation is usually denied "when the fight was caused by a quarrel between the employee's wives, when the argument was concerned with the assailant's misconduct with another employee's wife, or the employee's misconduct with the assailant's wife, and when the assault was occasioned by a remark to the co-employee's wife." 1 Larson § 11.21, at 3–254 to–255 (footnotes omitted).

10. Larson explains the concept of a neutral attack with this analogy:

There is a marked distinction between the holdup in which the robber says to himself, "I am going to track down Henry Davis wherever he may be and steal the gold watch which I know he has," and the holdup in which the robber says, "I am going to rob whoever happens to be on duty as night watchman at the Consolidated Lumber Company, or whoever happens to come down the dark, hidden path from the factory to the rear gate." The latter is not really personal to this victim at all.

1 Larson § 11.11(b), at 3–178 to–179 (footnotes omitted).

she at a place where her job expressly required her to be at that moment. ... Tolbert was on Martin Marietta premises walking from her work station to the employee cafeteria at the time of her assault. The parties agree that there are no facts or circumstances "tending to show that the attack was directed against [Tolbert] as opposed to any other woman who might have been present at the place and time." ... The undisputed facts and circumstances surrounding this attack meet the definition of a "neutral" attack.

This distinction is supported by the denial of compensation in *Velasquez v. Industrial Commission,* 41 Colo.App. 201, 581 P.2d 748 (1978). In *Velasquez,* the court of appeals upheld the commission's denial of compensation to two claimants shot by a co-employee whose anger was specifically directed at them. "[T]he shooting could have happened at any other time or place, wherever and whenever, the co-employee happened to find the petitioners." 41 Colo.App. at 202, 581 P.2d at 749; *see also Irwin v. Industrial Comm'n,* 695 P.2d at 766. *Compare In re McLaughlin,* 728 P.2d 337, 340 (Colo.App.1986) (An employee's widow is entitled to benefits when her husband and a co-worker were killed by the co-worker's husband. "His employment there created and sustained the co-worker relationship" and the attack was not imported to work from the employee's private life. *Id.*).

* * *

Because the time and place requirements are established, and the assault was "neutral" in the sense that it was not specific to Tolbert, we conclude that the particular facts of this case establish that this injury arose out of Ms. Tolbert's employment.

Notes

Knox v. Combined Insurance Company of American (Me.1988) 542 A.2d 363 held that mental injuries suffered by a worker as a result of sexual assaults and harassments perpetrated upon her by a supervisor could be compensable under the Maine workers' compensation act. But contrast Byrd v. Richardson–Greenshields Securities, Inc. (Fla.1989) 552 So.2d 1099, holding that employees with similar complaints as in *Knox* could sue the employer in tort. See chapter 11, infra.

SECTION 6. INJURIES CAUSED BY ON THE JOB ASSAULTS BY NON CO–WORKERS

WEISS v. CITY OF MILWAUKEE

Supreme Court of Wisconsin, 1997.
208 Wis.2d 95, 559 N.W.2d 588.

ANN WALSH BRADLEY, JUSTICE.

Holly Lynn Weiss seeks review of an unpublished court of appeals decision which affirmed a summary judgment dismissal of her complaint against the defendants, the City of Milwaukee and its employee, Yvette

Marchan (together, "the City"). Weiss argues that the court of appeals erred in determining that the Workers' Compensation Act (WCA) provides the exclusive remedy for her claim of emotional distress resulting from the City's disclosure of her home address and telephone number to her abusive former spouse. Because we conclude that Weiss has alleged injuries covered by the Worker's Compensation Act, and that the exclusive remedy provision of the WCA precludes her common law action against the defendants for negligent infliction of emotional distress, we affirm the decision of the court of appeals.

The relevant facts are not in dispute. On July 31, 1990, Weiss obtained a temporary restraining order against her abusive husband, Osama Abughanim. Shortly thereafter, she commenced a divorce action. Abughanim, forced to vacate the marital residence, began a campaign of harassing telephone calls and personal visits during which he would threaten the lives of Weiss and their two children. In October 1990, Weiss vacated the residence and moved in with her parents in order to escape her husband's harassment. Abughanim persisted in making threatening telephone calls, both to Weiss's parents' residence and to her place of employment. The calls to Weiss's employer were of such frequency that they resulted in her termination in December 1990.

In February 1991, Weiss obtained employment with the City of Milwaukee as an engineering technician. As an employee, she was required to establish residence in Milwaukee within one month of hiring. She therefore moved from her parents' residence in Waukesha County to an apartment located in Milwaukee. At that time, Abughanim did not know Weiss's Milwaukee address or telephone number.

Weiss was instructed by her supervisor to provide her address and telephone number to the City's payroll department. She contacted the payroll department, explained that she had an abusive former husband, and expressed her desire that her residential information remain confidential. A City payroll clerk assured Weiss that the City had a policy prohibiting the disclosure of such employee information to private individuals. Relying on the clerk's assurance, Weiss provided her address and telephone number to the payroll department.

On July 10, 1991, Abughanim contacted the City's Department of Employee Relations and spoke with Sheila Bowle, an employee of the department. Abughanim falsely represented to Bowle that he was calling on behalf of a bank and needed to confirm Weiss's address and telephone number for credit purposes. Bowle relayed the bogus inquiry to her supervisor, Yvette Marchan, who, without attempting to verify Abughanim's claimed credentials, authorized Bowle to disclose Weiss's residential information.

By this ruse, Abughanim obtained Weiss's home address and telephone number. Thereafter, Abughanim regularly telephoned Weiss at work to inform her that he now knew her home address and telephone number, and that he would kill her and their two children. Her awareness that Abughanim knew her address, and her then existing financial inability to change her residence, caused Weiss severe emotional distress arising from fear for her safety and that of their two children.

Weiss commenced a common law action in the circuit court against the City to recover damages for negligent infliction of emotional distress arising from the City's unwitting disclosure to Abughanim. The City filed a motion for summary judgment, asserting that the WCA covered Weiss's injuries, and the statute's exclusive remedy provision therefore barred Weiss's suit. The City also maintained that it had no duty to keep confidential Weiss's home address and telephone number, because such information was available to the public pursuant to Wisconsin's open records law.

The circuit court granted the City's motion for summary judgment, dismissing Weiss's complaint. . . . The court of appeals affirmed [Ed., on grounds that Weiss's] common law negligence action against the City was barred by the statute's exclusive remedy provision, Wis.Stat. s 102.03(2). . . .

We have repeatedly stated that the provisions of Chapter 102 must be liberally construed to effectuate the WCA's goal of compensating injured workers. * * * However, courts must also exercise care to avoid upsetting the balance of interests achieved by the WCA. . . .

Generally, an employer's obligation to pay worker's compensation accrues under Chapter 102 when all of the following conditions are present: 1) the employee sustains an injury; 2) at the time of the injury, both the employer and the employee are subject to the provisions of the WCA; 3) at the time of the injury, the employee is performing service growing out of and incidental to his or her employment; 4) the injury is not intentionally self-inflicted; and 5) the accident or disease causing injury arises out of the employment. Wis.Stat. ss 102.03(1)(a)-(e). For purposes of our review of summary judgment in this case, our inquiry is limited to determining whether, at the time of her injury, Weiss was performing service growing out of and incidental to her employment, and whether the accident causing injury arose out of her employment.

It is well settled that when the s 102.03(1) conditions of liability for worker's compensation are satisfied, the exclusive remedy provision, s 102.03(2), precludes an injured employee from maintaining a negligence action against his or her employer and fellow employees. . . . Jenson, 161 Wis.2d at 263, 468 N.W.2d 1 (plaintiff's "common law action is barred by the exclusivity provisions if she in all other respects is entitled to recovery under the Act"). Thus, Weiss's common law action against the City is barred if her alleged injuries are covered by Chapter 102.

The City asserts that Weiss meets each of the five criteria set out in ss 102.03(1)(a)-(e), and that the remedy for her injuries is therefore solely that which is provided under the WCA. [Ed., material from an omitted footnote states: "The legal positions of the employer and employee in this instance are the reverse of those found in many worker's compensation cases. Often it is the employer who resists coverage under the WCA, and the employee who desires such coverage. As Weiss candidly admits, she has filed a common law action because she feels that a recovery under the WCA would be inadequate compared to a jury award on her tort claim. Conversely, the City invokes the WCA in this instance in order to limit Weiss's potential recovery for its allegedly wrongful disclosure of her residential information."] In attempting to establish that her injury is not covered by Chapter 102, Weiss contends that at the time she was injured, she was not performing service growing out of and incidental to her employment. She also argues that the court of appeals erred when it determined that "the incident causing the injury arose out of Weiss's employment." Weiss, slip op. at 6–7.

We deal first with Weiss's claim that her injury is not encompassed within the WCA because at the time of the injury, she was not "performing service growing out of and incidental to . . . her employment," as required by s 102.03(1)(c). In essence, Weiss's argument is that an employee cannot satisfy s 102.03(1)(c) when receiving a personal telephone call at work. We disagree.

The statutory clause "performing service growing out of and incidental to his or her employment" is used interchangeably with the phrase "course of employment." . . . Both phrases refer to the "time, place, and circumstances" under which the injury occurred. Goranson v. DILHR, 94 Wis.2d 537, 549, 289 N.W.2d 270 (1980).

An injury is said to arise in the course of the employment when it takes place within the period of the employment, at a place where the employee reasonably may be, and while he [or she] is fulfilling his [or her] duties or engaged in doing something incidental thereto. 1 The Law of Workmen's Compensation s 14.00.

There is no dispute that Weiss's alleged injury occurred within the time and place of her employment. The question is whether receiving a personal phone call at work constitutes a "circumstance" of employment. We conclude that it does. Under the liberal construction given to Chapter 102, an employee acts within the course of employment when he or she is otherwise within the time and space limits of employment, and briefly turns away from his or her work to tend to matters "necessary or convenient to his [or her] own personal health or comfort." American Motors Corp. v. Industrial Comm., 1 Wis.2d 261, 265, 83 N.W.2d 714 (1957) (citations omitted). The personal comfort doctrine does not apply, and an employee is not within the course of employment, if the "extent of the departure is so great that an intent to abandon the job temporarily may be inferred, or . . . the method chosen is so unusual and unreasonable that the conduct cannot be considered an incident of the employment." Id. Applying the doctrine to the facts of this case, we conclude that regardless of the contents of a brief personal telephone call, the act of taking such a call at work constitutes a momentary departure from work duties to attend to a matter of personal comfort. Thus, when Weiss answered the personal telephone call from Abughanim, she was engaged in an activity incidental to employment, and was therefore within the course of employment.

Weiss next contends that the accident causing her injury did not arise out of her employment. s 102.03(1)(e). Citing

Goranson and cases from other jurisdictions, Weiss asserts that where, as here, an employee is injured at work by a non-employee for purely personal reasons, the injury is noncompensable under the WCA.

We agree with Weiss that Goranson stands for the proposition that injuries sustained in an assault occurring in the course of employment are generally noncompensable under the WCA when the assailant is motivated purely by personal animus, and the employment in no way contributes to the incident. We also agree that Weiss's employment did not create the initial threat posed to her by Abughanim. We nevertheless conclude that the accident did arise out of Weiss's employment with the City, because the conditions of Weiss's employment facilitated her eventual injury.

The "arising out of" language of s 102.03(1)(e) refers to the causal origin of an employee's injury. Goranson, 94 Wis.2d at 549, 289 N.W.2d 270. However, "arising out of his or her employment" is not synonymous with the phrase "caused by the employment." Id. at 555, 289 N.W.2d 270. In interpreting s 102.03(1)(e), we have adopted the "positional risk" doctrine: [A]ccidents arise out of employment if the conditions or obligations of the employment create a zone of special danger out of which the accident causing the injury arose. Stated another way, an accident arises out of employment when by reason of employment the employee is present at a place where he is injured through the agency of a third person, an outside force, or the conditions of special danger. Id. at 555, 289 N.W.2d 270. However, when the origin of the assault is purely private and personal, and the employment in no way contributes to the incident, the positional risk doctrine does not apply. Id. at 556–57, 289 N.W.2d 270 The Law of Workmen's Compensation s 11.21(c).

For example, in Goranson, a charter bus driver was injured after he drove a group of people to Green Bay. Upon arriving in Green Bay, the driver checked into a hotel along with his passengers. Later in the evening, he leaped from his third floor hotel room onto the roof of another section of the hotel two floors below, sustaining a broken hip and other injuries. There was evidence that the driver had been drinking throughout the evening with a woman, and that he had quarreled in his hotel room with the woman just prior to jumping from the hotel window.

This court upheld a denial of worker's compensation benefits. While there was no dispute that the driver was in the course of employment at the time of injury, the court determined that the accident did not arise out of the driver's employment, because the injuring force was purely personal to him. Goranson, 94 Wis.2d at 557, 289 N.W.2d 270.

The facts of this case are distinguishable from those in Goranson. In Goranson, the bus driver's employment did not contribute to or facilitate the accident causing the injury he suffered jumping from the hotel window. In this case, however, Weiss was required to provide her residential address and telephone number to the City as a condition of employment. If Weiss had never been required to provide the information to the City, the accident would not have occurred. The City's unwitting disclosure of that information to a private individual, Weiss's abusive former husband, was an accident that led to her injury. Because a condition of her employment facilitated the accident which caused her injury, we conclude that the accident arose out of her employment. See 1 The Law of Workmen's Compensation s 11.21(c) (privately motivated assaults generally do not arise out of employment, except where the employment facilitates the assault).

Weiss cites several cases from foreign jurisdictions for the proposition that when purely private animosity manifests itself in a workplace attack, the employment connection to the injury is so minimal that worker's compensation should be denied. Monahan v. United States Check Book Co., 4 Neb.App. 227, 540 N.W.2d 380 (1995); Ross v. Mark's, Inc., 120 N.C.App. 607, 463 S.E.2d 302 (1995). In both Monahan and Ross, a non-employee attacked and killed an ex-spouse at the ex-spouse's place of employment. Worker's compensation was denied in both cases, on the ground that assaults do not arise out of employment when they involve private quarrels imported into the workplace. In neither case did the court find evidence that the employment contributed to or facilitated the attacks.

We find unpersuasive the examples of worker's compensation denials cited by Weiss. Consistent with Goranson, we are of the view that in certain situations, "an injury from an admittedly private source should be compensable because it [is] facilitated or contributed to by the employment environment." 1 The Law of Workmen's Compensation s 11.23. For example, in Carter v. Penney Tire & Recapping Co., 261 S.C. 341, 200 S.E.2d 64 (1973), the claimant had previously quarreled with Crosby, a non-employee. On the date of the assault, Crosby threatened the claimant while the latter was engaged in repairing his employer's roof. Before returning to the roof, the claimant reported the threats to his employer, who responded that the claimant would be protected and should proceed with his work. Crosby later returned and shot the claimant, inflicting grievous injuries. The South Carolina Supreme Court determined that the claimant's injuries arose out of his employment, because: the employee was required to perform his duties under circumstances where he was endangered by a peril from a source outside of and unrelated to his actual work, which peril was known to the employer and against which the employer afforded no protection or relief. Id. 200 S.E.2d at 67.

Similarly, in Raybol v. Louisiana State University, 520 So.2d 724 (La.1988), superseded by statute as stated in Guillory v. Interstate Gas Station, 653 So.2d 1152 (La.1995), the Supreme Court of Louisiana awarded worker's compensation to a dormitory worker who was assaulted at work by her estranged former boyfriend. The court concluded that the worker's injuries arose out of her employment, based in part on its determination that "the employer's custodial workers contributed to the danger of the assault by informing the assailant of the plaintiff's work location in the building and by assisting him in gaining access to her by unlocking a door to the dormitory." Id. at 727.

In California Compensation & Fire Co. v. Workmen's Compensation Appeals Bd., 68 Cal.2d 157, 65 Cal.Rptr. 155, 436 P.2d 67 (1968), a worker at a table pad manufacturer was shot and killed by her ex-husband. The worker's employment required her to visit the homes of customers in order to measure the dimensions of tables. Upon learning that the worker intended to remarry, her ex-husband rented an apartment, ordered a table pad, and requested that someone be sent to measure the table. When his ex-wife arrived at the apartment, he murdered her and then committed suicide. The supreme court of California affirmed an award of death benefits in part on the grounds that the husband's elaborate plot was facilitated by the conditions of the worker's employment. Id. at 157, 436 P.2d at 69.

Finally, in Epperson v. Industrial Commission, 26 Ariz.App. 467, 549 P.2d 247 (1976), the claimant informed a security guard at her place of employment that she was having personal difficulties with her husband and did not wish to speak to him. Her husband later appeared at the building, observed the claimant, and proceeded unimpeded past the security guard's desk to confront the plaintiff. During the course of his ensuing conversation with the claimant, the husband shot her. The Arizona court of appeals concluded that the assault did not arise out of the course of her employment. However, it intimated that a different result would have been reached had the claimant informed the security guard of her fears and the dangers posed by her husband in a manner sufficient to justify reliance on the guard's protection. Id. 549 P.2d at 250.

None of the cited cases is on all fours with the one presently before us. However, each stands for the proposition that when an attack occurs during the course of employment and arises from personal animus imported from a private relationship, the incident arises out of the claimant's employment if employment conditions have contributed to or facilitated the attack. Weiss was required to provide her residential information to the City as a condition of employment. That condition of employment facilitated the City's subsequent accidental release of the information to a private individual, Weiss's abusive former spouse. The disclosure of the residential information in turn enabled Abughanim to threaten Weiss. We therefore conclude that the accident causing Weiss's injury arose out of her employment with the City.

In summary, Weiss has alleged an emotional injury which occurred in the course of employment and was caused by an accident arising out of that employment. Accordingly, we conclude that Weiss's complaint states a claim covered under s 102.03(1) of the WCA. Because the exclusive remedy provision of the WCA, s 102.03(2), bars Weiss's common law tort action against the City, the circuit court properly granted summary judgment dismissing the complaint, and the court of appeals correctly upheld the circuit court's decision.

The decision of the court of appeals is affirmed.

Notes

1. As noted in *Weiss*, in Raybol v. Louisiana State University, 520 So.2d 724 (La.1988) the Louisiana Supreme Court held that a former boyfriend's physical attack upon a maintenance employee at the employee's job site caused a compensable injury arising out of the employment. The rationale of the decision was that the worker was "squarely in the course of employment when the attack occurred and she had not invited the attack through any willful intention to injure another." Id. at 727. Thereafter, the Louisiana legislature amended the workers' compensation statute to include this provision:

> An injury by accident should not be considered as ! ·ving arisen out of the employment and thereby not covered by the ·rovisions of this Chapter if the employer can establish that the inju. arose out of a dispute with another person or employee over matters unrelated to the injured employee's employment.

La.R.S. 23:1031(D). The Louisiana supreme court applied this provision in Guillory v. Interstate Gas Station, 653 So.2d 1152 (La.1995) to deny coverage to a worker who was shot by her estranged husband while she was on the job in a retail gasoline station. The post-*Raybol* statutory change illustrates the ultimate control legislatures possess over workers' compensation policies.

2. In Bear v. Honeywell, Inc., 468 N.W.2d 546 (Minn.1991), an employee was raped by a man to whom she had given a ride from the company parking lot. She had mistakenly believed the rapist to be a co-worker whose car would not start. The employee brought a tort action against her employer alleging negligent security. The employer raised workers' compensation exclusivity as a defense. The Minnesota supreme court categorized the cases as follows:

> Compensation cases arising from assault fall mostly into three groups. Non-compensable are cases where the assailant was motivated by personal animosity toward his victim, arising from circumstances wholly unconnected with the employment.

> In contrast and compensable are injuries resulting from assault where provocation or motivation arises solely out of the activity of the victim as an employee.

> In a middle ground are cases * * * where the assault was directed against the victim, neither "as an employee" nor for "reasons personal to him." Injuries so arising are ordinarily compensable.

Id., at 547. Into which category does *Bear* fit?

3. Where the nature of the job or the working environment increases the risk of assault by a stranger to the employment, compensation is usually awarded. See, e.g., Williams v. Duplex Metal Corp., 60 A.D.2d 741, 400 N.Y.S.2d 905 (1977) (corporation president who frequently carried home large amounts of cash due to fear of theft in work premises was shot during robbery in driveway of his home); Town of Granite v. Kidwell, 263 P.2d 184 (Okl.1953) (Town Marshall shot during discharge of duties); Vivier v. Lum-

bermen's Indemnity Exchange, 250 S.W. 417 (Tex.Com.App.1923) (watchman killed at night in course of robbery in which only his personal property was taken; not necessary that assault be directed at victim in his capacity as employee); California Compensation & Fire Co. v. Workmen's Comp. Appeals Bd., 68 Cal.2d 157, 65 Cal.Rptr. 155, 436 P.2d 67 (1968) (deceased employee was directed by her employer to do work at a residence which had been leased by the employee's estranged husband as part of the husband's scheme to get her alone in isolation; she was shot; compensation awarded); Associated Vendors, Inc. v. Industrial Comm., 45 Ill.2d 203, 258 N.E.2d 354 (1970) (worker installing vending machines in tavern assaulted); Torosian v. Nash Cab., 27 A.D.2d 767, 277 N.Y.S.2d 112 (1967) (taxi driver assaulted in dispute over fare), and Walters v. American States Insurance Company, 654 S.W.2d 423 (Tex. 1983)(death benefits paid to employee who was murdered along with his employer while the two were on an trip to the airport to pick up a client). Contrast Gallimore v. Marilyn's Shoes, 292 N.C. 399, 233 S.E.2d 529 (1977) (shoe store employee kidnapped and murdered in course of robbery of her store; unknown to assailant she carried bank deposits for employer; compensation denied).

4. Where the employment merely happens to be the place where an assailant, who is not a co-worker, makes a non-employment, personally motivated attack upon an employee, compensation is commonly denied. Rice v. Revere Copper & Brass, Inc., 186 Md. 561, 48 A.2d 166 (1946) (assailant resented deceased's alleged misconduct with women in a dwelling occupied by both); Epperson v. Industrial Comm., 26 Ariz.App. 467, 549 P.2d 247 (1976) (marital difficulties led assailant to assault his wife while she was at work; compensation denied); and Ellis v. Rose Oil Co. of Dixie, 190 So.2d 450 (Miss.1966) (employee shot by jealous husband of employee's mistress). Contrast Livingston v. Henry & Hall, 59 So.2d 892 (La.App.1952) (worker assaulted by irate husband (not fellow worker) over love affair; compensation awarded under positional risk theory). Nevertheless, if the working environment enhances the opportunity or otherwise plays a causal part in what is otherwise an entirely personal, non-employment matter, compensation is more likely to be awarded. Brookhaven Steam Laundry v. Watts, 214 Miss. 569, 59 So.2d 294 (1952) (employee formed an alleged liaison with the wife of a customer; she placed laundry on her front porch as a signal that the coast was clear; employee was killed by irate husband when the signalling system went wrong; compensation initially awarded but reversed in reconsideration) and Todd v. Easton Furniture Mfg. Co., 147 Md. 352, 128 A. 42 (1925) (night watchman murdered for personal reasons while making his rounds; compensation awarded). Contrast Andrews v. Hoss, 286 Minn. 514, 174 N.W.2d 134 (1970) (use of gun supplied by employer as instrument of personally motivated assault did not cause it to arise out of employment).

Some statutes expressly exclude personally motivated physical attacks from coverage. See, e.g., Ga.Code Ann. § 34–9–1(4) (injury "shall not include injury caused by the willful act of a third person directed on employee for reasons personal to such employee.")

5. Injuries suffered by employees as a result of disputes with noncoworkers arising out of traffic incidents and collisions are commonly compensable, if the injured employees were within the course of employment. See, e.g., Augelli v. Rolans Credit Clothing Store, 33 N.J.Super. 146, 109 A.2d 439

(1954) (anger aroused on recalling traffic dispute of four weeks earlier prompted assault) and John Hancock Trucking Co. v. Walker, 243 Miss. 487, 138 So.2d 478 (1962).

6. If the motive for the assault can be attributed in substantial part to the employment, compensation is generally awarded despite any exacerbation by personal animosity. See, e.g., Brewster Motor Co. v. Industrial Comm., 36 Ill.2d 443, 223 N.E.2d 131 (1967) (auto salesman directed by sales prospect to bring truck to prospect's residence as excuse for opportunity to kill him over imagined romance with wife) and Crowder v. State Comp. Com'r, 115 W.Va. 12, 174 S.E. 480 (1934) (attendant at filling station left open a previously locked toilet in order to store his personal belongings; assaulted by next door neighbor who was incensed at violation of privacy).

7. Occasionally, an employee is battered by a still inflamed adversary sometime after the initial work connected dispute occurred. The mere intervention of a cooling off period does not break the causal relationship (i.e. "arising out of") with the employment, if it truly existed. See, e.g., Ward v. Typhoon Air Conditioning Co., 27 A.D.2d 785, 277 N.Y.S.2d 315 (1967); and Augelli v. Rolans Credit Clothing Store, 33 N.J.Super. 146, 109 A.2d 439 (1954) (claimant had traffic dispute with apparent stranger on the highway; in chance encounter five weeks later in the employer's plant the stranger gave employee a sound thrashing; compensation awarded).

8. Attacks by strangers, children, and insane co-workers, mistaken attacks, and other neutral risks associated neither with the employer's business nor with the employee's personal life, are often treated in line with the prevailing positional risk or street risk doctrine. Compare Belden Hotel Co. v. Industrial Comm., 44 Ill.2d 253, 255 N.E.2d 439 (1970) (shot by insanely jealous husband of co-employee; no basis for jealousy; compensation denied) with Mayo v. Safeway Stores, Inc., 93 Idaho 161, 457 P.2d 400 (1969) (attack by an apparently sane man but for no rational reason; positional risk doctrine applied to award compensation). Finally, what about completely unexplained attacks? Should these be regarded as arising out of the employment just as unexplained falls are usually so regarded? See, e.g., C.A. Dunham Co. v. Industrial Comm., 16 Ill.2d 102, 156 N.E.2d 560 (1959) (traveling employee on business trip killed when bomb planted in plane exploded, compensation awarded).

SECTION 7. INJURIES SUFFERED BY EMPLOYEES WHILE ATTEMPTING RESCUES

CHECKER TAXI CO. INC. v. INDUSTRIAL COMM.

Supreme Court of Illinois, 1965.
33 Ill.2d 264, 211 N.E.2d 273.

MR. JUSTICE SOLFISBURG delivered the opinion of the court:

This appeal is from an order of the former superior court of Cook County affirming an award entered by the Industrial Commission in favor of Lawrence H. Boyd against the Checker Taxi Company, Inc., his employer. The arbitrator found that the employee's injury arose out of and in the course of the employment, made an award for temporary total disability and an award of 47 weeks for 20% loss of use of the right arm, and medical and hospital expenses. Upon review the Commission confirmed the award of the arbitrator. * * *

The injury occurred on March 29, 1961, when Lawrence H. Boyd, a driver for the Checker Taxi Company, Inc., was operating his cab in the vicinity of 51st Street and Cottage Avenue in the city of Chicago. The employee testified, in essence, that he was stopped for a light when he saw two young white boys walking across the street in a northerly direction and that they passed three older colored boys on the corner, who began beating them. One of the white boys broke away and ran towards the cab. He stopped the cab and the boy had his hand on the right rear door of the cab when two of the colored boys ran over and grabbed him so that he couldn't get into the cab. Boyd got out of the cab, tried to push the one boy who had his hand on the cab behind him and to separate the fighting boys. The colored boys ran, but one stopped about 50 feet away and fired two shots at him—one hit him in the left hand and the other in the chest. Thereafter he drove his cab to a hospital where he was treated for his wounds.

Jesse Page, an eyewitness, testified on behalf of the employer, corroborating the testimony as to the shooting, but stating that he did not see either of the white boys approaching the cab. Three police officers also testified as to statements made by Boyd after the injury in which he did not state the details regarding the boy approaching his cab.

It is the contention of the employer that the employee must prove that the accident arose out of and in the course of his employment; that the injury was caused by the nature of his employment; and that the employer is not liable for compensation when the employee voluntarily exposes himself to a danger that is not incident to his employment.

Employee insists that his injury was sustained while going to the assistance of a passenger and that, even if the boy did not attempt to enter the cab, the injury is still compensable; and that the findings of the Industrial Commission are not against the manifest weight of the evidence.

In the case of Puttkammer v. Industrial Com., 371 Ill. 497, the employee, a driver of a coal truck, was on his way back to the coal yard when he came upon two automobiles which had collided. He stopped his truck, went over to one of the damaged cars and picked up an injured child. He was killed while walking back to his truck, when another auto struck one of the damaged cars, causing it to hit him. In awarding compensation to his widow under the Workmen's Compensation Act, the court considered the contention that the accident did not arise out of and in the course of the employment, and stated as follows:

> "If Puttkammer suffered an injury while driving, or while doing any act in connection with the use of his truck in the street, or any act that can reasonably and fairly be said to be incidental to his employment as a truck driver, his injury and death are compensable. The question is whether he broke the thread or chain of his

employment and went outside the course of that employment if, as plaintiffs in error assume from the facts stipulated, he went to aid those injured in the damaged automobiles and collision. Plaintiffs in error say the facts are equally applicable to an intention to give aid or to an intention to see whether his way was clear and that speculation as to what his real intention was cannot be resorted to to determine his purpose. In the view we take it is immaterial whether he went to the damaged cars for the one or for the other purpose. Neither would take him out of the course of his employment. Giving aid to an injured child on the highway is just as natural and is just as much to be expected from a driver of another vehicle as stopping to water horses drawing his dray or stopping to get liquid refreshment for himself." 371 Ill. at 503.

The doctrine of the *Puttkammer* case has been considered and approved by the Illinois courts, (Olson Drilling Co. v. Industrial Com., 386 Ill. 402; Boalbey v. Smith, 339 Ill.App. 466,) and the United States Supreme Court. O'Leary v. Brown–Pacific–Maxon, Inc., 340 U.S. 504, 95 L.Ed. 483.

The findings of the Industrial Commission are clearly not against the manifest weight of the evidence, but are amply supported by the record. Although there is some negative evidence contradicting employee's contention that one of the boys was attempting to become a passenger in the cab, in the light of the foregoing cases the injury received was nevertheless compensable under the Workmen's Compensation Act. * * *

Notes

1. Injuries suffered by an employee in attempting to rescue a fellow worker, a customer, or a passenger, or to preserve the employer's property are routinely compensated. Moreover, an injury suffered in an employee's attempt to rescue a stranger is compensable if the employer would be subjected to possible liability if the stranger were injured. Ocean Accident & Guarantee Corp., Ltd. v. Industrial Acc. Comm., 180 Cal. 389, 182 P. 35 (1919); Reilly v. Weber Engineering Co., 107 N.J.Super. 254, 258 A.2d 36 (1969) (death from attempt to rescue a stranger was held to be compensable under the positional risk theory where the duties brought the worker to the spot where the attempted rescue occurred); Matter of Babington v. Yellow Taxi Corp., 250 N.Y. 14, 164 N.E. 726 (1928) (policeman leaped on taxi driven by the decedent and directed him to pursue another car; driver killed in resulting collision; compensation awarded from taxi company); and O'Leary v. Brown–Pacific–Maxon, Inc., 340 U.S. 504, 71 S.Ct. 470, 95 L.Ed. 483 (1951) (employer maintained recreation center on island of Guam; employee drowned while attempting to rescue a swimmer in difficulty; compensation awarded).

2. Some decisions compensate injuries incurred in a rescue attempt on the basis that rescues are expectable human responses to the perception that someone needs help. See, e.g., D.L. Cullifer and Son, Inc. v. Martinez, 572 So.2d 1360 (Fla.1990) (compensation awarded fruitpickers injured while

helping push disabled vehicle of passing motorist from its position of imminent hazard to motoring public; response to emergency is incidental to employment), and Edwards v. Louisiana Forestry Comm., 221 La. 818, 60 So.2d 449 (1952) (observer in a fire tower attempted to rescue a child attacked by dog). Other decisions compensate the rescuer on the ground that the rescue accrues good will to the employer. Compare Carey v. Stadther, 300 Minn. 88, 219 N.W.2d 76 (1974) (feed salesman met death attempting to rescue a stranger from a cesspool; compensation awarded) with Weidenbach v. Miller, 237 Minn. 278, 55 N.W.2d 289 (1952) (employer riding with employee in truck urged the latter to stop when a drowning man was seen; employee was injured in rescue attempt; compensation denied). How can the latter decision be justified?

3. In Re D'Angeli's Case, 369 Mass. 812, 343 N.E.2d 368 (1976) illustrates decisions that tend to enlarge the compensability of the scope of coverage of rescue attempts. There, a travelling employee was struck by a passing car while he was gratuitously attempting to remove dangerous debris from the highway. In awarding compensation the court observed:

> It is our present view that when a conscientious citizen is in the course of his employment and perceives an imminent danger to the public, as would appear to have been the case this instance, his endeavor to alleviate the danger should be considered incidental to his employment. In holding that emergency public service may be warranted in the course of employment we are following good precedent. 369 Mass. 812, 343 N.E.2d 368, 371.

SECTION 8. UNEXPLAINED DEATHS

IN RE LEBLANC'S CASE

Supreme Judicial Court of Massachusetts, 1955.
332 Mass. 334, 125 N.E.2d 129.

RONAN, JUSTICE. This is an appeal from a decree awarding compensation to the dependent mother of Robert LeBlanc who was crushed to death between the platform of an elevator and one of the floors of a large department store where he had been employed as a stock boy.

The store occupied a corner building and also an adjoining building known as the Jefferson Building which was separated from the corner building by an alleyway, known as Norfolk Place. The main store was located in the corner building. Both buildings were connected by bridges over Norfolk Place. A freight elevator known as elevator numbered 3 was located in the Jefferson Building. It was used to take foodstuffs to the employees' cafeteria which was located on the sixth floor of this building and to remove the garbage from the cafeteria, but its principal duty was to receive the incoming merchandise at its Norfolk Place entrance and bring it up to the marking room on the third floor where the goods were sorted and price tags attached and the goods then placed in that part of the third floor known as the stock room. This elevator had a regular operator but it was usually operated only about four or five hours a day during the period when the bulk of incoming freight was received, which was usually within the first few hours in the morning. The elevator with the lock engaged was left at the Norfolk Place entrance for the receipt of any further goods that might arrive. The lock consisted of a clamp which prevented the movement of the shipper cable sufficiently to start the elevator. The lock could be released by pushing in the clamp by one in the elevator.

The duties of stock boys were to keep replenished the merchandise in the departments to which they were assigned in accordance with the instructions given to them by the heads of the respective departments. LeBlanc was assigned to the women's and children's shoe department which were located in the corner building and below the level of the stock room. The proper and convenient way for LeBlanc to take shoes for the children's department from the stock room, was to go to the rear of the stock room, cross over the bridge spanning Norfolk Place, and take elevator numbered 5 in the main building, and, if going to the women's department, to go to the front of the stock room, cross over the bridge nearest the front of the main building, and then descend by elevator numbered 15. Both of these elevators had operators and were available for the use of the stock boys.

At the time he was hired and on two subsequent occasions—once when he was operating a freight elevator under the immediate supervision of a licensed operator and once when he was preparing to use elevator numbered 3 for the transfer of merchandise to one of the departments in the store—he was warned that he was not permitted to operate the elevator.

About 1:30 o'clock on the afternoon of March 27, 1951, his dead body was observed on elevator numbered 3, crushed between the platform of the elevator and the third floor. The upper part of the body was on the floor of the elevator and his legs hung in the well. His body was a short distance from the elevator lock. So far as the record goes the accident was unwitnessed and unexplained. We do not know who started the elevator. If it had an operator on it as it approached the third floor there was no evidence that it was anyone other than LeBlanc. We do not know whether he was attempting to get off or to get on the elevator at the time he was fatally injured. We do not know in which direction the elevator was moving. There was no merchandise near the place of the accident that LeBlanc might be conveying to the shoe departments, nor were there any empty receptacles that he might be returning to the stock room. The record sheds no light as to the purpose he was intending to accomplish by being on the elevator. We cannot accept the inference of the single member adopted by the board that LeBlanc might have been caught by the elevator as he was looking down or up into the elevator shaft trying to locate the elevator for that rests on conjecture and surmise. The insurer contends that the death of the employee did not arise out of and in the course of his employment. The burden is, of course, upon a claimant to prove both elements before she is entitled to receive compensation. Barrette's Case, 312 Mass. 697, 45 N.E.2d 403; Flaherty's Case, 316 Mass. 719, 56 N.E.2d 880. The Legislature, however, has furnished a statutory presumption in aid of a claimant by G.L.

(Ter.Ed.) c. 152, § 7A, inserted by St.1947, c. 380, which in so far as material provides that where the employee is killed or unable to testify "it shall be presumed, in the absence of substantial evidence to the contrary, that the claim comes within the provisions of this chapter * * *." That section has been frequently construed by this court. * * * [citations omitted.] The statute does not mean that the death of an employee which occurs at the place of his employment and during his working hours, and which there is substantial evidence tending to show is disconnected from and unrelated to his employment, is compensable. Where, as here, such evidence exists, the statutory presumption disappears and the decision is to be based upon the entire evidence. Lapinsky's Case, 325 Mass. 13, 16, 88 N.E.2d 642; Lysaght's Case, 328 Mass. 281, 284–285, 103 N.E.2d 259.

The difficulty with the claimant's case is that the employee at the time of his death was in a place where all the evidence shows he had no right to be. He was forbidden to operate a freight elevator. The particular elevator upon which he was at the time he was killed was in the Jefferson Building, and it did not lead to the women's or children's shoe departments in connection with which the decedent was employed. It was not impossible to use elevator numbered 3 and cross the open Norfolk Place and go into the corner building where these departments were located, but there was no evidence that any such indirect route had ever been followed by any stock boy especially where the employer had furnished ample and direct means of access from the stock room to freight elevators, equipped with regular operators, which were located in the corner building and which went directly to the departments with which the decedent was connected. In the next place, in view of the evidence, there is no basis for the operation of the statutory presumption that his presence on the elevator was connected either directly or indirectly with his employment. We are of opinion that said § 7A does not apply as there was substantial evidence tending to show that his death was not caused by the performance of any duties he was hired to do or anything incidental thereto. * * *

The final decree is reversed and a decree is to be entered dismissing the claim.

So ordered.

Notes

1. The statutes of several states prescribe presumptions of coverage similar to the one in the principal case, including New York and Florida (N.Y.W.C.L. § 29; F.S.A. 440.26). Does it occur to you that these presumptions, if interpreted broadly, would do away with the statutory tests of compensability in many instances? The courts do not always read them that liberally. See, e.g. Pridgen v. International Cushion Co., 88 So.2d 286 (Fla.1956) (employee suddenly dropped dead from unexplained cause while at work; the court held that the statutory presumption is not a substitute for evidence of a causal connection between the employment and the death and stated that the purpose of the provision is to raise a presumption where the physical cause has been established and the remaining question is whether

death occurred during course of employment); and McCormack v. National City Bank of New York, 303 N.Y. 5, 99 N.E.2d 887 (1951) (same outcome in divided decision). As one court has stated:

> When substantial evidence is introduced by the party against whom a presumption operates controverting the presumed fact, then its existence or non-existence is to be determined from the evidence, exactly as if no presumption had been operative in the case. In other words, such presumptions are procedural (placing the burden upon the party denying their truth to produce evidence) and not for consideration of the trier of the facts who has the function of determining what facts are proved by the evidence produced.

Duff v. St. Louis Mining & Milling Corp., 363 Mo. 944, 948, 255 S.W.2d 792, 793 (1953). Other cases denying compensation include: Hunter v. American Steel & Wire Co., 293 Pa. 103, 141 A. 635 (1928) (body of worker found in river at place one hundred and twenty-five feet from toilet; compensation denied); Pinkerton's, Inc. v. Helmes, 242 Va. 378, 410 S.E.2d 646 (1991)(injuries to employee found unconscious in her wrecked car shortly after her shift as night security guard ended: held; in the absence of death, the court refused to presume injuries arose out of and within course of employment and denied benefits); and Green v. Simpson & Brown Constr. Co., 14 N.J. 66, 101 A.2d 10 (1953) (a night watchman on barge last seen at a gate leading to waterfront and place of work but was not missed until several days later; body found in water where it had floated downstream, but with no proof as to when or how it came to be in the water; compensation denied). Noted (1954) 8 Rutgers L.Rev. 100.

Nevertheless, other decisions award compensation in equally problematic situations. See, e.g., Downes v. Industrial Comm., 113 Ariz. 90, 546 P.2d 826 (1976); Slotnick v. Howard Stores Corp., 58 A.D.2d 959, 397 N.Y.S.2d 179 (1977) (store manager, whose duties compelled his presence on streets was discovered nude and unconscious with a two inch cut on his head and a beer can in his hand; compensation awarded because the statutory presumption that he was in the course of employment was not rebutted).

2. A similar but distinguishable issue arises if the evidence supports inferences of two competing possible causes of death, one of which would be definitely attributable to the employment, and the other not. Many decisions award compensation. See, e.g., Southwest Forest Industries v. Industrial Comm., 96 Ariz. 91, 392 P.2d 506 (1964) (the body of a worker who was hired to divert coal onto conveyor belt was found buried under four feet of coal at the end of the belt; did he die of heart attack and fall onto belt, or did the coal slide and bury him?; evidence supported award of compensation); American Sugar Refining Co. v. Ned, 209 F.2d 636, 638 (5th Cir.1954) (a worker on a barge fell into river; did he die of heart attack or drowning?; compensation awarded; "The death was accidental even though the man might have died a few minutes later from natural causes if he had not met with the accident"; and Southern Motor Lines Co. v. Alvis, 200 Va. 168, 104 S.E.2d 735 (1958) (unexplained death of worker found dead at place and at time work required his presence presumed to be compensable). Compare Henry v. Schenk Mechanical Contractors, Inc., 169 Ind.App. 178, 346 N.E.2d 616 (1976) (an employee's death was caused by the puncture of his temple with a Ram Set tool; was it an accident or suicide?; compensation denied because circumstantial evidence supported finding of suicide).

Chapter 6

ACCIDENT AND OCCUPATIONAL DISEASE

INTRODUCTION TO THIS CHAPTER

In the early days of the workers' compensation movement in England and most of the American states, it was the policy not to cover loss of wages caused by occupational disease. The goal of the new program was limited to providing an effective remedy for disability resulting from industrial accident. Occupational disease was not initially considered to be within the ambit of the workers' compensation statutes. This general limitation of purpose was reflected in the original statutes by terms restricting compensation to cases of "injury by accident" or "accidental injury," which as shown below, were not originally interpreted by the courts to include diseases.

As time passed, a variety of influences brought about a modification of the original approach. Occupational diseases did occur and no alternative means to compensate affected workers materialized. Problems of interpretation arose as to what constituted an "injury by accident" and it became difficult to determine where the outer boundaries of the limitation were to be fixed. It was found that accident and disease blend into each other by minute gradations. Furthermore, it became obvious that the exclusion of occupational disease left many disabled workers without assistance under circumstances economically identical to those of fellow workers disabled by accident, bringing into focus the arbitrariness of the restriction. For these and other reasons, England and almost all the American states amended their laws or passed new ones to provide compensation for losses caused by occupational disease.

In this chapter the student is directed to the legal issues surrounding the concept of "accident" and the application of the different types of occupational disease laws. The reader will recognize that these problems constitute another phase of the familiar general policy issue that underlies so many areas of workers' compensation law, namely, to what risks ought workers' compensation coverage be extended?

234

SECTION 1. THE CONCEPT OF "ACCIDENT"

MATTHEWS v. R.T. ALLEN & SONS, INC.

Supreme Court of Maine, 1970.
266 A.2d 240.

WEATHERBEE, JUSTICE. On May 1, 1969 an Industrial Accident Commissioner rendered a decree denying an award of compensation to the Petitioner.

[The opinion first discussed certain alleged irregularities in the post-decree procedure. After concluding that the case was reviewable as to questions of substantive law, it continued].

We must decide the single issue of whether the Petitioner suffered a personal injury arising out of and in the course of his employment.

The Petitioner, a 43 year old woodsworker, testified that on November 13, 1967 he was employed loading pulpwood onto trucks by hand. He had worked at this since 7:00 A.M. and the lifting evidently involved bending and straightening the back. The sticks were four feet long and from four inches to two feet in diameter. At about 10:30 or 11:00 A.M. he felt pain in his back but he continued to work. During his noon lunch period while he ate his lunch in the truck, the pain became worse. He worked one to one and a half hours after lunch at which time the pain was so great that he reported to his employer that he was unable to continue and went home. During the next four days the back pain continued to increase in severity and he could not go to work. On November 18 he was admitted to the Maine Coast Memorial Hospital in Ellsworth and on December 10 he was transferred to the Maine Medical Center in Portland where a herniated disc was removed. He returned to work the first of May, 1968.

On cross-examination he testified that the pain began that morning gradually and was not associated with any "specific lifting, slipping or tripping". He admitted he had told an insurance company investigator that the pain came on while he was sitting in the truck at noon but he testified that he had noticed the pain while working that morning " * * * [B]ut when I first noticed it why it didn't bother me to lift or anything. It was after when I started to straighten up to pull myself back." At noon it had become worse. He agreed that he told the doctors that the pain came on gradually and "got worse and worse and worse" as he worked. He also said that on previous occasions while doing woods work he had had low back pains but they were never disabling.

The doctors' reports and hospital discharge summaries add only that the Petitioner had been admitted to the Ellsworth hospital suffering such severe pain that he "could hardly move". During the next four days the pain increased in severity and also radiated down into his left leg and foot. After two weeks of conservative treatment his condition had only worsened. A myelogram showed a defect in the L4–5 interspace on the left and surgery disclosed an acutely herniated disc in that area, which was removed.

The doctors' reports expressed no opinion as to the precipitating cause of the injury, whether it may have developed prior to November 13, 1967 or, if so, whether the exertion of November 13 may have aggravated the condition except for one significant comment to be discussed later.

The Commissioner found:

"The evidence, we find, is insufficient to support a finding that Mr. Matthews sustained a personal injury by accident arising out of and in the course of his employment. We cannot conclude from the testimony that the disc condition which disabled him on November 13, 1967, resulted from any single episode, or traumatic incident. The medical history given by Mr. Matthews and his testimony on cross examination, indicate that the symptoms of the underlying disc condition became disabling on November 13, 1967, but that the herniated disc had developed prior to that time—probably gradually. It is our decision that the petition must be dismissed."

Our own findings lead us to an opposite conclusion.

The Petitioner has the burden of proving that he suffered a personal injury by accident arising out of and in the course of his employment. 39 M.R.S.A. § 52.

The Workmen's Compensation Law represents a relatively recent concept of responsibility without negligence. While the early cases usually concerned accidental injuries where an external force was applied to an external portion of the body, our own Court decided early in the development of our law that the term injury by accident includes incidents where internal parts of the physical structure break down under external force, including the stress of labor. While this may more dramatically occur as a result of a slip, a fall or a single unusual strained effort, we have found other such internal breakdowns to have resulted from the usual work which the workman was performing in his usual, normal way. In short, we have construed the term "accident" to include not only injuries which are the results of accidents but also injuries which are themselves accidents. 58 Am.Jur., Workmen's Compensation, § 195. In Brown's Case, 123 Me. 424, 123 A. 421 (1924) a fatal heart dilation resulted from the exertion of shovelling snow. In Patrick v. J.B. Ham Co., 119 Me. 510, 111 A. 912 (1921) the Petitioner's husband suffered a cerebral hemorrhage while performing his regular duties of lifting sacks of grain. In Taylor's Case, 127 Me. 207, 142 A. 730 (1928) the Petitioner's husband had been lifting heavy objects in the course of his usual work and a particularly vigorous straining caused a pulmonary embolism.

This position is in agreement with that taken by the great majority of American jurisdictions and follows the rule recognized in England which in many respects furnished the model for our own Act. Brzozowski's Case, 328 Mass. 113, 102 N.E.2d 399 (1951); Kacavisti v. Sprague Electric Co., 102 N.H. 266, 155 A.2d 183 (1959); Bryant Stave & Heading Co. v. White, 227 Ark. 147, 296 S.W.2d 436 (1956); Larson's Workmen's Compensation Law, Vol. 1A, 38.20. In England the Courts soon came to hold that an unexpected, unforeseen or unintended result from usual or customary exertion constitutes an injury by accident even though there is no unexpected or fortuitous cause. Fenton v. Thorley Co., Ltd., A.C. 443 (House of Lords) (1903); Clover, Clayton & Co. v. Hughes, A.C. 242, 3 B.W.C.C. 775 (1910); A Problem in the Drafting of Workmen's Compensation Acts by Francis H. Bohlen, 25 Harvard Law Review, 328 at page 337.

In some of the earlier decisions holding that the breaking down of internal parts might be accidents under the statute, the death or incapacity occurred suddenly as the internal part dramatically gave way. This furnished another similarity to the usual concept of accident occurring when an external force is applied violently to an external part and assisted this Court in arriving at its conclusion that the Legislature intended both situations to be considered industrial accidents.

> "If a laborer performing his usual task, in his wonted way, by reason of strain, breaks his wrist, nobody would question the accidental nature of the injury. If instead of the wrist it is an artery that breaks, the occurrence is just as clearly an accident." Brown's Case, supra, 123 Me. at 425, 123 A. at 422.

Certainly the sudden quality of a mishap often makes it more clearly distinguishable from the mere malfunctioning of an organ which develops through natural progression, unrelated to the employment.

This thinking led our Court in early decisions to describe an accidental injury as being "unusual, undesigned, unexpected, sudden" (*Brown's* Case, supra, where the employee "suddenly became dizzy, faint and short of breath" while shovelling snow). As recently as in Bernier v. Coca–Cola Bottling Plants, Inc., Me., 250 A.2d 820 (1969) in pointing out that the Petitioner need not prove that his back strain resulted from "any unusual slip, fall, etc., in other words, external injury" we quoted *Brown's* Case to hold that "an internal injury that is itself sudden, unusual, and unexpected is none the less accidental because its external cause is a part of the victim's ordinary work."

* * *

We find no significant dispute in the testimony. It reveals a 43 year old woodsworker who had had low back pains in the past, usually associated with his work, but never to the extent of being disabling. On this occasion the pain began while he was loading sticks of pulpwood, some very heavy. He continued to work several hours while the pain got "worse and worse and worse". After he stopped working the pain continued to increase in severity and to extend in area until relieved by surgery. Surgery disclosed that an extruding mass from the ruptured disc was pressing against the nerve and obviously bowing it outward and upward.

* * *

We are called upon to decide whether Petitioner's disability, hospitalization and surgery were causally connected with his activities while loading pulpwood that November 13. Whether Petitioner's disc ruptured abruptly the morning of November 13 or whether the defective condition developed gradually during his previous episodes of low back pain is not controlling here. The scanty facts presented to us lead us to the conclusion that in either case the heavy labor of November 13 constituted the critical episode which completely incapacitated the man with increasing and unrelieved crippling pain until surgery removed the ruptured part.

While we do not know the moment when the actual herniation occurred its causal connection with the labor of November 13 seems apparent. In other words the personal injury appears either to have been caused by the exertions of November 13 or aggravated by them. We have repeatedly held that if stress of labor aggravates or accelerates the development of a preexisting infirmity causing an internal breakdown of that part of the structure a personal injury by accident occurs. *Hull's* Case, supra; *Swett's* Case, supra. The point is dramatized by the language of the Court in Lachance's Case, 121 Me. 506 at page 510, 118 A. 370 at page 372 (1922):

> "If Lachance, but for the hurt, would not have died at the time at which, and in the way in which, he did die, then, within the meaning of the Workmen's Act the unfortunate occurrence, though it merely hastened a deep-seated disorder to destiny, must be held to have resulted in an injury causing death."

Although neither the Ellsworth orthopedic surgeon who originally treated Petitioner nor the Portland neuro-surgeon who performed the surgery was called to testify, the orthopedic surgeon (who also assisted in the operation) commented tersely in his written report:

> "Unfortunately, after the pain had developed he continued to work until the job was completed."

We infer from this that it was his opinion that Petitioner's exertion in loading the trucks at least contributed to his disability and to his need for surgery.

We find that Petitioner sustained a personal injury by accident arising out of and in the course of his employment on November 13, 1967.

* * *

Appeal sustained. Case remanded to the Industrial Accident Commission for determination of compensation. * * *

Notes

1. The issue presented in the foregoing case was perceived to be a potential source of difficulty at an early date in the development of workers' compensation in the United States. It constitutes one branch of a two-pronged problem that resulted from the use in workers' compensation statutes of the term "personal injury by accident" or "accidental injury" or some similar expression.

The nature of the problem was outlined by Professor Francis H. Bohlen in 1912. (25 Harv.L.Rev. 328) He wrote:

> "The term 'by accident' has been consistently construed to include two different ideas: the first is that of unexpectedness; the second, that of an injury sustained on some definite occasion, the date of which can be fixed with reasonable certainty. The first idea would be as well conveyed by the word 'accidentally' or by any phrase or phrases in which unforeseen harm is sharply contrasted with harm intended or expected to result. The latter idea, it is submitted, is not necessarily included in the term 'accidental' or 'accidentally'; such words, especially if the phrases employed in such legislation are to be construed in accordance with the popular meaning of the terms used, do not appear necessarily to indicate the existence of an accident, but would seem to relate solely to the injury being neither intended nor expected."

The *Matthews* case involves the first aspect of the term "accident", namely, unexpectedness. What unexpected event will satisfy that requirement? Is it necessary that, in addition to the unexpected injury, there be some contemporaneous occurrence of a causal nature such as a fall, a slip, a blow or similar incident? Or is the unexpected injury standing alone sufficient to constitute the "accident"?

The problem had been identified and solved in England long before any statute had come into effect in the United States. In 1903 it was held by the House of Lords in Fenton v. Thorley & Co., Ltd [1903] A.C. 443, that the unexpected injury itself could constitute the accident, reversing the position originally taken on this question by an English court in Hensey v. White [1900] 1 Q.B. 481. In the United States, however, the early holdings in many states having statutes containing the term "accident" or "accidental" required that there must be some external event other than the injury itself in order to bring the case within the purview of the statute. Some jurisdictions demanded that something unusual or out of the ordinary course of the employee's work must be shown to have occurred contemporaneously with the injury in order to comply with the requirement of "accidental personal injury". E.g., Kelly–Springfield Tire Co. v. Daniels, 199 Md. 156, 85 A.2d 795 (1952) (compensation denied for injury to intervertebral disc when lifting air bag and hooking it on a machine while in a stooping position). The majority of jurisdictions in the United States at the present time are in accord with the view expressed in *Matthews* and do not require an unusual event in addition to the unexpected injury. See, 2 A. Larson & L. Larson, Larson's Workers' Compensation § 38.00 (1997).

2. Some jurisdictions distinguish between usual and unusual exertion in construing the term "accident" or "accidental." If the injury occurs while the employee is engaged in the usual exertion called for by the job, there is

no "injury by accident"; but if the injury results from some special activity culminating in extraordinary strain, the injury is considered an accident. E.g., Virginia Electric and Power Co. v. Cogbill, 223 Va. 354, 288 S.E.2d 485 (1982) (gradual back injury is not an industrial accident since it was not caused by an employment-related activity requiring different or unusual exertion); Satrom v. North Dakota Workmen's Comp. Bureau, 328 N.W.2d 824 (N.D.1982) (hairdresser's acute disc syndrome held compensable under finding that it was caused by unusual exertion). Today, most courts will award compensation when usual exertion leads to some sort of "breakage" in the body, such as a herniated disc. E.g., Builders & Managers, Inc. v. Cortilesso, 608 A.2d 725 (Del.1992) (injuries to foot and ankle resulting from usual exertion are compensable); Wolfgeher v. Wagner Cartage Serv., Inc., 646 S.W.2d 781 (Mo.1983) (back injury is a compensable accident when caused by routine exertion of carrying a refrigerator at work); Village v. General Motors Corp., 15 Ohio St.3d 129, 472 N.E.2d 1079 (1984) (a back "injury caused by the performance of an employee's job duties, which develop gradually over a period of time, is a compensable injury...."); Allen v. Industrial Comm., 729 P.2d 15 (Utah 1986) (low back injury sustained while lifting milk crates is an "injury by accident" even if not the result of any unusual stress). Moreover, courts that adhere to the "unusual exertion" requirement often find that the exertion that produced the injury was "unusual." E.g., Ogden Allied Aviation Services v. Shuck, 18 Va.App. 756, 446 S.E.2d 898 (Va.App.1994) (airplane refueller whose neck "popped" while he looked at a fuel gauge under the wing of a plane was allowed to recover; incident was sufficiently unusual).

3. The National Commission of State Workmen's Compensation Laws recommended that the accident requirement be dropped as a test of compensability. See the Commission's Report, July 1972, page 49. Several states have since deleted the words "accident" or "accidental" from their workers' compensation statutes. Maine, the jurisdiction of the principal case, did so in 1973. 1973 Me.Laws Ch. 389. States that do not define coverage in terms of "injury by accident" include California, Colorado, Iowa, Maine, Massachusetts, Minnesota, Pennsylvania, Rhode Island, and South Dakota. See 2 A. Larson & L. Lawson, Larson's Workers' Compensation Law § 37.10 (1998).

4. The *Matthews* court recognized that the real issue presented in these cases is one of factual causation. Did the occupational activity of the employee have any substantial causal relation in a medical sense to the injury suffered? An example of this type of approach may be seen in Barrett v. Herbert Engineering, Inc., 371 A.2d 633 (Me.1977) in which claimant in the course of his employment was walking along to fetch some tools when one of his fellow employees yelled at him. He turned around to ask what was wanted and was requested to bring a special tool. Resuming his walk he "quickened his pace and while walking along at his normal gait he felt a sharp pain in the lower lumbar region of his back." The pain caused him to drop to his knees. He had had a long intermittent history of low back discomfort. Compensation was denied, the Supreme Court writing " ... the petitioner's lumbar-sacral strain did not spring into activity by reason of any work he was doing, but occurred while he was walking at his normal gait to fetch some tools." The injury " ... was not legally causally related to the employment." See also Caldwell v. John Morrell & Co., 489 N.W.2d 353

(S.D.1992)(claimant who sustained a herniated disc only needs to prove that employment was a contributing factor to his back injury rather than the existence of a specific accident).

PEORIA COUNTY BELWOOD NURSING HOME v. THE INDUSTRIAL COMMISSION

Illinois Court of Appeals, 1985.
138 Ill.App.3d 880, 93 Ill.Dec. 689, 487 N.E.2d 356 (1985), aff'd
115 Ill.2d 524, 106 Ill.Dec. 235, 505 N.E.2d 1026 (1987).

BARRY, PRESIDING JUSTICE.

The critical issue in this appeal is whether an injury sustained as the result of work-related repetitive trauma is compensable under the Workers' compensation Act absent one precise, identifiable incident which a court may label an "accident." Based upon the purpose of the Workers' Compensation Act (Ill. Rev. Stat. 1983, ch. 48, par. 138.1 et seq.) (hereafter the Act) and recognizing the new and changing nature of the employment environment, we hold that such injuries, when the claimant's burden of proof has been met, are compensable under the Act.

* * *

This appeal is brought by the claimant's employer, Peoria County Belwood Nursing Home (hereafter Belwood). The claimant, Wanda Cagle, filed a claim for compensation under the Act on August 24, 1979. The claimant alleged that she developed carpal tunnel syndrome in her left wrist in the course of her job in the laundry room of Belwood. She had been employed by Belwood for 12 years. She worked in the laundry room for the six years prior to her injury. Her duties in the laundry room consisted of sorting laundry and loading the laundry into two 200–pound capacity washing machines. Each machine was operated six times a day and was loaded by operating a spring-loaded door into each of three compartments. She was also required to carry laundry bags weighing from 25 to 50 pounds.

The claimant initially identified the date of her injury as October 5, 1976. At trial, she testified that she noticed pain, numbness and tingling for a substantial period of time prior to October 5. Her testimony was confused as to exactly how long she experienced symptoms, but she did experience symptoms on October 5, 1976. On October 5, 1976, she consulted Dr. McLean, a neurologist, regarding her symptoms. She continued to work until August 23, 1977, when she underwent outpatient surgery for carpal tunnel syndrome.

Based on this evidence, the arbitrator amended the application for benefits to reflect a date of injury of October 4, 1976. The arbitrator awarded benefits for temporary total disability and for 25% permanent total disability. The Industrial Commission affirmed the award. The circuit court of Peoria County confirmed the Commission's decision. Belwood brings the instant appeal.

Belwood raises two interrelated issues. It asserts, first, that the Industrial Commission's finding that the claimant sustained an accidental injury is contrary to the manifest weight of the evidence. In a related argument, the employer asserts that the claim for benefits is barred by the statute of limitations.

The arbitrator and Commission found that the claimant had sustained an accidental injury as a result of repeated trauma to her wrist in operating the two large washing machines. The employer argues that because there was no specific incident by which the claimant's injury could be traced to a definite time, place and cause, the injury was not an "accidental injury" under the Act. The Commission's finding that the claimant suffered an "accidental injury" is, according to Belwood, contrary to the manifest weight of the evidence.

The crux of this issue, then, is what constitutes an "accidental injury" under the Act. The Illinois Supreme Court has held that an injury is "accidental" within the meaning of the Act if it is traceable to a definite time, place and cause. (International Harvester Co. v. Industrial Com. (1973), 56 Ill.2d 84, 305 N.E.2d 529). The employee in *International Harvester* developed emphysema as a result of his employment. Barred from recovery under the Workmen's Occupational Diseases Act, the employee sought recovery under the Workmen's Compensation Act. The Illinois Supreme court noted that aggravation of a pre-existing disease was compensable under the Act where the "employee's existing physical structure, whatever it may be, gives way under the stress of his usual labor and he is suddenly disabled." ... The court thus reasoned that either the cause or the effect of the aggravation of disease must be traceable to a specific time, place and cause in order for an employee to recover under the Act.

* * *

The requirement that an accidental injury be traceable to a definite time, place and cause was reiterated in General Electric Co. v. Industrial Com. (1982), 89 Ill. 2d 432, 433 N.E.2d 671. The claimant in *General Electric* sought compensation for carpal tunnel syndrome sustained as the result of work-related repetitive trauma. General Electric argued that there was no accidental injury because the claimant's injury was not traceable to a definite time, place and cause. The supreme court held that the claimant sustained an accidental injury despite the fact that the injury was the result of repeated trauma because there was a precise identifiable incident in which her physical structure gave way under the stress of her usual work tasks.

Thus, the rule has evolved that in order to demonstrate an "accidental injury," a claimant must trace the injury either to a specific accident identifiable as to time and place or to the specific moment of collapse of one's physical structure, identifiable as to time and place. Under the present interpretation of the Act, it is not sufficient for a claimant to show that a bodily structure eroded over time to the point of uselessness as a result of employment. Instead, a claimant must demonstrate a precise moment of collapse and dysfunction.

We consider the implication of this rule for all of the employees, factory workers, supervisors, managers, secretaries, salesperson and others, working in Illinois in this technological age. In real life, the erosion of a bodily structure to the point of uselessness translates into arms that cannot lift, legs that cannot walk, knees that cannot bend, lungs that cannot breathe, and eyes chronically irritated or worse. But evidence of such work-related injuries alone is not sufficient under the prior interpretations of "accidental injury." Instead, useless limbs, damaged organs and disabled bodies must be pushed to a precise moment of collapse and dysfunction. Then, and only then, according to these interpretations, may a court of this State find an employee eligible for compensation under the Act.

The time has come to abandon an interpretation of "accidental" which fails to address documentable and medically recognizable risks faced by the individuals in connection with their employment. The risk of injury from repeated trauma and exposure endured by truck drivers, CRT operators, chemists and others must be recognized. The judicial interpretation of "accident" must be refined to reflect the purpose of the Act and the reality of employees obligated to perform repetitive tasks.

The purpose of the Act is that the burdens of caring for the casualties of industry be borne by industry and not the employees or the public.... The primary objective of the Act is to afford employees and their dependents a measure of financial protection while eliminating the vast costs of tens of thousands of potential common law actions filed against employers.... The Act represents the exchange of previously existing common law rights and remedies between employers and employee.... In construing the Act, courts must give its provisions the practical and liberal interpretation intended by the legislature.... [T]he Act is a humane law of remedial nature.

* * *

We concede that ... issues of law and fact will arise because we today recognize gradual injury due to repetitive trauma as compensable under the Act. However ... a claimant must fulfill his obligation of proof and show that his injury is work-related and not the product of the aging process.

An employee alleging injury based on repetitive trauma must meet the same standard of proof as claimants alleging a single, definable accident. The difficulty in proving that injury resulting from repeated trauma arose out of and in the course of employment will pose a serious burden for a claimant. The difficulty of resolving any such issues should not prevent this court, like Ohio, from considering just compensation for all employees so injured.

* * *

[T]his court finds that an employee may be "accidentally injured" under the Act as the result of repetitive, work-related trauma even absent a final, identifiable episode of collapse. We reject an interpretation of "accidental" which forces injured employees needing the protection of the Act to choose between foregoing that protection, "creating" one identifiable incident, or pushing their now-injured bodies to the point of collapse or dysfunction. The elimination of this too narrow definition of "accidental injury" will effectuate the purpose of the Act and provide equal protection for all manner of employees of this State.

Absent the narrow construction of "accident" in the case at bar, the evidence was sufficient to prove that the claimant sustained an accidental injury arising out of and in the course of her employment. Although the date of injury alleged by the claimant differed from the date of injury assigned by the arbitrator, the claimant established by her testimony that she was injured during her employment. The claimant testified that she experienced pain and tingling in her left arm. While she worked a regular work schedule on October 4, on October 5, she informed her physician that she experienced extreme difficulty in gripping the washer doors due to the severity of her symptoms. Both the claimant and Dr. Rivero related the symptoms to her employment. The medical testimony as to the claimant's conditions was uncontroverted. We find that the claimant proved that she sustained an "accidental injury" under the Act.

Because we so find, we must now consider whether the claim was timely filed. Belwood argues that the claim is barred by the statute of limitations.

Section 6(c)(2) of the Act provides, in relevant part, that a claim for compensation must be filed within three years after the date of the accident. (Ill. Rev. Stat. 1975, ch. 48, par. 138.6(c)(2).) To determine whether the filing of the claim was timely, we must first determine the date of the claimant's accident.

Professor Larson suggests that the date of an "accident" in cases of repetitive trauma be defined as "the date on which the disability, manifests itself." (1B Larson, Workmen's Compensation sec. 39.50 (1985.)* * *

Two alternative criteria are set forth by Larson for fixing the date when the injury manifests itself. The first is the time at which the employee can no longer perform his job. * * *

The alternate criteria set forth by Larson is the onset of pain which necessitates medical attention.* * *

We adopt the rule propounded by Larson and find that where an employee in Illinois suffers a work-related injury due to repeated trauma, the date of the accidental injury is the date on which the injury "manifests" itself. Manifest means to show plainly or make palpably evident. (Webster's Third New International Dictionary 1375 (1971).) We further find that an injury has manifested itself when both the fact of the injury and the causal relationship between the injury and the employment are plainly evident.

The time at which both the fact of the injury and the causal relationship became plainly evident will be a question of fact. The claimant may demonstrate the manifestation of the injury with divers facts. The criteria suggested by Larson, the onset of pain and the inability to perform one's job, are among the facts which may be introduced to establish the date of injury.

In sum, in the instant case the claimant experienced symptoms on October 4, 1976. On October 5, 1976, she sought medical attention, at which time the doctor confirmed that her injury was caused by the conditions of her employment. Thus, the arbitrator correctly set forth the date of claimant's injury as October 4, 1976, the last day on which she worked before the fact of the injury and the causal connection became apparent. On that date, both the fact of her injury and the causal relationship were plainly evident. The claimant filed her application of claim on August 24, 1979. The claim for benefits under the Act was, therefore, filed within the three-year statute of limitations.

The claimant was awarded benefits by the arbitrator and the Commission. The award of benefits was confirmed by the circuit court. We affirm the judgment of the circuit court of Peoria County.

Affirmed.

Presiding Justice Webber, dissenting:

I respectfully dissent from the principal opinion and suggest that it represents a usurpation of the legislative prerogative and purports to overrule many holdings of our supreme court while at the same time paying lip service to them.

* * *

[a lengthy discussion of Illinois cases is omitted]

All of this authority reiterates and reemphasizes the rule of *International Harvester*: to be compensable under the Workers' Compensation Act, an injury must be accidental; to be accidental, an injury must be traceable to a definite time, place, and cause. The term "accidental injury" subsumes and encompasses a cause-and-effect analysis; the accident is viewed as the cause and the injury as the result. Therefore, most cases may be analyzed in terms of causation. This appeared to be the basis of decision in the three carpal tunnel syndrome cases described above. In General Electric the sudden sharp pain coupled with the medical evidence supported the Commission's determination of accident; the opposite situation obtained in *Johnson* and *Caterpillar*; there was insufficient evidence to support a finding of accident. Thus, the cause of the injury is much narrower in scope than that posited by the repeated-trauma theory. It is not impossible for repeated trauma to lead up to an accident, but the accident, itself, the cause of the injury, must be pinpointed by clear evidence; it is not sufficient that a bodily structure eroded to the point of uselessness; there must be a precise moment of collapse and dysfunction.

There are a number of practical reasons for the rule. An exact time, place, and cause may be necessary to determine which employer and which compensation insurance carrier are on the risk; whether any statutory amendments are applicable; and, as in the case at bar, whether any limitations problem exists.

In the instant case, there was insufficient evidence of accidental injury within the meaning of the rule discussed above. There was no evidence of any unusual happening on October 4, 1976. Claimant testified that she worked a regular day on that date. She continued to work following her visit to Dr. McLean up to the time of her surgery in August 1977. Dr. McLean in his deposition described the surgery as elective, claimant's condition not having deteriorated to the point at which it might be described otherwise.

* * *

I would reverse the order of the circuit court of Peoria County.

Notes

1.   The foregoing case and many like it in the United States involve the second aspect of the term "accident" mentioned in the notes to the *Matthews* case, i.e., the idea of an injury sustained on some definite occasion, the time of which can be ascertained with reasonable certainty. As noted in the dissenting opinion, there are practical reasons why it is important to be able to specify the time when the injury was sustained. On that fact may turn various decisions, such as which of several employers should be held responsible for compensation, what wage rates were in effect at the time of injury, what other statutory provisions were then operative, what pertinent court decisions applied at that date, whether notice of injury and claim for compensation were timely, and similar matters.

2.   Wanda Cagle's injury was a type of cumulative trauma disorder (CTD). "CTDs are musculoskeletal disorders that result from tissue damage accumulating over time ... Common CTDs include localized muscle fatigue, tendon-related disorders such as tendinitis, nerve entrapment syndromes, carpal tunnel syndrome, and hand-arm vibration syndrome." David M. Repel et. al., Work–Related Cumulative Trauma Disorders of the Upper Extremity, 267 JAMA 838 (1992). CTDs are thought to be caused by the performance of repetitive tasks that over time injure soft tissue, ligaments, nerves and tendons. Certain occupations are thought to be especially susceptible to CTDs, including cashiers, secretaries, electricians, butchers, data entry clerks, textile sewing machine operators and construction workers. Id., 267 JAMA at 839.

CTDs may be the fastest growing type of workers' compensation claim. The Bureau of Labor Statistics estimates that the occurrence of CTDs increased 1,000% between 1982 and 1991. Theresa A. Cortese, Comment, Cumulative Trauma Disorders: A Hidden Downside to Technological Advancement, 11 J. Contemp. Health L. & P. 479 n. 2 (1995). OSHA reports that nearly one of every three dollars that employers spend on workers' compensation are due to repetitive motion injures and injuries due to overexertion. Charles N. Jeffress, Protecting the Lives of Working Americans (April 15, 1998) <http://www.osha-slc.gov/OshDoc/Speech_gif/rsi4.gif>. Aetna Life and Casualty found that 45% of its claim payments were for CTDs.

Emily A. Spieler, Perpetuating Risk? Workers' Compensation and the Persistence of Occupational Injures, 31 Hou. L. Rev. 119, 148 (1994). "Even with the large number and size of compensation claims currently associated with repetitive trauma, these claims are probably vastly under reported in the compensation systems." Id., at 149. The cost of an average CTD workers' compensation claim is twice that of an average non-CTD claim. Robert B. Reich Preventing Repetitive Stress Injuries (December 10, 1996), <http://www.osha-slc.gov/OshDoc/Speech_gif/rsi4.gif>.

See generally, Denise Paul Juge, et. al., Cumulative Trauma Disorders—"The Disease of the 90's": An Interdisciplinary Analysis, 55 La.L.Rev. 895 (1995); H. Douglas Jones and Cathy Jackson, Cumulative Trauma Disorders: A Repetitive Strain on the Workers' Compensation System, 20 N. Ky. L. Rev. 765 (1993); Theresa A. Cortese, Comment, Cumulative Trauma Disorders: A Hidden Downside to Technological Advancement, 11 J. Contemp. Health L. & Pol'y 479 (1995).

3. The states are divided on how to properly characterize CTD claims. Many states, perhaps a majority, are consistent with *Belwood* and classify CTD claims as accidents. E.g., Kraft v. Flathead Valley Labor & Contractors, 243 Mont. 363, 792 P.2d 1094, 1096 (Mont. 1990); In re Musick, 143 N.J. 206, 670 A.2d 11, 14–15 (1996); Barker v. Home–Crest Corp., 805 S.W.2d 373, 376 (Tenn.1991). A significant number of cases conclude that CTD is not an accident due to the absence of a specific time of injury and consider it an occupational disease. E.g., Kinney v. Tupperware Co., 117 Idaho 765, 792 P.2d 330, 333 (1990); Lettering Unltd. v. Guy, 321 Md. 305, 582 A.2d 996, 998–99 (1990). A Kansas court declared that CTD claims were "neither fish nor foul," falling somewhere between the definitions of disease and injury by accident, but concluded that they were compensable in any event. Berry v. Boeing Military Airplanes, 20 Kan.App.2d 220, 885 P.2d 1261, 1267 (Kan. App.1994). Virginia courts have concluded that CTD disabilities are not compensable under either the injury by accident provisions or as an occupation disease. Stenrich Group v. Jemmott, 467 S.E.2d 795 (Va. 1996). For citations to cases from various jurisdictions see Allied Fibers v. Rhodes, 23 Va.App. 101, 474 S.E.2d 829, 833–835 (1996); Scott Green, Note, Carpal Tunnel Workers' Compensation Claims in Iowa, 45 Drake L. Rev. 233, 237 n. 31 (1997).

4. Does it matter whether a claim is labeled an accident or an occupational disease? As will be seen in Section 3 of this chapter, most states have separate occupational disease provisions that often incorporate more rigorous standards of proof regarding work-relatedness than govern accidental injury claims. Thus, a claimant's attorney will generally try to pursue a claim as an accidental injury if possible. A recent series of cases illustrate this point. Some workers complain that occupational exposure to various chemicals produces a disabling condition known as Multiple Chemical Sensitivity Syndrome (MCS) and seek compensation benefits under the occupational disease provisions. Virtually every court to consider the issue has concluded that MCS does not meet the requirements of the statutory definition of occupational disease. Kelly Corbett, Comment, Multiple Chemical Sensitivity Syndrome: Occupational Disease or Work–Related Accident? 24 B.C. Envir. Aff. L.Rev. 395, 406 n. 94 (1997). Some commentators argue that the prospects for recovery would be greater if these claims were cast in

terms of an "accident," using CTD cases like *Belwood* as analogous authority. Id. at 414–23.

5. Even if a CTD is theoretically compensable as an accidental injury, the plaintiff must prove that the injury is sufficiently work-related. Courts deny benefits to workers who fail to present persuasive medical evidence linking the disability to the conditions of employment. In Stoner v. City of Lawton, 934 P.2d 340 (Ok.1997) a police officer presented testimony of a medical expert linking the carpal tunnel syndrome in his left hand and wrist to writing traffic citations. The employer countered with evidence of the claimant's hobbies of fishing, woodworking, building models, and working on a home computer. The employer's medical expert opined that the claimant's carpal tunnel syndrome was neither caused nor aggravated nor accelerated by his employment as a police officer. In the face of conflicting expert opinion, the lower court's denial of benefits was upheld. See also, Johnson v. Industrial Comm'n, 89 Ill.2d 438, 60 Ill.Dec. 607, 433 N.E.2d 649 (1982) (denying claim for bilateral carpal tunnel syndrome when there was no medical evidence that her condition could have been caused by her work).

6. A problem similar to that presented by CTDs arises in cases where an employee inhales a chemical or other substance on the job and later develops a disabling respiratory condition. Some courts will treat the disability as an accidental injury, at least if the occupational exposure occurred in a relatively short period of time. Campbell v. Heinrich Savelberg, Inc., 139 Vt. 31, 421 A.2d 1291 (1980) (four to six weeks exposure to varnish and paint fumes was a sufficiently specific trauma to constitute an accident); Texas Employers' Ins. Ass'n v. Murphy, 506 S.W.2d 312 (Tex.Civ.App.1974) (claimant inhaled fumes containing lead and zinc over a three day period aggravating a pre-existing emphysema and bronchitis condition which ultimately proved disabling; compensation granted); English v. Industrial Comm., 73 Ariz. 86, 237 P.2d 815 (1951) (inhalation of nitric acid and sulfur dioxide fumes for a period of less than one month caused injury of which claimant became aware some five years later; dismissal of claim reversed); Murch–Jarvis Co. v. Townsend, 209 Ark., 956, 193 S.W.2d 310 (1946)(employee's exposure to dust and fumes for a period of several days culminated in total disability from asthma five or six weeks later, held compensable); Industrial Comm. v. Ule, 97 Colo. 253, 48 P.2d 803 (1935) (unusual exposure for three days to "dope" spray used on airplane bodies caused death seven months later; held compensable). In this class of cases the brevity of the period during which the causal circumstances function enables the court to fix the time of injury with satisfactory certainty.

When the exposure is long term and the disabling condition develops gradually, courts may be more reluctant to find an injury by accident. E.g., Tegels v. Western Chevrolet Co., 81 S.D. 592, 139 N.W.2d 281 (S.D. 1965) (two years exposure to paint fumes produced headaches, instability, eye trouble, and hair loss; because his condition "developed gradually and progressively over a relatively long period of time" the injury was not compensable). On the other hand, some courts have found an injury by accident even under these circumstances. E.g., Jenkins v. Ogletree Farm Supply, 291 So.2d 560 (Miss.1974) (occupational exposure to fertilizer dust over a six year period aggravated Jenkins' asthma and eventually produced a total disability; disability was characterized as "an accidental injury").

SECTION 2. INFECTIOUS DISEASE AS AN ACCIDENTAL IN-JURY

CONNELLY v. HUNT FURNITURE CO.

Supreme Court of New York, 1925.
240 N.Y. 83, 147 N.E. 366.

CARDOZO, J. Claimant's son, Harry Connelly, was employed by an undertaker as an embalmer's helper. In the line of his duty, he handled a corpse, which by reason of the amputation of a leg had become greatly decayed and was full of gangrenous matter. Some of this matter entered a little cut in his hand, and later spread to his neck, when he scratched a pimple with the infected finger. General blood poisoning set in, and caused his death. His dependent mother obtained an award for death benefits. The Appellate Division reversed, and dismissed the claim.

" 'Injury' and 'personal injury' mean only accidental injuries arising out of and in the course of employment and such disease or infection as may naturally and unavoidably result therefrom." Workmen's Compensation Law (Consol.Laws, c. 67) § 2, subd. 7. A trifling scratch was turned into a deadly wound by contact with a poisonous substance. We think the injection of the poison was itself an accidental injury within the meaning of the statute. More than this, the contact had its occasion in the performance of the servant's duties. There was thus not merely an accident, but one due to the employment. We attempt no scientifically exact discrimination between accident and disease, or between disease and injury. None perhaps is possible, for the two concepts are not always exclusive, the one of the other, but often overlap. The tests to be applied are those of common understanding as revealed in common speech. Lewis v. Ocean Accident & Guarantee Corporation, 224 N.Y. 18, 21, 120 N.E. 56, 7 A.L.R. 1129; cf. Van Vechten v. Am. E.F. Ins. Co., 239 N.Y. 303, 307, 146 N.E. 432.

We have little doubt that common understanding would envisage this mishap as an accident, and that common speech would so describe it. Germs may indeed be inhaled through the nose or mouth, or absorbed into the system through normal channels of entry. In such cases their inroads will seldom, if ever, be assignable to a determinate or single act, identified in space or time. Matter of Jeffreyes v. Sager Co., 198 App.Div. 446; Id., 233 N.Y. 535, 135 N.E. 907. For this as well as for the reason that the absorption is incidental to a bodily process both natural and normal, their action presents itself to the mind as a disease and not an accident. Our mental attitude is different when the channel of infection is abnormal or traumatic, a lesion or a cut. If these become dangerous or deadly by contact with infected matter, we think and speak of what has happened as something catastrophic or extraordinary, a mishap or an accident (cf. Lewis v. Ocean A. & G. Corp., supra, at page 21, 120 N.E. 56), though very likely a disease also. "A common-sense appraisement of everyday forms of speech and modes of thought must tell us when to stop." Bird v. St. Paul F. & M. Ins. Co., 224 N.Y. 47, 51, 120 N.E. 86, 87, 13 A.L.R. 875.

If Connelly's death was the outcome of an accident, as we think indisputably it was, only a strained and artificial terminology would refuse to identify the accident with the pernicious contact and its incidents, and confine that description to the scratch or the abrasion, which had an origin unknown. On the contrary, when a scratch or abrasion is of itself trivial or innocent, the average thought, if driven to a choice between the successive phases of the casualty, would find the larger measure of misadventure in the poisonous infection. The choice, however is one that is needless and misleading. The whole group of events, beginning with the cut and ending with death, was an accident, not in one of its phases, but in all of them. If any of those phases had its origin in causes engendered by the employment, the act supplies a remedy. * * *

An argument is built upon the wording of the statute. Workmen's Compensation Law, § 2, subd. 7. The statute speaks, as we have seen of "accidental injuries arising out of and in the course of the employment," and also of "such disease or infection as may naturally and unavoidably result therefrom." The point is made that infection is here coupled with disease as something other than an accident or an injury, though a possible concomitant. We think the intention was by the addition of these words to enlarge and not to narrow. Infection, like disease, may be gradual and insidious, or sudden and catastrophic. It may be an aggravation of injuries sustained in the course of the employment and arising therefrom, in which event it enters into the award, though its own immediate cause was unrelated to the service. It may be an aggravation of injuries which in their origin or primary form were apart from the employment, in which event, if sudden and catastrophic and an incident of service, it will supply a new point of departure, a new starting point in the chain of causes, and be reckoned in measuring the award as an injury itself.

The order of the Appellate Division should be reversed and the award of the State Industrial Board affirmed, with costs in this court and the Appellate Division.

POUND, CRANE, and LEHMAN, JJ., concur.

HISCOCK, C.J., and McLAUGHLIN and ANDREWS, JJ., dissent, and vote to affirm the order of the Appellate Division on opinions of Kellogg and Van Kirk, JJ., below.

CITY OF NICHOLS HILLS v. HILL
Supreme Court of Oklahoma, 1975.
534 P.2d 931.

BARNES, JUSTICE:

This proceeding for review seeks to vacate an order awarding compensation for accidental injury from exposure to contaminated dust, which caused or aggravated histoplasmosis resulting in permanent partial disability.

Original claim for compensation alleged accidental injury by inhalation of dust July 1, 1970, causing illness and disability.

Petitioners, respondents herein, answered denying fact of injury in covered employment, and alleged claimant suffered from disease neither caused nor aggravated by employment. Further, claimant never requested medical treatment, or gave notice he suffered from condition within provisions of 85 O.S.1971, § 1, prior to filing claim, and failure to give notice prejudiced respondents.

At a hearing January 17, 1973, claimant was permitted to amend his claim to show injury occurred May 25, 1970, and that injury was to throat, lungs, and respiratory injury to body as a whole.

Respondents stipulated as to employment and compensation rate, but denied notice of injury, or that illness resulted from employment. Respondents also moved to amend answer by denial of jurisdiction of the court to adjudicate the claim, upon the ground claim was for an illness not enumerated in Section 3 of the Act, supra. This motion was denied.

Two extended hearings were held, which included both oral and deposition testimony from medical experts, hereafter summarized. The trial judge excused failure to give statutory written notice because respondents had knowledge of the occurrence and were not prejudiced by failure. The court found claimant sustained accidental personal injury during performance of work, from exposure to contaminated dust which caused or aggravated histoplasmosis and resulted in 50% permanent partial disability to the body as a whole. On appeal to State Industrial Court en banc, this order was affirmed by divided [3–2] vote.

Stedman's Medical Dictionary, [3rd L.Ed.], p. 581, defines histoplasmosis as a human infection acquired by inhalation of spores of the fungus in dust, particularly from soils contaminated by dejecta of fowls, birds, or bats.

Testimony of two physicians, and a doctor of veterinary medicine with doctorate in public health, reflects matters hereafter summarized. Histoplasmosis is a widely occurring common infection, but relatively uncommon as a clinical illness recognizable as causing disability. The disease was recognized in 1905 and first was cultured in 1934. Scope of the disease was recognized following development of a serum test in 1946, and it is estimated fifty million persons within the Mississippi Valley area presently are infected.

Causative organisms are located in soil contaminated by droppings of various animals, and particularly fowls and birds. The disease enters the human body by inhalation of dust which contains spores of fungi into the lungs, and remains associated with defensive [phagocytic] cells throughout the body. In a majority of cases the person is unaware of inhalation and suffers no debilitating illness. After a short incubation period following heavier inhalation, a mild flu-like or pneumonia-like illness may result. Ordinarily, even severe infections heal spontaneously with nothing more than supportive treatment required.

Although infection ordinarily is expelled from the body, the organisms can remain viable and capable of dissemination for years, when bodily resistance declines from other causes; i.e., leukemia, administration of drugs, or processes which interfere with physical resistance. When heavy exposure occurs the patient may suffer cyanosis, tightness of the chest, unproductive cough, fever, and shortness of breath for weeks or months. The disease attacks the lungs, but causes trouble in other parts of the body [brain, bones] as infection grows. Although chronic histoplasmosis may result in mild illnesses mentioned, the infection remains, and, in an acute or disseminated state incited by interference with bodily resistance, histoplasmosis can be fatal. The disease is treated by controlled intravenous injection of a highly toxic drug.

Respondent, hereinafter the claimant, was a 63–year–old maintenance worker, employed by petitioners, herein the respondents. Employment duties included operation of a Ford tractor [brush hog] mower, and on May 25, 1970, claimant was directed by the supervisor to mow specified lots which were overgrown with grass, sunflowers and high weeds. The weather was dry and windy, mowing created a great deal of dust, and there were many birds and bird nests in the area being mowed.

Prior to this occurrence, claimant never had difficulty with nose, throat, or lungs, and had not suffered breathing problems. During the afternoon, claimant began experiencing extreme thirst, drank excessive amounts of water, and suffered dryness and burning in his nose, throat and lungs, and difficulty in breathing. These difficulties continued through the night and necessitated claimant seeing a physician before reporting for work. Claimant told the foreman of his difficulty after the mowing episode and was advised to go in and see a doctor if feeling too bad. Claimant worked the following day with same complaints, but did not return to work thereafter. Treatment continued from this doctor for a week, during which injections for a cold were administered without relief. Claimant has never been able to work since the third day following this occurrence.

On July 1, 1970, claimant saw Dr. R.F.R., related history of occurrence on job, illness and treatment by other doctors, continuing complaints of sore throat and tongue, and general debility with progressively severe symptoms. Examination revealed lesions of tongue extending into posterior pharynx. Succeeding treatments were unsuccessful, cultures attempted to identify any organisms in area were unsuccessful, and by July 22nd claimant's deteriorating condition resulted in Dr. R.F.R. referring claimant to a specialist [Dr. R.M.]. Claimant was hospitalized for laryngoscopy and biopsy of nodules on right vocal cord and tongue lesions.

Claimant was discharged after three days and removed to another hospital for treatment. A specialist, Dr. H.G.M., was called into consultation following biopsy of tongue, which revealed presence of histoplasmosis. From tests and X–rays, this physician ascertained presence of calcification in the lungs, indicating existence of infection for six months. Upon this basis the physician testified it was possible, but considered improbable, claimant contracted the disease at the time and in the manner alleged.

Claimant introduced deposition testimony given February 14, 1972, by Dr. R.F.R., who first saw claimant July 1, 1970, and initiated consultation and research which established presence of this disease. This doctor continued to attend and treat claimant over entire period. Based upon history of exposure, subsequent diagnostic findings and ensuing treatment, this physician testified there was little doubt exposure and infection occurred as claimed. Subsequent course of illness, and eventual findings based upon diagnosis and biopsies from different sites, indicated dissemination of the disease was compatible with date of exposure, normal incubation period, and illness. As a result of exposure and disease, claimant was permanently totally disabled.

The only real conflict in the medical evidence concerning cause of illness results from evidence related to finding calcification in claimant's lungs. In the opinion of two experts, it would be unusual to find this condition in less than six months following infection. However, on cross-examination, one doctor stated the incubation period for acute histoplasmosis ranged between five to twenty days, and lung congestion should indicate something was wrong. The doctor also fixed two months minimum for calcification of the lungs. Neither expert evaluated extent of claimant's resulting disability.

Respondent also introduced a medical report of Dr. C.A.G., based upon physical examination and X-ray studies. This physician agreed both with diagnosis and treatment, but was of the opinion claimant had recovered, and had suffered no permanent partial disability as a result of this "rather remarkable disease."

Respondents first contend the Act, supra, was intended to provide compensation only for accidental injury in hazardous employment and occupational diseases enumerated in § 3(16), which cannot include diseases contracted in course of ordinary living. Thus, since claimant was afflicted by disease not mentioned in the statute, State Industrial Court had no jurisdiction to adjudicate this claim.

This argument need not be noted, other than to observe there was no claim of occupational disease, nor medical evidence supporting this theory. Medical testimony only suggested possible sources of infection. And, when viewed in proper context, particularly in view of wide-spread, infectious nature of histoplasmosis, the evidence negates consideration of the disease as an occupational hazard.

* * *

Under the Act [§ 11], and settled decisional law, compensation is allowable for accidental injury which results from accidental means which are unexpected or undesigned, or which result from miscalculation or mischance concerning effect of voluntary action. In determining whether accidental injury has occurred, the Act is not given a narrow, restricted meaning, but must receive a broad and liberal interpretation to effect intent of the Act. Armour & Co. v. Worden, 189 Okl. 106, 114 P.2d 173. Any reasonable doubt whether injury arose out of and in course of employment should be resolved in favor of an injured workman. In Re Martin [Okl.], 452 P.2d 785.

What constitutes accidental injury within meaning of the Act has been stated many times. An oft-quoted definition appears in Andrews Mining & Milling Co. v. Atkinson, 192 Okl. 322, 135 P.2d 960:

> "An 'accident' is an event happening without any human agency, or if happening through human agency, an event which, under the circumstances, is unusual and not expected to the person to whom it happens. In the term 'accidental injuries', the substantive 'injuries' expresses the notion of a thing or event, that is, the wrong or damage done to the person, while 'accidental' qualifies and describes the noun by ascribing to 'injuries' a quality or condition of happening, or coming by chance or without design, taking place unexpectedly or unintentionally."

* * *

Medical findings, ascertained from examination of claimant on July 1, 1970, were consistent with history of exposure to contamination and ensuing debilitating effects. This was basis of the physician's conclusion that there was little doubt exposure to histoplasmatic material was compatible with history of dust exposure, with the mouth and throat the likely site for entry of infection.

We have noted evidentiary matters concerning claimant's duties and working conditions, absence of prior physical difficulties, facts of exposure and immediate onset of difficulty, with ensuing progression of diagnostically established, disseminated histoplasmosis. This injury was not a designed or expected consequence of the work in which claimant was engaged, and was not categorized as an occupational disease by experts who testified. To the contrary, competent evidence established this injury resulted from unexpected exposure, which occurred at a definite time and caused infection and disability. This evidence measured by factors declared to constitute accidental injury under Atkinson, supra, clearly establishes correctness of the finding claimant sustained accidental injury within meaning and intent of the Act, supra.

See Victory Sparkler & Specialty Co. v. Francks, 147 Md. 368, 128 A. 635, 44 A.L.R. 363, at 371, which differentiates between occupational disease and accidental disease or injury.

Evidence which established disability resulted from histoplasmosis was sufficient to support an award based upon finding of accidental injury from exposure to contamination at a definite time. Respondents' evidence indicated claimant had been infected at least six months, but infection could remain dormant a long period before being triggered into activity by a variety of circumstances. The State Industrial Court resolved this conflicting evidence in claimant's favor. Weight and credibility of expert testimony is exclusively for determination of the trier of facts. Blue Bell, Inc. v. Owens [Okl.], 463 P.2d 969. Probative value of medical evidence is for State Industrial Court, which may accept all or part of such evidence, or reject this evidence entirely. Arnold v. J.F. Pritchard & Co. [Okl.], 399 P.2d 481.

We have determined the trial court was correct in finding occurrence of accidental injury. Under our decisions, the fact claimant suffered prior infection of the disease as reflected by respondents' evidence would not be decisive. Where accidental injury aggravates or lights up a pre-existing condition, the resulting disability is compensable. National Zinc Co. v. Cichon [Okl.], 364 P.2d 699, and cases cited. Under either hypothesis, the trial court's finding of accidental injury, which resulted in disability, is sustained by competent evidence.

* * *

Award sustained.

Notes

1. The question whether disability resulting from infectious disease is compensable has caused difficulty throughout the history of workers' compensation. It has been assumed from the beginning that workers' compensation laws are not intended to provide general health insurance. For this reason, courts were inclined originally to deny compensation in disease cases. As time went on, however, it has become clear that certain diseases are so closely related to the claimant's employment and are so similar to personal "injury" that they merit compensation. Yet in many states in which the statute contains the term "personal injury" and has no express provision on the subject of disease, there is a substantial question whether an infectious disease constitutes a "personal injury" within the contemplation of the law. If the statute also uses terms suggesting that the injury must be accidental, there may be problems on the two aspects of the concept of accident discussed above, namely the requirement of unexpectedness and that of definiteness in time of occurrence.

2. Some statutes specifically define "personal injury" in terms allowing compensation for a disease that *follows* an accidental injury but excluding all other diseases from the definition. E.g., Arizona Rev.Stats.Ann. § 23–901(12) (" 'personal injury by accident arising out of and in the course of employment' ... does not include a disease unless resulting from the injury."); Georgia Code Ann. § 34–9–1(4) (" 'Injury' and 'personal injury' ... shall not, except as hereinafter provided, include a disease in any form except where it results naturally and unavoidably from the accident ..."); S.C.Code Ann. § 42–1–160 (" 'Injury' and 'personal injury' ... shall not include a disease in any form, except when it results naturally and unavoidably from the accident ..."). States with statutes of the foregoing type have separate provisions in their acts for "occupational diseases" as discussed later in this chapter. Other statutes expressly require violence to or a change in the physical structure of the body, e.g., Neb.Rev.Stat. § 48–151(4); or "traumat-

ic" injury, e.g., Wash.Rev.Code Ann. 51.08.100. Such provisions present special obstacles to recovery for infectious disease as an accidental injury.

3. The *Connelly* case represents one of the first points of breakthrough in the disease field in holding that if the disease is caused by the entrance of germs into the body at a definite time through an abnormal channel, there is a personal injury and an accident. The decision has been widely approved and a number of state courts have followed it in awarding compensation for disabling infectious disease when it appeared that the disease-causing germs entered claimant's body through a cut or wound or were injected by the bite of an insect. Montgomery v. Industrial Comm'n, 173 Ariz. 106, 840 P.2d 282 (Ariz.App.1992) (Lyme Disease contracted through a tick bite); Baldwin v. Jensen–Salsbery Laboratories, 10 Kan.App.2d 673, 708 P.2d 556 (1985) (brucellosis contracted through cut on hand is compensable as an accidental injury); Okemah Pub. Co. v. Aaron, 285 P.2d 410 (Okl.1955) (death caused by tetanus contracted through a scratch on the finger); Roe v. Boise Grocery Co., 53 Idaho 82, 21 P.2d 910 (1933) and Smith v. McHan Hardware Co., 56 Idaho 43, 48 P.2d 1102 (1935) (Rocky Mountain spotted fever incurred through tick bites); Great Atlantic & Pacific Tea Co. v. Sexton, 242 Ky. 266, 46 S.W.2d 87 (1932) (tularemia or rabbit fever contracted while skinning and dressing a shipment of rabbits); Chicago Rawhide Mfg. Co. v. Industrial Comm., 291 Ill. 616, 126 N.E. 616 (1920) (anthrax contracted by foreman in hide tanning department when he scratched a pimple on his neck).

4. In the years that followed *Connelly,* the entrance of disease germs into the body through normal channels came to be recognized by many courts as an accidental injury. This result is frequently reached where claimant experienced some unusual occupational exposure to the disease. E.g., Jackson Township Volunteer Fire Co. v. Workmen's Comp. App. Bd., 140 Pa.Cmwlth. 620, 594 A.2d 826 (Pa. Comm. 1991) (volunteer ambulance worker's exposure to blood infected with hepatitis B and HIV was an "accident"); Olson v. Executive Travel MSP, Inc., 437 N.W.2d 645 (Minn. 1989) (claimant was infected with an Influenza Type B virus while traveling in the Orient for her employer; the virus led to pneumonia which resulted in chronic bronchiectasis; award of benefits under "personal injury" provision of compensation act affirmed); Middleton v. Coxsackie Correctional Facility, 38 N.Y.2d 130, 379 N.Y.S.2d 3, 341 N.E.2d 527 (1975) (a corrections officer who was in repeated and close contact with an inmate who coughed persistently and was later found to be tubercular was awarded compensation for tuberculosis as an "accident"); Cook County v. Industrial Comm., 54 Ill.2d 79, 295 N.E.2d 465 (1973) (claimant contracted tuberculosis working as a pathologist's assistant in hospital autopsy room); Industrial Comm. v. Corwin Hospital, 126 Colo. 358, 250 P.2d 135 (1952) (claimant contracted polio working in polio ward of hospital during epidemic).

5. In states that have separate occupational disease provisions in their statutes, a question may arise as to whether a given disability is compensable as a personal injury or as an occupational disease. In some instances it may be both, and in some neither. The former could be true in a state having a broad definition of occupational disease and court decisions that are not restrictive in delineating the concept of accidental injury. E.g., Bremer v. Buerkle, 223 Mont. 495, 727 P.2d 529 (1986) (contact dermatitis constituted both an injury and occupational disease). But in Stenrich Group v. Jemmott,

251 Va. 186, 467 S.E.2d 795 (Va. 1996) the court declared that cumulative trauma disorders are not compensable as an accident or as a disease. Similarly in Masterson v. Rutland Hospital, Inc., 129 Vt. 91, 271 A.2d 848 (1970) pulmonary tuberculosis contracted during work in a hospital was held not compensable either as an accident or occupational disease.

The possibilities of overlap on the one hand, and incomplete coverage on the other, under such state laws must always be kept in mind by the practicing lawyer. As to some aspects of the case it may make a great deal of difference whether the disabling condition is held to be an accident or an occupational disease; for example, the applicable statute of limitations, time of notice of injury, required period of employment prior to injury and similar requirements and limitations.

SECTION 3. OCCUPATIONAL DISEASE

a. *Introduction*

As it became apparent that the limitations associated with the concept of accidental injury left substantial gaps in the protection afforded disabled workers, states began to adopt statutes providing compensation for occupational disease. It was a slow process but ultimately all states afforded such coverage. Some do it by separate statutes. Some incorporate occupational disease provisions into their workers' compensation law by various devices such as expanding the definition of "injury."

In earlier years, some of the laws confined the protection to a specified list or schedule of diseases named in the statute and in some instances even described how the disease must be contracted. Difficult problems of interpretation were thereby created and sometimes anomalous decisions resulted. For example, in Ridley Packing Co. v. Holliday, 467 P.2d 480 (Okl.1970), claimant, a butcher, contracted brucellosis from killing and skinning cattle in the course of his employment. The occupational disease statute provided for compensation for "glanders and other diseased conditions caused by handling any equine animal or the carcass of any such animal." Compensation was denied because the disease was not contracted by handling a horse or its carcass but from cattle.

Following World War II, a trend developed toward general coverage. Some statutes retained a schedule of diseases but added a general clause affording coverage for any occupational disease. For example, the Ohio statute after a list of twenty-eight diseases contains the following provision: "All other occupational diseases: a disease peculiar to a particular industrial process, trade, or occupation and to which an employee is not ordinarily subjected or exposed outside or away from his employment." Ohio Rev.Code Ann. § 4123.68 (Baldwin 1989). Today, all states provide general compensation coverage for occupational disease.

There is reason to believe that occupational disease poses special challenges for the workers' compensation system. The number of potential occupational disease claims is quite large. One controversial but frequently cited report estimates that 100,000 workers die each year from occupational disease and an additional 390,000 workers contract some form of work related illness. The President's Report on Occupational Safety and Health 111 (1972). In a recent article reviewing available studies the authors stated: "[w]e estimated that 817,000 to 907,400 new cases of occupational illnesses and 46,900 to 73,700 deaths resulted from occupational disease in the United States in 1992." J. Paul Leigh et. al., Occupational Injury and Illness in the United States, 267 Arch. Intern. Med. 1157, 1562 (1997). The workplace is thought to be responsible for 6–10% of all cancers, 5–10% of all coronary heart disease, 5–10% of all cerebrovascular disease, and 10% of all chronic obstructive pulmonary disease in the United States. Id.

While the number of potential occupational disease claims is quite large, the percentage of potential claimants who receive compensation benefits is quite small. Only 2–3% of the total benefits paid under workers' compensation are for occupational disease claims and only about 5% of all occupational disease victims receive compensation. Thomas O. McGarity & Sidney A. Shapiro, OSHA's Critics and Regulatory Reform, 31 Wake Forest L. Rev. 587, 599–600 (1996). See also, George Freidman–Jimenez, Achieving Environmental Justice: The Role of Occupational Health, 21 Fordham Urban L. J. 605, 606 (1994) ("only three to five percent of occupational disease deaths and eleven to thirty-eight percent of new cases of occupational disease are actually reported as occupational.").

What explains the tremendous gap between the high estimates of incidences of occupational disease and the low number of claims in which compensation benefits are paid? Commentators offer two reasons. First, many workers and their physicians may fail to recognize that an illness is work related, so that no claim is made. Second, claims that are filed must overcome restrictive standards of recovery. Thomas O. McGarity & Sidney A. Shapiro, OSHA's Critics and Regulatory Reform, 31 Wake Forest L. Rev. 587, 600 (1996); Elinor P. Schroeder & Sidney A. Shapiro, Responses to Occupational Disease: The Role of Markets, Regulation, and Information, 72 Geo.L.Rev. 1231, 1246 (1984). Even for well recognized occupational diseases, such as those caused by exposure to asbestos, fewer than half of the potential beneficiaries file a claim for workers' compensation. R. Field & R. Victor, Workers' Compensation Research Institute, Asbestos Claims: The Decision to Use Workers' Compensation and Tort 12 (1988). The few occupational disease claims that enter the system are contested more frequently and take longer to resolve than claims involving accidental injuries. Schroeder, Legislative and Judicial Responses to the Inadequacy of Compensation for Occupational Disease, 49 Law & Contemp. Prob. (no. 4) 151, 157–58 (1986).

The following materials illustrate some of the practical and conceptual problems in processing occupational disease claims within the workers' compensation system. The first case addresses the definition of occupational disease, distinguishing it from ordinary diseases of life. The second set of cases address issues that arise when occupational and nonoccupational factors combine to produce a disabling disease.

b. Occupational Disease and Ordinary Diseases of Life

BOOKER v. DUKE MEDICAL CENTER
Supreme Court of North Carolina, 1979.
297 N.C. 458, 256 S.E.2d 189.

Stipulations and plaintiffs' evidence show the following facts:

Booker began working for Duke Medical Center on 24 October 1966. From that date until the first part of July 1971 he worked as a laboratory technician in the Clinical Chemistry Laboratory, where he performed various chemical determinations on serum blood, blood serum, whole blood, and other body fluids. In the process he manually tested blood samples and, although he was a careful and experienced employee, he routinely spilled blood upon his fingers. Each day one or more of the blood samples he tested was infected with serum hepatitis. These samples bore no diagnostic label when they came in or went out, and the lab technicians never knew whether the patient's blood was diseased. The blood samples tested were divided about equally between Duke's in-patients and out-patients. The first of July 1971 Duke began to label all diagnosed hepatic patients' blood which came to the lab, but not all infected blood had been diagnosed.

On 3 July 1971 Booker, who had been totally asymptomatic up until 3 or 4 days prior to that date, developed symptoms which caused him to consult Dr. Joe B. Currin, a specialist in internal medicine. Dr. Currin ascertained that Booker was suffering from serum hepatitis and hospitalized him for ten days. Thereafter Booker, who had worked continually with blood samples, ceased handling blood and worked in the lab as an "electronical engineer."

In July 1972 Dr. Michael E. McLeod of the Department of Medicine at Duke Hospital, Duke Medical Center, took Booker as a patient and treated him for serum hepatitis until Booker's death on 3 January 1974. During this interim Booker was "in and out" of the hospital on sick leave. About 1 October 1973 he became unable "to sustain his performance" at the lab, and on 15 October 1973 Dr. McLeod certified that Booker was no longer able to work. The autopsy, performed 3 January 1974 at Duke Medical Center, showed that Booker "died of a disease due to serum hepatitis." * * *

[Booker's dependents filed a claim for death benefits. Evidence presented at the hearing established that serum hepatitis is a virus disease of the liver which can be transmitted by contact with even microscopic amounts of infected blood.]

Serum hepatitis is not a disease limited to persons who handle blood. Members of the general public are from time to time afflicted with this disease. Thus, it was not possible for Booker himself or the medical experts and chemist who testified for plaintiffs to state with absolute certainty the time or place at which Booker became infected.

* * *

Mr. Robert F. Wilderman, the chemist in charge of the laboratory where Booker worked, testified that as far as he knew Booker was not exposed to hepatitis other than in his work at Duke; that in the performance of his work there he did know that Booker handled many samples of blood and that he came in contact with blood cells from hepatic patients.

In the opinion of Doctors Currin and McLeod there is a much greater likelihood that laboratory technicians in clinical labs at major medical centers will contract serum hepatitis than that persons working in other places will do so, for "the public is generally not nearly so exposed to the hazard." Booker's situation, Dr. Currin said, was such "that in all likelihood he contracted it through his employment." Dr. McLeod's testimony was that the conditions under which Booker worked put him "at a much, much higher risk to contract the disease serum hepatitis than other employees in the hospital and people who are not employed in the hospital." Public health surveys, he said, supported this conclusion. Further, "all the evidence [Dr. McLeod] could gather did not indicate any other contacts" by Booker "with anybody with hepatitis, jaundice or liver disease."

* * *

SHARP, CHIEF JUSTICE.

For an injury or death to be compensable under our Workmen's Compensation Act it must be either the result of an "accident arising out of and in the course of the employment" or an "occupational disease." The Court of Appeals concluded that Booker's injury was not the result of an "accident" because no specific incident could be identified which led to his contracting the disease. *Booker v. Medical Center,* 32 N.C.App. 185, 231 S.E.2d 187 (1977). None of the parties to this appeal assigned that conclusion as error. The question before us therefore is whether or not his death was the result of an "occupational disease." Because serum hepatitis is not expressly mentioned in the schedule of diseases contained in G.S. 97–53, it is a compensable injury only if it falls within the general definition set out in G.S. 97–53(13) [which provides as follows:]

* * *

"Any disease, other than hearing loss covered in another subdivision of this section, which is proven to be due to causes and conditions which are characteristic of and peculiar to a particular trade, occupation or employment, but excluding all ordinary diseases of life to which the general public is equally exposed outside of the employment."

* * *

Because serum hepatitis is not a disease which develops gradually through prolonged exposure to harmful conditions but instead is an illness caused by a single exposure to a virus, the Court of Appeals concluded that it was not compensable as an occupational disease. For the reasons which follow we disagree.

We begin by noting Professor Larson's admonition that "[d]efinitions of 'occupational disease' should always be checked against the purpose for which they were uttered." 1B A. Larson, Workmen's Compensation Law § 41.31 (1978). Because the first workmen's compensation acts usually provided coverage for accidental injuries while denying or limiting it for victims of occupational disease, the tendency in early court decisions construing these acts was to expansively define the term "accident" while narrowly construing the term "occupational disease." As jurisdictions amended their laws to provide coverage for all occupationally related illnesses, these older definitions became less viable * * *

* * *

In all of the North Carolina cases cited earlier, the term "occupational disease" was defined solely for the purpose of distinguishing it from an "injury by accident." In *Watkins v. Murrow,* supra, for example, claimant was a truck driver who was permanently disabled by carbon monoxide poisoning when he parked his truck and went to sleep with the motor running. The carbon monoxide entered the cab from a faulty exhaust pipe. Noting that an occupational disease is one which "develops gradually over a long period of time," the Court agreed with the Industrial Commission that claimant had suffered an accidental injury. 253 N.C. at 661, 118 S.E.2d at 11–12. In none of these cases was any attempt made to inclusively define the term "occupational disease." To use the definitions for that purpose is to carry them beyond their intended scope.

The Court of Appeals' construction, moreover, would work a judicial repeal of a portion of the statute. In holding that an illness is compensable only if it falls within prior judicial definitions of the term "occupational disease," the Court noted that even a disease listed by name in G.S. 97–53 would be noncompensable under that statute if it were the result of "a single event" as opposed to being the "cumulative effect of [a] series of events." 32 N.C.App. at 192–93, 231 S.E.2d at 192–93. Of the occupational diseases listed by name in the statute, however, at least three—anthrax, psittacosis, and undulant fever—are infectious diseases which are contracted, like serum hepatitis, by a single exposure under optimum conditions to the virus or bacteria causing the disease. Stedman's Medical Dictionary (22nd ed. 1972); G.S. 97–53(1), (26), (27). The Court of Appeals' construction would in effect read these diseases out of the statute.

Finally, the Court of Appeals' interpretation must be rejected as inconsistent with the overriding legislative goal of providing comprehensive coverage for occupational diseases. Except for those diseases specifically named in the statute, it is our view that the legislature intended the present version of G.S. 97–53(13) to define the term "occupational disease." To the extent that this statute conflicts with prior judicial definitions of the term "occupational disease," the older definitions must give way.

As Professor Larson points out, the "element of gradualness, so heavily stressed in definitions contrived to distinguish accident, loses its importance when the sole question is the inclusiveness of an occupational disease statute. If the inherent conditions of employment produce outright infection, . . . it may be treated as an occupational disease although the process is much more sudden than that described in the older definitions." 1B A. Larson, Workmen's Compensation Law § 41–40 (1978).

If an employee contracts an infectious disease as a result of his employment and it falls within either the schedule of diseases set out in the statute or the general definition of "occupational disease" in G.S. 97–53(13), it should be treated as a compensable event regardless of the fact that it might also qualify as an "injury by accident" under G.S. 97–2(6).

* * *

Having concluded that G.S. 97–53(13) is to be interpreted independently of any prior definitions of "occupational disease," we turn now to its construction. To be compensable under subsection (13) a disease must, *inter alia,* be "characteristic of and peculiar to a particular trade, occupation or employment."

A disease is "characteristic" of a profession when there is a recognizable link between the nature of the job and an increased risk of contracting the disease in question. *See Harman v. Republic Aviation Corp.,* 298 N.Y. 285, 82 N.E.2d 785 (1948). Appellees argue, however, that serum hepatitis is not "peculiar to" the occupation of laboratory technician since employees in other occupations and members of the general public may also contract the disease.

Statutes similar to G.S. 97–53 have been examined by the courts of many states. Conn.Gen.Stat. § 5223, for example, defined an occupational disease as "a disease peculiar to the occupation in which the employee was engaged and due to causes in excess of the ordinary hazards of employment as such." (Current version at Conn.Gen.Stat.Ann. 31–275 (West 1972)). In *LeLenko v. Wilson H. Lee Co.,* 128 Conn. 499, 503, 24 A.2d 253, 255 (1942) that statute was construed as follows:

> "The phrase, 'peculiar to the occupation', is not here used in the sense that the disease must be one which originates exclusively from the particular kind of employment in which the employee is engaged, but rather in the sense that the conditions of that employment must result in a hazard which distinguishes it in character from the general run of occupations (see Oxford Dictionary; Funk & Wagnalls Dictionary). . . . To come within the definition, an occupational disease must be a disease which is a natural incident of a particular occupation, and must attach to that occupation a hazard which distinguishes it from the usual run of occupations and is in

excess of that attending employment in general. *Glodenis v. American Brass Co.,* 118 Conn. 29, 40, 170 A. 146, 150."

In *Ritter v. Hawkeye–Security Insurance Co.,* 178 Neb. 792, 795, 135 N.W.2d 470, 472 (1965) the Nebraska Supreme Court examined a statute almost identical to our own. *See* Neb.Rev.Stat. § 48–151 (1974). In upholding a disability award to a dishwasher who developed contact dermatitis as a result of the use of cleansing chemicals in his work, the court made the following remark:

> "The statute does not require that the disease be one which originates exclusively from the employment. The statute means that the conditions of the employment must result in a hazard which distinguishes it in character from employment generally."

Similarly, in allowing an award to a nurse's aide who contracted tuberculosis from her patients, the Supreme Court of Maine in *Russell v. Camden Community Hospital,* 359 A.2d 607, 611–12 (Me.1976) said:

> "The requirement that the disease be 'characteristic of or peculiar to' the occupation of the claimant precludes coverage of diseases contracted merely because the employee was on the job. For example, it is clear that the Law was not intended to extend to an employee in a shoe factory who contracts pneumonia simply by standing next to an infected co-worker. In that example, the employee's exposure to the disease would have occurred regardless of the nature of the occupation in which he was employed. To be within the purview of the Law, the disease must be so distinctively associated with the employee's occupation that there is a direct causal connection between the duties of the employment and the disease contracted."

* * *

It is clear from this evidence that a distinctive relation exists between Mr. Booker's occupation and the disease serum hepatitis. The evidence amply supports the Commission's determination that Booker's job exposed him to a greater risk of contracting the disease than members of the public or employees in general. This finding of fact supports its legal conclusion that serum hepatitis is a disease "characteristic of and peculiar to his occupation of lab technician." We note that many other states have similarly recognized that hospital employees may face an increased risk of contracting communicable diseases. See Note, *Occupational Diseases and the Hospital Employee—A Survey,* 5 Mem.St. U.L.Rev. 368 (1975) and cases cited therein.

Appellees also argue that serum hepatitis is an "ordinary disease of life" and is therefore noncompensable. They cite in particular Dr. Michael McLeod's statement on cross-examination that "[s]erum hepatitis is not a disease which is limited to persons who handle blood. Members of the general public from time to time are [also] afflicted with this disease." Clearly, serum hepatitis is an "ordinary disease of life" in the sense that members of the general public may contract the disease, as opposed to a disease like silicosis or asbestosis which is confined to certain trades and occupations. Our statute, however, does not preclude coverage for all ordinary diseases of life but instead only those "to which the general public is *equally exposed* outside of the employment." G.S. 97–53(13) (Emphasis added). The testimony of Dr. McLeod and Dr. Currin cited earlier supports the Commission's conclusion that the public is exposed to the risk of contracting serum hepatitis to a far lesser extent than was Mr. Booker.

As the Michigan Supreme Court observed when faced with a similar argument in *Mills v. Detroit Tuberculosis Sanitarium,* 323 Mich. 200, 209, 35 N.W.2d 239, 242 (1948): "[T]he statute does not place all ordinary diseases in a non-compensable class, but, rather those 'to which the public is generally exposed outside of the employment.' The evidence in this case indicates that the plaintiff was exposed in his employment to the risk of contracting tuberculosis in a far greater degree and in a wholly different manner than is the public generally." The greater risk in such cases provides the nexus between the disease and the employment which makes them an appropriate subject for workmen's compensation.

The final requirement in establishing a compensable claim under subsection (13) is proof of causation. It is this limitation which protects our Workmen's Compensation Act from being converted into a general health and insurance benefit act. *Bryan v. Church,* 267 N.C. 111, 115, 147 S.E.2d 633, 635 (1966).

* * *

In the case of occupational diseases proof of a causal connection between the disease and the employee's occupation must of necessity be based on circumstantial evidence. Among the circumstances which may be considered are the following: (1) the extent of exposure to the disease or disease-causing agents during employment, (2) the extent of exposure outside employment, and (3) absence of the disease prior to the work-related exposure as shown by the employee's medical history.

Evidence on each of the foregoing three points was presented at the hearing before the Commissioner and may be summarized as follows: Serum hepatitis is a liver disease transmitted most often through injections, blood transfusions, by nicks and scratches on the skin, or by handling fecal materials. A person cannot contract serum hepatitis unless he comes in direct contact with the virus, which must enter his blood stream in one of the manners set out above. Only one contact is necessary to produce the disease. The maximum incubation period is six months.

During the four years he worked at the laboratory, Booker handled and tested blood samples, some of which would routinely spill on his fingers. Each day one or more of these samples showed a positive diagnosis of serum hepatitis. Booker's hobby was gardening and from time to time he would nick or cut his fingers. It was not unusual for him to work in the laboratory with unhealed nicks or scratches on his hands.

For more than six months prior to diagnosis of his disease Booker had no injections of any type and no illnesses. The only time a needle was inserted in his body during this period was when he donated blood at the Duke Blood Bank. All such donations were obtained by disposable needles; that is, the needles were used once and then destroyed. So far as Booker and his wife knew and as far as his physicians could ascertain, at no time or place outside of the Duke Medical Center lab where he worked had Booker ever come into contact with any person, blood or blood product infected with serum hepatitis.

The Commission's findings of fact based on the foregoing evidence substantially exclude the possibility that Booker contracted the disease outside of his employment. It is also perfectly obvious that his occupation exposed him to a greatly increased risk of contracting serum hepatitis for each day he handled unmarked vials of blood infected with the disease. These findings are sufficient to sustain the Commission's conclusion that Booker's disease was caused by his employment.

* * *

For the reasons stated, the decision of the Court of Appeals is reversed and the case is returned to the Court of Appeals with directions that it be remanded to the North Carolina Industrial Commission for the implementation of its award.

Reversed and Remanded.

BRITT and BROCK, JJ., took no part in the consideration or decision of this case.

Notes

1. The *Booker* case illustrates the central problem of distinguishing occupational from nonoccupational disease. Why is it considered both theoretically and practically necessary to maintain a distinction between occupational and nonoccupational diseases? Do any of the assumptions underlying the compensation principle discussed in Chapter 2 provide guidance on how to make this distinction?

2. The starting point for analysis is the statutory definition of occupational disease, which often provides specific criteria for inclusion and exclusion. Many statutes, such as that construed in *Booker,* define occupational disease to exclude "ordinary disease of life." E.g., N.D.Cent.Code § 65–01–02(8)(a)(1), S.C.Code Ann. § 42–11–10(4); Va.Code Ann. § 65.1–46. Others include only those diseases caused by conditions "characteristic of and peculiar to" the employment. E.g., Ala.Code § 25–5–110(1); Mich.Comp. Laws Ann. § 418.401(2)(b); Okla.Stat.Ann. tit. 85, § 3(10). As was the case in *Booker,* the definition often will include several standards. Consider the definition contained in Ga.Code Ann. § 34–9–280(2) which provides:

" 'Occupational disease' means those diseases which arise out of and in the course of a particular trade ... provided the employee ... first proves ... all the following:

(A) A direct causal connection between the conditions under which the work is performed and the disease;

(B) That the disease followed as a natural incident of exposure by reason of the employment;

(C) That the disease is not of a character to which the employee may have had substantial exposure outside of the employment;

(D) That the disease is not an ordinary disease of life to which the general public is exposed;

(E) That the disease must appear to have had its origin in a risk connected with the employment and to have flowed from that source as a natural consequence."

Is this five-part definition any improvement over the "arising out of and in the course of" test of work connectedness used in accident cases?

3. In determining whether a particular illness is a non-compensable ordinary disease of life or is a covered occupational disease, courts often compare the level of risk created by the work environment with that existing outside the job. If a worker is exposed to a known dangerous substance primarily encountered during employment, the resulting illness is most likely to be covered. Reynolds Metals Co. v. Stults, 532 So.2d 1035 (Ala.Civ. App.1988) (occupational exposure to asbestos); United Electrical Coal Co. v. Industrial Comm., 74 Ill.2d 198, 23 Ill.Dec. 535, 384 N.E.2d 329 (Ill. 1978) (evidence of claimant's exposure to coal dust for 28 years supported finding that pneumoconiosis is an occupational disease); Al's Radiator Service v. Workmen's Comp. App. Bd., 157 Pa.Cmwlth. 432, 630 A.2d 485 (Pa. Comm. 1993)(auto repair worker exposed to lead fumes; lead poisoning); Service Adhesive Co. v. Industrial Comm'n, 226 Ill.App.3d 356, 168 Ill.Dec. 366, 589 N.E.2d 766 (Ill.App.1992) (leukemia caused by exposure to benzene).

Other conditions, such as contagious diseases and various respiratory ailments, may appear to be work related but also could be contracted by the general public. These diseases lie at the borderline separating occupational from ordinary diseases of life. As reflected in *Booker*, coverage frequently hinges on whether the work conditions increased the employee's chances of contracting the particular illness. Accordingly, tuberculosis and emphysema have been considered occupational diseases where the incidence of those diseases was greater among workers than in the general population. Nathan v. Presbyterian Hospital, 66 A.D.2d 933, 411 N.Y.S.2d 419 (1978) (tuberculosis as an occupational disease); Borovich v. Colt Industries, 492 Pa. 372, 424 A.2d 1237 (1981) (emphysema). Conversely, where evidence of increased risk was lacking, these same diseases have been labeled ordinary diseases of life. Lindenfeld v. City of Richmond, 25 Va.App. 775, 492 S.E.2d 506 (Va.App. 1997) (deputy sheriff denied compensation for tuberculosis; ordinary disease of life); Brawn v. St. Regis Paper Co., 430 A.2d 843 (Me.1981) (emphysema). See also, Fulton–DeKalb Hosp. Auth. v. Bishop, 185 Ga.App. 771, 365 S.E.2d 549 (1988) (emergency medical technician who contracted Hepatitis B was denied compensation where evidence indicated that the general public was exposed to the disease and the record was silent on whether the claimant had substantial exposure to the disease outside the employment). The strength of expert testimony and the discretion of the fact finder are often determinative of such claims.

4. An increased risk analysis will lead to the denial of compensation in cases where there is only a fortuitous causal relationship between the workplace and the disease. E.g., Paider v. Park East Movers, 19 N.Y.2d 373, 280 N.Y.S.2d 140, 227 N.E.2d 40 (1967) (truck driver contracted tuberculosis from a co-worker; compensation denied); Young v. City of Huntsville, 342 So.2d 918 (Ala.Civ.App.1976) (compensation denied when claimant's employment as a nurse did not expose her to a danger of developing thrombophlebitis materially in excess of that to which people not so employed); Snir v. S.W. Mays, Inc., 19 N.Y.2d 373, 280 N.Y.S.2d 140, 227 N.E.2d 40 (1967) (a cashier claiming her myositis of the neck and shoulder was caused by a cold draft from the air conditioning at work was denied compensation). If a jurisdiction has adopted positional risk analysis for determining whether accidents are sufficiently work related, what is the justification for applying an increased risk standard for disease claims? See, Crossett School District v. Gourley, 50 Ark.App. 1, 899 S.W.2d 482 (Ark.App.1995) (awarding benefits to a school teacher whose sinus surgery was rendered necessary by mold in her employer's heating and air conditioning system.).

5. Some diseases might satisfy the increased risk test of *Booker,* yet coverage is still disputed. The controversy often centers around nonoccupational factors in the diseases' etiology. The next two cases explore the issues presented by diseases having multiple causal factors.

c. *Dual Causation*

OLSON v. FEDERAL AMERICAN PARTNERS
Supreme Court of Wyoming, 1977.
567 P.2d 710.

RAPER, JUSTICE.

From a judgment of the district court denying claimant-appellant's claims for herself as a widow and on behalf of the dependent child of an employee covered by Wyoming's Occupational Disease Law, § 27–288, et seq., as amended, (repealed, § 4, Ch. 149, S.L.Wyo.1975), arising out of the death of her husband, allegedly by malignancy caused by radiation, she appeals. We will affirm.

Section 27–290, of the Occupational Disease Law, stated in pertinent part:

"(a) The list of authorized compensable occupational diseases shall include:

. . .

"(xxii) ionizing radiation, radiation poisoning or malignancy caused thereby . . ."

* * *

Section 27–293 provided:

"When an employee has suffered a compensable occupational disease covered by this act, the employer's account in whose employment said employee was last injuriously exposed to the hazards of the disease at the time of exposure shall alone be liable therefore, without right to contribution from any prior employer."

Section 27–297(a) covered burden of proof:

"The burden in contested cases shall be upon the employee to make proper proof of his claim by a preponderance of the evidence, and to likewise prove by competent medical authority that this claim arose out of and in the course of his employment by showing by a preponderance of such evidence that:

"(i) there is a direct causal connection between the condition under which the work is performed and the occupational disease,

"(ii) the disease can be seen to have followed as a natural incident of the work as a result of the exposure occasioned by the nature of the employment,

"(iii) the disease can be fairly traced to the employment as the proximate cause,

"(iv) the disease does not come from a hazard to which workmen would have been equally exposed outside of the employment,

"(v) and the disease is incidental to the character of the business and not independent of the relation of employer and employee."

The claimant's husband had been employed as an underground uranium miner, as follows:

Jan. 3, 1958–Feb. 27, 1970	Continental Uranium Co.
Mar. 4, 1970–Sept. 10, 1970	Federal American Partners
Oct. 11, 1970–Jan. 15, 1971	Continental Uranium Co.
Jan. 18, 1971–Dec. 29, 1971	Federal American Partners

The appellee-employer was Olson's last employer. While in that employment, he became ill and on May 23, 1973, died of lung cancer. The claimant at the trial asserted that her husband died of a lung cancer induced by occupational radiation exposure arising out of his last employment. The last employer denied liability, claiming that Olson had not been subjected to injurious radiation exposure during his employment by it, so there was no causal connection between the employment with it and the lung cancer and, additionally, that there was no certainty that his cancer developed in his employment as a uranium miner. It was admitted that the deceased was an habitual cigarette smoker, having smoked daily at least a package to a package and a half from 1949 until 1971. The record evidence indicates he may have smoked even more.

The court's findings were:

"1. That it is unable to find that the Claimant has established by competent medical authority by a preponderance of the evidence that the disease of the decedent, Ralph R. Olson, did not come from a hazard to which the workman would have been equally exposed outside of his employment.

"2. That it is unable to find on the evidence in this case that the Claimant has established by the prescribed burden of proof that the disease in this case is not independent of the relation of Employer and employee.

"3. That it is unable to find that the Claimant has established that the disease is not independent of the relation of this particular Employer and this particular employee involved in these proceedings.

"4. That it is unable to find from the evidence that this Employer is the one in which the last injurious exposure occurred, neither is it able to make a contrary finding, and so that portion of the resolution of this case against the Claimant is made on the failure of the Claimant to carry the burden of proof prescribed by statute."

We see the only issue to be whether the trial judge erred in holding that the claimant failed in her statutory burden of proof.

Since the case is fact-oriented for disposition, the case has been predominantly studied and decided, having in mind the appellate rule that we will examine the evidence in the light most favorable to the prevailing party. *P & M Cattle Company v. Holler,* Wyo.1977, 559 P.2d 1019. Strangely enough here, the evidence most persuasive in support of the trial court's position came from the claimant's own expert witness. The employer's expert witness, a medical doctor, with a considerable experience in the study and treatment of cancer in uranium miners, was not in substantial disagreement. * * *

Dr. Victor E. Archer, a nationally recognized expert in the field of cancer induced by radiation, associated with the mining of uranium, testified for the claimant. He was commendably frank in his appraisal of the dead miner's disease and its connotations.

It was Dr. Archer's testimony that there is a high incidence of lung cancer amongst uranium miners. In order to determine the amount of radiation to which decedent had been exposed in his lifetime, his body was disinterred and parts, particularly bones, removed for testing. The results of inhaling air laden with an inert gas, radon, a decay product of radiation, ends up as a further radiation decay product in the bones of a human being as lead–210. The amount of that end product in the bones can be measured and with adjustments for periods of nonexposure or noninjurious exposure will reveal with accuracy the amount of radon gas taken into the lungs during a lifetime of uranium mining.

As previously indicated, Olson had been employed by Continental Uranium Company upon his entry into his occupation as a miner in 1958 and worked for that company continuously until 1970, a period of about 12 years. He was with his last employer here intermittently for a total period of about 18 months. Clinical appearance of the cancer developed after 13 years of uranium mining. There is what is known as an induction-latent period, a length of time between when a man first starts uranium mining, and the advent of cancer. This period is usually around 15 years though the cancer may appear at any time after five years, here 13 years.

According to Dr. Archer, tobacco use to the extent engaged in by Olson can either be the cause of the cancer here involved or it may promote the development of cancer induced by radiation. The latter is referred to as a synergizing effect. Tobacco use also leaves lead–210 in the body. Dr. Archer explained that the incidence of lung cancer amongst uranium miners is greater to a definite extent among smoking miners than nonsmoking miners.

While the trial judge may have been able, at the most, to find that the cancer of which decedent died might have been induced by radiation from uranium mining in the first employer, the proof completely breaks down as far as "injurious exposure" with the last employer, with whom we are concerned, is involved. There was no proof that the working level of radiation in the Federal American Partners mine was not within practical prescribed limits of safety.[1] The evidence in that regard fails also to show that Olson was even working in areas of the mine where radiation at any level was present. There was no proof that Olson was "injuriously exposed" to the hazards of radiation-induced cancer with the employer here.

The clincher, however, was when the following question and answer by Dr. Archer went into the record:

"Q. Can you tell from your records with medical certainty that the death of Mr. Olson occurred or was caused solely by radiation exposure?

---

1. The standard of measurement is "Working Level Months" (abbreviated "WLM"), a term incorporating a particular fixed quantity of radiation exposure over a work period of one month. The federal government standard of maximum exposure at the time in issue was four "Working Level Months" per year. The only acceptable proof of exposure with the employer party here was a total of around three WLM (.76 in 1970 and 2.31 in 1971) over a period of 18 months, not regarded an injurious exposure. The government-established standard, if followed during a working life as a uranium miner, would not induce cancer by radiation.

"A. No. I don't think we could be that certain about it."[2]

Dr. Archer specifically testified that if the working level exposure of Olson was within the United States Government permissible limits, there would not be injurious exposure; it would not contribute to or promote a cancer induced several years earlier with a different company but not discovered until later. The proof of the employer was that the exposure was within the safe limits. The claimant furnished no acceptable proof to the contrary.

If there is any reasonable basis for the findings of the trial judge as the fact finder, we must affirm. The outline we have just undertaken demonstrates the correctness of the district court and we likewise, as did the district court, hold there to have been a failure of proof under the applicable statutes, §§ 27–293 and 27–297, then in effect. * * *

Affirmed.

ROSE, JUSTICE, dissenting.

* * *

The majority opinion, as I read it, seems to treat the instant case as purely fact-oriented. I, on the other hand, would view the appeal as representing a misunderstanding or, if you will, a misapplication of the law as it relates to the facts presented. Once the proper legal standards are applied, it would have been my holding that the appellant did in fact satisfy her statutory burden of proof. This being so, I would direct that she should have been awarded appropriate compensation for the death of her husband, out of the fund established by his last employer, the appellee.

* * *

In a contested occupational-disease case, I see the claimant's burden as twofold: (1) He or she must show by competent medical evidence that his or her claim arose out of and in the course of the worker's employment—this burden is discharged if the five factors set forth in § 27–297(a) [Section 10(a)], supra, are satisfied; and (2) the claimant must show for which employer the worker was working when he received his last injurious exposure.

CONNECTION TO EMPLOYMENT

In satisfying the burdens of the first step, as they relate to § 27–297(a) [Section 10(a)], supra, the meaning of the word "employment" becomes critical. It is here that I would hold the trial court to have first erred in delineating or construing the appropriate legal standards. * * *

* * * Where there is a direct causal connection between the worker's several employments and his disability or death, the occupational

---

2. There must be a direct causal connection between the causal conditions under which the work is performed and the occupational disease. Section 27–297(a)(i). While statistically the risk of a uranium miner is increased, that does not rise to the standard of reasonable medical certainty to establish causal connection. *O'Connor v. Industrial Commission,* 19 Ariz.App. 43, 504 P.2d 966 (1972).

disease is compensable as "arising out of and in the course of the employment." This test in no way detracts from the express language set forth by the legislature—it merely places that language in its proper perspective. There seems to be no question but that a malignancy caused by radiation poisoning and exposure is a compensable occupational disease. § 27–290(a)(xxii) [Section 3(a)(xxii)] of the Occupational Disease Law, supra. The problem during the first stage of proof is to show that the malignancy had a direct causal connection with the worker's several employments.

The hazard with which the instant case is concerned is radiation exposure. The claimant's husband worked as an underground uranium miner from January 3, 1958 to December 29, 1971—a period of some 13 years. The record discloses that during the course of such employment his exposure to radiation was equivalent to at least 926 Working Level Months. After the worker's body was disinterred, a radiometric analysis of his bone specimens revealed an adjusted concentration of lead–210 of 1.63 picocuries lead per gram of tissue. The normal concentration of lead–210 in the dead bone tissue of the general non-mining public ranges from .01 to .05 picocuries lead–210 per gram of tissue, according to studies disclosed by expert witness Dr. Archer's testimony. These studies also disclosed that among the general non-mining public, extremely heavy smoking would only raise the concentration to about .06 to .08 picocuries lead–210 per gram of tissue. Dr. Archer, as pointed out in the majority opinion, testified under cross-examination that he could not be certain that the worker's death "occurred or was caused *solely* by radiation exposure." [Emphasis supplied] But Dr. Archer later went on, under cross-examination, to state:

"One cannot be absolutely sure in a situation like this, but I would say most probably his [Mr. Olson's] lung cancer resulted from his occupational exposure to radiation."

* * *

The burden of the claimant, under § 27–297(a) [Section 10(a)], supra, is to prove his or her claim by a preponderance of the evidence. This can be taken to mean that there must be proof which leads the trier-of-fact to find that the existence of a contested fact is more probable than its nonexistence, as distinguished from proof which is clear and convincing. In my judgment, the medical evidence here is sufficient to show that the claimant's husband "most probably" (Dr. Archer, supra) died as a result of radiation exposure which occurred during his several employments. The existence of heavy cigarette smoking cannot be discounted, but in this case the appellee has offered no reason to believe that the likelihood of contracting lung cancer from smoking was more than a mere possibility. See *McAllister v. Workmen's Compensation Appeals Board*, 69 Cal.2d 408, 71 Cal.Rptr. 697, 702–703, 445 P.2d 313, 318–319 (1968). I think a claimant has proven his or her claim according to the statute's burden-of-proof requirements when a medical expert states without direct contradiction that the worker "most probably" died of an occupational exposure to radiation—as opposed to testimony to the effect that there is a "possibility" that death was otherwise causally connected. See *McAllister v. Workmen's Compensation Appeals Board*, supra, 71 Cal.Rptr. at 701, 445 P.2d at 317. We cannot demand that experts be more certain, since the industrial causation itself need only be more probable than not.

* * *

I would have held, therefore, that the claimant sustained her burden of proof under § 27–297(a) [Section 10(a)], supra.

LAST INJURIOUS EXPOSURE

During the second stage of proof, the claimant need not prove that the worker's occupational disease was contracted or induced while he was working for a particular employee, but the proof-burden will be deemed satisfied when it is established by a fair preponderance of evidence in whose employ he was "last injuriously exposed." * * *

The Occupational Disease Law defines "injurious exposure" as:

> "... an exposure to such disease which is reasonably calculated to *bring on* the disease in question." § 27–289(d) [Section 2(d)], supra. [Emphasis supplied]

Virginia's definition of "last injuriously exposed" is substantially identical to our definition. In *Pocahontas Fuel Co. v. Godbey*, supra, at 864, the court observed that

> "... the phrase 'last injuriously exposed', as used in the statute, means an exposure or contact with the dangers of the disease which proximately causes the malady, or *augments or aggravates the pre-existing disease. Haynes v. Feldspar Producing Co.*, 222 N.C. 163, 22 S.E.2d 275, *Bye v. Interstate Granite Co.*, supra, ..." [Emphasis supplied]

Since the claimant need not necessarily show that the disease was caused while in the employment of the party from whom he seeks compensation, emphasis should properly be placed on *aggravation* of the disease in cases such as the one at Bar. ... Where the occupational disease is characterized as being gradual in development, and where several employers have been involved, it is incumbent upon the claimant to show that the disease was promoted or accelerated during his employment with the particular employer from whom compensation is sought. We are not concerned with an exposure which would cause the disease, only one which would be reasonably calculated to *aggravate, promote or accelerate* the disease.[7] Once some such contributing exposure is shown,

---

7. This is not a case, therefore, like *Climax Uranium Company v. Death of Smith*, 33 Colo.App. 337, 522 P.2d 134, where the claimant must show an exposure to a concentration of toxic material which would eventually cause an occupational disease. See also *Mathis v. State Accident Insurance Fund*, 10 Or.App. 139, 499 P.2d 1331; and *White v. Scullin Steel Company*, Mo.App. 435 S.W.2d 711—where a claimant must show conditions which are conclusive to the development of the disease, as opposed to aggravation of the disease.

the employer making that contribution is charged with full liability for the condition, even though it may have developed over a number of years. 4 Larson's Workmen's Compensation Law, § 95.21, at 77–87 (1976); and § 27–293 [Section 6] of the Occupational Disease Law.

* * *

The record is replete with testimony as to the promoting or accelerating effect of any radiation exposure. Dr. Archer explained this effect in the following discourse:

"Q. (By Mr. Zollinger) Taking the one unit or one measure of radiation, which we'll call Working Level, each unit that the human being receives is not greater nor less injurious than any other unit that person has received; is that correct?

"A. Yes. That's probably true on a theoretical basis; but in actual practice there, the effects might well be different because of the time element. The time element for the first unit received might be compatible with the development of cancer, whereas the last one received might not be.

"Q. Could you elaborate on that or explain that?

"A. The length of time for the induction, induction-latent period between when the man first started mining and when he developed cancer, among uranium miners is usually around 15, 16 or 17 years average time. The minimum time of this period, it's been noted in uranium miners, is somewhere around four or five years. So that the unit of radiation which the man received, say, 15 or 20 years earlier would be more likely to be associated with his present cancer than a comparable unit received one year before cancer developed. But even this isn't completely true because even though the last units of radiation received—even though it might not be held responsible for initiating his cancer, it still might be of help in promoting or speeding up the cancer, because there are many things which act as promoting agents for tumors. Sometimes the same agent which induces them may also promote them.

* * *

"Q. So that referring now to our hypothetical case, if the miner's disease, which is diagnosed as small-cell carcinoma, is diagnosed within two or three years of employment from mining company 'B' then would you say that would be circumstantial evidence that the cause of the carcinoma was not the exposure received from employment with mining company 'B'?

"A. Yes. I would say that most probably. However, one could not completely dismiss that last radiation because, although it's pretty certain it did not induce the cancer, it still might have had some sort of promoting effect to cause it to appear a little sooner.

* * *

"Q. Your statement that the period in which the claimant received the greatest amount of exposure is the probable cause of the induction of cancer, does that statement preclude the possibility of further injurious exposure subsequent to the induction of cancer?

"A. No, because it can't exclude the possibility that the later radiation acts as a promoting agent for the tumor which was induced at an earlier date.

* * *

"Q. Could exposure to radiation subsequent to the induction of a tumor be described as injurious?

"A. Under some circumstances, it could, yes.

"Q. Could that exposure promote or accelerate a clinical tumor?

"A. I think the answer to that depends somewhat on the amount of that exposure. I would say it's—if it was a substantial amount, then yes."

The only response to this testimony came in an exchange to which Dr. Connell responded as follows:

"Q. So in all cases, and I assume your testimony to be about latency—in all cases in which the carcinoma is found in a uranium miner, it would be your testimony that the carcinoma was essentially developed several years prior to that?

"A. Essentially developed, yes.

"Q. And that all of the exposure that occurred subsequent to the beginning of the initiation of that latent period is just kind of water over the dam, it doesn't have any effect whatever on the carcinoma?

"A. Yes, I think that's right.

I do not view Dr. Connell's observation as a direct contradiction of the testimony of Dr. Archer, but rather as a statement which indicates that once the carcinoma is induced, then further exposure to radiation will not have a *causative* effect. This is not to say that some subsequent radiation exposures will not have a *promoting* effect. The subsequent exposures need not have a *substantial* effect—only *some* effect is required. 4 Larson's Workmen's Compensation Law, § 95.21, supra. I am convinced by a reading of the entire record that there was sufficient evidence presented which would indicate that the radiation exposure received at the appellee's mine promoted or accelerated the cancer which killed the claimant's husband. * * *

Had I been writing for the majority, I would have reversed the trial court's judgment.

RUTLEDGE v. TULTEX CORP./KINGS YARN

Supreme Court of North Carolina, 1983.
308 N.C. 85, 301 S.E.2d 359.

EXUM, JUSTICE.

The questions for decision are whether the Industrial Commission applied the wrong legal standard in its order denying benefits to claimant and whether there is evidence from which the Commission could have made findings, using the correct legal standard, that would support a conclusion that claimant contracted an occupational disease. We answer both questions affirmatively.

After hearing evidence for claimant and defendants, Deputy Commissioner Denson concluded that claimant had not contracted an occupational disease. This conclusion was based in part on the following factual findings, which are summarized unless quoted, to which no exception has been taken: Plaintiff, born 8 August 1935, has a tenth grade education and now lives in Georgia. She has smoked cigarettes from about age fifteen until February 1979 at the rate of approximately one pack per day. She has worked for four textile mills: (1) United Merchants in Buffalo, South Carolina, from 1953 until 1971 as a weaver; (2) Milliken at Union, South Carolina, from 1971 to 1973 as a "dry cleaner"; (3) Aleo Manufacturing, Rockingham, North Carolina, from 1975 to 1976 as a weaver; and (4) for defendant from 25 October 1976 until 12 January 1979 as a winder and then as a spinner. She was absent "for bronchitis" from 28 January 1977 until 13 May 1977. She "retired" on 12 January 1979.

All the plants where plaintiff worked "had a lot of cotton dust and lint" but defendant's premises, both in the weaving and spinning areas, were "relatively clean." Defendant's mill processed essentially 50 percent cotton blend materials and occasionally blends made of even a smaller percentage of cotton. "Although there was respirable cotton dust in [defendant's] weave room, there was much less than ... in other premises." Plaintiff began developing a cough at work in 1969 or 1970. "[H]er cough was associated with her presence at work. Her shortness of breath became severe in December of 1976 and she has had various bouts with it since that time having to be out of work. ... Plaintiff suffers from chronic obstructive pulmonary disease [with elements] of pulmonary emphysema and chronic bronchitis.... Plaintiff is disabled, because of her pulmonary impairment from all but sedentary ... work which must be in a clean environment because of her reaction to cotton dust and other such irritants."

Deputy Commissioner Denson also made certain findings to which claimant excepted. The first was that in 1971 claimant "began developing a shortness of breath." Second was the following which the Deputy Commissioner included in the findings of fact:

> 6. ... Cigarette smoking and recurrent infection have played prominent roles in the pulmonary impairment. Cotton dust may

aggravate it, but since plaintiff was showing her symptomatology in problems prior to her employment with defendant employer, *exposure at defendant employer has neither caused nor significantly contributed to plaintiff's chronic obstructive pulmonary disease.*

* * *

8. Plaintiff has not contracted chronic obstructive lung disease *as a result of any exposure while working with defendant employer.* [Emphasis added.]

The Full Commission, with one commissioner dissenting, adopted Deputy Commissioner Denson's findings, conclusions, opinion and award as its own.

The Court of Appeals concluded that although the Commission erred "in requiring plaintiff to prove that her last employment was the cause of her occupational disease," the error was harmless since there was insufficient evidence before the Commission to show that plaintiff had ever contracted an occupational disease during her working life. *Rutledge v. Tultex Corp./Kings Yarn,* 56 N.C.App. 345, 350, 289 S.E.2d 72, 74 (1982).

Because of the italicized portions of findings 6 and 8, it does appear that the Commission thought that in order successfully to claim against defendant, claimant's last employer, claimant must establish that her exposure there either caused or significantly contributed to her chronic obstructive pulmonary disease. This is not the law. That part of G.S. 97–57 pertinent to this case provides:

> In any case where compensation is payable for an occupational disease, the employer in whose employment the employee was last injuriously exposed to the hazards of such disease, and the insurance carrier, if any, which was on the risk when the employee was so last exposed under such employer, shall be liable.

Under this statute, consequently, it is not necessary that claimant show that the conditions of her employment with defendant caused or significantly contributed to her occupational disease. She need only show: (1) that she has a compensable occupational disease and (2) that she was "last injuriously exposed to the hazards of such disease" in defendant's employment. The statutory terms "last injuriously exposed" mean "an exposure which proximately augmented the disease to any extent, however slight." *Haynes v. Feldspar Producing Company,* 222 N.C. 163, 166, 169, 22 S.E.2d 275, 277, 278 (1942).

* * *

The Court of Appeals correctly concluded, therefore, that the Industrial Commission applied the wrong legal standards to this claim.

We hold that the Court of Appeals erred, however, in concluding that there is no evidence that plaintiff had contracted an occupational disease. We think there is evidence from which the Industrial Commission could have made findings which in turn would have supported a conclusion that claimant's chronic obstructive lung disease was an occupational disease. Dr. Williams, after a lengthy recitation of certain assumed facts, was asked the following question:

> Now, based upon these facts and upon your examination and testing of Ms. Rutledge, do you have an opinion satisfactory to yourself to a reasonable medical certainty as to whether Ms. Rutledge's exposure to cotton dust for in excess of 25 years in her employment was probably a cause of her chronic obstructive lung disease which you diagnosed in your report?

When he replied, "Yes," the following colloquy occurred:

> Q. What is that opinion?
>
> A. Yes. That it probably was a cause. Based upon the same facts and upon my examination and testing of Mrs. Rutledge, I have an opinion as to whether her impairment with respect to her ability to perform labor is related to her pulmonary disease. That opinion is that it is.

* * *

[The defendants argued that Dr. Williams' opinion was not competent evidence since the hypothetical question posed by claimant's counsel did not expressly refer to claimant's history of cigarette smoking. The court rejected this argument noting that (1) the defendants did not object to the question nor move to strike the answer; (2) Dr. Williams based his opinion, in part, on his examination of the claimant which included taking a history that revealed claimant's smoking; and (3) the effect of claimant's smoking on Dr. Williams' opinion was explored by defendants' counsel on cross-examination.]

The thrust of Dr. Williams' entire testimony, then, seems to be that both her exposure to cotton dust over her working life and her cigarette smoking were causative factors in claimant's chronic obstructive lung disease. He also said other components of the lung disease were "pulmonary emphysema" and "chronic bronchitis" and that "chronic obstructive lung disease includes pulmonary emphysema, chronic bronchitis, and possibly asthma."

After relating his considerable experience in the treatment and study of respiratory diseases among textile workers, such as claimant here, Dr. Williams testified that these workers are "at an increased risk of contracting chronic obstructive pulmonary disease." Dr. Williams also testified that when claimant began such work in October 1976 "she was suffering from pulmonary emphysema, chronic bronchitis and chronic obstructive pulmonary disease ... caused by circumstances which existed prior to her employment by Kings Yarn." Although testifying that claimant's exposure to cotton dust at Kings Yarn's plant would have "minimal" effect on her condition and that she would not have had there a "very substantial exposure" to cotton dust, Dr. Williams did say that such exposure as she had at Kings Yarn "could have some aggravating effect on [her] underlying condition" and that removal from the

Kings Yarn "environment would probably improve her symptoms ... primarily, her symptoms of cough." Dr. Williams testified flatly that claimant's exposure to respirable cotton and synthetic dust at Kings Yarn "would have aggravated her condition." Medical records offered in evidence tended to show that claimant's lung function had decreased some 25 to 30 percent during the period from January 1977 to March 1979, while she worked for defendant employer.

Claimant, herself, described in some detail the dusty conditions under which she had worked for twenty-five years in various textile mills. She said she developed a breathing difficulty in 1971 which by 1977 had begun "affecting my ability to do my job" because it caused her to be too fatigued to work. She said she stopped work in January 1979 "because I was unable to perform my duties on my job. From tiredness, short of breath, cold sweats, headaches and I felt I was not being fair to myself or the company. I did not just quit, I was advised by my doctor ... to quit." Claimant testified that when she quit work "my symptoms were difficulty breathing, wheezing, tiredness, cold sweats, [and] stiffness in my neck. I coughed so hard until the [neck] muscle, you know, it's ruptured in the left side." By January 1979 claimant said that she did not have the "strength or ability to do my housework, my shopping or any of those things. I am able to do my daily routine, I can make a bed, at which time I have to rest.... I help [my mother] watch dinner and the rest of my day consists of soap operas and rest. I crochet, anything to pass time. I just cannot be exerted because if I do I just don't have the breath. I do drive. I don't have any training for jobs besides working in the mill."

For a disease to be occupational under G.S. 97–53(13) it must be (1) characteristic of persons engaged in the particular trade or occupation in which the claimant is engaged; (2) not an ordinary disease of life to which the public generally is equally exposed with those engaged in that particular trade or occupation; and (3) there must be "a causal connection between the disease and the [claimant's] employment." *Hansel v. Sherman Textiles,* 304 N.C. 44, 52, 283 S.E.2d 101, 105–06 (1981); *Booker v. Duke Medical Center,* 297 N.C. 458, 468, 475, 256 S.E.2d 189, 196, 200 (1979). To satisfy the first and second elements it is not necessary that the disease originate exclusively from or be unique to the particular trade or occupation in question. All ordinary diseases of life are not excluded from the statute's coverage. Only such ordinary diseases of life to which the general public is exposed equally with workers in the particular trade or occupation are excluded. *Booker v. Duke Medical Center, supra,* 297 N.C. at 472–75, 256 S.E.2d at 198–200. Thus, the first two elements are satisfied if, as a matter of fact, the employment exposed the worker to a greater risk of contracting the disease than the public generally. *Id.* "The greater risk in such cases provides the nexus between the disease and the employment which makes them an appropriate subject for workmen's compensation." *Id.* at 475, 256 S.E.2d at 200.

This Court has had little difficulty either articulating or applying the first two standards in occupational disease cases generally. They were articulated and properly applied in *Booker,* a hepatitis case, and reiterated and properly applied in *Hansel,* a lung disease case. We have had some difficulty in the lung disease cases, however, in both articulating and applying a factual standard for determining whether there is an appropriate causal connection between the employment and the disease. . . .

This difficulty in the lung disease cases stems largely from the complex medical picture often presented by chronic obstructive lung disease and chronicled in the medical testimony in *Walston, Hansel* and *Morrison.* This disease, as we understand it from the medical testimony presented in these cases and the literature to which we have been referred * * * has several components. Some of these components are seemingly not, in their incipience at least, work related, for example, bronchitis, emphysema and asthma; while at least one component, i.e., Byssinosis, is work related. Byssinosis may be understood as the adverse effect on the lungs resulting from the inhalation of cotton dust, a substance generally present in the work environment of textile mill employees. Other complicating factors are that chronic obstructive lung disease may apparently be brought on by just the continuous inhalation of cotton dust, just the continuous inhalation of other substances, such as cigarette smoke, or by the inhalation of both kinds of substances together. It is apparently medically impossible even on autopsy objectively to distinguish the effect on the lungs of cigarette smoke inhalation and the inhalation of cotton dust, or between the effects of bronchitis and the inhalation of these substances. Thus when a textile worker who is also a habitual cigarette smoker and who suffers from bronchitis, emphysema, or asthma, contracts disabling, chronic obstructive lung disease, the medical experts and, in turn, the Commission and the courts are presented with a difficult factual question on the causation issue. Since courts generally develop principles of law to deal as justly as possible with the facts of given cases, complex facts which the experts themselves have difficulty unraveling make the articulation of appropriate legal principles correspondingly difficult for the courts.

* * *

Our answer to the question posed is that chronic obstructive lung disease may be an occupational disease provided the occupation in question exposed the worker to a greater risk of contracting this disease than members of the public generally, and provided the worker's exposure to cotton dust significantly contributed to, or was a significant causal factor in, the disease's development. This is so even if other non-work-related factors also make significant contributions, or were significant causal factors.

Significant means "having or likely to have influence or effect: deserving to be considered: important, weighty, notable." Webster's Third New International Dictionary (1971). *Significant* is to be contrasted with *negligible, unimportant, present but not worthy of note, minuscule, or of little moment.* The factual inquiry, in other words, should be whether the occupational exposure was such a significant factor in the disease's development that without it the disease would not have developed to such an extent that it caused the physical disability which resulted in claimant's incapacity for work.

* * *

[T]he significant contribution principle which we adopt puts upon the claimant in these lung disease cases a somewhat heavier burden than our sister states seem to require or that we require in industrial accident cases. Our purpose in adopting this principle is to strike a fair balance between the worker and the employer in the administration of our Workers' Compensation Act as it is applied to the difficult lung disease cases. To hold that the inhalation of cotton dust must be the sole cause of chronic obstructive lung disease before this disease can be considered occupational establishes too harsh a principle from the standpoint of the worker and the purposes and policies of our Workers' Compensation Act. This Act "should be liberally construed so that the benefits under the Act will not be denied by narrow, technical or strict interpretation." *Stevenson v. City of Durham,* 281 N.C. 300, 303, 188 S.E.2d 281, 283 (1972). On the other hand, to hold the causation requirement is satisfied if cotton dust exposure contributes to the slightest extent, however minuscule or insignificant, to the etiology of chronic obstructive lung disease, places too heavy a burden on industry. This holding would compromise the valid principle that our Workers' Compensation Act should not be transformed into a general accident and health insurance law.

In determining whether a claimant's exposure to cotton dust has significantly contributed to, or been a significant causative factor in, chronic obstructive lung disease, the Commission may, of course, consider medical testimony, but its consideration is not limited to such testimony. It may consider other factual circumstances in the case, among which are (1) the extent of the worker's exposure to cotton dust during employment, (2) the extent of other non-work-related, but contributing, exposures and components, and (3) the manner in which the disease developed with reference to the claimant's work history. *See Booker v. Duke Medical Center, supra,* 297 N.C. at 476, 256 S.E.2d at 200.

* * *

From [the] evidence the Commission could have found as facts, although it would not have been compelled to find, that: (1) claimant has chronic obstructive lung disease; (2) the two primary causes of this disease are the inhalation of cotton dust for twenty-five years while claimant was a textile worker and the inhalation of cigarette smoke over a similar period of time; (3) the disease also has components of chronic bronchitis and emphysema; (4) the disease developed gradually over the period of claimant's working life until by 1971 claimant had developed a breathing difficulty; (5) by 1977 her breathing difficulty began to affect her ability to do her job because it caused her to be too fatigued to work; (6) by January 1979 claimant's disease had rendered her physically unable to work in the textile industry; (7) the disease would not have developed to this extent had it not been for her exposure to cotton dust and her inhalation of cigarette smoke, both of which significantly contributed to, or were significant causative factors in, the development of the disease; (8) because of her age, limited education, and her lifetime of employment in the textile industry, claimant is neither trained nor qualified to do other kinds of work and, at this time, is not able to be gainfully employed; (9) claimant's chronic obstructive lung disease was aggravated to some extent by her exposure to cotton dust at Kings Yarn; and (10) claimant's job in the textile industry exposed her to a greater risk of contracting chronic obstructive lung disease than members of the public generally.

These findings of fact, if made by the Commission, would support the following legal conclusions: (1) claimant's chronic obstructive lung disease is due to causes and conditions characteristic of and peculiar to the textile industry under G.S. 97–53(13); (2) claimant's chronic obstructive lung disease is not an ordinary disease of life to which the general public not employed in the textile industry is equally exposed under G.S. 97–53(13); (3) claimant's chronic obstructive lung disease is, therefore, an occupational disease under G.S. 97–53(13); (4) claimant is totally incapacitated for work under G.S. 97–29, 97–54, and 97–2(9); (5) claimant's total incapacity for work results from her occupational disease under G.S. 97–52; and (6) claimant's last injurious exposure to the hazards of her occupational disease were in the employment of defendant Kings Yarn under G.S. 97–57. These conclusions of law would, in turn, support an award against defendants and in favor of claimant for workers' compensation benefits for total incapacity for work by reason of an occupational disease.

On the other hand there is some testimony from Dr. Williams which would have supported a finding that claimant's exposure to cotton dust played an insignificant causal role in, or did not significantly contribute to, the development of Ms. Rutledge's lung disease. If the Commission so finds, it would have to conclude that the disease is not an occupational disease in this case.

* * *

* * * The only question for reconsideration by the Commission is whether the pulmonary disease is an occupational disease when the legal principles set out in this opinion are applied to the facts.

Affirmed in part; reversed in part and remanded.

MEYER, JUSTICE, dissenting.

I respectfully dissent.

* * * The majority obviously believes that the testimony of Dr. Williams to the effect that the mere exposure to cotton dust creates an increased risk of lung disease somehow establishes that all of Mrs. Rutledge's diseases (including, we must assume, her many non-lung related diseases) are "occupational diseases" provided any "significant contribution" to those diseases by the cotton dust can be established. This position was rejected by the majority opinion in *Morrison [v. Burlington Industries,* 304 N.C. 1, 282 S.E. 2d 458 (1981)]. I find it shocking that a disability from this range of diseases and conditions, most of which are ordinary diseases of life, would be fully compensable because of the "significant contribution" to only the lung conditions by the inhalation of cotton dust. While her non-lung related conditions did not contribute to her pulmonary conditions, it is inescapable that they contributed to her disability.

Nor do I find it unusually significant, as does the majority, that Dr. Williams was of the opinion that textile workers are "at an increased risk of contracting chronic obstructive pulmonary disease," which according to Dr. Williams includes "pulmonary emphysema, chronic bronchitis and possibly asthma" as well as byssinosis. We are repeatedly told by expert medical witnesses that the same is true of cigarette smokers and others who may be in no way connected with the textile industry. We are even told that the same is true of those exposed to concentrations of ordinary household or yard dust. It is interesting that in this very case Dr. Williams testified: "I think that exposure to *any type of dust* in someone with pre-existing chronic bronchitis could have some aggravating effect on the underlying condition." He also said "I stated that exposure to *any* kind of dust in an individual with underlying lung disease would have an aggravating effect." (Emphasis added). It is indeed on the basis of the last quoted sentence that the majority opinion characterizes Dr. Williams as saying "that such exposure as she had at Kings Yarn 'could have some aggravating effect on [her] underlying condition.' "As is obvious, this characterization of that testimony is completely misleading.

* * *

The case should *not* be remanded for the purpose of applying the new "substantial contribution" principle—if it is to be remanded at all it should be for the purpose of apportionment of Mrs. Rutledge's disability to work-related and non-work-related causes.

I agree with the majority's conclusion that it is not necessary that Mrs. Rutledge show that the conditions of her last employer's workplace were the *sole* causes of her disability and that it is only necessary for her to show that the conditions of her last employer's workplace "augmented the disease to any extent, however slight."[2] I vote to affirm the opinion

---

2. I must point out, however, what I consider to be a significant omission in the majority's statement that "She need only show: (1) that she has a compensable occupational disease and (2) that she was 'last injuriously exposed to the hazards of such disease' in defendant's employment." The omission from (1) that the occupational disease be the cause of her disability is fatal and will come back to haunt us. The first requirement should be accurately stated as

of the Court of Appeals and to modify it to the extent necessary to correct this error.

BRANCH, C.J., and COPELAND, J., join in this dissent.

Notes

1. Are the different outcomes reached in *Olson* and *Rutledge* best explained in terms of differences in facts, statutory language, or policy? Can you identify precisely where the majority and dissent disagree in both cases?

2. Establishing a causal connection between employment and disease is especially difficult in cases like *Olson* and *Rutledge* where the employee's life style or personal habits are suspected to be a significant contributing factor. The term "dual causation" is often used to describe such cases. *See* 3 A. Larson & L. Larson, Larson's Workers' Compensation Law § 41.64(a) (1998). Workers who smoke and are exposed to industrial irritants present the paradigm dual causation problem. These workers may develop lung cancer, emphysema, bronchitis or other respiratory ailments. As one might expect, the evidence of industrial causation presented by the claimant and employer is frequently conflicting. This is an especially fact-sensitive inquiry and the record often contains testimony that could support either the grant or denial of compensation benefits. The finder of fact enjoys substantial discretion in such cases. Compare Dunn v. Vic Mfg. Co., 327 N.W.2d 572 (Minn.1982) (claimant was a pack-a-day smoker for twenty-five years who was employed as a sandblaster for nine or ten years. He died of respiratory problems. In light of conflicting medical testimony, referee's finding that the death was caused by work-related exposure to dust was affirmed) with Howard v. Johns–Manville Sales Corp., 420 So.2d 1190 (La.App.1982) (claimant was a heavy smoker who was exposed to asbestos fibers during his twenty-one years of employment. The denial of benefits was affirmed where medical testimony was divided on whether the claimant's respiratory ailment was asbestosis or cigarette induced emphysema). Occasionally, however, an appellate court will reverse findings on the basis that they are not supported by the evidence. E.g., Home Insurance Co. v. Davis, 642 S.W.2d 268 (Tex.App.1982). The more common ground for appeal, as reflected in *Olson* and *Rutledge,* is that the lower court or administrative agency applied an incorrect legal standard. In this regard, what are the practical effects of the "significant causal factor" test approved by the majority opinion in *Rutledge* as compared to the standard applied in *Olson?*

3. The detail with which both the *Olson* and *Rutledge* courts analyzed the medical testimony emphasizes its central importance in resolving occupational disease claims. The expert witnesses for the respective sides are called upon to give their opinions as to the cause of the claimant's condition. This opinion, moreover, often must be expressed in terms of a "reasonable medical certainty." See note 6 following *Lancaster v. Gilbert Development* in the next section. Unfortunately little is "certain" regarding the cause of most diseases. The etiology of many diseases is simply unknown. The long latency period between industrial exposure and the onset of symptoms hinders efforts to isolate and identify particular occupational hazards. Even when there is a suspected linkage between occupational exposure to a

---

follows: "that she has an occupational disease which caused her disability."

particular substance and disease, proving causation in specific cases remains a formidable task. A great deal of the current scientific knowledge about occupational diseases is based on aggregate statistical data. Workers' compensation claims, however, are adjudicated on a case by case basis. Data indicating that the cancer rate for workers in a particular industry is higher than the national norm, for example, does not tell us which individual cancers are work induced. A large number of suspected carcinogens are plentiful in our nonindustrial environment and can cause illness and death of persons who are out of the work force. The dilemma facing the workers' compensation system was summed up by one expert as follows: "Workers' compensation judges may be asked to extrapolate causes in specific claims based on animal experiments or on isolated and often ambiguous epidemiological studies. Aside from the lack of competence that such hearing officers often have to reach decisions that as yet have no definitive answers, the record is replete with inconsistencies and capriciousness." Barth, A Proposal For Dealing With the Compensation of Occupational Diseases, 13 J.Legal Stud. 569, 572 (1984). For a more technical discussion of the etiological and diagnostic issues in occupational disease claims, see P. Barth & H. Hunt, Workers' Compensation and Work–Related Illnesses and Diseases 61–89 (1980).

4. In cases involving both occupational and nonoccupational causal factors there are several possible ways to allocate the cost of diseases. One option, reflected in *Olson,* is to deny compensation and thereby allocate such costs in the first instance to the worker. It should be obvious, however, that many workers will not be capable of shouldering those costs without assistance. A likely source of support is the Social Security system. Indeed, more workers disabled by occupational disease receive income benefits from Social Security than from workers' compensation. A. Packer, Assistant Secretary for Policy, Evaluation, and Research, Department of Labor, An Interim Report to Congress on Occupational Diseases 85 (1980). *Rutledge,* with its more relaxed "significant causal factor" test, effectively lumps many of these costs within the workers' compensation system. A third option is to apportion the costs between the worker and employer. States are divided on whether compensation awards should be reduced to reflect the nonoccupational contributions to the illness. Compare Fry's Food Stores v. Industrial Comm'n, 177 Ariz. 264, 866 P.2d 1350 (Ariz. 1994) (claimant who was exposed to flour dust on the job for seven years and smoked two packs of cigarettes a day for thirty seven years developed chronic obstructive pulmonary disease; apportionment was not allowed because the smoking did not disable the claimant prior to his occupational exposure to the flour dust; discussing cases) with Bolivar County Gravel Co. v. Dial, 634 So.2d 99 (Miss. 1994) (claimant smoked between one and one-half and two packs of cigarettes a day for 25–28 years and was exposed to welding fumes on the job; permanent total disability benefits were reduced by 90% to account for preexisting obstructive lung disease); Colorado Mental Health Inst. v. Austill, 940 P.2d 1125 (Colo.App.1997) (award for permanent total disability should be apportioned to account for claimant's preexisting pulmonary condition). Where apportionment is permitted, the burden rests with the employer to prove what percentage of the disability is attributable to nonoccupational factors. E.g., Watkins Engineers and Constructors v. Wise,

698 So.2d 294 (Fla.App.1997). What is the ideal allocation of costs when employment and nonoccupational factors combine to produce a disabling disease? What practical, theoretical or doctrinal problems do you see in achieving such an allocation?

5. Is the problem of allocating disease costs significantly different when work conditions aggravate a preexisting allergy? The problem of allergies and their disabling consequences has been treated in several different ways by the courts. At a time when there was little coverage of occupational disease, several courts treated allergic reactions to workplace chemicals as compensable accidents. E.g., Webb v. New Mexico Pub. Co., 47 N.M. 279, 141 P.2d 333 (1943) (allergy to soap causing disabling skin disorder); Hardin's Bakeries, Inc. v. Ranager, 217 Miss. 463, 64 So.2d 705 (1953) (contact dermatitis caused by allergy to baker's mitten); Vogt v. Ford Motor Co. 138 S.W.2d 684 (Mo.App.1940) (asthma and other ailments brought on by inhalation of chemicals and paint fumes).

A majority of states today compensate for disabling allergic reactions to workplace substances under the occupational disease statute if the causation and other required elements are present. E.g., Aleutian Homes v. Fischer, 418 P.2d 769 (Alaska 1966) (allergic reaction to paper and other office supplies); Ross v. Baldwin Filters, 5 Neb.App. 194, 557 N.W.2d 368 (Neb. App. 1996) (same); A New Leaf, Inc. v. Webb, 26 Va.App. 460, 495 S.E.2d 510 (Va.App. 1998)(contact dermatitis is compensable as an occupational disease); Revere Copper & Brass, Inc. v. Industrial Comm., 97 Ill.2d 388, 73 Ill.Dec. 560, 454 N.E.2d 657 (1983) (allergic reaction to nickel); Greger v. United Prestress, Inc., 180 Mont. 348, 590 P.2d 1121 (1979) (contact dermatitis due to allergic reaction to chromate and nickel ions present in cement additive). A minority of courts hold that an allergic reaction is not a compensable occupational disease. E.g., Pearce v. Reintjes Co., 493 So.2d 892 (La.App.1986) (allergic condition aggravated by work environment but producing no permanent disability); Thompson v. Burlington Industries, 59 N.C.App. 539, 297 S.E.2d 122 (1982) (asthma exacerbated by work conditions but no permanent functional impairment).

6. Another type of apportionment issue is raised in cases where a worker is exposed to disease producing conditions in several employments over many years. Recall, for example, that Mr. Olson worked in two different uranium mines and Ms. Rutledge was employed in four textile mills before becoming disabled. Where disability benefits are awarded, should responsibility be divided among the prior employers? A variation of this problem presents itself when a single employer was insured by several different carriers during the time the disabled worker was exposed to the harmful substance. Which insurance carrier is responsible for payment of benefits? A majority of jurisdictions apply what is known as the "last injurious exposure" rule in these situations. Under this rule, the employer and insurance carrier at the time the claimant was last injuriously exposed to the disease producing substance are responsible for payment of the benefits. E.g., CES Card Establishment Services v. Doub., 104 Md.App. 301, 656 A.2d 332 (Md. 1995); McSpadden v. Big Ben Coal Co., 288 N.W.2d 181 (Iowa 1980); Carter v. Avondale Shipyards, Inc., 415 So.2d 174 (La.1981); Bertrand v. API, Inc., 365 N.W.2d 222 (Minn.1985). The responsible employer/insurer is determined by fixing the date of disability and the last time the claimant was

injuriously exposed to the disease-producing substance. Hull v. Aetna Ins. Co., 247 Neb. 713, 529 N.W.2d 783 (Neb. 1995). The last injurious exposure rule is justified primarily on the basis of administrative efficiency. It allows agencies or courts to award benefits quickly without becoming bogged down in efforts to identify and assess all the exposures to toxic substances a claimant might have had during a work life.

Although the rule generally facilitates the processing of disease claims, problems in administration do arise. The last injurious exposure may have been with an out of state employer against whom the claimant cannot proceed. In such cases, several courts have applied the rule to the last in-state employer. E.g., Wolfer v. Veco, Inc., 852 P.2d 1171 (Alaska 1993); Garner v. Vanadium Corp., 194 Colo. 358, 572 P.2d 1205 (1977); Hamilton v. S.A. Healy Co., 14 A.D.2d 364, 221 N.Y.S.2d 325 (1961). Other states, however, will deny benefits when the last injurious exposure occurred outside the court's jurisdiction. E.g., Grice v. Graniteville Co., 278 S.C. 461, 298 S.E.2d 446 (1982).

Problems may also arise in determining whether the last exposure was "injurious." Most courts assign liability to the last employer so long as there was some exposure of a kind that could have caused, aggravated, or promoted the disease. See 9 A. Larson & L. Larson, Larson's Workers' Compensation Law § 95.26(a) (1998). This standard can result in one employer being charged with full liability for diseases that most probably developed in prior employments. E.g., Union Carbide Corp. v. Industrial Comm., 196 Colo. 56, 581 P.2d 734 (1978) (claimant worked for Union Carbide eight days before becoming disabled. During that time he was exposed to radiation which amounted to 1/10,000 of his total exposure during his entire mining career. Union Carbide was held solely responsible for death benefits under the last injurious exposure rule); Caudle–Hyatt, Inc. v. Mixon, 220 Va. 495, 260 S.E.2d 193 (1979) (claimant's husband died of asbestos-induced cancer after having worked with insulation for many years, including four months with his last employer. The last employer was liable for the entire claim). Some decisions require that the last exposure be a "substantial contributing cause" of the disease. In these cases, it may be the next to last or some earlier employer who ultimately must provide compensation. E.g., Scott Co. v. Workers Comp. App. Bd., 139 Cal.App.3d 98, 188 Cal.Rptr. 537 (1983) (claimant was exposed to asbestos while working for various employers from 1938–1970. An award of benefits against the employer for the period 1959–66 was affirmed where there was medical testimony that exposures after 1963 did not cause or aggravate the tumor); Halverson v. Larrivy Plumbing & Heating Co., 322 N.W.2d 203 (Minn.1982) (second to last employer was held solely liable for compensation benefits when medical testimony indicated that subsequent exposures to asbestos would not result in any measurable injury for another five years or more). Only a few states, either by statute or judicial opinion, allow apportionment between two or more employers. Me.Rev.Stat.Ann. tit. 39, § 104 B; R.I.Gen.Laws § 28–34–8; Cooper v. Chrysler Corp., 125 Mich.App. 811, 336 N.W.2d 877 (1983) (benefits awarded an auto worker exposed to fumes and dust were apportioned between General Motors and Chrysler). Where apportionment is allowed, the shares of each employer are usually based on the employee's length of time in each employer's service.

See Russell G. Donaldson, Annot., Workers' Compensation: Liable of Successive Employers for Disease or Condition Allegedly Attributable to Successive Employment, 34 A.L.R. 4th 958 (1984).

7. Several occupational disease statutes contain time-based restrictions on coverage. Some states impose minimum exposure limitations as a condition of coverage. A disease will not be compensable under these statutes unless the employee proves he was exposed to a particular substance on the job for the specified period of time. E.g., S.C.Code Ann. § 42–11–60 (Law.Co-op.1985) (worker must be exposed to organic or inorganic dust for seven years to recover for byssinosis); Nev.Rev.Stat. § 617.460(4) (1987) (no compensation for disease related to asbestos or silicosis unless the worker was exposed to the harmful substance at least one year while working in state for the employer against whom recovery is sought). A different type of time-based restriction is in the nature of a statute of repose. Compensation benefits for occupational disease may be awarded under these statutes only if the death or disability occur within a specified period after the last day of work or the last injurious exposure. E.g., Ind. Code Ann. § 22–3–7–9 (f) (Three years from last exposure for silica, coal, and asbestos dust cases, and two years for other occupational diseases); Kan.Stat.Ann. § 44.5aO1(e) (One year from last exposure, three-year period for silicosis, and no limitation for radiation).

These time-based restrictions on coverage are intended to guarantee that a particular death or disability is genuinely work related. In practice, however, they often serve to deny compensation claims even when the disabling disease was clearly caused by job conditions. The problem is that occupational diseases rarely develop according to a legislatively prescribed time table. In Magma Copper Co. v. Gonzales, 62 Ariz. 9, 152 P.2d 618 (1944), for example, the claimant indisputably became disabled by silicosis as a result of his four and one-half year employment in the defendant's mine. The employee was denied workers' compensation benefits, however, because he became disabled too soon. The Arizona statute then in effect conditioned coverage of silicosis on a minimum five year exposure to silicon dioxide dust. Conversely, statutes of repose may bar the compensation claims of employees who die or become disabled too slowly. The widow of a Texas worker who died from occupationally induced cancer was denied benefits because her husband's death occurred more than three years after his last day of employment. Legate v. Bituminous Fire & Marine Ins. Co., 483 S.W.2d 488 (Tex.Civ.App.1972).

Such restrictions are roundly criticized by commentators. See, 3 A. Larson & L. Larson, Larson's Workers' Compensation Law § 41.82 (1998); Schroeder, Legislative and Judicial Responses to the Inadequacy of Compensation for Occupational Disease, 49 Law & Contemp.Probs. (No. 4) 151 (1986); Locke, Adapting Workers' Compensation to the Special Problems of Occupational Disease, 9 Harv.Envtl.L.Rev. 349 (1985). Legislatures in several states have repealed or modified time based restrictions to give greater coverage for occupational disease. Courts in many of these states have given retroactive effect to such legislation. E.g., Puckett v. Johns–Manville Corp., 169 Cal.App.3d 1010, 215 Cal.Rptr. 726 (1985) (retroactive application given to statute extending time period in which to file claims for asbestosis); Long v. North Carolina Finishing Co., 82 N.C.App. 568, 346 S.E.2d 669 (1986) (statute extending limitation period for asbestos claims applied to pending cases). Other courts have invalidated repose type restrictions under provisions of the state constitution. E.g., Walters v. Blair, 120 N.C.App. 398, 462 S.E.2d 232 (N.C.App. 1995) aff'd 344 N.C. 628, 476 S.E.2d 105 (N.C. 1996)(minimum exposure provision for silicosis and asbestosis violate state and federal equal protection clauses); Alvarado v. Industrial Comm., 148 Ariz. 561, 716 P.2d 18 (1986) (statutory provision that barred the claim of the widow of a miner who died of silicosis more than five years from his last day of employment was held to deny the claimant the right to a remedy for work related injuries guaranteed by Arizona constitution); Caruso v. Aluminum Co. of America, 15 Ohio St.3d 306, 473 N.E.2d 818 (1984) (denial of death benefits to the widow of an employee who died more than eight years after last injurious exposure to silica dust was held to be an unconstitutional denial of equal protection under both federal and state constitutions); Wrolstad v. Industrial Comm'n, 786 P.2d 243 (Utah App.1990) (one year statute of repose as applied to a worker disabled ten years after his occupational exposure to asbestos was found to violate the open courts provision of the Utah constitution). But see, Bunker v. National Gypsum Co., 441 N.E.2d 8 (Ind.1982) (upholding the constitutionality of a statute that barred occupational disease claims unless brought within three years of the claimant's last exposure to asbestos).

SECTION 4. HEART CONDITIONS, MENTAL AND NERVOUS INJURY, AND OTHER SPECIAL CASES

LANCASTER v. GILBERT DEVELOPMENT

Supreme Court of Utah, 1987.
736 P.2d 237.

DURHAM, JUSTICE:

The claimant, James Lancaster, seeks review of the denial of workers' compensation benefits by the State Industrial Commission for injuries from a heart attack that occurred while he was clearing snow with a backhoe at Brian Head Ski Resort. We examine the evidence on this writ of review to determine if the claimant's heart attack is the result of an injury "by accident arising out of or in the course of his employment." U.C.A., 1953, § 35–1–45 (Supp.1986). We recently established the analytical framework for internal injury cases such as this in *Allen v. Industrial Commission,* 729 P.2d 15 (Utah 1986). Using the analysis in *Allen,* we affirm the decision of the Industrial Commission.

On February 17, 1984, the claimant, aged 43, arrived for work at Brian Head Resort at his usual hour of 7:00 a.m. The elevation at Brian Head Resort is approximately ten thousand feet. Claimant's first task was to clear snow using a backhoe. Although the temperature outside was cold, the cab of the backhoe was heated. All of the backhoe controls were hydraulically operated and required no unusual effort to operate. During the morning's work, the claimant climbed in and out of the backhoe two or three times.

The claimant experienced chest pains, which became more severe as the day progressed. These pains were more severe than similar pains he had experienced four days earlier. When the pains became debilitating, he informed his supervisor, who then called paramedics; the claimant was transported to a hospital in Cedar City, Utah. The treating physician determined that the claimant was suffering from acute anterior myocardial infarction. After one week at the hospital, the claimant was released to the care of his personal physician, Dr. Chanderraj. Although this was the claimant's first heart attack, he had several preexisting risk factors that predisposed him to heart attacks: a twenty-year smoking history, an elevated serum cholesterol level, an elevated uric acid level, and borderline diabetes.

On August 10, 1984, the Industrial Commission held a hearing in which one doctor, Dr. Perry, was appointed to a medical panel. A hearing on the medical panel finding was held on March 24, 1985. On April 5, 1985, the administrative law judge issued his findings of fact, conclusions of law, and order. The administrative law judge reviewed the conflicting medical evidence and then adopted the medical findings of the medical panel as his own. The administrative law judge found:

> [T]he Applicant's work activities and the myocardial infarction of [February 17, 1984] do not constitute an injury by accident. The Applicant's heart attack was unexpected, but there was nothing about his work activities that could constitute an unanticipated, unintended occurrence different from what would normally be expected to occur in the usual course of events. His heart attack appears to have been a mere coincidence, and his work activities did not contribute significantly to its occurrence. At best, it is conjectural as to whether it even precipitated his heart attack, but it clearly was not a significant precipitating cause. There was no evidence that the Applicant's work activities on February 17, 1984 were particularly different from the activities he had been performing for many weeks prior thereto.

The administrative law judge ultimately denied the claim on the ground that the claimant failed to show that the heart attack was "by accident" and that the heart attack was medically caused by an exertion in the workplace.

Our scope of review of factual findings in Industrial Commission cases is limited. We have explained in prior cases:

> The reviewing court's inquiry is whether the Commission's findings are "arbitrary and capricious" or "wholly without cause" or contrary to the "one [inevitable] conclusion from the evidence" or without "any substantial evidence" to support them. Only then should the Commission's findings be displaced.

Kaiser Steel Corp. v. Monfredi, 631 P.2d 888, 890 (Utah 1981). * * * At the time of his decision, the administrative law judge did not have the benefit of our analytical framework for accident cases involving internal failures set forth in *Allen v. Industrial Commission,* 729 P.2d 15 (Utah

1986). Nevertheless, the record is sufficiently developed for us to apply *Allen* to the facts and conclusions in the case before us.

In *Allen v. Industrial Commission,* we explained that the Utah Workers' Compensation Act, section 35–1–45, requires proof that an injury occurred "by accident" and proof of a causal connection between the accident and the activities or exertions required in the workplace. 729 P.2d at 18. The administrative law judge's ruling shows that he found the evidence insufficient to meet both the accident and the causation elements.

In *Allen,* we embraced the definition of "by accident" first formulated in *Purity Biscuit Co. v. Industrial Commission,* 115 Utah 1, 201 P.2d 961 (1949). We rejected the position that an accident requires an unusual event or occurrence. 729 P.2d at 20. An ordinary or usual exertion is sufficient to meet the "by accident" definition if "the result of an exertion was different from what would normally be expected to occur, the occurrence was unplanned, unforeseen, unintended and therefore by accident." 729 P.2d at 22. The critical factor when determining whether an incident is by accident is unexpectedness. 729 P.2d at 22.

Despite a finding that the heart attack was unexpected, the administrative law judge concluded there was no accident primarily because the claimant was undertaking his usual work duties. That conclusion cannot stand in light of the standard set forth in *Allen.* Although the claimant had experienced similar pains four days earlier, he had not been advised of the etiology of those pains and he had no forewarning that they would occur again on February 17. Moreover, there is nothing in the claimant's job duties to suggest that he would suffer a heart attack. There is overwhelming evidence that the claimant did not intend to have a heart attack, nor did he anticipate one. These factors, taken together with the finding that the myocardial infarction was the "unexpected" result of an exertion in the workplace, require the conclusion that the heart attack was "by accident."

The next step requires us to analyze the causal connection between the heart attack and the working conditions. *See Hone v. Shea,* 728 P.2d 1008, 1011 (Utah 1986). We adopted Professor Larson's two-step causation analysis in *Allen v. Industrial Commission,* 729 P.2d at 25. In order to meet the causation requirement, there must be sufficient evidence of legal cause and medical cause. Under the legal cause test, "a claimant with a preexisting condition must show that the employment contributed something substantial to increase the risk he already faced in everyday life because of his condition." 729 P.2d at 25. When a claimant has no preexisting risk factors, any exertion connected with the employment and causally connected with the injury as a matter of medical fact will satisfy the legal causation test. 729 P.2d at 26.

In addition to proving legal causation, the claimant must also prove medical causation. "Under the medical cause test, the claimant must show ... that the stress, strain or exertion required by his or her occupation led to the resulting injury or disability." 729 P.2d at 27.

In this case, the administrative law judge did not distinguish in his causation analysis between legal and medical causation. However, it is clear from the medical testimony and other evidence presented to the administrative law judge that his decision was based on the failure to prove medical causation. Because the result in this case turns on the issue of medical causation, we will not examine the issue of legal causation.

The claimant argues that his work activities in cold weather and at a high altitude precipitated the myocardial infarction. The medical evidence before the administrative law judge was less than conclusive. The claimant's physician, Dr. Chanderraj, was the doctor most certain that the working conditions at Brian Head contributed to the injury. His opinion, however, was not unequivocal. He stated that the altitude, cold, and working conditions "probably" precipitated the heart attack. Dr. Chanderraj answered questions by the claimant's counsel as follows:

Q. Let me ask you, Doctor, during all of the time that Mr. Lancaster has been your patient, have you had an opportunity to form an opinion as to whether or not the elevation, the cold, and the working conditions at the time of Mr. Lancaster's myocardial infarction precipitated that heart attack?

A. This is a very difficult question to answer because it's a gray area in the field of cardiology; the exact role of precipitating factors in producing the event, but it is well known that high altitude, where the oxygen content of the air is low, especially in cold weather, can induce a myocardial event * * *.

Q. Would it be your opinion that the cold, exposure, and the altitude, and the work conditions played a significant role or would be the trigger or the lighting up process of the myocardial infarction?

A. I think we did go over this. I do feel it triggered—let me put it another way. If he had not been working up on that particular day in the cold atmosphere, operating the heavy equipment, in spite of having—in spite of five days history of chest pain, he probably would not have sustained a myocardial infarction.

Dr. Perry, the chairman of the medical panel and a cardiologist, testified it was "likely" that the conditions under which Mr. Lancaster was working aggravated his preexisting heart condition. However, Dr. Perry also was less than certain about the causal connection between the work conditions and the myocardial infarction. In his report to the administrative law judge, Dr. Perry identified and ranked the role of various risk factors, including those associated with work, in precipitating the claimant's myocardial infarction. He stated in his report:

Mr. Lancaster has mild diabetes mellitus, smokes cigarettes, has an elevated uric acid and an elevated serum cholesterol level, all of which increase risk of coronary artery disease. In very rough terms the cigarette smoking, diabetes and high cholesterol approximately each double the risk of coronary artery disease such that with these three plus the uric acid elevation, his risk for coronary artery disease is 8–10 times higher than another male of his same age. From information gleaned from the records, summary of testimony and talking to Mr. Lancaster himself, I did not view his work as a risk factor for a myocardial infarction. While it was apparently cold, he was not involved in any unusual exertion, neither was he subjected to any unusual stress.

* * *

* * * While it is possible the cold exposure and his exertion had a role in precipitating the myocardial infarction, it is my opinion that it is unlikely they played a significant role. His 5 days of unstable angina lead me to believe that the patient was about to have a myocardial infarction, and the rather moderate amount of exertion and the length of time spent working simply offered an appropriate time and place for this event.

When asked to quantify the contribution of preexisting risk factors and work factors to the claimant's myocardial infarction, Dr. Perry assigned a value of 90 percent to preexisting conditions and 10 percent to work conditions. Dr. Perry explained, however, that his assessment of the factors was "a fairly random guess."

In addition, the State Insurance Fund had its doctor, Frank Dituri, review the claimant's medical records. Dr. Dituri opined that there was no evidence to indicate that the claimant's myocardial infarction was caused by his work or the altitude and cold at his place of work. Dr. Dituri concluded, "The type of work activities described could not precipitate any acute myocardial infarction." According to Dr. Dituri, the claimant's injury was "due to the normal progression of arteriosclerotic coronary artery disease that had been present for several years and was due to such factors as his smoking, his hypercholesterolemia, his poorly controlled diabetes and his prior history of alcohol abuse."

Thus, although there may have been some connection between the heart attack and the cold weather and high altitude, the evidence of any such connection is inconclusive. Not one of the doctors was willing to state with medical certainty that the claimant's injury was caused by work-related factors. Thus, there is competent and comprehensive medical evidence in the record upon which the administrative law judge could rely in concluding that medical causation was lacking. Although the medical evidence was conflicting, it is the responsibility of the administrative law judge to resolve factual conflicts.

We hold that the Industrial Commission's conclusion that there was no medical causal connection between work conditions and the claimant's heart attack is neither "arbitrary or capricious" nor "without any substantial evidence to support it." We therefore affirm the order of the Industrial Commission.

HALL, C.J., and HOWE and ZIMMERMAN, JJ., concur.

STEWART, ASSOCIATE C.J., concurs in the result.

Notes

1. The compensability of death or disability from diseases of the heart or blood vessels has been described as "probably the most prolific and troublesome problem in workers' compensation law." Larson, The "Heart Cases" in Workmen's Compensation: An Analysis and Suggested Solution, 65 Mich.L.Rev. 441 (1965). The problem exists because diseases of the heart and blood vessels are capable in their normal course of causing incapacity or death without any work connected activity whatsoever. Almost everyone has known someone who suffered a heart attack while asleep or while physically inactive. On the other hand, heart attacks may be precipitated by the physical and emotional stress of the job. Thus, the "heart" cases present another variation of the now familiar question of how to allocate injury costs when occupational and nonoccupational causal factors are difficult to separate.

2. Many courts, perhaps a majority, award compensation for heart attacks caused by ordinary job stress. E.g., Grainger v. Alaska Workers' Compensation Bd., 805 P.2d 976 (Alaska 1991) (awarding benefits to obese workers whose heart disease was triggered by ordinary stress); Bush v. Industrial Comm., 136 Ariz. 522, 667 P.2d 222 (1983) (compensation awarded to an accountant whose heart attack was triggered by the stress of an increased work load without regard to whether the stress was labeled unusual); Wynn v. Navajo Freight Lines, Inc., 654 S.W.2d 87 (Mo.1983) (benefits awarded to the family of a truck driver who died from a heart attack while driving a normal run); Kirnan v. Dakota Midland Hospital, 331 N.W.2d 72 (S.D.1983) (awarding compensation to an employee whose heart attack was triggered while performing ordinary housekeeping duties).

3. A substantial number of courts require a showing of "unusual" physical exertion or emotional stress to support an award for a job related heart attack. E.g., State Industrial Ins. System v. Foster, 110 Nev. 521, 874 P.2d 766 (Nev. 1994) (heart attacks triggered by ordinary stress are not compensable); Landis Office Center v. Barefield, 73 Md.App. 315, 533 A.2d 1332 (1987) (awarding compensation to a typewriter salesman whose heart attack was triggered by the unusual strain of removing old typewriters from client's office in 85–degree heat and pushing them up a 150 foot 30 degree incline); Grace v. North Dakota Workmen's Comp. Bureau, 395 N.W.2d 576 (N.D.1986) (denying compensation to masonry foreman with history of heart disease who suffered heart attack while working in 120–degree heat; no unusual stress). Cf. Fiore v. Consolidated Freightways, 140 N.J. 452, 659 A.2d 436 (N.J. 1995) (claimant must show that heart disease is due in "material degree" to work conditions that "substantially" contributed to the development of the disease).

An implicit question lurking within the "unusual" exertion or stress standard is: unusual as compared to what? Some jurisdictions compare the occupational emotional or physical strain that triggered the heart attack with that encountered by other employees in similar jobs. E.g., Matter of Desotell, 767 P.2d 998 (Wyo.1989) (denying compensation to widow of truck driver whose heart attack was triggered by stress of having to reload improperly balanced trailer). Occasionally the comparison is made between the claimant's job stress and that of workers generally. E.g., Ryan v. Connor, 28 Ohio St.3d 406, 503 N.E.2d 1379 (1986) (heart attack induced by job related emotional distress is compensable only if the emotional strain is greater than that to which all workers are occasionally subjected). Other courts look to whether the heart attack was caused by stress that was unusual for that particular employee. E.g., Matter of Carr v. Industrial Comm., 709 P.2d 52 (Colo.App.1985) (awarding compensation to the widow of a water commissioner whose heart attack was precipitated by the physical strain of turning water control equipment; this was seasonal activity, but more strenuous than his ordinary duties). Which comparison is the most appropriate?

Once the proper point of comparison is selected, there remains the formidable task of measuring relative levels of physical and emotional stress. Which is the more "unusual" stress for a police officer, forcibly removing from a public bar the disorderly date of the officer's daughter, or responding to a major fire? Compare Creek v. Town of Hulett, 657 P.2d 353 (Wyo.1983) with Town of Kaycee v. Van Buskirk, 721 P.2d 570 (Wyo.1986).

4. A third approach, favored by Professor Larson and illustrated in *Lancaster,* distinguishes between claimants with preexisting heart conditions and those with no such preexisting risk factors. The latter may receive compensation for heart attacks caused by ordinary occupational exertion or stress, while the former must prove that the heart attack was caused by unusual stress or exertion. What policy considerations might support such a distinction? A number of jurisdictions have adopted this approach. E.g., Trinity Industries Inc. v. Cunningham, 680 So.2d 262 (Ala.1996); Briar Cliff College v. Campolo, 360 N.W.2d 91 (Iowa 1984); Guidry v. Sline Indust. Painters, 418 So.2d 626 (La.1982); Cheshire Toyota/Volvo, Inc. v. O'Sullivan, 129 N.H. 698, 531 A.2d 714 (1987).

5. Allocation of injury costs under any of the aforementioned approaches is on an all-or-nothing basis. Either the employer or the employee bears the entire cost of the heart attack. Would it be theoretically preferable to apportion injury costs in cases where occupational and nonoccupational factors combine to produce a disabling condition? How should the loss be apportioned? Is such a division practical? See Rootenberg & Getz v. Workers' Compensation Appeals Bd., 94 Cal.App.3d 265, 156 Cal.Rptr. 314 (1979) (discussing the potential apportionment of disability benefits for a heart attack under Cal.Labor Code § 4663); Road Maintenance Supply, Inc. v. Dependents of Maxwell, 493 So.2d 318 (Miss.1986) (employee with a history of heart disease suffered a fatal heart attack on the job; compensation to be reduced by the proportion which the preexisting heart disease contributed to the heart attack pursuant to Miss.Code Ann. § 71–3–7 (1972)). Are there ways to provide complete compensation to the disabled worker and still limit the employer's liability to the occupational share of causal responsibility? See Yocom v. Loy, 573 S.W.2d 645 (Ky.1978) (apportioning compensation benefits for a heart attack between employer and statutory Special Fund). The use of special funds is explored in more detail in Chapter 8.

6. Regardless of which measure of comparative stress controls, the claimant must always prove a causal connection between that stress and the

heart attack. Even when ordinary occupational stress is sufficient to support coverage, compensation will be denied if the claimant fails to prove medical causation. E.g., Deuschle v. Bak Construction Co., 443 N.W.2d 5 (S.D.1989) (upholding a finding that the claimant's heart attack was not caused by occupational factors on the strength of evidence that the worker smoked and had a history of heart disease in his family). Causation is most often established through the opinion testimony of expert witnesses who must express their opinions in terms of probabilities or reasonable medical certainty. Equivocal expert testimony may not support an award of benefits. E.g., Wiedmaier v. Robert A. McNeil Corp., 718 S.W.2d 174 (Mo.App.1986) (expert opinion that physical and emotional strain of work "could or might have caused" the heart attack does not discharge the claimant's burden of proof). Would the testimony of Dr. Perry and Dr. Chanderraj regarding causation have been sufficient to uphold an award of benefits in *Lancaster* if the Commission had ruled for the claimant? *Lancaster* suggests that there are significant differences between legal and medical standards of causation. What are they? See, Danner and Sagall, Medicolegal Causation: A Source of Professional Misunderstanding, 3 Am.J.L. & M. 303 (1977); Small, Gaffing at a Thing Called Cause: Medicolegal Conflicts in the Concept of Causation, 31 Tex.L.Rev. 630 (1953). How far can or should an attorney go ethically in preparing a prospective expert witness to testify on the issue of causation? See, Piorkowski, Professional Conduct and the Preparation of Witnesses for Trial: Defining the Acceptable Limitations of "Coaching", 1 Geo.J. Legal Ethics 389 (1987).

SPARKS v. TULANE MEDICAL CENTER HOSPITAL & CLINIC

Supreme Court of Louisiana, 1989.
546 So.2d 138.

CALOGERO, JUSTICE.

The Louisiana Worker's Compensation Act provides coverage to any employee who suffers "*personal injury* by accident arising out of and in the course of his employment." La.R.S. 23:1031 (emphasis added). We have previously determined that mental injury induced by physical trauma and physical injury induced by mental stress are compensable "personal injuries" under the Act.

The primary issue presented in this case, heretofore not addressed by this Court, is whether a mental injury induced by mental stress is compensable when it is caused by a significant employment incident and is not accompanied by any apparent signs of physical trauma * * *.

[Claimant Sparks worked in a supervisory capacity for Tulane Medical Center. In 1982, she incurred the resentment of her co-workers by initiating a program to eliminate illegal drug use by employees on the hospital premises. Sparks soon thereafter became the victim of a series of thefts and vandalism, including urination into her coffee pot and waste basket. The court stated that many of these incidents appeared to be intentional and designed to harass or intimidate the claimant. No one was ever apprehended in connection with these incidents.

On April 6, 1987, Sparks suspended two employees who failed to stock the supply room. That same day, Sparks was informed that "a lot of people round here want to kick your butt." She became upset at the threat and left work. On April 7, 1987, Sparks was examined by an internist who diagnosed her as suffering from "tension headaches, which were probably related to ... stress she was encountering at work." When Sparks' condition did not improve, the internist referred her to a psychiatrist. The psychiatrist diagnosed Sparks as suffering from an "adjustment disorder" that was "definitely job related". Over the course of several months Sparks received counseling from a clinical social worker who also found that Sparks' condition was both disabling and work related.

Defendant, while presenting no medical witnesses, produced evidence that plaintiff was diagnosed with depression in 1970, and that she was treated for sinus headaches in 1985. The plaintiff's medical records also revealed a one-time doctor's visit in 1986 for headaches she suffered after a blow to the head.]

* * * The trial court denied the plaintiff's claims for benefits. The trial judge concluded that the plaintiff had been temporarily mentally disabled, but that she had not suffered the requisite "accident" under La.R.S. 23:1031. The court of appeals reversed and awarded plaintiff benefits for a five month period of disability. 537 So.2d 276 (La.App. 1988). * * *

In summary, then, we have a plaintiff who was diagnosed with a psychological adjustment disorder, depression and tension headaches, and who also complained of anxiety, loss of appetite, insomnia and nightmares. Three experts, an internist, a psychiatrist and a clinical social worker, related these problems to plaintiff's employment. Defendant presented no medical testimony but attempted to establish that plaintiff had pre-existing medical problems.

(II) Law and Analysis

Defendant argues that there are a number of reasons why the events described above do not provide a basis for recovery under the Louisiana Worker's Compensation Act. First, defendant argues that plaintiff did not prove that her injury resulted from an "accident" as that term is defined in the Act, because there was no "unexpected or unforeseen event happening suddenly or violently ... and producing at the time objective symptoms of an injury." La.R.S. 23:102(1). Secondly, defendant argues that because any injury suffered by plaintiff was not induced by physical trauma, there was not a compensable injury under the Act which involved "violence to the physical structure of the body." La.R.S. 23:1021(7). As a third and alternative contention, defendant argues that even if injuries are compensable absent evidence of physical trauma, this plaintiff failed to show that her medical problems were causally related to her employment.

* * *

(A) The Accidental "Event" Requirement

La.R.S. 23:1021(1) defines "accident" as "an unexpected or unforeseen event happening suddenly or violently, with or without human fault, and producing at the time objective symptoms of an injury."

The "event" which qualifies as an accident can be and often is a forceful and readily identifiable occurrence which *causes injury* to the employee, e.g., an automobile collision, a fall, an explosion, an assault, etc. However, under the jurisprudence, the sudden and unexpected appearance of a *physical injury*, such as a heart attack or stroke, is also viewed as an "accident." See, e.g., *Ferguson v. HDE, Inc.*, 270 So.2d 867, 869–70 (La.1972) (stroke). In such cases, the onset of the illness or injury is viewed as the accident because, from the employee's perspective, the injury was an unforeseen event which occurred suddenly or violently. *Ferguson v. HDE, Inc., supra*, 270 So.2d at 870.

The "event" which triggers coverage, then, may be an unexpected and sudden or violent occurrence which *causes injury*, or it may be an unexpected change in the employee's *physical condition*, which renders him incapable of working, a change caused at least in part by an employment incident. *See* Malone & Johnson, 13 Louisiana Civil Law Treatise, Worker's Compensation, § 214 (1980 & 1989 Supp.).

(B) The "Injury" Requirement

The terms "injury" and "personal injuries" are defined by the Act as "injuries by violence to the physical structure of the body and such disease or infections as naturally result therefrom." La.R.S. 23:1021(7). "These terms shall in no case be construed to include any other form of disease or derangement, however caused or contracted." *Id.*

The definition of "injury" contains a requirement of "violence to the physical structure of the body," but the statutory definition does not use the terms "physical injury" or "mental injury." Nor does the statutory definition attempt to provide any basis or method for distinguishing between "physical" and "mental" injuries.

Nevertheless, in attempting to determine the types of injuries covered by the Act, Louisiana courts have often drawn distinctions between physical and mental injuries. In Louisiana, as well as in other jurisdictions, worker's compensation cases involving mental injury or trauma have been grouped by courts and commentators into three general categories: (1) cases in which observable physical trauma causes mental injury ("physical-mental" injury cases); (2) cases in which mental stress or stimulus causes observable physical trauma ("mental-physical" injury cases); and (3) cases in which mental stress or stimulus causes so-called "purely mental" injuries, that is, injuries unaccompanied by any observable or apparent physical trauma ("mental-mental" injury cases). *See* Larson, 1B Workmen's Compensation Law, § 42.20 (1986 & 1988 Supp.). *See also Jordan v. Southern Natural Gas Co.*, 455 So.2d 1217, 1223–26

(La.App. 2d Cir.1984). While the distinction between these categories may often be less than precise,[2] the categories provide a helpful basis for reviewing the jurisprudence pertinent to mental injuries and for resolving the issues presented by this case.

In so-called "physical-mental" injury cases, where a mental injury or illness develops secondary to an ascertainable physical injury, Louisiana courts have uniformly found that the employee is entitled to compensation benefits for any disability resulting from the mental injury and to reimbursement for medical expenses incurred in the treatment of that condition. *See, e.g., Westley v. Land & Offshore,* 523 So.2d 812 (La.1988) (employee suffered post traumatic stress syndrome secondary to physical injury caused by fall); *Droddy v. Cliff's Drilling, Inc.,* 471 So.2d 223 (La.1985) (employee suffered depressive neurosis as "emotional overlay" to physical injury caused by fall). *See also Jordan v. Southern Natural Gas Co., supra,* 455 So.2d at 1222 ("[W]hen a plaintiff develops a disabling anxiety syndrome, traumatic neurosis, or other mental disorder as a result of a work related physical injury, he can recover compensation benefits even if he has recovered physically from the injury."). Allowance of coverage in these "physical-mental" injury cases seems clearly appropriate under the Act's definition of "injury," which covers not only the initial injury suffered by the employee but also "such disease or infections as naturally result therefrom."

We have also recognized that coverage is appropriate where mental stress or strain related to employment causes physical trauma ("mental-physical" injury cases). The leading Louisiana case in this area is *Ferguson v. HDE, Inc.,* 270 So.2d 867 (La.1972), wherein coverage was allowed for an employee who suffered a stroke while arguing with his supervisor. Noting that the claimant unquestionably would have been entitled to compensation if the stroke had been brought on by physical stress, however minimal, we found no basis for denying recovery when the injury was precipitated by mental stress.

* * *

In the third category are the "mental-mental" injury cases, in which there is no indication of apparent physical trauma but the claimant sustains disability due to mental illness precipitated by work-related mental stress. We have never considered whether such injuries are compensable, and our courts of appeal are divided on the issue.[3] This

---

2. "It must be understood that this use of such words as mental, nervous, emotional, stress, stimulus, psychic, and the like is only a rough expedient adopted in order to sort out an almost infinite variety of subtle conditions and relationships for compensation law purposes, and especially in order to narrow down the range of situations where controversy seems to persist." Larson, 1B Workmen's Compensation, *supra,* § 42.20 at 7–586.

3. Courts throughout the country are also divided on this issue. While the majority of jurisdictions permit recovery in "mental-mental" injury cases, a substantial minority do not. *See* Larson, *supra* § 42.23. On the other hand, almost all jurisdictions permit recovery in "physical-mental" injury and "mental-physical" injury cases. *Id.* §§ 42.21–22.

case, which concerns an injury that was not precipitated by any observable physical trauma, squarely presents that issue.

The Louisiana court of appeal decisions which have denied coverage in this area have done so primarily on the ground that the statutory requirement of an injury "by violence to the physical structure of the body" is not satisfied unless the injury was caused by some blow or physical force which causes observable physical injury. For example, in *Sutherland v. Time Saver Stores, Inc.,* 428 So.2d 972 (La.App. 1st Cir.1983), the employee, a convenience store clerk, suffered mental complications after she was robbed at gunpoint. The robber ordered the plaintiff to disrobe, and as she was doing so the police arrived and arrested the perpetrator. Although plaintiff was not physically assaulted in any way, expert testimony established that she suffered from a disabling anxiety syndrome as a result of the incident. The court of appeal affirmed summary judgment in favor of the employer, holding that the employee was not entitled to compensation because "in order to recover in workmen's compensation for a mental disability there must first exist a physical detriment as a causative or contributory factor." 428 So.2d at 972.

* * *

On the other hand, Louisiana court of appeal decisions which have permitted recovery for these types of injuries have concluded that when an employee suffers from a mental disability which is serious enough to render that employee unable to work, then the injury has done "violence to the physical structure of the body." For example, in *Jones v. City of New Orleans,* 514 So.2d 611 (La.App. 4th Cir.1987) *writ denied,* 515 So.2d 1111 (La.1987), compensation benefits were awarded to an employee who suffered from post traumatic stress syndrome as a result of threats to her safety that were made during the course of her employment. In allowing coverage, the court of appeal stated that "[w]e cannot ignore the scientific fact that mental disorders constitute an injury to the physical capabilities of a worker." 514 So.2d at 814.

* * *

Thus, the essential issue over which our courts of appeal are divided, and which we are called upon to resolve here, is whether the statutory requirement of injury "by violence to the physical structure of the body" is satisfied when the employee suffers a mental disability that is not accompanied by apparent physical trauma or physiological damage. In resolving this issue, we will consider both the requirement of "violence," as interpreted by well-established jurisprudence, and the meaning and scope of the phrase "physical structure of the body."

The statutory requirement of violence is satisfied when the injury has a violent or harmful *effect* on the employee's physical condition, even if the *cause* of that change was not in itself violent. Under the jurisprudence, there need not be a blow or visible application of force in order for the "violence" aspect of the statutory definition to be satisfied. *See, e.g.,*

Parks v. Insurance Co. of North America, 340 So.2d 276 (La.1976) (inhalation of fumes and lint caused chronic bronchitis, which in turn caused "violence" to the employee's body); *Cannella v. Gulf Refining Co.,* 154 So. 406, 413 (La.App.Orl.1934) (lead poisoning from fumes caused "violence . . . to both the blood and the intestines"); *Rochell v. Shreveport Grain & Elevator Co.,* 188 So. 429 (La.App. 2d Cir.1939) (small particle lodged in employee's eye and caused blindness); *Smith v. Brown Paper Mill Co.,* 152 So. 700 (La.App. 2d Cir.1934) (infection resulting from hypodermic injection); *Woodward v. Kansas City Bridge Co.,* 3 So.2d 221 (La.App. 1st Cir.1941) (inflammation of skin by creosote and poison ivy).

Thus, there is an "injury" when there is "violence," i.e., a harmful effect, to the "physical structure of the body." One possible interpretation of the phrase "physical structure of the body" is that it refers only to those physical component parts which make up the body, e.g., bones, tissues, organs, etc. We note, however, that the Texas Supreme Court, when interpreting a statutory definition in the Texas worker's compensation act that is similar to our own, rejected this interpretation and held that the "physical structure of the body" refers to:

> the *entire* body, not simply to the skeletal structure or to the circulatory system or to the digestive system. It refers to the *whole,* to the complex of perfectly integrated and interdependent bones, tissues and organs which function together by means of electrical, chemical and mechanical processes in a living, breathing, functioning individual. To determine what is meant by "physical structure of the body," the structure should be considered that of a living person—not as a static inanimate thing. *Bailey v. American General Ins. Co.,* 154 Tex. 430, 279 S.W.2d 315, 318 (1955) (emphasis by the court).

In *Bailey,* the claimant was working on a high-level scaffold with another worker. The scaffold collapsed and plaintiff, who was able to avoid injury to himself because he was caught in a cable, watched his co-employee plunge to this death. Afterward plaintiff claimed inability to work because of a disabling neurosis. The Texas court determined that plaintiff was entitled to benefits because the medical testimony established that as a result of his disabling neurosis, "plaintiff's body no longer functions properly." *Id.* 279 S.W.2d at 318. The court found itself unable to conclude that "though a 'physical structure' no longer functions properly, it has suffered no 'harm.' "*Bailey,* 279 S.W.2d at 318.

We agree with the analysis employed by the Texas Supreme Court in *Bailey,* while interpreting a statutory definition of injury similar to our own, as well as the reasoning used by the Louisiana Fourth Circuit Court of Appeal in *Jones, supra,* and *Taquino, supra.* An individual's mental health is an essential component to the overall operation of the physical structure of his body. If an injury so disables the mental machinery of a worker that "his body no longer functions properly," *Bailey, supra,* and he is unable to perform his employment duties, then the statutory requirement of violence (harm) to the physical structure of the body is satisfied. This is true regardless of whether the injury was prompted by observable physical trauma and regardless of whether the injury might be characterized as more "mental" in nature than "physical."

* * *

Furthermore, it has been persuasively argued that there is no bright-line distinction between "physical" and "mental" injuries, either in medicine or in law, which provides a reliable basis for awarding or denying workmen's compensation benefits. Many injuries which appear essentially mental in nature may actually be caused or accompanied by physiological change.[6]

* * *

Finally, we note that by rejecting the "nineteenth century approach" of making the availability of benefits dependent upon a rigid and absolute distinction between physical and mental injuries, Larson, *supra* at 7–651 n. 82, we reach a result that has been approved by a majority of the jurisdictions in this country. *Id.* at 7–639.

We emphasize, however, that a mere showing that a mental injury was related to *general conditions* of employment, or to incidents occurring over an extended period of time, is not enough to entitle the claimant to compensation. The mental injury must be precipitated by an accident, i.e., an unexpected and unforeseen event that occurs suddenly or violently.[7]

Among the cases involving work-related disabilities which appear to be essentially mental in nature, there are a number of examples of the type of sudden and unusual *event* which can truly be considered an "accident." *See, e.g., Bailey v. American General Ins. Co., supra* (plaintiff

---

6. That the distinction between physical and mental injury is often obscure is demonstrated by two recent worker's compensation cases, *Davis v. Oilfield Scrap & Equipment Co.,* 482 So.2d 970 (La.App. 3d Cir. 1986) and *Guillot v. Sentry Insurance Co.,* 472 So.2d 197 (La.App. 5th Cir.1985). Seemingly, the facts of *Davis* present a classic "mental-mental" injury case. The plaintiff suffered a mental disability after her supervisor shot himself at work and died in her arms. While plaintiff suffered from no apparent physical injury or trauma, medical evidence established that plaintiff's mental disability was accompanied by a physiological change in her body that could be measured by electroencephalograms (EEG) and chemical analysis. Because of this evidence, the court of appeal was satisfied that an "injury" had been proven, and allowed compensation. In *Guillot, supra,* the claimant alleged that he suffered a nervous

breakdown as the result of job related stress. There was no evidence of injury by physical trauma, but medical testimony established that the "breakdown" was accompanied by "physiological changes in brain cells along with biochemical changes that could be measured chemically," and recovery of benefits was allowed.

7. While the sudden onset of physical injury may qualify as the compensable "accident" in some cases, *see Ferguson v. HDE, Inc., supra,* (stroke), an employee's subjective assertion that he had a sudden onset of symptoms of mental injury, such as depression or anxiety, is not alone sufficient to show that an accident occurred. The employee must be able to point to a discernible employment-related event which caused the mental injury, an event separate and apart from the onset of the symptoms of that mental injury.

watched co-employee fall to death after collapse of scaffold); *Sutherland v. Time Saver Stores, Inc., supra* (robbery and fear of imminent sexual abuse); *Davis v. Oilfield Scrap & Equipment Co.,* 482 So.2d 970 (La.App. 3d Cir.1986) (co-employee suicide, see discussion in note six, *supra*). In cases involving such readily identifiable, unusual and dramatic events, compensation is appropriate when there is sufficient evidence that the sudden event caused the disabling mental condition. On the other hand, absent an identifiable accident of this type, an employee's general allegation that he is unable to work due to stress or tension caused by working conditions would not give rise to a compensable claim.

* * *

(C) Application of the Accidental Event and Injury Requirements to This Case; Causation

Defendant argues that there was no "accident" under the Act because "plaintiff never alleged a single, unexpected, unforeseen and catastrophic event which gave rise to her injuries," but rather alleged "a series of events which took place over the course of six and one-half years...." Under the Act, defendant argues, there must be a single, identifiable "event" which produces injury, and separate events which occurred over a six year period cannot constitute an accident.

We find, however, that the communication of the threats to plaintiff on April 6, 1987 was the event which produced injury in this case, not the incidents which occurred in the years prior to the threats. The accident thus occurred on April 6, 1987, and the events prior to that date are relevant simply to the extent that they reinforce the seriousness of the threats and lend credibility to plaintiff's assertion that the threats caused her severe anxiety and distress.

It is evident from the record that plaintiff suffered a temporarily disabling mental injury as a result of learning of the threats that had been made against her. Prior to April 6, 1987, plaintiff had an excellent seven-year work record at the medical center, a record which included a promotion to a supervisory position of substantial responsibility and highly favorable annual evaluations. Prior to April 6, 1987, plaintiff had missed some work due to illness but never for any significant period of time. And prior to April 6, 1987, plaintiff had been able to perform her employment duties in an able and competent manner. Yet after the events on the morning of April 6, 1987, when plaintiff learned of a physical threat to her safety, she experienced an unexpected and sudden inability to perform her normal employment duties. The breakdown or adjustment disorder which she experienced was accompanied by the immediate onset of headaches, tension and loss of appetite. The record evidences that the threats of harm precipitated a change in plaintiff from an able and competent worker to a person who was unable to engage in any meaningful activity, including employment, for almost five months.

All three of the experts called by plaintiff agreed that she was unable to work during the period that they treated her, because of her mental injury, and also because of the related headaches, insomnia and loss of appetite. All three of the experts also expressed the view that the disabling mental condition was caused by the fear and anxiety plaintiff had regarding returning to her job. The defendant presented no medical testimony to the contrary. In fact, the defendant presented no expert testimony at all regarding plaintiff's condition after April 6, 1987.

* * *

Finally, while there was evidence that plaintiff had some prior medical problems, including sinus headaches in 1985 or 1986 and depression in 1970, there is no indication in the record that whatever problems she experienced prior to April 6, 1987 were related to the disability which she suffered after that date.

In summary, since three experts affirmatively testified that plaintiff's disability was related to her employment, since defendant produced no testimony to the contrary, and since whatever previous medical problems plaintiff experienced were clearly not of the same severity and scope as those brought on by the events of April 6, 1987, we find that plaintiff established by a preponderance of the evidence that her injury was precipitated by the threats to her safety.

Decree

For the foregoing reasons, we agree with the court of appeal that this plaintiff suffered a compensable "injury by accident" under the Louisiana Worker's Compensation Act. Therefore, we affirm the court of appeal's judgment, ordering defendant to pay plaintiff $7,303.24 in benefits and medical expenses, plus legal interest and court costs.

AFFIRMED.

[Three justices dissented in two opinions that argued that Sparks was not entitled to compensation because: (1) the events leading to Sparks' disability could not be characterized as an "accident"; (2) Sparks had not suffered any damage to the "physical structures of the body"; (3) the statute excluded coverage of any "disease" other than "that naturally resulting from injuries by violence to the physical structure of the body"; and (4) any expansion of coverage for mental disabilities should come from the legislature.]

Notes

1. Medical science has identified a broad spectrum of mental disorders, each with its own diagnostic nomenclature and characteristic symptoms. The primary source for standard psychiatric diagnosis is the American Psychiatric Association, Diagnostic and Statistical Manual of Mental Disorders (4th ed. 1994) (DSM–IV revised). Three types of psychological disorders appear with some frequency in workers' compensation cases. The first is commonly referred to as post traumatic stress disorder. This condition is marked by symptoms of stress exhibited more than a month following an especially traumatic event, such as a serious workplace accident. A second type of common psychological injury is known as psychogenic pain disorder. A

person experiencing psychogenic pain disorder expresses genuine sensations of pain for which no organic explanation can be found. The third common claim involves a conversion disorder in which the patient suffers a loss of physical function unconsciously caused by a psychological conflict or need rather than any physical injury.

2. Workers seeking compensation for such psychological disorders face two recurring questions: is the injury genuine and, if so, is it sufficiently work related? The fundamental problem was succinctly described by one commentator as follows:

> The precise etiology of most mental disorders is inexplicable. Mental disorders result from an extraordinarily complex interrelation between an individual's internal or subjective reality and his external or environmental reality.... The precise psychogenesis of an individual's subjective reality is impossible to determine ... When mental disorder symptoms appear in parts of the body other than the brain, medical science is able, in most cases, to attach a quantitative or qualitative etiological probability. Scientists cannot make this determination, however, when the symptoms manifest themselves subjectively. An individual who suffers a mental disorder has an *a priori* personal subjective vulnerability or predisposition to the disorder.... Although mental injuries medically are as genuine as physical disorders, their subjective quality creates the possibility that the individual may feign a mental disorder. The specter of fraud has influenced judicial attitudes toward mental injuries.

Joseph, The Causation Issue in Workers' Compensation Mental Disability Cases: An Analysis, Solutions, and a Perspective, 36 Vand.L.Rev. 263, 271–273 (1983).

The potential number of claims for stress-related disabilities is enormous. A study conducted by the California Workers' Compensation Institute (CWCI) documented a 700% increase in the number of pure mental stress claims between 1979 and 1988. The benefit costs of such claims filed in California in 1987 alone was estimated to be $383 million. Peter S Barth, Workers' Compensation for Mental Stress Cases, 8 Behavioral Sci. & L. 349, 358 (1990). Other states have experienced similar increases in stress claims. See Nugent, Workers' Compensation and Stress, 14 Employee Rel.L.J. 239, 240 (1988). Cf. Aya V. Matsumoto, Comment, Reforming the Reform: Mental Stress Claims Under California's Workers' Compensation System, 27 Loy. L.A. L. Rev. 1328, 1335 (1994) (mental disorders currently rank among the top ten work-related injures and illnesses in the nation).

3. Professor Larson organizes his analysis of the cases by characterizing the cause and effect of disability as either physical or mental. 3 A. Larson and L. Larson, Larson's Workers' Compensation Laws § 42.20 (1998). This framework was utilized by the court in *Sparks* and is followed in many jurisdictions. Courts and administrative agencies are most likely to award compensation for mental injuries in cases in which the disabling mental disturbance is caused by some work related physical injury (so-called physical-mental cases). E.g., Southwire Co. v. George, 266 Ga. 739, 470 S.E.2d 865 (Ga. 1996) (benefits awarded truck driver for post-traumatic stress disorder following an accident in which the claimant observed a person crushed to

death on the grill of the truck; the driver also suffered physical injury to his knee, hip and chest; physical injury need not be the "precipitating cause" of the psychic trauma so long as it "contributes" to its continuation); Hollar Oil Co. v. Bryant, 644 So.2d 951 (Ala.1994) (compensation awarded for mental disorder caused by industrial accident in which the claimant lost a testicle); Harrison v. Osco Drug, Inc., 116 Idaho 470, 776 P.2d 1189 (1989) (employee awarded compensation for "foot drop" caused by "conversion hysteria" following work related slip and fall). Similarly, compensation is generally awarded for disabling pain following a physical work injury even if the pain is linked to psychological factors. E.g., Bruce v. Clear Springs Trout Farm, 109 Idaho 311, 707 P.2d 422 (1985) (psychogenic pain syndrome following on-the-job slip and fall); Gutierrez v. Amity Leather Products Co., 107 N.M. 26, 751 P.2d 710 (N.M.App.1988) (upholding award for psychogenic pain disorder following work related shoulder injury).

4. Courts and agencies also generally award compensation when nervous shock brings about a disabling physical reaction (so-called mental-physical cases). E.g., Reeser v. Yellow Freight System, 938 S.W.2d 690 (Tenn.1997) (stroke precipitated by unusual stress of driving through an ice storm; compensation awarded); Snyder v. San Francisco Feed & Grain, 230 Mont. 16, 748 P.2d 924 (1987) (reversing the denial of compensation to employee who suffered a ruptured aneurysm following a period of unusual stress in her job); Ferguson v. HDE, Inc., 270 So.2d 867 (1972) (claimant engaged in angry altercation with superiors over his pay and suffered either cerebral thrombosis or cerebral hemorrhage which disabled him; compensation awarded). This type of fact pattern frequently arises in the context of heart conditions, such as those reflected in *Lancaster* and ensuing notes.

5. The most difficult cases involve workers who suffer psychological disabilities as a result of some work related nervous shock or protracted stress (so-called mental-mental cases). A substantial majority of states now compensate employees for this type of claim under some circumstances. There is considerable variation, however, in how far courts will go in awarding compensation for a mental disability produced by a mental stimulus. Perhaps the fact pattern in which compensation is most frequently awarded involves a psychological disability brought about by a specific and sudden precipitating event. E.g., Pathfinder Co. v. Industrial Comm., 62 Ill.2d 556, 343 N.E.2d 913 (1976) (employee suffered emotional disorder after rescuing fellow worker whose hand was amputated by punch press); Belcher v. T. Rowe Price, 329 Md. 709, 621 A.2d 872 (Md. 1993) (compensation awarded to an office worker who suffered post traumatic stress disorder after a three ton steel beam crashed through the office wall); Wolfe v. Sibley Lindsay & Curr Co., 36 N.Y.2d 505, 369 N.Y.S.2d 637, 330 N.E.2d 603 (1975) (employee psychologically disabled after discovering the body of her supervisor who had committed suicide). Some states limit compensation to this type of fact pattern. E.g., Henley v. Roadway Express, 699 S.W.2d 150 (Tenn. 1985) (refusing to compensate injuries caused by chronic stress or emotional strain and instead requiring fright, shock or excessive unexpected anxiety); Transportation Insurance Co. v. Maksyn, 580 S.W.2d 334 (Tex.1979) (newspaper production manager disabled by anxiety depression triggered by years of stress was not entitled to compensation because he could not pinpoint a definite time, place and cause of mental trauma).

The most controversial cases involve psychological disabilities brought on by gradual stress. The trend is to award compensation in such cases. Courts disagree, however, whether the disabling stress must be "unusual" in some manner. Some decisions limit coverage to disabilities brought about by gradual stress that is greater than that normally encountered by similarly situated employees. E.g., Dunlavey v. Economy Fire & Casualty Co., 526 N.W.2d 845 (Iowa 1995) (adopting an "unusual stress" standard; excellent discussion of cases); Bedini v. Frost, 165 Vt. 167, 678 A.2d 893 (Vt. 1996) (stress caused by increased job responsibilities is not "unusual"; benefits denied).

The most liberal position is to award compensation to those disabled by the effects of ordinary occupational stress. E.g., Ann Marie Robinson's Case, 416 Mass. 454, 623 N.E.2d 478 (Mass. 1993) (stress occasioned by reduction in workforce can support a disability claim under an "ordinary stress" standard); Hansen v. Von Duprin, Inc., 507 N.E.2d 573 (Ind.1987) (stress related disability caused by "horseplay" is compensable; proof of unusual stress is not required).

6. A significant minority of states deny benefits to workers who suffer a psychological disability caused by stress or nervous shock. E.g., Abernathy v. City of Albany, 269 Ga. 88, 495 S.E.2d 13 (Ga. 1998) (park maintenance supervisor disabled by psychic trauma caused by having to retrieve caskets and cadavers lifted from a cemetery by a flood; mental-mental claims are not covered); Frantz v. Campbell County Memorial Hospital, 932 P.2d 750 (Wyo.1997) (worker disabled by protracted stress related to job security is not entitled to compensation; mental injuries are not compensable unless they are the result of physical injuries); Stratemeyer v. Lincoln County, 259 Mont. 147, 855 P.2d 506 (Mont. 1993) (sheriff who suffered psychological disability after responding to a suicide and witnessing the aftermath is denied compensation; mental disability must be caused by a physical injury).

7. Increasingly, states are amending their workers' compensation statutes to explicitly address the compensability of psychological disabilities. Legislation of this type generally limits the circumstances where compensation can be awarded, often in response to a more liberal judicial decision. E.g., Alaska Stat. § 23.30.395.17 (adopting a "extraordinary and unusual" stress standard in mental-mental cases); Ark. Code Ann. § 11–9–113(a) (excluding coverage of mental injury unless diagnosed by a licensed psychiatrist or psychologist using criteria contained in the DMS); Mont. Code Ann. § 39–71–119 (limiting coverage of mental disabilities to those caused by physical injury); W. Va. Code § 23–4–1f (limiting coverage of mental disability; "the purpose of this section is to clarify that so-called mental-mental claims are not compensable").

Should such legislation apply retroactively? See Ann Marie Robinson's Case, 416 Mass. 454, 623 N.E.2d 478 (Mass. 1993) (amendment increasing plaintiff's burden of proof in mental-mental cases does not apply to claims arising prior to the effective date of the legislation); Conley v. Workers' Compensation Division, 199 W.Va. 196, 483 S.E.2d 542 (W.Va.1997) (amendments intended to exclude mental-mental claims from coverage are not retroactive).

Constitutional challenges to statutes that erect greater barriers to coverage for mental disabilities than for physical disabilities have been largely unsuccessful. Courts tend to find that the distinction between physical and mental injuries is rational given the greater uncertainty in verifying the genuineness and work-relatedness of mental injuries. E.g., Williams v. Department of Revenue, 895 P.2d 99 (Alaska 1995); Stratemeyer v. Lincoln County, 259 Mont. 147, 855 P.2d 506 (Mont. 1993); Frantz v. Campbell County Memorial Hospital, 932 P.2d 750 (Wyo.1997).

8. A worker's predisposition to emotional or psychological disorders will not lessen the compensability of a mental injury if the evidence otherwise satisfies the standard for compensability. As in instances of preexisting physical weaknesses, the employer is said to take the employee as "he finds him." E.g., Amoco Oil Co. v. Industrial Comm'n, 218 Ill.App.3d 737, 161 Ill.Dec. 397, 578 N.E.2d 1043 (Ill.App.1991) (affirming an award of benefits to a worker whose preexisting emotional instability was aggravated by compensable physical injury); Federal Mogul Corp. v. Campbell, 494 So.2d 443 (Ala. App. 1986) (awarding compensation to a borderline mentally retarded worker who suffered a mental breakdown following a serious fall). Cf. Bedini v. Frost, 165 Vt. 167, 678 A.2d 893 (Vt. 1996) (reaffirming the principle that the employer takes his employees as he finds them, but upholding the denial of benefits because the Commissioner found no "unusual" stress).

When the legal standard allows compensation for mental injures, the claim will be denied if the worker fails to convince the finder of fact that the mental disability was caused by the work environment. Sometimes a claimant's predisposition to mental illness may be relevant to the determination of causation. E.g., Kuklok v. North Dakota Workers' Compensation Bureau, 492 N.W.2d 572 (N.D.1992) (worker with history of mental illness sought benefits for psychological disability allegedly related to compensable physical injury; Bureau's denial of benefits was affirmed on the strength of expert testimony that the claimant's current psychological problems were not related to the compensable physical injuries; Bureau to resolve conflict between experts). Cf., Branscum v. RNR Construction Co., 60 Ark.App. 116, 959 S.W.2d 429 (Ark.App.1998) (affirming the denial of benefits for post traumatic stress disorder following a 35 foot fall on strength of Commission's findings that diagnosis did not meet standards set forth in the DSM IV).

Of course, compensation will not be awarded to a claimant whose alleged traumatic neurosis is found to be nothing more than malingering. E.g., Sinegal v. Louisiana Blasters, Inc., 546 So.2d 308 (La.App.1989) (claimant alleged to be disabled by pain in the lower back was observed "moving freely" at a local night club and described by five physicians as exhibiting some kind of "inappropriate illness response," "malingering," or "exaggeration"; compensation denied).

9. Regardless of the controlling legal standard, the two most basic problems with cases like *Sparks* are determining the genuineness of the disability and its causal relationship with the employment. In this and most of the cases examined in this chapter, courts and administrative agencies are invariably thrust into a classic battle of experts. How is the fact finder to resolve the conflict among expert witnesses? Consider the testimony in

Ladner v. Higgins, 71 So.2d 242, 244 (La.App.1954). In response to the question "Is [it] your conclusion that this man is a malingerer?", the expert responded, "I wouldn't be testifying if I didn't think so, unless I was on the other side, then it would be a post traumatic condition."

10. Claims for "heart" and psychological disabilities are considered difficult because of the uncertainty of their underlying work relatedness. Other disabling conditions that present similar difficulties are sometimes addressed by specific statutory provisions. Several states have enacted statutes containing criteria for establishing the compensability of a hernia alleged to have arisen in the course of employment. The Wyoming statute is fairly representative. It provides:

> (c) If an employee suffers a hernia, he is entitled to compensation if he clearly proves that:

> > (i) The hernia is of recent origin;

> > (ii) Its appearance was accompanied by pain;

> > (iii) It was immediately preceded by some accidental strain suffered in the course of employment; and

> > (iv) It did not exist prior to the date of the alleged injury. Wyo.Stat. § 27–14–603.

See also, Ga.Code Ann. § 34–9–266; Mo.Ann.Stat. § 287.195; N.C.Gen. Stat. § 97–2(18). Under such statutes "the character and quantum of evidence necessary in hernia claims is perhaps somewhat stricter than is required in other claims" for compensation. Hagan v. Mayflower Transit Co., 483 S.W.2d 119. For a compilation of special hernia statutes see, 3 A. Larson & L. Larson, Larson's Workers' Compensation § 39.70 (1997).

Another special problem area is occupational loss of hearing. There are divergent views whether hearing loss should be treated as an "accidental injury" or occupational disease. Compare, Peabody Galion Corp. v. Workman, 643 P.2d 312 (Okl.1982) (hearing loss is not an occupational disease, but is compensable as an accidental injury under the "repeated-impact" theory) with Clinchfield Coal Co. v. Barton, 6 Va.App. 576, 371 S.E.2d 39 (1988) (hearing loss compensable under the recently amended occupational disease statute). Many states have specific statutory provisions addressing occupational hearing loss. This legislation often establishes minimum levels of noise exposure necessary to support compensation. The threshold exposure is commonly expressed in terms of decibels and time. E.g., Ill.Ann.Stat. ch. 820.310/7(c); Iowa Code Ann. 85B.5; Wis.Stat.Ann. 102.555. These provisions are designed to ensure that the hearing loss is sufficiently work related to justify coverage under workers' compensation. See, 3 A. Larson & L. Larson, Larson's Workers' Compensation § 41.50 (1997). In this respect, these hearing loss provisions are similar to minimum exposure requirements that sometime govern claims for silicosis related disabilities. See note 7 following *Rutledge*.

Chapter 7

EFFECT OF CAUSES AND CONDITIONS INDEPENDENT OF THE WORK RELATION

INTRODUCTION TO THIS CHAPTER

This chapter considers the extent to which compensation is or should be awarded for injuries enhanced by the employee's preexisting condition and injuries brought about by some incident or force which comes into operation after the original compensable accident has been sustained. The employee who has suffered a work injury that is covered by the workers' compensation law may have the injury aggravated or may suffer a new injury as a result in part of antecedent or subsequent conditions or events for which the employer is not responsible but which bring about an increase or prolongation of disability or even cause death. For example, the original injury may become infected and the infection may lead to an amputation, or some third party may treat the injury negligently and make the condition worse, or a weakened bodily member may cause a fall, or the employee's mind may give way leading to self-inflicted injury or suicide. Should compensation be awarded for such additional disability or death?

The question is reminiscent of the problem of "proximate cause" or "legal cause" in tort law, and the workers' compensation tribunals quite often employ terminology such as "proximate cause," "direct or natural cause," "intervening cause," or "superseding cause" in disposing of the cases in this category. The reader should recognize that, as in the common law area of proximate cause, the issues must be resolved by resorting to fundamental policy considerations underlying compensation law in order to enlighten the decision as to how far and to what kinds of risks compensation liability ought to extend.

Courts and administrators sometimes fail to differentiate between cases presenting the question of whether or not the injury "arose out of the employment" and those presenting the issue considered in this chapter. An example may be found in the cases of Saenger v. Locke, 220 N.Y. 556, 116 N.E. 367 (1917) (employee fainted following dispute with her superior and was injured when a well-meaning co-worker mistakenly threw ammonia in her face, compensation denied) and Fishman v. S.W. Layton, Inc., 284 App.Div. 165, 130 N.Y.S.2d 656 (1954) (employee became drowsy from working in dark place, co-worker advised her to take mixture of Coca–Cola and benzedrine, resulting rupture of blood vessels held compensable). Neither of the foregoing cases actually involved aggravation of a previous work-connected injury. By contrast, a true post-accident risk situation is found in Mackin & Assoc. v. Harris, 342 Md. 1, 672 A.2d 1110 (1996) (former employee fell on ice while traveling to physical therapist's office for treatment of a prior compensable injury; held compensation denied). A clear understanding of the basic issue requires differentiation between the two types of cases.

In addition, no subsequent injury or exacerbation is properly compensable if the claimant fails to establish a cause-in-fact relationship between the initial work injury and the antecedent condition or the second injury. See, e.g., Dutton v. Industrial Commission of Arizona, 140 Ariz. 448, 682 P.2d 453 (1984); Schulle v. Texas Employers' Insurance Association, 787 S.W.2d 608 (Tex.App.1990). If the cause-in-fact relationship exists, the question becomes how and where to establish the outer limits of workers' compensation coverage.

SECTION 1. RESULTS OF PREEXISTING WEAKNESS OR DISEASE

BRAEWOOD CONVALESCENT HOSPITAL
v. WORKERS' COMPENSATION
APPEALS BOARD

Supreme Court of California, 1983.
34 Cal.3d 159, 193 Cal.Rptr. 157, 666 P.2d 14.

RICHARDSON, JUSTICE.

Braewood Convalescent Hospital and its workers' compensation carrier, Cypress Insurance Company (hereinafter collectively referred to as employer), seek annulment of a decision of the Workers' Compensation Appeals Board (WCAB) awarding Eugene Bolton (applicant) compensation for (1) the cost of a self-procured, out-of-state weight reduction program, (2) temporary disability during his participation in that program and (3) expenses for his future participation therein. We conclude that the WCAB acted within its authority in making the challenged awards and will affirm its decision.

STATEMENT OF THE CASE

On January 6, 1978, applicant, while employed as a cook for employer, slipped and sustained injuries to his back and right elbow. At that time applicant, who had been chronically overweight since childhood, weighed approximately 422 pounds. Employer provided temporary disability benefits while applicant undertook treatment for his back injury.

Dr. Wells, applicant's personal treating physician, and two of employer's physicians joined in recommending that applicant lose weight in order to facilitate his recovery from his injuries. Applicant unsuccessfully had undertaken numerous weight reduction programs throughout his life, and at the time of the accident, was participating in a weight loss program; he claimed, however, not improbably, that this latest program "had not been too successful." None of the physicians recommended a specific weight reduction program, nor had the employer offered to pay for any such program. Upon the recommendation of a close friend, who had participated successfully in a regimen of the Duke University Medical Center obesity clinic in Durham, North Carolina (hereinafter Clinic), applicant enrolled in the Clinic in February 1979. Applicant described the Clinic, which provides closely supervised, live-in treatment, as the "number one obesity clinic in the world." With the consent and support of Dr. Wells, applicant participated in the Clinic until November 1979. During that period he lost approximately 175 pounds. Dr. Wells, in a letter dated June 29, 1979, reiterated that it is "imperative [applicant] lose weight to obtain relief from his industrial injury ... [and that Dr. Wells] is in total agreement with the program and believes it is an integral part of his treatment."

By November 1979, applicant could no longer afford to continue with the Clinic. He returned to California and commenced work as a parttime security guard, continuing with a modified version of the Clinic program under local medical supervision. During the two month period from November 10, 1979, to January 8, 1980, he regained 16 pounds.

Applicant filed a claim for reimbursement of his Clinic's expenses, including requests for medical, lodging, special diet and transportation costs. The workers' compensation judge (WCJ) made awards, inter alia, for applicant's temporary disability prior to his enrollment in the Clinic, for the cost of the Clinic and for future participation therein, observing that reimbursement for the Clinic costs was justified by the employer's failure to provide applicant with any alternative weight reduction program.

Employer sought reconsideration, challenging the award for past and future self-procured medical treatment. On its own motion, the WCAB granted reconsideration of the WCJ's failure to award temporary disability benefits during the time of applicant's treatment at the Clinic. (See Lab.Code, § 5906; all further statutory references are to this code.) After reconsideration, the WCAB affirmed the WCJ's award for self-procured past and future medical treatment and extended the temporary disability award to include the period of treatment outside California.

On appeal employer contends that the WCAB erred in awarding (1) reimbursement for the expenses of any self-procured weight reduction program, (2) temporary disability for the time that applicant spent in the Clinic, and (3) compensation for future medical treatment in the form of a continuing weight reduction program.

* * *

We turn to the merits: * * *

1. Reimbursement for Self-procured Treatment

* * *

It is a long accepted workers' compensation rule that the employer takes the employee as he finds him. (Lamb v. Workmen's Comp. Appeals Bd. (1974) 11 Cal.3d 274, 282, 113 Cal.Rptr. 162, 520 P.2d 978; Ballard v. Workmen's Comp.App.Bd. (1971) 3 Cal.3d 832, 837, 92 Cal.Rptr. 1, 478 P.2d 937.) Thus, an employee who suffers from a pre-existing condition and is thereafter disabled by an industrial injury is entitled to compensation and reimbursement of medical expense, even though a healthy person would not have been injured by the event (Ibid.) This is so even though the specific treatment is for a nonindustrial condition which must be treated in order to cure or relieve the effects of the industrial injury. (Granado v. Workmen's Comp. App. Bd. (1968) 69 Cal.2d 399, 405B406, 71 Cal.Rptr. 678, 445 P.2d 294; Dorman v. Workers' Comp. Appeals Bd. (1978) 78 Cal.App.3d 1009, 1020, 144 Cal.Rptr. 573; McGlinn v. Workers' Comp. Appeals Bd. (1977) 68 Cal.App.3d 527, 535, 137 Cal.Rptr. 326; 2 Hanna, Cal.Law of Employee Injuries and Workmen's Compensation, § 16.03[1], [2].) While such expenses, in order to be compensable, must be reasonably necessary to cure or relieve the effects of an industrial injury, the statutes do not require any finding of disability, temporary or permanent, as a condition to such recovery. (Cedillo v. Workmen's Comp. Appeals Bd. (1971) 5 Cal.3d 450, 454, 96 Cal.Rptr. 471, 487 P.2d 1039.) Here, applicant was injured on the job and employer was fully aware of the injury. Applicant was directed by three physicians, including two of employer's physicians, to lose weight in order to obtain relief from, and to aid in the cure of, his industrial injury. He was advised to participate in a careful program of weight reduction. All three physicians acknowledged that applicant had been extremely overweight all his life, had unsuccessfully participated in many weight loss programs and was, at that time, involved in such a program with only limited success. At no time did any of the physicians recommend a specific weight reduction program, nor did the employer ever offer to reimburse applicant for the expenses incurred in such program. Thus, while employer initially had the right to direct applicant to a specific program, that right was lost as a result of employer's failure to act by identifying and offering such an alternative program. At that point applicant acquired the right to choose for himself which program he reasonably might undertake. The right to appropriate reimbursement was a part and parcel of the proper exercise of applicant's right to choose.

* * *

Consistent with section 4600 applicant presented evidence which demonstrated that his cost of attending the Clinic itemizing his expenses for medical treatment, food, shelter and transportation, was in the aggregate sum of $7,725.91 for 10 months' treatment. Employer, in response presented neither evidence that the cost of the Clinic was unreasonable nor testimony as to the reasonable cost for such treatment.

Thus, no comparative costs were introduced and the board was justified in relying entirely on the testimony and documentation presented by applicant. * * *

While section 4600 requires that the applicant's medical treatment choice be located within a reasonable geographic area, as defined by the Administrative Code, in the present case employer has produced no comparative evidence contradicting applicant's claim that the Clinic's location is geographically reasonable in light of his needs. Applicant testified that he had a life-long obesity problem which he had been unsuccessful in treating with traditional weight loss methods. He further testified that to his knowledge, the Clinic was a unique facility. The record establishes that, in fact, the Clinic achieved remarkable results in his case.

We have consistently held that the Workers' Compensation Act is to be construed liberally for the purpose of extending its benefits for the protection of persons injured in the course of their employment (McCoy, supra, 64 Cal.2d at p. 86, 48 Cal.Rptr. 858, 410 P.2d 362). Because applicant's evidence has not been impeached, we conclude that the WCAB's award for reimbursement of Clinic expenses is based upon substantial evidence and, therefore, was proper.

2. Temporary Disability During Participation in the Program

Employer urges that applicant is not entitled to an award of temporary disability for the period during which he participated in the program because such participation was not reasonably necessary to facilitate applicant's recovery. An employer is under a statutorily imposed duty to pay temporary disability compensation for the period during which an injured employee who, while unable to work, is undergoing medical diagnostic procedure and treatment for an industrial injury. (§ 4600; Granado, supra, 69 Cal.2d at p. 403, 71 Cal.Rptr. 678, 445 P.2d 294.) The primary purpose of a temporary disability award being to compensate for wage loss, (ibid.; Allied Compensation Ins. Co. v. Industrial Acc. Com. (1963) 211 Cal.App.2d 821, 831, 27 Cal.Rptr. 918) that purpose was served by the award here. Employer presented no evidence demonstrating that applicant should not be considered to be temporarily disabled during his participation in the Clinic. On the other hand, applicant did present evidence demonstrating that he was unable to work while being treated at the Clinic. He also submitted a letter from Dr. Wells, dated December 13, 1979, commenting on his "remarkable progress," but noting that applicant still was experiencing limited motion of the lumbosacral spine, concluding that he should be considered temporarily disabled until the completion of the weight reduction program. While this letter reflects the conclusion of only one physician, it is well established that the relevant and considered opinion of one physician may constitute substantial evidence in support of a factual determination of the WCAB. [citing cases] We uphold WCAB's award of temporary disability.

3. Future Medical Treatment

We are also unable to accept employer's final contention that applicant is not entitled to future medical treatment because his industrial injury has become permanent and also because his weight problem is incurable. Employer essentially argues that the purpose of section 4600 is to provide benefits until the employee's ailment is cured, and that if such ailment is not curable, then the disability should be deemed permanent and medical treatment benefits should cease.

Employer, however, overlooks the wording of section 4600, which authorizes treatment required to "cure or relieve from the effects of the injury...." (Italics added; see Fidelity etc. Co. v. Dept. of Indus. Relations (1929) 207 Cal. 144, 150, 277 P. 492.) Applicant presented the recommendations from both Dr. Wells and Dr. Compton that he continue losing weight in order to relieve him from the effects of the industrial injury. Such evidence is sufficient to support the board's award of future medical treatment. (LeVesque, supra, 1 Cal.3d at p. 639, 83 Cal.Rptr. 208, 463 P.2d 432.) The present treatment aimed at affording applicant relief from the effects of an industrial injury represents a compensable expense under section 4600.

On the evidentiary record before us, we affirm the WCAB's award in its entirety.

BIRD, C.J., MOSK, BROUSSARD, REYNOSO, GRODIN and RICKLES, JJ., concur.

Notes

1. The central problem in Braewood is related to the claimant's preexisting obesity. The classification of obesity as a serious disease is well supported by the professional literature. The disease meets all of the accepted criteria for definition of a chronic illness (1. gradual, not acute, onset; 2. long duration with frequent recurrence; 3. definite morbid process which affects the entire body; and 4. identifiable pathology and prognosis). Sachiko St. Jeor, New Trends in Weight Management, 97 Journal of the American Dietetic Assoc. 1096 (1997). It has been estimated that obesity is responsible, on an annual basis, for 300,000 premature deaths. Charles Quesenberry et al., Obesity, Health Services Use and Health Care Costs Among Members of a Health Maintenance Organization, 158 Archives of Internal Medicine 466 (1998). Tens of billions of dollars in health care costs are expended annually treating obesity and related problems. Joseph Scherger, Obesity as a Chronic Disease, 167 The Western Journal of Medicine 178 (1997).

Obesity is a complex phenomenon which has its roots in biological, behavioral, and environmental components. So persistent is the problem that even treatment modalities which are targeted directly at the sources of obesity have extremely high recidivism rates. The majority of people who participate in lifestyle modification programs regain all of the weight lost within three to five years. Most pharmacotherapy patients return to their original weight within one year of completing their course of medication. Gary Egger, et.al. An Ecological Approach to the Obesity Pandemic, 315 British Medical Journal 477 (1997).

The following notes outline the typical judicial analysis of the relationship between pre-existing conditions and work related injuries. Consider the decision in *Braewood* against this backdrop. Is there something inherent in the condition of obesity which would call for courts to approach it differently than they do other types of pre-existing diseases?

2.   The general principle of compensation law that the employer "takes the employee as he finds the employee," i.e. with the employee's weaknesses, predispositions and personal susceptibilities is well established. See, e.g., Colonial Ins. Co. v. Industrial Accident Comm., 29 Cal.2d 79, 172 P.2d 884, 887 (1946); and Patterson v. Clarke County Motors, Inc., 551 So.2d 412 (Ala.Civ.App.1989). This is acknowledged not only in those cases in which the preexisting condition makes the employee peculiarly susceptible to injury, such as the case of the idiopathic fall exemplified in the *George* case in Chapter 5, but also in instances where the employee, having sustained a compensable injury that was not due to any special personal condition or weakness, suffers disabling consequences that are greater or more extensive than would have been suffered normally by a person who did not labor under the preexisting weakness or peculiarity. Workers in this category are at abnormally high risk of disability from the accident. This issue is often addressed in the lexicon of tort law as involving the plaintiff with the "eggshell skull." See Prosser & Keeton, The Law of Torts' 43 (5th Ed.1984)."

3.   Although an employee is generally taken by the employer "as is", such employee must always prove the existence of a casual relationship between the ultimate disability and the workplace. Among the states, this requirement is cast in different forms. Statutes such as the one in Oregon mandate that the workplace injury be the predominate cause of the disability. O.R.S.§ 656.005(7)(a)(B)(1997). The Massachusetts statute allows compensation so long as the workplace injury is a major but not necessarily predominate cause of the combined disability. Ma. St. 152 § 1 (7A)(1997). Some states address the problem by restricting the employee's recovery to that portion of the disability attributed solely to the workplace. See e.g. Ballard v. Workmen's Compensation Appeals Board, 3 Cal.3d 832, 92 Cal. Rptr. 1, 478 P.2d 937 (1971); Hardin's Bakeries v. Harrell, 566 So.2d 1261 (Miss.1990); Escambia County Council on Aging v. Goldsmith, 500 So.2d 626 (Fla.App. 1 Dist.1986); and see, West's Ann. Cal. Labor Code § 4750 (1997); and Wests F.S.A. § 440.02(1) (1997); and see Georgia's statute allowing compensation only for so long as the employment aggravation of the pre-existing condition causes the disability, O.C.G.A. 34–9–1 (4).

4.   A number of issues are implicated when the claimant suffers from a pre-existing condition. See, e.g., Bailey v. Reynolds Metals, 153 Or.App. 498, 959 P.2d 84 (Or.App.) (requirement that claimant prove that job-related factors were the major contributing elements of her injury held not to violate the Americans with Disabilities Act); Caldwell v. Aarlin / Holcombe Armature Co., 267 Ga. 613, 481 S.E.2d 196 (1997) (employee provided, false information in his employment application regarding his pre-existing back condition. Employer defended claim for disability based on the false representation. Even if application questions violated Americans with Disabilities Act provisions prohibiting pre-offer inquiries, employer could still rely on false representation defense; held compensation denied); Brown v. SAIF, 154 Or.App. 244, 961 P.2d 280 (Or.App.) (the natural effects of the aging process

can be considered a pre-existing weakness or condition thus placing the burden of satisfying the predominate cause hurdle upon the claimant). Of course, as was seen in chapter 5, risks which are purely personal to the employee and not enhanced by the employment generally are not compensable. This is typically the result in idiopathic fall cases. See, e.g., Svehla v. Beverly Enterprises, 5 Neb.App. 765, 567 N.W.2d 582 (1997) (employee had pre-existing gait imbalance. Employee fell on employer's sidewalk. Neither the positional risk nor idiopathic fall doctrines allowed death benefits where claimant failed to prove employment enhancement or contribution); Kovatch v. A.M. General, 679 N.E.2d 940, (Ind.Ct.App.1997) (employee found dead as result of head trauma caused by fall. Compensation denied due to failure of claimant to prove employment increased the risk of injury or enhanced the severity of the injury).

5. Should compensation be awarded for the abnormal consequences (even death) of an admittedly compensable injury, assuming, of course, that factual cause is established? The answer is frequently in the affirmative, at least in the absence of statutory provisions to the contrary. Where a latent or weakened but not disabling condition resulting from disease or prior injury is activated or accelerated by a compensable injury and the result is death or prolonged or disproportional disability, compensation is awarded. See, e.g., Chicago, Wilmington & Franklin Coal Co. v. Industrial Comm., 400 Ill. 60, 78 N.E.2d 104 (1948) (miner suffered injury to tip of index finger, infection followed ultimately causing amputation of finger, which weakened him so that tuberculosis germs latent in his body became active and he died of tuberculosis; held death compensable); Storie v. Taylor Supply Co., 190 Tenn. 149, 228 S.W.2d 94 (1950) (injuries in automobile accident activated a pre-existing "mild form of syphilis" which ultimately caused decedent's death, held death compensable); Pettit v. Austin Logging Co., 9 Or.App. 347, 497 P.2d 207 (1972) (back strain masked existence of multiple sclerosis thereby delaying treatment and aggravating the disease, results held compensable); Champion Home Builders v. Industrial Commission, 703 P.2d 306 (Utah 1985) (pre-existing ulcer perforated while claimant was lifting heavy beam, held compensable); Jameson v. SAIF, 63 Or.App. 553, 665 P.2d 379 (1983) (a work injury to the shoulder caused a pre-existing lipoma to become larger leading to disabling pain in back, held compensable); Jackson v. True Temper Corp., 151 Vt. 592, 563 A.2d 621 (1989) (pre-existing encephalopathy due to malnourishment and alcohol abuse was aggravated by a rip saw injury at work; resulting disability due to periodic seizures, held compensable); Conway v. Blackfeet Indian Developers, Inc., 205 Mont. 459, 669 P.2d 225 (1983) (pre-existing multiple sclerosis aggravated by work related fall became symptomatic, held compensable). But, cf. Giles v. Bozeman Public Schools, 257 Mont. 289, 849 P.2d 180 (1993) (unlike Conway, supra, medical testimony indicated no connection between trauma and onset of multiple sclerosis symptoms, held not compensable).

6. In cases in which the employee was suffering from a fatal disease that would have caused death eventually and where it appears that the work-connected injury weakened the employee's resistance or otherwise hastened the time of death, compensation is often awarded. See, e.g., Murphy's Case, 328 Mass. 301, 103 N.E.2d 267 (1952) (worker with carcinoma of the bladder that "would be fatal in any event, that was certain death"

suffered coronary thrombosis at work that shortened the employee's life, held compensable); McCann Steel Co. v. Carney, 192 Tenn. 94, 237 S.W.2d 942 (1951) (employee suffering from leukemia injured his hand and contracted "blood poisoning", medical testimony was that his inevitable death from leukemia was hastened, held death compensable); Oswald v. Connor, 16 Ohio St.3d 38, 476 N.E.2d 658 (1985) (pre-existing heart disease which would eventually cause death was hastened by avian tuberculosis, an occupational disease, which caused unusual stress and fatal heart attack; held death compensable); Bradford v. Workers' Compensation Commissioner, 185 W.Va. 434, 408 S.E.2d 13 (1991) (worker died of metastatic cancer. His severe occupational pneumoconiosis had prevented surgical treatment for the cancer. The occupational pneumoconiosis was found to have been a major contributing factor of his death, held widow entitled to death benefits); But see Schulle v. Texas Employers' Insurance Association, 787 S.W.2d 608 (Ct. App. Tx. 1990) (employee was in pain and confined to bed following a compensable back injury. Employee was subsequently diagnosed with lung cancer. His doctor stated that the back pain led to employee's loss of will to live and to rejection of aggressive cancer treatment. Doctor concluded while cancer would have been terminal in any event, the refusal of aggressive treatment hastened the death. Court found connections between back injury and death too weak to support award, held death benefits denied).

7. The general rule in this area applies as well to cases in which a claimant's mental, emotional or other personality traits at time of injury cause consequences from a work injury that would not ordinarily be expected. In Bullington v. Aetna Cas. & Sur. Co., 122 Ga.App. 842, 178 S.E.2d 901 (1970) decedent had a "moderate drinking problem" prior to injury; thereafter pain and enforced idleness aggravated his drinking until it finally caused death which was held compensable. Reversed for procedural irregularities, 227 Ga. 485, 181 S.E.2d 495 (1971), vacated 123 Ga.App. 781, 182 S.E.2d 487 (1971). In Ballard v. Workmen's Compensation Appeals Board, 3 Cal.3d 832, 92 Cal.Rptr. 1, 478 P.2d 937 (1971), the claimant with a preexisting psychological susceptibility to drug dependency became addicted to various drugs following a work related back injury. The aggravation of the previously asymptomatic condition was held to be compensable. In Globe Machine v. Yock, 79 Or.App. 9, 717 P.2d 1235 (1986), the claimant who suffered from preexisting alcoholism had apparently stopped drinking for two years prior to his disability, but, as a result of job related stress, began drinking again. The worsening of his preexisting condition caused total disability which was held to be compensable. In Matter of Compensation of Gygi, 55 Or.App. 570, 639 P.2d 655 (1982), claimant, an attorney, who suffered from preexisting mental health problems became depressed and alcoholic as a result of stress in his law practice. The court held that the aggravation of the preexisting condition was compensable. See also Jackson v. True Temper Corp. supra, note 5. Some jurisdictions address by statute the compensability of alcoholism and drug addiction following a work related injury. See, e.g., OCGA 34-9-1(4).

8. Issues in *Braewood* related to the reasonableness and necessity of medical benefits are treated in Chapter 8, section 1, infra. The "second injury" problem is considered in Chapter 8, section 3, infra, with observations that are instructive in resolving some of the apportionment issues

raised in this chapter. Various options include apportioning the pre-existing condition (1) fully to the employer, (2) fully to the employee or (3) to a "second injury" fund. See 2 Larson's Worker's Compensation Law §§ 59.20, 59.21 and 59.22(a).

SECTION 2.   FALLS AND SIMILAR MISHAPS

WILLIAMS CONSTR. CO., INC. v. GARRISON

Court of Special Appeals of Maryland, 1979.
42 Md.App. 340, 400 A.2d 22.

LISS, JUDGE.

Williams Construction Company, Inc., employer and American Automobile Insurance Company, insurer (hereinafter jointly designated as appellants), have filed this appeal from an order of the Circuit Court for Baltimore County which granted a summary judgment in favor of the claimant, Jesse R. Garrison, Jr. (hereinafter designated as appellee).

Appellants contend that the trial court erred in affirming an order of the Workmen's Compensation Commission dated August 9, 1977 by which the Commission found that the appellee was entitled to additional temporary total disability and was permanently totally disabled as a result of an accidental injury sustained by the appellee on July 25, 1974, which arose out of, and in the course of, his employment.

Appellants raise the following issues in support of their contention that the trial judge should not have granted appellee's motion for summary judgment:

(1) That the injuries and disability suffered by the appellee were caused by the claimant's own reckless and unreasonable conduct; and (2) that the initial compensable injury of July 25, 1974 was not the proximate cause of the injuries sustained by the appellee on December 28, 1974, and that the appellee's permanent total disability occurred by reason of appellee's own intervening unreasonable conduct.

The facts in the case are virtually undisputed. On August 13, 1974, appellee filed a claim for compensation with the Workmen's Compensation Commission in which he stated that on July 25, 1974, while in the employ of Williams Construction Company as a bulldozer operator, he fell from the tracks of a pusher-tractor and sustained injuries to his back. The appellants did not contest the claim and the Commission found the claim to be compensable. The insurer paid temporary total benefits for the period the appellee did not attend work and for the medical expenses incurred. No claim for permanent partial benefits was filed by the appellee. Appellee returned to his same employment with Williams Construction Company on August 13, 1974 and worked for an additional four months as a bulldozer operator until December 6, 1974, when he was laid off. Appellee then began to work for himself as a tree trimmer. On December 28, 1974, the appellee, while carrying a chain saw, ascended a forty-foot ladder and was engaged in trimming a tree when he fell from the ladder, struck the ground and sustained extremely serious injuries. In the latter part of 1976, after extensive medical treatment, the appellee requested that the claim involving his accident of July 25, 1974 be reopened on the theory that the injuries sustained by the claimant in his fall from the ladder on December 28, 1974, were caused by the disability which resulted from his accident of July 25, 1974. Appellants raised issues before the Commission as to whether the appellee sustained an accidental personal injury arising out of, and in the course of, employment with Williams Construction Co. on December 28, 1974. They also raised the issue of whether the disability of the employee was the result of an accidental personal injury arising out of, and in the course of, employment on July 25, 1974. The Commission held that the appellee was entitled to additional temporary total benefits and was permanently totally disabled as a result of the accident of December 28, 1974, and that that accident was attributable to the disabilities he sustained as a result of his injury on July 25, 1974. An award of benefits was made reflecting the Commission's decision, and the appellants appealed from the award to the Circuit Court for Baltimore County. Depositions were taken and filed with appropriate affidavits by the parties, and after a hearing, the trial judge granted appellee's motion for summary judgment affirming the decision of the Workmen's Compensation Commission. It is from this action that this appeal was taken.

The depositions and affidavits submitted in support of the several motions for summary judgment filed respectively by the appellants and appellees established that shortly after the original fall by the appellee in the accident of July 25, 1974, the claimant began to experience dizzy spells intermittently which required him to take medication prescribed by the treating physician, but which were not so severe as to prevent claimant from working. Although the claimant complained of dizziness to the attending physician on three separate visits, the doctor allowed him to return to work and placed no restrictions on the appellee. The claimant testified that when he returned to work for Williams Construction he noticed that he would from time to time suffer dizzy spells in which everything would "go round and round" and during which he would hang on to something until the dizzy spell subsided.

Appellants admit they have no evidence to contradict the appellee's contention that the dizzy spells which ultimately resulted in his fall from the ladder were related to the dizzy spells he experienced as a result of the original fall in July. They urge, however, that the appellee was aware of his condition; that he acted in a reckless and unreasonable manner in climbing the ladder knowing that he was having dizzy spells; and that if, in fact, the dizzy spells did cause his fall, then his reckless and unreasonable conduct in climbing the ladder amounted to a break in the direct causal relationship between the accident of July 1974 and the injuries sustained in the fall in December of 1974.

Appellants rely for legal sustenance on Watts v. Young Co., 245 Md. 277, 225 A.2d 865 (1967), a case which is factually distinguishable from the case *sub judice.* In *Watts,* the Court of Appeals had before it the case of a claimant who had sustained injuries and who refused to undergo corrective surgery. The Court, in holding that the refusal to undergo surgery justified the withholding of an award for permanent partial disability, gave as one of its reasons the conclusion that the claimant's intentional and unreasonable conduct broke the chain of causation between his employment and his injury. It held that to the extent the claimant's disability was found to relate to his arbitrary refusal to assent to treatment, such disability did not arise out of his employment. In support of this holding, the Court cited 2 Larson, Workmen's Compensation Law sec. 13.22 (1952).

In a discussion of the range of compensable consequences, Larson suggests the rule should be that when the primary injury is shown to have arisen out of, and in the course of, employment every natural consequence that flows from the injury likewise arises out of the employment, unless the injury is the result of an independent intervening cause attributable to claimant's own intentional conduct. The employee's own contributory negligence with regard to the primary injury is ordinarily not an intervening cause preventing initial compensability. But when the question is whether compensability should be extended to a subsequent injury or aggravation related in some way to the primary injury, Larson suggests the basic rule should be that a subsequent injury, whether an aggravation of the original injury or a new and distinct injury, is compensable if it is the direct and natural result of a compensable primary injury. He then suggests that when a subsequent injury arises out of what he designates a "quasi-course" activity, such as a trip to the doctor's office, the chain of causation should not be deemed broken by mere negligence in the performance of that activity, but only by intentional conduct which may be regarded as expressly or impliedly prohibited by the employer. Larson further develops his legal theory by stating that when the injury following the initial compensable injury does not arise out of a "quasi-course" activity, as when the claimant with an injured hand engages in a boxing match, the chain of causation may be deemed broken by either intentional or negligent claimant misconduct. 2 Larson, supra, sec. 13.11.

Although our courts have not expressly adopted the proposition that Larson posits, the law in Maryland, by statute and case law has considered the effect of the conduct of a claimant on his right to compensation benefits.

The Court of Appeals, in Dayton v. Davis, 218 Md. 614, 618, 147 A.2d 699, 701 (1959), speaking through Chief Judge Brune, said: "There are very few unavoidable accidents; negligence produces most of them and an employee's non-wilful negligence-his lapse from care-does not keep an injury-producing occurrence from being an accident nor bar his right to compensation."

Pursuant to the Workmen's Compensation Law, the right to compensation exists without reference to the care of the employee, and compensation is not denied by reason of contributory negligence on his part.

The Legislature of Maryland has explicitly stated the circumstances under which an employee otherwise eligible for compensation benefits will be denied those benefits in Article 10, Section 45 of the Annotated Code of Maryland (1957, 1979 Repl.Vol.):

> Notwithstanding anything hereinbefore or hereinafter contained, no employee or dependent of any employee shall be entitled to receive any compensation or benefits under this article on account of any injury to or death of an employee caused by self-inflicted injury, the willful misconduct, or where the injury or death resulted solely from the intoxication of the injured employee or solely from the effect upon him of any narcotic, depressant, stimulant, hallucinogenic or hypnotic drug or from the effect upon him of any other drug which renders him incapable of satisfactorily performing his job, except when such drug has been administered or taken in accordance with a physician's prescription.

The only portion of this section which might even remotely be applicable in this case is the segment involving the willful misconduct of an employee. 99 C.J.S. Workmen's Compensation § 258 (1958) defines willful misconduct as the intentional doing of something either with the knowledge that it is likely to result in serious injury or with a wanton and reckless disregard of its probable consequences.

* * *

In Karns v. Liquid Carbonic Corporation, 275 Md. 1, 338 A.2d 251 (1975), the Court of Appeals said willful misconduct may be found where the employee intended to place himself in a position whereby he might expect to meet with injury or death, and in carrying out his intention meets his death as a result of the injuries sustained. The actions of the employee must be such as to show that he intended thereby to place himself in such a hazardous position that injury or death might result as the reasonable consequence of his act.

We do not reach the conclusion that the appellee's conduct in this case amounted to such willful misconduct as to create an intervening superseding cause which was sufficient to break the chain of causation between the original injury and the subsequent injury so as to preclude the claimant from being entitled to compensation benefits flowing from the original accident.

We note from the testimony of the various witnesses included in the record extract that there is no evidence that the employer imposed any restrictions on the appellee's performance of his duties for the employer subsequent to the claimant being able to return to work. The appellee performed essentially the same climbing duties in the operation of the tractor bulldozer during the four months he remained employed by the appellant after the initial injury. The attending physician had knowledge of the appellee's complaint of giddy spells and dizziness. He was also aware of the circumstances of the fall from the bulldozer and that the claimant had struck his head in the fall. In addition, the doctor had made a notation in his records that several days after the accident the appellee had attempted to return to work but was too dizzy to continue to perform his duties. Although the complaints of giddiness continued on three separate visits to the doctor, the doctor, nevertheless, felt the appellee was ready to return to work by August 13, 1974. The doctor did not place any restrictions on the claimant's activities. And although the doctor felt that the dizzy spells were caused by a cerebral contusion, he did not feel it was warranted to send the appellee to anyone for additional tests. The attending physician indicated that he felt the appellee was capable of performing his functions when he discharged him. Not only were there no work restrictions placed on the appellee by the doctor, but the doctor's advice was also devoid of any restrictions whatsoever regarding any other activities in which the claimant might engage. In the light of this factual situation, the conduct of the employer and paucity of instructions by the physician, we think it totally unreasonable to hold that the actions of the appellee were of such a reckless and unreasonable nature as to amount to conduct which would break the chain of causation between the initial injury and the subsequent injury.

Thus it is clear that in the case *sub judice*, as there were no restrictions placed on the employee's activities either by the prior employer or the attending physician, the appellee's conduct in ascending the ladder in view of his prior episodes of dizziness was, at the most, poor judgment rather than willful misconduct.

The trial judge in his consideration of the depositions and exhibits filed in support of the motion for summary judgment by the appellee concluded that there was no disputed issue of fact as to whether the accident of December 28, 1974 was the direct result of the injuries sustained by the appellee, and that as a matter of law and of fact that the appellee's conduct in climbing the ladder, in view of his prior episodes of dizziness, was not sufficient to be an intervening cause so as to destroy the chain of causation between the original injury and the subsequent fall which resulted in the appellee's paralysis.

As a reviewing body, we are bound by our own Maryland Rule 1086 which states that this Court will review the case upon both the law and the evidence, but the judgment will not be set aside unless clearly erroneous. We find that the conclusions of fact by the trial judge are not erroneous and are correct as to the law.

Judgment affirmed; costs to be paid by appellants.

SULLIVAN v. B & A CONSTR., INC.
Court of Appeals of New York, 1954.
307 N.Y. 161, 120 N.E.2d 694.

FULD, JUDGE

Claimant, a painter by trade, sustained, in the course of two different employments, compensable injuries to his right knee. In March of

1948, while in the employ of appellant B & A Construction, Inc., he slipped on a paint brush and caught his right leg on a step; again, in June, 1949, while employed by appellant A.L. Turner, a ladder which he was climbing broke and he struck and twisted the same leg. As a result of these injuries, his right knee, previously sound, acquired a pronounced tendency to "lock," so that claimant, until he could "shake" it back into place, found himself-as he put it-"paralyzed * * * from my knee to my hip," and deprived of all use and control of his right leg. From the report of a doctor, made after the second accident, it appears that "even mild trauma such as that caused by stepping over a small stone on the road or a high place in the sidewalk * * * [created] the sensation of the 'knee giving away.' "

Claimant suffered this locking, and the accompanying pain and paralysis, frequently, not only while walking but, indeed, whenever he put pressure on his knee. Driving an automobile became particularly hazardous; claimant himself testified that "once or twice a week," in applying pressure to the brake, his knee slipped into such a position that "he would have to stop and unlock it." Nevertheless, he continued to operate his car.

On June 30, 1950, a year after the second injury, claimant was hurt in an automobile accident, and it is solely from that accident that the present award stems. He was driving in the state of Maryland, at a speed of between forty and forty-five miles an hour, when "something [went] haywire with" the steering wheel; the tie rod, by which the front wheels are controlled, had, it subsequently appeared, broken. Although in the past claimant had always succeeded in stopping his car, on this occasion, when he tried to press down on the brake, nothing happened. His knee "locked," it was "paralyzed" and useless, and the car, out of control, careened off the highway, into the woods, and struck a tree. Claimant lay unconscious for some time and, when taken to a local hospital, was found to have suffered a comminuted fracture of the right femur.

Having previously received an award for his earlier injuries, claimant now seeks compensation for the injuries sustained in the automobile accident. This latest mishap did not arise in the course of his employment, for, concededly, claimant was driving on his own personal business. An award is, therefore, warranted only if the automobile accident and the consequent injuries resulted directly and naturally from claimant's prior injuries and the disability thereby produced. * * * If such injuries only remotely caused or contributed to the accident on the road, then claimant is not entitled to compensation; or, to express it somewhat differently, if claimant is to recover, the disability occasioned by the earlier accidents must have been a proximate not simply a "but for," cause of his latest mishap.

Here, quite obviously, it was claimant's own temerity, not the physical handicap resulting from the industrial accidents, that was primarily responsible for the later, 1950, accident. Despite his serious infirmity and despite the obvious risk involved—to innocent passers-by as well as to himself—he persisted in operating a car, indeed, in driving at what was, for him, the immoderate speed of over forty miles an hour. Even the simple precaution of adding an auxiliary hand or left-foot brake, such as those used by others who are disabled, was omitted. Eventually, the inevitable accident occurred. While the earlier injuries may have been a "but for" cause of the accident, they certainly did not constitute the requisite legal or proximate cause. When claimant ignored his locking knee and, without justification, continued to drive, responsibility for the accident and its consequences could no longer be ascribed to his employment-created disability.

Had claimant been ignorant of the extent of his disability, had his knee not previously locked while driving, the case might conceivably have been different. In the light of the record before us, however, it is indisputable that claimant's own act of driving, supervening between the industrial accidents and the car crash, broke the essential chain of causation.

The order of the Appellate Division should be reversed, the award of the Workmen's Compensation Board annulled and the claim dismissed, with costs in this court and in the Appellate Division against respondent Workmen's Compensation Board.

Lewis, C.J., and Conway, Desmond, Dye, Froessel and Van Voorhis, JJ., concur.

Notes

1. As the foregoing cases suggest, subsequent injuries caused by falls or other mishaps due to the handicapped physical condition resulting from the original work accident are compensable consequences of the original injury, at least where the employee's unreasonable conduct is not the primary cause. Many cases have awarded compensation. See, e.g., Randolph v. E.I. Du Pont De Nemours & Co., 130 N.J.L. 353, 33 A.2d 301 (1943) (original injury to eyes required claimant to wear dark glasses as a result of which he lost his footing and fell down stairs, held injury from fall compensable); Mondillo v. Ward Baking Co., 73 R.I. 473, 57 A.2d 447 (1948) (claimant suffered injury to right leg and foot causing weakness, was inducted into army where marching caused development of club foot, held compensable); Great Atlantic & Pacific Tea Co. v. Hill, 201 Md. 630, 95 A.2d 84 (1953) (fracture of lower leg caused weakness which caused another fall three years later, held second fall compensable); Carabetta v. Industrial Comm., 12 Ariz.App. 239, 469 P.2d 473 (1970) (injury to claimant's knee caused it to give way or "buckle" at irregular intervals; injury suffered from fall at a funeral, held compensable); Barre v. Roofing and Flooring, Inc., 83 A.D.2d 681, 442 N.Y.S.2d 246 (1981) (first injury caused residual dizziness; dizziness caused claimant to fall causing second injury, held second injury compensable); Erwin v. Harris, 474 So.2d 1125 (Ala.Civ.App.1985) (work related knee injury; while on vacation, claimant fell due to weakened knee, held compensable); Pellerin v. New York State Dept. of Corrections, 215 A.D.2d 943, 627 N.Y.S.2d 147 (1995) (work related injury in 1980 caused claimant's leg to buckle periodically; in 1990, claimant's leg buckled and he fell from a

hunter's tree stand; court concluded employee's conduct was not too rash or irresponsible and thus did not break the chain of causation, held compensable).

2.   As the *Sullivan* case demonstrates however, if a claimant's subsequent injury results from intentional involvement in behavior of a kind that is inappropriate for a person with such an injury, compensation may be denied. See, e.g., Yarbrough v. Polar Ice & Fuel Co., 118 Ind.App. 321, 79 N.E.2d 422 (1948) (claimant had a weak knee caused by compensable work injury; while negligently attempting to carry a load of trash down stairs at home, his knee gave way and he fell fracturing his jaw; held fractured jaw not compensable); Johnnie's Produce Co. v. Benedict & Jordan, 120 So.2d 12 (Fla.1960) (claimant who suffered broken right ankle in a compensable accident later negligently jumped from a truck; due to the weakened condition of the ankle employee fell sustaining a back injury; held back injury not compensable); Brown v. State Industrial Insurance System, 106 Nev. 878, 803 P.2d 223 (1990) (employment related carpal tunnel syndrome to both wrists was treated surgically; two months after the last surgery while claimant's hands were still weak, claimant fell and broke both wrists while riding a horse through a barrel racing course; the fall occurred due to insufficient strength in hands to hold on to saddle horn; held claimant's negligent conduct was a superceding cause of the second injury and compensation denied).

3.   Contrast State Comp. Ins. Fund v. Industrial Acc. Comm., 176 Cal.App.2d 10, 1 Cal.Rptr. 73 (1959), in which an employee suffering "double vision", due to a work related accident, decided to cut some "junk lumber" at his home for use in his fireplace. While the off duty worker did this with an electric power handsaw, the saw "jumped and kicked" amputating one of his fingers. An award of compensation for the loss of the finger was affirmed in an opinion that warns "against atavistic attempts to retain common law concepts for tort and negligence in the compensation field." The cases are reviewed and disagreement expressed with the approach in the *Sullivan* case, supra. According to the court, "the employee's negligence actually is irrelevant in the second injury as it admittedly is in the first." The California Supreme Court declined to review the decision. On the topic of the relationship of the employee's negligence in the second injury see also the *Hallisey* case infra, note 5. The *Hallisey* court agrees that the negligence of the employee does not break the causal chain.

Larson asserted that the California decision went too far and as noted in the *Williams* case, supra, suggested a distinction along the following lines: if the employee is engaged in what he called a "quasi-course (of employment) activity," e.g. going to the doctor or taking medication for the work related injury, the employee's negligence should have no significance; but if the employee is not engaged in a quasi-course activity, e.g. taking part in an after work boxing match, then the negligence should bar compensation. 1 Larson's Workers' Compensation Law §§ 13.11(c) and 13.11(d) (1997).

4.   In response to judicial precedents such as those summarized in notes 1 and 3, supra, the state of Florida enacted legislation in 1991 seeking to restrict recovery in the "subsequent injury" cases. F.S.A. § 440.092(5) provides: "Injuries caused by a subsequent intervening accident arising from

an outside agency which are the direct and natural consequence of the original injury are not compensable unless suffered while traveling to or from a health care provider for the purpose of receiving remedial treatment for the compensable injury." Nevertheless, one Florida appellate court opinion has interpreted the statute narrowly. See U–Haul of South Florida v. March, 645 So.2d 581 (Fla.App.1994) (claimant wearing a short leg cast and using crutches following a compensable fracture of his right foot, fell injuring his shoulder while descending a flight of stairs at his home; employee testified he lost his balance and his left food slipped out from under him due to the cast and crutches and his resulting awkward effort to descend the stairs; court concluded the claimant's own left foot could not be considered an "outside agency"; held compensable).

5. In a related but factually distinguishable context, the original work injury in no way causes or contributes to the happening of the subsequent non-work accident but the original injury is aggravated by or implicated in the subsequent occurrence. Results, in terms of compensability, vary depending upon one or more of the following: (1) policy considerations; (2) the nature of the employee's conduct in relation to the subsequent accident; (3) the jurisdiction's apportionment statute; or (4) the applicable burden of proof. See, e.g., Kill v. Industrial Comm., 160 Wis. 549, 152 N.W. 148 (1915) (employee who suffered work related wrist injury later engaged in a boxing match against physician's advice and suffered a bacterial infection at the site of the original injury; resulting loss of use of hand found not compensable due to employee's conduct); Amick v. National Bottle, 507 A.2d 1352 (Sup. Ct. R.I. 1986) (over three year period, employee suffered two work related back injuries and two non-work related back injuries; after the fourth injury, which was non-work related, claimant became severely depressed and sought benefits for psychiatric care; court concluded under Rhode Island law claimant had burden of proving emotional disability resulted solely from work injuries; held compensation denied); Schaefer v. Williamston Community Schools, 117 Mich.App. 26, 323 N.W.2d 577 (1982) (work related injury to claimant's back was exacerbated when he lifted boxes at his home, "something I shouldn't have done"; court held this could be a compensable aggravation if the board concluded the activity of moving the household goods was not negligent in light of employee's knowledge of his pre-existing condition); Amey v. Friendly Ice Cream Shop, 231 N.J.Super. 278, 555 A.2d 677 (1989) (work related injury to flexor tendon of claimant's right hand; hand re-injured while employee was working on his car at home; doctor had warned claimant not to put pressure on the hand; held compensation denied); Webb v. Industrial Commission of Ohio, 76 Ohio App.3d 701, 602 N.E.2d 1265 (1991) (employee had work related knee injury surgically repaired; two years later, employee injured the same knee while playing touch football; doctor testified the knee was prone to such later injury due to the earlier work injury; court held employee must show a direct and substantial causal relationship between the first and second injuries but that the work injury need not be the sole cause of the ultimate disability); Aragon v. State of New Mexico Corrections Dept., 113 N.M. 176, 824 P.2d 316 (1991) (employee suffered work related back injury in 1983; in 1988 employee aggravated the back injury while repairing his personal truck at home; court reasoned an employee is entitled to benefits for disability arising immediate-

ly from a work related accident and for disability which develops later as a result of the normal activities of life; but the worker is not provided an insurance policy of indefinite duration to cover every non-work related accident that magnifies the original injury; held compensation denied); Kroh v. American Family Insurance, 487 N.W.2d 306 (N.D.1992) (employee suffered work related back injury; two months later claimant injured back again in non-work related vehicle accident; court applied North Dakota's aggravation apportionment statute and concluded that benefits are to be awarded only for work injuries and not for aggravation thereof by a non-work injury); Rogers v. Cascade Pacific, 152 Or.App. 624, 955 P.2d 307 (1998) (employee who suffered work related back injuries later suffered a neck injury while doing exercises as part of his preventative physical therapy regimen; court found the work injuries were not a "major contributing cause" of the neck injury as required by O.R.S. § 656.05(7)(a)(A); held compensation denied); Addington Resources v. Perkins, 947 S.W.2d 421 (Ct. App. Ky. 1997) (employee suffered work related injury at the C5–C6 level of the spine; five years later employee suffered a non-work injury at the C6–C7 level; court concluded the work related injury caused the part of the back which was subsequently injured to be more susceptible to injury; held second injury compensable); Benton v. Winn–Dixie Montgomery, Inc., 705 So.2d 495 (Ala.Civ.App. 1997) (work related back injury required surgical fusion of several vertebrae; five years later claimant was involved in non-work related vehicle accident; after car accident, fractures were detected in the previously fused vertebrae; held compensable); and Hallisey v. Fort Howard Paper Co., 268 Ga. 57, 484 S.E.2d 653 (1997) (employee suffered work related back injury; two days later during a day off from work after his tee shot on the twenty-fourth hole of golf, his back pain became so severe that he had to quit and seek medical treatment; ALJ awarded compensation but Court of Appeals reversed due to claimant's negligence in playing golf; Supreme Court reinstated the award holding that Georgia's Workers' Compensation Act does not treat an employee's negligence in aggravating an injury as an intervening cause).

6. In 1998, Georgia passed legislation which purports to codify existing case law in the "subsequent injury" case. See O.C.G.A. § 34–9–204(a) which provides: "No compensation shall be payable for the death or disability of an employee if his or her death is caused by or, insofar as his or her disability may be aggravated, caused or continued by a subsequent nonwork related injury which breaks the chain of causation between the compensable injury and the employee's disability."

SECTION 3. COMPLICATIONS AND ACCIDENTS DURING MEDICAL TREATMENT

Notes

1. Is disability or death compensable if not a normal effect of the original compensable injury but rather a consequence of adverse medical developments that follow it or transpire during its treatment? Most decisions award compensation. The development of an infection following an injury that delays recovery or even causes death is compensable as part of the original injury. Magnus v. Krug Electric Co., Inc., 271 App.Div. 761, 64 N.Y.S.2d 624 (1946) (trauma to thumb in November, subsequent infection

necessitating amputation in January; held compensable); Allen v. Industrial Commission, 110 Utah 328, 172 P.2d 669 (1946) (bruise on leg, resulting in septicemia and pulmonary embolism and death; held compensable); Herre Bros., Inc. v. W.C.A.B. ex rel. Mumma, 75 Pa.Cmwlth. 499, 462 A.2d 907 (1983) (broken ribs in employment related truck accident; employee died at home seven days later of pneumonia; held compensable). In American Smelting & Refining Co. v. Industrial Comm., 25 Ariz.App. 532, 544 P.2d 1133 (1976) compensation was awarded for death resulting from an infection that developed 30 years after the original injury.

2.   Further injury resulting from both the normal and unusual hazards of medical treatment required by a compensable injury are almost always compensable. In Beech Creek Coal Co. v. Cox, 314 Ky. 743, 237 S.W.2d 56 (1951), an employee convalescing at home from a compensable leg fracture fell, breaking the same leg in a different place. Death suffered during surgery required by the second injury, held compensable. Many other cases have awarded compensation. See, e.g., Paul Constr. Co. v. Powell, 200 Md. 168, 88 A.2d 837 (1952) (injury to back required operation which precipitated attack of acute toxic hallucinations, held death compensable); Abney and Eaves, Inc. v. Redeker, 303 P.2d 417 (Okl.1956) (as treatment for compensable work injury, claimant was injected with medicine that caused her to faint and fall; held injuries from fall compensable); Royal Palm Market v. Lutz, 126 So.2d 881 (Fla.1961) (operation for work connected hernia caused stroke; held compensable); Elmore's Variety Store v. White, 553 S.W.2d 350 (Tenn.1977) (claimant was being treated for a compensable puncture wound when a brain aneurysm ruptured; held both injuries compensable); Elizabethtown Sportswear v. Stice, 720 S.W.2d 732 (Ky.App.1986) (employee injured back and suffered death from allergic reaction to dye used in myelogram; held death compensable); City of Buford v. Thomas, 179 Ga.App. 769, 347 S.E.2d 713 (1986) (employee, hospitalized due to compensable work injury, fell while out of bed against doctor's orders; held, getting out of bed was not an independent intervening cause and death due to fall compensable); Eagle v. State of Nebraska, 237 Neb. 961, 468 N.W.2d 382 (1991) (a screw, implanted as part of surgery for a compensable injury, became loose and caused damage to the claimant's hip, held additional award granted for hip trauma); American Filtrona Co. v. Hanford, 16 Va.App. 159, 428 S.E.2d 511 (1993) (employee contracted hepatitis C from blood transfusion given during treatment of work related knee surgery, held compensation awarded for hepatitis C infection); Barrett v. Hames, 130 Or.App. 190, 881 P.2d 816 (1994) (worker suffered compensable shoulder injury; aggressive physical therapy injured ulnar nerve; held, additional compensation awarded for the injury to the nerve); Spacal v. Marietta, 642 So.2d 46 (Fla.App.1994) (even where the connection between the original compensable injury and the subsequent surgery is unclear, the employer will be liable for any complications that arise from that surgery if the employer has authorized it); Transport Associates v. Butler, 892 S.W.2d 296 (Sup. Ct. Ky.1995) (employee consulted physicians for treatment of compensable back injury. One recommended surgery while other did not. Employer held responsible for additional injury caused by unnecessary surgery due to employer's failure to exercise its statutory right to request that claimant be treated by another physician).

3. If the claimant fails to establish a cause-in-fact connection between the original injury or its treatment and the subsequent injury, compensation for the subsequent injury will be disallowed. See, e.g., Sicker v. Karl Schroll & Associates, Inc., 19 A.D.2d 925, 244 N.Y.S.2d 20 (1963) (death caused by cancer unrelated to employment, held compensation denied); Bauman v. Lord Electric Co., 79 A.D.2d 806, 435 N.Y.S.2d 98 (1980) (auto accident injured knee, buttock and thigh; frustration and inactivity arguably led to obesity; intestinal bypass surgery to ameliorate obesity resulted in surgical complications and death; held obesity not shown to be caused by accident and compensation denied); Matter of Injury to Loveday, 711 P.2d 396 (Wyo.1985) (compensable back injury treated surgically; back pain continued so a second surgery was performed; heart attack occurred two days after second surgery; held not compensable because of failure in proof of causation); Rogers v. Cascade, 152 Or.App. 624, 955 P.2d 307 (1998) (claimant completed course of treatment for a compensable back injury and was instructed to perform exercises in order to avoid future injury. Injury to back occurred while performing exercises. Held, exercises were not part of treatment of compensable injury and compensation denied).

To the contrary is Vanecek v. Greeley Square Bldg. Co., 278 App.Div. 869, 104 N.Y.S.2d 214 (1951) which permitted compensation under extended circumstances. The employee suffered a compensable scalp laceration which resulted in headaches and dizziness. Because of possible post-traumatic bleeding, two exploratory operations of the cranium were performed. No bleeding was found, but the second operation revealed a tumor that was not a result of the work accident. The tumor was removed and as a result of the surgery the patient died. An award of compensation was affirmed on the theory that the purpose of the operation was to determine the effect of the original injury.

4. The cause in fact issue also appears in cases which involve a distinction between medical care for a compensable injury and medical care for a condition which, although not work related, must be addressed before the work injury can be safely treated. See, e.g. Rank v. Lindblom, 459 N.W.2d 247 (S.D.1990) (claimant, a ranch hand, suffered knee injury by stampeding calves; during pre-operative workup, doctors discovered pulmonary disorder which required surgical correction before knee surgery could be safely done. Board awarded compensation for lung surgery. Supreme Court reversed holding that the pulmonary surgery would have been needed even in absence of the knee surgery); State of Wyoming v. Girardot 807 P.2d 926 (Wyo.1991) (claimant hospitalized for surgical repair of compensable hernia; during pre-operative examination severe arterial blockage of the heart was diagnosed; heart by-pass surgery was required before hernia repair. Held, compensation awarded ($3,790) for hernia repair but denied ($35,000) for heart by-pass); and see Beasley v. Industrial Commission of Arizona 175 Ariz. 521, 858 P.2d 666 (1993) holding where an unrelated condition would require treatment irrespective of the compensable injury, treatment of that condition is not covered by workers' compensation. Further, the unrelated condition does not become compensable even when treatment for it is a pre-requisite to treatment for a compensable injury, or when left alone, the unrelated condition would cause a worsening of the covered injury. Compare Forni v. Pathfinder Mines, 834 P.2d 688 (Wyo.1992)

claimant who suffered from work related back injury had preexisting diabetes and depression. Doctors concluded the preexisting conditions needed treatment before the back surgery could be accomplished. Both preexisting conditions required post surgery treatment as well. Held compensation awarded for treatment of the preexisting conditions. See also the *Braewood* Case, supra.

5. Should an accident which happens while the employee is visiting a health care provider for treatment of a compensable injury be compensable? Larson considers this a compensable quasi-course of activity injury unless the claimant's conduct leading to the injury is characterized as intentional rather than merely negligent; see summary of Larson's position in *Garrison* supra at pp. 311–312. Suppose an ambulance, hastening from the scene of an industrial accident, crashes into a tree and kills the injured worker. Would the result be different if there were no haste? Contrast Kiger v. Idaho Corp., 85 Idaho 424, 380 P.2d 208 (1963) (compensation denied) with Immer and Co. v. Brosnahan, 207 Va. 720, 152 S.E.2d 254 (1967) (automobile accident while going to doctor's office; compensation awarded). See also, All American Wheel World, Inc. & FAWA v. Gustafson, 499 So.2d 876 (Fla.App. 1 Dist. 1986) (employment related back injury; claimant, passenger in friend's car, injured in auto accident en route to chiropractor's office; held compensable); Case of McElroy, 397 Mass. 743, 494 N.E.2d 1 (1986) (back injury on assembly line; additional injuries in a car crash while driving for treatment; held compensable; street risk rule applied); D.O.T. v. King, 554 So.2d 1192 (Fla.App.1989) (claimant suffered work related injuries to her leg; doctor told claimant to walk for physical therapy; while walking, claimant was struck by auto; held compensable); Green v. Coca–Cola Bottling Co., 329 Ark. 345, 948 S.W.2d 92 (1997) (employee was driving to the doctor for treatment of work related injury when he stopped to assist an elderly driver whose car had broken down. Claimant's car was struck by another motorist injuring claimant. Applying Larson's prohibited conduct test, the court held that the claimant had not deviated from his journey. Such conduct could not be classified as expressly or impliedly prohibited by the employer). If the claimant had terminated the employment relationship prior to the auto accident, compensation might be denied. Contrast Bankers Investment Co. v. Boyd, 560 P.2d 958 (Okl.1977) with Telcon, Inc. v. Williams, 500 So.2d 266 (Fla.App. 1 Dist.1986). See also, Barrett Business Services v. Hames, 130 Or.App. 190, 881 P.2d 816 (1994) in which the court discussed changes to the Oregon statute which replaced the but-for causation standard with a "major contributing cause" test. The court quoted from the legislative debate which preceded this statutory change "... you have a broken arm [from a compensable accident] ... and you're crossing the street on the way to see your doctor, and the doctor's office is right over there ... and a car runs you down ... you got hurt on the way to the doctor. Requiring major contributing cause means that no, being run down crossing the street on the way to the doctor is not covered."

6. Exacerbation of the consequences of a compensable injury caused by subsequent acts of third persons are frequently compensable, particularly exacerbation caused by bad medical treatment of the original injury. See, e.g., Flanagan v. Charles E. Green & Son, 122 N.J.L. 424, 5 A.2d 742 (1939) (claimant hospitalized with a compensable injury broke arm while cooperat-

ing with nurses in changing the bed clothes; broken arm held compensable); McAvoy v. Roberts & Mander Stove Co., 173 Pa.Super. 516, 98 A.2d 231 (1953) (claimant underwent surgery as a result of a work injury; while still under anesthesia she was dropped from a litter and sustained a concussion; held disabling post-concussion syndrome compensable); Mallette v. Mercury Outboard Supply Co., Inc., 204 Tenn. 438, 321 S.W.2d 816 (1959) (claimant, hospitalized due to work injury, was paralyzed when a nurse "threw him around and twisted him" while bathing him; held, compensation awarded); Heumphreus v. State, 334 N.W.2d 757 (Iowa 1983) (claimant, a prisoner, suffered possible work related heart attack; jailor negligently delayed transport to hospital causing death; held death compensable); Sutherland v. Illinois Employers Ins. Co., 696 S.W.2d 139 (Tex.App.1985) (claimant fell at work injuring neck and back; in preparation for myelogram, medical staff negligently strapped claimant to the examination table; claimant fell to floor causing further injury; held compensable).

7.   The foregoing principle has been applied to award compensation for the consequences of a physician's negligent treatment of a compensable injury if the claimant used due care in the selection of the physician. The medical negligence may be in prescribing medication, in setting fractures and in performing other types of medical and surgical procedures. See, e.g., City of Lakeland v. Burton, 147 Fla. 412, 2 So.2d 731 (1941) (negligent prescription of narcotic caused death, held death compensable); Mitchell v. Peaslee, 143 Me. 372, 63 A.2d 302 (1948) (negligence in setting fracture; held compensable); Houston General v. Campbell, 964 S.W.2d 691 (Tex.App.1998) (claimant's compensable injury aggravated by doctor's malpractice; employer paid claimant additional compensation due to malpractice and would have subrogation interest in employee's common law malpractice action against doctor).

If the employee negligently selects an incompetent physician, compensation for the doctor's aggravation of the work injury may be denied. See, e.g., Cross v. Hermanson Bros., 235 Iowa 739, 16 N.W.2d 616 (1944) (Chiropractor broke claimant's vertebra during treatment of work related injury; no negligence found in selection of chiropractor); and Spencer v. Department of Industry, Labor and Hum. Rel., 55 Wis.2d 525, 200 N.W.2d 611 (1972) (claimant is not to be faulted for following erroneous medical advice, as long as he did so in good faith). Under Larson's "quasi-course" approach how would the employee's conduct in selecting a physician be assessed?

The method of selecting a physician or other health care provider is often dictated by the state's workers' compensation act. See Chapter 8. Failure to follow the statute may cause a loss of medical benefits including, it would seem, loss of any compensation due to malpractice by the improperly selected health care provider. See, e.g., Johnson Drug Co. v. Thaxton, 121 So.2d 158 (Fla.1960) first holding the employer not liable for the malpractice and, on rehearing, reversing itself by a closely divided vote. In Armstrong v. Stearns–Roger Electrical Contractors, Inc., 99 N.M. 275, 657 P.2d 131 (App. 1982), cert. denied 99 N.M. 226, 656 P.2d 889 (1983), the employee did not resort to the employer's list of approved physicians but rather sought care from his family doctor who employed treatment that interfered with the decedent's heart pacemaker causing cardiac arrest and death. Death benefits were denied because of the decedent's failure to follow the employer's procedures. In Crews v. WCAB, 123 Pa.Cmwlth. 610, 554 A.2d 190 (1989) claimant's recovery was apparently slowed because claimant followed his personal physician's prescribed exercise program at the YMCA rather than physical therapy at a rehab center as prescribed by the employer provided physician. This choice was held to be unreasonable.

8.   Many statutes include an express statutory provision that damages resulting from medical malpractice shall be deemed part of the injury resulting from the accident. See, e.g. Ga. Code Ann. § 34–9–203 (1988).

Common law suit against the physician as a "third party" for damages for the tortious treatment of the claimant is considered in Chapter 11.

SECTION 4. NEW INJURY OR RECURRENCE OF OLD INJURY

When a work related injury is followed by a subsequent injury, as typified by the cases in the previous two sections, the most recent injury may be considered either as a new injury or a recurrence of the old injury. The classification may be important in determining, among other things, which of two or more successive employers or insurance carriers is liable to the employee for the resulting disability; the relevant date of the injury so as to determine the appropriate rate of compensation to which the employee is entitled; whether the claimant is time barred from seeking additional compensation for a "change in condition"; and, perhaps, even whether or not the same tribunal has jurisdiction to resolve the successive claims. The following case and note materials are illustrative.

LOCKHEED MISSILES & SPACE COMPANY, INC. v. BOBCHAK

Court of Appeals of Georgia, 1990.
194 Ga.App. 156, 390 S.E.2d 82.

BANKE, PRESIDING JUDGE.

The claimant in this workers' compensation case sustained an osteochondral fracture to his left knee on August 10, 1987, while employed as a laborer for W.H. Gross Construction Company. He underwent arthroscopic surgery as treatment for this injury and was paid disability benefits until October 12, 1987, when he began working for Lockheed Missiles & Space Company. On February 25, 1988, he noticed a "tired and weak feeling" in the knee after climbing and descending a ladder at Lockheed. By that evening the knee had become painful and swollen, resulting in further disability and, eventually, the need for additional surgery.

At issue in this appeal is whether the knee impairment which the claimant experienced at Lockheed must, as a matter of law, be considered the result of a new accident, with the result that Lockheed would be required to provide compensation for it, or whether it may instead be treated as a change in condition for which Gross Construction Company would be responsible. Based on findings that the claimant's "employment duties at Lockheed were not more strenuous as compared to the heavy labor type work he engaged in with W.H. Gross" and that "[n]o incident occurred that aggravated claimant's prior injured knee," the administrative law judge concluded that the claimant had experienced a change in condition. The full board affirmed; however, the superior court reversed, concluding that the record was "totally devoid of any evidence of a gradual worsening of claimant's condition as a result of the activity connected with his normal duties for the four and one-half month period immediately prior to the ladder incident," and further concluding that there was "no evidence whatever ... to support the board's conclusion that no specific incident occurred aggravating the claimant's previous injury." The case is before us pursuant to our grant of Lockheed's application for discretionary appeal. See generally OCGA § 5–6–35. Held: 1. "[W]here there is no actual new accident, ordinarily the distinguishing feature that will characterize the disability as either a 'change of condition' or a 'new accident' is the intervention of new circumstances. If the claimant leaves the old employer and goes to work in a different environment with a new employer, there are new circumstances with a new employer; and this is particularly true when the activity performed for the new employer exceeds the limits of the light duty offered by the old employer." Certain v. U.S. Fidelity & Guaranty Co., 153 Ga.App. 571, 573, 266 S.E.2d 263 (1980). The claimant in Certain had been injured while performing strenuous work for his original employer. He was later given a light-duty job assignment by that employer but left that assignment almost immediately to begin working for a new employer. "For [the next] five months, he worked at the same type strenuous work which he had been medically forbidden to do at the first employer's, and from which he had been relieved to perform light work duties. After five months, although he did not have an actual new accident, his condition worsened so that he again became totally disabled...." Id. at 572, 266 S.E.2d 263. We held that under these circumstances his disability must, as a matter of law, be considered the result of a fictitious "new accident" rather than a change in condition.

Subsequently, in Beers Constr. Co. v. Stephens, 162 Ga.App. 87, 90, 290 S.E.2d 181 (1982), we emphasized that "[t]he decision in Certain that the claimant had suffered a new accident and not a change of condition was not controlled by the mere fact that the claimant was employed by a new employer in a different environment but by the additional new circumstances that the work performed for the second employer exceeded the limits of light work duties offered by the previous employer." We also emphasized in Beers that "a 'specific incident' is not [a] prerequisite to a finding of new accident...." Id. at 91, 290 S.E.2d 181, citing Blackwell v. Liberty Mut. Ins. Co., 230 Ga. 174, 175, 196 S.E.2d 129 (1973). By the same token, we do not believe that in all cases where the worsening of a pre-existing condition can be traced to a "specific incident" occurring on the new job, that incident must necessarily be considered a "new accident." Rather, the determinative inquiry is whether the circumstances associated with the incident and with the new employment in general were "such as to independently aggravate the condition" or whether the renewed impairment instead resulted from the "wear and tear of ordinary life in connection with performance of normal duties...." Beers, supra, 162 Ga.App. at 90–91, 290 S.E.2d 181. As previously indicated, the administrative law judge in this case found that "[c]laimant's employment duties at Lockheed were not more strenuous as compared to the heavy labor type work he had performed for W.H. Gross." Furthermore, although the claimant stated that his knee had been improving prior to the ladder incident, he acknowledged that he had continued to experience pain and stiffness in it; and one of the physicians who examined him subsequent to the incident testified: "My experience with those people who have sustained large osteochondral fractures is that they never return to their steady state and may periodically need an arthroscopic debridement every two to five years." As for the ladder-climbing incident itself, it appears to have been completely uneventful. There is no suggestion that the claimant was carrying a heavy object at the time, nor is there any indication that he twisted the knee or otherwise sustained any unusual trauma to it as a result of the climbing. We hold that even though the administrative law judge may have been authorized under these circumstances to conclude that the claimant had experienced a "new accident," he was also authorized to conclude that the claimant had undergone a change in condition, with the result that the superior court erred in substituting its judgment on this issue for that of the board. See generally Atkinson v. Home Indem. Co., 141 Ga.App. 687, 234 S.E.2d 359 (1977).

2. The appellees urge that in the event the judgment of the superior court is reversed, the case should be remanded for a determination of whether or not the administrative law judge made a misstatement of significant testimony when he found as a fact that "[t]he ladder climbing was a part of claimant's ordinary work." It is contended that this finding conflicts with the claimant's undisputed testimony that he had not previously climbed any ladders in connection with his work at Lockheed but had climbed only stairs. However, we do not interpret this statement by the administrative law judge as a finding that the claimant was routinely required to climb ladders at Lockheed; rather, we interpret it to mean simply that the incident occurred while he was engaged in the performance of his ordinary and usual duties there. In any event, regardless of how many ladders the claimant had climbed at Lockheed, there was no indication that the demands placed on his weakened knee by his job responsibilities at Lockheed exceeded those which would have been placed on the knee had he returned to work for his prior employer, where he had also been required to climb ladders. Consequently, we do not believe the administrative law judge's finding in this regard can be considered unfavorable to the appellees, regardless of how it is interpreted.

Judgement reversed.

SOGNIER and POPE JJ. concur.

Notes

1. In Gonzales v. Stanke–Brown and Associates, Inc., 98 N.M. 379, 648 P.2d 1192 (1982), the issue concerned which of two successive insurance carriers was liable for two injuries suffered in the same employment. The court held that the injury was compensable by the compensation carrier at the time of the second accident.

2. In Fisher v. K Mart Corp., 174 Mich.App. 669, 436 N.W.2d 434 (1989), a claimant who suffered an initial injury to his foot in 1976 reinjured the foot and fractured his wrist in 1977. In 1978, the claimant's foot pain became so severe he left work, underwent surgery and remained disabled. The ensuing workers' compensation claim raised the issue of whether he was entitled to compensation at the rate provided for in the 1976 statute or at the rate provided by 1978 legislation. The workers' compensation appeal board, in a split decision, held the 1978 disability to be a recurrence of the 1976 injury not a "new injury" and applied the 1976 rate. The Michigan Court of Appeals reversed and applied the 1978 rate on the ground that the 1978 disability constituted a "new injury." The new injury was held to have occurred on the date that the pain from the 1976 accident became so great that the claimant was no longer able to work. The Gonzales case, note 1, supra, also addressed the issue of which rate of compensation was appropriate for the second injury. See also Harris v. District of Columbia Office of Workers Compensation, 660 A.2d.404 (D.C.Ct.App.1995) (First injury occurred before the effective date of the workers' compensation statute. Second event took place after the law was in force. The hearing officer found the second event was a re-occurrence of the first injury and, thus, non-compensable. The court reversed finding that the second event was an aggravation of the prior injury and that the employee was entitled to an award for the aggravation.).

3. Andras v. Donovan, 414 F.2d 241(5th Cir.1969) raised a dispute as to whether compensation should be paid under the Longshore and Harbor Workers' Compensation Act or under a state workers' compensation law. The claimant suffered the first injury, a traumatic neurosis, and was compensated under the Longshore Act. As part of the treatment for his psychiatric injuries, his physician directed him to return to work in the shipyards. Claimant subsequently injured his back in the course of his land-based employment duties. The deputy commissioner refused jurisdiction under the Longshore Act for the second injury because, being a land-based injury, it was beyond the jurisdiction of the statute. The fifth circuit reversed and remanded for the deputy to determine whether there was any causal connection between the two injuries. If such connection was found, the deputy could properly award compensation for both injuries. See also, Insurance Co. of N.A. v. U.S. Department of Labor, Office of Workers' Compensation Programs, 969 F.2d 1400 (2d Cir.1992) (Employee died of lung cancer after on-the-job exposure to asbestos. The question of compensation hinged on whether the version of the Longshore and Harbor Workers' Compensation Act in effect on the date of last exposure or the amended version in place on the date of first manifestation of illness controlled. The answer would determine whether the employee had met the situs requirement of the statute and, thus, whether his widow would receive death benefits.

4. As to these issues, see Generally 4 Larson's Workmen's Compensation Law § 95.11 et seq. (1997), and as to the "change of condition" issue, see Chapter 10, infra, pp. 455–457.

SECTION 5. REFUSAL TO ACCEPT MEDICAL TREATMENT

COMMONWEALTH, DEPT. OF HIGHWAYS v. LINDON

Court of Appeals of Kentucky, 1964.
380 S.W.2d 247.

DAVIS, COMMISSIONER. Following an accident in the course of his employment with the Kentucky Department of Highways in which he sustained a minor, temporary injury to his left foot, William A. Lindon, Jr., developed a condition described by one doctor as a "psychoneurosis conversion hysteria which was superimposed on a minor foot injury." Lindon became convinced in his mind that he had constant pain in his foot and leg and as a result he was unable to work. The Workmen's Compensation Board gave him an open-end award for total permanent disability, based on a finding that he was suffering from "compensation neurosis" (a medically recognized mental aberration distinguished from conscious malingering). On appeal to the circuit court judgment was entered upholding the award. The Department of Highways has appealed here from that judgment.

We find merit in the appellant's contention that the compensation board erred in holding that Lindon's refusal to submit to certain psychiatric treatment was not unreasonable. (KRS 342.035 provides that no compensation shall be payable for disability of an employee "in so far as his disability is aggravated, caused or continued, by an unreasonable failure to submit to or follow any competent surgical treatment or medical aid or advice.")

A psychiatrist who treated Lindon recommended that he submit to a sodium amytal interview, which would involve administering a sedative similar to "truth serum," would make the patient drowsy and less resistant and more amenable to suggestion. The purpose would be to overcome the neurosis by suggestion. The psychiatrist stated that if the treatment were successful a cure could be effected in two or three sessions. Lindon refused to take the treatment. His personal physician stated that he did not believe the psychiatric treatment alone would effect a cure.

The compensation board expressed the views that the proposed treatment might further deter Lindon's improvement, and that the treatment would be of no good effect if Lindon resisted its purpose. There is no evidence in the record to sustain these views. No doctor testified that the treatment might be harmful, or that Lindon's resistance would make the treatment completely ineffectual.

The appellee argues that the board's ruling should be upheld under the rule that if there is a difference of expert opinion as to the danger *or* *efficacy* of medical or surgical treatment the employee's refusal to submit is not unreasonable. * * * However, the cases stating that rule all involved *operations,* where there was some degree of physical suffering involved from the operation. Here there is nothing to indicate that the treatment would involve any suffering or even material discomfort. Under such circumstances, in our opinion, the mere fact that there is a difference of expert opinion as to the possible success of the treatment is not sufficient to support a refusal to take the treatment. We think this is particularly so in the case of mental disturbances, where the methods of treatment have not yet reached the stage of development where successful results can accurately be predicted.

It is our conclusion that the compensation board erred in finding that Lindon's refusal to submit to the proposed treatment was not unreasonable. Upon remand of the case the board will enter an order withholding compensation payments until Lindon submits to the treatment.

The appellant makes a further contention that the evidence does not support the board's finding that there was a causal connection between the traumatic injury and the disability. We believe there was adequate proof of causal connection. Dr. Maddox stated in a written report that the accident was the only cause of Lindon's condition. Dr. Wiesel testified that the injury precipitated the condition. It no doubt is true, as stated by Dr. Maddox, that Lindon's psychoneurotic tendencies existed before the injury; however, he had no disability until the tendencies were activated by the injury. We agree with the authorities holding that the injury is the cause of the compensation neurosis disability in such circumstances. See Larson, Workmen's Compensation, Volume I, sec. 42.24.

* * *

The judgment is reversed with directions to enter judgment remanding the case to the Workmen's Compensation Board for further proceedings in conformity with this opinion.

Notes

1. The Kentucky statute set out in the principal case is similar to that in many other states. See, e.g., Ariz. Rev. Stats. Ann. Volume 8A, § 23–1027; Ga. Code Ann. § 34–9–200 (1988) Purdon's Pa. Stats. Ann. 531(4) (1991); 9A Tenn. Code Ann. § 50–6–204(7) (1990); and Code of Va. § 65.1–88.

2. In the absence of specific statutes, courts commonly apply the same general principle on the theory that an injury caused by an employee's unreasonable refusal of needed treatment "is not proximately caused by the accident, but is the direct result of such unreasonable refusal." Lesh v. Illinois Steel Co., 163 Wis. 124, 157 N.W. 539 (1916). Larson suggests that because the employee's conduct in accepting or rejecting medical treatment for a work related injury involves a "quasi-course-of-employment" activity, compensation should be suspended only if the employee's conduct is inten-

tional and "clearly unreasonable" and not merely negligent. 1 Larson's Workmen's Compensation Law § 13.22 et seq. (1997).

3. Applying this principle is sometimes troublesome particularly because of a convention that forfeiture statutes, such as these, must be "strictly construed." See, e.g., Wood v. Wagner Electric Corp., 192 S.W.2d 579 (Mo.App.1946), opinion modified 355 Mo. 670, 197 S.W.2d 647 (1946) (claimant over sixty years of age with high blood pressure, refused to undergo hernia operation, held not unreasonable). Some statutes require that the workers' compensation tribunal mandate the treatment before the employee's refusal will preclude further benefits (see, e.g., (1988) Ga. Code Ann. § 34–9–200) and some decisions require the employer to prove the claimant's conduct was unreasonable. See, e.g., Smiley v. Foremost–McKesson, 708 S.W.2d 330 (Mo.App.1986).

Once compensation is awarded, the award ordinarily will not be terminated in the absence of strong justification. See, e.g. Stump v. Norfolk Shipbuilding & Dry Dock Corp., 187 Va. 932, 48 S.E.2d 209 (1948) (employee refused medication for infected abrasion of skin, ultimate loss of leg held not compensable); Skidmore v. Drumon Fine Foods, Inc., 119 So.2d 523 (La.App. 1960) (claimant with persistent pain following amputation of a finger was required to submit to simple, minor surgery or lose his compensation); Sanderson v. Secrest Pipe Coating Co., 465 S.W.2d 65 (Ky., 1971) (failure to follow a course of exercises); Byrd v. WCAB, 81 Pa.Cmwlth. 325, 473 A.2d 723 (1984) (claimant cancelled eight of twelve physical therapy sessions and suffered second injury because of failure to complete therapy; held unreasonable); Menges v. WCAB, 93 Pa.Cmwlth. 395, 501 A.2d 347 (1985) (leg surgery was refused by claimant because "some people told [him] it wouldn't help any"; evidence showed surgery would reduce disability by one half, would reduce pain and had a 80 percent success rate; held refusal unreasonable); Dabney v. Boh Brothers Construction Co., 710 So.2d 1106 (La.App. 1998) (Court found the statute to be mandatory, clear and unambiguous in its call for a fifty percent reduction in benefits when a claimant refuses to participate fully in a vocational rehabilitation program).

4. What criteria should courts invoke in determining whether the medical procedure is "reasonably required" so that the employee's refusal to undergo the treatment is "unreasonable" or "unjustifiable"? The principal considerations seem to be: the prospect of success of the surgical procedure or medical treatment; the amount of pain and suffering it entails; and, the danger to the claimant's health or life. Where the prospects for success are poor or uncertain, courts commonly hold that the claimant's refusal to accept the treatment is not unreasonable. The Kentucky court has upheld claimant's refusal where "the result of his operation would be speculative." Melcher v. Drummond Mfg. Co., 312 Ky. 588, 229 S.W.2d 52 (1950) (hernia); and see Couch v. Saginaw Malleable Iron Plant, 42 Mich.App. 223, 201 N.W.2d 681 (1972) (50 per cent chance of success; held, refusal not unreasonable). Contrast the following cases: K. Lee Williams Theatres, Inc. v. Mickle, 201 Okl. 279, 205 P.2d 513 (1949) ("a minor operation, simple, safe, and reasonably certain to effect a cure"); Sultan & Chera Corp. v. Fallas, 59 So.2d 535 (Fla.1952) ("an operation of a simple character not involving serious suffering or danger of death"); and Joyce Western Corp. v. WCAB, 518 Pa. 191, 542 A.2d 990 (1988) ("If the evidence establishes that the

recommended surgery involves minimal risk to the patient and offers a high probability of success, the proposed surgery is reasonable.'').

5. An employee's age, general physical condition, and specific medical circumstances, such as high blood pressure, are all taken into account. In Parker v. Mead Corp., 91 F.Supp. 960 (E.D.Tenn.1949), affirmed 183 F.2d 952 (6th Cir.1950), a sixty-two year old claimant who suffered from "smothering spells," tortuosity and enlargement of descending aorta, enlargement of the liver, calcification in the left lung and near spleen, arthritic lipping in the spine, and arthritic spurs in the lumbar region was held justified in refusing a herniotomy. In Waldroup v. J.C. Penney Co., 30 Or.App. 443, 567 P.2d 576 (1977), a claimant, suffering from a low back injury, refused myelography and surgery because she was receiving treatment from a chiropractor who reported she was "responding very satisfactorily." The court held that the refusal was reasonable. Reef v. Willamette Industries, 65 Or.App. 366, 671 P.2d 1197 (1983), held that reasonableness is a question of fact and the determination must be based upon all relevant factors including the worker's present physical and psychological condition.

In Flaherty v. Industrial Comm., 73 Ariz. 74, 237 P.2d 806 (1951), the court took into account the immediate economic necessity of the employee who refused treatment that would have disabled him from continuing to do some work and bring in as much income as possible to support his family.

6. Courts are unlikely to require an employee to submit to repeated tests where the first one proves negative. See, e.g., Zanotti v. New York Telephone Co., 61 A.D.2d 861, 401 N.Y.S.2d 911 (1978).

Where an operation has been performed previously and has not been successful, courts are not likely to require claimant to endure a second one. See, e.g., City of Olive Hill v. Parsons, 306 Ky. 83, 206 S.W.2d 41 (1947) (hernia); and Dudansky v. L.H. Sault Const. Co., 244 Minn. 369, 70 N.W.2d 114 (1955) (disc). Contrast, Muse v. W.C.A.B., 514 Pa. 1, 522 A.2d 533 (1987) (first surgery to repair hernia resulted in complications and need for second corrective surgery which offered high probability of success and little risk, held, second surgery reasonable and refusal thereof unreasonable).

7. An employee's fear of the operation may be sufficient ground to hold refusal not unreasonable. See, e.g., Morgan v. Sholom Drilling Co., 199 Kan. 156, 427 P.2d 448 (1967) (85 to 90 percent chance of success but fear present; held refusal reasonable); American Asbestos Textile Corp. v. Ryder, 111 N.H. 282, 281 A.2d 53 (1971) (fear of laminectomy); Fluor Alaska, Inc. v. Mendoza, 616 P.2d 25 (Alaska, 1980) (fear of dying during laminectomy); Small v. Combustion Engineering, 209 Mont. 387, 681 P.2d 1081 (1984) (manic-depressive claimant refused knee surgery out of fear of detrimental consequences; held refusal not unreasonable because of mental disorder) and Grandinetti v. Syracuse University, 134 A.D.2d 683, 521 N.Y.S.2d 343 (1987) (claimant refused myelogram and back surgery because of attendant serious dangers and because claimant's wife and brother-in-law had experienced adverse results from myelogram; held refusal reasonable).

8. Should the reasonableness of an employee's refusal of treatment be examined objectively or subjectively? States differ in their approach. See, e.g., Genuardi Supermarkets v. WCAB, 674 A.2d 1194 (Pa.Cmwlth.1996) (The standard for determining whether a claimant's refusal to accept medi-

cal services is whether the services themselves are reasonable, not whether the claimant's refusal is reasonable); Schwab Construction v. McCarter, 25 Va.App. 104, 486 S.E.2d 562 (1997) (the test employed ... [in an unjustified refusal of treatment case] is a subjective one–whether the claimant acted reasonably in refusing the medical treatment) ; Johnson v. Jones, 123 N.C.App. 219, 472 S.E.2d 587 (1996) (Test is whether a reasonable person who is motivated to improve his or her health would accept the proffered treatment); Dorris v. Mississippi Regional Housing Authority, 695 So.2d 567 (Miss. 1997) (included in the court's reasons for finding the refusal to undergo surgery justifiable was claimant's subjective fear).

9.   Sometimes an employee's refusal of medical services may be less direct but will nevertheless raise similar problems. Suppose, for example, that in the *Braewood* case, supra, the doctors had ordered the claimant to lose weight before proceeding with rehabilitative therapy. Would the claimant's refusal or failure to lose weight be tantamount to a refusal of medical services? What if a claimant needs surgery but is ordered to stop smoking in order for surgery to be safely performed. Should claimant's inability or refusal to cease smoking be deemed an unreasonable refusal of medical care? In this context, should addiction to food or drink or tobacco be treated differently than traditional refusal of medical care? Is addiction solely a matter of will power? If the claimant makes a good faith effort, achieves substantial progress but is not completely successful in the attempt to break the addiction, should this still be treated as refusal of medical care? Does it matter whether or not the addiction exists prior to the accident in question. See Shawnee Management Corp. v. Hamilton 24 Va.App. 151, 480 S.E.2d 773 (1997) (claimant's continued smoking was refusal of treatment precluding right to compensation); reversed on rehearing 25 Va.App. 672, 492 S.E.2d 456 (1997) (evidence was sufficient to support Commission's finding that claimant's unsuccessful attempt to quit smoking was not wilful refusal of medical services).

10.   Should a refusal to accept medical treatment because of religious convictions be a basis for terminating or denying compensation? Is an individual at liberty to practice a faith of choice if to do so will result in the loss of a workers' compensation award which the employee or the employee's family needs in order to survive financially. Do statutes which authorize a forfeiture so chill the concept of free exercise as to render it illusory? On the other hand, should an employer be required to bear the increased disability costs which may result from an employee's refusal of reasonable medical care? Is the companion of freedom the responsibility to pay the costs which one's choices entail? See Martin v. Industrial Acc. Comm., 147 Cal.App.2d 137, 304 P.2d 828 (1956) (member of Jehovah's Witnesses refused to accept blood transfusion and died; held death not compensable). See, however, Montgomery v. Board of Retirement, 33 Cal.App.3d 447, 109 Cal.Rptr. 181 (5th Dist.1973), citing Sherbert v. Verner, 374 U.S. 398, 83 S.Ct. 1790, 10 L.Ed.2d 965 (1963) and holding that the principles set forth in *Martin* no longer represented the law in this field; but see Walter Nashert and Sons v. McCann, 460 P.2d 941 (Okl.1969) holding that an employee who suffered multiple work related heart attacks and then refused, because of his religious beliefs, to take doctor prescribed medicines was entitled to compensa-

tion for his heart injury attributable to the work but not for the disability attributed to his refusal of medication.

If a religious based refusal of medical treatment is permitted, an accompanying issue may be whether all religions, faiths and equivalent belief systems must be treated similarly. The court in Kemp v. Workers' Compensation Dept., 65 Or.App. 659, 672 P.2d 1343 (1983) review denied 296 Or. 638, 678 P.2d 739 (1984), held that a Workers' Compensation Department rule and a virtually identical provision in the workers' compensation statute which authorized compensation for workers who chose to be treated by "a duly accredited practitioner of a well-recognized church" violated the First Amendment to the U.S. Constitution as well as Article I sections 2 and 3 of the Oregon constitution. The court held that the state cannot extend a benefit to one person and withhold it from another because the former belongs to an established religious denomination while the latter does not. The court further reasoned that in deciding whether a principled refusal of medical treatment will work a forfeiture of workers' compensation coverage, the State must treat people equally regardless of whether they belong to recognized churches, are members of little known denominations, or are individuals "whose personal conscience without the dictates of a formal religious belief mandate no medical treatment." Compare the 1984 amendment to the Longshore and Harbor Workers' Compensation Act (1986) 33 U.S.C.A. § 907 (K)(*l*) "nothing in this chapter prevents an employee whose injury or disability has been established under this chapter from relying in good faith on treatment by prayer or spiritual means alone, in accordance with the tenets and practice of a recognized church or religious denomination." How does this statute fare in the light of the Kemp analysis?

SECTION 6. SUICIDE AS AN INTERVENING ACT OR CAUSE

FOOD DISTRIBUTORS v. ESTATE OF BALL
24 Va.App. 692, 485 S.E.2d 155 (1997).

FITZPATRICK, JUDGE

Food Distributors and its insurer (collectively referred to as "employer") contend that the Workers' Compensation Commission ("commission") erred in finding that (1) Kenneth Merrill Ball's (decedent) death by suicide was causally related to his compensable September 5, 1989 injury by accident; and (2) Code § 65.2–306(A)(1) did not bar compensation for the decedent's suicide. We conclude that the suicide was causally related to the earlier injury and that compensation was not barred.

I. BACKGROUND

On September 5, 1989, decedent suffered a compensable injury to his left shoulder when he tripped over a phone cord in his employer's office. His claim was accepted by employer and he underwent successive surgeries to his shoulder in October 1989, February 1990, and October 1990. Ultimately, decedent was diagnosed with post-traumatic impingement syndrome and with a permanent thirty-three percent "impairment of the upper extremity or twenty percent of the whole person." Despite the three operations, rehabilitation, and medication, decedent remained incapacitated, in pain, and depressed.

Following the injury, due to his chronic pain, decedent was unable to work full time or to engage in simple, repetitive tasks. He also suffered from insomnia. The pain began immediately after his injury and continued throughout the rest of his life. Decedent described his pain as an aching in his left shoulder, accompanied by the sensation of pins and needles and numbness throughout his left arm and hand. Decedent's inability to work and to provide for his family led to low self-esteem and depression. He went from being an "outgoing, vibrant person" prior to his injury to becoming "someone who was very morose, moody, and at times angry." Decedent's treating orthopedic surgeon, Dr. Thomas W. Daugherty, referred decedent to Dr. Bernard J. Lewis for psychological counseling.

Before he was seen by Dr. Lewis, decedent's depression worsened, and he attempted suicide in December 1990. He was hospitalized at the Winchester Medical Center and treated by Dr. Bob Lizer. Following his release from the hospital, decedent began individual and group counseling with Dr. Lewis, who became his treating psychologist at the Chronic Pain Program of Psychological Health Associates, Ltd. Decedent continued treatment with Dr. Lewis until his death. Decedent continually took pain medication and antidepressants following his first suicide attempt. Five years later, decedent committed suicide by taking a drug overdose. He was fifty-six at the time of his death, and he is survived by his wife, Mrs. Ball, and two daughters.

Decedent's estate and widow (claimant) filed a claim for benefits with the commission on February 22, 1995 and requested death and other benefits pursuant to the Workers' Compensation Act. In an opinion dated April 16, 1996, the commission relied on Dr. Lewis' opinion regarding causation and the doctrine of compensable consequences to find decedent's action outside the scope of the bar of Code § 65.2–306(A)(1). The commission reviewed the history of decedent's injury, pain, depression, and treatment, as well as evidence presented by Dr. Lewis, Mrs. Ball, Dr. Daugherty, and Dr. Bruce M. Smoller. Based on this review, the commission determined that:

> From this record the Deputy Commissioner concluded that the evidence preponderates in establishing a direct and proximate causal connection between the decedent's September 5, 1989, industrial accident and his death on February 12, 1995. We agree. Dr. Lewis has been the treating psychologist since 1990. His extensive reports over the course of his treatment document overwhelmingly the fact that the most significant stressor in the claimant's life was his "intractable pain" resulting in incapacity and depression. Dr. Lewis' unequivocal opinion linking the decedent's death to his chronic pain and resulting depression is supported repeatedly by Dr. Lewis'

ongoing assessments. Dr. Smoller's opinion attributing the depression and suicide to other factors has minimal support in the record.

The employer argues that Code § 65.2–306(A)(1) bars compensation for suicide. However, as the Deputy Commissioner noted, Mr. Ball's industrial accident in 1989 was not self-inflicted. His suicide was a consequence of the depression resulting from the compensable accident. Therefore, the claim is not barred by this section of the Act. Employer appeals the commission's award of benefits to claimant.

II. DOCTRINE OF COMPENSABLE CONSEQUENCES

Employer argues that the commission erred in awarding benefits to claimant because decedent's suicide was an independent and willful act that barred compensation. Code § 65.2–306(A)(1) provides in pertinent part that "[n]o compensation shall be awarded to the employee or his dependents for an injury or death caused by: (1) The employee's willful misconduct or intentional self-inflicted injury." Employer's argument presents an issue not yet addressed by this Court.

It is undisputed that decedent's initial injury in 1989 was compensable. It is also undisputed that "[t]he doctrine of compensable consequences is well established and has been in existence for many years" in Virginia. Williams Industries, Inc. v. Wagoner, 24 Va.App. 181, 480 S.E.2d 788 (1997). This doctrine, also known as the chain of causation rule, provides that " 'where ... the chain of causation from the original industrial injury to the condition for which compensation is sought is direct, and not interrupted by any intervening cause attributable to the [employee's] own intentional conduct, then the subsequent [condition] should be compensable.' " Leadbetter, Inc. v. Penkalski, 21 Va.App. 427, 432, 464 S.E.2d 554, 556 (1995) (quoting American Smelting & Refining Co. v. Industrial Comm'n, 25 Ariz.App. 532, 544 P.2d 1133, (1976)). Moreover, [o]nce an injury is compensable, the employer is liable for the full extent of the injury: the fact that complications arise or the injury worsens does not alter the compensable nature of the injury. "When the primary injury is shown to have arisen out of and in the course of employment, every natural consequence that flows from the injury likewise arises out of the employment, unless it is the result of an independent intervening cause attributable to claimant's own intentional conduct." Imperial Trash Service v. Dotson, 18 Va.App. 600, 445 S.E.2d 716, 720 (1994) (quoting Morris v. Badger. Powhatan/Figgie Int'l, Inc., 3 Va.App. 276, 348 S.E.2d 876 (1986)). "In other words, where a causal connection between the initial compensable injury and the subsequent injury is established, the doctrine of compensable consequences extends the coverage of the Workers' Compensation Act to the subsequent injury because the subsequent injury is treated as if it occurred in the course of and arising out of the employee's employment." American Filtrona Co. v. Hanford, 16 Va.App. 159, 428 S.E.2d 511, 513 (1993) (quoting Bartholow Drywall Co. v. Hill, 12 Va.App. 790, 407 S.E.2d 1, 3 (1991)).

Although we have long accepted the doctrine of compensable consequences, we have yet to examine its application in the context of death by suicide. However, we are guided by the decisions of our sister states that have considered this issue. Initially, we note the West Virginia Supreme Court of Appeals' observation that "[m]ost [suicide] cases ... present the same pattern of facts: a severe, or extremely painful, or hopelessly incurable injury, followed by a deranged mental state ranging from depression to violent lunacy, followed in turn by suicide." Hall v. State Workmen's Compensation Commissioner, 172 W.Va. 87, 303 S.E.2d 726 (1983). In addressing such circumstances, other states generally apply one of two rules.[1]

Under the minority rule, known as the rule in Sponatski's Case, 220 Mass. 526, 108 N.E. 466 (1915) or the "voluntary wilful choice test," the requisite mental derangement is defined as: "[A]n insanity of such violence as to cause the victim to take his own life through an uncontrollable impulse or in a delirium of frenzy without conscious volition to produce death, having a knowledge of the physical consequences of the act." 1A Arthur Larson, Workmen's Compensation Law § 36.21.

Additionally, this rule proscribes the following behavior: "[W]here the resulting insanity is such as to cause suicide through a voluntary willful choice determined by a moderately intelligent mental power which knows the purpose and the physical effect of the suicidal act, even though choice is dominated and ruled by a disorderly mind, then there is a new and independent agency which breaks the chain of causation arising from the injury." Id. This minority rule is steadily losing ground.[2]

The rule adopted by the majority of states is known as the "chain of causation" rule , which provides that suicide is compensable if the injury produces mental derangement and the mental derangement produces suicide. Larson, supra § 36.00.

This theory focuses not upon any particularized state of mind or mental disease, but upon the causal link between a work-related injury and ultimate death by suicide. The rationale ... of the rule is grounded in advances in modern psychiatry and a recognition that volition may be negated by a deterioration in mental health short of insanity or derangement. Where a direct causal link can be established between a work-related injury and a disturbance of the mind which leads to suicide, compensation will not be barred. Wells v. Harrell, 714 S.W.2d 498 (Ky.Ct.App.1986).

Applying this rationale, the Supreme Court of Oklahoma held that the applicable statute did not preclude payment of death benefits to the

---

1. Two other rules have been developed, the New York rule and the English rule. The New York rule "is generally a chain of causation test but with the possible requirement of physical damage to the brain itself." State v. Ramsey, 839 P.2d 936, 940 (Wyo.1992). The English rule states that the "insanity must be a direct result of the injury itself or the shock produced by it, and not an indirect result caused by brooding over the injury and its its conse-

quences." Id. As these two rules are rarely, if ever, applied, we do not address them for the purposes of this opinion.

2. The Sponatski case itself was reversed legislatively, as Massachusetts amended its statute to provide for compensation when "due to the injury, the employee was of such unsoundness of mind as to make him irresponsible for his act of suicide." Larson, supra § 36.21.

surviving spouse and dependents of an injured worker who committed suicide after incurring a work-related injury. See Stroer v. Georgia Pacific Corporation, 672 P.2d 1158 (Okla.1983).[3] In Stroer, a factually similar case, decedent injured his shoulder. Despite surgery and extensive therapy, he never regained the full use of his shoulder. Approximately eighteen months following his injury, decedent shot himself. His widow, daughter, best friend, and attending physician testified that after the accident, decedent became unhappy, depressed, antisocial and unstable, and that his depression was caused by his inability to continue to work, earn a living, or be physically active. Id. at 1160. As in the instant case, the employer in Stroer presented the testimony of an expert witness, who formed his opinion based on his review of decedent's medical records without ever having seen the decedent. The expert opined that it was possible that decedent's depression was caused by factors other than his injury. Id. at 1160–61. The court disagreed. It analyzed the statute denying benefits for an employee's intentionally self-inflicted injury, and observed that "[t]he majority of jurisdictions whose workers' compensation statutes contain an exclusion for wilful or intentional injury have adopted the chain of causation test as the criterion for interpreting the term 'wilful', 'purposeful' or 'intentional.' " The court then articulated the chain of causation rule in detail:

> [A]n employee's death by suicide is compensable if the original work-related injuries result in the employee's becoming dominated by a disturbance of mind directly caused by his/her injury and its consequences, such as extreme pain and despair, of such severity to override normal or rational judgment. The act of suicide is not an intervening cause of death and the chain of causation is not broken in cases where the incontrovertible evidence reflects that, but for the injury, there would have been no suicide. A suicide committed under these circumstances cannot be held to be intentional even though the act itself may be volitional. The chain of causation rule places the burden on the claimant to prove by a preponderance of the evidence that there was an unbroken chain of causation between the compensable injury, the disturbance of mind, and the ultimate suicide. The direct causal connection between the work-related injury and the suicide must not be overpowered and nullified by influences originating solely outside the employment. Id at 1161.

Accordingly, the court affirmed the award to decedent's widow. See also Estate of Jenkins v. Recchi America, 658 So.2d 157 (Fla.App.1995) (finding that suicide was not willful within the meaning of the statute; thus, it was compensable); Wells v. Harrell, 714 S.W.2d 498 (Ky.Ct.App. 1986) ("[w]here a direct causal link can be established between a work-related injury and a disturbance of the mind which leads to suicide, compensation will not be barred"); Campbell v. Young Motor Co., 211 Mont. 68, 684 P.2d 1101 (1984) (finding a causal connection; stating that

---

3. The statute allowed compensation for the work-related death of an employee "except where the injury is occasioned by the willful intention of the injured employee to bring about injury to himself...." Id. at 1160.

"the injury and the post-injury trauma, mental as well as physical, may take a path anticipated by no one, but nonetheless [be] traceable to the injury itself"); Schell v. Buell ECD Co., 102 N.M. 44, 690 P.2d 1038, (App.1983) ("once causation has been established, ... the act of suicide cannot then be said to be wilful or intentional within the meaning of the statute"); Hall v. State Workmen's Compensation Commissioner, 172 W.Va. 87, 303 S.E.2d 726 (1983) (employee's suicide is compensable provided injury sustained arose in the course of and resulted from covered employment). See also George W. Jackson Mental Health Center v. Lambie, 49 Ark.App. 139, 898 S.W.2d 479, (1995) (allowing compensation for suicide caused by stress rather than by physical injury).

Additionally, the commission has followed this rationale in deciding suicide cases. See, e.g., Confer v. Arban & Carosi, Inc., 63 O.I.C. 66 (1984) (a case in which the issues were whether decedent's suicide was statutorily barred and whether the suicide was caused by decedent's initial injury.)[5] In Confer, the commission adopted the majority rule:

> [T]he appropriate test to be adopted in Virginia is that designated as the chain-of-causation rule, wherein where the injury and its consequences directly result in the worker's loss of normal judgment and domination by a disturbance of the mind causing the suicide, his suicide is compensable, with a suicide committed by the worker suffering from this degree of disturbance not to be considered "willful" or an "intentional" injury even though the action is volitional since the suicide relates back to the original injury rather than existing independently of the injury. Id. at 80.

Additionally, the commission explained as follows:

> [W]e agree with the basic tenet behind those cases adhering to the chain of causation, that recent psychiatric advances point to the fact that the consequences of an accidental injury can be so devastating that they influence the employee's mind to the point that the employee understands the consequences of the act of destruction but the employee is unable to resist the impulse to take his own life. Under such circumstances we do not find that the act is independent of the accident nor that it is willful within the meaning of [the statute]. Id. at 80–81.

" 'It is well settled that where the construction of a statute has been uniform for many years in administrative practice, and has been acquiesced in by the General Assembly, such construction is entitled to great weight....' " Holly Farms v. Carter, 15 Va.App. 29, 422 S.E.2d 165, (1992) (quoting Dan River Mills, Inc. v. Unemployment Compensation Comm'n, 195 Va.997, 81 S.E.2d 620, (1954)). The commission consistently has affirmed its adoption of the chain of causation rule in suicide cases. See, e.g., Ball v. Food Distributors, VWC File No. 1447752 (April 16, 1996); Stone v. Formex, Inc., VWC File No.1652559 (May 15,

---

5. This case was decided under Code § 65.1 which read that "[n]o compensation shall be allowed for an injury or death: (1) Due to the employee's willful misconduct, including intentional self-inflicted injury...."

1996); Wheeler v. Pomalco Corporation, VWC File No. 1529329 (October 7, 1992); Confer v. Arban & Carosi, Inc., 63 O.I.C. 66 (1984). Accordingly, we find both the commission's construction of the statute and rationale of the majority rule compelling.

III. FINDING OF CAUSATION

Lastly, employer argues that the commission relied on less than credible evidence in finding that decedent's suicide was a compensable consequence of his original industrial accident. Specifically, employer contends that the commission improperly relied on Dr. Lewis' opinion and disregarded the opinion of Dr. Smoller. Additionally, employer asserts that the evidence failed to substantiate that decedent suffered a "loss of normal judgment and domination by a disturbance of the mind."

On appeal, we view the evidence in the light most favorable to the prevailing party below. R.G. Moore Bldg. Corp. v. Mullins, 10 Va.App. 211, 390 S.E.2d 788 (1990). We will not disturb the factual determination of causation if credible evidence supports the finding, even if the record contains evidence to the contrary. Ingersoll–Rand Co. v. Musick, 7 Va.App. 684, 376 S.E.2d 814 (1989); Wagner Enters., Inc. v. Brooks, 12 Va.App. 890, 407 S.E.2d 32, (1991). Additionally, "[q]uestions raised by conflicting medical opinions will be decided by the commission," Penley v. Island Creek Coal Co., 8 Va.App. 310, 381 S.E.2d 231, (1989); and "when an attending physician is positive in his diagnosis..., great weight will be given by the courts to his opinion." Pilot Freight Carriers, Inc. v. Reeves, 1 Va.App. 435, 339 S.E.2d 570 (1986).

In the instant case, the record demonstrates that the commission reviewed substantial medical and other evidence to conclude that decedent's suicide was causally connected to his original compensable injury. The commission considered the testimony of decedent's widow, Mrs. Ball, and reviewed records kept by decedent's treating orthopedic surgeon, Dr. Daugherty. Included in Dr. Daugherty's records is his final diagnosis of decedent's condition as a "thirty-three percent impairment of the upper extremity, or twenty percent of the whole person." Dr. Daugherty's records also reflect his opinion that "Mr. Ball has a post traumatic reactive depression leading to hospitalization ... [which] is directly and causally related to the injury which he sustained and for which he has been under the care of Winchester Surgical Clinic physicians...."

Additional medical records were made part of the record in this case. Dr. Lizer, decedent's treating physician at Winchester Medical Center, described decedent's depression as follows: "[T]his patient reported increasing depression over the past year. He had multiple stressors. Most significantly, he had had a shoulder injury resulting in a significant period of disability." Included in Dr. Lewis' medical records and correspondence is his opinion regarding decedent's depression. Dr. Lewis opined that "Mr. Ball's current condition is clearly and directly related to his left shoulder and subsequent surgery.... The psychological factors we are dealing with are directly related to the pain and the depression which frequently accompanies this [condition]." Following decedent's suicide, Dr. Lewis wrote:

> [I]n my opinion, Mr. Ball's suicide is directly related to the chronic pain he struggled with in both shoulders.... [T]his pain resulted in considerable depression and several periods of suicidal ideation as the only way out of his pain and depression.... [H]is death is clearly a direct result of the chronic pain and depression associated with his original work related injury.

At employer's request, a psychiatrist, Dr. Smoller, reviewed decedent's records, interviewed decedent's widow, and issued an opinion regarding the cause of decedent's suicide. The commission summarized Dr. Smoller's findings as follows:

> Dr. Bruce M. Smoller, M.D., psychiatrist, concluded that "shoulder injuries of this type do not ordinarily cause depression which would end in suicide." He surmised that a number of factors had a bearing on the suicide, including a possible biological component, loss of position in the family business, personality factors, and marital problems. Dr. Smoller stated these other factors were as important as or more important than the chronic pain.

In weighing the testimony of Dr. Lewis and Dr. Smoller, the commission specifically found:

> Dr. Lewis has been the treating psychologist since 1990. His extensive reports over the course of his treatment document overwhelmingly the fact that the most significant stressor in the claimant's life was his "intractable pain" resulting in incapacity and depression. Dr. Lewis' unequivocal opinion linking the decedent's death to his chronic pain and resulting depression is supported repeatedly by Dr. Lewis' ongoing assessments. Dr. Smoller's opinion attributing the depression and suicide to other factors has minimal support in the record.

Viewing the evidence in the light most favorable to claimant, we find that credible evidence supports the commission's determination that decedent's death was causally related to his earlier compensable injury and that Code § 65.2–306(A)(1) does not bar recovery under these circumstances.

Affirmed.

Notes

1. The *Ball* opinion provides a review of the varying approaches taken by the states in the work related suicide cases. As *Ball* illustrates, the issue of suicide raises difficult questions regarding the proper relationship between causation (as developed in the criminal law and tort law contexts) and the goals of the workers' compensation system. When the employee is the victim, not of an outside agent, but of his own self destructive act, can logic support the claim that "the act causing death [is] an intervening act but not an intervening cause." See State v. Ramsey, 839 P.2d 936, 940 (Wyo.1992).

Would it be better to recognize that the traditional understanding of legal causation is not as relevant because of the humane objectives of workers' compensation which favor payment of death benefits when an employee chooses to end life rather than live with the consequences of work related injuries? See, e.g., Globe Security Systems Co. v. WCAB, 518 Pa. 544, 553, 544 A.2d 953, 957 (1988) in which the court found the chain of causation test consistent with the humanitarian purposes of the workers' compensation system.

2.   While usually, as in the *Ball* case, the suicide occurs as a consequence of a compensable physical injury, compensation is also awarded on occasion where the original work injury is a mental or emotional disturbance attributed to the stress or demands of the job. See, e.g., Wilder v. Russell Library Co., 107 Conn. 56, 139 A. 644 (1927) (a temperamentally overconscientious librarian whose work was demanding and highly frustrating committed suicide; held compensation awarded); Anderson v. Armour & Co., 257 Minn. 281, 101 N.W.2d 435 (1960) (truck driver with a 25 year record of safe driving, while in the course of employment, ran into a pedestrian; after six weeks of brooding he took his life; held death compensable); Fitzgibbons' Case, 374 Mass. 633, 373 N.E.2d 1174 (1978) (employee suffered severe mental shock when fellow worker whom he had ordered to quell an inmate disturbance was killed by inmates; employee's mental condition deteriorated for three weeks at which time he killed himself; death held compensable); Globe Security Systems Co. v. WCAB, 518 Pa. 544, 544 A.2d 953 (1988) (employee, security guard at a liquor store, thwarted a store robbery but in process accidentally shot one of the would be robbers; apparently upset by this, the employee then turned the gun on himself taking his own life; held death compensable); and Chu v. WCAB, 49 Cal.App.4th 1176, 57 Cal.Rptr.2d 221 (1996) (employee, a police sergeant, suffered from severe work related stress which lead to depression and eventual suicide; held death compensable).

Chapter 8

COMPENSATION FOR NON-FATAL INJURY

INTRODUCTION TO THIS CHAPTER

At the outset, the student must bear in mind that the intent of a workers' compensation law is not to furnish damages for physical injury in the common law sense. The ultimate purpose is to provide for payments of money to, or for the benefit of, an injured employee, which payments are intended to mitigate the disastrous economic effects of a work injury. These payments are usually called "benefits". If the injury does not cause death, they fall into two general categories: (1) medical and rehabilitation benefits; and (2) disability benefits.

Provisions pertaining to medical and rehabilitation benefits involve fewer legal disputes than do disability benefits provisions. Section 1 highlights judicial efforts to define the scope of the employer's obligation to provide medical care and rehabilitation for the injured worker. Section 2 surveys a variety of issues pertaining to disability benefits. Specifically, the student's attention is directed to kinds of disability, the general concept of disability, disputes that arise in applying that general concept, the amount of and method of determining compensation, and proof of disability. It is in this area that the states have met some of the most difficult practical problems in the administration of the workers' compensation system. The third section of this chapter considers possible ways to apportion responsibility for the cumulative effect of successive injuries. Section 4 concludes this chapter with a discussion of how to coordinate an award of workers' compensation benefits with other payments that may be available from public or private sources.

SECTION 1.   MEDICAL AND REHABILITATION BENEFITS

SQUEO v. COMFORT CONTROL CORP.
Supreme Court of New Jersey, 1985.
99 N.J. 588, 494 A.2d 313.

Garibaldi, J.

The primary issue in this workers' compensation case is whether the construction of a self-contained apartment attached to the home of an injured worker's parents may constitute "medical, surgical or other treatment ... necessary to cure and relieve" or "other appliance" under N.J.S.A. 34:15–15 of the Workers' Compensation Act (Act); and if so, whether there is sufficient credible evidence in the record to support the finding that the construction of the apartment addition was necessary and that its cost was reasonable.

The petitioner, Eugene M. Squeo (Squeo), is a quadriplegic. He was injured in 1978 when he fell from a roof while working for respondent, Comfort Control Corp. (Comfort Control). He is totally and permanently disabled. In 1979, a judgment ordering disability payments was entered by a judge of the Division of Workers' Compensation.

In February, 1982, Squeo filed an Application for Review or Modification of Formal Award seeking, *inter alia,* an order requiring Comfort Control to construct a self-contained apartment attached to the home of his parents. [Instead of the usual addition of a room and bath, with ingress to and egress from the home, the plan contemplated a separate apartment attached to the home. The apartment would contain a bedroom, kitchen, living room, bathroom, carport, basement, and hydraulic lift, and would require its own electricity, plumbing and heating. The architect estimated the cost to be in excess of $65,000.] The compensation court ordered that such construction be undertaken. [It ordered that Squeo be charged with the cost of constructing any additions to the standard apartment and with the care, maintenance, capital repairs, insurance, and any taxation to be associated with the construction.] The Appellate Division affirmed the Order of the compensation court 194 N.J.Super. 366, 476 A.2d 1265. [The Appellate Division instructed that the "cost of the apartment not go beyond providing for petitioner's basic need for independent living quarters." It ordered that the employer be secured by a mortgage executed by Squeo's parents so that if Squeo should no longer use the apartment, the employer would be compensated for any significant value the apartment may add to the property in the event it is sold, rented, or mortgaged.] We granted Comfort Control's petition for certification. 99 N.J. 148, 491 A.2d 664 (1984).

. . .

N.J.S.A. 34:15–15 in pertinent part provides:

> The employer shall furnish to the injured worker such medical, surgical and *other treatment,* and hospital service *as shall be necessary to cure and relieve the worker of the effects of the injury* and to restore the functions of the injured member or organ where such restoration is possible; ... the Division of Workers' Compensation after investigating the need of the same and giving the employer an opportunity to be heard, shall determine that such physicians' and surgeons' treatment and hospital services *are or were necessary and that the fees for the*

same are reasonable and shall make an order requiring the employer to pay for or furnish the same.

* * *

When an injured employee may be partially or wholly relieved of the effects of a permanent injury, by use of an artificial limb or *other appliance,* which phrase shall also include artificial teeth or glass eye, the Division of Workers' Compensation, *acting under competent medical advice, is empowered to determine the character and nature of such limb or appliance, and to require the employer or the employer's insurance carrier to furnish the same.* [Emphasis added.]

Pursuant to N.J.S.A. 34:15–15, it is evident that an employer must provide an injured worker with "other treatment" or "other appliance" that serves to cure and relieve a worker of the effects of his work-connected injury. The employer contends, however, that "other treatment" or "appliance" under N.J.S.A. 34:15–15 is not intended to encompass the construction of a self-contained apartment.

There is no express legislative or judicial definition of these terms in New Jersey. However, it has long been recognized that the Act is remedial social legislation and as such is to be liberally construed so that its beneficent purposes may be accomplished. * * *

The expansion in coverage since the Act's inception, as evidenced by the legislative history of N.J.S.A. 34:15–15, supports a liberal interpretation of the Act.

When N.J.S.A. 34:15–15 was first enacted in 1911 it simply provided:

During the first two weeks after the injury the employer shall furnish reasonable medical and hospital services and medicines, as and when needed, not to exceed one hundred dollars in value, unless the employee refuses to allow them to be furnished by the employer. [L.1911, c. 95, § 14.]

The Act was amended in 1913, and again in 1919. The latter amendment extended recovery under the Act beyond medical and hospital services and medicines.

[I]n severe cases requiring unusual medical or surgical treatment or calling for artificial limb or other mechanical appliances, the employee or his representative shall be authorized to present a petition to the Workmen's Compensation Bureau, and the Commissioner, deputy commissioner or referee thereof is hereby empowered, when warranted by the evidence produced, to order additional services, artificial limbs or other appliances not to exceed in total the sum of two hundred dollars, or to extend over a period not to exceed in total seventeen weeks. This paragraph shall apply only to nonfatal cases. [L.1919, c. 93, § 4]

In 1922, the statute was amended again and its coverage expanded. The 1922 amended statute, virtually identical to the present version, is especially pertinent to our analysis. The 1922 amendment removed the monetary limitation on benefits to be paid by the employer and authorized the Workmen's Compensation Bureau to allow such treatment or services as it found to be "necessary." Moreover, the words "unusual medical surgical treatment" were omitted and in lieu thereof appeared the words "medical, surgical and *other treatment,* and hospital services as shall be necessary to cure and relieve the workman of the effects of the injury." (Emphasis added).

* * *

Although this Court has liberally construed the Act to promote its beneficent purposes, we have always imposed the limitation that no expense incurred may be recovered that is not shown to be reasonable and necessary by sufficient competent medical evidence. . . .

We have also emphasized that claimant bears the burden thus to establish his claim. *Kahle v. Plochman, supra,* 85 N.J. at 548, 428 A.2d 913.

II

Other jurisdictions have also liberally construed the terms "treatment" and "appliance" so as to allow such expenses as may be said to be reasonable and necessary for the cure of an ailment or relief of its symptoms. Courts have been generous in allowing recovery as "treatment" not only the cost of medical and hospital services, but also of necessary incidentals such as transportation, apparatus, and even nursing care furnished by a member of claimant's own family. 2 A. Larson, *Workmen's Compensation Law* § 61.00 (1983).

For instance, under the Florida Workmen's Compensation Statute, an act similar to ours, an employer was required to reimburse claimant for expenses incurred for child care. Claimant's inability to care for her child due to a work-connected injury resulted in the development of a severe depressive neurosis. In light of the extreme circumstances, the court held it medically necessary for treatment of her psychiatric condition and hence for claimant's recovery, that her daughter be placed in a nursery school. *Doctors Hosp. of Lake Worth v. Robinson,* 411 So.2d 958 (Dist.Ct.App.1982).

In *Talas v. Correct Piping Co., Inc.,* 435 N.E.2d 22, 27 (Ind.1982), the Supreme Court of Indiana awarded benefits for the palliative care of claimant, a quadriplegic, provided through nonprofessional nursing services while claimant's wife was working. The Court found that the nursing care was required to prevent the development of life-threatening disease, such as pneumonia; therefore the care could be said to be within the statutory requirement of being "necessary to limit or reduce the amount and extent of such impairment." * * *

[I]n *Haga v. Clay Hyder Trucking Lines,* 397 So.2d 428 (Fla.Dist.Ct. App.), review denied, 402 So.2d 609 (Fla.1981), the employer of a double amputee who had suffered numerous complications after his injury was ordered to assume the reasonable costs for installation and maintenance of an in-ground pool with access facilities for the handicapped, or, in the alternative, to provide the claimant with daily access, along with reimbursement expenses, to a pool within a reasonable distance from claimant's home. In reliance upon the testimony of claimant's treating physicians and because of the claimant's severe and unusual injuries, the court held that the installation of a swimming pool was medically necessary to provide him with needed cardiovascular exercise as part of his rehabilitation program and to control his weight. * * *

In *Peace River Elec. Corp. v. Choate,* 417 So.2d 831 (Fla.Dist.Ct.App. 1982), petition for review dismissed, 429 So.2d 7 (Fla.1983), the court ordered that claimant be awarded rent-free use of a wheelchair-accessible modular home to replace the dilapidated wood shed he had been occupying. All title and right of ownership would remain in the employer, as would the responsibility to provide adequate maintenance. The claimant would assume responsibility for real estate taxes and assessments. The court there rejected the employer's suggested alternative of remodeling claimant's existing dwelling since "nothing short of bulldozing the dwelling would serve to remedy the situation." *Id.* at 832.

In *Pine Bluff Parks and Recreation v. Porter,* 6 Ark.App. 154, 639 S.W.2d 363 (1982), although the relevant statute made no express provision for rental payments, the court ordered the employer of a paraplegic to assume liability for part of the rental cost of living in a project designed for paraplegics. The Workers' Compensation Commission, after hearing testimony from claimant's treating physician and from a hospital administrator, who himself was a quadriplegic, determined that the requested program in the special facility for the claimant was reasonable and necessary under the Arkansas Compensation Law. That law requires that an employer supply an employee with "services and apparatus" as necessitated by an employee's injuries. *Id.* at 366. Accordingly, the court held that the Commission should determine what portion of the total cost to the claimant of living in the special facility was attributable to those services and apparatus required to be furnished by the employer under the compensation law and what portion was noncompensable under that statute;[3] ... *Contra, Low Splint Coal Co., Inc. v. Bolling,* 224 Va. 400, 297 S.E.2d 665 (1982) (court's decision to disallow claimant's request for an improved entrance ramp at rear of residence and modifications to bathroom turned on language of particular statute. Court found that such structural improvements could not be considered to be either "other necessary medical attention" or "reasonable and necessary vocational rehabilitation training services" within purview of Virginia Compensation Statute).

. . .

3. The court recognized that the employer had a statutory obligation to furnish ramps, rails, wheelchairs, widened doors, special commodes, and shower facilities and other *apparatus* required by claimant. However, it questioned whether there existed any liability for custodial care, lodging, or other non-medical services such as housekeeping. *Pine Bluff Parks, supra,* 639 S.W.2d at 366.

It is important to note that in those cases in which courts have allowed recovery for unusual requests, for example, the construction of a swimming pool or use of a modular home, they have premised their decision on the unique circumstances of the particular case. ...

In view of the remedial nature of the New Jersey Workers' Compensation Act and the liberal construction accorded to it, we conclude that under certain unique circumstances, when there is sufficient and competent medical evidence to establish that the requested "other treatment" or "appliance" is reasonable and necessary to relieve the injured worker of the effect of his injuries, the construction of an apartment addition may be within the ambit of N.J.S.A. 34:15–15. We caution however that it is only the unusual case that may warrant such extraordinary relief.

III

We find this to be such an "unusual case," and, consequently, the apartment addition is to be considered "other treatment" within the intendment of N.J.S.A. 34:15–15. The facts before us support this conclusion.

Dr. Sullivan testified that instead of the usual eight weeks required by most quadriplegics to recover, Squeo was unwell for about two and one-half years. He had "just about every complication that God ever put on earth for him." Squeo's living arrangements were further complicated by the fact that he had been living independently of his parents prior to his accident. As Dr. Sullivan testified, this "*is an unusual case* where the individual is twenty-five years old when he sustains the injury and he is already out on his own and now he has to be reintroduced into the family picture." (Emphasis added).

Apart from his quadriplegia, which cannot be reversed, and physical complications, which are treated as they arise, Squeo has suffered serious psychological setbacks. No one disputes that these emotional problems are a result of his work-connected injury and its consequences. Nor is it disputed that Squeo's depression is so aggravated by living in the nursing home that he has tried to kill himself on three occasions. We find these three factors—Squeo's unremitting physical ailments, his age and his having lived independently of his parents for several years prior to the accident, and his psychological dread of institutional living, culminating in three suicide attempts—are sufficient to consider this an unusual case calling for unusual relief.

Moreover, we find that competent medical testimony exists on this record to hold that the construction of the apartment addition was reasonable and necessary treatment to relieve Squeo of his severe mental depression. *See Howard v. Harwood's Restaurant Co., supra*, 25 N.J. at 93, 135 A.2d 161.

It is undisputed that the nursing home is the worst place in the world for Squeo. Dr. Crain testified that Squeo's depression was rooted in the resentment and frustration he experienced while living in the nursing home, where he felt his life was neglected. He stated that continuous living in that nursing home environment would certainly lead to yet another suicide attempt, and perhaps a successful one. Other witnesses, Anthony and Davis, testified that it was extremely important to the functional well-being of a disabled person that he be permitted to choose his own living environment. Anthony testified that lack of options makes the disabled "angry, frustrated and depressed." Davis opined that confining Squeo to a nursing home would condemn him "to a fate worse, worse than death." Further, the witnesses' testimony indicates that relegating Squeo to a state-sponsored facility would neither fulfill Squeo's psychological need for independent living, nor assuage his fear of institutional living, nor lessen his suicidal inclinations. . . .

We stress that in determining what is reasonable and necessary, the touchstone is not the injured worker's desires or what he thinks to be most beneficial. Rather, it is what is shown by sufficient competent evidence to be reasonable and necessary to cure and relieve him. Here, that relief is of a psychological nature. The source of Squeo's severe mental depression is his fear of institutionalization. The testimony of all witnesses substantiates that this psychological disturbance can be relieved only by Squeo's living in an independent setting. Thus, we find sufficient credible evidence on the record to establish that construction of the apartment addition is necessary to cure and relieve the mental depression caused by Squeo's work-related injury.

There is also sufficient credible evidence to establish that the cost of the addition is reasonable. While there are no monetary limitations on the cost of treatment set forth in the statute, the cost must be reasonable. Both the compensation court and the Appellate Division were careful to restrict the cost of the proposed construction. Further, the Appellate Division provided the employer with protection against Squeo's failure to use the apartment by ordering Squeo's parents to execute a mortgage in the employer's favor. 194 N.J.Super. at 371, 476 A.2d 1265.

We agree with the restrictions on the cost of the construction of the apartment imposed by both the compensation judge and the Appellate Division. We find that within the limits of such restrictions the cost of the construction of the apartment will be reasonable.

The award also appears reasonable when viewed in comparison to the cost of the available alternatives which the employer was willing to pay. Although the employer indicates that the cost of the apartment would be greater than that of the other alternatives, no such evidence was submitted. In fact, while the cost of the proposed addition initially may be greater, in the long run it is likely to be far less than the expense of maintaining a young man in a nursing home or rental unit for the rest of his life.

We affirm the judgment of the Appellate Division. At oral argument we learned that the Squeos have constructed the apartment. Accordingly, we remand to the Division of Workers' Compensation for a determination as to the portion of the cost of the construction of the apartment for which the employer will be liable, within the restrictions set forth by the Division and the Appellate Division.

Notes

1. The most immediate need of an injured worker is medical attention and in many cases hospitalization. In recognition of this, all workers' compensation statutes require medical aid to be furnished to injured employees. In earlier days this class of benefits was closely circumscribed and limited as to time and amount. All states but a few now provide for medical aid on an "unlimited" basis or authorize the administrative body to extend the time of medical aid indefinitely. See, U.S. Dept. of Labor, Employment Standards Administration, Office of Workers' Compensation Programs, *State Workers' Compensation Laws* table 5a (January 1998).

2. Medical benefits cover the reasonable cost of physicians, hospitalization, medication and other necessary treatment. As illustrated by *Squeo,* a variety of incidental care and equipment may also be covered by workers' compensation. Professional nursing services are routinely covered. See, Hopson v. Hickman, 182 Ga.App. 865, 357 S.E.2d 280 (1987); Currier v. Hruska, 228 Neb. 38, 421 N.W.2d 25 (1988). Though once a point of controversy, a majority of states today require employers to pay family members who provide medically necessary nursing services. See, Close v. Superior Excavating Co., 166 Vt. 318, 693 A.2d 729 (Vt. 1997) (collecting cases). Transportation costs incurred in connection with medical treatment are generally compensable. Sigman Meat Co. v. Industrial Claim Appeals Office, 761 P.2d 265 (Colo.App.1988) (taxi fare to and from doctor's office); Miceli v. Industrial Comm., 135 Ariz. 71, 659 P.2d 30 (1983) (out of town travel to consult a specialist). Child care expenses may be compensable if incidental to needed medical treatment. Bellone v. Industrial Claim Appeals Office, 940 P.2d 1116 (Colo.App.1997). However an employee cannot recover the cost of an airline ticket to fly in her sister to take care of her children during a one week hospitalization. Kuziel v. Pet Fair, Inc., 931 P.2d 521 (Colo.App.1996). A weight loss program was approved as part of a medical/rehabilitation plan, but the court denied approval of compensation for a stomach-stapling procedure when the claimant failed to maintain weight loss. Shepherd v. Van Ohlen Trucking, 49 Ark.App. 36, 895 S.W.2d 945 (Ark.App.1995).

Courts are divided on whether employers are obligated to modify automobiles for physically disabled workers. Compare, McDonald v. Brunswick Elec. Membership Corp., 77 N.C.App. 753, 336 S.E.2d 407 (1985) (statutory authorization of "other treatment or care" or "rehabilitative services" did not include "tangible, non-medically related items such as a van") with Terry Grantham Co. v. Industrial Comm., 154 Ariz. 180, 741 P.2d 313 (App.1987) (a van equipped for a paraplegic is an "other apparatus" whose cost is a proper medical benefit since it replaces a bodily function). See also Petrilla v. Workmen's Compensation Appeal Bd., 692 A.2d 623 (Pa. Cmwlth. 1997) (employer is not responsible for cost of vehicle, but must pay for modifications to make it wheelchair accessible).

Universal limitations on coverage are the medical necessity and reasonableness of the cost of the treatment or apparatus. An employer is not required to pay for treatment or equipment that might be medically appropriate in some instances if the medical need in the particular case is attenuated. E.g., R & T Construction Co. v. Judge, 323 Md. 514, 594 A.2d 99 (1991) (refusing to order the remodeling of the quadriplegic employee's house when the requested changes would give the claimant "a sense of increased independence and self-worth", but were not needed to provide medical "necessities"); Glinka v. Workmen's Compensation Appeal Board, 104 Pa.Cmwlth. 175, 521 A.2d 503 (1987) (disapproving medical expenses of $1,080 for weekly rubdowns when employer's physician testified that such treatment was no longer necessary).

3. One of the most controversial issues in the medical benefits area involves the selection of the treating physician. Several considerations bear on this controversy. Employees, like other patients, have an interest in choosing their own physicians. The intimate and fiduciary nature of the doctor-patient relationship suggests that a patient should be free to choose a greatly trusted doctor. This interest transcends the personal compatibility of doctor and patient. The selection of a physician may also affect the range of treatment options as well. A patient with a back injury, for example, may prefer chiropractic care to that offered by an orthopedist. These interests are advanced by giving employees great latitude in selecting their physicians. A patient's ability to select his or her physician has eroded with the rise of managed care. As discussed in note 5, infra, managed care is also an important feature of the workers' compensation system. Employers and their insurers have an interest in controlling costs. This objective can be accomplished most effectively if the party that pays the bills also selects the health care provider. Both the employer and employee have an interest in ensuring that the treating physician is competent and qualified to treat the underlying injury or illness. Yet, they may honestly disagree whether the orthopedist or the chiropractor is best qualified to treat the employee's back injury. Finally, but perhaps most importantly, each party may seek a tactical advantage in the compensation claim by selecting a physician who tends to sympathize with its side in evaluating the extent of the worker's injury.

States have found various ways to balance the competing interests of employers and employees in selecting the treating physician. The most prevalent approach is to allow the employee to make the initial selection. E.g., 820 Ill.Comp.Stat.Ann. 305/8(a); Or.Rev.Stat. § 656.245; R.I.Gen.Laws § 28–33–8. Some states require that the employee select a physician from a list prepared by a state agency or maintained by the employer. E.g., N.Y. Work.Comp. Law § 13–a (state agency); Ga.Code Ann. § 34–9–201 (employer list). A significant number of states give the employer the right to select the physician. E.g., Fla.Stat.Ann. § 440.13; N.J.Stat.Ann. § 34:15–15; N.M.Stat. Ann. § 52–1–49. In states where the employer controls the initial selection, the employee may petition the agency for a change in physicians. E.g., Colo.Rev.Stat. § 8–43–501. See also, Cal.Labor Code § 4600 (employee may change physician after a specified period of time); Ga.Code Ann. §§ 34–9–200, 34–9–201 (employee may select another physician from among those listed on the employer's list, but must petition the Board for permission to make a second change or select a physician not listed); Vt.Stat.Ann. tit. 21, § 640 (if the employee is dissatisfied with the physician selected by the employer, the employee shall have the right to select his own physician upon giving written notice to his employer). For a listing of positions of the states, see U.S. Department of Labor, Employment Standards Administration, Office of Workers' Compensation Programs, *State Workers' Compensation Laws*, Table 5b (January 1998).

4. Employers are not responsible for medical expenses incurred through unauthorized treatment. This issue often arises in jurisdictions that give employers the initial control over the selection of physicians and the employee obtains treatment from an unapproved physician. E.g., ITT–Continental Baking Co. v. Powell, 182 Ga.App. 533, 356 S.E.2d 267 (1987) (employer is not responsible for expenses of podiatrist who was not included on employer approved list of physicians), and Lavine v. SAIF Corp., 79 Or.App. 511, 718 P.2d 1391 (1986) (claimant is not entitled to payment for cost of unauthorized thermogram test).

5. The cost of medical benefits increased dramatically during the 1980's. By 1993, approximately $17.5 billion were expended for workers' compensation medical benefits. United States Chamber of Commerce, 1996 Analysis of Workers' Compensation Law vii (1996). While medical benefits once accounted for less than 25% of the total workers' compensation benefits package, they accounted for approximately 40% of all workers' compensation payments in 1993. Id .. Medical costs have risen at a faster rate for workers' compensation than in the general health care system. Between 1985 and 1990 the annual average percentage increase for workers' compensation medical costs was 15.1% while the comparable figure for non-workers' compensation medical costs was 9.9%. Stacey M. Eccleston, Managed Care and Medical Cost Containment in Workers' Compensation 4 (Workers' Compensation Research Institute 1995). Some researchers attribute the faster rise of workers' compensation medical costs to two factors. First, unlike conventional medical insurance, workers' compensation does not utilize deductibles or coinsurance that might deter patients from over-utilizing medical services. Second, historically, employers and their insurers have had little bargaining power regarding physician and hospital fees. Leslie I. Bodon and Charles A. Fleishman, Medical Costs in Workers' Compensation: Trends and Comparisons 18–19 (Workers' Compensation Research Institute 1989).

Beginning in the late 1980's, states began experimenting with various cost containment strategies. Among the common strategies in place by the mid–1990's were: limiting employee choice of medical providers; limiting changes in physicians; use of physician fee schedules; hospital payment regulation; development of treatment guidelines for common injuries; and facilitating, or in some cases mandating, the use of managed care. See Stacey M. Eccleston, Managed Care and Medical Cost Containment in Workers' Compensation 13–14 (Workers' Compensation Research Institute 1995). A few states have imposed deductibles or co-payment requirements on employee. United States Dept. Labor, Employment Standards Administration, Office of Workers' Compensation Programs, *State Workers Compensation Laws*, Table 5a (1998). More than half the states now regulate or mandate managed care in workers' compensation. Stacey M. Eccleston, Managed Care and Medical Cost Containment in Workers' Compensation 67 (Workers' Compensation Research Institute 1995). For a detailed discussion of how a "public health" model of managed care might be structured to optimize a reduction in workplace accident costs, see Dean M. Hashimoto, The Future

Role of Managed Care and Capitation in Workers' Compensation, 22 Am. J. L. & Med. 233 (1996). Many states have intensified their efforts to combat fraud as a means of containing workers' compensation costs, including medical costs. E.g. Fla. Stat. Ann. § 440.105. This development is discussed in Chapter 10.

Pennsylvania purports to control medical costs by authorizing insurers to suspend payments for medical treatment pending an independent review of whether the treatment is "reasonable and necessary". Payments can be suspended without prior notice to the worker or a hearing. The Supreme Court recently held that private compensation carriers who invoke these procedures are not "state actors" under the Fourteenth Amendment and that the Pennsylvania regime does not deprive injured workers of "property" within the meaning of that amendment. American Manufacturers Mutual Insurance Co. v. Sullivan, 119 S.Ct. 977 (1999).

Most of these reforms have been in place for only a short time, so their effect on cost and quality of care have not been systematically assessed. One early effort at such an assessment concluded that "traditional approaches to health care cost containment in workers' compensation programs have not effectively restrained medical cost growth." Silvana Pozzebon, Medical Cost Containment Under Workers' Compensation, 48 Indus. & Labor Rel. Rev. 153 (1994). More specifically, Professor Pozzebon found that states with limits on choice of providers have higher medical benefit expenditures than other states, the effect of fee schedules on medical costs is "less clear," and that regulation of hospital costs is "the only cost containment strategy that appears to effectively decrease medical benefit spending ..." Id., 48 Indus. & Labor Rel. Rev. at 164. Notwithstanding this cautious appraisal, medical costs have decreased in recent years. Medical benefit costs for 1994 and 1995 were $17.1 billion and $16.7 billion respectively. National Academy of Social Insurance, Workers' Compensation: Benefits, Coverage and Costs 1994–95, Table 5 (1997).

SMITH v. HASTINGS IRRIGATION PIPE CO.

Supreme Court of Nebraska, 1986.
222 Neb. 663, 386 N.W.2d 9.

GRANT, JUSTICE.

This action was brought by appellee, Linda K. Smith, to recover workmen's compensation benefits from the appellant, Hastings Irrigation Pipe Co. (Hastings Pipe). Smith was injured while working for Hastings Pipe on October 10, 1983, and filed a petition with the Nebraska Workmen's Compensation Court on July 12, 1984. After rehearing, a three-judge panel of the Workmen's Compensation Court, with one judge dissenting, modified a single-judge order and found that Smith was entitled to the costs of certain medical treatment by Dr. John L. Greene, together with temporary total disability payments during that treatment, and that Smith was entitled to rehabilitation services. Hastings Pipe appeals from that order, assigning as error the findings set out above.

* * *

[Smith suffered the amputation of several fingers while operating a punch press.]

In its other assignment of error, Hastings Pipe contends the Workmen's Compensation Court erred "In finding that the plaintiff [Smith] was entitled to vocational rehabilitation services." The record shows that Smith has a 12th–grade education and is currently attending Hastings Central Community College and taking classes which will enable her to do managerial-type duties in the retail horticultural field.

In *Evans v. American Community Stores,* 222 Neb. 538, 540, 385 N.W.2d 91, 93 (1986), we held:

> The right of an injured workman to vocational rehabilitation depends upon his inability to perform work for which he has previous training and experience. § 48–162.01; *Behrens v. Ken Corp.,* 191 Neb. 625, 216 N.W.2d 733 (1974). This is ordinarily a question of fact to be determined by the compensation court. *Pollock v. Monfort of Colorado, supra* [221 Neb. 859, 381 N.W.2d 154 (1986)].

Smith testified her arm still is essentially useless. Prior to her employment at Hastings Pipe, Smith held jobs which required two good hands and arms. Most, if not all, of these jobs were minimum-wage-type jobs. Smith's vocational training will allow her to obtain a job which will not require constant use of two good hands and arms. The Workmen's Compensation Court found vocational rehabilitation training was authorized under Neb.Rev.Stat. § 48–162.–01(6) (Reissue 1984).

The dissenting judge of the three-judge panel felt that the "loss of her long and ring fingers ... is [not] sufficient to entitle her to vocational rehabilitation ... particularly ... in view of the plaintiff's work history which shows that she has experience and training in several jobs that she can do." It is true that in her 10 years in the work force, Smith had jobs as a worker in the kitchen and dining room of a retirement home, as a filing clerk with an insurance company, as a waitress in bars and a restaurant, and as a sales clerk in various retail establishments. Smith testified, however, that each of these jobs required the use of both hands and both arms and that, although she had done such jobs in the past, she was unable to do them after her injury. Smith's testimony as to the physical requirements of each of her jobs, and her inability to perform the jobs after her injury, constituted sufficient evidence to support the findings of the majority of the panel, which found that Smith had suffered a reduction in her earning power as a result of her accident and injury and determined that Smith was entitled to rehabilitation in an effort to increase her earning capacity. The evidence before the panel was sufficient to support these findings.

We determine that the evidence before the three-judge panel was sufficient to support the award entered by the court. The judgment of the compensation court is affirmed, and Smith is allowed the sum of $1,000 for the services of her attorney in this court.

AFFIRMED.

Notes

1. Vocational rehabilitation and its relationship to medical benefits has been described by one expert as follows:

> Operationally, rehabilitation consists of a range of services bracketed by the two mentioned above—medical management and formal education. Among these services are counseling, guidance, evaluation, retraining, and job placement. Rehabilitation may involve job redesign and modifications to the work place or even to the home environment, although, most commonly, rehabilitation services are directed toward improving the individual and his job chances, rather than the environment in which he functions.

> Rehabilitation is said to be a team effort involving the physician, allied health professionals, and persons from a host of assorted disciplines—vocational education, social work, work evaluation, etc. The coordinator of the team may be a professional rehabilitation counselor. It is a continuous integrated progress, with one service melding into and flowing from the other. The focus is on the client and the accomplishment of the stated objectives, be they return to the worker's old job, or possibly some more ambitious objective such as restoration of the maximum capabilities of the person given his residual functioning capacities. If the process is truly a continuous one, then there is no real dividing line between medical and vocational rehabilitation. Yet one of the difficulties of bringing rehabilitation into workers' compensation is that the laws of some jurisdictions require such a distinction, since they provide for different payers for the different types of services.

Berkowitz, *Rehabilitation and Workers' Compensation: Incompatible or Inseparable?,* in Benefits, Costs, and Cycles in Workers' Compensation 80–81 (P. Borba and D. Appel eds. 1990).

2. The importance of vocational rehabilitation in a workers' compensation scheme has long been recognized. As early as 1916, the International Association of Industrial Accident Boards and Commissions (IAIABC) called for greater provision of rehabilitation services to the injured worker. Yet, until recently, workers' compensation statutes guaranteed few rehabilitation benefits. Today, every state has some kind of rehabilitation provision in its statute. These statutes vary widely in terms of the scope of coverage. A survey of twelve states found that awards for rehabilitation benefits are made in approximately 10% of the claims involving permanent partial disability. Variations among states in the frequency of awards are considerable. Rehabilitation benefits were awarded in 50% of the Florida claims surveyed while such benefits were awarded in only 3% of the claims surveyed in New York and Wisconsin. See, Berkowitz, *Rehabilitation and Workers' Compensation: Incompatible or Inseparable,* in Benefits, Costs, and Cycles in Workers' Compensation 79, 87–88 (P. Borba and D. Appel eds. 1990).

3. How far should states go in mandating vocational rehabilitation under workers' compensation laws? Most statutory rehabilitation provisions condition benefits on an administrative finding that rehabilitation would be "feasible," "desirable," or "necessary." See, 5 A. Larson & L. Larson,

Larson's Workers' Compensation Law § 61.23 (1998). Some courts apply these terms liberally so that rehabilitation may be considered "necessary" if it will materially assist in restoring the employee's impaired earning capacity. E.g., Norby v. Arctic Enterprises, Inc., 305 Minn. 519, 232 N.W.2d 773 (1975). Other courts adopt more restrictive interpretations and find that rehabilitation is not "necessary" unless the employee's disability rises nearly to the level of total incapacity. E.g., McInnis v. Town of Bar Harbor, 387 A.2d 739 (Me.1978).

Whether a specific rehabilitation plan will be found to be feasible or necessary often depends on the facts of the particular case. In evaluating a claim for rehabilitation benefits, courts commonly consider the relative costs and benefits of the program, the employee's worklife expectancy, and the ability and motivation of the employee. See, National Tea Co. v. Industrial Comm., 97 Ill.2d 424, 73 Ill.Dec. 575, 454 N.E.2d 672 (1983). Vocational rehabilitation benefits will not be granted when the plan is too vague, or the employee is untrainable, or the employee is capable of earning pre-injury wages without additional training. E.g., Madonna v. Industrial Comm., 171 Ill.App.3d 301, 121 Ill.Dec. 469, 525 N.E.2d 275 (1988) (rehabilitation not necessary when laborer is able to perform pre-injury work and plans for rehabilitation are vague); Hewson v. Stevenson, 225 Neb. 254, 404 N.W.2d 35 (1987) (66 year old mechanic with severe physical limitations and no other training or skills was not entitled to rehabilitation). See also, Rydwell v. Anchorage School Dist., 864 P.2d 526 (Alaska 1993) (claimant with a 0% impairment rating under the AMA Guides is not entitled to rehabilitation benefits); Ward v. Bonne Idee Aero Service, Inc., 687 So.2d 629 (La.App. 1997) (claimant who can perform old job is not entitled to rehabilitation); Bishop v. Town of Barre, 140 Vt. 564, 442 A.2d 50 (Vt. 1982) (disapproving rehabilitation plan that would cost $2,500 but would produce only $200 in annual income). On the other hand, substantial rehabilitation services will be provided when the anticipated impact on the claimant's earning capacity is great. E.g., Howlett's Tree Service v. Industrial Comm., 160 Ill.App.3d 190, 111 Ill.Dec. 836, 513 N.E.2d 82 (1987) (awarding rehabilitation benefits including a one-year course in agricultural business to a highly motivated worker with a 30 year worklife expectancy); Thom v. Lutheran Medical Center, 226 Neb. 737, 414 N.W.2d 810 (1987) (approving a two-year training course in business and computer studies for a nurse whose physical injury substantially reduced employment potential as a nurse); Held v. North Dakota Workers Compensation Bureau, 540 N.W.2d 166 (N.D.1995) (approving plan to retrain an auto service technician to work as an account clerk). Should it matter whether the proposed rehabilitation plan might give the employee a greater earning capacity than existed before the injury? Is *Smith* such a case?

When appropriate, incidental expenses are included as part of the rehabilitation award. E.g., Mosley v. Bank of Delaware, 372 A.2d 178 (Del.1977) (rehabilitation benefits include the costs of travel to and from training center); Grover v. Industrial Comm., 759 P.2d 705 (Colo.1988) (child care expenses of worker undergoing vocational training are compensable).

4. The employer may have a positive interest in vocational rehabilitation as when restoring an employee's pre-injury earning capacity would reduce the employer's liability for disability benefits. Thus, employers may

support rehabilitation efforts and press for incentives to encourage employee cooperation. In some states, disability benefits of an employee who unreasonably refuses rehabilitation may be denied or suspended. E.g., Stone v. Industrial Comm., 286 Ill.App.3d 174, 221 Ill.Dec. 373, 675 N.E.2d 280 (Ill.App.1997) (terminating temporary total disability benefits to worker who did not cooperate with rehabilitation); Paris v. J.A. Baldwin Mfg. Co., 216 Neb. 151, 342 N.W.2d 198 (1984) (disability benefits could be terminated when employee failed to cooperate with vocational training); Ga.Code Ann. § 34–9–200.1(d) ("the refusal of the employee without reasonable cause to accept rehabilitation shall entitle the board in its discretion to suspend or reduce the compensation otherwise payable . . ."). Cf. Fuhrman v. North Dakota Workers Compensation Bureau, 569 N.W.2d 269 (N.D.1997) (expense of commuting between Bismarck and Minneapolis to receive training was "good cause" for not complying with rehabilitation plan).

SECTION 2. DISABILITY BENEFITS

a. *Introduction: Duration and Degree of Disability*

Disability benefits are money payments made directly to injured workers to compensate for earnings lost as a result of compensable injuries. These benefits are sometimes also referred to as "income," "indemnity" or "cash" benefits, and are most commonly calculated as a percentage of the recipient's average weekly wage, subject to a specified dollar limit. In New York, for example, total disability is compensated at the rate of 66⅔% of the worker's average weekly wage, but no more than $400.00 per week. N.Y. Work.Comp. Law § 15. While the percentage of wages payable as compensation varies among the states, the 66⅔% figure is common. In a different approach, Michigan and Iowa define disability benefits in terms of 80% of a worker's "spendable earnings". Iowa Code Ann. § 85.34 (but not more than 184% of the average statewide weekly wage for permanent partial disability); Mich.Comp.Laws Ann. § 418.351 ("after-tax" average weekly wage). The maximum benefit payable ranges widely among the states. For example, in 1998, a totally disabled worker in Alaska could receive as much as $700 per week, Alaska Stat. § 23.30.175, whereas in Georgia, the maximum was $325. Ga.Code Ann. § 34–9–261.

Under section 104(a)(1) of the Internal Revenue Code, workers' compensation benefits are excluded from the definition of "gross income" and hence are not subject to federal income tax.

Some statutes express the maximum weekly payment as a flat dollar amount. E.g., Ga.Code Ann. § 34–9–261. In these states the maximum weekly payment remains constant until the legislature amends the statute. Other states tie the maximum weekly payment to some index, such as the state's "average weekly wage," which allows adjustment in compensation levels without legislative amendment. E.g., 820 Ill.Comp. Stat.Ann. 305/8(b)(4) (maximum weekly compensation payment is 100% of state's average weekly wage as adjusted annually.)

Benefits are often classified according to the degree and duration of disability. The degree of disability refers to its extent. A disability may be total (i.e., the worker is completely unable to work) or partial (i.e., the worker is injured, but is capable of performing some work). The duration of the disability may be temporary or permanent. These variables produce the four common categories of disability benefits: temporary total disability, temporary partial disability, permanent total disability, and permanent partial disability.

The vast majority of compensable work injuries involve a temporary total disability rendering the injured employee unable to work for the time being. Whether in the hospital or healing and recuperating at home, the worker is expected to recover fully. Accordingly, disability benefits are payable until the worker has recovered and returned to work, subject to statutory limitations as to amount and duration. While accounting for the greatest number of claims, only 18–19% of the total cost of disability payments is for temporary total disabilities. Worrall and Appel, *Some Benefit Issues in Workers' Compensation,* in Workers' Compensation Benefits 4 (Worral and Appel eds. 1985).

Permanently and totally disabled employees are not able to do any substantial work and are not expected ever to do so. Some states limit permanent total disability benefits by amount and duration, e.g., S.C.Code Ann. § 42–9–10 (limiting benefits to 100% of state average weekly wage per week for 500 weeks with some limited exceptions) but many pay them for the duration of the disability or life. 820 Ill.Comp. Stat.Ann. 305/8 (benefits payable for life). Claims for permanent total disability are fewer in number, but greater in average cost. Only 2 or 3 of every 1,000 workers' compensation claims involve permanent total disability, but these claims account for 9% of all the disability benefits paid under the system. Worrall and Appel, *Some Benefit Issues in Workers' Compensation,* in Workers' Compensation Benefits 5 (Worrall and Appel eds. 1985).

More dollars are paid out for permanent partial disability benefits than in any other category of disability. In fact, 65% of all the disability benefits paid to injured workers are for permanent partial disabilities. Worrall and Appel, *Some Benefit Issues in Workers' Compensation,* in Workers' Compensation Benefits 4–5 (Worrall and Appel eds. 1985). This class of cases involves employees who are permanently impaired in some manner, but are able to perform some fairly substantial kind of work. In most states, certain types of permanent partial disabilities are compensable according to a statutory "schedule". The statute specifies the amount of benefits for particular injuries, such as the loss of an arm, a leg, or an eye. For example, a worker in Tennessee who loses a hand in an occupational accident is entitled to a maximum payment of $73,800 for permanent partial disability. Tenn.Code Ann. § 50–6–207 (150 weeks of benefits at a maximum of $492 per week). As the following subsections illustrate, the standards for determining disability and the widespread use of schedules are points of controversy within the workers' compensation system. With this background, the student may now address the issue of determining what constitutes a "disability".

b. Disability as Impaired Earning Capacity

FLETCHER v. DANA CORPORATION
Court of Appeals of North Carolina, 1995.
119 N.C.App. 491, 459 S.E.2d 31.

OPINION: JOHN, JUDGE.

Defendants appeal an award to plaintiff by the North Carolina Industrial Commission (the Commission) of temporary total disability accrued during the period between 7 November 1989 and 1 April 1991. Defendants contend the Commission erred by basing its determination of disability upon plaintiff's inability to obtain employment during the period in question.

We find defendants' argument unpersuasive.

Relevant background information includes the following: Plaintiff was injured 27 January 1989 in the course of his employment with defendant Dana Corporation (Dana). He was struck in the left arm by a steel chip buggy, part of a train of carts containing scrap metal moved by a tow motor.

After undergoing surgery on his shoulder, plaintiff returned to work 24 July 1989.

On 8 September 1989, plaintiff was assessed by Dr. Larry G. Anderson, his treating physician, as having 20% permanent partial disability of the left arm.

Plaintiff received temporary total disability compensation until returning to work as well as compensation for the permanent disability rating.

On 17 October 1989, plaintiff reinjured his shoulder while attempting to move a basket containing approximately one dozen 60–pound axle tubes. He thereafter was restricted by Dr. Anderson from lifting more than 40 pounds and from lifting overhead.

However, neither plaintiff's job nor any other position then available at Dana was consistent with the limitations imposed by Dr. Anderson.

Plaintiff consequently was discharged 7 November 1989.

Despite extensive efforts, he was unable to secure employment until 1 April 1991.

On 1 February 1991, plaintiff's claim for disability benefits was heard by Deputy Commissioner Charles Markham who ruled plaintiff was not entitled to temporary total disability benefits for the period subsequent to 7 November 1989.

Plaintiff appealed the decision to the full Commission. In an Opinion and Award filed 28 September 1993, the Commission reversed the Deputy Commissioner and ordered defendants to pay temporary total disability accrued during the period of 7 November 1989 through 1 April 1991. In pertinent part, the Commission specified the following findings and conclusions:

10. Dr. Anderson believed that as of October 25, 1989, when he gave plaintiff the written restriction as to the 40 pound weight limitation, plaintiff had essentially reached the maximum point of medical improvement. It was his opinion that as of October 25, 1989, Mr. Fletcher could work with the restrictions given him, that is, not lifting anything above 40 pounds. From a medical point of view, plaintiff would have been able to perform sales work or administrative work as of October 25, 1989.

11. Dana Corporation had no jobs available which met plaintiff's physical restrictions. Therefore, he was terminated on November 7, 1989. . . .

12. After his termination November 7, 1989 and until the time of the hearing [before the Deputy Commissioner], plaintiff made extensive but unsuccessful efforts to gain employment. Plaintiff did not limit himself in this search to industrial work but included supervisory positions and jobs in state government. He was involved with the Employment Security Commission. While he was initially somewhat selective in terms of the pay expected, he lowered his sights, and finally was willing to take anything he could find (except selling insurance). Plaintiff had and sought no medical treatment after November, 1989 except that he received pain medications from his family physician. He did not re-apply for a position with [Dana] as far as its personnel director was aware.

. . . .

17. Despite reasonable efforts, the plaintiff was not able to actually obtain employment from his discharge on November 7, 1989 until returning to work on April 1, 1991.

. . .

CONCLUSION OF LAW

As a result of the compensable injury, the plaintiff was unable to obtain employment, despite reasonable efforts, until April 1, 1991, and plaintiff is entitled to temporary total disability benefits from the time of his discharge from defendants' [sic] employment on November 7, 1989 until obtaining employment on April 1, 1991, and such other and further medical compensation as may effect a cure, give relief or shorten the period of the claimant's disability.

Defendants gave notice of appeal to this Court 8 October 1993.

* * *

Defendants and amicus counsel argue the Commission committed error of law by awarding temporary total disability benefits to plaintiff under circumstances wherein he possessed the capacity to earn wages and thus was not totally disabled. Defendants assert the Commission thereby "stretched [the Workers' Compensation Act] to provide unemployment insurance for workers ready, willing and able to work, who have qualifications to obtain employment, but who are unemployed because of economic conditions." We disagree.

A claimant seeking to recover under the Workers' Compensation Act (the Act) bears the burden of proving both the existence and extent of disability ... Under the Act, an employee injured in the course of his employment is "disabled" if the injury results in an "incapacity ... to earn the wages which the employee was receiving at the time of injury in the same or any other employment." N.C. Gen. Stat. § 97–2(9) (1991). Disability as defined in the Act is thus the impairment of the injured employee's earning capacity rather than physical disablement ...

A claimant may meet the burden of proving inability to earn the same wages earned before injury by showing "he is capable of some work, but that he has, after a reasonable effort on his part, been unsuccessful in his effort to obtain employment." Russell v. Lowes Product Distribution, 108 N.C. App. 762, 765, 425 S.E.2d 454, 457 (1993) (citation omitted).

Defendants assert the Commission misinterpreted Russell and "erroneously focused on whether plaintiff was able to actually obtain employment" instead of whether plaintiff was capable of earning the same wages. Amicus counsel maintains an injured employee in the circumstance of plaintiff must demonstrate "he is unable to work and not merely that he unsuccessfully sought work." In addition, counsel reiterates defendants' contention that the holding of the full Commission in reliance upon Russell "in effect converted temporary total disability into unemployment compensation."

However, the Court in Russell did not address the causes of plaintiff's inability to obtain employment, but rather focused upon evidence of plaintiff's reasonable efforts to obtain employment as being one means of meeting his burden of showing incapacity to earn the same wages earned prior to injury. Id. at 764–65, 425 S.E.2d at 456–57.

"The so-called 'work search' test is merely the evidentiary vehicle by which employability, or lack of it, is proven," Flesche v. Interstate Warehouse, 411 So. 2d 919, 922 (Fla. 1st DCA 1982), and "there are a number of criteria by which wage-earning capacity must be measured, and 'no single factor is conclusive.' "

Anderson v. S & S Diversified, Inc., 477 So. 2d 591, 594 (Fla. 1st DCA 1985), disc. review denied, 486 So. 2d 597 (Fla.1986) (quoting Walker v. Electronic Products & Engineering Co. 248 So. 2d 161, 163 (Fla.1971)) ...

As opposed to Russell, the issue in the case sub judice is whether plaintiff, having met the Russell test with credible (as determined by the Commission) evidence of diligent efforts to find employment, is entitled to receive compensation benefits where his inability to earn the same wages was caused in part by unavailability of area jobs consistent with his physical limitations. Not only this Court, but a leading workers' compensation scholar and courts from other jurisdictions suggest an affirmative response.

In Bridges v. Linn–Corriher Corp., 90 N.C. App. 397, 368 S.E.2d 388, disc. review denied, 323 N.C. 171, 373 S.E.2d 104 (1988), this Court observed:

> the Workers' Compensation Act was enacted to ameliorate the consequences of injuries and illnesses in the workplace and one of those consequences, at least on occasion, is that a recuperated worker capable of holding a job cannot get one. A capable job seeker whom no employer needing workers will hire is not employable.

Id. at 399–400; 368 S.E.2d at 390.

Additionally, in the opinion of Professor Larson:

> Inability to get work, traceable directly and substantially to a compensable injury, may be as effective in establishing disability as inability to perform work.... The two essentials [of disability are]: wage loss, and causation of the wage loss by work-connected injury. The fact that the wage loss comes about through ... unavailability of employment rather than through incapacity to perform the work does not change the result [of disability].

1C Arthur Larson, Larson's Workmen's Compensation Law § 57.61(a), 10—389–397.

Moreover, other jurisdictions support the proposition that compensation is allowable where unavailability of jobs prevents a claimant from earning the same wages received prior to injury. In Regency Inn v. Johnson, 422 So. 2d 870 (Fla. 1st DCA 1982), disc. review denied, 431 So. 2d 989 (Fla.1983), for example, the claimant was injured during the course of her occupation as a housekeeper and consequently was required to seek lighter work. Id. at 872–73. Although she actively pursued other employment in the area, including seeking assistance from the Florida State Employment Office, her efforts were unsuccessful and she was subsequently awarded wage loss benefits for the period of her unemployment. Id. at 873.

As in our jurisdiction, the Florida statute then in effect placed the burden on the employee "to establish that any wage loss claimed is the result of the compensable injury." Fla. Stat. § 440.15(3)(b)(2) (1979).

The Florida Court of Appeals, in the en banc portion of the Regency opinion, pointed out that

> whether the nonavailability of jobs due to economic conditions is a factor to be considered or ignored in determining the after-injury wages an employee is 'able to earn,' is not immediately apparent from a literal reading of the statute itself.

422 So. 2d at 875 (citation omitted). Relying on prior case law, the court went on to state that

in the broadest sense, 'able to earn' takes into account many factors, including the availability of jobs, and such a broad interpretation is consistent . . . with the principle which requires a liberal construction in favor of the injured employee.

Id. The full court upheld the original panel's conclusion that since the claimant would not have suffered wage loss if the injury had not occurred, the statutory requirement of causation was satisfied. 422 So. 2d at 872.

In other words, "but for" the work-related injury she sustained, the Florida claimant, like plaintiff herein, would not have become unemployed and suffered wage loss in consequence of the unavailability of other employment. Her wage loss was thus caused by and resulted from the injury she sustained within the scope and course of her employment.

The employer in Regency Inn had insisted that a work search which is unsuccessful due to unavailability of employment precludes compensation because such evidence does not prove a wage loss due to a compensable disability. Id. The panel disagreed:

> For wage loss the statute provides simply for general causal relation by covering such loss which 'is the result of the . . . injury.' If the intent had been to require wage loss from physical incapacity for work (independent of job availability) as an absolute condition to compensation for wage loss, the alternative language would surely have been used.

422 So. 2d at 873. We note again that disability under our Act relates to impairment of the injured employee's earning capacity rather than physical infirmity. Peoples, 316 N.C. at 434–35, 342 S.E.2d at 804 (citations omitted).

In a similar vein, the full Florida court emphasized that

> had the legislature intended 'able to earn' to be further qualified so as to preclude consideration of non-availability of jobs because of economic conditions, it would have been a simple matter for this to have been written into the law.

* * *

The rationale of the en banc opinion in Regency Inn also addresses the assertion of defendants and amicus counsel herein that the Commission in effect converted workers' compensation benefits into unemployment benefits.

First, the court observed that the Florida workers' compensation act contained no indication its legislature "devised and enacted a system of reparations for injured workers that would fulfill its purposes in time of relative economic prosperity, but would automatically withhold or suspend such reparations in time of economic depression." 422 So. 2d at 878. We likewise find no such legislative indication in our workers' compensation law. Whatever the health of the economy at any given time, workers' compensation statutes are to be liberally construed to give full effect to their humane purpose and remedial character. See Hartley v. Prison Department, 258 N.C. 287, 290–91, 128 S.E.2d 598, 600–01 (1962) (citations omitted).

Next, the court continued, employees receiving unemployment compensation "do not suffer compensable industrial accidents; only employed workers do." Regency, 422 So. 2d at 878.

> The employed worker is an integral part of the productive machinery of society and he is entitled to be treated as still belonging to that segment of the economy after a compensable accident, rather than categorized as a member of the unfortunate group whose unemployed status is due solely to economic conditions.

Id. Thus, workers who would not be unemployed but for a work-related injury should be compensated by workers' compensation, a system "intended to relieve society of the burden of caring for injured workers and to place the responsibility on the industry served." Id. (citation omitted).

The court concluded by pointing out that unemployment compensation is of "more limited amount and duration than workers' compensation benefits, and these benefits are not provided as an alternative to any other form of legal redress, as is true of workers' compensation." Id. (citation omitted) . . .

In Michigan, moreover, the Supreme Court, in Sobotka v. Chrysler Corporation, 447 Mich. 1, 523 N.W.2d 454 (1994), considered the implications of the circumstance that, as in North Carolina, "worker's compensation benefits in Michigan are payable on the basis of wage loss and not on the basis of physical impairment." Id. at 15, 523 N.W.2d at 459 (citation omitted). The court determined as follows:

> Where, on account of an injury, an employee is, in fact, unemployed, the employee is entitled to [workers' compensation benefits] because the employee is not "able to earn" wages postinjury.

447 Mich. at 7–8, 523 N.W.2d at 455.

> [A] disabled worker does not bear the burden of unfavorable economic conditions that further diminish his ability to find suitable work.

Id. at 25, 523 N.W.2d at 463.

> This means that the partially disabled employee's only burden is to show he is unable to earn wages because of his injury, not that he must show that the economy or other factors are not the cause of unemployment.

Id. at 8 n.5, 523 N.W.2d at 455 n.5.

> The court went on to hold that while

> it is the employee's burden to show a link between wage loss and the work-related injury . . ., once the employee shows a work-related

injury and subsequent wage loss, the factfinder may infer that the employee cannot find a job because of the injury.

Id. at 25, 523 N.W.2d at 463.

Finally, the courts in Maine have adopted a similar approach:

> To be entitled to compensation for total incapacity when only partially disabled in the medical sense, the employee must show "that he has engaged in a good faith effort to obtain work within the tolerance of his physical condition, and ... that he failed in his effort, either because employers in his community would not hire people with such a limited capacity to do the type of work within his tolerance, or because there was no reasonably stable market in his community for that restricted work of which he was capable.

Theriault v. Walsh Const. Co., 389 A.2d 317, 320 (Me.1978) (quoting Bowen v. Maplewood Packing Co., 366 A.2d 1116, 1119 (Me.1976)).

The rationale of the foregoing authorities is sound and consistent with our statements in Russell and Bridges. We therefore hold that an employee who suffers a work-related injury is not precluded from workers' compensation benefits when that employee, while employable within limitations in certain kinds of work, cannot after reasonable efforts obtain employment due to unavailability of jobs.

Based on the foregoing, the Commission's award to plaintiff of temporary total disability is affirmed.

Affirmed.

Judges Greene and Martin, John C. concur.

Notes

1. The principal case reflects the historical view that "disability" in the workers' compensation field means more than the physical impairment sustained by the employee as a result of his injury. The ultimate question is to what extent has the employee lost his or her capacity to earn wages as a result of the injury. Physical condition is an important factor and may be decisive for a particular case, but it is by no means the only consideration.

The earliest workers' compensation cases defined disability in terms of impaired earning capacity. In 1912, the House of Lords decided Ball v. William Hunt & Sons, Ltd., 1912 A.C. 496, in which the claimant lost an eye in a work-related injury and thereafter was unable to obtain employment despite his physical ability to perform his usual type of work. A judgment denying compensation was reversed with Lord Atkinson commenting: "The earning of wages depends as much on the demand for the workman's labor as it does upon his physical ability to work. If because of his apparent physical defects no one will employ him, however efficient he may be in fact, he has lost the power to earn wages as completely as if he were paralyzed in every limb." For an early American case reaching the same result, see Fennell's Case, 289 Mass. 89, 193 N.E. 885 (Mass. 1935) ("when one is unable to obtain other employment because of visible, physical results of an industrial accident, that person's earning capacity is as impaired as if he were physically disabled to the extent that he could do no work'').

Defining disability in terms of impaired earning capacity allowed the claimants to recover in *Fletcher* and *Fennell's Case*. It can also lead to the denial of benefits to workers who suffer significant physical injury but no wage loss. E.g., City of Philadelphia v. Workmen's Compensation Appeal Board, 695 A.2d 910 (Pa.Cmwlth.1997) (denying benefits to worker whose job related hearing loss did not affect his ability to earn a wage).

2.   Defining disability in terms of impaired earning capacity is often referred to as a "wage loss" system. The Michigan Supreme Court explained the philosophy underlying a wage loss system as follows:

> [t]he central idea is that each worker will be treated individually, and will receive, in addition to necessary medical expenses, a percentage of his or her actual wage loss (or more precisely, loss of earning capacity), however short or long that loss may continue. The key advantage of this approach, of course, is that it adapts much more readily to the widely varying circumstances of given cases. The lawyer who has lost the little finger on his left hand will receive little or nothing; the concert pianist with the same injury will be entitled to benefits until reasonable alternative employment is made available . . .

Sobotka v. Chrysler Corporation, 447 Mich. 1, 523 N.W.2d 454, 459 (Mich. 1994) (quoting St. Antoine, Workers' Compensation in Michigan, Cost, Benefits, and Fairness 25–26).

3.   The issue in *Fletcher* was whether the claimant could be considered totally disabled when he could not find employment consistent with his physical restrictions. Are there explanations other than the claimant's work injury that might explain his inability to secure employment? Who has the burden of proof? See Padgett v. Waffle House, Inc., 269 Ga. 105, 498 S.E.2d 499 (Ga. 1998)(burden of proof is on the employer to prove that a suitable job is available when the employee was terminated for reasons related to a disability). What sort of evidence is needed to establish or refute a claim of impaired earning capacity? These issues are explored in more detail in the case below.

KARR v. ARMSTRONG TIRE & RUBBER
Supreme Court of Mississippi, 1953.
216 Miss. 132, 61 So.2d 789.

[Claimant suffered a compensable injury by inhaling chemical smoke. It caused painful irritation of his chest, face and throat. He was unable to work for 4 weeks and suffered an 80% loss of his voice. The administrative officer allowed compensation for the 4 weeks. He disallowed any compensation for the voice loss, although he found it was caused by the smoke. Claimant testified that he did not use his voice in his work "too much" but that "You can't work without saying something sometime"; that when he did say something above a hoarse whisper "it'll tire me."]

ROBERDS, PRESIDING JUSTICE. * * *

The Attorney–Referee also had before him the fact that when the injury occurred claimant was earning $45.12 per week working 6 days and at the time of the hearing he was making $60.40 a week working five days at the same employment for the same employer. And that, of course, is strong evidence he had suffered no loss in earning capacity. That comparative actual wage pay, we take it from the arguments, was the test applied at the hearing to determine whether the earning capacity of applicant had been decreased by the eighty percent impairment in his speech. And some of the authorities seemingly hold that such comparative actual wage pay is the correct and only test. The statutes vary. Our statute does not test the earning capacity by the comparative wages received by applicant before and after the injury. It is not a comparison of actual wage with actual wage. The benefits are figured on a percentage of applicant's average weekly wages at the time of the injury as compared to "his wage-earning capacity thereafter in the same employment or otherwise ...". Chapter 354, Sec. 8(c)(21) General Laws of Miss. 1948. In determining the wage-earning capacity of claimant after the injury a number of factors are to be considered in addition to the actual pay received by him when injured as compared to his actual earnings thereafter. Larson has a very good discussion of the elements of proof entering into the question. Vol. 2, Sec. 57.21, page 4:

"Degree of disability is calculated under most acts by comparing actual earnings before the injury with earning capacity after the injury.

"It is at once apparent that the two items in the comparison are not quite the same. Actual earnings are a relatively concrete quantity; rules for their measurement, for this purpose and for the general purpose of fixing claimant's benefit level, are set out in a later section. Earning capacity, however, is a more theoretical concept. It obviously does not mean actual earnings, since the legislature deliberately chose a different phrase for the post-injury earnings factor. Even under those statutes which compare, for example, 'average monthly wages before the accident' with 'the monthly wages he is able to earn thereafter', the test remains one of capacity. If the legislature had spoken of the wages 'he has earned thereafter', or even the wages 'he has been able to earn thereafter', the comparison of actual wage with actual wage would be indicated. But the concept of wages he 'is able' to earn cannot mean definite actual wages alone, especially in the absence of a fixed period of time within which post-injury wages are to be taken as controlling.

"In essence, the problem is one of tying earnings to a period of time. The relevant period of time for prior earnings can be made relatively short and definite, such as the six months preceding the accident. Once an arbitrary past period is specified as setting the basis for computing an average weekly wage, there can be little argument about what wages were in fact earned. But the relevant period for post-injury earnings melts away into the indefinite future. Obviously we cannot take an arbitrary period of, say, six months after the injury as conclusive, since for a multitude of reasons that period might be entirely nonrepresentative. On the other hand, we cannot wait out the rest of claimant's life to see what his average weekly wage loss ultimately turned out to be, for by then it would be too late for the award to do him any good. An award must be made now and paid now. The only possible solution is to make the best possible estimate of future impairment of earnings, on the strength not only of actual post-injury earnings but of any other available clues.

"It is uniformly held, therefore, without regard to statutory variations in the phrasing of the test, that a finding of disability may stand even where there is evidence of actual post-injury earnings equalling or exceeding those received before the accident. The position may be best summarized by saying that actual post-injury earnings will create a presumption of earning capacity commensurate with them, but the presumption may be rebutted by evidence independently showing incapacity or explaining away the post-injury earnings as an unreliable basis for estimating capacity. Unreliability of post-injury earnings may be due to a number of things: increase in general wage levels since the time of accident; claimant's own greater maturity or training; longer hours worked by claimant after the accident; payment of wages disproportionate to capacity out of sympathy to claimant; and the temporary and unpredictable character of post-injury earnings.

"The ultimate objective of the disability test is, by discounting these variables, to determine the wage that would have been paid in the open labor market under normal employment conditions to claimant as injured, taking wage levels, hours of work, and claimant's age and state of training as of exactly the same period used for calculating actual wages earned before the injury. Only by the elimination of all variables except the injury itself can a reasonably accurate estimate be made of the impairment of earning capacity to be attributed to that injury."

There was no proof on a number of these elements. For instance, it is not shown whether the increase in wages being paid claimant at the time of the hearing, as compared to his wages at the time of the injury, was the result of a general rise in wage scales, or was influenced by sympathy of the employer for the injured employee, or the result of enlarged experience of the applicant. A general discussion of the factors entering into this question, taken from cited cases, will be found in the annotation in 149 A.L.R. beginning at page 413. Everything considered we believe that justice requires that this matter be reconsidered. By this we do not mean to adjudicate, or intimate, what the result of another hearing should be.

Reversed and remanded.

HALL, KYLE, ARRINGTON and ETHRIDGE, J.J., concur.

Notes

1. *Karr* illustrates the generally accepted principle that a determination of earning capacity involves more than a comparison of post and pre-injury earnings. Such a comparison yields relevant, but not conclusive, evidence of earning capacity. See, Johnson v. Industrial Comm., 40 Ohio St.3d 384, 533 N.E.2d 775 (1988) (evidence of increased or decreased wages may be considered in determining the impact of an injury on earning capacity, but such evidence is not by itself determinative of the issue); Fairbanks North Star Borough School Dist. v. Crider, 736 P.2d 770 (Alaska 1987) (in evaluating the claimant's earning capacity, the Board should consider increases in salary that would have taken place if claimant had not been injured); Mountainside Medical Center v. Tanner, 225 Ga.App. 722, 484 S.E.2d) 706 (Ga.App. 1997) (Board should consider evidence of what the claimant is *able* to earn, not simply *actual* earnings).

2. Earnings, however, serve as an effective presumption of earning capacity. 4 A. Larson and L. Larson, Larson's Workers' Compensation Law § 57.20 (1998). Some states presume a worker has not suffered any impairment of earning capacity when post-injury earnings equal or exceed pre-injury wages. E.g., Jim Walter Resources, Inc. v. Hall, 576 So.2d 673 (Ala.Civ.App.1991) (unrebutted evidence of higher post-injury earnings mandated a reversal of compensation award); Bragg v. Evans–St. Clair, Inc., 15 Ark.App. 53, 688 S.W.2d 956 (1985) (evidence that the employee returned to work at an equal or higher wage creates a presumption of no loss in earning capacity); Ruddy v. I.D. Griffith & Co., 237 A.2d 700 (Del.1968) (returning to same job at the same pay raised a rebuttable presumption that there was no loss of earning capacity).

A worker may be considered disabled despite earning more after the accident, however, if the higher pay can be explained by other factors. E.g., Cherokee Electric Coop. v. Lecroy, 587 So.2d 351 (Ala.Civ.App. 1991) (evidence that claimant needed help by co-workers to perform job duties supported finding of impaired earning capacity despite evidence of greater post-injury earnings); Twiggs v. Municipality of Anchorage, 938 P.2d 1046 (Alaska 1997) (evidence of greater post-injury earnings not dispositive when the claimant alleged the compensable injury caused him to lose a second promotion); Don Ward & Co. v. Industrial Comm., 722 P.2d 1026 (Colo.App. 1986) (claimant who increased post-accident earnings by working longer hours for a lower hourly wage could be considered disabled).

Similarly, evidence of lower post-accident earnings does not conclusively establish impaired earning capacity. Occasionally, a worker who accepts employment at lower wages will be found not to have suffered any impairment of earning capacity. E.g., Wilde v. Taco Bell Corp., 531 So.2d 918 (Ala.Civ.App.1988) (claimant returned to work at same pay, but was fired for reasons unrelated to his injury; he secured a similar job paying less money; based on the testimony of the vocational expert and its own observations, the court determined that claimant had not suffered any loss of earning capacity). Cf. Mountainside Medical Center v. Tanner, 225 Ga.App. 722, 484 S.E.2d 706 (Ga.App.1997) (claimant with no actual post-injury earnings may not be disabled if the employer proves that suitable jobs were available within the claimant's work restrictions).

3. Impaired earning capacity is usually measured in terms of the ability to perform or obtain work "suitable" to claimant's qualifications and training. Thus, workers who are unable to secure employment for which they are qualified may be considered disabled. E.g., Moore v. RPM Industries, Inc., 144 A.D.2d 135, 534 N.Y.S.2d 463 (1988) (cement worker disabled by asthma may be considered totally disabled if not qualified to perform other work); Reust v. State Accident Insurance Fund, 60 Or.App. 9, 652 P.2d 884 (1982) (back injury prevented claimant from performing any work previously performed; error to reduce award for permanent partial disability); Posey v. State Workmen's Compensation Commissioner, 157 W.Va. 285, 201 S.E.2d 102 (1973) (nearly illiterate manual laborer who suffered knee injury is entitled to permanent total disability benefits since he is unable to perform any work for which he is qualified). Workers who are unable to return to their former jobs may nevertheless be able to secure employment in unrelated areas. Most jurisdictions consider post-injury earnings in unrelated employments in determining whether and to what extent a claimant is disabled. E.g., Lusietto v. Industrial Commission, 174 Ill.App.3d 121, 123 Ill.Dec. 634, 528 N.E.2d 18 (1988) (iron worker who is physically unable to perform manual labor is not entitled to permanent total disability benefits because he had been performing sedentary work at his wife's company); Smith–Gruner v. Yandell, 768 P.2d 388 (Okl.App.1989) (securing employment in a different line of work creates a rebuttable presumption that claimant was not totally disabled).

4. Evidence that the claimant is able to secure occasional employment does not preclude a finding of total disability. As stated by the Minnesota Supreme Court,

> An employee who is so injured that he can perform no services other than those which are so limited in quality, dependability, or quantity that a reasonably stable market for them does not exist, may well be classified as totally disabled.

Lee v. Minneapolis St. Ry., 230 Minn. 315, 41 N.W.2d 433, 436 (1950). This principle dates back to an early English decision that referred to this type of worker as an "odd lot" in the labor market. Cardiff Corporation v. Hall, [1911] 1 K.B. 1009, 1021. Judge Cardozo quoted from *Cardiff* with approval in describing the "odd lot man" as "nondescript in the labor market. Work, if he gets it, is likely to be casual and intermittent . . ." Jordan v. Decorative Co., 230 N.Y. 522, 525, 130 N.E. 634, 635 (1921). What has now become known as the "odd lot doctrine" is accepted in virtually all jurisdictions. It instructs agencies and courts to look beyond any intermittent employment the claimant might secure when determining total disability. The court or agency must also consider whether the claimant's residual physical limitations, mental capacity, age, experience, education, skills and training, considered collectively, preclude regular employment. Accordingly, the odd lot doctrine justifies an award of total disability benefits to workers who may be able to secure occasional jobs. E.g., Guyton v. Irving Jensen Co., 373 N.W.2d 101 (Iowa 1985) (40 year old, mildly retarded, illiterate manual laborer with residual back injury); Piggly Wiggly v. Houston, 464 So.2d 510 (Miss.1985) (claimant with a fractured kneecap found totally disabled when she lacked the skills or training to obtain a job that would not require lifting and/or standing); Swanson v. Westport Lumber Co., 4 Or.App. 417, 479 P.2d 1005

(1971) (63 year old sawmill worker with an eighth grade education and no specialized skills found to be totally disabled). The critical question is whether suitable work is regularly and continuously available to the claimant. In many jurisdictions, the employer bears the burden of proving that regular and continuous employment is available once the worker is shown to be in the odd-lot category. *Guyton,* supra; *Swanson,* supra. See generally, 4 A. Larson and L. Larson, Larson's Workers' Compensation Law § 57.51 (1998).

5. Certain kinds of physical injuries may be defined or presumed by statute to constitute total and permanent disability. In California, for example, permanent total disability is "conclusively presumed" whenever a worker suffers the loss of both eyes, both hands, total paralysis, or insanity as a result of a compensable injury. Cal. Labor Code § 4662. Such presumptions are quite common. See, e.g., Ga.Code Ann. § 34–9–263(g)(rebuttable presumption); Mich.Comp.Laws Ann. § 418.361(3)(conclusive presumption). Conclusive presumptions of permanent total disability obviate the need for evidence of impaired earning capacity. In this respect, they are similar to scheduled permanent partial disabilities discussed in the next subsection.

c. *Disability as Physical Impairment*

BISHOP v. TOWN OF BARRE
Supreme Court of Vermont, 1982.
140 Vt. 564, 442 A.2d 50.

OPINION BY: HILL

OPINION: This case concerns the proper standard for computing benefits under the Vermont Workmen's Compensation Act, 21 V.S.A. §§ 601–709. The claimant, Leroy Bishop, challenges the amount of compensation he was awarded by the Commissioner of Labor and Industry. . . .

I.

The facts in this case are straightforward. On October 3, 1973, the claimant suffered an injury to his back while employed as a laborer by the Town of Barre. Although he returned to work for short periods of time, he has not worked since October of 1977. From December 15, 1973, to April 8, 1974, and from October 3, 1977, to January 22, 1979, the claimant received temporary total disability benefits. On January 22, 1979, the defendants discontinued temporary benefits on the ground that the claimant had reached the "end result" of the healing process.

The claimant filed for permanent disability and vocational rehabilitation benefits. At the hearing on these claims, the medical testimony stood uncontradicted: the claimant's back impairment would not improve, resulting in a thirty-five to forty per cent permanent impairment of the spine, and a twenty per cent impairment to the whole man. The claimant also adduced testimony that, taking account of his age, training, and educational background, he would be unable to work again. . . .

The Commissioner found that the claimant was entitled to sixty-six weeks of permanent partial disability benefits, computed on the basis of a twenty per cent impairment to the whole man. The Commissioner based this decision on medical evidence alone, and did not address the claimant's age, education, or training. . . .

The claimant appealed the Commissioner's decision to the Washington Superior Court, which certified the following questions to this Court under V.R.A.P. 5(a):

(1) Did the Commissioner of Labor and Industry err in concluding that claimant was only 20% permanently disabled?

(2) Is the Commissioner of Labor and Industry's conclusion of 20% permanent partial disability in error because it is based only on permanent physical impairment and not permanent economic impairment?

(a) Did the Commissioner of Labor and Industry err in not finding that the claimant has sustained permanent economic impairment?

(3) Was it error for the Commissioner of Labor and Industry to conclude the claimant is only 20% permanently partially disabled in light of Dr. Felix Callan's testimony that claimant sustained a 20% permanent partial disability to the "whole man" and 35–40% permanent partial disability to his spine?

* * *

We answer questions one [and] three . . . in the affirmative, and two [and] two(a) . . . in the negative, for reasons which will be discussed in the remainder of this opinion.

II.

A.

The Vermont Workmen's Compensation Act provides two distinct classes of benefits. Temporary disability benefits are provided for workers who suffer a "disability for work," 21 V.S.A. §§ 642, 646, during the period between their injury and final recovery. Once the recovery process has ended, or the worker has achieved the maximum possible restoration of his earning power, he is no longer entitled to temporary disability benefits. At this point, the worker has reached the "end result" of the healing process. . . . Because the claimant's condition has reached an "end result," claims for benefits are then treated under the permanent disability sections, 21 V.S.A. §§ 644, 648. . . .

Our case law has established different criteria for computing temporary, as opposed to permanent, benefits. Temporary disability benefits are awarded on the basis of an individual's incapacity for work. . . . This involves consideration of not only physical injury, but also of other factors restricting the claimant's capacity to obtain work. . . . In contrast, permanent disability benefits are calculated solely on the basis of physical impairment: "[The permanent disability] statute has arbitrarily fixed the amount of compensation to be paid for scheduled specific injuries regardless of loss of present earning power." Beane v. Vermont Marble Co., 115 Vt. 142, 145, 52 A.2d 784, 786 (1947). . . .

The claimant challenges the validity of these different standards set forth in Vermont case law. He asserts that permanent disability, like temporary disability, should be evaluated by reference to any factor which restricts capacity for work. In support of this position, he advances several arguments. First, he contends that the Act's use of the word "disability" connotes more than physical impairment, thereby requiring evaluation of ability to work. Second, he asserts that by allowing compensation for unscheduled injuries, see 21 V.S.A. §§ 644(b), 648(20), the Act sanctions consideration of factors other than physical injury. Third, he argues that the purpose of the statute is to compensate for lost wages, which requires consideration of capacity for work. Thus, he concludes that the Commissioner erred in failing to consider the claimant's ability to work, and in relying solely on physical impairment in setting compensation.

The claimant's arguments do not persuade us to reject our precedent. Earning capacity is significant to the Workmen's Compensation Act, but it performs a far different function than envisioned by the claimant.

The claimant correctly assigns protection against wage loss as one of the Act's purposes. The Act, however, also seeks to establish an expedient, efficient remedy for injured workers.... Simplifying the elements of recovery is the Act's mechanism for achieving efficiency. To be entitled to benefits, a claimant need only establish that he suffered "a personal injury by accident arising out of and in the course of his employment by an employer subject to [the Act]." 21 V.S.A. § 618. The employee need not show that the employer was negligent ... or that he actually suffered a wage loss.... Because resolution of these issues on a case by case basis would impede the process, thereby delaying awards to needy beneficiaries, the legislature has chosen a "scheduled benefits" system. The rate of compensation for listed injuries has been conclusively determined in the Act. See 21 V.S.A. §§ 644, 648. The system still protects against wage loss, but it fulfills this aim by awarding permanent disability benefits on the basis of physical impairment as a means to insure against wage loss. Professor Larson explains how a scheduled benefits system, such as Vermont's, insures against wage loss:

> [Exclusion of individual wage loss evidence] is not, however, to be interpreted as an erratic deviation from the underlying principle of compensation law—that benefits relate to loss of earning capacity and not to physical injury as such. The basic theory remains the same; the only difference is that the effect on earning capacity is a conclusively presumed one, instead of a specifically proved one based on the individual's actual wage-loss experience.

2 A. Larson, Workmen's Compensation Law § 58.11, at 10–173 to 174 (1981) (footnotes omitted).

The yardstick is general, not particular. The total disability section compensates for injuries which, as a general rule, tend to have the most severe impact on earning capacity. The partial disability section compensates for injuries which generally have a less serious impact, and rates the scheduled impairments accordingly.

The claimant's arguments that the plain meaning of disability and the presence of compensation for unscheduled injuries compel consideration of individual wage loss must be rejected in light of the elaborate and carefully drawn scheme of scheduled benefits.... The Act enumerates "partial disabilities" in 21 V.S.A. § 648, and "total disabilities" in 21 V.S.A. § 644. Yet, each of the "partial disabilities" could, depending upon a person's age, occupation, and training, prevent a worker from obtaining employment. Similarly, a worker could suffer a disability listed as "total," yet return to his or her previous job.[4] If we were to inject individual wage loss into this scheme, as urged by the claimant, we would effectively collapse the distinctions between total and partial benefits explicitly drawn by the legislature.

The claimant also points to the statutory definition of "partial disability" as supporting his position. Subsection ten of 21 V.S.A. § 601 states: " 'Partial disability' may be held to include diminished ability to obtain employment owing to disfigurement resulting from an injury." Thus, the claimant argues, individual ability to work is, by definition, a factor in computing benefits. This analysis collapses under careful scrutiny. First, it ignores the theory of a scheduled benefits act and the carefully drawn distinction between partial and total disability, subjects previously discussed in this opinion. Second, there is a more plausible application of the definition: it only addresses the award of temporary benefits under 21 V.S.A. § 646, the temporary disability section. As previously discussed, ability to work is a crucial factor in awarding temporary disability benefits. The section dealing with temporary disability awards compensation "[where] the disability for work resulting from an injury is partial." 21 V.S.A. § 646. The permanent disability section awards compensation on the basis of "sixty-six and two-thirds percent of the average weekly wages ... for the periods stated against such injuries respectively." 21 V.S.A. § 648. Thus, although the headnote to the permanent disability section contains the defined term, its text does not. This contrasts with the quoted portion of the temporary disability section.

Given the Act's history and structure, we must reject the claimant's contention that individual wage loss should be considered in computing permanent benefits. The plain meaning of the statute precludes consideration of individual wage loss. We reaffirm the distinction between temporary and permanent benefits.

---

4. For example, a typist might be able to work after losing both feet, yet be "totally disabled" under 21 V.S.A. § 644(a)(2). The loss of one hand would prevent the same typist from returning to work, yet, the injury would be a "partial disability" under 21 V.S.A. § 648(4). Indeed, the claimant himself would be unable to resume work as a laborer if he suffered any one of several of the impairments scheduled in 21 V.S.A. § 648.

* * *

III.

Certified questions one and three present the same issue: whether, based on the evidence in the record, the Commissioner's decision, finding the claimant to be twenty per cent permanently partially disabled, correctly computes his physical impairment. The issue can be narrowed considerably. Our holding concerning the effect of an individual's economic impairment on the award of benefits precludes our finding the claimant to be totally disabled. There is no medical evidence that the claimant suffers an impairment approaching the severity of those listed in 21 V.S.A. § 644. Thus, it is clear that the claimant is only entitled to partial disability. Furthermore, there is no dispute concerning the medical evidence, which was uncontradicted. The only remaining question is the legal effect of that evidence.

The medical testimony indicated, and the Commissioner found, that the claimant suffered a thirty-five to forty per cent impairment of the spine, resulting in a twenty per cent impairment of the "whole man." The Commissioner awarded compensation on the basis of the twenty per cent figure, which yielded sixty-six weeks of benefits. The claimant argues that it was error not to use the thirty-five to forty per cent figure, which would yield 115.5 to 132 weeks of benefits.

The issue is whether impairment to the "whole man" or impairment to the affected part of the body is the proper standard. Back injuries are not scheduled under 21 V.S.A. § 648. Rule 10(a)(3) [of the Rules Pertaining to Workmen's Compensation and Occupational Disease] addresses the level of compensation for back injuries:

> The back. In the event an employee receives a personal injury by accident arising out of and in the course of his employment resulting in the permanent and complete loss of the use of his back the employee shall be entitled to 330 weeks of compensation. If the loss of the use of his back is partial he shall be entitled to that percentage of 330 weeks of compensation which is represented by the loss.

In assessing what figure is "the percentage ... represented by the loss," the Commissioner used the whole man figure. His reasoning was that the maximum recovery allowable for total disability is 330 weeks. See 21 V.S.A. § 645. Therefore, benefits for back impairments are calculated on the basis of the percentage of disability caused to the "whole man." The claimant argues that the percentage of loss to the back is the appropriate standard. We agree with the claimant.

Interpretations of their own regulations by administrative agencies are usually given great weight by this Court. See In re Brooks, 130 Vt. 83, 85–86, 286 A.2d 279, 281 (1971). Yet, in this case, we believe that the Commissioner's interpretation of Rule 10(a)(3) is clearly erroneous. The Act, in providing compensation for unscheduled injuries, focuses solely upon the injuries themselves. The statute allows benefits for "all other cases in this class, or where the *usefulness of a member or any physical function is permanently impaired.*" 21 V.S.A. § 648(18) (emphasis added). Similarly, the rule itself only makes reference to "loss of the use of [the] back." Rule 10(a)(3). Nowhere, in either the rule or the statute, is reference made to any criterion other than impairment to the injured body part. Using 330 weeks as the basis for calculating benefits does not, as the Commissioner apparently held, alter the plain language of the rule. If a claimant completely lost the use of his back, he would be totally disabled within the meaning of 21 V.S.A. § 644(b). The 330–week figure simply reflects the severity of back injuries, and assures that compensation for back impairments will be proportional to the scheduled benefits. See Part II A of this opinion, supra.

Given these factors, the Commissioner erred in interpreting Rule 10(a)(3) by reference to a "whole man" standard. The claimant's benefits should have been calculated on the basis of his back impairment, which is thirty-five to forty per cent. It is axiomatic that an administrative agency must follow its own substantive regulations in deciding contested cases ... Thus, the Commissioner's decision must be reversed. On remand, the Commissioner should award benefits on the basis of the claimant's thirty-five to forty per cent back impairment.

* * *

Certified questions one [and] three ... are answered in the affirmative. Certified questions two [and] two(a) ... are answered in the negative. The case is remanded for the entry of an award consistent with this opinion.

* * *

Notes

1. Most workers' compensation acts include provisions similar to sections 644 and 648 of the Vermont statute at issue in *Bishop*. Such statutes specify a precise and uniform measure of benefits for loss of certain mentioned members of the body. These are commonly referred to as "scheduled benefits". Thus, the loss of a leg or a foot or an eye is a "scheduled loss" in most states. The precise amount of the scheduled benefits is commonly expressed in terms of a number of weeks to which the claimant is entitled to receive income benefits. Scheduled benefits are often payable in an immediate lump sum. The number of weeks specified in the statute to calculate the amount of the award varies with the particular loss. In 1998 in Georgia, for example, a worker is entitled to 225 weeks of income benefits for the loss of an arm or leg, 160 weeks of income benefits for the loss of a hand, and 135 weeks of income benefits for the loss of a foot. Ga.Code Ann. § 34–9–263(c). There is considerable variation among states with regard to the number of weeks used in the schedule for the same loss. The loss of an arm entitles the employee to benefits for 312 weeks in Rhode Island, 269 weeks in Michigan, and 500 weeks in Wisconsin. R.I.Gen.Laws § 28–33–19; Mich.Comp.Laws Ann. § 418.361; Wis.Stat.Ann. § 102.52. The combination of variations in the maximum weekly income benefit and the number of weeks to which a

claimant is entitled to receive benefits, produces significant differences among the states in the amount of compensation a worker will receive for a particular scheduled injury. For example, the Wisconsin worker who loses an arm will receive a maximum of $89,500 under the schedule, while a Pennsylvania counterpart will receive a maximum of $230,010. A comprehensive comparison of benefit levels for certain common scheduled losses can be found in U.S. Dept. of Labor, Employment Standards Administration, Office of Workers' Compensation Programs, *State Workers' Compensation Laws* table 9a (January 1998).

2. Scheduled benefits are payable without proof of actual wage loss or impairment of earning capacity. In effect, the schedule provides a conclusive presumption that a worker will sustain wage loss that justifies compensation in the prescribed amount. The Supreme Court explained the rationale underlying the use of schedules as follows: "The lump-sum awards for total and permanent disability under [the Alaska] Compensation Act ignore wage losses. Whatever the employee may have made before, whatever his wages may be after the injury, the award is the same. To that extent it is an arbitrary amount. But it is the expression of a legislative judgment that on the average there has been a degree of impairment, and whatever may be the fact in a particular case, the lump-sum should be paid without more." Alaska Industrial Board v. Chugach Electric Ass'n., Inc., 356 U.S. 320, 323–24, 78 S.Ct. 735, 737–38, 2 L.Ed.2d 795 (1958). Schedules also do not distinguish between different occupations or how the loss of the specific member might effect a particular worker's job. "The schedule . . . awards the same benefit to a piano player as to a night watchman for the loss of a finger, hand, or arm." Hise Construction v. Candelaria, 98 N.M. 759, 652 P.2d 1210, 1211 (1982). Why would the legislature award the same benefits to these two workers when the effect of the injury on their respective earning capacities is so very different?

3. The use of schedules under the earliest workers' compensation statutes was quite limited. Only a few major appendages, such as arms and legs, were included in the statutory schedule, and the concept of "loss" was strictly construed to require an actual severance or its functional equivalent. Over time, the scheduled injury principle expanded greatly. An increasing number of smaller members, such as portions of fingers and toes, were added to the statutory schedule. The more inclusive "loss of use" concept replaced amputation as the degree of physical impairment necessary to trigger the schedule. Providing scheduled benefits for "partial loss of use" vastly expanded the number of injuries compensable without proof of wage loss. The most recent expansion of the schedule injury principle has been to move beyond specific members to "the body as a whole" or the "whole person". This addition to the list of scheduled injuries allows physicians to express the claimant's non-specific residual physical limitations as a percentage loss of the "body as a whole". Injuries to internal organs and the back, for example, are compensable under the body as a whole provision without proof of wage loss. E.g., Thom v. Callahan, 97 Idaho 151, 540 P.2d 1330 (1975) (restaurant worker with back injury awarded permanent partial disability benefits for 25% impairment of "the whole person"); Bess v. Tyson Foods, Inc., 125 N.C.App. 698, 482 S.E.2d 26 (N.C.App.1997) (loss of sense of taste and smell

is compensable as a permanent injury to an "important external or internal organ").

4. The expansion of the scheduled injury principle is discussed and criticized in Larson, *The Wage–Loss Principle in Workers' Compensation,* 6 Wm. Mitchell L.Rev. 501 (1980). Larson states that when lump sum payments are routinely provided under vastly expanded schedules, "all resemblance to a wage-loss system is lost. If a worker is given $20,000 for some internal organ damage that has no conceivable effect, actual or presumptive, on earning capacity, it is no longer possible to pretend that the statute is still somehow only an extrapolation of the wage-loss principle aided by the conclusive presumption of eventual wage loss." 6 Wm. Mitchell L.Rev. at 512.

Professor Larson advocated the abandonment of schedules and a return to wage-loss as the guiding standard for awarding disability benefits. Florida enacted such a system in 1979. The Florida law eliminated the use of schedules for virtually all permanent partial disabilities. Benefits were awarded in most instances exclusively on the basis of wage-loss. Florida's return to a wage-loss approach to compensating permanent partial disability was expected to reduce both the cost of processing and number of claims. These savings, in turn, were supposed to be channelled to workers who suffer actual wage loss by increasing the level of maximum weekly benefits. Reviews of the Florida system were mixed. Professor Larson reported that "on the whole, the Florida reforms are succeeding in achieving the improvements that had been hoped for. Litigation has been reduced; total claims have been sharply cut, and the great majority of these have been disposed of without hearings; legal costs and insurance rates have decreased; and general surveys show that claimants are satisfied with the system." Larson, *Tensions in the Next Decade,* in New Perspectives in Workers' Compensation 34 (Burton ed. 1988). Professor Burton, on the other hand, was less certain that cost reductions are inherent in the wage-loss approach. Burton, *Introduction,* in New Perspectives in Workers' Compensation 5 (Burton ed. 1988). A Florida study concluded that "the current system of paying workers under the wage loss system is not working as originally perceived and intended." Governor's Task Force on Workers' Compensation, *Florida Workers' Compensation System Part III: Recommendations for Solving Problems* 20 (March 1, 1989). In 1990, Florida returned to an impairment schedule. See Timothy A. Watson and Michael J. Valen, A Historic View of Workers' Compensation Reform in Florida, 21 Fla. St. L. Rev. 501 (1993).

5. An important practical issue is the extent to which the schedule provides the exclusive measure of compensation. This issue commonly presents itself in two contexts. The first involves the loss of a smaller member that might also be viewed as a fractional loss of a larger member, as when the loss of a finger might also be considered the partial loss of a hand. The second context involves a worker who claims to suffer a permanent total disability as the result of a scheduled injury. The common question presented by these types of cases is whether the worker is limited to the benefits authorized by the most specific provisions of the schedule.

There is widespread agreement that if the loss of a scheduled member adversely affects another part of the body, benefits are not limited to those prescribed for the scheduled member. If the other part of the body affected by the scheduled injury is not itself a scheduled injury, the schedule does not provide the exclusive measure of benefits. E.g., A.M.R. Services v. Butler, 697 So.2d 472 (Ala.Civ.App. 1997) (injury to finger causing pain in hand and forearm is compensable as a 50% permanent partial disability to the body as a whole); Mountain City Meat Co. v. Oqueda, 919 P.2d 246 (Colo.1996) (when an employee suffers a work-related accident that results in both a scheduled and non-scheduled injury, the scheduled injury must be converted to a whole person impairment rating and combined with the non-scheduled injury's whole person rating in calculating permanent disability benefits); Dye v. Industrial Comm., 153 Ariz. 292, 736 P.2d 376 (1987) (injury to the arm bone (a scheduled injury) produced residual impairment of the shoulder (an unscheduled injury); benefits are not limited to the schedule for the arm bone); Harrison v. Animas Valley Auto & Truck Repair, 107 N.M. 373, 758 P.2d 787 (1988) ("implicit" finding that injuries extended beyond the wrist, hand and arm authorized an award of benefits based on 80% permanent partial disability of the "whole man"). If the other part of the body affected by the scheduled injury is also a scheduled injury, the worker may recover the greater of the two. E.g., United Parcel Service v. Outlaw, 190 Ga.App. 840, 380 S.E.2d 310 (1989) (claimant whose three toes were amputated as a result of a work injury was rated as suffering a 100% loss of the three toes, a 25% impairment of the foot, and a 15% impairment of the leg; claimant could recover under whichever calculation produced the greatest recovery, but could not cumulate all three); Onley v. National Union Fire Ins. Co., 785 S.W.2d 348 (Tenn.1990) (worker suffered a broken bone in thumb that resulted in a 60% residual impairment of thumb (60 weeks of benefits) and a 50% residual impairment of hand (150 weeks of benefits); benefits may be awarded under the schedule for impairment of the hand).

The more difficult cases are those in which the only physical injury is to a scheduled member, but when combined with other factors, produces an impairment of earning capacity that exceeds the schedule. Van Dorpel v. Haven–Busch Co., 350 Mich. 135, 85 N.W.2d 97 (Mich. 1957) was an early and influential decision that upheld an award of benefits that exceed those authorized under the schedule. This position has been adopted by a number of other courts. E.g., McNeely v. Clem Mill & Gin Co., 241 Ark. 498, 409 S.W.2d 502 (1966) (worker who suffered the loss of a leg (a scheduled injury) awarded benefits for total disability); Whitley v. Columbia Lumber Mfg. Co., 318 N.C. 89, 348 S.E.2d 336 (1986) (cabinet maker who suffered a 75% impairment to right hand and 30% impairment to left hand (both scheduled injuries) could be awarded benefits for permanent total disability); Jensen v. Zook Bros. Const. Co., 178 Mont. 59, 582 P.2d 1191 (1978) (left-handed construction worker who had his left hand crushed could be awarded permanent total disability benefits despite having been given only a 5% partial disability rating by an orthopedic surgeon).

When the physical injury is confined to the scheduled member, however, some courts view the schedule as the exclusive basis for the award of benefits. E.g., Potomac Electric Power Co. v. Director, Office of Workers' Compensation Programs, 449 U.S. 268, 101 S.Ct. 509, 66 L.Ed.2d 446 (1980) (clear statutory language and legislative history supports limiting worker to scheduled benefits notwithstanding his greater impairment of earning capacity; the Court notes the trend to the contrary); Ratliff v. Alaska Workers' Compensation Bd., 721 P.2d 1138 (Alaska 1986) (claimant is limited to compensation for a scheduled injury to knee in the absence of a finding that the knee injury had an effect on any other portion of the body).

6. A work-connected injury that disfigures the victim with scars or distorted appearance may impair wage-earning capacity. In that case an award of compensation is entirely consistent with the principles on which the workers' compensation system is founded. People engaged in certain occupations, e.g., receptionist, model, television performer, are more likely to be adversely affected by these injuries than others who do not encounter the public in their occupations.

Where there is no evidence that the disfigurement has had an impact on the claimant's ability and opportunity to work and earn, the workers' compensation principle would suggest that no award be made. In the absence of a special statute such is the result reached in the case of the so-called "cosmetic injury". McPherson v. American Mut. Liability Ins. Co., 208 S.C. 76, 37 S.E.2d 136 (1946) (award for injury to hand for disfigurement disallowed because earning capacity not impaired); Wengler v. Grosshans Lumber Co., 173 Neb. 839, 115 N.W.2d 415 (1962) (award refused for scar, loss of teeth and speech defect).

Most states have enacted special statutory provisions governing compensation for disfigurement. Although these statutes differ widely in scope and method of operation, some relate the award directly to loss of earning power. In Jolly v. J.M. Hampton & Sons Lumber Co., 234 Ark. 574, 353 S.W.2d 338 (1962), the statute provided:

> The Commission shall award compensation for serious and permanent facial or head disfigurement in a sum not to exceed two thousand ($2,000.00) dollars, based solely upon the effect such disfigurement shall have on the future earning capacity of the injured employee in similar employment.

Claimant suffered an electrical burn that caused loss of facial tissue which was repaired by plastic surgery leaving permanent scars on his face and ear. Although the claimant testified that he was embarrassed when meeting people, there was no evidence that he could not work or that he had been refused employment. Compensation was denied. This type of statute is entirely consistent with the wage-loss principles underlying workers' compensation systems.

Other statutes authorize the administrative agency to make awards for disfigurement of certain parts of the body such as "serious facial or head disfigurements", but do not expressly condition the disfigurement award on a reduction of earning capacity. These statutes presume that certain disfigurements impair earning capacity. In upholding the validity of such a statute, the New York court said: "But one of the truths of life is that serious facial disfigurement has a tendency to impair the earning power of its victims." Sweeting v. American Knife Co., 226 N.Y. 199, 123 N.E. 82 (1919), affirmed 250 U.S. 596, 40 S.Ct. 44, 63 L.Ed. 1161 (1919). See also, 820 Ill.Comp.Stat.Ann. 305/8(c) (employee is entitled to compensation "for any serious and permanent disfigurement to the hand, head, face, neck, arm, leg below the knee, or chest above the axillary line"); Del.Code Ann. tit. 19

§ 2326 (employee may receive compensation for permanent disfigurement that is "visible and offensive when the body is clothed normally").

If the state allows compensation for disfigurement, benefits may be awarded for the medical expense of cosmetic surgery. Thus in Akers Auto Salvage v. Waddle, 394 P.2d 452 (Okl.1964), in which claimant suffered marked disfigurement of the right ear, compensation was allowed for the medical expense of reconstructive surgery. Conversely, if compensation for the disfigurement is not allowable, the expenses of corrective plastic surgery are not recoverable. Eckert v. Yellow Freight Systems, Inc., 170 Ind.App. 196, 351 N.E.2d 924 (1976).

Should compensation be allowed for both bodily impairment and disfigurement? Compare, Ind.Code Ann. § 22–3–3–10 (no compensation for disfigurement where benefits are payable under other provisions) with Mass.Gen. Laws Ann., ch. 152, § 36 (employee may receive compensation for disfigurement "in addition to all other sums due").

For a summary of state laws providing disfigurement benefits see U.S. Dept. of Labor Employment Standards Administration, Office of Workers' Compensation Programs, *State Workers' Compensation Laws*, Table 11 (1998).

SLOVER MASONRY, INC. v. INDUSTRIAL COMMISSION

Supreme Court of Arizona, 1988.
158 Ariz. 131, 761 P.2d 1035.

FELDMAN, VICE CHIEF JUSTICE.

Claimant seeks review of a court of appeals' opinion denying his workers' compensation award. The court vacated the award because the administrative law judge (ALJ) did not strictly adhere to the American Medical Association's *Guides to the Evaluation of Permanent Impairment* (the AMA Guides) when determining the percentage of claimant's permanent impairment. We must decide whether an administrative law judge is bound to follow the AMA Guides as the sole measure of impairment.

FACTUAL AND PROCEDURAL SUMMARY

The operative facts are undisputed. Thaddeus J. Williamson (claimant) was a hod carrier employed by Slover Masonry (respondent). On December 3, 1984, claimant fell off a scaffold at work, fracturing the tibial condyle of his right knee. James Alway, M.D., a board-certified orthopedic specialist, performed five surgical operations on claimant's leg. The surgeries did not entirely repair the damage, and claimant continued to suffer cramping, pain, loss of balance, foot drop, numbness, tingling, and restricted extension and flexion of both the right leg and right foot.

On January 7, 1986, the Industrial Commission (the Commission) issued a Notice of Permanent Disability Benefits (Scheduled) stating that claimant had suffered a fifty percent loss of function in his right leg. The fifty percent loss entitled claimant to fifty percent of his average monthly wage for twenty-five months. A.R.S. § 23–1044(B)(15) and (21). Claimant requested a hearing to prove that his permanent disability was greater than fifty percent.

The Commission held hearings on July 25 and August 16, 1986 to determine the correct percentage of permanent disability for claimant's injury. * * *

Claimant explained that ... he could not complete [five of the seven] tasks related to his hod carrier job, which constituted about seventy-eight percent of his job when measured by time allotted each task. A labor market consultant confirmed that claimant's injury disabled him from performing sixty-five percent of a hod carrier's job.

Dr. Alway testified that he evaluated claimant's permanent injuries under the AMA Guides and concluded that claimant had a fifty percent functional loss of his right lower leg. However, Dr. Alway made it clear that the AMA Guides did not actually measure ability to perform a specific job or occupation: ...

> On August 26, 1986, the ALJ conducting the hearing summarized Dr. Alway's testified money in his decision:

>> Dr. Alway opined that the A.M.A. Guidelines do not attempt to take into consideration the applicant's impairment in terms of his job functions. Stated another way, Dr. Alway said that the working disability the applicant suffers is not totally covered by the Guides. Dr. Alway agreed with the applicant's assessment of which job functions he can no longer do.

Decision Upon Hearing, August 26, 1986 (Findings), at para. 4.

The ALJ recognized that the "effect [of the injury] on earning capacity is not a factor to be considered," but concluded also that the AMA Guides did "not provide a fair, accurate measure of the degree of impairment." *Id.* at para. 8 and 9. After making an "independent evaluation of the record," the ALJ found that claimant had sustained a seventy-percent permanent impairment of function. *Id.* at para. 9 and 11. He awarded claimant fifty percent of his average monthly wage for a period of thirty-five months, a total of $23,187.50. A.R.S. § 23–1044(B)(15) and (21).

Pursuant to the employer's request, the ALJ reviewed his decision and affirmed the award. *See* A.R.S. §§ 23–942(D),–943(A) and (B). The employer and compensation carrier then sought special action reviewed by the court of appeals. A.R.S. §§ 23–951(A); 12–120.21(B); Rule 1, Ariz.R.P.Spec.Act., 17B A.R.S.

Court of Appeals

The court of appeals set aside the award, concluding it was "inconsistent" with the medical testimony and with Arizona Supreme Court decisions. The court reasoned that *unless* a medical expert determines that the AMA Guides do not "adequately" rate claimant's impairment, an ALJ cannot consider a claimant's inability to perform his job in determining the correct disability rating.

* * *

THE ISSUES

This case presents two interrelated issues:

1. When may an ALJ reject the AMA Guides in determining a claimant's percentage of permanent impairment?

2. Did the ALJ here abuse his discretion in concluding that the AMA Guides did not accurately reflect the true percentage of claimant's leg impairment?

DISCUSSION

The Arizona workers' compensation program provides benefits to covered employees disabled by industrial accidents. The program attempts to accurately ascertain the worker's disability and promptly distribute his benefits. To streamline procedures, the legislature created standard compensation percentages for specific ("scheduled") injuries. For instance, for the loss of a leg, the state compensation fund will pay fifty-five percent of a covered employee's average monthly wage for fifty months. A.R.S. § 23–1044(B)(15). This sum is in addition to compensation for any temporary total disability. A.R.S. § 23–1044(B). If the impairment is only partial, the fund will pay fifty percent of the worker's average monthly wage for the proportionate number of months that the partial loss bears to the total loss of use. A.R.S. § 23–1044(B)(21). Thus, if a leg is fifty percent impaired, the fund will pay benefits for only twenty-five months (fifty percent x fifty months). If the leg is seventy percent impaired, the payments are for thirty-five months (seventy percent x fifty months).

Normally the Commission determines the percentage of the leg's loss based on the treating physician's rating of the impairment resulting from the injury. When the physician discharges a claimant, the physician rates the percentage of functional impairment in accordance with the AMA Guides, if they apply, with a clinical report sufficiently detailed to support the percentage rating. *See* A.C.R.R. R4–13–113(D). The AMA Guides measure the clinical or physiological percentage of impairment without regard to how the injury affects a person's ability to perform his job. *See Adams v. Industrial Commission,* 113 Ariz. 294, 295, 552 P.2d 764, 765 (1976).

If a claimant is dissatisfied with the Commission's initial rating, he may seek a hearing before an ALJ. An ALJ determines the correct percentage of a claimant's disability and may consider a wide range of evidence to ensure "substantial justice." A.R.S. § 23–941(F). Although the AMA Guides are important in the disability rating, they are not the philosopher's stone: . . .

Indeed, non-medical factors may be vital when assessing a disability, despite the AMA Guides. *See Jaske v. Murray Ohio Manufacturing Co., Inc.,* 750 S.W.2d 150, 151 (Tenn.1988). In fact, sometimes the AMA Guides do not apply. *See, e.g., Dayron Corp. v. Morehead,* 509 So.2d 930 (Fla.1987) (AMA Guides inadequately gave a rating of zero to five percent permanent impairment for a machinist who could no longer perform his craft because of acute contact dermatitis to cutting oils); *OBS Co., Inc. v. Freeney,* 475 So.2d 947 (Fla.Dist.Ct.App.1985) (AMA Guides gave no ratable permanent impairment for journeyman plasterer who developed severe contact dermatitis to wet plaster and cement); *Kroeplin v. North Dakota Workmen's Compensation Bureau,* 415 N.W.2d 807 (N.D.1987) (employee entitled to industrial award even though the AMA Guides did not substantiate subjective pain symptoms). Therefore, when other evidence requires a different result, a medical expert cannot bind the ALJ to unreasoning adherence to the AMA Guides.

Here, claimant sought a hearing to establish the correct rating of his permanent disability. Using the AMA Guides as his only criterion, Dr. Alway concluded that claimant has a fifty percent impairment in his right leg. However, Dr. Alway also testified that the AMA Guides provided a fair measure of claimant's medical impairment "but not his disability as far as his former occupation." Claimant testified, on the other hand, that he could only perform about twenty-two percent of his duties as a hod carrier. Dr. Alway agreed with this assessment. The labor consultant concurred in the general range, stating that claimant could perform about thirty-five percent of his job.

The ALJ is responsible for determining the percentage of disability, not simply the percentage of physiological impairment in the functioning of limbs and organs. The AMA Guides measure only clinical, physical impairment expressed in percentage of loss of motion. The ALJ, however, must determine the degree of functional loss or impairment, and thus may consider claimant's inability to pursue the specific craft, job, or profession he or she practiced at the time of the incapacitating industrial injury. *Dutra,* 135 Ariz. at 61, 659 P.2d at 20.

Therefore, the individual claimant's occupation, viewed in light of the physical impairment, affects the ALJ's determination of the claimant's "disability." Each craft, calling, or job places unique demands on the body. Thus, a five percent loss of leg movement might slightly disable a lawyer or computer programmer but could markedly disable a laborer or professional dancer. Of course, we leave undisturbed the rule that in no event should the ALJ consider the actual loss of individual earning capacity in establishing the correct percentage of scheduled disability. *See* A.R.S. § 23–1044(H); *Gomez,* 148 Ariz. at 569, 716 P.2d at 26. . . .

The AMA Guides are only a tool adopted by administrative regulation to assist in ascertaining an injured worker's percentage of disability. Thus, when the AMA Guides do not truly reflect a claimant's loss, the ALJ must use his discretion to hear additional evidence and, from the whole record, establish a rating independent of the AMA recommendations. *W.A. Krueger Co.*, 150 Ariz. at 68, 722 P.2d at 236. That is why A.C.R.R. R4–13–113(D) states that the AMA Guides "should" be used to establish a rating of functional impairment *"if applicable"* (emphasis added). If an injury has resulted in a functional impairment not adequately reflected by clinical measurement under the AMA Guides, then an ALJ must consider impact on job performance. *See Gomez*, 148 Ariz. at 569, 716 P.2d at 26.

Conclusion

An ALJ may properly consider the impact of the industrial accident on a claimant's ability to perform his or her job. Here, the AMA Guides gave only a fifty percent rating when the medical expert, the labor consultant, *and* the claimant all agreed that the impact on claimant's ability to perform his job was greater than fifty percent. The ALJ's resulting seventy percent rating reasonably conformed to the testimony. Thus, the award was supported by the evidence.

We vacate the court of appeals' opinion and reinstate the Commission's award.

Notes

1. The American Medical Association created a committee on the topic of rating permanent impairment in 1956. Over the next fifteen years, the committee developed guides for rating particular impairments. In 1971, the AMA compiled and published the standards that had been developed at that time. This work become known as the American Medical Association *Guides to the Evaluation of Permanent Impairment* (AMA *Guides*). The AMA *Guides* are revised periodically and the fourth edition was published in1993.

Each chapter of the *Guides* prescribes specific means for measuring impairment of particular organs or bodily system and translating such measurements into percentage ratings. The percentage is calculated on both an organ and "whole person" basis. The knee injury involved in *Slover Masonry,* for example, would be covered in Chapter 3. The AMA *Guides* instruct the examining physician to measure the degree of lost flexion in the knee by the use of an instrument called a goniometer; and then provides a chart that translates that measurement into a "percentage impairment of the lower extremity" and "percentage impairment of the whole person". The actual application of the *Guides* can be quite complex. See, e.g., Deschampe v. Arrowhead Tree Service, 428 N.W.2d 795 (Minn.1988) (calculating impairment rating for brain injury); York v. Burgess–Norton Mfg. Co., 803 P.2d 697 (Okl.1990) (calculating impairment rating for injury to lung and respiratory system).

2. In 1972, *The Report of the National Commission on State Workmen's Compensation Laws* recommended that states use the AMA *Guides* as a source of standardized and medically justified criteria for measuring physical impairment. *Id.*, at 69. The Report cautioned, however, that physical "impairment" was a more limited concept than "disability"; and that disability should be the primary basis for awarding permanent partial disability benefits. At first, states were slow to adopt the AMA *Guides* as standards.

During the 1980's, a number of states embraced the AMA *Guides*. Today, more than thirty states either mandate or approve the use of the AMA *Guides* in calculating disability benefits. See Steven Babitsky and James J. Mangraviti, Jr., *Understanding The AMA Guides in Workers' Compensation* (2d ed. 1996) (listing jurisdictions). Proponents of the use of the AMA *Guides* maintain that they will "establish more certainty and uniformity" to the rating of permanent impairment. E.g., Tenn. Code Ann. § 50–6–204(d)(3); Kroeplin v. North Dakota Workmen's Compensation Bureau, 415 N.W.2d 807, 808 (N.D.1987).

3.   The use of the AMA *Guides* to calculate an award of benefits under workers' compensation has been criticized on several grounds. One commentator questions the degree of objectivity in the *Guides*. Any standardized measurement of impairment requires a comparison of the injured worker to some "norm." The comparisons used in the AMA *Guides* for measuring impairment of the "whole person" are based on assumptions about what constitutes normal activities and abilities. The assumptions about the norm are inherently subjective and often controversial. Indeed, many of the examples used in the guidelines reflect gender differences. In the reproductive system chapter, for example, a man may receive a 5–10% whole-person impairment rating for an injury that diminishes his sexual "sensation", but a woman would receive an impairment rating of 0% so long as sexual intercourse "is possible". See, Pryor, *Flawed Promises: A Critical Evaluation of the American Medical Association's Guides to the Evaluation of Permanent Impairment,* 103 Harv.L.Rev. 964, 970 (1990). Others criticize the *Guides* for utilizing a conservative approach to rating individual impairments and then further reducing the rating by combining instead of cumulating multiple impairments. S. Babitsky and G. Shapiro, *The Use of the AMA Guides to the Evaluation of Permanent Impairment in Workers' Compensation Cases* 30–40 (1986).

Constitutional challenges to the mandated use of the AMA *Guides* have generally failed. E.g., Texas Workers' Compensation Comm'n. v. Garcia, 893 S.W.2d 504 (Tex.1995); Brown v. Campbell Bd. of Educ., 915 S.W.2d 407 (Tenn.1995); Allen v. Natrona County School Dist., 811 P.2d 1 (Wyo.1991).

4.   Most jurisdictions adhere to the approach reflected in *Slover Masonry,* that the AMA *Guides* are not the exclusive measure of disability. In addition to the authorities cited in the principal case, see City of Aurora v. Vaughn, 824 P.2d 825 (Colo.App.1991) (hearing loss); Sutton v. Quality Furniture Co., 191 Ga.App. 279, 381 S.E.2d 389 (1989) (claimant may be awarded disability benefits for physical impairment caused solely by pain, despite *Guides* failure to provide a methodology for evaluating impairments based solely on pain).

5.   The court in *Slover Masonry* noted that scheduled benefits for permanent partial disability are payable in addition to whatever benefits have been paid for temporary total disability. The cumulation of temporary total and permanent partial disability benefits is quite common. E.g., Md. Code Ann., Lab. And Emp. § 9–639; Ohio Rev.Code Ann. § 4123.57. A few states reduce the award for permanent partial disability by the amount paid for temporary total or temporary partial disability. E.g., La.Rev.Stat.Ann. § 23:1223. See U.S. Dept. of Labor, Employment Standards Administration,

Office of Workers' Compensation Programs, *State Workers' Compensation Laws*, Table 9b (January 1998) (listing jurisdictions).

The line separating "temporary" from "permanent" is often expressed in terms of the claimant's physical condition. An employee who has not reached "maximum medical improvement" may be eligible for temporary disability benefits (total or partial), but is not entitled to permanent disability benefits (total or partial). E.g., J.A. Riggs Tractor Co. v. Etzkorn, 30 Ark.App. 200, 785 S.W.2d 51 (1990) (payments made during the "healing period" are classified as temporary total disability benefits and are not credited against the maximum permanent total disability benefits to which the employee is entitled; payment of permanent total disability begins only after the "healing period" is completed); State v. Birditt, 181 Ga.App. 356, 352 S.E.2d 203 (1986) (nurse who sustained a head injury returned to work but continued to experience stuttering, loss of memory and loss of concentration; since the claimant had returned to work at full pay, she was not eligible for temporary disability benefits; in light of physician's testimony that claimant's condition might improve over the next 6 to 9 months, claimant was not eligible for permanent partial disability benefits). Conversely, entitlement to temporary disability benefits (total or partial) ceases upon the claimant's reaching maximum medical improvement. E.g., Coca–Cola Bottling Co. v. Tunson, 534 So.2d 910 (Fla.App.1988) (since all the medical testimony established that the claimant had reached maximum medical improvement, no award could be made for temporary total disability benefits).

Should factors other than the claimant's physical condition influence the classification of a disability as permanent or temporary? Consider, for example, the role of vocational rehabilitation discussed in Section 1 of this chapter. Vocational rehabilitation may reduce the long range impact of an injury on earning capacity without improving the worker's physical condition. It is also apparent that a worker's medical condition might stabilize before vocational rehabilitation is complete. Should a worker who has reached maximum medical improvement be eligible for temporary disability benefits while undergoing vocational rehabilitation? Compare, Allee v. Contractors, Inc., 783 P.2d 273 (Colo.1989) (worker who had reached maximum medical improvement is entitled to temporary partial disability benefits while enrolled in a vocational rehabilitation program) with Wroten v. Lamphere, 147 Vt. 606, 523 A.2d 1236 (1987) (employee who had reached maximum medical improvement is not entitled to receive temporary total disability benefits while completing vocational rehabilitation).

SECTION 3.   THE "SECOND INJURY" PROBLEM

LAWSON v. SUWANEE FRUIT & STEAMSHIP CO.

Supreme Court of the United States, 1949.
336 U.S. 198, 69 S.Ct. 503, 93 L.Ed. 611.

Mr. JUSTICE MURPHY delivered the opinion of the Court.

This is a workmen's compensation case, under the Longshoremen's and Harbor Workers' Compensation Act, 44 Stat. 1424, 33 U.S.C. § 901 et seq., 33 U.S.C.A. § 901 et seq. A narrow and difficult question of statutory construction confronts us.

John Davis lost the sight of his right eye in an accident unconnected with industry or his employment. He was later hired by respondent. An injury occurred during this employment, and he is now blind in both eyes. The parties agree that he is totally disabled within the meaning of the Act; they also agree that the employer is liable for compensation for the loss of the left eye. The dispute is narrowed to this question: should the employer or the statutory second injury fund, administered by petitioner, be liable for the balance of payments to equal compensation for total disability?

Petitioner concluded that the employer was liable. The employer secured a reversal of this determination in the District Court for the Southern District of Florida, 68 F.Supp. 616, and the Court of Appeals for the Fifth Circuit affirmed the judgment of the District Court. 166 F.2d 13. Because this decision conflicted with that of the Court of Appeals for the District of Columbia in National Homeopathic Hospital Association of District of Columbia v. Britton, 79 U.S.App.D.C. 309, 147 F.2d 561, certiorari denied 325 U.S. 857, 65 S.Ct. 1185, 89 L.Ed. 1977, we granted certiorari.

Section 8(f)(1) of the Act provides that "If an employee receive an injury which of itself would only cause permanent partial disability but which, *combined with a previous disability,* does in fact cause permanent total disability, the employer shall provide compensation only for the disability caused by the subsequent injury: *Provided, however,* That in addition to compensation for such permanent partial disability, and after the cessation of the payments for the prescribed period of weeks, the employee shall be paid the remainder of the compensation that would be due for permanent total disability. Such additional compensation shall be paid out of the special fund established in section 44." The court below [166 F.2d 13, 14] held that this section is "clear and unambiguous, and therefore needs no construction. When read in its ordinary sense it can have but one meaning": liability for the second injury fund.

But the word "disability" is defined in the statute. Section 2 provides that "when used in this Act . . . (10) 'Disability means incapacity because of *injury* . . . ." (Emphasis supplied.) The word "injury" is, in turn, defined as "accidental injury or death arising out of and in the course of employment . . . ." § 2(2). If these definitions are read into the second injury provision, then, it read as follows: "If an employee receive an injury which of itself would only cause permanent partial disability but which, combined with a previous *incapacity because of accidental injury or death arising out of and in the course of employment,* does in fact cause permanent total disability, the employer shall provide compensation only for the disability caused by the subsequent injury." Because Davis' previous injury was nonindustrial, this reading points to liability for the employer.

If Congress intended to use the term "disability" as a term of art, a shorthand way of referring to the statutory definition, the employer must pay total compensation. If Congress intended a broader and more usual concept of the word, the judgment below must be affirmed. Statutory definitions control the meaning of statutory words, of course, in the usual case. But this is an unusual case. If we read the definition into § 8(f)(1) in a mechanical fashion, we create obvious incongruities in the language and we destroy one of the major purposes of the second injury provision: the prevention of employer discrimination against handicapped workers. We have concluded that Congress would not have intended such a result.

Chief Justice Groner, dissenting in the National Homeopathic case, supra, 147 F.2d at page 565, noticed that the "interreplacements of words" we have set out above "produces a manifest incongruity, for . . . it would literally result in this: ' . . . a previous *incapacity* because of accidental injury or *death*'—And if to avoid this it be argued that only a portion of the definition of injury should be inserted, the result would be to change or at least to limit the statutory definition only to produce a desired result, which no one would urge or defend. It is evident, therefore," that the definition of disability was "not made with watch-like precision" and should not be so applied in § 8(f)(1). If the intent of Congress had been to limit the applicability of this subsection in the fashion for which petitioner contends, "it could easily have accomplished this by the insertion of the word 'compensable' between the words 'previous' and 'disability'. . . ." And see Atlantic Cleaners & Dyers v. United States, 286 U.S. 427, 52 S.Ct. 607, 76 L.Ed. 1204.

More important, perhaps, is the disservice we would do to the purpose of the second injury provision. We must look to the explanation of congressional intent behind the subsection. A witness at a hearing on the measure outlined his reasons for favoring the provision in the following manner: "The second injury proposition is as much to the advantage of the employer and his interests as it is for the benefit of the employee. It protects the employer who has hired, say, a one-eyed worker who goes and loses his other eye and becomes a total disability. The employer without this sort of thing would have to pay total permanent disability compensation. Then, on the other hand, this also protects the worker with one eye from being denied employment on account of his being an extra risk. Now, by simply taking this up in this way it is possible to protect both the employer and to protect the one-eyed employee also."

Petitioner relies on the statement of another witness before the Senate Committee, who favored inclusion of the second injury provisions because "they have become a commonplace . . . in State compensation legislation and ought to be included in the Act." And petitioner states that "we may appropriately refer, therefore, to the second injury provisions in other statutes and to the evaluations made by administrative experts in the field for guidance with respect to the manner in which opposing policy considerations have been resolved." But our search for guidance in the sources suggested by petitioner convinces us that petitioner's theories are not well-founded.

From the attitude of experts in the field, one would not expect Congress to distinguish between two types of handicapped workers. The annual conventions of the International Association of Industrial Accident Boards and Commissions provide the most helpful considerations of the problem. At the 1931 convention, Mr. Joseph Parks of the Massachusetts Commission spoke as follows of workmen's compensation legislation without a second injury provision: "I little knew that this great piece of legislation . . . would become an instrument of persecution, as I may call it, of men who are physically handicapped, but that is what it has become. Men who are physically handicapped are being discriminated against in our Commonwealth."

This attitude has been echoed by Mr. Charles Sharkey of the United States Bureau of Labor Statistics; Miss Frances Perkins, then Industrial Commissioner in New York; and others. Perhaps the most impressive evidence of the force behind these statements is that offered by Mr. I.K. Huber of Oklahoma. Nease v. Hughes Stone Co., 114 Okl. 170, 244 P. 778, held the employer liable for total compensation for loss of the second eye. After the decision, Mr. Huber reports, "thousands of one-eyed, one-armed, one-handed men in the State of Oklahoma were let out and can not get employment coming under the workmen's compensation law of Oklahoma. . . . Those . . . court decisions put us in bad shape. . . . The decision displaced between seven and eight thousand men in less than 30 days in Oklahoma."

A distinction between a worker previously injured in industry and one handicapped by a cause outside of industry has no logical foundation if we accept the premise that the purpose of the fund is that of aid to the handicapped. This is the conclusion of Mr. Fred Wilcox, then Chairman of the Wisconsin Commission: "Wisconsin takes no account of where the injured man may have gotten his first injury. It makes no difference where he got it. It is just as serious to him, when he has the second injury, as if he had gotten the first one in industry." We cannot attribute the illogic of petitioner's position to Congress.

Our conclusion is reinforced by the administrative practice under the New York statute. The federal statute is based upon New York law. In New York "the commission holds that if the man loses his second eye in an industrial accident it is immaterial how he lost his first eye. The loss of eyesight in one eye may have been congenital; it may have occurred when the child was two years old, or it may have occurred after he was grown, but not in an industrial accident. Nevertheless, at the time he loses his second eye he has suffered total disability." . . .

Petitioner's most strenuous argument is that the fund will soon be insolvent if we open liability to a nonindustrial previous injury, and that therefore Congress could not have contemplated the result we reach. Petitioner's worries seem exaggerated in the light of Wisconsin and New York experience. From 1919 to 1933, Wisconsin's fund had only 50 second injury cases charged against it. Second–Injury Funds as Employment Aids to the Handicapped, U.S. Division of Labor Standards (1944) p. 7. From 1919 to 1943, only 99 cases were charged against the New York fund. Id., p. 5. In 1930 Miss Frances Perkins told her associates that the problem is "not so large ... as it appears."

On the basis of the incongruity involved in applying the definition mechanically, the unmistakable purpose of the second injury fund, and the interpretation of the State statute on which the federal act is based, we conclude that the term "disability" was not used as a term of art in § 8(f)(1), and that the judgment must be affirmed.

Affirmed.

Mr. Justice Douglas dissents.

[Footnotes to the opinion have been omitted.]

Notes

1. How should a worker be compensated when successive injuries produce a total disability greater than the sum of the individual effects of the two or more injuries? There are at least three possible solutions to the problem.

One is to require the last employer to bear the entire compensation burden for the total disability that was brought into existence by the last injury. For example, if the employee had previously lost one eye, and while working for the last employer lost the second eye, the last employer, under this plan, would pay compensation for total blindness. This is the general rule where there is no statute providing for a "second injury" or "subsequent injury" fund, or where the case is not covered by such a statute. Schwab v. Emporium Forestry Co., 216 N.Y. 712, 111 N.E. 1099 (1915) (claimant, who had previously lost his left hand, lost his right hand at the wrist as a result of an industrial injury, held entitled to compensation for permanent total disability); Polston v. Ready Made Homes, 171 Kan. 336, 232 P.2d 446 (1951) (claimant suffered loss of eye in industrial accident but previous injury to other eye did not bring case within second injury statute, employer held liable for permanent total disability). This method of handling the matter may seem unfair to the employer, but may be even more harmful to handicapped employees if, as suggested in the principal case, it results in discrimination against them in employment policies.

Another solution is apportionment under statutes that limit the liability of employers in whose employment the last injury was sustained to only the compensation that would normally be payable for that injury standing alone. If there is no second injury fund statute coupled with such an apportionment provision, the worker receives compensation only for the second injury. E.g., Georgia Ins. Service v. Lord, 83 Ga.App. 28, 62 S.E.2d 402 (1950) (employee who was blind in his right eye lost the sight in his left eye in second injury, held compensation limited to loss of one eye).

The most common solution to the problem is the so-called second injury or subsequent injury plan which apportions responsibility for compensating the worker between the employer and a fund. Almost every state, the

District of Columbia, Puerto Rico and the Longshore and Harbor Worker' Compensation Act now employ this kind of apportionment scheme.

2. In many states the Fund's contribution to the final award is the difference between the compensation that would be payable for the second injury alone and the compensation payable for the combined injuries. E.g., 820 Ill.Comp.Stat.Ann. 305/8(f); N.J.Stat.Ann. § 34:15–15. Other states utilize a more rigid formula to apportion disability costs between the employer and the Fund. E.g., Haw.Rev.Stat. § 386–33 (employer pays disability benefits for the first 104 weeks of disability and the Fund pays any benefits beyond 104 weeks).

In some states the employer pays only for the disability attributable to the second injury and the employee must apply directly to the Second Injury Fund for additional compensation. E.g., Cal.Labor Code § 4750; Ark.Stat. Ann. § 11–9–525. In other states the employer compensates the employee for the entire disability and seeks reimbursement from the Fund for a portion of its payments. E.g., Ga.Code Ann. § 34–9–360; N.Y. Work. Comp. Law § 15(8)(d). What difference does it make whether the employer or the employee applies for payment from the Second Injury Fund? Which approach do you think is preferable?

Second Injury Funds commonly are financed by payments from workers' compensation insurance carriers in cases of work-related deaths where there are no dependents to collect death benefits. A portion of the death benefits that would have been payable to dependents is paid to the Fund. See, Colo.Rev.Stat. § 8–46–102; N.Y. Work. Comp. Law § 15(h). Other common sources of funding include small percentage assessments against all compensation carriers or other special assessments.

3. What type of preexisting injury or condition is necessary to trigger recourse to the Second Injury Fund? The primary issue addressed in *Lawson* concerns the origin of the preexisting condition. A variation of this issue was addressed in McLean's Case, 326 Mass. 72, 93 N.E.2d 233 (1950). McLean had a congenital dislocation of the lens of his right eye, and later suffered a work injury that detached the retina of his left eye. The work injury in combination with the congenital condition left the worker with the industrial loss of both eyes. The employer sought reimbursement from the Second Injury Fund. The specific statutory provision in effect at that time covered employees who had "previously suffered a personal injury." The court interpreted this phrase as excluding congenital conditions. Consequently, the employer was not entitled to reimbursement from the Fund and had to pay full compensation for the loss of both eyes. The Massachusetts second injury fund statute was later amended to include congenital conditions. See, Fireman's Fund Ins. v. Commonwealth, 18 Mass.App.Ct. 129, 463 N.E.2d 582 (1984). Today, most second injury fund provisions cover preexisting congenital conditions. E.g., Second Injury Fund v. Conrad, 947 S.W.2d 278 (Tex.App. 1997) (Fund is liable when claimant's work-related injury combined with birth defect to produce permanent total disability); Fierro v. Stanley's Hardware, 104 N.M. 411, 722 P.2d 662 (App.1986) (second injury fund is responsible for a portion of benefits paid to a worker who had a preexisting congenital condition in the right eye and suffered a work injury to the left eye); Whiteside v. Morrison, Inc., 799 S.W.2d 213 (Tenn.1990) (apportioning

compensation between employer and Fund for disability resulting from work injury and congenital vascular malformation).

Many states limit the application of the second injury fund to specific preexisting conditions, such as the loss of a hand or eye. If the employee's prior impairment is not included on the list of covered conditions, neither the employer nor the worker may resort to the second injury fund. E.g., Golden Bay Earthquakes v. W.C.A.B., 129 Pa.Cmwlth. 236, 565 A.2d 212 (1989) (claimant had lost the hearing in one ear as a child and lost the hearing in the other ear as the result of being hit in the head while playing professional soccer; since the preexisting hearing loss was not a covered condition under the statute, claimant could not secure additional benefits from second injury fund). Second injury funds in other states are less rigidly limited and usually cover an array of preexisting general injuries. See generally, 5 A. Larson and L. Larson, Larson's Workers' Compensation Law § 59.32(e) (1998).

Two other common limitations based on the nature of the preexisting condition are worth noting. The first limitation is the permanence of the employee's prior condition. Virtually all states require that the preexisting condition have been "permanent" in order to trigger second injury fund liability. If the prior condition was not permanent, the Fund bears no liability and the employer pays for the entire disability. E.g., D.A. Netzel, Inc. v. Special Disability Trust Fund, 681 So.2d 874 (Fla.App.1996) (claimant's obesity was not a permanent physical impairment entitling employer to reimbursement); Todd Shipyards v. Director, Office of Workers' Compensation Programs, 793 F.2d 1012 (9th Cir.1986) (employer is not entitled to reimbursement by Fund when employee's prior back injury produced no permanent impairment). The second limitation is whether the preexisting condition actually or potentially impaired the claimant's earning capacity prior to his second injury. As a general matter, the prior impairment needs to have been of a physical quality that did or reasonably could have interfered with the claimant's securing employment. Compare Hettenhausen v. Gene Jantzen Chevrolet, 499 S.W.2d 785 (Mo.1973) (Second Injury Fund should not provide additional compensation to worker whose preexisting condition (surgical removal of testicle) did not impair his earning capacity) with Archer v. Bonners Ferry Datsun, 117 Idaho 166, 786 P.2d 557 (1990) (Second Injury Fund must contribute to permanent total disability award made to employee whose preexisting knee injury "constituted a hindrance or obstacle to obtaining employment for the particular claimant").

4. It is not enough that the preexisting permanent impairment actually or potentially impaired the worker's ability to secure employment. The preexisting condition must contribute in some significant way to the disability resulting from the second injury. This requirement is defined by Ga.Code Ann. § 34–9–351(1) as follows:

(a) Had the preexisting permanent impairment not been present, the subsequent injury would not have occurred;

(b) The disability resulting from the subsequent injury in conjunction with the preexisting permanent impairment is materially, substantially, and cumulatively greater than that which would have resulted had the preexisting permanent impairment not been present, and the employer has been required to pay and has paid compensation for that greater disability; or

(c) Death would not have been accelerated had the preexisting permanent impairment not been present.

If the preexisting condition did not significantly contribute to the final disability, no claim against the second injury fund can be made. E.g., Norris v. Iowa Beef Processors, Inc., 224 Neb. 867, 402 N.W.2d 658 (1987) (Second Injury Fund is not liable for any portion of claimant's work related injuries when preexisting conditions (blindness in one eye) neither caused nor enhanced the subsequent injuries to arm, knee, and shoulder).

5. *Lawson* explains that one of the primary purposes of second injury funds is to remove some of the economic disincentives that might discourage employers from hiring persons with permanent disabilities. Because only employers who are aware of a worker's preexisting condition would be so discouraged, most statutes condition the application of the second injury fund upon proof of the employer's awareness of the employee's preexisting permanent disability. The degree of awareness demanded varies among jurisdictions. The most demanding states require written documentation of the employer's knowledge of the employee's preexisting condition. E.g., Sea–Land Services, Inc. v. State, Second Injury Fund, 737 P.2d 793 (Alaska 1987) (employer who had actual knowledge of employee's prior back surgery could not make a claim against the Second Injury Fund when the employer's written record did not clearly reflect that the employee suffered from a permanent impairment). Other states condition second injury fund liability on proof that the employer had "actual knowledge" of the employee's preexisting condition, although proof of actual knowledge may be circumstantial. E.g., Whiteside v. Morrison, Inc., 799 S.W.2d 213 (Tenn.1990) (employer who had actual knowledge of employee's physical limitations may make a claim against the Second Injury Fund despite ignorance of the underlying medical cause of the limitation). Perhaps the most common approach is to require that the prior impairment be "obviously manifested." This standard is met when the preexisting permanent disability would be "obvious and apparent from observation and examination by an ordinary layman." Special Indemnity Fund v. Scott, 652 P.2d 278 (Okl.1982) (preexisting congenital pilonidal cyst was sufficiently manifest to fall within the second injury fund statute). The broadest second injury fund coverage is found under statutes that apportion liability between the employer and the Fund even when the preexisting condition was not known or manifest. E.g., Flores v. Honolulu Dept. of Parks & Recreation, 67 Hawaii 663, 701 P.2d 1282 (1985) (second injury fund liable for 80% of disability even though worker's preexisting heart condition was not manifest).

6. The second injury fund cases raise questions concerning the apportionment of disability costs that are reminiscent of those explored in Chapter 6 dealing with occupational disease, heart conditions, and psychological disabilities and in Chapter 7 dealing with the effect of independent causes after the accident. Collectively, these materials have examined several alternative apportionment schemes that might be employed when factors other than the claimant's last employment contributed to producing a disability. What are the most important considerations to take into account in appor-

tioning disability costs? In light of those considerations, what is the ideal method of apportionment when factors other than the claimant's last employment help produce the disability?

7.   The Americans With Disabilities Act (ADA), 42 U.S.C.A. § 12101 et. seq., prohibits employment discrimination against physically disabled persons. This federal statute raises a number of issues pertaining to state workers' compensation laws, including second injury funds. As discussed in note 5 above, many state second injury fund statutes require some evidence that the employer was aware of the worker's pre-existing disability as a prerequisite for asserting a claim against the fund. The ADA, however, prohibits employers from asking prospective employees about their workers' compensation history and greatly restricts pre-employment medical examinations. How is an employer to obtain the kind of information needed to assert a claim under the state second injury fund provision without violating the federal ADA?

A common purpose of both state second injury fund laws and the ADA is to facilitate the employment of workers with pre-existing disabilities. Second injury funds advance this goal by reducing one economic disincentive to hiring the disabled. The ADA acts more directly by prohibiting discrimination. In light of the direct prohibitions of the ADA, are second injury funds needed to make employment opportunities available to those with pre-existing permanent impairments? For an argument that second injury funds are no longer needed, see Catherine M. Dowd, Comment, Oklahoma's Special Indemnity Fund: A Fund Without a Function?, 30 Tulsa L. Rev. 745 (1995). The availability of remedies under the ADA was one of the reasons given in support of the prospective repeal of the Colorado and Kansas second injury fund laws. Id., at 765.

The ADA intersects with other provisions of state workers' compensation laws. In some states, an employer may not have to pay compensation benefits to an employee who falsely answers questions about prior injuries on his employment application. E.g, Georgia Electric Co. v. Rycroft, 259 Ga. 155, 378 S.E.2d 111 (Ga. 1989). The ADA now prohibits employers from asking the type of question that gave rise to the misrepresentation defense in *Rycroft*. Is the workers' compensation defense of misrepresentation abrogated by an employer's violation of the ADA? The Georgia Supreme Court answered this question in the negative. Caldwell v. Aarlin/Holcombe Armature Co., 267 Ga. 613, 481 S.E.2d 196 (Ga. 1997). The court reasoned that state workers' compensation and the federal ADA were separate sets of laws. If the employers' conduct violated the ADA, the employee can pursue remedies under the ADA.

Two other sets of issues merit brief mention. Under the "employment-at-will" doctrine, a few states allow employers to terminate employees who file workers' compensation claims. E.g., Evans v. Bibb Co., 178 Ga.App. 139, 342 S.E.2d 484 (Ga.App.1986); Kelly v. Mississippi Valley Gas Co., 397 So.2d 874 (Miss.1981). The ADA obligates employers to accommodate workers with disabilities who are nonetheless able to do their job. How does the duty to accommodate under the ADA affect workers who have been injured on the job? For a discussion of what constitutes "reasonable accommodation" of workers who suffered repetitive stress injuries on the job, see Dalton v.

Subaru–Isuzu Automotive, Inc., 141 F.3d 667 (7th Cir.1998). The ADA only protects "qualified" workers with disabilities, i.e., those who can perform the essential job functions with or without reasonable accommodation. 42 U.S.C.A. § 12111(8). Can a worker who claims to be "disabled" for purposes of workers' compensation be considered "qualified" for purposes of the ADA? Some courts have concluded that employees who seek disability benefits under state workers' compensation laws cannot be considered "qualified" workers under the ADA. E.g., Hensley v. City of Punta Gorda, 686 So.2d 724 (Fla.App.1997); Jackson v. County of Los Angeles, 60 Cal. App.4th 171, 70 Cal.Rptr.2d 96 (Cal.App.1997). See Maureen C. Weston, The Road Best Traveled: Removing Judicial Roadblocks that Prevent Workers From Obtaining Both Disability Benefits and ADA Civil Rights Protection, 26 Hofsta L. Rev. 377 (1997).

For a more detailed discussion of the interplay of the ADA and workers' compensation, see Alison Steiner, The Americans With Disabilities Act of 1990 and Workers' Compensation: An Employee's Perspective, 62 Miss. L.J. 631 (1993); Scott A. Carlson, Comment, The ADA and the Illinois Workers' Compensation Act: Can Two "Rights" Make a "Wrong"?, 19 S. Ill. U. L. J. 567 (1995); Catherine M. Dowd, Comment, Oklahoma's Special Indemnity Fund: A Fund Without a Function?, 30 Tulsa L. Rev. 745 (1995); 5 A. Larson and L. Larson, Larson's Workers' Compensation Law § 59.33(g) (1998).

SECTION 4. COORDINATING WORKERS' COMPENSATION WITH OTHER SOURCES OF BENEFITS

DEPARTMENT OF PUBLIC HEALTH v. WILCOX

Reprinted in Chapter 1, section 3.

Notes

1. Should the disabled worker be allowed to recover both social security disability and workers' compensation benefits? If some sort of adjustment is to be made, is it preferable to reduce social security benefits by reason of receipt of workers' compensation benefits, or visa versa?

2. Approximately one-third of the states reduce workers' compensation benefits in some manner when the employee also receives social security disability benefits. These setoff provisions vary widely in their scope and method of operation. For example, some states apply the social security setoff against both permanent and temporary disability benefits while others reduce only permanent total disability benefits. Compare State, Department of Transportation v. Jackson, 379 So.2d 1045 (Fla.App.1980) ("the setoff is applicable to all weekly benefits, whether permanent, temporary, total, or partial") with Huval Baking Co. v. Fontenot, 629 S.2d 431 (La.App.1993) (statute allows setoff for social security benefits only when the employee is permanently and totally disabled). In some states the setoff is limited to one-half the social security benefits received. E.g., Mich.Comp.Laws § 418.354; N.D.Cent.Code § 65–05–09.1. This limitation reflects the fact that employees and employers each contribute half of the payments into the social security system. Some consider it unfair to reduce an employee's workers' compensation benefits because of an "insurance policy" paid for by the employee. The intricacies of coordinating workers' compensation and social security are

discussed in 9 A. Larson and L. Larson, Larson's Workers' Compensation Law § 97.35 (1998).

3. Should workers' compensation benefits be reduced if the employee is receiving benefits under some private health, accident or disability insurance plan? Compare Varnell v. Union Carbide, 29 Ark.App. 185, 779 S.W.2d 542 (1989) (employee who injured her back had medical expenses paid by her employer's group health insurer and received income benefits under employer's sick pay plan; the injury was later ruled to be covered under workers' compensation; held that employer is not entitled to "credit" for payments made by group health carrier or sick pay plan) with Scriven v. Industrial Comm., 736 P.2d 414 (Colo.App.1987) (workers' compensation award properly reduced by amounts received under employer-financed pension plan) and Warsocki v. City of Omaha, 1 Neb.App. 874, 510 N.W.2d 446 (Neb.App.1993) (workers' compensation may be offset by employer's proportional share of service-connected disability pension benefits).

4. Should workers' compensation disability benefits be adjusted when the disabled worker reaches the normal retirement age? Some states make adjustments. E.g., Mont.Code Ann. § 39–71–710 (terminating permanent total disability benefits when employee is eligible to receive "full social security retirement benefits"); Mich.Comp.Laws § 418.354(1)(a) (reducing permanent total disability benefits by 50% of old age insurance benefits under social security); Polomski v. Mayor of Baltimore, 344 Md. 70, 684 A.2d 1338 (App.1996) (firefighter's workers' compensation benefits were reduced so that those benefits combined with retirement benefits would not exceed his weekly wage). But see State ex rel. Boan v. Richardson, 198 W.Va. 545, 482 S.E.2d 162 (W.Va. 1996) (statute mandating setoff of permanent total disability benefits when the claimant receives old age benefits under Social Security Act violates equal protection by not treating all social security recipients equally).

5. For a comprehensive listing of various offset provisions, see U.S. Dept. of Labor, Employment Standards Administration, Office of Workers' Compensation Programs, *State Workers' Compensation Laws*, Table 17 (January 1998).

Does continuing payment of disability benefits past the age of normal retirement force the workers' compensation system to do more than protect against wage-loss? Does the answer to this question depend on whether there is any legally enforceable mandatory retirement age? See, C. Williams and P. Young, *Workers' Compensation Disability Benefits During Retirement Years: Proper and Present Role,* in Benefits, Costs, and Cycles in Workers' Compensation (Borba and Appel eds. 1990).

Chapter 9

DEATH BENEFITS

INTRODUCTION TO THIS CHAPTER

One of the purposes of the workers' compensation law in cases in which the work injury results in death of the employee, is to provide funds to cover burial expenses. This is true in all states except Oklahoma and even there a specified amount may be paid to decedent's estate in no-dependency cases. The amount provided for such expense varies from one state to another from $800.00 to $7,5000.00[1]. Many states also provide additional funds to cover the costs of transporting the employee's body from the place of death to the place of burial. No substantial legal problems arise in connection with these provisions.

The other purpose of providing benefits in cases of death from work injury is to take care of the members of the decedent's family and other individuals who were economically dependent upon the decedent's capacity to earn income. This chapter examines a substantial number of legal problems that arise in this connection. Among the subjects considered are the nature of dependency; what persons are included in certain statutory descriptions or terms such as "widow," "widower," and "children"; who are "members of the family"; what is the relationship, if any, between the right of the injured employee to compensation during lifetime and the right of the dependents to compensation after the decedent's death; priorities among different dependents or classes of dependents; and the legal status of accrued and unaccrued benefits at the time of the death of the employee.

SECTION 1. NATURE OF DEPENDENCY

DURBIN v. ARGONAUT INSURANCE CO.
Court of Appeal of Louisiana, 1980.
393 So.2d 385.

LOTTINGER, JUDGE.

The parents of a deceased employee brought this action for death benefits against the employer's workmen's compensation insurance car-

---

1. For details see Table 13, Maximum Burial Allowances, U.S. Department of Labor, Employment Standards Administra- tion, Division of State Workers' Compensa- tion Standards, January 1, 1998.

rier. The insurer appeals the trial court judgment awarding the plaintiffs $25.00 per week for 400 weeks. The plaintiffs have not appealed the trial court judgment rejecting their tort suit against the employer's executive officers. That matter is now final.

The sole issue on appeal is whether the plaintiffs proved they were actually dependent upon the deceased at the time of death. La.R.S. 23:1252, 1254. Eddie Durbin suffered a compensable fatal injury in 1976 while in the course and scope of his employment with Dibert Bancroft & Ross, Limited. At the time of death and for the two or three months he was working for the company, Eddie lived at home. Both parents testified that Eddie gave them $10.00 to $20.00 per week, depending upon the size of his check, up to a month before his death. His mother told him he need not continue contributing the money because he was getting married and he needed the money to establish his new apartment. Eddie's mother fixed him two meals a day while he lived at home and she fixed him a lunch to take to work. She washed his clothes and took care of his room. In his spare time, Eddie helped around his family's 110–acre farm by feeding the animals and getting the corn ground for about 100 head of cattle. He also occasionally helped out at a family restaurant. The father claimed the deceased on the father's income tax during the year of death. Both parents testified that the money given to them by Eddie was not in return for his living at the house.

In written reasons for judgment, the trial court found that there was a "partial actual dependency" on the part of the plaintiffs attributable to Eddie's earnings and to his work on the farm. The court explicitly took into account Eddie's contributions through work on the farm in finding under La.R.S. 23:1231 that Eddie contributed 20% of his total weekly wages to the plaintiffs.[2]

The defendants contend on appeal that the plaintiffs failed to prove that they were dependent either partially or fully on contributions from the deceased for their support. They cite the following facts to back up their claim: The parents' testimony regarding the contributions was self serving; The parents instructed the deceased to stop payments one month before the fatality since the son was soon to be married; The father claimed the son on his income tax return; The father occasionally gave Eddie money for work Eddie did on the farm or at the restaurant.

Under La.R.S. 23:1252 the question of legal and actual dependency in cases in which conclusive dependency does not exist shall be determined "in accordance with the facts as they may be at the time of the accident and death." La.R.S. 23:1254 provides that "the relation or

2. Eddie earned $3.26 per hour on the date of death which computes to $130.40 for a 40–hour week. A contribution of $10.00 to $20.00 per week out of that amount would represent 7.5% to 15% of the total weekly wage. The trial court apparently found that the work on the farm accounted for the remainder of the 20% which the deceased contributed to the plaintiffs.

dependency must exist at the time of the accident and at the time of death, and the mere expectation or hope of future contribution to support of an alleged dependent by an employee, shall not constitute proof of dependency as a fact."

In its latest discussion of the dependency issue, the Louisiana Supreme Court in Hurks v. Bossier, 367 So.2d 309 (La.1979), cited with approval Larson's definition of dependency.

"The general test of dependency may be stated as follows: A showing of actual dependency does not require proof that, without decedent's contributions, claimant would have lacked the necessities of life, but only that decedent's contributions were relied on by claimant to maintain claimant's accustomed mode of living." The Law of Workmen's Compensation, Matthew Bender, Volume 2, 1976, § 63.11.

As to partial dependency, Larson states at 63:12:

"Partial dependency may be found when, although the claimant may have other substantial sources of support in his own work, from property, or from other persons on whom claimant is also dependent, the contributions made by the decedent were looked to by the claimant for the maintenance of his accustomed standard of living."

The court in Hurks held that the contributions by the deceased of $50.00 to $60.00 a week to his mother who lived in poverty with her invalid mother and with the deceased supported a showing of dependency. The Hurks court cited McDermott v. Funel, 258 La. 657, 247 So.2d 567 (1971), where the Supreme Court held that a mother proved dependency by showing that her son contributed $15.00 to $20.00 a week out of a $55.00 paycheck. The mother earned about $40.00 a week as a domestic worker.

The defendants assert that the rule fashioned in Hurks and McDermott, supra, requires the plaintiffs to show that Eddie's contributions were relied on by his parents to maintain their accustomed mode of living. They also claim that the fact that the payments had ceased one month before the time of death shows that the Durbin family did not rely on Eddie's contributions to maintain their accustomed mode of living.

In 14 Louisiana Civil Law Treatise, Workers' Compensation, Section 309 (West, 2nd Ed.1980), Professors Wex Malone and H. Alston Johnston, III, comment that: "... in all cases (except where the dependency of the spouse and child is conclusively presumed), the claimant must prove dependency by establishing both a need for support and also the fact that contributions to his support were actually made by the deceased during the latter's lifetime...

"Thus, it is commonly held that neither need for support nor the existence of a moral or legal obligation to support is sufficient proof of dependency if there is not showing that the deceased in fact contributed to the claimant's support...."

"The dependency must have existed at the time of the accident and death. Proof of prior dependency is not sufficient, and contributions made by the deceased to a partial dependent more than a year before the death cannot be included in determining the amount of compensation to which a partial dependent is entitled."

We think the law of this state is clear that for a dependency relationship to be shown the relationship must exist at the time of death. Additionally, a decedent's contributions must be relied upon by the claimant to maintain the claimant's accustomed mode of living. The fact that the decedent in this case stopped making the payments to his mother about one month prior to his death and the fact that his parents were adequately supporting themselves without the decedent's contribution leads us to the conclusion that the decision of the trial court must be reversed. See Darrow v. Travelers Ins. Co., 175 So. 98 (La.App. 2d Cir.1937), writ denied, June 21, 1937, wherein termination of contributions more than a year prior to death was used by the court to hold that the decedent was not supporting his parents at the time of death. Therefore, for the above and foregoing reasons, the decision of the trial court is reversed, and plaintiffs' petition is dismissed with prejudice. All costs in both the trial court and this court are assessed against plaintiffs-appellants.

Reversed and rendered.

Notes

1. Statutes often provide for a conclusive presumption of dependency as to certain relatives of the decedent, usually the surviving spouse, and children under a specified age. See, for example, Code of Laws of S.C. § 42–9–110 (1998); Ky. Rev. Stat. Ann. § 342.750 (1997); and N.D. Century Code § 65–05–17 (1997).

Sometimes the conclusive presumption of dependency is on condition that the relatives named were living with the decedent at the time of the fatal accident or, if living apart from, were doing so because of the decedent's misconduct. See, for example, Code of Ala. § 25–5–61 (1997); 19 De. Code Ann. § 2330 (d) (1997); Mn. St. Ann. § 176.11 (1998); Tenn. Code Ann. § 50–6–210(1) (1998). Compare, 77 Pa. St. § 562 (1998) (if a wife was not living with her husband at the time of his death, she must show that she "... was then actually dependent upon him and receiving from him a substantial portion of her support"). Does the payment of a mutual debt such as a mortgage qualify as support? The answer depends on several factors which include which spouse is living in the former marital home and which partner, if either, repudiated the marriage. Compare S and S Associates, Inc. v. W.C.A.B., 77 Pa.Cmwlth. 11, 465 A.2d 57 (1983) (decedent, husband, lived in the home after the separation and had instituted divorce proceedings on grounds of desertion; held, benefits from the payment of the mortgage had flowed to the husband and, consequently did not constitute support for the wife); and M.D.S. Laboratories v. W.C.A.B., 111 Pa.Cmwlth. 541, 534 A.2d 844 (1987)(wife left husband because of his alcoholism; neither party disavowed marriage; court affirmed referee's findings that : (1) husband and wife had agreed that payment by husband of mortgage and taxes on marital home, in which he resided, would be in lieu of court-ordered spousal support; (2) payment of the mortgage and taxes protected the interests of the wife and children in the home; and (3) the mortgage payment was a form of a substantial support for the wife).

As to such persons who enjoy the conclusive presumption, there is no necessity to analyze the "nature of dependency." In Adkins v. Comcar Industries, 323 S.C. 409, 475 S.E.2d 762 (1996) the statute provided for payment of death benefits to parents, regardless of need, if decedent left no dependents. Even though the father had abandoned his son, the decedent, many years earlier, he was still entitled to death benefits because the statute did not qualify the word "father."

The conclusive presumption of dependency may result sometimes in twice the usual recovery. Thus, in United States Nat. Bank of Denver v. Industrial Comm., 128 Colo. 417, 262 P.2d 731 (1953), the claimants' mother and father, both of whom were employed and contributed their earnings to the support of the family, were killed in the same accident. It was held that in view of the statutory presumption of the dependency of a child on its parents, the claimants were entitled to an award for each death. A similar result was reached in State ex rel. Olsen v. Industrial Comm., 9 Ohio St.2d 47, 223 N.E.2d 362 (1967);

2. It has been held that statutory creation of a conclusive presumption of dependency of a surviving wife is within the power of the legislature. State ex rel. London & Lancashire Indemnity Co. v. District Ct., 139 Minn. 409, 166 N.W. 772 (1918); Shahan v. Beasley Hot Shot Service, Inc., 91 N.M. 462, 575 P.2d 1347 (1978). Prior to 1980, a number of state workers' compensation acts created a conclusive presumption of dependency as to widows but required widowers to prove actual dependency. The U.S. Supreme Court in Wengler v. Druggists Mutual Insurance Co., 446 U.S. 142, 100 S.Ct. 1540, 64 L.Ed.2d 107 (1980), held such a provision of the Missouri Statute to be unconstitutional as prohibited gender-based discrimination under the Equal Protection Clause of the Fourteenth Amendment. The court apparently left it to the states to determine whether the violation should be remedied by extending the conclusive presumption of dependency to widowers or by removing such presumption for widows. Both approaches have been followed by the states.

3. As to persons not presumed to be dependent, questions often arise as to what constitutes dependency. How great must have been the reliance of the claimant upon the deceased employee? The principal case reflects the rule in most states that dependency does not mean destitution or poverty in the sense that the survivor would have been on the welfare rolls without the financial help of the decedent. It means that the survivor was receiving financial aid from the decedent and relied on the support in maintaining the usual mode of living; see also, Lineal Industries v. W.C.A.B., 542 Pa. 595, 669 A.2d 329 (1995) (the test for dependency of parents is "[I]f contributions of the deceased child were necessary to maintain the parents in an established standard of living"; monthly expenditures must be reasonable given the circumstances as of the date of child's death; whether a particular debt of parent's is reasonable is determined by the life situation at time debt was incurred); Chevron USA v. W.C.A.B., 51 Cal.App.4th 1553, 60 Cal.Rptr.2d 165 (1997)("dependency in fact or the amount annually devoted to the

[partially dependent widow] and the [marital] community must be calculated according to amounts that terminated with the death of the decedent....");
Oil Transport v. Jordan, 22 Va.App. 633, 472 S.E.2d 291 (1996) (parent who has only enough resources for bare survival is "financially vulnerable" and considered destitute by code § 65.2–515(A)(4) and, thus conclusively presumed to be wholly dependent for support upon deceased employee). As to expectation of support, see Maryland House of Correction v. Jenkins, 228 Md. 146, 178 A.2d 892 (1962). (Decedent was a prisoner at the time of death; had contributed to claimant's support prior to incarceration and expected to do so after release; death benefits granted.);

As to the effect of claimant's other means of support, many cases in which the survivor had some income from sources other than the deceased still found a state of dependency had existed. Zelizer v. Prospect Inn, 28 A.D.2d 1034, 283 N.Y.S.2d 736 (1967) (parents of college student held dependent on him though father was employed); Paul Spellman v. Spellman, 103 So.2d 661 (Fla.App.1958) (deceased and two working sisters lived with mother and deceased made regular contributions to the "family pot"). But see, Terrinoni v. Westward Ho!, 418 So.2d 1143 (Fla.App.1982) (mother held dependent upon son at time of death; three months after son's death, mother received $155,000 from a combination of sources; held no longer dependent), and Miller & Long Co. of Virginia, Inc. v. Frye, 215 Va. 591, 212 S.E.2d 258 (1975) (decedent was one of nine children, lived with his parents, received food, housing and the use of telephone and car; contributed about $67 out of his $110 weekly wages to help pay for food, telephone and entertainment of his sisters; his father's net weekly earnings were $396; benefits denied on the ground that this was "a situation of mutual assistance and not one of unilateral reliance".); and see, Federico v. Industrial Comm. Of Arizona, 186 Ariz. 382, 923 P.2d 848 (1996) (a parent is entitled to death benefits only during the period of dependency; mother's dependency ceased when she received $200,000 as beneficiary of son's life insurance policy); and Roanoke Belt v. Mroczkowski, 20 Va.App. 60, 455 S.E.2d 267 (1995) (in determining whether mother was destitute and thus presumptively wholly dependent upon deceased son, court held mother's receipt of unemployment benefits were status based not need based and thus had to be considered as part of mother's income);

4. Adults who are not in the categories of persons presumed to be dependent must offer evidence as to why the claimed dependency exists, Gherardi v. Connecticut Co., 92 Conn. 454, 103 A. 668 (1918), and the explanation cannot be simply that the claimant does not like the work available locally. Ferriter's Case, 269 Mass. 267, 168 N.E. 747 (1929). A justifiable explanation may be incapacity to work because of physical or mental illness or deficiency. Reilly v. Weber Engineering Co., 107 N.J.Super. 254, 258 A.2d 36 (1969); Columbus Mining Co. v. Pelfrey, 237 S.W.2d 847 (Ky.1951); and Currie v. Workmen's Compensation Appeal Board, 102 Pa. Cmwlth. 398, 518 A.2d 348 (1986). Another acceptable explanation is that the decedent's domestic arrangements were sufficient evidence of the dependency of the adult survivor. Steverson v. Struck Constr. Co., 243 S.W.2d 494 (Ky.1951); Milwaukee Casket Co. v. Kimball, 201 Wis. 516, 230 N.W. 627 (1930) (daughter divorced or separated, resided with her father and kept house for him, held a dependent). Inability to find work because of economic

depression was held to be sufficient to support a finding of dependency in Northern Hotel Co. v. Industrial Comm., 223 Wis. 297, 270 N.W. 66 (1936). The Longshore and Harbor Workers' Compensation Act as well as most state workers' compensation statutes permit a child 18 or over who is a student, as defined in the statutes, to be considered dependent. 33 U.S.C.A. § 902, paragraphs 14 and 18.

5. Whether dependency is established as of the date of the accident or as of the date of death can have an outcome determinative effect. See, National Corporation for Housing Partnership v. Keller 119 Md.App. 566, 705 A.2d 142 (1998), cert. granted, 350 Md. 280, 711 A.2d 871 (1998) (standard techniques of statutory interpretation (plain meaning given to words, consideration of legislative intent, attention to section within statutory scheme as a whole) indicate that the legislature meant to give the Workers' Compensation Commission the discretion to decide the date upon which dependency should be calculated).

6. To establish dependency, the contributions by the decedent must have been something more than occasional irregular gratuities. American Fuel Co. of Utah v. Industrial Comm., 60 Utah 131, 206 P. 786 (1922) (brother occasionally sent sister cash to purchase clothing and other items for school; held dependency not established); Rhoden v. Smith & Decker Electric Co., 107 Ind.App. 152, 23 N.E.2d 306 (1939) (occasional gifts by brother to sister to enable her to dress as did other students at her school; held dependency not established); Fernwood Industries, Inc. v. Mitchell, 219 Miss. 331, 68 So.2d 830 (1953) (deceased's only contributions over a four-year period for support of his illegitimate son consisted of three pairs of pants, a shirt, and now and then a nickel, dime, or quarter; held dependency not established); Lopez v. Schultz & Lindsay Construction Co., 79 N.M. 485, 444 P.2d 996 (1968) (son living at home made one contribution during 1 1/2 month period he worked for employer; parents held not dependent on him; dissent; compare with principal case); and see to the same effect, Gallegos v. Homestake Mining Co., 97 N.M. 717, 643 P.2d 281 (1982). Cf. Union Camp, Inc. v. Dependents of McCall, 426 So.2d 796 (Miss.1983).

Ordinarily, the evidence to prove regular contributions consists of conventional records such as checks, account books, and similar means, although in sympathetic cases appellate courts have permitted the administrative body to find dependency on the basis of testimony of claimant alone with very little substantiation. Thus, in Bridges v. Merritt–Chapman and Scott Corp., 11 A.D.2d 854, 203 N.Y.S.2d 132 (1960), the claimant testified that her son sent her money from time to time and that it came by check and money order "although she was vague as to the times and amounts." The president of her bank stated that he knew that she received money from her son. The court sustained a finding of dependency. Contrast, Oil Transport v. Jordan, supra, note 3 (mother "produced no tax returns, no documentation of bills being paid by her son, nor any other tangible objective evidence" and, consequently, failed to prove that she had been dependent upon her son).

PARTIAL DEPENDENCY

Although the receipt of income other than the contributions of the decedent may not completely negate the existence of dependency, it may change the case from one of "total dependency" to one of "partial dependency." Partial dependency is said to exist "when the dependent receives less than all of his support from the deceased employee." Schneider, Workmen's Compensation Text, vol. 9, p.21, sec.1906(b), Thomas Law Book Co. (1950). Thus, Rose v. Paper Mills Trucking Co., 47 Mich.App. 1, 209 N.W.2d 305 (1973) granted only partial dependency to a surviving child who was receiving $105 per month social security benefits at the time his stepfather was killed. His mother was saving these payments for his education. Similarly, Mario Anello & Sons, Inc. v. Dunn, 217 Md. 177, 141 A.2d 731 (1958) awarded only partial dependency benefits to a widow who was employed and earning about $30 per week at the time of the decedent's death. The decedent had earned $90 per week and the two pooled their money and used it to pay their bills.

The determination that a survivor's dependency is partial rather than total will affect the amount of compensation awarded. The methods by which the different states compute compensation for partial dependency vary. Some states award the part of a total dependency award that is proportional to the percentage that the decedent's contribution bore to the decedent's total earnings; thus if the decedent contributed one-half of earnings, the partial dependent would get one-half of the amount of a total dependency award. Burns Ind.Stats.Ann. § 22–3–3–18 (1998). In some states the amount of a partial award is related to the proportion that decedent's contribution bore to the total income of the dependent; thus if the dependent had a total income of $100 per month of which the deceased contributed $25, the claimant would be entitled to one-fourth of the amount of a total dependency award. Minn.Stats.Ann. § 176.111, subd. 17 (1998). Some states delegate broad discretion to workers' compensation administrators in the determination of the amounts of partial dependency awards. See, e.g., Wis.Stats.Ann. § 102.48 (1997):

> ". . . (2) In all other cases the death benefit shall be such sum as the department shall determine to represent fairly and justly the aid to support which the dependent might reasonably have anticipated from the deceased employee but for the injury."

SECTION 2. "WIDOW" "WIDOWER" "CHILD" "MEMBER OF THE FAMILY"

SPALDING COUNTY COMMISSIONERS v. TARVER
Court of Appeals of Georgia, 1983.
167 Ga.App. 661, 307 S.E.2d 58.

CARLEY, JUDGE.

On November 17, 1963, James Tarver married Mary Tarver. This ceremonial marriage ended by divorce on September 17, 1964. Nine days later, on September 26, 1964, James Tarver entered into a ceremonial marriage with Patricia Jo Tarver. On April 3, 1966, while James Tarver was ostensibly married to Patricia Jo Tarver, a child, Barry Tarver, was born to Mary Tarver and James Tarver. James Tarver and Patricia Jo

Tarver were divorced in 1968 and remarried in 1969. In April of 1974, Patricia Jo Tarver and James Tarver were again divorced. Subsequently, James Tarver married and divorced again. Thereafter, in January of 1976, James Tarver married Revia Tarver and this marriage also ended in divorce on April 26, 1979.[1]

[James Tarver, a Spalding County Deputy Sheriff, on December 24, 1980, while in the course of his employment with Spalding County, was struck and killed by a truck driven by Mark Martin, a third-party tortfeasor. A wrongful death action was brought against Martin and his employer. In that action, the plaintiffs were two of Tarver's sons[2] and two women alleging they were his widow—Mary Tarver and Revia Tarver. The trial court joined all plaintiffs in order to allow the jury to determine the proper party. The plaintiffs sought immediate review. The Georgia Court of Appeals accepted the interlocutory appeal and held that the trial court should have determined the proper party plaintiff(s) by declaratory judgment because if such were left to the jury the decedent's colorful marital history would have a prejudicial effect on their deliberations. Tarver v. Martin, 175 Ga.App. 689, 334 S.E.2d 18 (1985).]

Three separate [workers' compensation] claims were made for dependency benefits pursuant to OCGA § 4-9-13 (Code Ann. § 114-414).

At the time of the hearing, one claimant [Mary Tarver as common law wife of James] was dismissed as a party.[3] The two remaining individuals making claims for dependency benefits were: Revia Tarver, who was claiming entitlement as the alleged common law wife of James Tarver at the time of his death, and Mary Tarver, acting solely as appointed guardian of Barry Tarver, the minor child of James Tarver. The administrative law judge awarded compensation benefits to Barry Tarver and denied the claim of Revia Tarver. The award was premised upon the finding that, prior to James Tarver's ceremonial marriage to Patricia Jo on September 26, 1964, James Tarver and Mary entered into a common law marriage. The administrative law judge further found that because the common law marriage created between James and Mary Tarver was never dissolved by divorce, all subsequent marriages entered into by James Tarver were not valid, including the common law marriage with Revia Tarver. A de novo hearing was held before the full Board and the award of the administrative law judge was adopted and affirmed with minor modifications.

1. Editor's Note: At the time of death, decedent was living with Revia, who claimed their relationship constituted a common law marriage (Brief for Appellant at 2–3, Tarver v. Martin, 175 Ga.App. 689, 334 S.E.2d 18) (1985).

2. Editor's Note: James M. Tarver, Jr. and Jeffrey Tarver, were born during James and Patricia Jo Tarver's first marriage of May 27, 1954. Both were over 18 years of age at decedent's death and did not claim dependency benefits. (Brief for Appellant at

2, Spalding County Commissioners v. Tarver, 167 Ga.App. 661, 307 S.E.2d 58) (1983).

3. Editor's Note: At time of death, decedent was living apart from Mary, who was not actually dependent upon him and thus not entitled to dependency benefits under Georgia's Workers' Compensation Act, O.C.G.A. § 34-9-13 (Brief for Appellant at 2, Spalding County Commissioners v. Tarver, 167 Ga.App. 661, 307 S.E.2d 58) (1983).

On appeal, the superior court found there was no evidence to support the finding of the existence of a common law marriage between James Tarver and Mary Tarver. The case was remanded for additional findings concerning the existence of such a common law marriage. This court granted a discretionary appeal. In case number 65807, the Spalding County Commissioners appeal from the order of the superior court remanding the case to the Board of Workers' Compensation. In case number 65808, Revia Tarver cross-appeals, asserting that OCGA § 34–9–13 (Code Ann. § 114–414) is unconstitutional and that the superior court erred in failing to admit certain records into evidence.

CASE NUMBER 65807

OCGA § 34–9–105(a) (Code Ann. § 114–710) provides, in relevant part, that an award of the State Board of Workers' Compensation "shall be conclusive and binding as to all questions of fact." Neither the superior court nor the Court of Appeals has any authority to substitute itself as the fact-finding body in lieu of the Board of Workers' Compensation. "Even though the evidence is conflicting, or not altogether complete and satisfactory, an award must be affirmed if there is any evidence to support it." Depart. of Public Safety v. Rodgers, 149 Ga.App. 683, 255 S.E.2d 139 (1979). There is evidence in the instant case which would support the finding that a common law marriage was created between James and Mary Tarver subsequent to the entry of their divorce decree on September 17, 1964, and prior to James Tarver's marriage to Patricia Jo Tarver nine days later, on September 26, 1964. There is some evidence that, during this period, the deceased and Mary Tarver mutually agreed to be husband and wife, that they held themselves out as such, and that there was a consummation of that relationship. Askew v. Dupree, 30 Ga. 173, 178 (1860). Prior to the entry of the divorce decree on September 17, 1964, Mary Tarver moved into her sister's apartment. Also prior to September 17, 1964, James Tarver informed Mary that he had stopped the divorce proceedings, and he then moved his clothes and possessions into the apartment with Mary. Mary Tarver testified that subsequent to the entry of the divorce decree, of which she had no knowledge, she and the deceased continued to share a room in her sister's apartment, shared the same bed, and held themselves out as man and wife. Mary Tarver's sister testified that at all times when Mary and the deceased were living in the apartment with her, they held themselves out as man and wife, and, in fact, she did not even know that a divorce had been obtained during that time. When James Tarver did inform Mary of the divorce, he told her that a lawyer had pressed him to complete the case and that he had made the divorce between them final, but told her "that we were still married, it didn't make no difference." Several other witnesses testified that at all times during the period in question Mary Tarver and the deceased held themselves out as man and wife. "While a proven ceremonial marriage will prevail over a presumption of marriage founded on cohabitation and repute, yet such a ceremonial marriage will not prevail over a properly proven previous common-law marriage." Carter v. Graves, 206 Ga. 234, 56 S.E.2d 917 (1949). The evidence was sufficient to support a finding of a common law marriage. See Kickasola v. Jim Wallace Oil Co., 144 Ga.App. 758(1), 242 S.E.2d 483 (1978).

Accordingly, the superior court erred in finding that there was no evidence to support the finding of the Workers' Compensation Board that a common law marriage between Mary and James Tarver had been created but never terminated by divorce, and that, therefore, all subsequent marriages entered into by James Tarver were invalid, including the alleged common law marriage to Revia Tarver.

CASE NUMBER 65808

* * *

Judgment in Case Number 65807 reversed. Judgment in Case Number 65808 affirmed.

Notes

1. The use of the terms "wife", "widow", "husband" and "widower" in the workers' compensation statutes brings into operation the law of domestic relations of the particular state in which the case arises. As illustrated by the principal case, some involved situations have come before the courts from time to time where the lives of the decedent and intermittent domestic helpmates have been uninhibited and unconventional. See, for example, Mims v. Hardware Mut. Cas. Co., 82 Ga.App. 210, 60 S.E.2d 501 (1950), in which claimant, at the time she married the decedent, was already married to X, who was already married to A, who was already married to H, no divorce having been previously secured by any of the parties at the time that they married each other. The court found the key to the puzzle in the fact that at the time A married H, she (A) was only twelve years old; hence her marriage to H was invalid and her later marriage to X was valid, thus making X's marriage to claimant invalid and claimant's marriage to the decedent valid, with the result that claimant could be allowed compensation as a widow. See also, Ritchie v. Katy Coal Co., 313 Ky. 310, 231 S.W.2d 57 (1950) (Bertha, wife of decedent, was given dependency benefits as was Lonnie who had entered into a bigamous marriage with decedent).

In cases of alleged bigamous marriages, the courts sometimes resort to the presumption that the last marriage is the legal one. Annotation (1977) 81 A.L.R.3d 97. Parker v. American Lumber Corp., 190 Va. 181, 56 S.E.2d 214 (1949) (testimony of first wife was that she had never divorced deceased and had never had notice of any divorce obtained by him; nevertheless, she had married someone else within two and one-half years of her separation from deceased; held, presumption of validity of most recent marriage not rebutted); Denson v. C.R. Fish Grading Co., Inc., 28 N.C.App. 129, 220 S.E.2d 217 (1975) (burden of proof was on the first wife to produce evidence of the invalidity of the second marriage. Mere proof that the first wife had not obtained a divorce and that first wife was never served with papers of divorce proceeding was not sufficient to overcome the presumption of validity of the second marriage); Newburgh v. Arrigo, 88 N.J. 529, 538, 443 A.2d 1031 (1982) (". . . irrespective of the factual context in which the issue may arise, the last of two or more marriages is presumptively valid. The presumption ... may be overcome only by clear and convincing evidence that (1) there was a prior marriage, (2) the prior marriage was valid, and (3) the prior marriage was not terminated by death or divorce before the latest marriage."); See also, Heuer v. Heuer, 152 N.J. 226, 234, 704 A.2d 913, 917 (1998); Estate of Allen, 738 P.2d 142 (Okla.1987) (wife left husband and, without divorcing him, established a common law marriage with another man; after first husband died, she filed for death benefits as his widow; held, "... appellee is estopped from asserting her continual marital status with the decedent ... if this court ... allow[ed] appellee to participate in decedent's estate, this would prejudice those who are rightfully entitled to share in the estate. Because of her previous conduct, appellee should have no right to share in the estate.").

The presumption can be rebutted, however, by appropriate evidence. See, e.g., Harmes v. Industrial Comm., 40 Ill.2d 488, 240 N.E.2d 674 (1968) (inquiry is limited to whether, at time of death, decedent had legal obligation to support wife; it is irrelevant that wife may have been living apart from husband for many years and not been dependent upon him); Metropolitan Life Insurance Co. v. Jackson, 896 F.Supp. 318 (S.D.N.Y.1995) ("Under New York law, the presumption in favor of a second marriage is rebutted when diligent record searches, in the counties where both parties to the first marriage resided, fail to show evidence of the dissolution of the first marriage.") See also, Daniels v. The Retirement Board of the Policeman's Annuity and Benefit Fund, 106 Ill.App.3d 412, 62 Ill.Dec. 304, 435 N.E.2d 1276 (1982) and 29 Am. Jur.2d Evidence § 220 (1994) (current through 1997 supp.) Equitable Considerations Affecting Standing to Raise the Presumption and § 222 Rebutting the Presumption.

2. Where the domestic arrangements in which claimant was involved with the decedent were actually illicit but this aspect of the relationship was not known to claimant, the court may give weight to the claimant's good faith and allow an award to claimant as widow or widower or as a dependent "member of the family." Dawson v. Hatfield Wire & Cable Co., 59 N.J. 190, 280 A.2d 173 (1971) (good discussion of the issue); see also Parkinson v. J. & S. Tool Co., 64 N.J. 159, 313 A.2d 609 (1974); and see Burton v. Chater, 1996 WL 310299 (E.D.Ark.1996) (state law holds a person who goes through a ceremonial marriage and lives with another in good faith belief that the marriage is valid is "a putative spouse with all the rights of a legal spouse." But if good faith is not found, the individual will not be accorded the status of a putative spouse and will not have the legal rights thereof); and Visconti v. Secretary of Health, Education and Welfare, 374 F.Supp. 1272 (W.D.Pa. 1974), affd. 556 F.2d 570 (3d Cir.1977) (benefits will be awarded to a 'good faith' widow unless, if at the time of her application, another person has filed for benefits and that other person is (or is deemed to be) the widow of the decedent). See 42 U.S.C. § 416 (h)(1)(A) and (B), Social Security Act § 216(h)(1)(A) and (B).

If the arrangements and conduct of the parties resulted in a valid common law marriage, the survivor's claim as surviving spouse is valid. In addition to the principal case see Parker v. 36 South Oxford St., Inc., 28 A.D.2d 1031, 283 N.Y.S.2d 700 (1967). If, however, it appears that claimant was aware of the unlawful nature of the cohabitation, and no common law marriage is established or recognized, most courts deny compensation to the survivor in any capacity. Powell v. State Compensation Ins. Fund, 496 F.2d 1248 (9th Cir.1974), certiorari denied 419 U.S. 1032, 95 S.Ct. 514, 42 L.Ed.2d 307 (1974); Reichert v. Sunshine Mining Co., 95 Idaho 647, 516 P.2d 704 (1973); Tatum v. Tatum, 736 P.2d 506 (Okl.1982), rehearing denied 736 P.2d 506 (Okl.1982); and Williams v. Corbett, 260 Ga. 668, 398 S.E.2d 1 (1990). In McDonald v. Kelly Coal Co., 335 Mich. 325, 55 N.W.2d 851 (1952) the Michigan Supreme Court stated: "Public policy does not sanction the payment of compensation arising out of a meretricious cohabitation." Contrast West v. Barton–Malow Co., 394 Mich. 334, 230 N.W.2d 545 (1975) which awarded compensation to a claimant who had lived with decedent for 13 years and held herself out as his wife although during that time she was legally married to another man. The court held "[s]he did bear to Clarence West the relationship of a wife for the 13 years preceding his untimely death. During those years plaintiff was responsible for maintaining their household while the deceased undertook the responsibility for furnishing them both with monetary support." *West* distinguished *McDonald* on the ground that the *McDonald* relationship was "of short duration based on meretricious cohabitation." *West* is consistent with the cases that take the position that "dependency" has no moral attributes or requisites but should be found in accordance with the fact. See, e.g., Henderson v. Travelers Ins. Co., 354 So.2d 1031 (La.1978); Winn v. Thompson–Hayward Chemical Co., 522 So.2d 137 (La.App.1988); Kendall v. Housing Authority of Baltimore City, 196 Md. 370, 76 A.2d 767 (1950); and Russell v. Johnson, 220 Ind. 649, 46 N.E.2d 219 (1943) (Neither statute nor public policy excludes a woman who has shared an adulterous relationship with a man from receiving compensation as his dependent.) In Burgess Constr. Co. v. Lindley, 504 P.2d 1023 (Alaska 1972) the concurring opinion suggests that the distinction between a "legal wife" and one sharing an illicit relationship is an unconstitutional denial of equal protection of law.

3. Courts ordinarily interpret the term "child" as used in a workers' compensation law in light of the local domestic relations law as they do with respect to the words "wife", "widow", "husband" or "widower". Ellis v. Henderson, 204 F.2d 173 (5th Cir.1953) (Applying Longshore and Harbor Workers' Act and determining meaning of "child" on basis of Louisiana law). This approach has not escaped criticism. In Albina Engine and Machine Works v. O'Leary, 328 F2d. 877, 879 (9th Cir.1964) the court said, "The application of state domestic relations law, developed in other contexts, to the solution of problems under Workmen's Compensation statutes, produces results which at best have only a fortuitous relation to the remedial purposes of the compensation acts, and often are in direct conflict with them." See also, In the Matter of the Adventure Bound Sports, 1994 WL 510892 (S.D.Ga.1992) for a discussion of the different objectives served by wrongful death; inheritance, and support statutes.

In determining the rights of dependent children, courts are less captive to conventional family law then in determining marital relationships. But cf. Ryan–Walsh Stevedoring Co., Inc. v. Trainer, 601 F.2d 1306 (5th Cir.1979). The statutes of some states contain provisions expressly defining "child" or "children" to include a stepchild, an adopted child, and an illegitimate child. Some require acknowledgment of the latter. See, e.g., Longshore Act, 33 U.S.C.A. § 902(14). One of the most inclusive definitions is in the Wyoming statute which provides: " 'child' means any unmarried minor or physically or mentally incapacitated individual receiving court ordered support or substantially all of his financial support from the employee at the time of injury or death of that employee and includes an adopted child, stepchild, posthumous child or acknowledged illegitimate child but does not include a parent or spouse of the employee" Wyo. Stat.§ 27–14–102(iii) (1998).

The treatment of posthumous children varies. See, e.g., Renard v. Security Protection Services, 692 So.2d 9 (La.App. 4th Cir.1997) (posthumous child is not a member of the family "... for that term connotes a living person ... the right to compensation is determined upon the basis of facts existing at the time of death of the employee and not deferred to await the contingency of live birth"). Contrast State Compensation Insurance Fund v. W.C.A.B., 19 Cal.App.4th 1645, 24 Cal. Rpt. 2d 67 (1993) (posthumous child included in statutory definition of dependent).

The status of illegitimate children varied widely among the states until Weber v. Aetna Cas. § Sur. Co., 406 U.S. 164, 92 S.Ct. 1400, 31 L.Ed.2d 768 (1972), held that the Louisiana workers' compensation statute which denied coverage to unacknowledged illegitimate children violated the Equal Protection Clause of the Fourteenth Amendment. Post–Weber decisions, however, suggest greater constitutional tolerance. See, e.g., Mathews v. Lucas, 427 U.S. 495, 96 S.Ct. 2755, 49 L.Ed.2d 651 (1976); Wittig v. Shalala, 852 F.Supp. 613 (1994) (child born as a result of an adulterous relationship is not a stepchild of the innocent spouse so as to be eligible for child's benefits under the Social Security Act); Hendrix v. Secretary of Health and Human Services, 156 F.3d 1229 (6th Cir.1998)(42 U.S.C. § 416 (h)(2)(A) of the Social Security Act provides that an illegitimate child is entitled to death benefits if he or she would have been deemed to be an intestate heir of the deceased under the law of the state in which the decedent was domiciled. "... where state intestacy law provides that a child may take personal property from a father's estate, it may reasonably be thought that the child will more likely be dependent during the parent's life and at his death.") See generally, Ellman, Kurtz & Scott, *Family Law Cases, Text, Problems* 3rd Edition, 1136–1142 (Lexis Law Publishing, 1998). Of course, the sometimes difficult task of proving that the decedent was the father of the child remains.

4.   Many workers' compensation statutes use the term "member of the family" to describe the persons or classes entitled to death benefits. The usual provision grants compensation only to claimants who prove actual dependency and actual status as a member of the family of the decedent. Applying the statute poses no great difficulty as to such close relatives as parents, or children under the statutory age (if not otherwise expressly covered), as long as the evidence supports actual dependency. Caporoz v. Labor Commission, 945 P.2d 141 (Utah App.1997) (when statutory presumption does not apply, one prerequisite to a finding of dependency is the existence of "some family or other social relationship giving rise to a legal or moral obligation to support.") In addition, there should be a determination that the claimant relied wholly or partially on the decedent or that the claimant would most likely have received assistance from the decedent but for the death.) Other close relatives often brought within the term are brothers. See, e.g., Park Utah Consol. Mines Co. v. Industrial Comm., 84 Utah 481, 36 P.2d 979 (1934); Leigh Coal Co., Inc. v. Cantrell, 434 S.W.2d

315 (Ky.1968), and Sawyer v. Dependents of Head, 510 So.2d 472 (Miss. 1987); and sisters. See, e.g., Clark v. White, 197 Wis. 597, 222 N.W. 823 (1929); Reese v. Beshel, 10 La.App. 347, 120 So. 530 (1929); Peterson v. Industrial Acc. Comm., 188 Cal. 15, 204 P. 390 (1922); Mile High Masonry v. Industrial Commission, 718 P.2d 257 (Colo.App.1986); and Corbin v. Industrial Commission, 724 P.2d 677 (Colo.App.1986). Contrast Tisdale v. Wilson & Co., 141 Kan. 885, 43 P.2d 1064 (1935) (married sister whose husband had deserted her, supported by deceased but not living with him, denied compensation). Other relatives that have been awarded compensation include aunts, Peay v. Fred Kulow & Co., 226 Mich. 512, 197 N.W. 1020 (1924) and Harlan v. Industrial Acc. Comm., 194 Cal. 352, 228 P. 654 (1924); but contrast, Stafford's Case, 238 Mass. 93, 130 N.E. 109 (1921) which denied compensation to the aunt who was the actual head of the household; nephews, A.E. Peterson v. Industrial Acc. Comm., 188 Cal. 15, 204 P. 390 (1922); and Franklin v. Jackson, 231 Miss. 497, 95 So.2d 794 (1957); cousins, Holmberg v. Cleveland–Cliffs Iron Co., 219 Mich. 204, 189 N.W. 26 (1922); and grandparents, London Guarantee & Acc. Co. v. Industrial Comm., 78 Colo. 478, 242 P. 680 (1925); Howard v. Lenhart & Bennett, 663 P.2d 386 (Okl.App.1983); and grandchildren, Farmer v. Metro Light and Electrical Services, Inc. 708 So.2d 1251 (La.App.1998).

In-laws are frequently included. In Goshorn v. Roger Sherman Transfer Co., 131 Conn. 200, 38 A.2d 585 (1944) claimant was the mother-in-law of decedent. She had lived with decedent for about 20 years after he and his wife (her daughter) separated, had raised his child and managed the household as "the mother of the family". Decedent had taken her as a dependent on his income tax returns and had promised he would maintain a home for her as long as she lived and would provide for her in his will. For 7 years prior to his death she had been wholly dependent on him. It was held that while she was not "next of kin" she was a member of decedent's family and entitled to death benefits. See also Archibald v. Employers' Liability Assur. Corp., 202 La. 89, 11 So.2d 492 (1942) (father-in-law, mother-in-law and two sisters-in-law); Larsen v. Industrial Acc. Comm., 34 Cal.2d 772, 215 P.2d 16 (1950) (mother-in-law).

5. Even persons not having any blood or other legal relationship to the decedent may qualify for benefits in the absence of statutory prohibition. Lumbermen's Underwriting Alliance v. Teague, 521 So.2d 820 (La.App.1988) (despite the lack of blood relations or legal obligation, the woman with whom the decedent lived and her child were awarded death benefits to exclusion of the decedent's natural children); Housley v. Everts' Commercial Transport, Inc., 4 Or.App. 80, 475 P.2d 977 (1970), and Blair v. Keller, 16 Ohio Misc. 157, 241 N.E.2d 767 (1968) (unadopted children of decedent's widow); Southern Motor Car Co. v. Patterson, 168 Tenn. 252, 77 S.W.2d 446 (1935) (nephew of decedent's wife); and Patin v. T.L. James & Co., Inc., 218 La. 949, 51 So.2d 586 (1951) (child of another couple taken at infancy into home of decedent and reared there).

6. What significance attaches to the existence or lack of a legal obligation on the part of decedent to support the claimant? In general, in the absence of a statutory requirement, the basis of beneficial status is determined by dependency in fact and not by legal obligation. Leigh Coal Co., Inc. v. Cantrell, 434 S.W.2d 315 (Ky.1968) (brother supported his siblings). In

some states, the statute attaches a conclusive presumption of dependency to the legal obligation to support. See, e.g., Holley v. Mississippi Lime Co. of Missouri, 266 S.W.2d 606 (Mo.1954) (affirming an award of compensation to a child under eighteen even though mother had remarried after divorce and her second husband supported the child); and Rocky Mountain Helicopter v. Carter 652 P.2d 893 (Utah 1982).

In the converse situation, the courts are divided as to whether an unfulfilled legal obligation to support claimant is enough to base a finding of dependency. See, e.g., Ladner v. Mason Mitchell Trucking Co., 434 A.2d 37 (Me.1981) (employee's legal obligation to support the minor children of a prior marriage was not alone sufficient to make the children "dependents"); C.W. Wright Constr. Co., Inc. v. Brannan, 217 Md. 397, 142 A.2d 574 (1958) (decedent separated from wife and made payments for her support for eleven months but for twenty months thereafter made no payments and disappeared; wife divorced him and remarried; compensation for child denied); and Yanofchick v. State Workmen's Ins. Fund, 174 Pa.Super. 182, 100 A.2d 387 (1953) (decedent and wife separated and wife obtained a court order of support; decedent never complied with the order fully but would occasionally send small sums to her, and for more than ten years claimant wife did not try to enforce the court order; compensation denied). Contrast State ex rel. Wright v. Industrial Comm., 141 Ohio St. 187, 47 N.E.2d 209 (1943) (divorce decree obligated father to support child but he never complied with it during his lifetime; child awarded compensation); Snodgrass v. AMF Bowling Center, 1997 WL 343087 (Ohio App. 10 Dist.1997) ("Under the Workers' Compensation Act, dependency is based upon the right to support rather than the actual fact of support.... Thus, the fact that [father] Roy, Jr. had not been ordered to provide support, nor had he actually provided support, does not determine whether [son] Eric is entitled to workers' compensation benefits"); and Menard v. Fairchild, 254 Ga. 275, 328 S.E.2d 721 (1985) (dependency under workers' compensation act was not eliminated by previous judicial termination of parental rights; the termination of parental rights "... merely terminates the rights and obligations flowing between a parent and a child. They remain parent and child." The statutory presumption of dependency is a status, not a dependency, based determination).

SECTION 3. SPECIAL ASPECTS OF CLAIMS OF SURVIVORS

BUCHANAN v. KERR–MCGEE CORPORATION

Court of Appeals of New Mexico 1995.
121 N.M. 12, 908 P.2d 242.

Bustamante, Judge.

Muriel Buchanan (Claimant), widow of Henry Buchanan (Worker), appeals an order denying her claim for death benefits under the New Mexico Occupational Disease Disablement Law (the Occupational Disease Law). NMSA 1978, § 52–3–13 to–60 (Repl.Pamp.1991 & Cum.Supp. 1995). Claimant raises two issues on appeal: (1) is Claimant's claim for death benefits barred by a settlement and release made by Worker during his lifetime, and (2) did the Workers' Compensation Judge (WCJ) err in deciding Worker's lung cancer was noncompensable because of the presence of a non-occupational risk factor? Deciding that there is no bar and that the WCJ applied an incorrect standard of proof to the facts, we reverse and remand.

FACTS AND PROCEEDINGS

Worker was an underground uranium miner employed by Kerr–McGee Corporation d/b/a Quivira Mining Company (Employer) and its subsidiaries for more than twenty years. In 1985, Worker suffered a work-related back injury for which he filed a claim for workers' compensation benefits. In addition, Worker joined a silicosis claim under the Occupational Disease Law to the back injury action. In 1987, the district court awarded Worker compensation benefits for his back injury. Contemporaneously, Worker and Employer entered into a settlement agreement with regard to the silicosis claim which required Employer to pay Worker $15,000 in exchange for a release (the Release) in full of all claims under the Occupational Disease Law. Worker signed the Release in January 1987. The Release included the following language:

["]However, if it should develop that I did receive any other injuries or damages or was involved in any other accident or suffered any other exposure which might hereafter lead to another occupational disease disablement while employed by KERR–McGEE CORPORATION or QUIVIRA MINING COMPANY, f/k/a KERR–McGEE NUCLEAR CORPORATION, at any time, then this Release forever releases and discharges KERR–McGEE CORPORATION, QUIVIRA MINING COMPANY, f/k/a KERR–McGEE NUCLEAR CORPORATION, and their subsidiaries, insurers, successors and assigns, and their officers, agents, servants and employees who or which could or might possibly be liable for any such injuries, disablement or damages whether discovered or latent or otherwise.["]

Worker and Employer stipulated that the settlement would bind Worker and "his dependents". Claimant did not read or sign the Release and she took no part in the negotiation and settlement of Worker's claims under the Occupational Disease Law.

In January 1993, Worker was diagnosed with lung cancer. Worker filed an occupational disease claim against Employer. In September 1993, Worker died of " '[m]etastatic squamous cell carcinoma of the lung' "while his Claim was pending. Claimant eventually filed her own complaint seeking death benefits and medical expenses.

The WCJ ordered the case to be submitted on briefs and stipulated facts. After briefing, the WCJ dismissed Claimant's complaint on two grounds, each independently fatal to Claimant's course of action: (1) the Release bars Claimant's claim; and (2) Worker's disablement and death were not caused by an occupational disease arising out of his employment.

DISCUSSION

With regard to issues of fact, we review this case using the whole record standard of review. See Herman v. Miners' Hosp., 111 N.M. 550, 552, 807 P.2d 734, 736 (1991); Tallman v. ABF (Arkansas Best Freight), 108 N.M. 124, 126–30, 767 P.2d 363, 365–69 (Ct.App.), cert. denied, 109 N.M. 33, 781 P.2d 305 (1988). Whole record review is not an excuse for an appellate court to reweigh the evidence and replace the fact finder's conclusions with its own, although it does allow the reviewing court greater latitude to determine whether a finding of fact was reasonable based on the evidence. Herman, 111 N.M. at 553, 807 P.2d at 737. With regard to issues of law, this Court determines whether the WCJ correctly applied the law to the facts, viewing the facts in the light most favorable to the determination below. See Golden Cone Concepts, Inc. v. Villa Linda Mall Ltd., 113 N.M. 9, 12, 820 P.2d 1323, 1326 (1991); see also Texas Nat'l Theatres, Inc. v. City of Albuquerque, 97 N.M. 282, 287, 639 P.2d 569, 574 (1982).

Issue 1. Does the Release Bar Claimant's Recovery for Death Benefits?

The WCJ determined that the express language of the Release bars Claimant's recovery of death benefits. The WCJ reached her decision by applying broadly accepted concepts of contract interpretation and public policy, with which we have no quarrel in the abstract. For example, the WCJ noted that the courts of New Mexico favor settlement and that settlements will be enforced in accordance with their terms absent an ambiguity in the terms of the settlement agreement or release. See Ratzlaff v. Seven Bar Flying Serv., Inc., 98 N.M. 159, 163, 646 P.2d 586, 590 (Ct.App.), cert. denied, 98 N.M. 336, 648 P.2d 794 (1982). In addition, a settlement agreement or release can be challenged if there is a lack of consideration, fraud, misrepresentation, duress, mistake, undue influence, overreaching, or other factors supporting unenforceability. Id. Hendren v. Allstate Ins. Co., 100 N.M. 506, 508, 672 P.2d 1137, 1139 (Ct.App.1993). Claimant did not assert that there was any ambiguity in the Release, and the WCJ found no evidence of fraud, misrepresentation, duress, or other grounds for challenging the Release. Absent a direct challenge to the facial validity of the Release, the WCJ held that Worker had released Employer from all claims arising under the Occupational Disease Law.

The WCJ's decision presupposes that Worker's valid release is also effective to release Claimant's cause of action as a surviving dependent under the Occupational Disease Law. We disagree with this premise and the conclusion that follows from it. We hold that Claimant, as Worker's widow and dependent, has independent statutory rights to death benefits which arise upon Worker's death, and Claimant is not bound by Release. The claim of a dependent arising from the death of a worker is a new and separate claim and is not derivative of the worker's claim. See Gonzales v. Sharp & Fellows Contracting Co., 48 N.M. 528, 537–38, 153 P.2d 676, 681–82 (1944); 2 Arthur Larson, The Law of Workmen's Compensation § 64.10 (1995). A unilateral settlement or release by a worker of his or her own claims does not bar the surviving dependent's claim even if the release signed by the worker explicitly purports to release the dependent's claim, as was the case here. Brown v. General Aniline & Film Corp., 127 N.J.Super. 93, 316 A.2d 478, 480 (Ct.App.Div. 1974), aff'd per curiam, 65 N.J. 555, 325 A.2d 689 (1974); Fossum v. State Accident Ins. Fund, 289 Or. 787, 619 P.2d 233, 237 (en banc), reh'g denied and modified, 290 Or. 267, 624 P.2d 1074 (1980); 2 Larson, supra, § 64.12 (1995). Our holding is in accord with the great weight of authority from other jurisdictions. See Kay v. Hillside Mines, Inc., 54 Ariz. 36, 39, 91 P.2d 867, 870 (1939); American Steel Foundries v. Industrial Comm'n, 361 Ill. 582, 198 N.E. 687, 690 (1935); Routh v. List & Weatherly Const. Co., 124 Kan. 222, 257 P. 721, 724 (1927); In re Cripp, 216 Mass. 586, 104 N.E. 565, 566 (1914); Smith v. Kiel, 115 S.W.2d 38, 41 (Mo.Ct.App.1938); Viersen & Cochran Drilling Co. v. Ford, 425 P.2d 965, 967–68 (Okla.1967).

Restated in the language of contract law, Claimant's cause of action under the Occupational Disease Law is a new and separate claim, and it is not barred by the Release because Claimant was not a party to the Release and received no consideration for relinquishment of her dependent's claim for death benefits. See Fleet Mortgage Corp. v. Schuster, 112 N.M. 48, 49, 811 P.2d 81, 82 (1991) (it is a general rule that one who is not a party to a contract cannot maintain suit upon it, nor is bound by it).

The Occupational Disease Law does not directly address the issue before us. That is, there is no specific provision of the Occupational Disease Law which explicitly states that survivor's benefits constitute a claim completely separate and apart from the worker's claim. In addition, there is no provision in the statute which addresses in any fashion the effect of a broadly worded release form executed by a worker but not signed by any of worker's dependents. We can glean, however, the outcome most compatible with the intent and purpose of the Occupational Disease Law by comparing its treatment of the worker's disability benefits with the treatment accorded dependent's death benefits.

Section 52–3–10(A) provides:

A. There is imposed upon every employer a liability for the payment of compensation to every employee of such employer who suffers total disablement by reason of an occupational disease arising out of his employment, subject to the following conditions[.]

In contrast, Section 52–3–10(B) provides:

B. There is imposed upon every employer a liability for the payment of compensation to the dependents of every employee in cases where death results from an occupational disease arising out of his employment, subject to the following conditions[.]

The Occupational Disease Law thus draws a clear distinction between an employer's obligation to its employees for benefits during their lifetime and an employer's obligation to "the dependents" of its employees for death benefits.

Similarly, Section 52–3–14(A), (B), and, (G) distinguish between the benefits payable to the worker and those payable to the worker's dependents upon the worker's death. The benefits payable to dependents are: (1) funeral and medical expenses, (2) such other sums as the deceased may have been paid for disability, and (3) 700 weeks of death benefit payments. The language of Section 52–3–14(G) itself does not provide for a deduction, credit or setoff against an employer's liability to dependents for death benefits on account of payments to a worker during his lifetime under the Occupational Disease Law. We conclude, therefore, that it was the intent of the legislature to award death benefits to a worker's dependents if death arises or proximately results from an occupational disease notwithstanding what the worker received or was deemed entitled to receive during his lifetime. It follows that surviving dependents are entitled benefits notwithstanding any release worker may execute during his or her lifetime.

Employer argues that Hubbs v. Sandia Corp., 98 N.M. 389, 648 P.2d 1202 (Ct.App.), cert. denied, 98 N.M. 478, 649 P.2d 1391 (1982), undercuts Claimant's position that worker and survivor benefits are independent of each other. Hubbs is distinguishable, however, because it dealt specifically with a statute of limitations issue. In Hubbs, the employer asserted the independence of disablement and death benefits in support of its argument that a disablement claim filed within the ten-year period of NMSA 1978, Section 52–3–10(C), could not be used to make a death claim timely when the death claim was filed after the statutory ten-year period had elapsed. The Court and the parties in Hubbs did not disagree that disablement and death claims are distinct and separate. Id. at 391, 648 P.2d at 1204. The only issue was whether their independence affected the statute of limitations issue presented. We held it did not because of the internal wording of the statute, but we did not compromise the distinction between employee's disablement benefits and the surviving dependent's death benefits.

Accordingly, we reverse the WCJ's determination that the Release acted to bar Claimant's recovery. Claimant's recovery of death benefits is, however, also contingent upon whether Claimant can show that Worker died from an occupational disease. We turn now to that issue.

Issue 2. Did the WCJ Error in Concluding that Worker's Death was Not Caused by an Occupational Disease Arising out of his Employment?

* * *

Based on the foregoing, we conclude that the occupational Disease Law does not require Claimant to prove that Worker's exposure to uranium was the only factor causing Worker's fatal lung cancer or even the major factor, as the WCJ apparently concluded. Rather, the occupational Disease Law only requires Claimant to show that as a matter of medical probability there is a recognizable, non-negligible link between Worker's exposure to radiation as a miner for over twenty years and his risk of contracting lung cancer.

* * *

Accordingly, we reverse the WCJs finding that Claimant failed to prove that Worker suffered total disablement or death by reason of an occupational disease arising out of his employment, and remand for reconsideration in light of our opinion.

* * *

IT IS SO ORDERED.

ALARID and WECHSLER, JJ., concur

DUNI v. UNITED TECHNOLOGIES COR-PORATION/PRATT AND WHITNEY AIRCRAFT DIVISION ET. AL.

Supreme Court of Connecticut 1996.
239 Conn. 19, 682 A.2d 99.

PALMER, JUSTICE

The dispositive issue raised by this appeal is whether a stipulation entered into by an employee and his employer in full and final settlement of the employee's workers' compensation claim can bar a claim for survivor's benefits by the employee's widow after the death of the employee. The employee, William Duni (decedent), filed a workers' compensation claim against his former employer, United Technologies Corporation/Pratt and Whitney Aircraft Division (Pratt & Whitney), the named defendant. The decedent, Pratt & Whitney, the defendant Liberty Mutual Insurance Company (Liberty) and the defendant Second Injury and Compensation Assurance Fund (fund) entered into a stipulated settlement agreement that purported to bind the decedent and anyone else who might ever have a claim against the defendants on account of the decedent's work-related injuries. After the decedent's death, his widow, the plaintiff, Beatrice Duni, filed a claim for survivor's benefits under General Statutes § 31–306. Pratt & Whitney and Liberty sought dismissal of the claim on the ground that it was barred by the settlement agreement. The workers' compensation commissioner (commissioner) denied the motion to dismiss. On appeal, the workers' compensation review board (review board) reversed the decision of the commissioner, concluding that the settlement agreement was binding on the plaintiff. The plaintiff appealed from the decision of the review board to the Appellate Court, and we transferred the appeal to this court pursuant to Practice Book § 4023 and General Statutes § 51–199(c). We affirm the decision of the review board.

The facts relevant to this appeal are undisputed. The decedent was employed by Pratt & Whitney from 1941 to December, 1982. On December 3, 1984, the decedent filed a workers' compensation claim asserting that during the course of his employment with Pratt & Whitney he had been exposed to various substances that had caused injury to his lungs, heart, eyes, nose and other body parts, leaving him disabled.

The decedent and the defendants subsequently agreed to settle the claim and entered into an agreement entitled "Stipulation for Full and Final Settlement" (stipulation). Under the terms of the stipulation, the defendants agreed to make a lump sum payment to the decedent in return for his agreement to release them from any further liability in connection with his claim. The stipulation purported to "constitute a complete satisfaction of all claims due or to become due at any time in favor of anybody on account of the claimed injuries or on account of any condition in any way resulting out of the said injuries."[4] The parties' stipulation was approved by the commissioner on September 15, 1986.

On December 14, 1991, the decedent died. Approximately two months later, the plaintiff submitted to Pratt & Whitney a claim for survivor's benefits pursuant to § 31–306. The plaintiff alleged that the decedent's death was the result of the injuries that he had sustained during the course of his employment with Pratt & Whitney and, consequently, that she was entitled to survivor's benefits.

Pratt & Whitney and Liberty contested the claim and, thereafter, sought its dismissal on the ground that the stipulation barred the plaintiff's recovery. The commissioner denied the motion, concluding that the plaintiff's right to survivor's benefits was independent of the decedent's claim and that the plaintiff was not bound by the stipulation because she was not a signatory to it. The defendants appealed to the review board, which reversed the commissioner's decision on the ground that the plaintiffs application for survivor's benefits was precluded by the stipulation. This appeal followed.

On appeal, the plaintiff contends that the review board improperly concluded that she was not entitled to seek survivor's benefits under § 31–306. Specifically, the plaintiff maintains that her right to compensation under § 31–306 is completely independent of the decedent's rights to compensation for work related injuries under the Workers' Compensation Act (act), and, accordingly, that the decedent lacked the authority to settle any claim for survivor's benefits that she might later have arising from his work-related injuries. Alternatively, the plaintiff argues that the stipulation cannot reasonably be construed to bar her right to make a claim under § 31–306. We disagree with both of these claims.

The plaintiff first contends that the stipulation entered into by the decedent does, not bar her claim for workers' compensation benefits because her rights under § 31–306 are entirely independent of the

---

4. The stipulation provides in relevant part: "The payment of SEVENTY-TWO THOUSAND DOLLARS ($72,000) of which the respondent employer and insurer shall pay $36,000 and the respondent Second Injury and Compensation Assurance Fund shall pay $36,000, shall be made and accepted as a full and final settlement for all compensation including specific[ally] for said injuries and for all results upon the claimant past, present and future and for all claims for medical, surgical, hospital and incidental expenses to the end that the payment of such sum shall constitute a complete satisfaction of all claims due or to become due at anytime in favor of anybody on account of the claimed injuries or on account of any condition in any way resulting out of the said injuries."Neither Pratt & Whitney nor the fund admitted any liability for the decedent's injuries.

decedent's compensation rights and, consequently, that the decedent had no authority to compromise her right to seek benefits under § 31–306 after his death. We disagree.

Our resolution of this issue is guided by well established principles of statutory construction. "Our fundamental objective is to ascertain and give effect to the apparent intent of the legislature.... In seeking to discern that intent, we look to the words of the statute itself, to the legislative history and circumstances surrounding its enactment, to the legislative policy it was designed to implement, and to its relationship to existing legislation and common law principles governing the same general subject matter...." (Citations omitted; internal quotation marks omitted.) State v. Metz, 230 Conn. 400, 409, 645 A.2d 965 (1994); Fleming v. Garnett, 231 Conn. 77, 92, 646 A.2d 1308 (1994). "We have previously recognized that our construction of the Workers' Compensation Act should make every part operative and harmonious with every other part insofar as is possible.... In applying these principles, we are mindful that the legislature is presumed to have intended a just and rational result...." (Citations omitted; internal quotation marks omitted.) Dos Santos v. F.D. Rich Construction, Inc., 233 Conn. 14, 20–21, 658 A.2d 83 (1995).

"It is well established that [a]lthough not dispositive, we accord great weight to the construction given to the workers' compensation statutes by the commissioner and review board.... A state agency is not entitled, however, to special deference when its determination of a question of law has not previously been subject to judicial scrutiny." (Citation omitted; internal quotation marks omitted.) Davis v. Norwich, 232 Conn. 311, 317, 654 A.2d 1221 (1995).

As is often the case in the context of workers' compensation legislation; see Dos Santos v. F.D. Rich Construction, Inc., supra, 233 Conn. at 20, 658 A.2d 83; the statutory language provides little guidance for our determination of whether the decedent, in settling his own workers' compensation claim, also had the authority to compromise whatever right the plaintiff might have to survivor's benefits. Furthermore, the pertinent legislative history is silent on the question. Several considerations persuade us, however, that, under our statutory scheme, a surviving dependent's right to compensation is subordinate to an employee's right to settle his or her workers' compensation claim.

First, the availability of survivorship benefits under § 31–306 is inextricably linked to, and wholly dependent upon, the existence of a compensable injury or illness suffered by the employee. Thus, in the absence of a work related injury or illness, a surviving dependent of the employee has no claim whatsoever under § 31–306. Moreover, a dependent has no compensation rights unless and until the employee dies as a result of the occupational injury or disease. Further, the calculation of the amount of survivor's benefits to which a dependent may be entitled is determined as of the date of the employee's injury and not as of the date on which the dependent becomes eligible to receive such benefits.

General Statutes § 31–306(a)(2). Similarly, a person who has not attained dependent status until after the date of the employee's injury is not entitled to bring a claim under § 31–306. See General Statutes § 31–275(6). Thus, a surviving dependent's compensation rights under § 31–306 flow directly from the work-related injury or disease suffered by the employee.

Second, our conclusion advances the public policy favoring the pretrial resolution of disputes. As we have long recognized in the context of civil actions, "the pretrial settlement of claims is to be encouraged because, in the vast number of cases, an amicable resolution of the dispute is in the best interests of all concerned. 'The efficient administration of the courts is subserved by the ending of disputes without the delay and expense of a trial, and the philosophy or ideal of justice is served in the amicable solution of controversies.' Krattenstein v. G. Fox & Co., 155 Conn. 609, 614, 236 A.2d 466 (1967). . . . At a time when our courts confront an unprecedented volume of litigation, we reaffirm our strong support for the implementation of policies and procedures that encourage fair and amicable pretrial settlements." Grayson v. Wofsey, Rosen, Kweskin & Kuriansky, 231 Conn. 168, 174, 646 A.2d 195 (1994). We see no reason to eschew this sound public policy in connection with claims arising under our workers' compensation statutes.

To conclude, as the plaintiff urges, that an employee may not compromise his or her dependent's future rights under § 31–306 would unduly undermine the public interest in the prompt and comprehensive resolution of workers' compensation claims. Under the plaintiff's view, a full, final and global settlement of a workers' compensation claim involving a potentially fatal work-related injury or illness would be impossible without the express authorization of all the employee's dependents. Under such circumstances, it is less likely that a comprehensive settlement would be reached. An employer who is faced with the prospect of litigating additional claims upon the employee's death is less apt to be willing to settle the employee's claim.[9]

Finally, the statutory interpretation advanced by the defendants promotes the public policy in favor of administrative simplicity. As we have noted in a related context, the plaintiffs statutory construction would require employers to maintain records for a considerable period of time after each disability compensation claim had been settled, an interpretation that "would undermine the statutory purpose of adminis-

---

9. We also note that stipulations in settlement of workers' compensation claims must be approved by the commissioner, a requirement that serves to protect interested parties against settlements that are not fair and equitable. As we have recently stated regarding such stipulations, "[t]he commissioner decides whether to approve a stipulation only after thoroughly reviewing it, along with all the pertinent medical bills and reports, and after evaluating employment possibilities and any concurrent claims. The commissioner undertakes such exhaustive inquiry in order to judge properly whether the stipulation is fair and comprehensive. . . . We can therefore assume that a commissioner is well acquainted with the terms generally used in stipulations and the proper authority conferred upon commissioners by the legislature." (Citation omitted) Muldoon v. Homestead Insulation Co., 231 Conn. 469, 480 n. 9, 650 A.2d 1240 (1994).

trative simplicity." Davis v. Norwich, supra, 232 Conn. at 323, 654 A.2d 1221. This construction would also frustrate the related public interest in the finality of administrative determinations.

The plaintiff cites Muldoon v. Homestead Insulation Co., 231 Conn. 469, 650 A.2d 1240 (1994), in support of her contention that the act should not be read to permit an employee to settle any possible claim that his or her dependent may have under § 31–306 after the employee's death. In Muldoon, the employee and employer entered into a stipulated settlement of the employee's claim for compensation stemming from injuries suffered as a result of exposure to asbestos. Id., at 472, 650 A.2d 1240. Several years after the stipulation was approved, the employee filed a second workers' compensation claim, alleging that, in the interim, additional exposure to asbestos had caused him further injuries. Id., at 473, 650 A.2d 1240. We concluded that the stipulation's preclusion of " 'future ... claims ... resulting out of the said injury ...' "did not foreclose a future claim based upon a subsequent, although similar, injury. Id., at 479, 650 A.2d 1240. We did so in part "because to decide otherwise would conflict with public policy and the remedial purpose of the act. Except in very rare instances, the settlement and release of a claim does not cover claims based on events that have not yet occurred.... The usual general release, then, is not ordinarily construed to include in its coverage claims based upon occurrences which have their beginning after the instrument is executed.... For that reason, language covering 'future claims' and 'unknown claims' in releases is ordinarily construed to cover only inchoate claims that are in being at the time of release but which have not yet manifested themselves." (Citations omitted; internal quotation marks omitted.) Id., at 481–82, 650 A.2d 1240.

Contrary to the plaintiff's contention, Muldoon does not support a conclusion that an injured employee who settles his or her workers' compensation claim is without authority to compromise any claims that his or her surviving dependents might have under § 31–306. In fact, the claim asserted by the plaintiff is much more analogous to an "inchoate (claim] that [is] in being at the time of release but which [has] not yet manifested [itself]" than it is to the unforeseeable subsequent injury that was suffered by the employee in Muldoon. Id., at 481–82, 650 A.2d 1240. Although it is true, of course, that the plaintiff's rights under § 31–306 did not arise until after the stipulation had been signed, the decedent's death was a reasonably foreseeable consequence of the disabling occupational injuries that he had suffered and, accordingly, such a consequence was likely within the contemplation of the parties when they agreed to bar all claims "on account of any condition in any way resulting out of the said injuries."[10]

10. The plaintiff points to cases from other jurisdictions, cited in 2 A. Larson, Workmen's Compensation (1996) § 64. 11, pp. 11–195–11–203, to support her contention that the stipulation does not bar her claim under § 31–306. Each of the cases relied on by the plaintiff, however, is distinguishable from the present case, because in none of those cases had the employee en-

In light of the derivative nature of the rights created under § 31–306 and the public policy considerations involved, we agree with the review board that, under our workers' compensation scheme, an employee, in settling his or her claim for disability compensation, may also compromise his or her surviving dependents' rights under § 31–306.[11] Having determined that the decedent had the authority to extinguish the plaintiff's rights under § 31–306, we now turn to the question of whether the review board properly concluded that the stipulation accomplished that end.

The plaintiff maintains that even if the decedent had the authority to extinguish her rights under § 31–306, the stipulation was ineffective in doing so. We disagree.

In the context of workers' compensation, "[a] stipulation is a compromise and release type of settlement similar to settlements in civil personal injury cases where a claim is settled with a lump sum payment accompanied by a release of the adverse party from further liability.... Although the act does not explicitly provide for this type of settlement, we have consistently upheld the ability to compromise a compensation claim as inherent in the power to make a voluntary agreement regarding compensation...." (Citation omitted; internal quotation marks omitted). Muldoon v. Homestead Insulation Co., supra, 231 Conn. at 479–80, 650 A.2d 1240.[13]

The stipulation entered into by the decedent and the defendants provides that it is in "complete satisfaction of all claims due or to become due at any time in favor of anybody on account of the claimed injuries or on account of any condition in any way resulting out of the said injuries." There is no doubt that the stipulation was intended to be broad in scope and, by its plain terms, purported to foreclose any and all workers' compensation claims arising out of the decedent's alleged injuries. On its face, then, the stipulation clearly encompasses a workers' compensation claim filed under § 31–306.

Notwithstanding the unambiguous breadth of the stipulation, the plaintiff argues that the word "anybody" in the stipulation reasonably can be construed to include only the estate of the decedent and his creditors but not his surviving dependents. As the review board stated in

tered into a full, final and comprehensive settlement of his claim prior to his death.

11. As the review board stated, "[a]ll existing rights to compensation for [the decedent's] compensable injuries were vested in [him] at the time he signed the stipulation. No claim then existed that was not personal to him. Therefore, [the decedent] had the authority at the time the settlement was reached to release the [defendants] from liability for future claims arising out of his allegedly compensable injuries."

13. "There are three types of stipulations [in workers' compensation cases]: (1) a full and final stipulation that closes all aspects of the claim whether they are for past, present or future wages and medical expenses, known and unknown; (2) a stipulation to date that is used to close out only a portion of a claim with the remainder left open or that is used to close out an entire claim but only up to a certain date; and (3) an open medical stipulation that closes all aspects of the claim except for medical expenses that are related to the accident or the disease." Muldoon v. Homestead Insulation Co., supra, 231 Conn. at 480, 650 A.2d 1240.

reversing the decision of the commissioner, however, " '[a]nybody' is a far more general term that simply refers to any person, and we will not favor a strained interpretation of that term over a straightforward one. We think it evident that the parties to the agreement contemplated the release of all claims that might result from the [decedent's] previous injuries, including those arising in favor of a third party." Because we agree with the conclusion of the review board, we reject the plaintiff's argument regarding the scope of the stipulation.

The decision of the review board is affirmed.

In this opinion the other justices concurred.

Notes

1. As between *Buchanan* and *Duni*, which result is preferable? In a *Buchanan* type jurisdiction, is it ever possible for an employer to settle an employee's claim so as to preclude later claims by dependents for death benefits?

While *Buchanan* expresses the majority view, other cases, either by statutory construction or common law analysis, take the approach espoused in *Duni*. See, e.g., Pigeon v. Department of Industry, Labor and Human Relations, 109 Wis.2d 519, 326 N.W.2d 752 (1982)("... subject to the provisions of [Wis. Stats.] Sec. 102.16(1), a compromise of all liability entered into by an employee shall be binding upon his dependents"); Condoll v. Johns–Manville Sale Corp., 448 So.2d 169 (La.App.1984)(a compromise settlement of the worker's disability claim simultaneously compromised and settled the widow's claim).

2. The *Buchanan* and *Duni* decisions agree that from one event (the compensable accident or disease) flows two distinct sets of injuries. One is incurred by the employee, the other by the dependents. *Buchanan* and *Duni* come to very different conclusions, however, about the ways in which the two sets of harm relate to each other and to the core policy objectives of providing economic assistance to the decedent's family.

It may be helpful, when examining these connections, to look at how courts have characterized the bonds between personal injury actions, wrongful death claims, and the goals of the common law tort system. Many of the problems are the same.

As with claims for disability and death benefits under workers' compensation, both personal injury actions and wrongful death claims are intended to address the two separate sets of interests that emerge from the single act of the tortfeasor. Similar tensions between protecting unvested interests, avoiding double recoveries, and promoting the swift resolution of disputes are present. Frequently, it is the emphasis which a particular court gives to one or the other of these factors that determines the outcome of a case. See, e.g., Alfone v. Sarno, 87 N.J. 99, 432 A.2d 857, 870 (1981) ("The policy favoring settlement and finality of claims ... cannot defeat statutory rights created for the protection of survivors of one wrongfully killed."); and Schwarder v. United States 974 F.2d 1118, 1123 (9th Cir.1992) (affirming that "California does not permit a decedent to compromise by contract the survivors' rights to wrongful death recovery). Contrast, Garde v. Wasson,

251 N.J.Super. 608, 598 A.2d 1253, 1258 (1991) (A personal injury claimant may release the inchoate rights of his or her potential beneficiaries. To hold otherwise would be counter to the public policy favoring settlement and finality of claims); and Variety Children's Hospital v. Perkins, 445 So.2d 1010, 1014 (Fla.1983) (The primary purpose of a wrongful death claim is to prevent a tortfeasor from avoiding liability for the consequences of his harmful actions. "The majority of courts have held that a judgement for or against the decedent in an action for his injuries commenced during his lifetime or the compromise and release of such action, will operate as a bar to any subsequent suit founded upon his death").

3. Generally, in the workers' compensation context, the rights of the injured worker and those of the dependents are regarded as separate and independent. The worker's rights originate in the compensable injury and consequent disability whereas those of the dependents originate in the death of the worker as a result of the compensable injury. This independence is reinforced by workers' compensation statutes in several states which explicitly provide that none of an employee's dependents shall be considered parties in interest to any actions undertaken by the employee for the collection or compromise of a compensation claim. See, e.g., Col. Rev. Stat. Ann § 8–41–504 (1998), Neb. Rev. Stat. § 48–124 (1998), and Mich Comp. Laws Ann. § 418.341 (1998).

4. Several consequences follow from this independence one of which is illustrated in *Buchanan*. A worker's release or compromise of a claim does not bar the dependents from claiming death benefits. See also, Brown v. General Aniline and Film Corp., 127 N.J.Super. 93, 316 A.2d 478, affirmed, 64 N.J. 428, 316 A.2d 689 (1974); and Roberts v. All American Engineering Co., 104 N.J.Super. 1, 248 A.2d 280 (1968).

5. Another consequence of the independence of the worker's claim and that of the dependents is that decisions and findings in any proceeding to which the worker was a party during the worker's lifetime are not binding as to dependents who survive the death. Thus in Wolanin v. Chrysler Corp., 304 Mich. 164, 7 N.W.2d 257 (1943) the employee suffered two injuries, one in 1934 and the other in 1935. He filed two claims. Compensation proceedings while he was alive determined that the 1934 injury was compensable but that the 1935 injury was not because it was merely a result of the 1934 incident. No appeal was taken. The claimant received compensation until he died in 1940 and his survivors then claimed death benefits. If the death was attributable to the 1934 injury, the dependents' claim was barred by the then existing statute; if it was attributable to the 1935 injury the claim was valid. The court held, first, that the death could be found to be a result of the 1935 injury and, second, that, pursuant to code section 17.157, the unappealed finding in the prior proceeding (i.e., that the compensable injury occurred in 1934) was not binding on the survivors. Similarly, in Claimants of Hampton v. Director of Division of Labor, 31 Colo.App. 141, 500 P.2d 1186 (1972), the deceased worker's dependents' rights were held to be independent from the rights of the employee, thus the statute of limitations applicable to the worker's claim could not bar subsequent claims for death benefits. In Wade & Richey v. Oglesby, 251 Ala. 356, 37 So.2d 596 (1948) (a decree fixing 100 weeks as the period of disability and specifying the amount of compensation did not bind the widow's claim for death benefits. "... the

causes of action by the workman and his dependents on his death under the workmen's compensation act, are separate and distinct. Final determination of his rights under the statute could not conclude their rights under the statute."); and see, Mikolich v. State Industrial Accident Comm., 212 Or. 36, 316 P.2d 812 (1957), a prior finding that decedent was temporarily disabled did not preclude a finding of permanent disability in the post death proceeding, thereby making possible a claim by the widow who was entitled to compensation only if the deceased had died during the period of permanent disability."); and see, Singleton v. Kenya Corp., 961 P.2d 571 (Colo.App. 1998)(while Col. Rev. Stat.§ 8–42–116 predicates the recovery of death benefits upon proof that an industrial injury caused the deceased employee to suffer a permanent disability, the statute does not foreclose such posthumous proof when the employee dies of unrelated causes before reaching maximum medical improvement.).

Occasionally this principle works to the disadvantage of the claimant. For example, Chuplis v. Steve Shalamanda Coal Co., 192 Pa.Super. 76, 159 A.2d 520 (1960), denied a widow's claim for death benefits on the ground that the decedent was not an employee of the employer even though benefits had been awarded the decedent before his death. Contrast Card v. Lloyd Mfg. Co., 82 R.I. 182, 107 A.2d 297 (1954), in which the court held that a finding that decedent's injury arose out of and in the course of his employment was binding as to a claim filed by the decedent's widow

6.   A different case is presented, however, if the statutory conditions for compensation are affected by the employee's actions. See, e.g., Bennett Properties Co. v. Industrial Comm., 165 Colo. 135, 437 P.2d 548 (1968)(where death-causing injury resulted from violation of a safety rule for which the statutory penalty was 50% reduction of benefits, survivors were subject to the same reduction). See to the same effect, Aragon v. Anaconda Mining Co., 98 N.M. 65, 644 P.2d 1054 (1982); and if during the lifetime of the employee, the employer's compensation obligations are fully discharged by payment and the employee thereafter dies due to the injury, the survivors may be limited to funeral and medical expenses of the last illness. See, e.g., Tidey v. Riverside Foundry and Galvanizing Co., 381 Mich. 551, 164 N.W.2d 3 (1969). Moreover, if the employee rejects the compensation law pursuant to statutory provisions authorizing rejection, the statute may thereafter be inapplicable to the worker and the worker's survivors. Coyner v. Industrial Comm., 77 Ariz. 210, 269 P.2d 712 (1954)(dependents' benefits while distinct from the rights of the employee, are contingent upon the existence of a compensable injury; if employee has elected to forgo coverage under the workers' compensation act, then the employee's dependents cannot receive death benefits under the act). When, however, the employee simply fails to seek injury benefits during his lifetime, his dependents may nevertheless recover death benefits. See, e.g., Conley–Slowinski v. Superior Spinning and Stamping Co., 1998 WL 351875 (Ohio App. 6th Dist. 1998). See also, Jones v. Multi–Color, 108 Ohio App.3d 388, 670 N.E.2d 1051 (1995)(an employee may forgo his right to compensation by signing a pre-activity waiver; however, the waiver does not change the nature of the subsequent injury and it remains a compensable event within the workers' compensation system; the signing of the waiver merely precludes the employee from receiving a workers' compensation award and the dependents may still maintain an

action for death benefits). As to the employee's waiver of rights under the workers' compensation act, see Watts v. Newberg, 920 S.W.2d 59 (Ky.1996)(employee given the option of maintaining his workers' compensation coverage and accepting a 20% reduction of wages or choosing an employer sponsored insurance plan and retaining regular salary; held, freedom of choice and an understanding of the consequences are prerequisites to a valid waiver of workers' compensation coverage; the choice presented was coercive and against public policy; therefore, compensation granted for injury which occurred after date invalid waiver was signed).

7. The law in effect at the time of the decedent's injury may differ from that which existed at the time of death. As a result, courts may have to resolve which law is applicable to the survivor's death benefit claim. In Sizemore v. State Workmen's Compensation Com'r., 159 W.Va. 100, 219 S.E.2d 912 (1975), the statute in effect at the date of the decedent's injury conditioned survivor's benefits upon the occurrence of death within six years. The worker survived for nine years , but in the meantime the law had been changed to allow claims for death occurring within 10 years after injury. The court held that the law at the time of death controlled and allowed the claim. See also, Richards v. Richards and Richards, 664 P.2d 254 (Colo.App.1983)(widow's dependency benefits should have been calculated based on percentage of the state average weekly wage at the time of employee's death rather than at the time of his disablement); To the same effect see, Kisco v. Industrial Commission of Arizona, 190 Ariz. 389, 949 P.2d 49, (App.1997)(where injury causes death, death is the ultimate injury; accordingly, the class of beneficiaries and the amount of death benefits are determined as of the date of death). Contrast Cogswell v. Max Silverstein & Sons Inc., 488 A.2d 732 (R.I.1985)(determination of employee's rate of compensation was res judicata in the subsequent action for death benefits even though death benefits had been increased by legislature by the time of the employee's death).

8. Each state's law provides a fixed maximum death benefit, which may be stated in terms of: (1) limited duration; (2) dollars per week; (3) total dollars; or (4) a combination of the three. Many states also provide for a minimum weekly payment. Because the number of eligible beneficiaries varies from one case to another, the statutes prescribe means to fix priorities among beneficiaries and to divide benefits among them. Commonly, if the beneficiaries consist only of a surviving spouse and children, the entire award goes to them and may increase according to the number of children. Code of Ala. Sec. 25–5–62 and Sec. 25–5–64 (1998); Mich.Comp. Laws Ann. Sec. 418.331 (1998); McKinney's N.Y. Workers' Compensation Law, Sec. 16, par. 2 (1998)(sliding scale based on number of dependents, not necessarily children).

Another common priority method provides that persons who were wholly dependent on the decedent take to the exclusion of others, sharing the maximum benefits among themselves. (For a good discussion see Pinecrest Memorial Park v. Miller, 7 Ark.App. 185, 646 S.W.2d 33 (1983)). If there is no wholly dependent person, then those partially dependent take the benefits. N.C.Gen.Stats. Sec. 97–38 (1997). A survivor is wholly dependent within the meaning of the statute if conclusively presumed so or if dependency is proved as a fact by appropriate evidence. Shealy v. Associated Transport, Inc., 252 N.C. 738, 114 S.E.2d 702 (1960)(statute gave priority to those wholly dependent over those partially dependent. Widower, who enjoyed conclusive presumption of total dependency, stood on equal footing with decedent's mother who was wholly dependent in fact.) In Duffy v. Walsh–Kaiser Co., 75 R.I. 170, 64 A.2d 863 (1949), a surviving widow was accorded priority over a son of decedent by a former marriage who was living with his mother but was receiving partial support from decedent under a divorce decree.

Under some statutes close relatives have priority in varying degrees over others, the closeness of relationship usually being the governing consideration. See, e.g., Robinson v. First Nat. City Bank of New York, 6 N.Y.2d 944, 190 N.Y.S.2d 1010, 161 N.E.2d 221 (1959) (award to mother approved even though spouse and minor child survived); Johnson v. Johnson, 477 So.2d 21 (Fla.App.1985) (the entire benefit awarded to decedent's three children as members of a preferred class to exclusion of decedent's dependent mother); and Aragon v. Anaconda Mining Co., 98 N.M. 65, 644 P.2d 1054 (1982).

These issues are wholly resolved by statutory interpretation and cannot be generalized in outcomes.

9. Most workers' compensation statutes terminate a surviving spouse's weekly death benefits upon remarriage. Frequently, however, the surviving spouse is entitled to a lump sum payment that is equivalent to the present day value of a prescribed number of weeks worth of benefits. See, e.g., Utah Stat. § 2–414(6)(a) (1998); S.D. Codified Laws Sec. 62–4–12(1998); Kan. Stat. Ann § 44–510(b) (1997). This award is separate from the weekly benefits and the employer may not credit the amounts already paid thereto against it. In Fort Smith v. Tate, 311 Ark. 405, 844 S.W.2d 356, 359 (1993) the statute provided that employer was liable for first $50,000 in weekly benefits and the Death and Permanent Total Disability Trust Fund for amounts in excess of $50,000. In holding the employer liable for the lump sum payment even though employer had already satisfied the $50,000 maximum in weekly benefits, the court reasoned, "The obvious purpose of the lump sum benefit provision upon remarriage is to lessen the disincentive to remarry that would be inherent in a flat cutoff of dependency benefits. This disincentive . . . does not cease to exist when the employer reaches his maximum liability in weekly benefits; it continues indefinitely because the widow continues to receive benefits from the Fund. Therefore, the need for the reduction of the disincentive in the form of a lump sum payment is still needed even after the employer reaches this maximum liability." See also, Self v. Industrial Commission of Arizona, 192 Ariz. 399, 966 P.2d 1003 (Ariz.App.1998) ("The surviving spouse's periodic benefit terminates upon remarriage and the lump sum benefit is an independent payment rather than an advance on monthly compensation. Therefore, when the surviving spouse's monthly benefits terminate, the dependent children's monthly death benefits should be recalculated immediately without consideration of the lump sum benefit."); Todd v. W.C.A.B., 547 Pa. 687, 692 A.2d 1086 (1997)(statute authorized termination of weekly benefits and the payment of a lump sum when a widow remarried. If the widow entered into a meretricious relationship, she forfeited both her weekly benefits and her future entitlement to the lump sum. Claimant lived with her fiancé for two years prior to marrying him. Hearing Officer, Appeals Board, and the Commonwealth Court all held that the

widow had forfeited her right to the lump sum. State Supreme Court reversed holding, the date on which the employer filed the petition to terminate benefits was the date upon which the widow's status was evaluated. As the widow had remarried one month prior to the employer's petition, she retained her right to the lump sum payment.).

10.   In the absence of a controlling statute, courts generally hold that no right to unaccrued installments of a compensation award survives the death of the entitled worker. Rozales v. Peerless Welder, Inc., 311 Minn., 6, 246 N.W.2d 851 (1976) (permanent partial disability benefits are personal to the employee. Consequently, they do not survive when the death of the employee is from causes unrelated to the compensable injury.) County of Spotsylvania v. Hart, 218 Va. 565, 238 S.E.2d 813 (1977) (decedent's claim for schedule injury had not accrued because his condition had not reached the point of maximum improvement at time of his death from other cause). Contrast, Singleton, supra, note 5, (benefits accrue at time that employee may first assert an enforceable claim. Proof may be made posthumously that the employee had reached maximum medical improvement (MMI). If employee had reached MMI, his dependents were entitled to accrued, but unpaid, permanent disability benefits.); and see, Estate of Peterson v. J.R. Simplot Co., 83 Idaho 120, 358 P.2d 587 (1961) (acknowledging that compensation for permanent partial disability, according to statutory schedule, was in the nature of liquidated damages and payable to dependents); Parker v. Walgreen Drug Co., 63 Ariz. 374, 162 P.2d 427 (1945) (schedule award is a vested right); and Pfefer v. Winer & Saroff Comm. Co., 227 Mo.App. 280, 49 S.W.2d 293 (1932) (award to a dependent child survives his death and his personal representative is entitled to the unpaid portion of the award).

Payments accrued but unpaid prior to the death of the employee usually are payable either to the dependents or to the estate. Breen v. Industrial Acc. Bd., 150 Mont. 463, 436 P.2d 701 (1968) (injured employee died from intoxication; widow entitled to accrued unpaid compensation installments but not death benefits). When an injured worker has filed no claim for a compensable injury suffered prior to death from a cause unrelated to the injury, or an award has been made but is on appeal, some courts permit the survivors to file the claim or pursue the award. See, e.g., Kozielec v. Mack Mfg. Corp., 29 N.J.Super. 272, 102 A.2d 404 (1953) (employee had not filed a claim during his lifetime; held, his surviving widow could file an original claim after his death from cause not related to the compensable accident); Turner v. Southern Wheel and Rim Service, Inc., 332 So.2d 770 (La.1976); Falcon Coal Co. v. Sweet, 518 S.W.2d 343 (Ky.1974); Brandner v. Myers Funeral Home, 330 Mich. 392, 47 N.W.2d 658 (1951) (employee died while award was on appeal in which it was affirmed; administrator of employee's estate entitled to amounts accrued between date of award and date of employee's death) . Others do not permit the post-death claims. See, e.g., Ferguson v. State Workmen's Compensation Comm., 152 W.Va. 366, 163 S.E.2d 465 (1968); and State of Wisconsin v. Labor and Industry Review Commission, 136 Wis.2d 281, 401 N.W.2d 585 (1987).

A number of states have enacted statutes providing that unaccrued installments of an injury award are to be paid after death of the employee (from a cause unrelated to the injury) to named persons, usually dependents who would have received support from the payments if the employee had lived. For example, Snyder v. Wickwire Spencer Steel Co., 277 App.Div. 233, 98 N.Y.S.2d 1006 (1950), applied Mckinney's Workers' Compensation Law Sec.15(4), to allow a surviving widow to maintain two claims after the death of her husband-one for death benefits and the other for a post mortem schedule award. See also, Ala. Code Sec. 25–5–57(5) (1998).

Chapter 10

ADMINISTRATION OF WORKERS' COMPENSATION LAWS

INTRODUCTION TO THIS CHAPTER

For Forms of Government Let Fools Contest;
Whate'er Is Best Administered Is Best:[1]

It would be impossible to overemphasize the importance of effective administration to the success of any workers' compensation law. No such statute, regardless of the high quality of its substantive content, can accomplish or even approach the objectives of the workers' compensation system, if that statute is poorly administered. Some of the disappointments experienced in the past by those interested in the workers' compensation movement are the results of inept administration.

The main purposes of administration are to insure that the law is understood by workers and employers affected by it, that workers are aware of their rights and obligations, and that those rights and obligations are enforced. The fulfillment of these purposes involves many functions entirely apart from the resolution of disputes between contesting parties. Indeed, most compensation claims are uncontested. Included among the necessary administrative functions are dissemination of information to employees and employers; supervision of benefit payments in uncontested cases; surveillance of compromises in cases in which disputes exist; continuing supervision of awards, sometimes over a long period of time; and the encouragement of and assistance in rehabilitation of injured employees. Good administration also includes keeping accident records and related data, compiling statistics about the law's operation and its defects, and making recommendations to the executive and the legislative branches of the state government. These tasks call for the highest caliber of public service, but unfortunately, many of them have not always received the attention, effort, and legislative support they should have had.

This chapter briefly considers some of the more important aspects of workers' compensation administration. Most workers' compensation sys-

1. Alexander Pope, An Essay on Man,
Epistle III, Lines 303–4, 1733–34.

tems are administered by special agencies. The manner in which these agencies handle uncontested cases has great practical significance, although often its importance is not realized by lawyers accustomed to thinking in terms of adversary proceedings. In contested cases, a number of procedural matters have considerable substantive significance in the functioning of the law. These include notice of injury, statutes of limitation, rules of evidence, judicial review, compromise of disputed claims, lump-sum settlements, and modification and reopening of awards. In these areas each state's laws, practices, customs and traditions are more peculiarly its own than in any other.[2] Consequently, the brief review in this chapter is limited to pointing up the sources and nature of the most common controversies.

SECTION 1. ADMINISTRATION BY SPECIAL AGENCY

The administrative arrangements of the state, federal, and territorial workers' compensation laws vary greatly in detail, but fall into patterns of identifiable general categories. In most jurisdictions administrative responsibility and authority are vested in a special state agency, but a few states still rely on substantial court involvement in the administration of the law. Students of workers' compensation generally deem court administration to be inferior to agency administration and to reduce the effectiveness of the law substantially.[3] This view holds that courts are not equipped to handle all aspects of workers' compensation administration effectively. For example, injured workers often need the type of help in the early stages of their distress that the initiative of a properly functioning administrative agency can best provide. A court on the other hand must await the initiative of the parties. Moreover, courts generally do not have facilities or staff for following up initial determinations as to disability, insuring prompt payments, keeping statistics, publishing information needed by both employer and employees, and performing the many other tasks that must be done.

Arrangements for administration of the law by special agency may take any one of several forms. Two specific examples are, first, a single administrative officer responsible directly to a state cabinet officer such as the Commissioner of Labor, and, second, a commission or board responsible directly to the governor.

---

2. For a state-by-state survey of various aspects of administrative practices, see U.S. Dept. of Labor, Employment Standards Administration, Office of Workers' Compensation Programs, *State Workers' Compensation Laws* (January 1998); United States Chamber of Commerce, 1998 Analysis of Workers' Compensation Laws.

3. In 1936 Dodd concluded "Where attempted in the United States, it may safely be said that court administration of workmen's compensation has failed." Dodd, Administration of Workmen's Compensation 98 (1936). See also Somers & Somers, Workmen's Compensation 143–150 (1954). In 1973 the authors of one study stated, "With their expanded responsibilities, court administration as practiced by the States of Alabama, Louisiana, New Mexico, Tennessee, and Wyoming is inadequate." National Commission on State Workmen's Compensation, Compendium on Workmen's Compensation 217 (1973). Louisiana and New Mexico have since adopted an agency administration system.

In the early part of the century it was common to create an administrative tribunal with legislative (rule-making), administrative, and adjudicative powers and authority. This concept rested on the premise that the bulk of the work in administering a workers' compensation law was to render decisions of contested claims. In fact, however, the vast majority of cases are not disputed and the primary need is for an administrative structure that insures the system efficiently and speedily gets benefit payments into the hands of injured workers and their medical attendants. In light of this need most states now employ a system in which an executive officer and staff administer the ordinary non-contested bulk of the payments, and in which appeals from the decisions of hearing officers are reviewed by a separate independent appeals board. This system is recommended by the National Commission on State Workmen's Compensation Laws.[4]

In some states, advisory committees composed of groups representing labor, industry and the public meet regularly to consider compensation issues and make recommendations for improvement or reform. These recommendations are often submitted to the legislature as agreed bills and thus are not the subject of dispute and debate on the legislative floor. To the extent that this approach permits non-controversial bills to be enacted without unnecessary political battling it serves a highly useful function of keeping the workers' compensation laws up to date. Nevertheless, matters that affect the cost of the plan to employers, such as coverage and benefits, rarely are enacted without extensive consideration by the legislatures. Despite this, an advisory committee composed of conscientious members of good will interested in improving the effectiveness of the law can accomplish a great deal.

SECTION 2. WAITING PERIOD

The workers' compensation acts of every state provide that a specified period of time must elapse after an injury occurs before the employee has a right to receive disability benefits to offset lost earnings. What this means is that a work injury is not compensable unless the resulting disability continues longer than the stipulated waiting period. For example, an employee who loses three days of pay as a result of an injury will receive no workers' compensation benefits to make up the lost wages in a state with a five day waiting period. (Of course, nothing keeps the employer from voluntarily maintaining the wages.) A waiting period is not normally required for medical benefits.

The purposes of the waiting period are to exclude minor injuries from the compensation scheme, to discourage malingering and to avoid excessive costs and administrative overhead. Initially, the customary length of the period was two weeks, but it has steadily diminished until today waiting periods vary among the states from three to seven days.[5]

4. The Report Of the National Commission On State Workmen's Compensation Laws 101–103 (1972).

5. U.S. Dept. of Labor, *State Workers' Compensation Laws,* supra note 2 at table 14.

All states provide that if the disability continues more than a specified length of time, compensation benefits are retroactive to the date of injury. The length of that period varies from five to twenty-nine days.[6]

Varying the lengths of the waiting and retroactivity periods substantially affects benefits. Consider two workers, each earning $250 a week. Worker A is employed in a state with a three day waiting period and a seven day retroactivity period; worker B is employed in a state with a seven day waiting period and a 21 day retroactivity period. Each state's rate of compensation is 66⅔ percent of the weekly wage. The two suffer identical injuries and are disabled for two weeks. Worker A would receive $330 in income benefits while the worker B would receive $165.

SECTION 3. UNCONTESTED CASES

In 70 to 90 percent of the cases of work-connected injury or disease, liability is not disputed either as to matters of fact or questions of law.[7] With them no adversary proceeding is necessary and the paramount administrative task is to see to it that compensation is promptly paid the injured workers. To achieve this most states prescribe that the claim is made directly to the employer or the employer's insurer. In the few states that employ exclusive state funds to pay benefits the claim is made to the agency administering the fund.[8] In the eighteen states that currently employ a competitive state fund the claim is made against either the employer or employer's insurer or the state body administering the fund, depending on which is carrying the risk.[9] Thus, in uncontested cases the prime function of agency administering the workmen's compensation act is to insure that the employers and those required to pay the compensation fulfill their obligations under the law. The states have two kinds of payment systems to accomplish this function.

a. The Agreement System

The earliest workers' compensation systems employed what is known as the "agreement system" for handling uncontested cases. It assumed that the administration of workers' compensation would be largely an automatic, self-executing and inexpensive process. Under the agreement system an employer or insurer proposes a settlement to the employee. If the proposal is accepted, the employee signs an agreement and payments begin after a somewhat routine approval by the state administrative body. If no dispute arises, state officials neither investi-

---

6. For a listing of various state provisions on this point see U.S. Dept. of Labor, *State Workers' Compensation Laws,* supra note 2 at table 14.

7. 8 A. Larson and L. Larson, Larson's Workers' Compensation Law § 82.10 (1998).

8. U.S. Department of Labor, *State Workers' Compensation Laws,* supra note 2 at table 1 (listing Nevada, North Dakota,

Ohio, Washington, West Virginia and Wyoming; Nevada, Ohio, Washington and West Virginia also permit self insurance in proper cases.)

9. Id. (listing Arizona, California, Colorado, Hawaii, Idaho, Maryland, Michigan, Minnesota, Montana, New York, Oklahoma, Oregon, Pennsylvania, Tennessee, Texas and Utah).

gate nor intervene. This system currently remains in effect in eleven states.[10]

Critics of the agreement system deem it to be unsatisfactory for two reasons; first, workers often are not able to protect their own interests; and, second, initial payments are delayed for substantial periods. As to the first point, critics observe that many workers do not read well or understand complicated documents and explanations of the technicalities of the law. By contrast, employers routinely employ experienced representatives who are able to bargain skillfully. Furthermore, employers gain economically from any delays in the commencement of payments, whereas injured workers usually need money quickly. Thus the bargaining position of workers is relatively poor.[11] Whether or not this bargaining disparity actually results in undue delay is harder to verify because of the lack of data demonstrating the facility or sluggishness of the system. Nevertheless, anecdotal evidence supports the criticism. For example, Michigan employed the agreement system for some thirty years before changing to the direct payment plan. One experienced observer concluded that the change immediately increased the number of workers receiving compensation within two weeks of the date of injury by a considerable margin.[12]

b. The Direct Payment System

The second basic method used in administering uncontested cases is known as the "direct payment" system. It was initially developed in Wisconsin to shorten the amount of time elapsing between the occurrence of an injury and the time the first benefit payment is made and to subject workers to the least formal procedure. Most states now employ direct payment systems.[13]

Under the direct payment plan, employers report the occurrences of compensable injuries directly to the state administrative body. The initial report is followed by a second report, filed either by the employer or the insurer, verifying the commencement of payments or stating why no payment has been made. Finally, another report is filed when payments are discontinued stating why, and describing the nature of any dispute that may exist between the parties. Final settlements are promptly reported with a copy of the final receipt signed by the injured employee.

In many states, the administrative agency informs the injured worker in writing of the rights and duties under the statute as soon as it

---

10. U.S. Dept. of Labor, *State Workers' Compensation Laws,* supra note 2 at table 16 (listing Connecticut, Delaware, Indiana, Iowa, Massachusetts, Mississippi, North Carolina, Rhode Island, South Carolina, Vermont and Virginia).

11. Harry J. Burczyk, Commissioner Wisconsin Industrial Commission (1947)

Bull. No. 87, p. 129, U.S. Department of Labor, Bureau of Labor Standards.

12. Betty W. Allie, Chairman Michigan Compensation Commission, Ibid., p. 131.

13. U.S. Dept. of Labor, *State Workers' Compensation Laws,* supra note 2, at table 16.

receives notice of a compensable accident. The agency makes a public record of how promptly insurers make payments and may impose penalties on employers and carriers who are guilty of unreasonable delays.

The agency ordinarily does not pass upon the validity of undisputed final settlements and these cases may be reopened within a specified period after the settlements are filed. When settlement is reached after genuine dispute, the agency does approve it and the right to reopen often is limited to a shorter period.

Experienced observers claim that the direct payment system has speeded up payments and created a cordial atmosphere between employees and employers and carriers. One report concluded that it tends to "eliminate contests which otherwise might arise and to prevent hearings and appeals."[14]

SECTION 4.   CONTESTED CASES

a.   *General Approach*

States that utilize an administrative agency to adjudicate disputed workers' compensation claims generally employ informal and expeditious procedures[15] that avoid the sometimes technical and cumbersome procedures that govern civil litigation.[16] The obvious purpose is to facilitate prompt and inexpensive resolution of claims. Nevertheless, the resolution of a contested compensation claim is essentially a judicial function[17] and adherence to prescribed formalities is necessary to ensure fairness and uniformity in the application of the law. Thus, fact finders must be impartial[18] and must base decisions on appropriate evidence that appears in the record.[19] The following subsections address some of the procedural and evidentiary aspects of a contested workers' compensation claim.

---

14. U.S. Department of Labor, Division of Labor Standards, Bull. No. 80, p. 39 at 44 (1946) (statement of Harry A. Nelson, Director, Workmen's Compensation, Wisconsin Industrial Commission); See also comments by James L. Hill quoted in Somers and Somers "Workmen's Compensation" 155 (1954).

15. E.g., Mo.Rev.Stat. § 287.550 ("All Proceedings before the commission or any commissioner shall be simple, informal and summary, and without regard to the technical rules of evidence . . .").

16. See generally, 7 A. Larson and L. Larson, Larson's Workers' Compensation Law §§ 77A and 79 (1998).

17. E.g., Reck v. Whittlesberger, 181 Mich. 463, 148 N.W. 247 (1914) (a compensation commission is a judicial as well as an administrative body and should observe the elementary principles governing judicial inquiry); Fremont Indem. Co. v. Workers'

Compensation Appeals Board, 153 Cal. App.3d 965, 200 Cal.Rptr. 762 (1984) (the Board acts "in legal effect" as a court and must observe the constitutional mandates of due process, including the prohibition on receiving unsworn testimony).

18. E.g., Delta Air Lines, Inc. v. McDaniel, 176 Ga.App. 523, 336 S.E.2d 610 (1985) (reversing an award made to employee when one of the directors of the State Board of Workers' Compensation that heard the employer's appeal was the son-in-law of the employee's attorney); Vayiar v. Vic Tanny Int'l., 114 Mich.App. 388, 319 N.W.2d 338 (1982) (the composition of the appeals panel violated employer's due process rights when 2 of its 3 members were representatives of employee interests).

19. E.g., Crowell v. Benson, 285 U.S. 22, 52 S.Ct. 285, 76 L.Ed. 598 (1932) (award cannot be upheld on the basis of evidence that was not placed in the record).

b. *Notice of Injury*

As a condition precedent to entitlement to benefits, most workers' compensation statutes require employees to notify employers of work injuries "forthwith" or within a period of time specified in the statute.[20] Notice serves two purposes. One is to afford the employer an opportunity to mitigate the effects of the injury by furnishing medical treatment without delay, and the other is to afford the employer an opportunity to investigate the circumstances under which the injury occurred.[21]

In deciding whether the failure to give notice should defeat the claim, courts regularly take into account both the remedial aims of the law and the purposes of the requirement. Lack of notice is often excused, especially if the employer has not demonstrated prejudice. For example, prompt notice is commonly excused if the employee could not reasonably have realized that the injury was one likely to lead to a compensable disability. In this situation, many courts have adopted something akin to the "discovery rule" in civil litigation, under which the time for giving notice does not begin to run until the employee should reasonably recognize the nature, seriousness, and probable compensatory character of the claim. In Slater v. United Parcel Service,[22] for example, a seasonal employee suffered a back injury on his last day of work. At that time he thought he had suffered only a mild back strain. The full extent of his injury was not known until a CAT–Scan was performed several months later. The court held that the claimant's failure to give notice within 30 days of the accident did not bar the claim because the disabling character of the injury was not reasonably known until the CAT–Scan had been performed. This is but one of innumerable decided cases in which administrative bodies and courts, guided by the foregoing principles, have been willing to overlook technical non-compliance with notice of injury requirements.

Another set of "notice" issues focuses on how and to whom notice is given. Strict compliance with formal procedure is not required.[23] No matter how acquired, actual knowledge of the accident by the employer is sufficient to constitute notice,[24] and, most jurisdictions impute notice to the employer when a supervisor or other representative employee is aware of the accident or injury.[25]

20. E.g., Ariz.Rev.Stat.Ann. § 23–908(d) ("forthwith"); Mich.Comp.Laws Ann. 418.381(1) (within 90 days); Kan.Stat.Ann. § 44.510 (within 10 days); Utah Code Ann. 34A–2–407(2) (within 180 days).

21. See generally, Bucuk v. Edward A. Zusi Brass Foundry, 49 N.J.Super. 187, 139 A.2d 436 (1958).

22. 507 So.2d 1146 (Fla.App.1987).

23. E.g., Ziegler v. Workmen's Compensation Appeals Board, 101 Pa.Comwlth. 392, 516 A.2d 128 (1986) (employee did not have to comply with employer's internal reporting procedures; notice to the foreman sufficed).

24. E.g., Moon v. Auto–Owners Ins. Co., 736 S.W.2d 92 (Tenn.1987) (Notice was given when an officer of the corporate employer witnessed the trench cave-in, even though the officer did not believe the claimant had been injured).

25. E.g., Williams v. Travelers Ins. Co., 153 Ga.App. 443, 265 S.E.2d 354 (1980) (employer had notice because the foreman was aware of the accident); Ross v. Oxford Paper Co., 363 A.2d 712 (Me.1976) (treatment of workplace injury by company doctor is notice to employer); Thompson v. Monfort of Colo., Inc., 221 Neb. 83, 375 N.W.2d 601 (1985) (notice may be satisfied

Nevertheless, because the notice of injury requirement is imposed by statute, claims are occasionally denied because of lack of notice. For example, an employer's awareness that a worker has congenital problems that often cause pain is not notice of an alleged work-related aggravation;[26] and simply telling co-workers of an alleged injury does not constitute notice if those co-workers have no supervisory or representative responsibilities.[27]

c. *Statutes of Limitations*

All workers' compensation statutes require that claims be filed within a specified period of time, usually one or two years from the date of injury or accident. This time-based restriction on filing is in the nature of a statute of limitations and is intended to protect employers against claims too old to be successfully investigated and defended. While noncompliance with notice provisions is sometimes excused when there is no showing of prejudice to the employer, statutes of limitations are not as easily avoided. Courts, in effect, construe statutes of limitations as carrying a conclusive presumption that an employer is prejudiced by a late filing.[28]

Disputes pertaining to workers' compensation statutes of limitations are most likely to arise in claims involving latent or progressive conditions in which the key issue is determining when the limitation period began to run. In most states, either by statute or judicial opinion, the time period for filing a claim does not begin to run until the claimant reasonably should recognize the nature, seriousness and probable compensable character of the injury or disease.[29] This approach is often referred to as the "discovery rule" and enables a worker to file a claim even if the disabling condition does not become manifest until several years after the work related "accident." The discovery rule is especially important in occupational disease claims involving a long delay between exposure and manifestation of the disability.[30] Where a discovery rule

by informing foreman, plant supervisor, or company nurse of injury).

26. Reil v. Billings Processors, Inc., 229 Mont. 305, 746 P.2d 617 (1987).

27. E.g., Wallace v. Gentry, 150 So.2d 66 (La.App.1963) (co-workers). Cf. Masters v. Industrial Garments Mfg. Co., 595 S.W.2d 811 (Tenn.1980) (telling Union president of back pain is not notice to the employer).

28. E.g., Cecil W. Perry, Inc. v. Lopez, 425 So.2d 180 (Fla.App.1983) (claim filed one day after the expiration of the limitation period must be dismissed); Asato v. Meadow Gold Dairies–Hawaii, 68 Hawaii 111, 706 P.2d 13 (1985) (untimely claims are barred even if the employer does not allege that lateness impaired its ability to investigate and defend).

29. E.g., Ariz.Rev.Stat.Ann. § 23–1061(A); Wis.Stat. § 102.12; Dafermo v.

Municipality of Anchorage, 941 P.2d 114 (Alaska, 1997).

30. A majority of states today employ a discovery rule for occupational disease claims. E.g., Cal.Labor Code § 5412; Del. Code Ann. tit. 19, § 2361(c); N.J.Stat.Ann. § 34:15–34. Some states have a separate (and generally longer) limitation period for a few particular diseases, such as asbestosis and silicosis. E.g., Ark.Stat.Ann. § 11–9–602. A state by state summary of occupational disease limitation provisions can be found at 2 A. Larson and L. Larson, Larson's Workers' Compensation Law § 41.83(b) (1998). The student is reminded that other aspects of time-based restrictions on occupational disease claims are discussed in Chapter 6 at note 7 following *Rutledge v. Tultex Corp./Kings Yarn.*

applies, decisions often turn on the fact-specific question of when this claimant *should* have recognized the presence of a potentially compensable injury or disease. For example, a worker may not be expected to attribute a stomach rash and infectious bone inflammation to an on-the-job back injury until so advised by a treating physician,[31] but may be expected to see the connection between a convulsion requiring hospitalization and an earlier compensable head injury.[32]

In a few states, the statute of limitations begins to run from the date of the "accident." This may lead to the denial of benefits when there is a substantial gap between the time of the "accident" and the onset of "disability." In Ingram v. Land–Air Transportation Co.,[33] for example, the worker fell off a truck injuring his shoulder. Because his treating physician said the injury was not serious, the employee did not file a workers' compensation claim and continued to work. The employee's shoulder gradually deteriorated, reaching the point of "disability" more than two years later. Although recognizing its distinct minority position and the harshness it produces, the court dismissed the employee's claim because it had not been filed within two years of the "accident." Leading commentators[34] criticize as unjust a rule that starts the limitation period at the date of accident regardless of the worker's lack of knowledge that an injury has occurred.

Although some early workers' compensation decisions held that timely commencement of compensation proceedings was "jurisdictional" and could not be waived,[35] only a few states currently give limitations periods that conclusive effect.[36] Instead, most states treat an objection to the timeliness of a claim as a defense that may be forfeited by waiver or estoppel. For example, many courts have held that payments made by an employer under group health or nonoccupational disability insurance policies toll the limitation period for filing a workers' compensation claim,[37] especially in "heart attack" and occupational disease cases where

---

31. Sherman v. Industrial Commission, 158 Ariz. 177, 761 P.2d 1081 (App.1988).

32. Bowers v. Wayne Lovelady Dodge, Inc., 80 N.M. 475, 457 P.2d 994 (App.1969).

33. 537 N.E.2d 532 (Ind.App.1989). See also, Latino v. Binswanger Glass Co., 532 So.2d 960 (La.App.1988) (The claimant was injured on the job when metal particles blew and implanted into his eyes. This accident did not produce any permanent or temporary disability at the time and no workers' compensation claim was filed. More than two years later, however, the implanted particles rusted, leading to the loss of one eye. The worker was denied compensation under a statute that required all claims to be filed within two years of the original accident).

34. 7 A. Larson and L. Larson, Larson's Workers' Compensation Law § 78.42(c)–(e) (1998).

35. E.g., American Car and Foundry Co. v. Industrial Commission, 335 Ill. 322, 167 N.E. 80 (1929).

36. E.g., Seckman v. Wyo–Ben, Inc., 783 P.2d 161 (Wyo.1989) (since limitation periods pertain to the subject matter jurisdiction, a court may properly dismiss, *sua sponte,* compensation claim filed outside the period even if the issue was not raised by the defendant).

37. E.g., New Castle County v. Goodman, 461 A.2d 1012 (Del.1983) (payment of two medical bills by employer tolled the limitation period for filing claim); Caterpillar Tractor Co. v. Industrial Comm., 33 Ill.2d 78, 210 N.E.2d 215 (1965) (payments made under group insurance plan covering nonoccupational disabilities effectively tolled the workers' compensation limitations period); Jaeger v. Stauffer Chem. Co., 198 Mont. 263, 645 P.2d 942 (1982) (payment of claimant's salary for a year and a

the work-relatedness of the disability is uncertain. These payments are most likely to toll the statute of limitations if they offset compensation liability or are reasonably viewed as remuneration in lieu of compensation.[38] Furthermore, employers are estopped from asserting a limitation defense if their actions mislead or prevent an employee from filing a timely claim.[39] Finally, in most jurisdictions lack of timeliness of filing a claim is waived as a defense if it is not raised in a timely fashion.[40]

The limitation period for compensation claims arising from the death of an employee usually runs from the date of death.[41] The dependent's right to death benefits is not derived from the rights of the deceased employee but is created directly by statute and does not accrue until the death of the employee. Thus, it is no defense to a dependent's claim for death benefits that the deceased employee failed to file a timely claim for injuries resulting from the occupational disease or accident that led to death.[42]

d. Evidence

As a general proposition, the rules of evidence are applied in a relaxed fashion in workers' compensation hearings. Indeed, many statutes expressly provide that the hearing is not governed by the technical rules of evidence that apply in civil litigation.[43] The emphasis on informality undoubtedly reflects both the remedial purposes of workers' compensation and the prevalence of professional administrative factfinders. Administrative law judges are more likely to receive hearsay

half following injury tolled the statute of limitations).

38. Compare, Frost v. Anaconda Co., 198 Mont. 216, 645 P.2d 419 (1982) ("Compensation, to toll the statute, must be sufficient to convince the recipient that he is receiving such a large percentage of workers' compensation benefits available to him that to seek further benefits would be a wasted effort.") with Maxey v. Fremont Dept. of Utilities, 220 Neb. 627, 371 N.W.2d 294 (1985) (payments for wages or medical services under an employee benefit plan does not toll the statute unless they clearly indicate that they constitute payment of compensation). See also, Caterpillar Tractor Co. v. Industrial Comm., 33 Ill.2d 78, 210 N.E.2d 215 (1965) (payments received under group nonoccupational disability insurance plan tolled the statute of limitations and the employer was entitled to a credit for the group insurance payments).

39. E.g., Stines v. Winter Haven Hospital, 548 So.2d 818 (Fla.App.1989) (statute of limitation did not bar claim when employer sent "entitlement of rights" letter to wrong address); Hutcherson v. Dawn Trucking Co., 107 N.M. 358, 758 P.2d 308 (App.1988) (claimant's testimony that insurance adjuster assured him that everything will be taken care of raises a fact issue whether claimant had been lulled into letting the statute of limitations elapse).

40. E.g., Priedigkeit v. Industrial Comm., 20 Ariz.App. 594, 514 P.2d 1045 (1973) (statute of limitations defense was waived when it was not raised at the first hearing); Maryland Casualty Co. v. Smith, 122 Ga.App. 262, 176 S.E.2d 666 (1970) (statute of limitation defense was waived by failing to raise the issue at the administrative hearing).

41. E.g., N.Y. Work.Comp. Law § 28; Ohio Rev.Code Ann. § 4123.84.

42. E.g., Berkebile v. Workers' Compensation Appeals Board, 144 Cal.App.3d 940, 193 Cal.Rptr. 12 (1983) (widow could file claim for death benefits even if her husband never filed an occupational disease claim arising from lingering illness); Mentzer v. Westinghouse Corp., 10 Ohio App.3d 198, 461 N.E.2d 24 (1983) (widow's claim for death benefits is timely even if her deceased husband's claim was not). See also note 5 following Deeni v. United Technologies Corp. reprinted in Chapter 9, section 3.

43. E.g., N.Y. [Work.Comp.] Law § 118; Utah Code Ann. § 34A–2–802.

evidence and give a more generous scope to the exceptions to the hearsay rule than would their counterparts on the trial bench. The most striking example of this may be the routine admission of letters and reports of physicians without the rigorous foundation ordinarily required in civil trials.[44] Rarely is an award or denial of workers' compensation benefits reversed because of the improper admission of evidence, but the exclusion of competent evidence is sometimes reversible error.[45] Consequently, hearing examiners and administrative law judges tend to err on the side of admitting disputed evidence.

Evidentiary disputes most frequently arise regarding proof of medical facts. Many of these medical issues have been discussed in earlier chapters. For example, the extent of disability, and hence the amount of compensation, is often determined by reference to the A.M.A. *Guides to the Evaluation of Permanent Impairment.*[46] Under the *Guides,* impairment ratings are generally considered a medical fact. Proof of causation is also a frequently disputed medical issue. Did the claimant's work-related trauma cause the subsequent cancer?[47] Did workplace stress cause the disabling heart attack?[48] Was the claimant's disabling respiratory ailment caused by occupational exposure to cotton dust?[49] In short, because medical evidence may be probative of whether a disability is compensable and, if so, to what extent, its admission is often controversial.

A recurring question is whether medical evidence, often in the form of expert opinion, is indispensable to support an award of benefits. Many workers' compensation awards have been upheld despite the absence of strong supporting medical evidence. Thus, benefits have been awarded for heart attacks and occupational diseases when expert opinions regarding causation were equivocal or even totally lacking.[50] On the other hand, many decisions have denied compensation because of lack of supporting

44. E.g., Foster v. Continental Casualty Co., 141 Ga.App. 415, 233 S.E.2d 492 (1977) (it was proper for the workers' compensation board to consider a letter from a doctor even though the signature was not authenticated); Forrest v. Industrial Commission, 77 Ill.2d 86, 32 Ill.Dec. 346, 395 N.E.2d 576 (1979) (letter from claimant's chiropractor to claimant's attorney was properly admitted into evidence).

45. E.g., Gill v. Workers' Compensation Appeals Board, 167 Cal.App.3d 306, 213 Cal.Rptr. 140 (1985) (reversing the board's finding of only a partial disability when the board improperly refused to consider report of vocational counselor); Tradewinds Mfg. Co. v. Cox, 541 So.2d 667 (Fla.App.1989) (reversible error not to permit the employer to prove that it made overpayments by calling the claimant as a witness).

46. See Slover Masonry, Inc. v. Industrial Comm'n., Chapter 8, supra.

47. E.g., Cox v. Ulysses Cooperative Oil & Supply Co., 218 Kan. 428, 544 P.2d 363 (1975).

48. See, Lancaster v. Gilbert Development, Chapter 6, supra.

49. See, Rutledge v. Tultex Corp./Kings Yarn, Chapter 6, supra.

50. E.g., Guye v. Home Indemnity Co., 241 Ga. 213, 244 S.E.2d 864 (1978) (a "natural inference" of causation based on common experience can support an award of benefits to laborer who suffered a heart attack after digging a ditch and lifting a 250 pound pole); King v. Oregon Steel Mills, Inc., 25 Or.App. 685, 550 P.2d 747 (1976) (occupational causation of pulmonary disease may be inferred when claimant's condition improved after quitting his job in the furnace area of a steel plant).

medical evidence proving causation.[51] The cases do not definitively prescribe when expert testimony is essential. Perhaps the most that can be said is that medical evidence is highly desirable in all cases, but is more likely to be indispensable if the issue of causation is thought to lie beyond the expertise of the administrative factfinder.

Some cases have called the qualifications of expert witnesses into question, but most administrative agencies and courts allow the parties considerable latitude in this regard. Thus, chiropractors are commonly allowed to testify about the nature and extent of back injuries[52] and physicians who are not expert in psychiatric disorders have been allowed to diagnose traumatic neuroses.[53] An objection to the qualifications of the opposing party's expert witness is often dismissed with the observation that such matters bear more on the weight to be given an opinion than on its admissibility.

e. *Administrative and Judicial Review*

In the few states in which courts administer the workers' compensation law, an award or denial of compensation is subject to judicial review in the same manner as other court judgments.[54] In the great number of jurisdictions in which the law is administered by an agency or commission, special provisions for judicial review are provided and commonly incorporate a review procedure at the administrative level. The original hearing is usually held before an administrative law judge or hearing officer who makes an initial decision that is binding if unappealed. If appealed, the initial decision is reviewed administratively by the full workers' compensation board, a commission, or a board of appeals within the compensation system.[55] In most jurisdictions, the reviewing administrative body is not bound by the hearing officer's findings of fact, but is free to reconsider evidence and adopt or reject the initial findings or conclusions. The reviewing administrative body may also order additional testimony, but this is rarely done. The full board or commission usually limits its review to the record made before the hearing officer or administrative law judge.[56]

---

51. E.g., Maness v. Industrial Comm., 102 Ariz. 557, 434 P.2d 643 (1967) (claimant fell from a roof and later developed an ulcer; since the causal connection between the fall and the ulcer was not apparent to a layman, compensation for the ulcer could not be made in the absence of medical testimony); Interlake Steel Co. v. Industrial Comm., 136 Ill.App.3d 740, 91 Ill.Dec. 493, 483 N.E.2d 979 (1985) (reversing an award of benefits when there was no expert medical evidence to establish that the disabling tumors were work related).

52. E.g., Chalupa v. Industrial Comm., 109 Ariz. 340, 509 P.2d 610 (1973); Vallejos v. KNC, Inc., 105 N.M. 613, 735 P.2d 530 (1987). But see, Weis v. Division of Work-

ers' Compensation, 232 Mont. 218, 755 P.2d 1385 (1988) (upholding an administrative rule restricting medical evaluations to licensed physicians, thereby excluding chiropractors from the field).

53. E.g., Guillory v. Travelers Ins. Co., 326 So.2d 914 (La.App.1976); Barrett v. Coast Range Plywood, 294 Or. 641, 661 P.2d 926 (1983).

54. E.g., Ala.Code § 25–5–81; Tenn. Code Ann. § 50–6–225(e).

55. E.g., Ga. Code. Ann. § 34–9–103(a).

56. See, 3 A. Larson and L. Larson, Larson's Workers' Compensation Law § 80.12(g) (1998).

After a final decision is concluded within the administrative system, judicial review is available in one of several forms. In a few states, the case is taken to a court for a trial de novo.[57] In these jurisdictions, the reviewing court has greater power to reexamine and reweigh the evidence than is typically allowed in judicial review of administrative decisions, but the particular scope of de novo review varies widely. Most states that allow de novo review limit the appeal to a review of the administrative record.[58] The decision resulting from the de novo review may then be appealed through conventional avenues of appellate jurisdiction. In recent years, several states have abandoned or substantially modified the de novo appeal procedure.[59]

In most states, judicial review is limited to an appellate court's examination of the record to ensure that the agency correctly applied the law and that its findings of fact are supported by sufficient evidence.[60] This more limited scope of judicial review pays great deference to the discretion of the final administrative factfinder. The administrative body is entrusted to make findings of fact that appellate courts may review only under the "substantial evidence"[61] rule. If sufficient evidence exists, the appellate court must accept the board's findings of fact. Thus, courts will generally defer to the administrative agency's resolution of the "battle of experts" regarding medical causation, the extent of the claimant's disability, and any other disputed issue of fact.

In some states judicial review of the agency's decision is first made by a trial court with any additional appeals proceeding as a matter of discretion by writ of certiorari.[62] As a practical matter, this process usually makes the trial court the tribunal of last resort. Furthermore, because most states do not publish trial court decisions, this procedure produces a body of significant but unreported case law. By contrast, the

---

57. E.g., Md. Labor and Employment §§ 9–742, 737. Other states that employ some form of de novo review are Hawaii, Louisiana, New Hampshire, Ohio, Tennessee, and Washington. See, United States Chamber of Commerce, 1998 Analysis of Workers Compensation Laws, chart XV.

58. U.S. Chamber of Commerce, 1998 Analysis of Workers' Compensation Laws, chart XV.

59. E.g., McAlear v. Arthur G. McKee & Co., 171 Mont. 462, 558 P.2d 1134 (1976) (after the repeal of Mont.Code Ann. §§ 92–834 and 92–835 Montana adopted the substantial evidence review standard); Or.Rev. Stat. § 656.298 (amended in 1987 to not allow any new evidence to be admitted at the court of appeals); Tex.Lab.Code Ann. § 410–306 (amended in 1990 to limit the issues and evidence to be considered by review).

60. See, 8 A. Larson and L. Larson's, Larson's Workers' Compensation Law § 80.00 (1998).

61. The most common articulation of the standard of review is in terms of "substantial evidence". E.g., Armstrong v. Iowa Bldgs. & Grounds, 382 N.W.2d 161 (Iowa 1986); Hess Bros. v. Workmen's Compensation Appeal Board, 128 Pa.Cmwlth. 240, 563 A.2d 236 (1989). Other jurisdictions invoke different terminology. E.g., Skelton v. Department of Transportation, 191 Ga. App. 835, 383 S.E.2d 162 (1989) ("any evidence"). The common substantive thrust of these variously phrased standards is to prevent the reviewing court from substituting its judgment for that of the administrative factfinder on contested issues of fact. Variations on the "substantial evidence" standard are discussed in 8 A. Larson and L. Larson, Larson's Workers' Compensation Law § 80.26(a)–(h) (1998).

62. E.g., Ga.Code Ann. §§ 34–9–105(e) and 5–6–35.

many jurisdictions that employ appellate court review as the final stage of the process accumulate a mass of published decisions explicating the law.

f. Recent Efforts to Reduce Litigation Costs and Fraud

Although the workers' compensation system processes contested claims more efficiently than does the tort system, many critics maintain that litigation costs are too high. Reduction of the litigation costs has been a primary objective of recent workers' compensation reform efforts. Proponents of such reforms argue that a reduction of litigation costs will reduce insurers' and employers' costs and make more money available for benefits. Two common types of reforms are restriction on claimants' attorneys' fees and mandatory informal claims processing.

In the 1990's many states imposed limits on claimants' attorneys' fees.[63] Some reform measures shifted payment of claimants' attorneys' fees from insurers to injured workers.[64] The impact of some of these reforms on attorneys' fees can be dramatic. In Florida, for example, reforms of this type were reported to result in cuts in attorneys' fees from $15,750 to $10,750 in cases where the benefits were $100,000. For a claim involving benefits of $20,000 a claimant's attorney would have been paid $3,750 before the reform and $2,750 after.[65] This reduction in fees is reportedly making it more difficult for some claimants to secure representation.[66]

A second type of reform involves increased use of informal dispute resolution processes. Several states require mediation or some other informal dispute resolution process prior to a hearing.[67] While such processes can facilitate the resolution of contested claims in many instances, in others it can add delay and cost. In Florida, a worker who has been denied benefits by an employer/insurer must apply to a state ombudsman for informal assistance in resolving the dispute before becoming eligible to file a formal claim.[68] If the worker's claim is not resolved by the ombudsman, the worker may then file a formal claim but it will not be resolved by hearing and legally binding decision until after the disputed claim has been submitted to mediation before a professional state mediator.[69] The parties may be represented by lawyers in the

---

63. E.g., Kan. Stat. Ann. § 44–536(a) (reducing attorneys' fees from 25% of award to 15% for benefits greater than $20,000); Me. Rev. Stat. Ann. Tit 39–A § 325(3) (capping attorney fees at 30%); S.D. Codified Laws § 62–7–36 (capping fees at 25% of settlements, 30% for benefits awarded after a hearing, and 35% in cases appealed to the highest state court).

64. E.g., Me. Rev. Stat. Ann, tit. 39–A § 325(1).

65. Martha T. McCluskey, The Illusion of Efficiency in Workers' Compensation "Reform," 50 Rutgers L. Rev. 657, 863 n. 874 (1998).

66. Id., at 864.

67. E.g., Me. Rev. Stat. Ann. Tit. 39–A § 313 (mandatory mediation); New York Work. Comp. Law § 25(2–b) (claims for benefits of 52 weeks or less to be submitted to informal conciliation process); Tex. Labor Code Ann. § 410.024 (no hearing until informal benefit review conference is conducted).

68. Fla. Stat. Ann. § 440.191(2).

69. Fla. Stat. Ann. §§ 440.182(1), 440.25(1).

mediation except that an employer may not be represented by legal counsel if the worker is unrepresented. Only if the mediation is unsuccessful will the claim be resolved in formal proceedings conducted by an administrative hearing officer. Does it appear to you that this system systematically favors either employees as a class or employers as a class?

Another popular target for reform is fraud. Since 1989, a majority of states have enacted new laws designed to combat claims of fraud. Such legislation often provides for stronger penalties for fraud, create fraud investigative units vested with enforcement authority, and provides protection for persons reporting fraud.[70]

For a comprehensive description and critique of these and other recent reform efforts, see Martha T. McCluskey, The Illusion of Efficiency in Workers' Compensation "Reform," 50 Rutgers L. Rev. 657 (1998).

SECTION 5. COMPROMISE (SETTLEMENTS) AND COMMUTATION (LUMP SUM PAYMENTS)

Should an employer and employee be permitted to settle a workers' compensation claim for less than the worker might be entitled to under the law? Just as in tort litigation, uncertainties regarding coverage and the extent of disability often set the stage for compromise. Yet the social insurance aspect of workers' compensation is thought by some to be inconsistent with tort-like settlement practices.

Many workers' compensation acts expressly prohibit contractual waivers or compromises of entitlements under workers' compensation laws.[71] Such provisions reflect a concern that employers would exploit their superior economic position to extract waivers or compromises of statutory rights from employees. Decisions under these statutes are mixed: some invalidate compromises for less than full benefits and some decisions uphold the compromises.

The argument for restricting settlement of workers' compensation claims was expressed by the New Jersey Supreme Court as follows: "[t]he fulfillment of the statutory policy is of concern to the State. The parties themselves are not free to bargain for a surrender of a right of compensation under the statute. * * * The compensation act provides social insurance in the common interest as well as [in] the interest of the injured workman. Indemnity for the risks of service, even without fault, is made to fall upon industry as an incident of the operation and

---

70. E.g., Ark. Code Ann. § 11–9–106 (making willful false statements or representations with respect to workers' compensation claims a felony; creating a fraud investigation unit; granting immunity from employers or employees to an employee who has reported fraud). For a description of other state laws, see Martha T. McCluskey, The Illusion of Efficiency in Workers' compensation "Reform," 50 Rutgers L. Rev. 657, 873–74 (1998). For a survey of fraud investigation units, their powers and results, see Brian Zaidman & David Berry, State Workers' Compensation Anti–Fraud Activity: Survey Results, Workers' Compensation Year Book 1996, at I–172–I–176.

71. E.g., N.Y. Work.Comp. Law § 33 ("Compensation or benefits due under this chapter shall not be assigned, released or commuted except as provided by this chapter * * * ").

eventually upon the consumer."[72] The contrary view was expressed by the Kansas Supreme Court, as follows, "[w]orkmen are not in any respect under guardianship or other disability; they and their employers are free agents; they may release their employers from liability for injuries on any agreed terms satisfactory to both."[73]

Notwithstanding questions about theoretical propriety, settlement has become a practical reality in modern workers' compensation practice. Most state statutes permit settlement and compromise if approved by the board or commission.[74] Although the scope of permissible compromise varies considerably among jurisdictions, one common restriction prohibits or restricts the release of the employer's liability for future medical expenses.[75] Also, recall from the materials in Chapter 9 that in some states an employee's settlement of his claim may not necessarily bar the claims of survivors for death benefits.

A separate issue is whether to permit lump sum payments (or "washouts") when the parties agree on liability and the extent of benefits. When an award has been made, or the parties agree that an award should be made, the claimant may wish to receive a single lump sum payment instead of weekly payments of income benefits extended into the future. The lump sum thus involves a commutation of benefit payments rather than a compromise of amount.

Critics of lump sum awards point out that periodic (weekly) payment of income benefits advances the important objective of ensuring that workers regularly receive income support for the duration of disability and allows for adjustments if conditions change. Some observers fear that workers will dissipate a single lump sum before the disability ends, leaving the disabled workers with no income support.[76] Other considerations, however, favor awarding lump sum payments. Many claimants prefer having a larger sum of money in hand to the guarantee of smaller periodic payments in the future. This may enable workers to improve their earning capacity by financing retraining or capitalizing a new business. Insurers and employers tend to favor the lump sum option to reduce administrative costs in monitoring individual files, and claimants' attorneys prefer receiving fees in full out of the lump sum to being paid in smaller weekly installments over a period of time.

These arguments have been resolved in most states to permit lump sum awards in appropriate cases. Ordinarily the statutes provide only general standards[77] that charge the administrative agencies with the

---

72. Nagy v. Ford Motor Co., 6 N.J. 341, 78 A.2d 709 (1951).

73. Dotson v. Proctor & Gamble Mfg. Co., 102 Kan. 248, 169 P. 1136 (1918).

74. See, United States Chamber of Commerce, 1998 Analysis of Workers Compensation Laws, chart XI.

75. E.g., Brooks v. Arkansas–Best Freight System, Inc., 247 Ark. 61, 444 S.W.2d 246 (1969); Great Bay Distrib. v. Everett, 513 So.2d 187 (Fla.App.1987).

76. 8 A. Larson and L. Larson, Larson's Workers' Compensation Law § 82.71 (1998) ("Experience has shown that in many cases the lump sum is soon dissipated and the worker is right back where he or she would have been if workers' compensation had never existed.").

77. E.g., Alaska Stat. § 23.30.012 (authorizing lump sum award when in the "best interest of the employee); 820 Ill. Comp. Stat. 305/9 (authorizing lump sum

paternal responsibility of safeguarding the claimants' long term interests. Much of the litigation on this point concerns the agency's assessment of the purported need for a lump sum payment with the critical factor often being whether a lump sum payment can realistically be expected to improve the claimant's ability to earn a living.[78]

SECTION 6.   REOPENING AND MODIFYING AWARDS

Judgments in personal injury litigation and awards in a workers' compensation claims differ markedly in their finality. The trial of a tort claim is intended to resolve all factual disputes completely and conclusively, including those pertaining to the future consequences of the plaintiff's injuries. Courts do not monitor subsequent developments and will not modify a jury's award simply because the plaintiff's actual injuries turned out to be more or less severe than determined at trial. By contrast, the workers' compensation system is less embued with the notion of ultimate finality. Almost every state has some provision authorizing the administrative body to reopen cases and modify awards.[79] The statutes vary as to the period of time within which modifying action may be taken and the reasons for which modification is permitted.

The reopening period varies from as little as six months to no time limitation at all,[80] but the vast majority of jurisdictions places some fixed limit on the time to reopen an award. Some states calculate the limitation period by reference to the date of the injury, whereas others refer to the date of the original award or the date of the last payment.[81]

Many statutes incorporate specific grounds for modifying an award, such as fraud, mistake, or newly discovered evidence.[82] Others authorize modifications in expansive terms, such as for "good cause" or any

payment when it is in the "best interest of the parties"); Mich.Comp.Laws Ann. § 418.835 (authorizing lump sum payment if "special circumstances" exist). Cf. State ex rel. Kenner Products v. Industrial Comm., 21 Ohio App.3d 232, 486 N.E.2d 1280 (1985) (statute authorized lump sum payment if "special circumstances" existed, but administrative regulations prohibited the award of lump sum payments for the purchase of luxury items such as television sets; Commission award of lump sum payment for purchase of a television set, automobile, and air conditioner reversed).

78. Compare City of Miami v. Mercer, 513 So.2d 149 (Fla.App.1987) (approving a lump sum award to pay for aviation training) with Ventura v. Palm Springs General Hospital, 463 So.2d 414 (Fla.App.1985) (upholding the denial of a request for lump sum payment to be used to purchase rental property when claimant had no experience in real estate management and investment).

79. For a brief description of the practices of every state regarding the modifica-

tion of awards, see United States Chamber of Commerce, 1998 Analysis of Workers Compensation Laws, chart XI.

80. E.g., Neb.Rev.Stat. § 48–141 (6 months from the date of the award or agreement); Ga.Code Ann. § 34–9–104(b) (two years from the date of the last payment); Md. Code Ann., Lab. & Empl. § 9–736(b) (five years from the date of the last payment); N.D.Cent.Code § 65–05–04 ("any time").

81. E.g., Colo.Rev.Stat. § 8–43–303 (6 years from the date of the injury); 820 Ill. Comp. Stat. 305/19(h) (30 months from the date of the award); Ga.Code Ann. § 34–9–104(b) (2 years from the date of the last payment).

82. E.g., Ky.Rev.Stat.Ann. § 342.125 (change in condition, mistake, fraud or newly discovered evidence); Colo.Rev.Stat. § 8–43–303 (error, mistake, or change in condition and overpayment).

grounds "as may be justified."[83] Nevertheless, the most common reason for modifying an award is that the claimant's physical condition has changed in a way that affects the existence or extent of disability. Often the employee attempts to establish a worsened physical condition and entitlement to greater benefits. The worsening may be due to aggravation or deterioration of the original injury, discovery of a new and more serious condition, or simply the failure to heal as completely as predicted.[84] States are divided on the question of whether a change in economic conditions alone can justify a modification of an award.[85]

A considerable amount of litigation focuses on whether the worsening of the claimant's physical impairment should be considered a change in condition or a new injury. Consider, for example, the worker who suffers a back injury and receives an award for a 10% impairment to the body as a whole. The worker recuperates and returns to work, but later reinjures the back injury and becomes totally disabled. Is the second disability a change in condition or a new injury? Several important practical consequences flow from how this question is answered. If the injury is determined to be a change in condition, the claim might be untimely, whereas, if determined to be a new injury, it would not be. If the employee has changed jobs or if the employer has changed insurance carriers between the first and second injuries, the characterization will determine which employer or insurance company is responsible for payment of any benefits due.[86]

The line separating a change in condition from a new accident is sometimes hard to draw. Courts often invoke a quasi-causation analysis to resolve the issue. The closer the causal connection between the original compensable injury and the second disability, the more likely the second disability will be characterized as a change in condition. For example, the board may modify an award for a change in condition when a subsequent fall was plainly caused by a previously compensated leg

---

83. E.g., Cal. Labor Code § 5803 ("good cause"); Md. Code Ann., Lab. and Empl. § 9–736(b) (such modifications as the committee considers "justified"); N.Y. Work. Comp. Law § 123 (such modifications as "may be justified").

84. E.g., Pascucci v. Industrial Comm., 126 Ariz. 442, 616 P.2d 902 (App.1980) (an award may be increased in light of a previously undiscovered herniated disc caused by the work injury); Zachary v. Bituminous Cas. Corp., 371 So.2d 1249 (La.App.1979) (increasing award when the claimant did not recover from a work-related knee injury as originally predicted); Rightnour v. Kare-Mor, Inc., 236 Mont. 108, 768 P.2d 871 (1989) (previously settled claim may be reopened when subsequent aggravation of back injury produces total disability).

85. Compare Hartford Accident & Indemnity Co. v. Bristol, 242 Ga. 287, 248 S.E.2d 661 (1978) and Blacksmith v. All-American, Inc., 290 N.W.2d 348 (Iowa 1980)

(both cases increasing awards due to economic change in condition) with Petrie v. Industrial Comm., 160 Ill.App.3d 165, 111 Ill.Dec. 858, 513 N.E.2d 104 (1987) (limiting modifications to changes in physical condition).

86. E.g., Bryan County Emergency Medical Services v. Gill, 187 Ga.App. 125, 369 S.E.2d 495 (1988) (employee suffered a back injury in 1977 for which he received medical treatment paid for by his employer's workers' compensation insurance carrier; the claimant continued to work until 1985 when his back condition deteriorated to the point of requiring surgery; the court found the employee had suffered a "new accident" in 1985 when he became unable to work; the court held that the claim was not barred by the statute of limitations, and the now self-insured employer was responsible for the payment of benefits).

disability.[87] By contrast, the more tenuous the causal connection between the two events, or the greater the number of intervening factors, the more likely the second injury will be treated as a new injury. Thus, the second injury may be considered a new accident if it arises from a preexisting condition or an intervening cause not attributable to the claimant's first compensable injury.[88] Nevertheless, in workers' compensation, as in torts, the concept of causation is subject to shifting meanings. The extent to which a second injury may be considered attributable to the first is explored in more detail in Chapter 7.

SECTION 7. EVALUATING THE ADMINISTRATIVE PROCESS

Some of the observed differences between workers' compensation administration and tort litigation are substantive in nature, such as the standard of liability and the use of schedules to calculate standardized awards, and others are procedural, such as the workers' compensation notice of injury requirements. The "tort crisis" of the mid–1980's prompted a renewed interest in comparing the workers' compensation system and tort. Some critics of tort litigation have looked to workers' compensation as a more efficient mechanism for relieving the economic consequences of injury but have come away with mixed findings. For example, a comprehensive study on personal injury conducted under the auspices of the American Law Institutes drew the following conclusion about the relative administrative efficiencies of workers' compensation, tort litigation and other social insurance programs.

THE AMERICAN LAW INSTITUTE
REPORTER'S STUDY
ENTERPRISE RESPONSIBILITY FOR PERSONAL INJURY[89]

"In addition to these distinctive substantive policies of WC [workers' compensation], another major institutional step was taken in the general design of the program. Responsibility for at least front-line decision making about entitlement and the scope of compensation was taken from courts and juries because of concern about technical formalities that only lawyers could deal with effectively. That role was assigned

---

87. E.g., Burt v. Oklahoma National Bank, 632 P.2d 440 (Okl.App.1981).

88. E.g., Hawthorne v. Industrial Comm., 114 Ariz. 63, 559 P.2d 183 (App. 1976) (affirming the denial of worker's petition to reopen a claim when the hearing officer found that the worker's present back condition was not caused by his prior work injuries); Certain v. United States Fidelity & Guaranty Co., 153 Ga.App. 571, 266 S.E.2d 263 (1980) ("ordinarily the distinguishing feature that will characterize the disability as either a 'change in condition' or a 'new accident' is the intervention of *new circumstances*."); Board of Supervisors v. Martin, 3 Va.App. 139, 348 S.E.2d 540 (1986) (claimant suffered a compensable

knee injury and later reinjured the knee when slipping on a wet floor; the second fall was considered a new accident, in part, because the slippery floor and not the earlier injury was deemed to be the cause of the fall).

89. Copyright 1991 by The American Law Institute reprinted with the permission of the American Law Institute, vol. I, pp. 118–121 (April 15, 1991). (Footnotes in the quoted material have been renumbered to be sequential in this text.) (The American Law Institute has neither endorsed nor acted upon this Report as of the date of publication of this casebook).

instead to specialized administrative tribunals which would permit workers and employers to resolve the problems on their own, ideally more informally, expeditiously and economically. Under WC the courts serve essentially as a backstop to insure that the administrative tribunal acts in reasonable accord with its statutory mandate.

"In practice there have been major compromises in the non-legal cast of WC, which is perhaps to be expected in any serious liability system. Nevertheless, at least in aggregate terms WC is an administratively faster and cheaper system than tort litigation. In cases in which entitlement is not contested, benefits begin to be paid on average in three weeks. Even in contested cases, the average disposition time is roughly four months.[90] Abstracting from the business costs incurred by any private insurance system in selling insurance and collecting premiums, WC spends roughly 15 to 20 percent of its total claim costs on administrative expenses (as opposed to benefits), whereas tort litigation spends 50 to 55 percent on administration.[91]

"It is true that the majority of WC claims are made (though less than half of WC dollars are paid) for comparatively minor injuries. In contrast, product liability and medical malpractice litigation tend to screen out most of the smaller claims and to produce more incentive to litigate the sizable claims that remain. Still, this factor is largely controlled for in motor vehicle accident litigation, which spends between 45 and 50 percent of claims dollars on administration. However, in the motor vehicle context as well, the bulk of the claims are made (though not dollars paid) for smaller cases. The difference between WC and motor vehicle tort litigation provides some sense of the potential administrative payoff attainable by eliminating fault and using standardized benefit formulas.

"Yet WC looks somewhat less attractive along that dimension in comparison with a social insurance program such as SSDI [Social Security Disability Insurance], which has an administrative cost ratio under 5 percent, less than one-third that of WC. Even more important, the administrative burden of WC is attributable disproportionately to the two trouble spots * * * PPD [permanent, partial disability] and occupational disease claims.

"Empirical study of PPD cases found that more than half of these cases (compared with 10 percent in the overall program) were initially

---

90. See R. Conley and J. Noble, *Workers' Compensation and Reform: Challenge for the 80's* 57 (1979).

91. The figure for WC administrative costs is calculated in the ALI Working Paper by P. Weiler, [Legal Policy for Workplace Injuries (ALI Working Paper, 1986)] at 20, drawing on figures from the insurer and public claims administration costs contained in Price, ["Workers' Compensation: 1976–80 Benchmark Revisions," 47 *Social Security Bulletin* 7 (July, 1984)], and on

estimates of injured worker expenditures on lawyers presented by M. Bernstein, *Litigation, Representation and Claimant Protection and Workers' Compensation* (1979). The figures for the tort system are calculated in another ALI Background Paper, P. Weiler, *Legal Policy for Medical Injuries* 128–30 (1988), drawing primarily, although not entirely, on the data developed by J. Kakalik and N. Pace, *Costs and Compensation Paid in Tort Litigation* (1986).

contested by the employer or insurer. These percentages were even greater in cases with higher impairment ratings and larger wage losses. Consequently, the victims in such cases had to hire a lawyer and pay significant attorney's fees. This combination of delay and cost has led to a widespread practice of "compromise and release" settlements from lump-sum payments at only a fraction of the already too low levels of non-indexed PPD pensions.[92]

"The picture is even worse for occupational disease claims. A national survey of closed WC claims in the mid–1970's found that fully 90 percent of these cases were contested, three-quarters of them on the issue of cause and entitlement. This meant that 65 percent of these disease claimants had to hire or pay for a lawyer (versus 15 percent for accident victims). They then had to wait a year on average for resolution and payment of their claims (versus two months for accidents), and at the end of that time the average award was valued at $9,000, or only about 10 percent of the earnings lost.[93]

"Thus, systematic research about the performance of WC in these two settings corroborate the intuitive impressions of many observers that this version of the no-fault model has its own significant deficiencies as a solution to the problems in tort litigation."

92. See generally M. Bernstein, supra note 86.

93. The details of this survey are presented and analyzed in the U.S. Department of Labor [Interim Report to Congress On Occupational Diseases 69–71 (1980)], as well as in P. Barth, [and H. Hunt, Workers' Compensation and Work–Related Illnesses and Diseases (1980)].

Chapter 11

THE EXCLUSIVE REMEDY DOCTRINE AND THE THIRD PARTY SUIT

One of the cornerstones of the original workers' compensation compromise is the employer's immunity from tort suits by an injured employee. This immunity is reflected in what is commonly called the exclusive remedy doctrine, which provides that workers' compensation is the employee's exclusive remedy vis a vis the employer. While the exclusive remedy doctrine generally bars a tort claim against an injured worker's employer, it does not preclude tort claims against third parties who might be responsible for the injuries. Under the proper set of facts, the injured worker may pursue both remedies simultaneously. That is, the worker may recover workers' compensation benefits from the employer and at the same time sue a third party in tort. The intersection of tort and workers' compensation has been the source of much friction in recent years. Workers and third parties have pressed for greater employer accountability in tort. At the heart of the controversy is the continued vitality of the exclusive remedy doctrine. The materials in this chapter explore the contours of the exclusive remedy doctrine and its impact on third party actions.

SECTION 1. THE EXCLUSIVE NATURE OF WORKERS' COMPENSATION

New York Work. Comp. Law § 11

The liability of an employer prescribed by the [workers' compensation act] shall be exclusive and in place of any other liability whatsoever, to such employee, his personal representatives, spouse, parents, dependents or next of kin, or anyone otherwise entitled to recover damages, at common law or otherwise on account of such injury or death . . .

HYETT v. NORTHWESTERN HOSPITAL
FOR WOMEN AND CHILDREN

Supreme Court of Minnesota, 1920.
147 Minn. 413, 180 N.W. 552.

BROWN, C.J. Plaintiff was in the employ of defendant, a Minnesota corporation, in the capacity of fireman in charge of its heating plant. Both were within and subject to the Workmen's Compensation Act (Gen.St.1913, §§ 8195–8230). Plaintiff was injured while engaged in his employment, by reason of which he was disabled for a brief period from the discharge of his duties, in adjustment of which there was paid to him the sum of $44. There were, as we understand the matter, no compensation proceedings, but that is not of special importance. At the time of the accident resulting in the disability stated plaintiff received an additional independent injury, but not amounting to a disability to perform his work, for which the Compensation Act makes no express or other provision for compensation. The additional injury was to his left pubic nerve, totally destroying the functions thereof, rendering him permanently impotent. Finding no remedy under the Compensation Act for the particular injury, plaintiff brought this action at law to recover therefor, alleging that it was caused by the negligence of defendant. Defendant interposed in defense, among other things, that the parties were within the Compensation Act, and that the remedy there provided is exclusive. Plaintiff demurred to that part of the answer, and defendant appealed from an order sustaining the same.

The only question presented is whether an employe, within the Compensation Act, who suffers an injury in the course of his employment which results (1) in a disability, temporary or permanent, for which compensation may be had under the act; and (2) an associate injury not amounting to a disability, either temporary or otherwise and for which no compensation is provided, may maintain an action at law for the latter injury on the ground that it was occasioned by the negligence of the employer. We answer the question in the negative.

The question is of first impression in this state, though it has come before the courts of other jurisdictions. It is important, for a decision thereof will determine whether our Workmen's Compensation Act, as heretofore generally understood, furnishes the exclusive relief of an injured employe, or whether, in addition to the relief thus provided, he may resort to a common-law action for injuries not amounting to a disability. Every personal injury causes pain and suffering, measured in degree by the character of the injury; some result in the disfigurement of the person—the loss of a hand or other member of the body, an eye, scalds and burns upon the hands or face, all of which must be carried through life to the mental distress of the victim. And in given cases, like that at bar an injury, accidental or otherwise, may impair and totally destroy some function of the human body not of a character to incapacitate the employe from his usual employment, or affect his earning capacity, therefore not within the letter of the Compensation Act. Matters of that character are proper elements of damage in the negligence action, but our Compensation Act makes no provision for a consideration thereof in the award to an injured employe, even though they may constitute his major or principal grievance.

In some of the jurisdictions of this country, and in England, situations of the kind are expressly covered by statute. Bradbury, Compensation Acts (3d Ed.) 874. But not by the statute of this state. The whole scheme of our statute is one of reciprocal concessions by employer and employe, from which benefits and protection fall to each which without the law neither could demand or recover; of benefit to the employe for he is thereby given protection for injuries impairing his earning capacity, without regard to the culpability of the employer, when without the statute he would be remediless. In consideration of this insured compensation and protection by the acceptance of the act he by necessary implication relinquishes his common-law remedies, and thus places a limit on his rights to that measured and granted by the Compensation Act. Section 8204, G.S.1913. In return for the required payment of compensation for the accidental injury, for which the common law furnishes the employe no relief, the employer is protected from the suit at law for the negligent injury. Thus we have the reciprocal yielding and giving up of rights existing at common law for the new and enlarged rights and remedies given by the Compensation Act. That this comes about by force of compulsory legislation (section 8204) in no way alters the legal character of the relation of the parties. That the Legislature was within its authority in so enacting, in the interests of the general welfare and in regulation of rights, duties, and obligations between employer and employe as a class has been affirmed by all the courts where compensation acts have been sustained. Matheson v. Minneapolis Street Railway Co., 126 Minn. 286, 148 N.W. 71, L.R.A.1916D, 412; Jensen v. Southern Pacific Railway Co., 215 N.Y. 514, 109 N.E. 600, L.R.A.1916A, 403, Ann.Cas.1916B, 276.

That the remedy so given and provided is exclusive of all others seems to be the prevailing opinion of the courts where the question has received attention. Shanahan v. Monarch Engineering Co., 219 N.Y. 469, 114 N.E. 795; Gregutis v. Waclark Wire Works, 86 N.J.L. 610, 92 A. 354; Peet v. Mills, 76 Wash. 437, 136 P. 685, L.R.A.1916A,358, Ann.Cas. 1915D,154; King v. Viscoloid Co., 219 Mass. 420, 106 N.E. 988, Ann.Cas. 1916D, 1170. Connors v. Semet–Solvay Co., 94 Misc.Rep. 405, 159 N.Y.S. 431, in which it was said that Shinnick v. Clover Farms Co., 169 App.Div. 236, 154 N.Y.Supp. 423, holding to the contrary had been overruled by Jensen v. Southern Pacific, supra. If the case was not in effect there overruled, it clearly was so disposed of by the later decision of the Court of Appeals in the Shanahan Case above cited. The case of Boyer v. Crescent Paper Co., 143 La. 368, 78 So. 596, takes the other view of the Louisiana Compensation Act and supports plaintiff in the case at bar. But to follow that rule would in a large measure be destructive of the main purpose and scheme of the statute, and deprive the employer of a right expressly granted him in return for his concession of liability for the nonactionable injury. It would result also in opening wide the door to double litigation in a great majority of the compensation cases. With the opportunity presented the discovery of negligence in some respect contributing to a particular injury would not be difficult, and thus the employer exposed to a second suit in which recovery could be had for pain and suffering, disfigurement of person, in addition to a recovery of compensation for actual disability under the Compensation Act. A personal injury received at the hands of a wrongdoer constitutes but one right of action. It cannot be divided into several parts to accord with the elements of damages recoverable therefor. It presents a single controversy to be settled in a single action. Dunnell's Dig. 5167. That is elementary, and it is manifest that there was no intention on the part of the Legislature to change or abrogate it by the Compensation Act; and no such intention should be presumed by the court. On the other hand, it is clear that the intention of that body was to present to the employers and employes of the state a comprehensive act embracing their exclusive rights and remedies for accidental or other injuries suffered by the employe. Morris v. Muldoon, 190 App.Div. 689, 180 N.Y.S. 319. If the compensation so provided is deemed inadequate, or that the act should be made to include all or any of the common-law elements or ingredients of relief found in the negligence law, the change should come about by legislation and not by rule of court.

For the reasons stated the demurrer to the answer should have been overruled, and the order sustaining it is accordingly reversed.

Notes

1. Why is the employer's immunity from tort claims by an injured worker considered fundamental to the operation of the workers' compensation system? Is it a matter of fairness, economics, or constitutional necessity?

2. *Hyett* illustrates the general rule that the exclusive remedy doctrine bars a tort suit against the employer when the injury is covered by workers' compensation, even if it is not compensable because it does not impair earning capacity. This general rule has precluded tort actions seeking recovery for noncompensable injuries to reproductive organs, Kline v. Arden H. Verner Co., 307 Pa.Super. 573, 453 A.2d 1035 (1982), affirmed 503 Pa. 251, 469 A.2d 158 (1983), loss of sense of taste and smell, Swilley v. Sun Oil Co., 506 So.2d 1364 (La.App.1987), and mental anguish, Witty v. American General Capital Distributors, 727 S.W.2d 503 (Tex.1987). Even if the worker is not entitled to receive disability benefits for an injury that does not impair earning capacity, medical or rehabilitation benefits may be available. See, Regnier v. Industrial Comm., 146 Ariz. 535, 707 P.2d 333 (App.1985) (artificial spermatocele implant); Crain Burton Ford Co. v. Rogers, 12 Ark.App. 246, 674 S.W.2d 944 (1984) (penile implant). In some states, injuries that do not produce any demonstrable loss in earning capacity may be compensable under schedules that cover loss of use of any member or part of the body. See, Bess v. Tyson Foods, Inc., 125 N.C.App. 698, 482 S.E.2d 26 (N.C.App.1997) (loss of sense of taste and smell is compensable as a permanent injury to an "important external or internal organ"); Chrysler Corpora-

tion v. Chambers, 288 A.2d 450 (Del.Super.), affirmed 299 A.2d 431 (Del. 1972) (loss of testicle compensable under schedule for loss of member or part of the body).

3. Courts distinguish between injuries which are covered by workers' compensation but under the facts of the particular case do not produce a disability, and injuries which do not come within the fundamental coverage of the act. See generally, 6 A. Larson and L. Larson, Larson's Workers' Compensation Law § 65.40 (1998). *Hyett* is an example of the former type of case. The latter type of case might arise when an injury is excluded from coverage by some restrictive provision designed to protect employers from workers' compensation liability. Ironically, the effect of such restrictive provisions may be to expose employers to tort liability. For example, in McClendon v. Mid–City Discount Drugs, Inc., 876 S.W.2d 657 (Mo.App.1994) an intoxicated worker died after falling down some steps at his job. Injuries to intoxicated worker were expressly excluded from coverage under the Missouri workers' compensation statute. Since his death, by definition, did not arise from his employment, a wrongful death tort suit was not barred by the exclusive remedy doctrine. In Stratemeyer v. Lincoln County, 276 Mont. 67, 915 P.2d 175 (Mont. 1996) an employee's tort suit against his employer for mental distress was not barred by the exclusive remedy doctrine because "mental-mental" claims were excluded from workers' compensation coverage. Similarly, Washington's restrictive definition of occupational disease allowed a worker to sue her employer in tort for occupational exposure to second hand cigarette smoke. McCarthy v. Dept. of Social & Health Services, 110 Wash.2d 812, 759 P.2d 351 (Wash. 1988). Of course, such tort actions would be barred if the injury was covered by workers' compensation. E.g. Ate Fixture Fab v. Wagner, 559 So.2d 635 (Fla.App.1990); Pechan v. Dyna-Pro, Inc., 251 Ill.App.3d 1072, 190 Ill.Dec. 698, 622 N.E.2d 108 (Ill.App.1993) (injuries and diseases caused by workplace exposure to cigarette smoke are compensable; tort suit barred by exclusive remedy doctrine).

4. The exclusive remedy provision of most workers' compensation statutes also bars tort suits against employers brought by family members that arise from a compensable injury to the worker. Thus, claims for loss of spousal consortium are almost always precluded. E.g., Vallery v. Southern Baptist Hosp., 630 So.2d 861 (La.App.1993); Mardian Constr. Co. v. Superior Court, 157 Ariz. 103, 754 P.2d 1378 (App.1988); West v. Plastifax, Inc., 505 So.2d 1026 (Miss.1987); Young v. Prevue Products, Inc., 130 N.H. 84, 534 A.2d 714 (1987). Similarly, an employer is protected from claims by parents for the lost services of their injured or deceased minor children. E.g., Slagle v. Reynolds Metals Co., 344 So.2d 1216 (Ala.1977); Salin v. Pacific Gas & Electric Co., 136 Cal.App.3d 185, 185 Cal.Rptr. 899 (1982). Next of kin and others are barred from bringing a wrongful death action against an employer even if they are not entitled to death benefits under workers' compensation. E.g., Leech v. Georgia–Pacific Corp., 259 Or. 161, 485 P.2d 1195 (1971); Morrill v. J & M Construction Co., 635 P.2d 88 (Utah 1981). What is the quid pro quo for the family member who loses the right to bring a tort action but receives no benefits under workers' compensation?

5. Family members have been permitted to sue employers in tort when the alleged injury does not arise from a personal injury to a worker, but is based on their own personal injury. For example, in Raney v. Walter O. Moss

Regional Hosp., 629 So.2d 485 (La.App.1993) a hospital employee was exposed to hepatitis "B" on the job. As a result, her husband and children had to undergo a series of vaccinations. The children's tort suits against the employer for their fear of contracting the disease, medical expenses and pain and suffering were not barred by the exclusive remedy doctrine. Similarly, a number of courts have allowed children to sue their mothers' employers for injuries inflicted on the children while they were in utero. E.g., Snyder v. Michael's Stores, Inc., 16 Cal.4th 991, 68 Cal.Rptr.2d 476, 945 P.2d 781 (Cal. 1997) (unborn child exposed to hazardous levels of carbon monoxide); Pizza Hut of America v. Keefe, 900 P.2d 97 (Colo.1995) (death of child born prematurely allegedly caused by employer's insistence that the mother work in violation of her medical work restrictions); Hitachi Chem. Electro–Products v. Gurley, 219 Ga.App. 675, 466 S.E.2d 867 (Ga.App. 1995) (employees and minor children allowed to sue employer in tort for birth defects allegedly caused by the parents exposure to hazardous chemicals at the workplace prior to the birth of the children).

SECTION 2. LIMITATIONS ON THE EXCLUSIVE REMEDY DOCTRINE

TRAVIS v. DREIS AND KRUMP MANUFACTURING COMPANY

Supreme Court of Michigan, 1996.
453 Mich. 149, 551 N.W.2d 132.

BOYDE, J.

These consolidated cases involve the proper construction of the intentional tort exception to the exclusive remedy provision of the Worker's Disability Compensation Act, MCL § 418.131(1); MSA § 17.237(131)(1). The precise issues framed by the parties are (1) whether the facts alleged by the plaintiffs are sufficient as a matter of law to state a question for the jury regarding liability within the intentional tort exception of the WDCA, (2) whether it is a question for the court or the jury whether an intentional tort has been committed by an employer, and (3) the extent to which, if at all, plaintiff Stanislaw Golec may maintain his intentional tort claim against the individual coemployees.

* * *

FACTS AND PROCEDURAL HISTORY

* * *

[The first case involved the suit brought by Aimee Sue Travis against her employer, Greenville Wire Products Co .. Travis operated a "press brake" equipped with a "die" used to form refrigerator wires. She was instructed by her supervisor (Clarke) to place the wires into the die by hand and then activate the machine by pushing the "palm buttons" with both hands. She would remove the wires by hand after they were formulated by the machine. The machine was designed so that it could not be activated without the operator pushing both palm buttons. This design was intended to prevent the activation of the machine while the operator's hands were in the die. The machine that Travis operated, however, had a history of "double cycling," i.e., cycling two times when the palm buttons were pushed only once. The machine had been double cycling for about a month. The tool room supervisor (King) advised Clarke to shut down the machine so that it could be repaired. Clarke refused to shut down the machine because exterior adjustments temporarily corrected the problem; a shut down "would take too long"; and he felt that the cycle was so slow that "an operator could avoid injury even when it was double cycling. . . . Unfortunately, [Travis'] hands were in the die space when the press double cycled, and she was unable to remove her hands before the die came down. [Travis] suffered severe injuries to her hand, including the amputation of both of her fifth fingers."]

[The second case involved a suit brought by Stanislaw Golec against his employer, Metal Exchange Corporation. Golec used a tractor to load scrap metal into a furnace for smelting. Although the tractors were usually equipped with a plexiglass splash guard, Golec's tractor was not so equipped. Nor was Golec provided any protective clothing other than a helmet. Golec's employer allegedly was aware that wet scrap or scrap that contains closed aerosol cans could explode when placed in the furnace. The parties disputed whether Golec had been instructed to separate closed aerosol cans before loading scrap into the furnace. On the night in question, a minor explosion occurred in the furnace, splashing Golec with molten aluminum. Golec reported the incident to his shift leader (Mazur) saying that he thought the explosion was due to either wet scrap or the presence of closed aerosol cans in the pile of scrap. The shift leader notified his supervisor (Rziemkowski) who allegedly instructed Golec to return to work. Later that night there was a "huge explosion" resulting in severe burns to thirty percent of Golec's body.]

[Both Travis and Golec filed tort claims against their respective employers. The trial courts in both cases granted the employers' motions for summary judgment on the ground that the claims were barred by the exclusive remedy doctrine. The court of appeals reversed both cases reasoning that the facts alleged, if accepted as true, supported claims for intentional torts.]

ANALYSIS

I

INTRODUCTION

The present version of subsection 131(1) of the WDCA was enacted in 1987 PA 28. It indicates that an employee's exclusive remedy for a personal injury or occupational disease is the recovery permitted under the Worker's Disability Compensation Act. The one exception to this recovery scheme is when an employer commits an intentional tort. Subsection 131(1) provides:

The right to the recovery of benefits as provided in this act shall be the employee's exclusive remedy against the employer for a personal injury or occupational disease. The only exception to this exclusive remedy is an intentional tort. *An intentional tort shall exist only when an employee is injured as a result of a deliberate act of the employer and the employer specifically intended an injury. An employer shall be deemed to have intended to injure if the employer had actual knowledge that an injury was certain to occur and willfully disregarded that knowledge.* The issue of whether an act was an intentional tort shall be a question of law for the court. This subsection shall not enlarge or reduce rights under law. [MCL § 418.131(1); MSA § 17.237(131)(1) (emphasis added).]

The Court's primary task in this case is the proper construction of the intentional tort exception as set forth in 1987 PA 28.

II

Background of the Intentional Tort Exception

Before its amendment by 1987 PA 28, subsection 131(1) was silent regarding whether an employee could sue in tort for an intentional tort suffered at the hands of his employer. This Court construed the prior version of subsection 131(1) in Beauchamp v. Dow Chemical Co., 427 Mich. 1; 398 N.W.2d 882 (1986).

In *Beauchamp*, the plaintiff was exposed at work to the chemical "agent orange" and, as a result, suffered physical and mental injuries. He sued his employer, alleging in part that his employer intentionally misrepresented and fraudulently concealed potential danger, intentionally assaulted him, and committed the tort of intentional infliction of emotional distress. The first issue before the Court was whether intentional torts should be excluded from coverage under the WDCA. The Court determined that intentional conduct by an employer was not within the act's exclusivity provision. It reasoned, "because the Legislature intended to limit and diffuse liability for accidental injury by no means suggests the Legislature intended to limit and diffuse liability for intentional torts. Accidents are an inevitable part of industrial production; intentional torts by employers are not."

The *Beauchamp* Court's next task, then, was to construe the parameters of the newly created "intentional tort exception." The version of the WDCA before the Court was silent with regard to whether intentional torts were covered by its provisions. The Court reviewed other jurisdictions and recognized two lines of cases. Some jurisdictions required an actual intent to injure in order for conduct to fall outside the parameters of the worker's compensation system. Other jurisdictions defined intentional tort more broadly. The latter line of cases did not limit recovery to cases in which the consequences were intended, but rather allowed tort recovery where the employer knew that the consequences of his actions were certain, or substantially certain, to occur. The Court explained that under this latter line of cases, the employer may be deemed to possess the intent to injure if it is substantially certain that the injury will occur as a consequence of its actions.

Beauchamp adopted the "substantial certainty" standard, reasoning:

> The problem with the true intentional tort test appears to be that it allows employers to injure and even kill employees and suffer only workers' compensation damages so long as the employer did not specifically intend to hurt the worker.... Prohibiting a civil action in such a case "would allow a corporation to 'cost-out' an investment decision to kill workers."

Under *Beauchamp*, the substantial certainty standard is defined as:

> If the actor knows that the consequences are certain, or substantially certain, to result from his act, and still goes ahead, he is treated by the law as if he had in fact desired to produce the result. It does not matter whether the employer wishes the injury would not occur or does not care whether it occurs. If the injury is substantially certain to occur as a consequence of actions the employer intended, the employer is deemed to have intended the injuries as well.

Beauchamp held that the plaintiff's complaint had pleaded a prima facie case of the intentional tort exception to the WDCA, reversed the decision of the Court of Appeals, and remanded for further proceedings.

* * *

III

Legislative History of 1987 PA 28

Of relevance to these cases is the amendment of subsection 131(1), which occurred less than five months after *Beauchamp* was released. The parties in these cases do not dispute that the amendment is a legislative reaction to *Beauchamp*, and an attempt to clarify the intentional tort exception to the act's exclusive remedy provision....

* * *

[The court examined competing drafts of the legislation noting that a Senate version used the phrase "deliberately intended," while a House version would have defined intent in terms of actual knowledge that an injury was "likely" to occur. The court also quoted several Senators who had different understandings of the language ultimately adopted. Senator Dillingham, for example, understood the statute "to restore the integrity of the exclusive remedy provision and avoid a new window of litigation that would threaten the financial stability of Michigan business and government." Senator Cherry, on the other hand, commented that the "change in the standard although narrowing the substantial certainty test does not preclude the specific cases which the Supreme Court indicated were actionable under the *Beauchamp* decision."]

We interpret the statute's history as indicating that the language of the final bill was a compromise. Senator Cherry's comments indicate that although *Beauchamp* needed to be tightened, there was still room for tort recovery in this area. Senator Dillingham advocated a much more rigorous standard. The legislation finally adopted did not restrict recovery to "true" intentional torts. Our task is therefore to discover what compromise the Legislature struck.

IV

CONSTRUING THE STATUTE CONSISTENTLY WITH LEGISLATIVE INTENT

At issue are two sentences of subsection 131(1). . . .

The first sentence reads, "An intentional tort shall exist only when an employee is injured as a result of a deliberate act of the employer and the employer specifically intended an injury." MCL § 418.131(1); MSA § 17.237(131)(1). The two phrases in this first sentence we must construe are: "deliberate act" and "specifically intended an injury."

The Legislature's use of the phrase "deliberate act" may indicate either that the employer must have deliberated about the act[7] or that the act must be one of commission rather than omission. Although not free from doubt, we construe the phrase "deliberate act," to encompass both commissions and omissions. . . . The legislative history indicates that employer omissions may constitute the "act" necessary to establish an intentional tort. Senator Cherry cited several cases that indicate that events other than a traditional battery may fulfill the "deliberate act" requirement. . . . The interpretation is also supported by the second sentence in which the employer is deemed to have the requisite intent from the failure to act in certain circumstances. Therefore, we construe the phrase "deliberate act" to include a situation in which an employer consciously fails to act.

The more difficult issue is what the Legislature intended by the phrase "specifically intended an injury." The commonly accepted meaning of the word "intent" includes a state of mind in which the actor is substantially certain that his act will produce a certain result. . . .

* * *

[The court observed that the substantial certainty test is endorsed by both Prosser & Keeton, Torts § 8 (5th ed. 1984) and 1 Restatement (Torts) 2d § 8A]

It would be an absurd construction, however, to conclude that the Legislature meant to define "intended" to include when the actor was "substantially certain" of the consequences of his acts. That the Legislature intended a meaning other than the "substantially certain" language of Prosser and the Restatement is clear from the fact that the amendment was intended to reject *Beauchamp* and from the use of the word "certain," not "substantially certain," in the second sentence. Whatever else the Legislature intended, we are confident it intended to prohibit

---

7. For example, if an employer punches his employee, the punch could be considered deliberate; yet if the employer suffers an involuntary muscle spasm that causes his arm to make contact with his employee, the spasm cannot be considered deliberate.

tort liability if an employer is only substantially certain that injury will result from his acts. Therefore, we conclude that the phrase "specifically intended an injury" means that the employer must have had in mind a purpose to bring about given consequences.

* * *.

Construing the entire first sentence according to the Legislature's intent, to state a claim against an employer for an intentional tort, the employer must deliberately act or fail to act with the purpose of inflicting an injury upon the employee.

The most difficult problem of interpretation is ascertaining the intent of the Legislature under the second sentence defining the intentional tort exception. That sentence reads: "An employer shall be deemed to have intended to injure if the employer had actual knowledge that an injury was certain to occur and willfully disregarded that knowledge." MCL § 418.131(1); MSA § 17.237(131)(1)…. [T]he second sentence will be employed when there is no direct evidence of intent to injure, and intent must be proved with circumstantial evidence. It is a substitute means of proving the intent to injure element of the first sentence. The three phrases in this sentence that we must construe are: "actual knowledge," "certain to occur," and "willfully disregarded."

A

ACTUAL KNOWLEDGE

Because the Legislature was careful to use the term "actual knowledge," and not the less specific word "knowledge," we determine that the Legislature meant that constructive, implied, or imputed knowledge is not enough. Nor is it sufficient to allege that the employer should have known, or had reason to believe, that injury was certain to occur…. A plaintiff may establish a corporate employer's actual knowledge by showing that a supervisory or managerial employee had actual knowledge that an injury would follow from what the employer deliberately did or did not do.

B

INJURY CERTAIN TO OCCUR

Once we conclude that the employer must have actual knowledge that an injury would occur, the question becomes when does a dangerous condition rise to the level of "certain to occur"? … When an injury is "certain" to occur, no doubt exists with regard to whether it will occur. Thus, the laws of probability, which set forth the odds that something will occur, play no part in determining the certainty of injury. Consequently, scientific proof that, for example, one out of ten persons will be injured if exposed to a particular risk, is insufficient to prove certainty. Along similar lines, just because something has happened before on occasion does not mean that it is certain to occur again. Likewise, just because something has never happened before is not proof that it is not certain to occur.

Moreover, conclusory statements by experts are insufficient to allege the certainty of injury contemplated by the Legislature…. Under the

Michigan statute, ... even if the expert opined that the injury was "certain to occur," and not merely "substantially certain to occur," this affidavit would be insufficient. It merely parrots the language of the legal test and gives no scientific or factual support for its conclusion....

One case which is directly on point is Gulden v. Crown Zellerbach Corp., 890 F.2d 195 (C.A.9, 1989). In *Gulden*, the defendant's plant was contaminated with toxic levels of polychlorinated biphenyls (PCBs). After hazardous waste specialists were unsuccessful in reducing the level of PCBs on the plant floor, the defendant ordered the plaintiffs to scrub the floor on their hands and knees, with no protective clothing. This assignment continued for five days, during which time the plaintiffs' clothing was soaked with PCBs. The court held that under Oregon's narrow intentional tort exception,[10] the plaintiffs' complaint withstood summary judgment. The court found that the injury in question was the exposure to the PCBs itself, because the level of toxicity was sufficient to produce a body level of PCBs of six to ten times higher than normal and to trigger serious health concerns. The court then held that the injury was certain to occur. It reasoned that the defendant was aware that contact with the PCBs would injure the plaintiffs, yet deliberately ordered them to perform their task "in a manner requiring them to initiate and maintain contact with the PCBs." These facts would constitute allegations of certainty of injury under the Michigan statute.

A further question under the certainty requirement, closely related to the actual-knowledge requirement, is the level of awareness an employer must possess: is it enough that the employer know that a dangerous condition exists, or must the employer be aware that injury is certain to occur from what the actor does? We find the latter interpretation the proper one....

Despite the very high threshold required to deem an injury "certain to occur," some situations constitute examples of certain injury. For example, Professor Larson, in his treatise on worker's compensation, agrees that the *Film Recovery* case discussed in *Beauchamp*, constitutes an intentional tort.[12] He explains:

> The fumes ... were continuously operative, and the employer knew it.... The exposure to fumes did in fact occur. The only possible

---

10. Oregon's statute permits a civil tort claim to be filed "if injury or death results to a worker from the deliberate intention of the employer of the worker to produce such injury or death...." [Or Rev Stat 656.156(2).]

12. The facts of the case, as set forth by *Beauchamp*, are as follows,

Film Recovery Systems went into the business of recovering silver from film negatives. This was done by placing the negatives into vats of cyanide. Hydrogen cyanide gas would bubble up from the vats and there was inadequate ventilation. The employer knew about the dangers. The labels on the chemicals being used contained adequate warnings; as a result, the employer hired only employees who could not speak or read English. The workers complained about the fumes daily. In 1981, an inspector had warned that the operation had outgrown the plant. The employer's response was to move the executive offices while tripling the size of the operations. Eventually one worker died and several others were seriously injured because of hydrogen cyanide poisoning. The corporate officers were convicted of involuntary manslaughter.

"unknown" might have been the effect of inhaling the fumes, but this unknown was removed by the plain warning on the package. The hiring of only workers who could not read warning labels confirms that the employer wanted those employees to continue to inhale these and suffer these known consequences. A court could well say that this amounted to intending the injury. [2A Larson, Workmen's Compensation, § 68.15(e), pp 13–105 to 13–106.]

We agree with Professor Larson's reasoning. When an employer subjects an employee to a continuously operative dangerous condition that it knows will cause an injury, yet refrains from informing the employee about the dangerous condition so that he is unable to take steps to keep from being injured, a factfinder may conclude that the employer had knowledge that an injury is certain to occur.

C

Willfully Disregards

Finally, the term "willfully disregards" must be construed.... Because the purpose of the entire second sentence is to establish the employer's intent, we find that the use of the term "willfully" in the second sentence is intended to underscore that the employer's act or failure to act must be more than mere negligence, that is, a failure to act to protect a person who might foreseeably be injured from an appreciable risk of harm. An employer is deemed to have possessed the requisite state of mind when it disregards actual knowledge that an injury is certain to occur.

D

Inference of Intent

In short, under the second sentence, the Legislature has permitted the employer's state of mind to be inferred from its actions when there is no direct evidence of the employer's intent to injure....

If we read both sentences of the intentional tort exception together, it becomes evident that an employer must have made a conscious choice to injure an employee and have deliberately acted or failed to act in furtherance of that intent. The second sentence then allows the employer's intent to injure to be inferred if the employer had actual knowledge that an injury was certain to occur, under circumstances indicating deliberate disregard of that knowledge. The applications that follow are our attempt to give effect to the expressions of legislative intent contained in the statute: an intent to create a rigorous threshold for a claim of intentional tort, and an intent that the threshold created not be so rigorous as to preclude all claims of intentional torts.

Application

* * *

Conclusion

We would reverse the opinion of the Court of Appeals in Travis, and reinstate the trial court's order granting summary disposition for defendant. We would affirm the Court of Appeals opinion in Golec with regard to defendants Metal Exchange and Rziemkowski, and would remand to the trial court for further proceedings consistent with this opinion.

[concurring and dissenting opinions are omitted]

Notes

1. Should either Travis' or Golec's claim survive a summary judgment motion under the standards adopted by the court? A majority affirmed summary judgment against Travis. The majority concluded that evidence was insufficient as a matter of law to prove that the injury was certain to occur. "Although Clarke had actual knowledge that the press was malfunctioning, he did not have knowledge that an injury was certain to occur.... [I]n this case, unlike *Film Recovery*, supra, plaintiff was not required to confront a continually operating dangerous condition. The press double cycled only intermittently." A majority reversed the employer's summary judgment against Golec. "If the facts as alleged by the plaintiff are established at trial, then plaintiff has proved the existence of a continually operative dangerous condition. Accordingly, we conclude that a genuine issue of material fact is presented whether the injury was certain to occur."

Three justices agreed with the test adopted by the majority, but concluded that summary judgment was appropriate in both cases. In their view, there was insufficient evidence that Golec's employer had "actual knowledge that an injury was certain to occur." Two justices concluded that summary judgment was not authorized in either case. In their view, the majority placed too much importance on whether there was "a continuously operative dangerous condition that [the employer] knows will cause injury." They would draw from prior decisions in which the intended injury exception applied to "isolated but extremely dangerous activities."

2. Either by express statutory provision or judicial construction, every state allows employees to sue their employers in tort for intended injuries. See 6 A. Larson and L. Larson, Larson's Workers' Compensation Law § 68 (1998) for a compilation of cases. *Beauchamp*, quoted in the principal case, articulates the traditional doctrinal explanation for this exception to the exclusive remedy rule: intended injuries are not "accidental" within the meaning of workers' compensation coverage. Consider the following policy justification offered by the North Dakota Supreme Court:

> Other strong public policy considerations support permitting an intentional tort cause of action. An underlying objective of workers' compensation is to promote a safe work environment. Affording employers immunity for intentional acts does not promote that objective ... Employers would not be held individually responsible for their intentional actions. In effect, it would allow an employer to buy the right to hit an employee ... Furthermore, ... [p]roviding immunity to employers for intentional torts is inconsistent with [state] insurance law that generally denies coverage for willful acts.

Zimmerman v. Valdak Corp., 570 N.W.2d 204, 207 (N.D.1997). To what extent is exposure to tort liability needed to "promote a safe workplace"? Do employers have incentives to minimize occupational injury and disease other than liability concerns?

3. The early cases applying the intended injury exception to the exclusive remedy doctrine involved fist fights and similar traditional assaults and batteries. E.g., Heskett v. Fisher Laundry & Cleaners Co., Inc., 217 Ark. 350, 230 S.W.2d 28 (1950). Many recent cases like *Travis* explore the application of this exception to business decisions that consciously and systematically increase the employee's exposure to risk. This new line of cases force courts to come to grips with the meaning of "intent."

A majority of courts limit the intended injury exception to instances where the employer subjectively desires to injure the employee. Few claims other than those involving fist fights can satisfy this exacting standard. See, Zimmerman v. Valdak, Corp., 570 N.W.2d 204 (N.D.1997) (employer knew that a safety device was inoperable and was warned that an injury was "substantially certain" to occur if the machine was not repaired; employer deliberately chose not to shut down the machine for repair; no intent to injure); Miller v. Ensco, Inc., 286 Ark. 458, 692 S.W.2d 615 (1985) (knowingly exposing employee to polychlorinated byphenyls (PCB's) without adequate protection is not an intended injury); Kearney v. Denker, 114 Idaho 755, 760 P.2d 1171 (1988) (employer's failure to install safety guards and cut off switch was not "willful or unprovoked aggression" that would allow injured employee to maintain a common law tort action); Noonan v. Spring Creek Forest Products, 216 Mont. 221, 700 P.2d 623 (1985) (employer's failure to repair equipment known to violate OSHA safety standards does not constitute an intent to injure); Mullins v. Biglane Operating Co., 778 F.2d 277 (5th Cir.1985) (employer who deliberately withheld safety equipment did not actually intend to injure employee).

Several states look beyond subjective intent and allow employees to sue their employers in tort when the employer knew the injury was "substantially certain" to occur. E.g., Eller v. Shova, 630 So.2d 537, 539 (Fla.1993) (intentional act exception applies when the act is "designed to result in or that is substantially certain to result in injury or death to the employee."); Woodson v. Rowland, 329 N.C. 330, 407 S.E.2d 222 (N.C. 1991) (wrongful death action based on fatal trench cave-in; plaintiff's expert gave an affidavit attesting that given the height and slope of the trench, the cave-in was substantially certain to occur; jury issue as to intent); Mayer v. Valentine Sugars, Inc., 444 So.2d 618 (La.1984) (allegations that the employer knew to a substantial certainty that violations of safety regulations would produce an explosion are sufficient to state a cause of action for an intended injury). As a general proposition, employees are more likely to successfully assert tort claims against their employers under the substantial certainty standard of intent than they would under the subjective intent to injure test. Even in the former jurisdictions, however, courts will summarily dispose of tort claims if evidence of the likelihood of injury does not rise to the level of substantial certainty. E.g., Rose v. Isenhour Brick & Tile Co., 344 N.C. 153, 472 S.E.2d 774 (N.C. 1996) (employer had actual knowledge that employees routinely by-passed safety guards on machines; no serious injuries or deaths had occurred in six years prior to fatal incident; summary judgment for employer, affirmed); Millison v. E.I. du Pont de Nemours & Co., 101 N.J. 161, 501 A.2d 505 (1985) (evidence that employer deliberately concealed from employees the risk of exposure to asbestos did not establish knowledge that injury was substantially certain to occur; summary judgment for the employer, affirmed).

4. The substantial certainty standard is endorsed by Prosser and the Restatement and is used in most states in the context of non-workplace intentional torts. Yet, a majority of states reject this standard in the context of an exception to the exclusive remedy doctrine. Why would a state allow a non-workplace battery claim to proceed on the strength of evidence that the defendant knew to a substantial certainty that a harmful contact would occur, but require a worker to prove that her employer subjectively intended to injure her? What are the perceived stakes in selecting a subjective intent to injure or a substantial certainty standard?

5. Michigan is not the only state to attempt to statutorily define the scope of the intentional tort exception to the exclusive remedy doctrine. A West Virginia statute limits tort actions to cases where the employer acts with a specific intent to injure the employee, or if all of the following facts are proven:

> (A) That a specific unsafe working condition existed in the workplace which presented a high degree of risk and a strong probability of serious injury or death;

> (B) That the employer had a subjective realization and an appreciation of the existence of such specific unsafe working condition and of the high degree of risk and the strong probability of serious injury or death presented by such specific unsafe working condition;

> (C) That such specific unsafe working condition was a violation of a state or federal safety statute, rule or regulation, ... or of a commonly accepted and well-known safety standard within the industry ...;

> (D) That notwithstanding the existence of the facts set forth in subparagraphs (A) through (C) hereof, such employer nevertheless thereafter exposed an employee to such specific unsafe working condition intentionally; and

> (E) That such employee so exposed suffered serious injury or death as a direct and proximate result of such specific unsafe working condition.

W.Va. Code § 23–4–2(c)(2)(ii). In Blake v. Skidmore Truck Stop, Inc., 201 W.Va. 126, 493 S.E.2d 887 (W.Va. 1997) an employee sued her employer in tort after she was robbed, stabbed, and beaten by a third party robber. In support of her claim, the employee presented the following evidence:

> Among other things, Mrs. Blake testified that: (1) there were no limitations on the amount of money she should keep in the cash register; (2) customers could stand directly behind her when she using [sic] the register; (4) she could not see out any windows when she was standing at the register; (5) there was no "drop safe" in the Store; (6) the area was not well lit after dark; and (7) she did not recall being instructed by the manager of the Store that she was to hand over the money in the cash register in the event of the robbery.

> Appellants also presented evidence from Ira Somerson, an expert witness ... [who] testified that it is standard security practice in the

convenience store industry to have "a cash control or a cash management policy" ... That it is important to keep the cash register visible from the outside (by positioning it in front of a window and having proper lighting so those passing by the store can see it) and to train employees about what to do in case of a robbery. Mr. Somerson also commented that putting a barrier or counter between a cashier and a customer is "so automatic. . . . that's like cars have wheels."

493 S.E.2d at 895–96. Mrs. Blake's employer contended that as a matter of law injuries resulting from the criminal acts of a third party could never rise to a claim under W.Va. Code § 23–4–2 and, in any event, the evidence presented by the plaintiff did not satisfy the five-part test of § 23–4–2(c)(2)(ii). Should Blake's case be submitted to a jury?

The Ohio experience reflects a tug-of-war between the courts and the legislature. In the early 1980's, several cases expanded employer exposure to tort liability. In response to these decisions, the Ohio legislature enacted a statute that purported to limit the intentional tort exception to instances where the employer acts with the "deliberate intent to cause ... injury." A rebuttable presumption of such intent would arise if the employer deliberately removed safety guards from machinery or deliberately misrepresented toxic or hazardous substances. Ohio Rev. Code Ann. § 41.21.80. This statute also eliminated the right to a trial by jury, recognized certain defenses, and created a fund to pay for damages. This statute was declared unconstitutional in Brady v. Safety–Kleen Corp., 61 Ohio St.3d 624, 576 N.E.2d 722 (Ohio 1991). The legislature passed another statute in 1995 that states that the only suit an employee may bring against an employer is one for an "employment intentional tort" which is defined as "an act committed by an employer in which the employer deliberately and intentionally injures ... an employee." Ohio Rev. Code Ann. § 2745.01 (D)(1). The statute imposes a clear and convincing evidence standard of proof. Ohio Rev. Code Ann. § 2745.01 (C)(1). The explicit purpose of this statute is to supersede standards created in prior court decisions and replace them with a more limited cause of action. The Court of Appeals has ruled that this statute unconstitutionally deprives workers of equal protection by imposing on them different and more difficult standards for pursuing intentional tort claims. Johnson v. BP Chemicals., Inc., 1997 WL 729098 (1997). The Ohio Supreme Court has agreed to hear the appeal of this case. Johnson v. BP Chemicals, Inc., 81 Ohio St.3d 1500, 691 N.E.2d 1061 (Ohio 1998). For an overview of the Ohio experience, see Marc A. Claybon, Comment, Ohio's "Employment Intentional Tort": A Workers' Compensation Exception, Or the Creation of an Entirely New Cause of Action, 44 Clev. St. L. Rev. 381 (1996).

In California, workers may recover tort damages from their employers for injuries caused by the "knowing removal of or knowing failure to install, a point of operation guard on a power press." Cal.Labor Code § 4558.

What are the differences among these various statutes? Are statutory formulations of exceptions to the exclusive remedy doctrine preferable to judicially crafted rules? How would you articulate a standard for determining when an employee must accept workers' compensation benefits as her exclusive remedy and when she can sue her employer in tort? What standard would provide the best mix of societal objectives to create incentives to reduce occupational injuries, preserve the quid pro quo of the workers' compensation bargain, and achieve fairness for the parties?

6.   Employees sometimes couch their tort claims against their employers in terms of fraud. Several courts distinguish between fraudulent concealment of the risks of employment and the fraudulent concealment of an already-contracted disease or injury. The former is not actionable as a tort because it is said to "merge" with the subsequent compensable injury or disease for which workers' compensation provides the exclusive remedy. See, e.g., Wilkins v. West Point–Pepperell, Inc., 397 So.2d 115 (Ala.1981) (alleged fraudulent concealment of risk of "brown lung" disease in a textile plant); Johnson v. Kerr–McGee Oil Ind., Inc., 129 Ariz. 393, 631 P.2d 548 (App. 1981) (failure to warn of hazards of working in a uranium mine); Johnson v. Hames Contracting Co., 208 Ga.App. 664, 431 S.E.2d 455 (Ga.App.1993) (alleged intentional failure to warn of asbestos exposure). The fraudulent concealment of diseases already developed is considered a separate wrong that lies outside the scope of the exclusive remedy doctrine. See e.g., Millison v. E.I. du Pont de Nemours & Co., 101 N.J. 161, 501 A.2d 505 (N.J. 1985); Johns–Manville Prods. Corp. v. Contra Costa Superior Court, 27 Cal.3d 465, 165 Cal.Rptr. 858, 612 P.2d 948 (1980) (subsequently codified in Cal.Labor Code § 3602(b)(2)). In terms of the moral culpability of the employer or the nature of the injury, how convincing is the distinction between the fraudulent concealment of the initial workplace risk and the fraudulent concealment of an already-contracted disease? Which party should bear the burden of determining how much harm occurred after the fraudulent concealment? See Cal.Labor Code Ann. § 3602(b)(2) (the burden of proof respecting apportionment of damages rests upon the employer). The plaintiffs in *Millison* were ultimately successful in proving that the defendants had deliberately concealed the plaintiffs' asbestos-related diseases. See, Millison v. E.I. du Pont de Nemours & Co., 226 N.J.Super. 572, 545 A.2d 213 (1988), affirmed 115 N.J. 252, 558 A.2d 461 (1989).

7.   An alternative strategy for reducing risks posed by exposure to hazardous substances is reflected in what are commonly called right-to-know laws. On the federal level, the Occupational Safety and Health Administration (OSHA), adopted regulations that require employers in the manufacturing sector to implement a "hazard communication" program encompassing labeling, material safety data sheets, and employee training. See, 29 C.F.R. § 1910.1200 et. seq. Additionally, close to half the states have enacted right-to-know laws that mandate the identification of hazardous substances to which employees are exposed in the course of employment. Furthermore, right to know laws generally obligate employers to inform their employees of the potential health risks posed by such exposure. These laws vary in their degree of comprehensiveness. Some legislation simply requires the maintenance of lists of hazardous substances, while other statutes incorporate strict training procedures. For a listing of specific statutes, see O'Reilly, Driving a Soft Bargain: Unions, Toxic Material, and Right to Know Legislation, 9 Harv.Envtl.L.Rev. 307, 309 n. 13 (1985). For an insightful discussion of the difficulties in communicating information pertaining to risk, see Nordenstam and DiMento, Right to Know: Implications of Risk Communication Research for Regulatory Policy, 23 U.Cal.Davis L.Rev. 333 (1990). How might administratively regulated disclosure of information affect the level of risk in the

workplace? What role should workers' compensation and tort play in such a scheme?

BYRD v. RICHARDSON–GREENSHIELDS SECURITIES, INC.

Supreme Court of Florida, 1989.
552 So.2d 1099.

BARKETT, JUSTICE.

We have for review *Byrd v. Richardson–Greenshields Securities, Inc.*, 527 So.2d 899, 902 (Fla. 2d DCA 1988), which certified "the contention in this case concerning the exclusivity of worker's compensation benefits." The case presents the following question of law:

WHETHER THE WORKERS' COMPENSATION STATUTE PROVIDES THE EXCLUSIVE REMEDY FOR A CLAIM BASED ON SEXUAL HARASSMENT IN THE WORKPLACE.

We have jurisdiction. We answer in the negative and quash the opinion below.

The plaintiffs, all female employees, brought claims for assault and battery, intentional infliction of emotional distress, and negligent hiring and retention of employees. These claims were based on incidents in which male employees repeatedly touched the women and made verbal sexual advances on them in the workplace during work hours. In their suit, the women claimed this resulted in emotional anguish and stress.

The trial court dismissed the complaint on grounds that the workers' compensation statute provided the exclusive remedy for the women. On appeal, the Second District affirmed.

Our analysis must begin with the premise, now well established in our law, that workers' compensation generally is the sole tort remedy available to a worker injured in a manner that falls within the broad scope and policies of the workers' compensation statute. Indeed, section 440.11, Florida Statutes, provides that workers' compensation is the exclusive remedy and is "in place of all other liability of such employer ... on account of such injury or death." This statute expresses a plain legislative intent that any potential liability arising from "injury or death" is abolished in favor of the exclusive remedy available under workers' compensation. However, if the liability arises from something other than "injury or death," the other potential bases of liability remain viable.

Thus, the definition of the word "injury" is crucial to the determination of this case. That definition is provided in the statute itself. Section 440.02(14), Florida Statutes, states that "injury" means *"personal injury ... by accident* arising out of and in the course of employment, and such diseases or infection as naturally or unavoidably result from such injury" (emphasis added). Moreover, section 440.02(1), Florida Statutes, defines "accident" as "only an unexpected or unusual event or result, happening suddenly."

It is apparent, however, that the term "accident arising out of . . . employment" has been construed well beyond the more limited definition suggested by the statutory language. This judicial extension of the statutory language is in keeping with the liberal construction accorded the workers' compensation statute . . . and has affected both the terms "accident" and "arising out of."

As far back as the case of *Czepial v. Krohne Roofing Co.*, 93 So.2d 84, 85–86 (Fla.1957), for instance, the Court recognized that an injury was compensable under the statute even though caused by the gradual accumulation of otherwise insignificant injuries arising from repeated exposure to somewhat noxious substances at the workplace. This is true even though, strictly speaking, a cumulative injury of this type is not an "accident" within the dictionary definition of the word.[3]

In a similar manner, the Court has accepted that even a suicide precipitated by serious workplace injuries can be compensable. We have qualified this statement only by requiring that the suicide must arise from a mental disturbance directly attributable to an actual workplace injury.

An analogous line of cases has held that severe emotional disorders also may be compensable where caused by actual physical injury at the workplace. This is not true, however, where no physical injury has occurred, since the statute by its own terms excludes such matters. Indeed, the statute expressly prohibits a workers' compensation award for "[a] mental or nervous injury due to fright or excitement only." § 440.02(1), Fla.Stat.

Similarly, Florida courts have extended the definition of "accident arising out of . . . employment" to encompass a wide variety of injuries caused by intentional torts, provided there is a sufficient nexus with the activities of the workplace itself. This is true where workplace tensions lead one employee to assault another, where jealousy over a lovers' triangle causes one worker to attack another with a workplace tool, where an employee is robbed at the workplace by an armed gunman, and where a worker is robbed at home by persons seeking workplace cash register receipts.[5]

In a recent extension from this prior line of cases, the First District has held that sexual harassment claims are governed by the same general principles. Thus, in *Brown v. Winn–Dixie Montgomery, Inc.*, 469 So.2d 155, 159 (Fla. 1st DCA 1985), the district court concluded that the workers' compensation statute barred a claim for battery and intentional

3. Webster's Third New International Dictionary 11 (1981), for instance, defines "accident" as "a usu. sudden event or change occurring without intent or volition through carelessness, unawareness, ignorance, or a combination of causes and producing an unfortunate result."

5. However, an injury intentionally inflicted by the employer himself or his or her alter egos does not fall within these principles, since workers' compensation was not established to excuse misconduct of this type. *See Schwartz v. Zippy Mart, Inc.*, 470 So.2d 720, 724 (Fla. 1st DCA 1985).

infliction of emotional distress based on an incident in which a male supervisor grabbed the breast of a female employee.

The *Brown* decision in turn rested on the First District's prior analysis in *Schwartz v. Zippy Mart, Inc.*, 470 So.2d 720, 724 (Fla. 1st DCA 1985). *Schwartz* had held that sexual harassment falls outside the rule that, under workers' compensation, an employer remains liable in tort for his or her own intentional misconduct. The First District buttressed this rationale with the following quote from a treatise on the subject:

> "When the person who intentionally injures the employee is not the employer in person nor a person who is realistically the alter ego of the corporation, but merely a foreman, supervisor or manager, both the legal and the moral reasons for permitting a common-law suit against the employer collapse, and a substantial majority of modern cases bar a damage suit against the employer."

Id. at 724 (quoting 2A *Larson's Workmen's Compensation Law* § 68.21, 13–28 (1982)). Under this rationale, the First District held that claims for assault and battery were barred as a result of an incident in which two female workers had been subjected to pinching, grabbing, and other gestures of a sexual nature. *Id.* at 724–25.

We acknowledge and reaffirm the strong policies regarding workers' compensation that form the foundation of the decisions discussed above. As the Court often has noted, our obligation is to honor the obvious legislative intent and policy behind an enactment, even where that intent requires an interpretation that exceeds the literal language of the statute.

In this context, we cannot find that acts constituting sexual harassment were ever meant to fall under workers' compensation. Moreover, we have an equal obligation to honor the intent and policy of other enactments and, accordingly, may not apply the exclusivity rule in a manner that effectively abrogates the policies of other law. In this instance, we find that the First District in *Brown* and *Schwartz,* and the Second District in the instant case, have ignored an equally important expression of public policy emanating from both federal and state enactments.

There can be no doubt at this point in time that both the state of Florida and the federal government have committed themselves strongly to outlawing and eliminating sexual discrimination in the workplace, including the related evil of sexual harassment. The statutes, case law, and administrative regulations uniformly and without exception condemn sexual harassment in the strongest possible terms. We find that the present case strongly implicates these sexual harassment policies and, accordingly, may not be decided by a blind adherence to the exclusivity rule of the workers' compensation statute alone. Our clear obligation is to construe both the workers' compensation statute and the enactments dealing with sexual harassment so that the policies of both are preserved to the greatest extent possible.

Thus, we must examine the scope of the public policies regarding sexual harassment. The primary source of these policies, both historically and under the supremacy clause of the United States Constitution, article VI, clause 2, is a portion of Title VII of the Civil Rights Act of 1964, which provides in pertinent part:

> It shall be an unlawful employment practice for an employer ... to discriminate against any individual with respect to his compensation, terms, conditions, or privileges of employment, because of such individual's ... sex....

42 U.S.C. § 2000e–2(a)(1) (1982). This federal provision was the model of Florida's Human Rights Act of 1977, sections 760.–01–.10, Florida Statutes (1987), which uses virtually the same language in prohibiting the same practices. The Human Rights Act provides in pertinent part:

> "It is an unlawful employment practice for an employer ... to discriminate against any individual with respect to compensation, terms, conditions, or privileges of employment, because of such individual's ... sex...."

§ 760.10(1)(a), Fla.Stat.

In interpreting Title VII, the federal courts have stated unequivocally that any sort of workplace sexual harassment is unlawful under Title VII and contrary to public policy. So strong is this policy that the United States Supreme Court has stated that,

> [w]ithout question, when a supervisor sexually harasses a subordinate because of the subordinate's sex, that supervisor "discriminate[s]" on the basis of sex.... The phrase "terms, conditions, or privileges of employment" evinces a congressional intent " 'to strike at the entire spectrum of disparate treatment of men and women' "in employment.

Meritor Sav. Bank v. Vinson, 477 U.S. 57, 64, 106 S.Ct. 2399, 2404, 91 L.Ed.2d 49 (1986). Indeed, in *Meritor* the Supreme Court expressly rejected the notion that Title VII addresses only "economic discrimination." *Id.* The *Meritor* Court quoted with approval a statement by the Eleventh Circuit Court of Appeals that

> "Sexual harassment which creates a hostile or offensive environment for members of one sex is every bit the arbitrary barrier to sexual equality at the workplace that racial harassment is to racial equality. Surely, a requirement that a man or woman run a gauntlet of sexual abuse in return for the privilege of being allowed to work and make a living can be as demeaning and disconcerting as the harshest of racial epithets."

Id. at 67, 106 S.Ct. at 2405 (quoting *Henson v. City of Dundee,* 682 F.2d 897, 902 (11th Cir.1982)).

. . .

In light of this overwhelming public policy, we cannot say that the exclusivity rule of the workers' compensation statute should exist to shield an employer from all tort liability based on incidents of sexual harassment. The clear public policy emanating from federal and Florida law holds that an employer is charged with maintaining a workplace free from sexual harassment. Applying the exclusivity rule of workers' compensation to preclude any and all tort liability effectively would abrogate this policy, undermine the Florida Human Rights Act, and flout Title VII of the Civil Rights Act of 1964.

This, we cannot condone. Public policy now requires that employers be held accountable in tort for the sexually harassing environments they permit to exist, whether the tort claim is premised on a remedial statute or on the common law.

We find this conclusion harmonizes with the policies and scope of workers' compensation. As often has been noted, workers' compensation is directed essentially at compensating a worker for lost resources and earnings. This is a vastly different concern than is addressed by the sexual harassment laws. While workplace injuries rob a person of resources, sexual harassment robs the person of dignity and self esteem. Workers' compensation addresses purely economic injury; sexual harassment laws are concerned with a much more intangible injury to personal rights. To the extent these injuries are separable, we believe that they both should be, and can be, enforced separately.

Certainly, whenever a claim is based on the Human Rights Act, Title VII of the Civil Rights Act of 1964, the Educational Equity Act, or any other statute prohibiting sexual discrimination or harassment, that claim cannot in logic or fairness be barred by the exclusivity rule. Doing so would improperly nullify a statute by judicial fiat and, in the case of the Civil Rights Act of 1964, would defy the Constitution.

Similarly, to the extent that the claim alleges assault, intentional infliction of emotional distress arising from sexual harassment or the specific type of battery involved in this case,[8] the exclusivity rule also will not bar them. This is so because these causes of action address the very essence of the policies against sexual harassment—an injury to intangible personal rights.

For the foregoing reasons, we quash the opinion of the district court below and remand for further proceedings consistent with the views herein. We express no opinion as to whether petitioners in this case have alleged sufficient facts to state a cause of action under the common law, an issue we do not reach. To the extent they conflict with this opinion, we disapprove *Schwartz v. Zippy Mart, Inc.,* 470 So.2d 720, 724 (Fla. 1st DCA 1985), and *Brown v. Winn–Dixie Montgomery, Inc.,* 469 So.2d 155,

---

8. Because the battery involved in cases of this type differs significantly from that addressed in our prior case law, we distinguish this case factually from our opinions in *W.T. Edwards Hospital v. Rakestraw,* 114 So.2d 802, 803 (Fla.App.1959); *Tampa Maid Seafood Products v. Porter,* 415 So.2d 883, 885 (Fla.App.1982); *Prahl Brothers,* *Inc. v. Phillips,* 429 So.2d 386, 387 (Fla. 1st DCA 1983); and *Strother,* 383 So.2d at 623. That is, we do not perceive the battery alleged in this instance as involving wage loss or workplace injury, but an unlawful intrusion upon personal rights protected by remedial legislation such as the Florida Human Rights Act.

159 (Fla. 1st DCA 1985). We answer the certified question in the negative.

It is so ordered.

McDONALD, SHAW and KOGAN, JJ., concur.

EHRLICH, C.J., concurs in result.

OVERTON, J., dissents.

GRIMES, JUSTICE, concurring.

If the plaintiffs had suffered physical and emotional injuries as a result of sexual batteries perpetrated by the two employees whose conduct is complained of in this action, they would have a compensable workers' compensation claim and their lawsuit against the employer would be barred by virtue of the exclusiveness of the workers' compensation remedy. Here, because the plaintiffs incurred no physical injury, are they barred from recovery because the touching in a technical sense constituted a battery? Professor Larson suggests that the determination of the applicability of the workers' compensation law depends upon the nature of both the tort and the injury:

> To test ... the conclusion that the element of damage must be considered along with the legal components of the tort, we may adduce the tort of assault. Here, we are fortunate in having an actual decided case that makes the point. In *Ritter v. Allied Chemical Corporation,* [295 F.Supp. 1360 (D.S.C.1968), aff'd, 407 F.2d 403 (4th Cir.1969)] plaintiff brought suit against her employer for an assault by one of her superiors. She stated that the only result of the assault was a scratch on her hand and some soreness, and did not claim any disability or other elements which might have provided compensation under the workmen's compensation laws of South Carolina. Because the injuries for which plaintiff was suing were not those which were covered by the compensation act, the court held that, on defendant's motion for judgment on the pleadings, the tort action against the employer was not barred.

> This case is a reminder of the fact that, as every law student should know by his third week, the tort of assault does not require physical injury or even touching. Its minimal essence is putting the victim in fear of bodily harm. If bodily harm accompanies assault, as it usually does, the exclusiveness bar comes into play. If bodily harm does not accompany assault, the exclusiveness bar does not come into play. The conclusion must be that the test is not just the legal ingredients of assault, but also the results—specifically whether physical injury of the kind dealt with by the compensation act is produced.

> To summarize: If the essence of the tort, in law, is non-physical, and if the injuries are of the usual non-physical sort, with physical injury being at most added to the list of injuries as a make-weight, the suit should not be barred. But if the essence of the action is

recovery for physical injury or death, the action should be barred even if it can be cast in the form of a normally non-physical tort.

2A A. Larson, *The Law of Workmen's Compensation* § 68.34(a) at 13–116 to–117 (1989) (footnotes omitted).

Measured by the foregoing criteria, I concur that the plaintiffs' suit is not barred by the exclusive remedy of workers' compensation. Whether the amended complaint states a cause of action against the employer remains a question for the district court of appeal to decide.

Notes

1. Most courts have allowed workers to pursue common law tort or statutory civil rights claims under circumstances similar to those presented in *Byrd*. See, See e.g., Busby v. Truswal Systems Corp., 551 So.2d 322 (Ala.1989) (claim for intentional infliction of emotional distress is not barred by the exclusive remedy doctrine for emotional injuries caused by sexual harassment); Ford v. Revlon, 153 Ariz. 38, 734 P.2d 580 (Ariz. 1987) (claim for intentional infliction of emotional distress is not barred by the exclusive remedy doctrine for emotional injuries caused by sexual harassment); Byers v. Labor and Industry Review Comm'n., 208 Wis.2d 388, 561 N.W.2d 678 (Wis. 1997) (claim under state Fair Employment Act for sexual harassment is not barred by the exclusive remedy doctrine); Cox v. Brazo, 165 Ga.App. 888, 303 S.E.2d 71 (1983), affirmed 251 Ga. 491, 307 S.E.2d 474 (1983) (negligent supervision of sexually abusive supervisor); Boscaglia v. Michigan Bell Telephone Co., 420 Mich. 308, 362 N.W.2d 642 (1984) (sexual harassment violated state civil rights and fair employment practices acts); Kerans v. Porter Paint Co., 61 Ohio St.3d 486, 575 N.E.2d 428 (1991) (sexual harassment as a non-physical injury tort).

A number of jurisdictions have ruled that workers' compensation is the employee's exclusive remedy in a sexual harassment context. E.g., Konstantopoulos v. Westvaco, Corp., 690 A.2d 936 (Del.1996) (common law tort claims barred by the exclusive remedy doctrine); Green v. Wyman–Gordon Co., 422 Mass. 551, 664 N.E.2d 808 (Mass. 1996) (common law tort claims barred by the exclusive remedy doctrine); Knox v. Combined Ins. Co., 542 A.2d 363 (Me.1988) (assault, battery and intentional infliction of emotional distress claims barred); Loges v. Mack Trucks, Inc., 308 S.C. 134, 417 S.E.2d 538 (S.C. 1992) (assault, battery and intentional infliction of emotional distress claims barred, but claim for slander was actionable); Baker v. Wendy's of Montana, Inc., 687 P.2d 885 (Wyo.1984) (assault, battery and intentional infliction of emotional distress claims barred).

For a collection of cases see Linda A. Sharp, Workers' Compensation As Precluding Employee's Suit Against Employer For Sexual Harassment In The Workplace, 51 A.L.R. 5th 163 (1998).

2. A variety of explanations have been offered to explain why statutory and common law tort claims can be asserted by employees against employers for sexual harassment. Among the arguments that appear in the cases are: sexual harassment is not an "accident"; dignitary interests injured by sexual harassment are not covered by workers' compensation; the risk of sexual harassment is not incidental to the character of employment; acts of sexual

harassment are directed at employees for reasons personal to the employee; and public policy as reflected in state and federal civil rights laws support allowing such claims. Reasons given in support of the conclusion that workers' compensation is the exclusive remedy in the sexual harassment context include: workplace assaults are now commonly viewed to arise out of employment; insulating employers from tort liability is a central component of the workers' compensation principle; and exceptions to the exclusive remedy doctrine should come explicitly from the legislature.

Which of these arguments are most persuasive? Which are least persuasive? Is there a conflict between *Hyett*'s conclusion that the exclusive remedy doctrine bars a tort claim against an employer whose negligence causes noncompensable impotence and *Byrd*'s conclusion that an employer may be sued in tort for sexual harassment? How does one distinguish between assaults by co-workers that are compensable under workers' compensation and those for which workers' compensation is not the exclusive remedy?

3. Note that a majority of jurisdictions give a narrow scope to the intended injury exception to the exclusive remedy doctrine but allow tort suits against employers for sexual harassment. Why should workers' compensation be the exclusive remedy for the worker injured when his employer knowingly exposed him to asbestos, but the employee subject to sexual harassment is allowed to pursue a claim in tort? Consider the comments of Professor McCluskey:

> The reasoning in these cases points to a central issue underlying controversies over the bounds of the intentional tort exception. To distinguish "intentional" from "accidental" work injuries, we must decide the political and moral question of how much and what kinds of harm employers should be obligated to avoid (subject to more costly tort remedies). The willingness of many jurisdictions to exempt sexual harassment tort claims from exclusive remedy provisions reflects a change toward the value judgment that sexual harassment is neither necessary nor appropriate to a normal, productive economy. The unwillingness of most jurisdictions to exempt tort claims [from the exclusive remedy doctrine] for knowing exposure to occupational diseases (such as asbestos dust) reflects the persistence of the value judgment that such illnesses and injuries are a necessary part of productive workplaces.
>
> These judgments about the normal production process do not merely describe an economic fact about modern employment, nor do they merely reflect social norms about employment. Instead, they also implicitly prescribe what the normal conditions of employment should be. These courts insist that sexual harassment (unlike asbestos exposure) is a harm not reasonably connected to the production process. In theory, however, some employers might be able to increase profits or production (at least in the short run) by overlooking or condoning sexual harassment in the workplace ... The decision by some courts to view sexual harassment as outside the bounds of workers' compensation rests on an implicit determination that employers *should not* be allowed to profit from sexual harassment in the workplace, even if they could. In contrast, the perception that asbestos exposure has a productive purpose is the result of political decisions to allow employers to treat workers'

exposure to toxic materials as a cost of doing business. Unlike sexual harassment, then, employers can overlook or tolerate asbestos exposure in the pursuit of profit.

Martha T. McCluskey, The Illusion of Efficiency in Workers' Compensation "Reform," 50 Rutgers L. Rev. 657, 911–12 (1998) (footnotes omitted; emphasis in original).

4. In 1991 Congress enacted legislation that authorizes a limited damage remedy against employers who engage in or tolerate sexual harassment. See 42 U.S.C.A. § 1981A. Should the availability of a damage remedy under federal law affect whether the exclusive remedy doctrine precludes a tort action under state law? For a discussion of Title VII remedies see Mark Hager, Harassment as a Tort: Why Title VII Hostile Environment Liability Should Be Curtailed, 30 Conn. L. Rev. 375 (1998).

5. Justice Grimes' concurring opinion in *Byrd* refers to Professor Larson's distinction between physical injury and non-physical injury torts. Relying on this distinction, courts have held that workers' compensation is not the exclusive remedy for such torts as false imprisonment, libel, malicious prosecution, and intentional infliction of emotional distress. E.g., Fermino v. Fedco, Inc., 7 Cal.4th 701, 30 Cal.Rptr.2d 18, 872 P.2d 559 (1994) (false imprisonment claim is not barred by the exclusive remedy doctrine); Snead v. Harbaugh, 241 Va. 524, 404 S.E.2d 53 (1991) (law professor's suit against the dean and other members of the faculty for alleged defamation is not precluded by the exclusive remedy doctrine). Cf. Williams v. Caruso, 966 F.Supp. 287 (D.Del.1997) (claims for tortious interference with contract are not barred by the exclusive remedy doctrine). For a collection of cases see, 6 A. Larson and L. Larson, Larson's Workers' Compensation Law § 68.30 (1998). Is an exception to the exclusive remedy doctrine grounded in the type of injury any easier to justify or apply than one based on the employer's state of mind? See Love, Actions for Nonphysical Harm: The Relationship between the Tort System and No–Fault Compensation (With an Emphasis on Workers' Compensation), 73 Cal.L.Rev. 857 (1985).

6. The exclusive remedy doctrine may be preempted by federal legislation. See, Adams Fruit Co., Inc. v. Barrett, 494 U.S. 638, 110 S.Ct. 1384, 108 L.Ed.2d 585 (1990) (Florida exclusive remedy provision preempted by the Migrant and Seasonal Agricultural Worker Protection Act, 29 U.S.C.A. 1801 et seq.); McClary v. O'Hare, 786 F.2d 83 (2d Cir.1986) (civil rights claim brought under 42 U.S.C.A. 1983 is not barred by state exclusive remedy doctrine). How does a preemption analysis differ from that used by the court in *Byrd*? See Paul J. Zech, Federal Pre–Exemption and State Exclusive Remedy Issues in Employment Litigation, 72 N. Dak. L. Rev. 325 (1996).

7. Other circumstances occasionally arise in which the exclusive remedy doctrine will not apply. For example, employees may bring common law tort actions against their employers if their relationship is not covered by workers' compensation at the time of the injury. Thus, farm laborers may bring tort suits against their employers in states that exclude such employment from workers' compensation coverage. E.g., Eastway v. Eisenga, 420 Mich. 410, 362 N.W.2d 684 (1984); Baskin v. Worker's Compensation Division, 722 P.2d 151 (Wyo.1986). A worker who is not in the course of employment when injured may sue the employer in tort. E.g., Beckham v.

Estate of Brown, 100 N.M. 1, 664 P.2d 1014 (App.1983) (salesman died in plane crash on his way to attend a basketball game; trip was a prize for sales contest at work; widow allowed to proceed with wrongful death claim). In many states an employee may maintain a tort action against an employer who fails to secure workers' compensation insurance. E.g., Ehredt v. DeHavilland Aircraft Co., 705 P.2d 913 (Alaska 1985) (uninsured employer held liable for death of employee in air crash). The uninsured employer is typically stripped of traditional tort defenses such as assumption of risk and comparative negligence. E.g., Grothe v. Olafson, 659 P.2d 602 (Alaska 1983) (employee's 20% comparative negligence would not reduce tort recovery against uninsured employer); Arvas v. Feather's Jewelers, 92 N.M. 89, 582 P.2d 1302 (App.1978) (common law defenses not available to uninsured employer sued by an employee who fell through unprotected opening in attic).

8.   If it is unclear whether an injury is covered by workers' compensation or is actionable in tort under an exception to the exclusive remedy doctrine, must the employee "elect" one or the other remedy? The New Jersey Supreme Court spoke to this issue as follows:

> Our view is that in light of the Compensation Act's purpose of assisting disabled workers, the best approach is to allow a plaintiff to process his workers' compensation claim without forfeiting the opportunity to establish that he was injured as a result of conduct that amounted to an intentional wrong, entitling him to seek damages beyond those available in workers' compensation. If, however, a plaintiff should prevail in his suit based on intentional wrong, he would not be entitled to keep the entire amount of his compensation award as well as his civil suit remedy.... [I]f the trier-of-fact determines that du Pont and/or its doctors have been guilty of an intentional wrong as a result of their alleged fraudulent concealment of existing occupational diseases, du Pont or its insurance carrier will be able to offset compensation benefits previously paid to the extent that the civil damage award would serve as a double recovery.

Millison v. E.I. du Pont de Nemours & Co., 101 N.J. 161, 501 A.2d 505, 519 (N.J. 1985). Not all courts agree with *Millison* on this point. See Zurowska v. Berlin Indus., 282 Ill.App.3d 540, 217 Ill.Dec. 499, 667 N.E.2d 588 (Ill.App. 1996) (acceptance of compensation benefits barred claim for intentional tort); Werner v. State, 53 N.Y.2d 346, 441 N.Y.S.2d 654, 424 N.E.2d 541 (1981) (acceptance of workers' compensation benefits forecloses suit against employer for alleged intentional tort); Barrino v. Radiator Specialty Co., 315 N.C. 500, 340 S.E.2d 295 (1986) (employee who recovered workers' compensation benefits made a "binding election" of remedies that precluded tort claim against employer for alleged assault). See 6 A. Larson and L. Larson, Larson's Workers' Compensation Law § 67.30 (1998).

9.   In 1972 the National Commission on State Workmen's Compensation Laws identified the encouragement of safety conditions as one of the objectives of a workers' compensation system. To what extent do the cases in this section reflect a concern that the limited recovery under workers' compensation and the exclusive remedy doctrine too greatly dilute the employer's economic incentives to reduce accident costs? What factors other

than compensation costs might affect an employer's investment in workplace safety? What strategies might a law maker consider to regulate risk in the workplace?

10. Commentaries on the exclusive remedy doctrine and its exceptions include, King, The Exclusiveness of an Employee's Workers' Compensation Remedy Against His Employer, 55 Tenn.L.Rev. 405 (1988); Note, Exceptions to the Exclusive Remedy Requirements of Workers' Compensation Statutes, 96 Harv.L.Rev. 1641 (1983). For a state-by-state comparison of the scope of exceptions to the exclusive remedy doctrine, see International Association of Industrial Accident Boards and Commissions, Exclusive Remedy Survey (1990).

SECTION 3. THIRD PARTY ACTIONS: WHO IS A THIRD PARTY?

Cal.Labor Code Ann. § 3852

> The claim of an employee ... for compensation does not affect his or her claim or right of action for all damages proximately resulting from the injury or death against any person other than the employer.

WRIGHT ASSOCIATES, INC. v. RIEDER

Supreme Court of Georgia, 1981.
247 Ga. 496, 277 S.E.2d 41.

HILL, PRESIDING JUSTICE.

The Georgia Education Authority contracted with Wright Associates, Inc., for the construction of an academic building at Macon Junior College. Wright Associates, as the general or prime contractor, then contracted with Eastern Steel Erectors, Inc., an independent subcontractor, for certain on-site work. Thomas Rieder, an Eastern employee, was injured in an on-site accident and recovered worker's compensation benefits from Eastern. He then sued Wright Associates in April, 1978, alleging that his injury was caused by the negligence of a Wright employee. Nearly two years after answering, Wright moved for summary judgment on the ground, raised for the first time in its motion, that Rieder's tort action was barred by Code Ann. [§§ 34–9–11, 34–9–8]. The trial court denied the motion for summary judgment but certified the question for immediate review. After the Court of Appeals denied the application for interlocutory review, Wright Associates petitioned for writ of certiorari, which was granted.

. . .

Code Ann. [§ 34–9–8] ... provides that "A principal, intermediate, or subcontractor shall be liable for compensation to any employee injured while in the employ of any of his subcontractors engaged upon the subject-matter of the contract, to the same extent as the immediate employer. ..."

. . .

By this Code Section the principal or intermediate contractor is made the "statutory employer" of the subcontractor's employee.

Under the facts of this case [the] issue [is] whether an employee of an independent subcontractor can recover in tort against the principal contractor.

In *Blair v. Smith*, 201 Ga. 747, 41 S.E.2d 133 (1947), this court cited Code Ann. [§ 34–9–8], but held without discussion of it that the employee of an independent contractor who recovered worker's compensation benefits from his immediate employer could maintain an action in tort against the principal contractor. Subsequently the Court of Appeals reluctantly followed *Blair*.

. . .

In 1979, this court decided *Haygood v. Home Transportation Co.*, 244 Ga. 165, 259 S.E.2d 429 (1979), in which we held that a principal contractor is the statutory employer of the employee of a subcontractor who is an independent contractor. . . . Since Home Transportation Company was the statutory employer of Mrs. Haygood's deceased husband, Home was liable for worker's compensation benefits to Mrs. Haygood. In that case, Home did in fact pay benefits to Mrs. Haygood. This court held that as a statutory employer who had paid compensation benefits, Home was immune from suit in tort under Code Ann. [§ 34–9–8]. In a concurring opinion, Justice Jordan (now Chief Justice) contended that *Haygood* overruled *Blair v. Smith*.

In the case before us, we have the same facts as in *Haygood, supra,* except that here the employee recovered worker's compensation benefits not from the statutory employer, Wright Associates, but from his immediate employer, Eastern Steel Erectors. Wright Associates argues that as a statutory employer liable to pay worker's compensation benefits under Code Ann. [§ 34–9–8], it should receive the correlative benefit of tort immunity under Code Ann. [§§ 34–9–11, 34–9–8]. We agree and so hold. As one commentator has pointed out in his discussion of statutory employers, "Since the general contractor is thereby, in effect, made the employer for the purposes of the compensation statute, it is obvious that he should enjoy the regular immunity of an employer from third-party suit when the facts are such that he could be made liable for compensation; and the great majority of cases have so held." 2A Larson, The Law of Workmen's Compensation, § 72.31 at p. 14–47.

Rieder contends that even if a statutory employer is normally insulated from tort liability despite the fact that he has not paid worker's compensation benefits, he should not be where, as here, he has a contract with the subcontractor which provides that the subcontractor shall carry worker's compensation insurance and in the event that the statutory employer is held liable for worker's compensation benefits, he will be indemnified by the subcontractor. Because Code Ann. [§ 34–9–8] gives a right of indemnification absent a contract, this amounts to an argument that because of the statutory right of indemnification as to compensation benefits, a statutory employer should not be immune from tort liability. We cannot agree. The purpose of Code Ann. [§ 34–9–8] is to ensure that employees in construction and other industries are covered by worker's compensation. In order to do so, it places an increased burden, in the form of potential liability for worker's compensation benefits, on the statutory employer. This encourages the statutory employer to require subcontractors to carry worker's compensation insurance. The fact that the statutory employer reacts to the statute in the manner intended by the legislature should not result in a penalty on the statutory employer. Conversely, if the statutory employer does not require subcontractors to provide compensation benefits (as intended by the statute), the statutory employer may acquire tort immunity. See, *Haygood v. Home Transportation Co., supra.* The quid pro quo for the statutory employer's potential liability is immunity from tort liability. The fact that the statutory employer has a right to indemnification, statutory or contractual, does not strip him of his tort immunity. See 2A Larson, The Law of Workmen's Compensation, § 72.31, p. 14–55, 56, § 72.32, p. 14–66 n. 72.

. . .

Judgement reversed.

All the Justices concur, except UNDERCOFLER, J., who dissents.

UNDERCOFLER, JUSTICE, dissenting.

. . .

The majority here finds that since the general contractor is a statutory employer and has a potential liability for workers' compensation to the independent sub-contractor's employee, the general contractor is immune from tort liability to that employee. The majority reasons: "The quid pro quo for the statutory employer's potential liability is immunity from tort liability." In my view, it is not potential liability for workers' compensation which insulates a statutory employer from tort liability but actual liability. *Blair v. Smith,* 201 Ga. 747, 41 S.E.2d 133 (1947); *Haygood v. Home Transportation Co.,* 244 Ga. 165, 259 S.E.2d 429 (1979). Unless the general contractor is required to pay workers' compensation as a statutory employer there is no quid pro quo and he remains liable in tort for his wrong. Here the general contractor had no actual liability. The sub-contractor paid the workers' compensation. Thus the majority opinion has gratuitously relieved the general contractor of liability for his tort.

I would not overrule *Blair v. Smith, supra.* Its judgment is correct that a general contractor who has not been held liable for workers' compensation may be sued in tort. *Blair* has stood for thirty-three years unchanged by the legislature and stare decisis compels that we adhere to it.

Haygood v. Home Transportation Co., Inc., supra is not support for the majority opinion. In that case the general contractor scheduled Haygood as his employee with his compensation carrier which paid the benefits due.

Notes

1. *Wright* illustrates the prevailing view that statutory employers enjoy the protection of the exclusive remedy doctrine even if the immediate employer pays workers' compensation benefits. E.g., Edwards v. Price, 191 Colo. 46, 550 P.2d 856 (1976); Fireman's Fund Ins. v. Sherman & Fletcher, 705 S.W.2d 459 (Ky.1986); Parker v. Williams and Madjanik, Inc., 275 S.C. 65, 267 S.E.2d 524 (1980); Crowe v. Brasfield & Gorrie Contractors, Inc., 688 So.2d 752 (Miss.1996). A few jurisdictions treat statutory employers as third parties subject to suit unless they actually provide the workers' compensation insurance. E.g., Boettner v. Twin City Constr. Co., 214 N.W.2d 635 (N.D.1974); Bence v. Pacific Power and Light Co., 631 P.2d 13 (Wyo.1981). Some statutes have been construed to allow injured workers to bring suit against their statutory employer even when the statutory employer has paid compensation benefits. E.g., Webb v. Montana Masonry Constr. Co., 233 Mont. 198, 761 P.2d 343 (1988).

2. A similar problem is posed by the borrowed servant line of cases considered in Chapter 3. Workers' compensation is the exclusive remedy for the "borrowed servant" against his "special employer". E.g., Capps v. N.L. Baroid–NL Industries, Inc., 784 F.2d 615 (5th Cir.1986) (applying Longshore and Harbor Workers' Compensation Act); Santa Cruz Poultry v. Superior Court (Stier), 194 Cal.App.3d 575, 239 Cal.Rptr. 578 (1987); Six Flags Over Georgia v. Hill, 247 Ga. 375, 276 S.E.2d 572 (1981); Kidder v. Miller–Davis Co., 455 Mich. 25, 564 N.W.2d 872 (Mich. 1997); Vigil v. Digital Equipment Corp., 122 N.M. 417, 925 P.2d 883 (N.M.App.1996). Defendants sued in tort by injured workers usually raise the exclusive remedy defense by motion for summary judgment. If the defendant's status as special employer turns on disputed issues of material fact, the defense cannot be summarily established and the case is submitted to the jury. E.g., Whittington v. New Jersey Zinc Co., 775 F.2d 698 (6th Cir.1985); Barajas v. USA Petroleum Corp., 184 Cal.App.3d 974, 229 Cal.Rptr. 513 (1986); Food Giant, Inc. v. Davison, 184 Ga.App. 742, 362 S.E.2d 447 (1987). In a few jurisdictions, the special employer may be subject to suit as a third party if the general employer actually paid the compensation benefits to the injured worker. E.g., Lang v. Edward J. Lamothe Co., Inc., 20 Mass.App.Ct. 231, 479 N.E.2d 208 (1985).

A growing number of states address this issue in specific statutes. Most of these statutes confer immunity on the special employer. E.g., Colo. Rev. Stat. § 8–41–303; Conn. Gen. Stat. Ann. § 31–292; Wis. Stat. Ann. § 102.29. Hawaii allows the employee of a temporary employment agency to sue the special employer for negligence. Haw. Rev. Stat. § 366–1. See Brian C. Baugh, Comment, Workers' Compensation: Temporary Employees and the Exclusiveness-of-Remedy Provision, 86 Ky. L.J. 163 (1997–98).

3. Insurance carriers who conduct safety inspections are sometimes the target of tort actions by injured workers. The common allegation is that the insurance company undertook to inspect the work premises and failed to discover, warn of, or remedy the dangerous condition that caused the worker's injury. Insurance companies maintain that they should be afforded the same immunity from suit as the employer. The great majority of courts that have addressed this issue have concluded under varying rationales that the compensation carrier is immune from tort liability to the injured worker.

In some states, the insurance carrier enjoys an express statutory immunity from such claims. E.g., Mich.Comp.Laws Ann. § 418.827. Other states confer the protection of the exclusive remedy doctrine on "employers" who are statutorily defined to include the compensation carrier. E.g., Ga.Code Ann. § 34–9–1(3); Pa.Stat.Ann., tit. 77, § 501. A few courts discern from the overall structure of the workers' compensation act a legislative intent to immunize insurance carriers from such claims. E.g., Kifer v. Liberty Mutual Ins. Co., 777 F.2d 1325 (8th Cir.1985) (construing Arkansas law). Several jurisdictions, however, permit employees to sue workers' compensation insurers for negligent safety inspections. Silva v. Hodge, 583 So.2d 231 (Ala.1991); Thompson v. Bohlken, 312 N.W.2d 501 (Iowa 1981); Derosia v. Duro Metal Products Co., 147 Vt. 410, 519 A.2d 601 (1986). A few states distinguish between safety inspections conducted by workers' compensation carriers and those conducted by general liability insurers. Tort suits against the compensation insurer are barred, but general liability carriers are treated as third parties subject to suit. E.g., Latour v. Commercial Union Ins. Co., 528 F.Supp. 231 (D.R.I.1981) (applying Rhode Island law); Wilson v. Rebsamen Ins., Inc., 330 Ark. 687, 957 S.W.2d 678 (Ark. 1997); Sims v. American Casualty Co., 131 Ga.App. 461, 206 S.E.2d 121 (1974), affirmed sub nom. Providence Washington Ins. Co. v. Sims, 232 Ga. 787, 209 S.E.2d 61 (1974). Aside from legislative language, what policy considerations are relevant to deciding whether an insurance carrier should be subject to suit for an alleged negligent safety inspection?

4. Is the parent company of a wholly-owned subsidiary a "third party"? See, Boggs v. Blue Diamond Coal Co., 590 F.2d 655 (6th Cir.1979) (the survivors of miners killed in a mining disaster allowed to sue the parent company of their husbands' employer); Boswell v. May Centers, Inc., 669 S.W.2d 585 (Mo.App.1984) (employee of parent company allowed to sue wholly-owned subsidiary for its negligence in maintaining a parking lot). But cf. Beck v. Flint Construction Co., 154 Ga.App. 490, 268 S.E.2d 739 (1980) (parent company that so dominated the affairs of its wholly-owned subsidiary so as to be considered its "alter-ego" would be entitled to the subsidiary's immunity from tort suit).

5. In the absence of a special provision in the compensation statute, coworkers are generally considered third parties subject to suit by an injured employee. E.g., Vittum v. New Hampshire Ins. Co., 117 N.H. 1, 369 A.2d 184 (1977); Gorzalski v. Frankenmuth Mut. Ins. Co., 145 Wis.2d 794, 429 N.W.2d 537 (1988). A great majority of states, however, have extended the exclusive remedy doctrine to also preclude tort actions against coemployees. E.g., Alaska Stat. § 23.30.055; Cal.Labor Code § 3601(a); Conn.Gen.Stat.Ann. § 31–293a. Does the injured worker receive any quid pro quo in exchange for losing his right to sue a coemployee? Can it be argued that tort immunity is an additional benefit conferred upon the worker? Is a quid pro quo necessary to uphold the constitutionality of coemployee immunity? Compare Estabrook v. American Hoist & Derrick, Inc., 127 N.H. 162, 498 A.2d 741 (1985) (striking down a statute creating coemployee immunity, in part, on the absence of an off-setting quid pro quo) with Young v. Prevue Products, Inc., 130 N.H. 84, 534 A.2d 714 (1987) (quid pro quo is not required to uphold the constitutionality of bar on suit for loss of consortium). In view of the fact that an employer is universally entitled to indemnity against a "third party"

who wrongfully injured the worker, would tort liability of a coempl result eventually in relieving the employer's enterprise of the compens; cost and shifting this onto the shoulders of one of the workers? See, Ste: The Employer's Indemnity Action, 25 U.Chi.L.Rev. 465 (1958).

6. The "dual capacity doctrine" illustrates an attempt to characterize the employer as a third party. The leading early case applying this approach was Duprey v. Shane, 39 Cal.2d 781, 249 P.2d 8 (1952). The plaintiff in *Duprey* was a nurse who was injured on the job. Her chiropractor-employer further injured her in the course of treating her compensable injury. The court upheld the employee's right to sue her employer for malpractice since his negligence was performed in his "capacity" as a doctor, rather than in his capacity as her employer.

In the late 1970's and early 1980's, some courts expanded the concept of dual capacity. Employers who manufactured or modified equipment used on the job were held suable in tort in their capacity as product manufacturers. E.g., Bell v. Industrial Vangas, Inc., 30 Cal.3d 268, 179 Cal.Rptr. 30, 637 P.2d 266 (1981) (employer liable in capacity of manufacturer when employee was injured while delivering the gas that his employer had manufactured); Mercer v. Uniroyal, Inc., 49 Ohio App.2d 279, 361 N.E.2d 492 (1976) (truckdriver-employee could recover from his employer, Uniroyal, when injured in an on-the-job automobile accident caused by a defective Uniroyal tire). The dual capacity doctrine came under considerable attack. With only slight imagination, negligent employers could be cast in some other capacity, such as product manufacturer or premises owner. Critics maintained that the dual capacity doctrine threatened the basic structure of the quid pro quo compromise that underlies workers' compensation. See, 6A A. Larson and L. Larson, Larson's Workers' Compensation Law § 72.81(c) (1998). Jurisdictions that once warmly embraced the expansion of the dual capacity doctrine began to substantially limit its application. E.g., Bakonyi v. Ralston Purina Co., 17 Ohio St.3d 154, 478 N.E.2d 241 (1985) (employer who sold fertilizer to the public and used it in the workplace was not subject to liability for employee's injury under the dual capacity doctrine). California legislatively abolished this exception to the exclusive remedy doctrine. Cal.Labor Code § 3602(a).

Today, efforts to sue employers on the basis of their alleged dual capacities are often unsuccessful. E.g., Bowen v. Goodyear Tire & Rubber Co., 516 So.2d 570 (Ala.1987) (dual capacity doctrine did not apply when an employee injured his hand trying to fix a machine manufactured by his employer solely for use in the plant); Panaro v. Electrolux Corp. , 208 Conn. 589, 545 A.2d 1086 (Conn. 1988) (co-employee-nurse who told the plaintiff to rest and then to return to work after complaining about dizziness was not subject to suit under the dual capacity doctrine); Stewart v. CMI Corp., 740 P.2d 1340 (Utah 1987) (decedent's survivors barred from bringing wrongful death action based on employer's design and manufacturing of screw auger). Occasionally, however, this doctrine is invoked to allow a tort claim to proceed against the plaintiff's employer. E.g., Dalton v. Community General Hosp., 275 Ill.App.3d 73, 211 Ill.Dec. 433, 655 N.E.2d 462 (Ill.App.1995) (hospital employee could maintain a suit against the hospital for negligence in connection with surgery to treat work-related carpal tunnel syndrome). For a compilation of cases, see Michael A. DiSabatino, Modern States: "Dual

Capacity Doctrine" as a Basis for Employee's Recovery from Employer in Tort, 23 A.L.R. 4th 1151 (1997).

7. A similar concept, called dual persona, remains a viable doctrinal basis for avoiding the exclusive remedy doctrine in certain instances. In contrast to dual capacity, the concept of dual persona involves an employer who also has a distinctly different legal identity. This distinct legal identity may be considered a "third party" for purposes of the exclusive remedy doctrine. An example of the successful use of the dual persona idea lies in the corporate merger area. An employee injured by defective equipment manufactured by X Corporation has been allowed to sue the merged corporate employer in tort when the original employer's business merged with X Corporation after the sale of the product. E.g., Percy v. Falcon Fabricators, 584 So.2d 17 (Fla.App.1991); Kimzey v. Interpace Corp., 10 Kan.App.2d 165, 694 P.2d 907 (1985); Billy v. Consolidated Machine Tool Corp., 51 N.Y.2d 152, 432 N.Y.S.2d 879, 412 N.E.2d 934 (1980); Schweiner v. Hartford Acc. & Indem. Co., 120 Wis.2d 344, 354 N.W.2d 767 (App.1984). The defendant is subject to tort liability in such cases not because it is the plaintiff's employer, but because it is the successor in interest to the third party manufacturer. Through the law governing corporate mergers, the employer has taken on the additional legal identity as successor in interest to the merged manufacturer. Part of that identity includes acceptance of the former corporation's liabilities. Should it make any difference whether the former corporation manufactured the defective equipment only for use in its workplace? Compare Billy v. Consolidated Machine Tool Corp., 51 N.Y.2d 152, 432 N.Y.S.2d 879, 412 N.E.2d 934 (1980) (employer held liable) with Corr v. Willamette Indust., Inc., 105 Wash.2d 217, 713 P.2d 92 (1986) (no liability).

SECTION 4. THE RIGHTS OF EMPLOYER AND EMPLOYEE IN THIRD PARTY ACTIONS

CASTLEMAN v. ROSS ENGINEERING, INC.

Supreme Court of Tennessee, 1997.
958 S.W.2d 720.

REID, J.

* * *

I

On November 3, 1989, the plaintiff, Billy Castleman, an employee of a subcontractor, Jack Castleman d/b/a J.E.C. Electric Company, sustained a compensable injury under the workers' compensation law, for which the general contractor's workers' compensation insurance carrier, Hartford Accident and Indemnity Company, paid the plaintiff benefits in the approximate amount of $100,000.

A tort action for personal injuries was filed by the plaintiff against a third party, Ross Engineering, Inc., on April 3, 1990. Hartford filed an intervening petition, asserting a subrogation right and a lien pursuant to

Tenn. Code Ann. § 50–6–112(c) (1) (1991) on any recovery by the plaintiff from Ross Engineering.

The case was tried on March 4, 1993, 10 months after the release of the decision in *McIntyre v. Balentine*, 833 S.W.2d 52 (Tenn.1992).[9] The case was submitted to the jury on instructions that fault could be apportioned among the plaintiff, Castleman, the defendant, Ross Engineering, and the employer, J.E.C. Electric. The jury found damages of $1,500,000, and attributed 68 percent of the fault to the defendant, 16 percent of the fault to the plaintiff, and 16 percent of the fault to the employer. The court entered judgment against Ross Engineering for $1,020,000, 68 percent of the $1,500,000. The plaintiff did not appeal from the judgment on the jury verdict.

On May 26, 1993, the plaintiff acknowledged full satisfaction of the judgment, and the plaintiff received from Ross Engineering full payment of the amount of the judgment less $100,000, which was retained by consent pending resolution of Hartford's subrogation claim. By order entered on July 7, 1995, Hartford was awarded the $100,000 claimed, less attorneys fees and expenses incurred in pursuing the third-party claim, a net amount of $68,489.

On appeal to the Court of Appeals, the plaintiff contested the subrogation award to Hartford, insisting that Hartford's right to subrogation was conditioned on the plaintiff's recovery of the damages for fault attributed to the employer as well as fault attributed to Ross Engineering. The Court of Appeals rejected the plaintiff's contention and affirmed the trial court's decision.

II

The plaintiff does not deny that Hartford has a subrogation claim against the third party judgment for the total amount of workers' compensation benefits paid to the plaintiff Section 50–6–112 (1991) provides that when the injury compensated under the Workers' Compensation Law was caused by the negligence of a third party, the injured employee may pursue an action against the third party. Subsection (c) (1) provides as follows:

> In [the] event of such recovery against such third person by the worker, or by those to whom such worker's right of action survives, by judgment, settlement or otherwise, and the employer's maximum liability for workers' compensation under this chapter has been fully or partially paid and discharged, the employer shall have a subrogation lien therefor against such recovery, and the employer may intervene in any action to protect and enforce such lien.

The plaintiff insists, however, that the enforcement of that right is conditioned upon the employee, as the subrogor, being "made whole."

---

9. In *McIntyre v. Balentine*, 833 S.W.2d 52 (Tenn.1992), the "all-or-nothing rule of contributory negligence" was replaced with principles of comparative fault so that "so long as a plaintiff's negligence remains less than the defendant's negligence the plaintiff may recover; in such a case, plaintiff's damages are to be reduced in proportion to the percentage of the total negligence attributable to the plaintiff." Id. at 57.

The plaintiff defines "made whole" as being able to recover for all damages found by the jury except damages representing fault attributed to him. In this case, recovery making the plaintiff whole would include the approximately [$240,000] for damages attributed to the fault of the employer, J.E.C. Electric.

* * *

In the case of *Ridings v. Ralph M. Parsons Co.*, the tort defendants sought to assert as an affirmative defense that the employer contributed to the employee's injuries. The defendants argued that under *McIntyre*, "fault can be attributed to the employer, and the liability of the defendants [could] be decreased accordingly, without the imposition of liability upon the employer." *Ridings v. Ralph M. Parsons Co.*, 914 S.W.2d at 81. Though *Ridings* was a transitional case, the Court found that "application of comparative fault principles to this case requires no transitional procedure [because] the acts and omissions of an employer covered by the worker's compensation law neither enlarge nor limit the rights or liabilities of any party to a tort action by an employee governed by the doctrine of comparative fault." Id. at 80–81. The Court concluded that "fault may be attributed only to those persons against whom the plaintiff has a cause of action in tort." Id. at 81.

* * *

Under *Ridings*, the trial court erred in instructing the jury that fault could be attributed to the employer, and the plaintiff would have been entitled to relief from that error on appeal. However, the plaintiff did not appeal, but instead accepted payment of the judgment awarded against Ross Engineering as satisfaction in full for his cause of action. Of course, this Court cannot provide relief for errors that are not preserved on appeal.

The decisions governing the application of comparative fault principles have sought to achieve fairness to the parties within the constraints of statutory law providing immunity in particular situations:

> Limiting the parties to whom fault may be attributed to those subject to liability, accomplishes the policy objectives of fairness and efficiency. Since liability is several and is in direct proportion to legal fault, each defendant will be liable only for the percentage of the damages caused by it. Since fault is limited to the plaintiff and those against whom the plaintiff has a cause of action, the plaintiff is not denied the right to recover those damages to which it is entitled. However, the plaintiff will bear the loss for any liability that it fails or is unable to assert and any judgment that cannot be enforced.

Ridings v. Ralph M. Parsons Co., 914 S.W.2d at 83.

The plaintiff's rights as they existed prior to the release of the decision in *McIntyre* have not been adversely affected by the adoption of the principles of comparative fault; consequently, this is not a transitional case entitled to special consideration.

This conclusion also resolves the plaintiff's primary contention, that the insurer is not entitled to enforce its right of subrogation because the plaintiff has not been "made whole." The plaintiff acknowledges that Hartford has a subrogation claim for benefits paid under the workers' compensation law but, asserting principles of equitable subrogation, insists that the subrogation claim is not enforceable unless the employee has recovered the full amount of the damages not attributed to his own fault.

The statute creating the subrogation claim does not by its terms condition the claim upon the employee obtaining a full recovery of damages sustained. The subrogation lien attaches to "the net recovery collected" and secures the amount "paid" by the employer or the amount of the employer's "future liability, as it accrues."[6] It appears that, under the statute, the subrogation lien attaches to any recovery from the tort-feasor "by judgment, settlement or otherwise." Id. Consequently, even if under equitable principles of subrogation the employer was not entitled to assert the subrogation lien, the statute specifically creates that right.

The record does not support the premise on which the plaintiff bases his argument, that he has not been made whole. Further, the plaintiff has asserted no basis on which the subrogation claim created by statute should be denied.

The judgment of the Court of Appeals is affirmed.

Notes

1. All states recognize an employer's right to be reimbursed for compensation benefits from the proceeds from an employee's tort claim against a third party. There are several general legislative approaches to this area of the law. A few states unconditionally assign the employee's cause of action to the payor of compensation benefits. E.g., Colo.Rev.Stat. § 8–52–108; Idaho Code Ann. § 72–204; Okla.Stat.Ann. tit. 85, § 44. This approach gives the

---

6. Tenn. Code Ann. § 50–6–112(c) provides:

(1) In [the] event of such recovery against such third person by the worker, or by those to whom such worker's right of action survives, by judgment, settlement or otherwise, and the employer's maximum liability for workers' compensation under this chapter has been fully or partially paid and discharged, the employer shall have a subrogation lien therefor against such recovery, and the employer may intervene in any action to protect and enforce such lien.

(2) In the event the net recovery by the worker, or by those to whom such worker's right of action survives, exceeds the amount paid by the employer, and the employer has not, at the time, paid and discharged the employer's full maximum liability for workers' compensation under this chapter, the employer shall be entitled to a credit on the employer's future liability, as it accrues, to the extent the net recovery collected exceeds the amount paid by the employer.

(3) In the event the worker, or those to whom such worker's right of action survives, effects a recovery, and collection thereof, from such other person, by judgment, settlement or otherwise, without intervention by the employer, the employer shall nevertheless, be entitled to a credit on the employer's future liability for workers' compensation, as it accrues under this chapter, to the extent of the net recovery.

employer or its workers' compensation insurance carrier control over the tort claim against the third party tortfeasor. Other states allow both the worker and the employer to pursue claims against the third party tortfeasor simultaneously, with provision for joinder of the two claims. E.g., Rana v. Ritacco, 236 Conn. 330, 672 A.2d 946 (Conn. 1996); Hartford Casualty Ins. Co. v. Albertsons Grocery, 931 S.W.2d 729 (Tex.App.1996). The most common statutory scheme establishes a priority as to who may initiate the third party action. Priority is most often given to the employee as the party with the greater interest in the litigation. E.g., Ariz.Rev.Stat.Ann. § 23–1023; Haw.Rev.Stat. § 386.8; N.Y.Work.Comp.Law § 29. If the party having the first right to initiate the third party action fails to do so within a specified period of time, the other becomes authorized to do so. E.g., Fla.Stat.Ann. § 440.39. For a thorough discussion of the various forms of subrogation, see 6 A. Larson and L. Larson, Larson's Workers' Compensation Law § 74 (1998).

2. The amount of the employer's lien often is stated in terms of compensation benefits "paid or payable". Calculating the precise amount of the lien is complicated by two factors. The first is that the extent of the employer's liability for future compensation benefits often is unknown. Some states calculate the lien by computing the present value of the probable future compensation benefits. E.g., N.Y.Work.Comp.Laws § 29. Most states, however, merely treat the excess of a third party recovery over past compensation actually paid as a credit against future compensation liability. E.g., Moore v. General Foods, 459 A.2d 126 (Del.1983); Mastin v. Liberal Markets, 674 S.W.2d 7 (Ky.1984). For a discussion of whether courts or the administrative agency should determine the effect of future compensation benefits on the employer's lien, see Johnson v. Southern Industrial Constructors, Inc., 347 N.C. 530, 495 S.E.2d 356 (N.C. 1998) (agency is "better equipped ... to make the determinations and dispensations" contemplated by the statute).

The second complicating factor is allocating the expenses of the third party claim between the employer and employee. In many cases, it is the worker who incurs most of the expenses in maintaining the third party action. The employer or its insurer merely enforces its lien against any resulting judgment or settlement. Since the employer benefits financially from the employee's efforts, as in *Castleman* most states require the employer to bear a portion of the expenses of litigation, including attorney fees. One equitable approach to this problem is to base the employer's share of litigation expenses on the ratio of compensation benefits to the third party recovery. In Fitzgerald v. Challenge Cook Bros., 80 Mich.App. 524, 264 N.W.2d 348 (1978), for example, the employer's insurance carrier paid the worker $8,533.95 in compensation benefits. The worker then secured a judgment against a third party for $57,000. The expenses of securing that judgment, including attorney fees was $21,383. The court apportioned the expenses of the third party action according to the following formula:

$$\frac{\text{benefits paid}}{\text{Judgment}} = \frac{\$8,533.95}{\$57,000} = 14.84\%$$

Thus the employer's share of the litigation expenses was 14.84% of $21,383. Any sums actually expended by the employer in the third party action would be included in determining both the total expenses and the employer's proportionate share of those expenses. See Hodder v. Goodyear Tire & Rubber Co., 426 N.W.2d 826 (Minn.1988); Kindt v. Otis Elevator Co., 32 Cal.App.4th 452, 38 Cal.Rptr.2d 121 (Cal.App.1995) (burden on lienholder to prove it had actively participated in the lawsuit).

3.   The Tennessee Supreme Court in *Castleman* rejected the employee's argument that subrogation was conditioned on the employee being "made whole." Some statutes contain such a limitation. E.g., Ga. Code Ann. § 34–9–11.1(a) ("the employer's or insurer's [subrogation lien] ... shall only be recoverable if the injured employee has been fully and completely compensated...for all economic and noneconomic losses incurred as a result of the injury"). Why would a legislature place such a limit on the right of subrogation? How much of a limitation does it create? In Bartow County Board of Education v. Ray, 229 Ga.App. 333, 494 S.E.2d 29 (Ga.App.1997) a bus driver (Ray) was injured in a work-related motor vehicle collision. She received almost $40,000 in compensation benefits and sued the driver of the other vehicle in tort. The jury returned a general verdict for Ray for $175,000. Her employer sought to enforce its right of subrogation. The court held that the general verdict made it impossible to determine "what portion of the award applied to economic loss and what portion applied to noneconomic losses." 494 S.E.2d at 31. The third party defendant claimed that some of the plaintiff's damages were attributable to injuries sustained in a previous accident. The court concluded that the subrogation lien was properly denied, reasoning that "[g]iven that circumstance, reference to the general verdict alone ... cannot rule out the possibility that the jury reduced its award based on that defense." Id. What should an employer do to better protect its right of subrogation?

4.   Should the employers' lien attach to items of damages not covered by workers' compensation? Suppose the judgment or settlement of the third party action segregates items of recovery, such as pain and suffering. The prevailing view, based largely on the language of the subrogation statute, holds that the lien attaches to the entire judgment or settlement, regardless of how it is structured. E.g., United States v. Lorenzetti, 467 U.S. 167, 104 S.Ct. 2284, 81 L.Ed.2d 134 (1984) (lien under Federal Employees Compensation Act attaches to sums recovered in third party action limited to noneconomic damages); Barth v. Liberty Mut. Ins. Co., 212 Ark. 942, 208 S.W.2d 455 (1948) (third party suit limited to pain and suffering; subrogation lien attaches); Page v. Hibbard, 119 Ill.2d 41, 115 Ill.Dec. 544, 518 N.E.2d 69 (1987) (lien attaches to pain and suffering). Is the issue any different when the damages are earmarked for the employee's spouse's claim for lost consortium? See Page v. Hibbard, 119 Ill.2d 41, 115 Ill.Dec. 544, 518 N.E.2d 69 (1987) (lien does not attach to wife's recovery for loss of consortium); Rascop v. Nationwide Carriers, 281 N.W.2d 170 (Minn.1979) (subrogation does not extend to so much of a settlement as was earmarked for the wife's loss of consortium). How might this affect the structure of settlements? See Dearing v. Perry, 499 N.E.2d 268 (Ind.App.1986) (injured worker and spouse cannot negotiate settlement with third party that allocates substantial sums

to loss of consortium without participation of insurer); Nichols v. Cantara & Sons, 659 A.2d 258 (Me.1995) (although lien does not attach to portion of settlement earmarked for spouses' loss of consortium, such division must be clear in the settlement agreement). Courts have also split on whether the lien should attach to an award of punitive damages. Compare Mississippi Power Co. v. Jones, 369 So.2d 1381 (Miss.1979) (employer's lien attaches to "net proceeds" of third party action, including punitive damages) with Hodder v. Goodyear Tire & Rubber Co., 426 N.W.2d 826 (Minn.1988) (employer's right of subrogation does not reach amounts awarded as punitive damages in third party action).

5. Should a jury be permitted to apportion a percentage of fault against an employer in a tort suit brought by an employee against a third party? This question is of tremendous practical significance in those jurisdictions that have abrogated the rule of joint and several liability. *Castleman*, in reaffirming Ridings v. Ralph M. Parsons, Co., 914 S.W.2d 79 (Tenn.1996), reflects the view of a substantial number of states that juries should not apportion fault to the immune employer. E.g., Durniak v. August Winter and Sons, Inc., 222 Conn. 775, 610 A.2d 1277 (Conn. 1992); Varela v. American Petrofina Co., 658 S.W.2d 561 (Tex.1983); Seattle–First National Bank v. Shoreline Concrete Co., 91 Wash.2d 230, 588 P.2d 1308 (Wash. 1978). Several states have allowed juries to calculate the percentage of fault of the employer. E.g., Dietz v. General Electric Co., 169 Ariz. 505, 821 P.2d 166 (Ariz. 1991); Williams v. White Mountain Const. Co., 749 P.2d 423 (Colo. 1988); Powers v. Kansas Power & Light Co., 234 Kan. 89, 671 P.2d 491 (Kan. 1983); Sullivan v. Scoular Grain Co. of Utah, 853 P.2d 877 (Utah 1993). In these jurisdictions, should the employer's fault also effect its subrogation lien? See Utah Code Ann. § 36–1–62(5)(b) (subrogation claim is reduced if employer fault is 40% or more); Brabander v. Western Cooperative Electric, 248 Kan. 914, 811 P.2d 1216 (Kan. 1991) (subrogation claim reduced by employer's comparative percentage of responsibility multiplied by the amount of the subrogation claim).

We will return to the question of how to allocate responsibility among employees, employers and third parties in the next section. But first, consider how another common tort reform measure, modification of the collateral source rule, might affect an employer's right of subrogation.

SCHONBERGER v. ROBERTS

Supreme Court of Iowa, 1990.
456 N.W.2d 201.

Harris, Justice . . .

On July 22, 1987, the plaintiff, Rodney Schonberger, was driving west on U.S. Highway 30 in Carroll, Iowa. He had picked up his employer's mail and was headed to work when an accident occurred. Schonberger was preparing to turn into his employer's parking lot when he was struck by the defendant, Carroll John Roberts, who was driving a truck owned by defendant Buck Hummer Trucking, Inc.

As a result of the accident Schonberger was unable to return to work for three and one-half weeks. He suffered injuries to his neck, back, and knee. His medical bills totaled $7,625.40 at the time of trial. These expenses, as well as future medical expenses, are being reimbursed as part of the workers' compensation benefits Schonberger is receiving. Schonberger's injuries were permanent, and he will continue to incur medical expenses as a result of the accident.

Schonberger then brought this tort suit for his injuries which resulted in a jury verdict in his favor. The jury assessed eighty percent of the negligence to Roberts and twenty percent to Schonberger. It determined past damages were $18,000 and that future damages were $115,-000. The jury also found that Schonberger was not wearing a seat belt and determined the award should be reduced an additional two percent.

Although defendants assert the damage awards were excessive—a matter we later address—the preeminent issue in the case is defendants' challenge to a trial court ruling refusing to admit evidence. Defendants sought to introduce evidence regarding the payment of medical bills and other workers' compensation benefits to Schonberger. The trial court ruled the evidence inadmissible. This ruling is defendants' first assignment of error on appeal.

Since 1913 an Iowa statute, now Iowa Code section 85.22 (1989), has provided a right of indemnity to workers' compensation employers (or their insurers) for amounts paid under the Act from recoveries realized by the worker in tort actions for the same injuries. Without doubt Schonberger's workers' compensation insurer is entitled to be compensated from his recovery in this suit for any amounts paid to or for him on account of this injury. See, e.g., *Liberty Mut. Ins. Co. v. Winter,* 385 N.W.2d 529, 531–32 (Iowa 1986).

In 1987 the General Assembly amended the comparative fault Act, to include a special provision, Iowa Code at 668.14, also aimed at prohibiting an injured worker to recover twice for the same industrial injury. Both section 85.22 (in a limited situation) and section 668.14 (in a broader sense) are limitations on the collateral source rule, a principle long recognized as a part of our common law. Under the collateral source rule a tortfeasor's obligation to make restitution for an injury he or she caused is undiminished by any compensation received by the injured party from a collateral source. *Clark v. Berry Seed Co.,* 225 Iowa 262, 271, 280 N.W. 505, 510 (1938).

The trial court's rejection of the proffered evidence was in reaction to the obvious inconsistency between compelling the injured worker to pay back his benefits from his recovery and at the same time have the jury reduce his recovery because of them. To remedy this inconsistency the trial court rested its exclusion of evidence of workers' compensation benefits on Iowa Rule of Evidence 402 (all irrelevant evidence is inadmissible). Schonberger argues in support of the ruling in part by contending that the workers' compensation Act is, because of its design and regulated status, a state program. State programs are expressly exempted from the sweep of section 668.14.

I.   There are well-recognized limits to the extent to which courts will slavishly ascribe literal meanings to the words of a statute. Because legislative intent is the polestar of statutory interpretation

> it is clear that if the literal import of the text of an act is inconsistent with the legislative meaning or intent, or if such interpretation leads to absurd results, the words of the statute will be modified to agree with the intention of the legislature.

2A Sutherland, Statutory Construction at 46.07 (Sands 4th Ed. 1984) (citing *Graham v. Worthington,* 259 Iowa 845, 854, 146 N.W.2d 626, 633 (1966)).

In construing various statutes we have often applied this rule by refusing to attribute to the General Assembly an intention to produce an absurd result. *Harden v. State,* 434 N.W.2d 881, 884 (Iowa 1989).

. . .

A literal application of section 668.14 under the present circumstances would also lead to an absurd result. Under section 85.22 Schonberger must repay from his recovery his workers' compensation insurer any benefits he has received. The only conceivable purpose of informing the jury of those benefits is to invite the jury to reduce his recovery because of them. But, to any extent the jury does reduce the damage award because of the benefits, Schonberger is in effect paying, not once, but twice. We are convinced the legislature did not intend to call for this double reduction.

To avoid this unintended result we interpret the statute so as to deem its requirements satisfied when the requirements of section 85.22 are complied with. The case is remanded to district court for a proceeding in which it must be established that the proceeds of any recovery received by Schonberger are pledged to reimburse his workers' compensation insurer in accordance with Iowa Code section 85.22. Upon such a showing the judgment of the trial court shall stand as affirmed.

. . .

Affirmed and remanded.

All Justices concur except McGIVERIN, C.J., and NEUMAN, and ANDREASEN, JJ., who dissent.

McGIVERIN, C.J. (dissenting).

I respectfully dissent.

The majority opinion substantially sets aside the clear terms of Iowa Code section 668.14 and, as a practical matter, fully reinstates the judicially created collateral source rule by use of Iowa Rule of Evidence 402, at least in cases where collateral benefits are paid subject to a statutory right of subrogation.

Unlike the majority, I believe that the terms of section 668.14 can be respected without visiting inequity on Schonberger and others in his position.

. . .

Under the collateral source rule, damages awarded to a successful tort plaintiff against a tort defendant are not reduced by any sums which the plaintiff has received, or will receive, from another source (a "collateral source") on account of the plaintiff's injury. See *Groesbeck v. Napier,* 275 N.W.2d 388, 391–92 (Iowa 1979); 22 Am.Jur.2d Damages at 566 (1988). Typically these sources are insurance benefits of one form or another, such as the workers' compensation benefits in this case. As a common law rule of evidence, the collateral source rule bars evidence of such "collateral benefits." See, e.g., *Stewart v. Madison,* 278 N.W.2d 284, 293–94 (Iowa 1979). As a common law rule of damages, the rule provides that a damages award against a tort defendant will not be reduced by reason of such collateral benefits. See, e.g., *Rigby v. Eastman,* 217 N.W.2d 604, 609 (Iowa 1974).

One effect of the common law collateral source rule is that in cases where the plaintiff receives collateral benefits which are not paid subject to a right of subrogation in the payor, and also is compensated for the same injuries from a tort suit against the defendant, the plaintiff receives duplicate damages to the extent that the collateral benefits and tort recovery overlap. 22 Am.Jur.2d Damages at 566 (1988). This is commonly known as "double dipping" and is thought by tort defendants to unfairly overcompensate the plaintiff. Carlson, Fairness in Litigation or "Equity for All," 36 Drake L.Rev. 713, 719 (1987). The counterargument is that to allow collateral benefits to reduce the tort recovery would relieve the defendant of the consequences of tortious conduct. *Clark v. Berry Seed Co.,* 225 Iowa 262, 271, 280 N.W. 505, 510 (1938). As between the plaintiff and the tortfeasor, the common law deems it more just that the plaintiff profit from collateral benefits. See id.; 22 Am. Jur.2d Damages at 566 (1988).

On the other hand, in cases where collateral benefits are paid subject to a right of subrogation, the plaintiff is not double dipping because the subrogee will recover the collateral benefits out of the plaintiff's tort recovery from the defendant. Schonberger's case is a prime example of this situation because under Iowa Code section 85.22, the workers' compensation benefits he received will have to be repaid out of his tort recovery.

The majority of the study commission recommended that the legislature enact a statute which would allow the factfinder in a tort suit to hear evidence and argument on certain collateral benefits in cases where the plaintiff's losses were "replaced" or "indemnified" by a collateral source. Liability Report at 134. In those cases the factfinder would be allowed but not required to reduce the plaintiff's tort recovery by the amount of collateral benefits, presumably avoiding a double dipping situation whenever the factfinder took the collateral benefits into account. See id.; cf. Iowa Code at 147.136 ("damages awarded [in a medical malpractice action] shall not include actual economic losses ... to the extent that those losses are replaced or are indemnified [by certain collateral sources].")

II. The legislature apparently approved of this recommendation and enacted a statute—Iowa Code section 668.14—very similar to that recommended by the majority of the study commission. Iowa Code section 668.14 provides:

1. In an action brought pursuant to this chapter seeking damages for personal injury, the court shall permit evidence and argument as to the previous payment or future right of payment of actual economic losses incurred or to be incurred as a result of the personal injury for necessary medical care, rehabilitation services, and custodial care except to the extent that the previous payment or future right of payment is pursuant to a state or federal program or from assets of the claimant or the members of the claimant's immediate family.

2. If the evidence and argument regarding previous payments or future rights of payment is permitted pursuant to subsection 1, the court shall also permit evidence and argument as to the costs to the claimant of procuring the previous payments or future rights of payment and as to any existing rights of indemnification or subrogation relating to the previous payments or future rights of payment.

3. If evidence or argument is permitted pursuant to subsection 1 or 2, the court shall, unless otherwise agreed to by all parties, instruct the jury to answer special interrogatories or, if there is no jury, shall make findings indicating the effect of such evidence or argument on the verdict.

4. This section does not apply to actions governed by section 147.136. (Emphasis added.) For purposes of this opinion I will assume that workers' compensation benefits are not paid "pursuant to state or federal program" within the meaning of Iowa Code subsection 668.14(1).

Under subsection (1) of this statute, evidence of certain collateral benefits paid the plaintiff is clearly admissible. The statute says "the court shall permit" such evidence. Subsection (2) allows the plaintiff to counter this evidence by introducing evidence of the cost of obtaining the collateral benefits and evidence of any rights of subrogation relating to the benefits. The language could not be more clear. The evidence excluded by the trial court here should have been admitted.

By enacting section 668.14, the legislature intended to change the evidentiary portion of the judicially created collateral source rule. The statute allows the factfinder to consider all the facts concerning payment of the plaintiff's losses. Under the common law collateral source rule, the factfinder is not given all those facts.

III. I do not believe, however, that the legislature intended that a plaintiff in Schonberger's position should have his tort recovery reduced by the amount of collateral benefits and also have to repay the collateral benefits out of his remaining tort recovery. In this respect, I agree with the majority. In my view, however, the obvious inequity produced by such an application of section 668.14 is to be avoided in a jury case by appropriate jury instructions and interrogatories.

Under section 668.14 evidence of collateral benefits should be admitted pursuant to subsections (1) and (2). Then, pursuant to subsection (3), the jury should be instructed that if it finds liability it must find whether any of the plaintiff's claimed damages were or will be paid by collateral sources and, if so, how much. The jury should also be instructed to find whether any of those collateral sources are subrogated to the plaintiff's recovery from the tort defendant. Next, the jury should be instructed that if it finds that such rights of subrogation do exist, the plaintiff's recovery from the defendant may not be reduced by the amount of those collateral benefits. Finally, the jury should be asked to state the amount of economic losses of the plaintiff that were or will be paid by collateral sources and which are also included in its jury award to the plaintiff.

The result of this approach would be to prevent double dipping—which only occurs in cases where the plaintiff receives collateral benefits which are not subject to subrogation—but avoid the inequity correctly perceived by the majority. At the same time, the evidence called for by the legislature in section 668.14 would be admitted. Where the collateral benefits are not paid subject to rights of subrogation, it is left to the jury to prevent or allow double dipping.

. . .

The majority indicates that an absurd result, not intended by the legislature, would be reached by a literal application of section 668.14. When evidence made admissible in subsections 668.14(1) and 668.14(2) is accompanied by appropriate instructions pursuant to subsection 668.14(3), an absurd result is avoided and the entire statute is given effect.

V. I would reverse the trial court judgment and remand for a new trial on the issue of damages. The parties should be allowed to introduce evidence before the jury pursuant to Iowa Code section 668.14. Then the jury should be instructed appropriately and allowed to state the effect of such evidence on its verdict.

The court should work within the intent and language of section 668.14 rather than against it. Section 668.14 was the result of a studied decision by the legislature to abrogate the collateral source rule as a common law rule of evidence, and to prevent double dipping. The majority effectively refuses to acknowledge that fact. Therefore, I dissent.

Neuman and Andreasen, JJ., join this dissent.

Notes

1. More than a dozen states abolished or modified the collateral source rule as part of tort reform legislation enacted in the mid–1980's. See 4 Harper, James & Gray, The Law of Torts 25.22 n. 7 (2d ed. 1998 Cumulative

Supp.) for citations to and a discussion of this legislation. *Schonberger* illustrates the problem of reconciling a modification of the collateral source rule with the employer's right of subrogation. Both the right of subrogation and the abrogation of the collateral source rule have as a goal the prevention of a double recovery by the worker-plaintiff. There is widespread agreement, however, that both rules should not apply simultaneously. That is, the employee should not have a tort recovery reduced by the amount of workers' compensation received (modified collateral source rule) and then repay the employer for those benefits (subrogation) out of the reduced tort judgment. To prevent a double reduction of recovery, either the modified collateral source rule legislation or the employer's right of subrogation must yield to the other. Several jurisdictions do not apply the modified collateral source rule statute when the employer retains a right of subrogation. E.g., American Mut. Ins. Co. v. Decker, 518 So.2d 315 (Fla.App.1987); Rogers v. City of Detroit, 457 Mich. 125, 579 N.W.2d 840 (Mich. 1998); Western National Mutual Ins. Co. v. Casper, 549 N.W.2d 914 (Minn.1996); Nance by Nance v. Westside Hospital, 750 S.W.2d 740 (Tenn.1988).

2. Some tort reform statutes have been interpreted to disallow the employer's subrogation lien. In Toomey v. Surgical Services, P.C., 558 N.W.2d 166 (Iowa 1997) the employee's third party action was against a doctor for alleged malpractice committed in the course of treating a work related injury. Under an Iowa malpractice reform statute, damage awards in malpractice cases "shall not include" economic loss covered by workers' compensation. Under these circumstances, the court held that the employer's subrogation lien could not be enforced. Is *Toomey* consistent with *Schonberger*? See also, Graham v. W.C.A.B., 210 Cal.App.3d 499, 258 Cal. Rptr. 376 (Cal.App.1989) (pursuant to a medical malpractice reform statute, an employer's subrogation lien is eliminated when evidence of compensation benefits is admitted in the malpractice action).

From a policy standpoint, is it better to reduce the tort award against the third party by amounts recovered in workers' compensation, or to not reduce the tort award and reimburse the employer or its insurer from the tort recovery?

3. Recall from note 8 following *Byrd* that some states require an employee to elect between seeking compensation benefits and suing his employer in tort. Should an employee have to elect between seeking compensation benefits from his employer and bringing a tort claim against a third party? In a majority of states, an employee may seek remedies against the employer under workers' compensation and against a third party in tort. Historically, a few states required that an employee elect between claiming workers' compensation benefits and pursuing a tort claim against a third party. Under a "strict election," a worker who guessed wrongly about which was the appropriate remedy could end up with either. E.g., Ott v. St. Paul Union Stockyards, 178 Minn. 313, 227 N.W. 47 (Minn. 1929) (unsuccessful workers' compensation claim precluded later third party action). The few states that require an election today have adopted doctrine that allows employees who are unsuccessful in pursuing one remedy to seek the other. For a general discussion of these issues, see A. Larson and L. Larson, Larson's Workers' Compensation Law § 73 (1998).

SECTION 5. ADJUSTMENT OF RIGHTS OF THIRD PARTIES AND NEGLIGENT EMPLOYERS

LAMBERTSON v. CINCINNATI CORP.

Supreme Court of Minnesota, 1977.
312 Minn. 114, 257 N.W.2d 679.

SHERAN, CHIEF JUSTICE.

Cincinnati Corporation, defendant and third-party plaintiff in a personal injury/product liability action, appeals from a judgment of the district court which awarded a worker $34,000 in damages but denied defendant manufacturer contribution from an employer which was partly at fault for the accident. We reverse in part and remand with instructions.

Cincinnati is the manufacturer of a press brake, a large machine used for bending metal. The brake has a large vertical ram which moves up and down. Dies are placed on the ram and on the bed of the machine, and metal to be bent is placed between the ram and the bed. When the ram comes down onto the metal, a bend, or brake, is made in the metal at the point where the die on the ram matches the die in the bed. The movement of the ram is controlled by the operator by means of a single foot pedal at the base of the machine.

Cincinnati sold a press brake to Hutchinson Manufacturing and Sales, Inc., plaintiff's employer. On April 25, 1972, plaintiff was assisting a co-employee in the operation of the press brake. The co-employee was controlling the foot pedal, and plaintiff was placing long metal strips between the ram and the bed and removing them after they had been bent. As the ram was being raised after one cycle, a piece of metal which had been bent fell to the side of the bed opposite to the side where plaintiff was working. Plaintiff reached through the jaws of the machine to retrieve the piece of metal, but his co-employee had kept his foot on the pedal, thus permitting the ram to descend again, crushing plaintiff's arm between the ram and the bed.

After recovering workers' compensation from Hutchinson, plaintiff brought this action against Cincinnati. Plaintiff testified that he had never operated the press brake before and did not know it was capable of double cycling, i.e., continuing through another cycle without the ram's stopping at the top. He testified that he knew he should not have put his arm between the jaws, but that he did not know that his co-employee still had his foot on the pedal or that the ram would descend again before he could retrieve the piece of metal.

Plaintiff introduced expert testimony and safety rules and regulations from which the jury could have found that certain safety devices and features could have been installed on the press brake at the time of its manufacture and sale to Hutchinson in 1967, and that such devices would have prevented the accident. Sufficiency of this evidence to support a finding of negligence on the part of Cincinnati is not contested on this appeal. Cincinnati does, however, ask for indemnity from Hutchinson based on events occurring after 1967.

In 1969, after representatives of Cincinnati viewed the particular uses to which the press brake was put at Hutchinson, Cincinnati offered to Hutchinson (at Hutchinson's expense) two changes in the machine: (1) Operation by two or more palm buttons or foot switches; (2) automatic stoppage of the ram at the top of the cycle—i.e., no double cycling. These changes apparently were declined. In 1971, Cincinnati sent out a sales pamphlet to all owners of its press brakes describing a Waveguard safety device, an electronic sensing device designed to deter foreign matter in the press and stop the press if such matter were present. Hutchinson did not order or install such a device. There was testimony by plaintiff's expert from which one could conclude that the absence of two of these offered features—the automatic stop and the electronic sensor—constituted defects in the machine that were causally related to this accident.

When plaintiff's left forearm was crushed in the press brake, both bones were broken in such a way that the lower part of the arm was at a 90–degree angle to the upper part. It took 5 to 6 minutes to reverse the press and extricate his arm. He reported considerable pain. The fractures were surgically set and he was hospitalized initially for 10 days. During the succeeding 2 months his cast had to be removed and replaced 5 times so that the wound could be cleaned and X-rays taken. The fractures did not unite properly, and subsequent surgery was necessary. The bones were reset, using steel plates and screws. Plaintiff remained in a cast until February 1973, received medical for pain, and underwent physical therapy to regain the use of his arm. He was unable to work for a year after the accident and sustained an approximately $6,000 wage loss plus $2,600 in medical expenses.

The case was submitted to the jury on special verdict on a theory of negligence. The jury found all parties causally negligent and apportioned their comparative negligence as follows: Plaintiff—15 percent; Cincinnati—25 percent; Hutchinson—60 percent. The jury found damages of $40,000. The trial court ordered judgment against Cincinnati for $34,-000, the full amount of the verdict less 15 percent for plaintiff's negligence, and denied Cincinnati's claim for contribution or indemnity from Hutchinson.

* * *

4. The final and most important issue in this case concerns the claim of Cincinnati, a third-party tortfeasor, for indemnity or contribution from Hutchinson, plaintiff's employer. This issue is a troublesome one and has generated a substantial amount of debate in the bench and bar of this and other states. Arthur Larson, a leading commentator on workmen's compensation law, has called the controversy surrounding indemnity and contribution against employers in third-party actions "[p]erhaps the most evenly-balanced controversy in all of compensation law." 2A Larson, Workmen's Compensation Law, § 76.10. The essence

of the controversy is this: If contribution or indemnity is allowed, the employer may be forced to pay his employee—through the conduit of the third-party tortfeasor—an amount in excess of his statutory workers' compensation liability. This arguably thwarts the central concept behind workers' compensation, i.e., that the employer and employee receive the benefits of a guaranteed, fixed-schedule, nonfault recovery system, which then constitutes the exclusive liability of the employer to his employee. See, Minn.St. 176.031. If contribution or indemnity is not allowed, a third-party stranger to the workers' compensation system is made to bear the burden of a full common-law judgment despite possibly greater fault on the part of the employer. This obvious inequity is further exacerbated by the right of the employer to recover directly or indirectly from the third party the amount he had paid in compensation regardless of the employer's own negligence. Minn.St. 176.061, subds. 5, 6(d). See, *Nyquist v. Batcher,* 235 Minn. 491, 51 N.W.2d 566 (1952). Thus, the third party is forced to subsidize a workers' compensation system in a proportion greater than his own fault and at a financial level far in excess of the workers' compensation schedule.

The even balance in this controversy results from conflicts among the policies underlying workers' compensation, contribution/indemnity, and comparative negligence and the fault concept of tort recovery . . .

[T]he interests of the respective parties in the workers' compensation system are therefore as follows: The employer has a primary interest in limiting his payment for employee injury to the workers' compensation schedule and a secondary interest in receiving reimbursement when a third party has caused him to incur obligations to his employee. See, *Nyquist v. Batcher, supra.* The employee has a primary interest in receiving full workers' compensation benefits and, to the extent a third party has caused him injury, a common-law recovery from that third party.

In contrast, the third party's interest is that of any other co-tortfeasor—to limit its liability to no more than its established fault. This interest is vindicated through contribution or indemnity. Contribution and indemnity are variant common-law remedies used to secure restitution and fair apportionment of loss among those whose activities combine to produce injury. As this court stated in *Hendrickson v. Minnesota Power & Light Co.,* 258 Minn. 368, 370, 104 N.W.2d 843, 846 (1960):

.   .   .

"Contribution is the remedy securing the right of one who has discharged more than his fair share of a common liability or burden to recover from another who is also liable the proportionate share which the other should pay or bear. Contribution rests upon principles of equity. Indemnity is the remedy securing the right of a person to recover reimbursement from another for the discharge of a liability which, as between himself and the other, should have been discharged by the other. Indemnity is generally said to rest upon contract, either express or implied. However, there are numerous exceptions and situations in which a contract is implied by law, and contract, therefore, seems to furnish too narrow a basis. In the modern view, principles of equity furnish a more satisfactory basis for indemnity.

"Contribution and indemnity are variant remedies used when required by judicial ideas of fairness to secure restitution. Although similar in nature and origin and having a common basis in equitable principles, they differ in the kind and measure of relief provided. Contribution requires the parties to share the liability or burden, whereas indemnity requires one party to reimburse the other entirely. Differing thus in their effect, these remedies are properly applicable in different situations. Contribution is appropriate where there is a common liability among the parties, whereas indemnity is appropriate where one party has a primary or greater liability or duty which justly requires him to bear the whole of the burden as between the parties."

When one tortfeasor has paid or is about to pay more than his equitable share of damages to an injured party, he has an interest in obtaining indemnity or contribution from his fellow tortfeasors.

Comparative negligence, which is embodied in Minn.St. 604.01 and was substantially borrowed from our sister state of Wisconsin in 1969, introduces yet another dimension to the third-party tortfeasor's predicament. By abolishing the defense of contributory negligence in cases where plaintiff's percentage of total causal negligence is less than defendant's, it permits an injured workman to recover against the third party more frequently. In addition, Minn.St. 604.01, subd. 1, specifies a rule for contribution:

". . . When there are two or more persons who are jointly liable, contributions to awards shall be in proportion to the percentage of negligence attributable to each, provided, however, that each shall remain jointly and severally liable for the whole award."

Thus, a jointly liable tortfeasor has an interest, at least where the other tortfeasors are solvent and otherwise available for contribution, in contributing no more to the plaintiff's recovery than the percentage of negligence attributable to him.

. . .

In *Hendrickson v. Minnesota Power & Light Co.*, 258 Minn. 368, 104 N.W.2d 843 (1960), this court denied recovery to a third-party tortfeasor seeking contribution or indemnity from a negligent employer. The court held: (1) There was no right of contribution because there was no common liability to the employee, i.e., the employer was not liable in tort to the employee because of the exclusive-remedy provision of our workers' compensation law; (2) there was no right of indemnity because the facts did not fall within one of the exceptional situations in which indemnity is allowed, unlike the facts in *Lunderberg*.

In the years following *Hendrickson,* this court also upheld an award of indemnity against an employer who had breached contractual duties to observe safety rules and an express contract of indemnity. In *Keefer v. Al Johnson Construction Co.,* 292 Minn. 91, 100, 193 N.W.2d 305, 310 (1971), we commented that the negligence of the third party was imputed or vicarious as compared with the active negligence of the employer. But we reaffirmed, in *Froysland v. Leef Bros., Inc.,* 293 Minn. 201, 197 N.W.2d 656 (1972), the rule of *Nyquist v. Batcher,* 235 Minn. 491, 51 N.W.2d 566 (1952), and held that the employer's contributory negligence was not available to the third party as a defense, since the rights of the employee in the third-party action were primary. *Froysland* did not involve any claim of indemnity.

. . .

Cincinnati initially seeks indemnity from Hutchinson chiefly on the ground that it offered safety devices to Hutchinson which, if installed on the press brake, could have prevented the accident. The difficulty with this argument lies in the jury's unchallenged finding that Cincinnati was 25–percent negligent in the first instance, when it placed its press brake in the stream of commerce without certain kinds of safety devices. Since the independent acts of negligent manufacture and sale by Cincinnati and refusal of safety devices by Hutchinson combined to produce plaintiff's injury, liability should be apportioned between them, not shifted entirely to one or the other. Therefore, if Cincinnati is entitled to any remedy, that remedy is contribution.

Cincinnati's claim for contribution, however, confronts two further problems: (1) Our holding in *Hendrickson v. Minnesota Power & Light Co.,* 258 Minn. 368, 104 N.W.2d 843 (1960), that contribution is not available because of the absence of a common liability; and (2) the policy interest of the employer in paying no more than his workers' compensation liability because of an employee injury and the other conflicting policies and statute discussed earlier in this opinion.

Considering the first of these problems, we cannot find any continuing persuasive force in the reasoning of the court in *Hendrickson.* ... While there is no common liability to the employee in *tort,* both the employer and the third party are nonetheless liable to the employee for his injuries; the employer through the fixed no-fault workers' compensation system and the third party through the variable recovery available in a common law tort action. Contribution is a flexible, equitable remedy designed to accomplish a fair allocation of loss among parties. Such a remedy should be utilized to achieve fairness on particular facts, unfettered by outworn technical concepts like common liability.

The second problem confronting Cincinnati's claim is a more formidable one. The equitable merit in Cincinnati's claim is plain: It has been forced to bear the entire burden of plaintiff's recovery despite the fact that it was only 25–percent negligent and has a 60–percent employer joined in the action and available for contribution. In contrast, granting contribution would result in substantial employer participation in its employee's common-law recovery despite the exclusive-remedy clause. This problem is, in large part, a legislative one which demands a comprehensive solution in statutory form.

* * *

While the opinions of other jurisdictions must be read with caution on this issue because of different statutes and concepts of recovery in negligence cases, we have found direction in the approach taken by the Pennsylvania Supreme Court. That court has allowed contribution from the employer up to the amount of the workers' compensation benefits. *Maio v. Fahs,* 339 Pa. 180, 14 A.2d 105 (1940); *Brown v. Dickey,* 397 Pa. 454, 155 A.2d 836 (1959). See, also, *Stark v. Posh Construction Co.,* 192 Pa.Super. 409, 162 A.2d 9 (1960). This approach allows the third party to obtain limited contribution, but substantially preserves the employer's interest in not paying more than workers' compensation liability. While this approach may not allow full contribution recovery to the third party in all cases, it is the solution we consider most consistent with fairness and the various statutory schemes before us. If further reform is to be accomplished, it must be effected by legislative changes in workers' compensation third-party law.

For the reasons expressed above, the judgment is reversed and the case is remanded with instructions to grant contribution against Hutchinson in an amount proportional to its percentage of negligence, but not to exceed its total workers' compensation liability to plaintiff.

Affirmed in part, reversed in part and remanded with instructions.

Notes

1. *Lambertson* addresses the allocation of financial responsibility for workplace injuries between the tort and workers' compensation systems. This issue is germane to all types of third party tort actions, but is most acute in the products liability field. Consider the following commentary:

[S]ystemic differences [between workers' compensation and tort create] an incentive structure that explains why workplace product liability claims tend to be "high stakes" litigation. As explained by Professor Viscusi:

From the worker's standpoint there is little incentive to pursue a third-party suit unless these stakes are substantial. Collateral source rules prevent the courts from lowering a tort award because the injured worker has received workers' compensation benefits. The worker, however, cannot obtain a double recovery since in such contexts the employer or the insurer who paid the claim is generally surrogated to the worker's tort claim, up to the amount of workers' compensation benefit.... Thus, the injured party's financial incentive to file a product liability claim will be diminished by the extent of the workers' compensation benefits that have been already received. As a result, the cases for which litigation is worthwhile will tend to be only those with larger losses. [W. Kip Viscusi, *The Interaction Between Product Liability and Workers' Compensation as Ex Post Remedies for Workplace Injuries*, 5 J.L. Econ. & Org. 185, 187 (1989).]

This profile is supported by the limited available data. A frequently cited study from the 1970s estimates that while approximately 11% of all product liability suits are filed by injured workers, these cases account for more than 40% of total product liability payments. A 1980's study found that workplace product liability claims account for 60% of all payments exceeding $100,000. Workplace product liability claims are four times as likely to involve fatalities and twice as likely to go to trial than are other types of product liability claims.

Product-related injuries also appear to be "high stakes" from a workers' compensation perspective. This conclusion may be drawn inferentially from the limited available data regarding costs of claims. Employers in all states may obtain reimbursement of workers' compensation benefits paid to injured employees form tort damages the employee recovers from third parties, such as product manufacturers. This reimbursement procedure is generally referred to as a right of subrogation. Product-related injures for which subrogation is sought constitute a small percentage of all workers' compensation claims, but are the second largest category of claim in which subrogation rights are asserted. The average total cost for claims with subrogation is more than twice that of claims without subrogation.

Thomas A. Eaton, Revisiting The Intersection of Workers' Compensation and Product Liability: An Assessment of a Proposed Federal Solution to an Old Problem, 64 Tenn. L. Rev., 881, 884–86 (1997) (footnotes omitted).

With this background in mind, consider what adjustments should be made to achieve a "proper" allocation of injury costs between the workers' compensation and tort systems.

For other discussions of this topic see, William A. Drier, Injuries to Production Workers: Reform of the Workers' Compensation Product Liability Interface, 48 Rutgers L. Rev. 813 (1996); Weiler, Workers' Compensation and Product Liability: The Interaction of a Tort and a Non–Tort Regime, 50 Ohio State L.J. 825 (1989); Weisgall, Product Liability in the Workplace: The Effect of Workers' Compensation on the Rights and Liabilities of Third Parties, 1977 Wis.L.Rev. 1035.

2. Contrary to the result reached in *Lambertson,* most courts hold that a third party tortfeasor is not entitled to contribution from a negligent employer. E.g., Thompson v. Stearns Chemical Corp., 345 N.W.2d 131 (Iowa 1984); Diamond Int'l. Corp. v. Sullivan and Merritt, Inc., 493 A.2d 1043 (Me.1985); Downie v. Kent Products, Inc., 420 Mich. 197, 362 N.W.2d 605 (1984), clarified 421 Mich. 1202, 367 N.W.2d 831 (1985); Glass v. Stahl Specialty Co., 97 Wash.2d 880, 652 P.2d 948 (1982). See Nicholas B. Clifford, Jr., Kotecki v. Cyclops Welding Corp.: The Efficacy of a Limited Contribution Rule and Its Effect on Good Faith Settlement, 68 U.Chi.-Kent L. Rev. 479, 492 n. 84 (1992) (citing cases from 45 jurisdictions); Edward J. Kionka, Recent Developments in the Law of Joint and Several Liability and the Impact of Plaintiff's Employer's Fault, 54 La. L. Rev. 1619, 1630–35 (1994) (state by state summary). The primary justification for this result is that the exclusive remedy doctrine immunizes employers from tort liability to their

employees. Since the employer is not a tortfeasor vis a vis the injured worker, it shares no common liability with the third party upon which to base a claim for contribution. This traditional "no contribution" rule combined with the employers' right of subrogation effectively allocates all the costs of workplace injuries to the third party tortfeasor, even when the employer is more culpable. E.g., Stephenson v. R.A. Jones & Co., Inc., 103 N.J. 194, 510 A.2d 1161 (1986) (manufacturer who was held to be 5% negligent could not recover contribution from employer who was 95% at fault). Is a third party entitled to contribution when the employer intended to injure the employee? See Taylor v. Academy Iron & Metal Co., 36 Ohio St.3d 149, 522 N.E.2d 464 (1988) (only an employee can invoke the intended injury exception to the exclusive remedy doctrine).

3. New York and Illinois formerly permitted tortfeasors to bring a third party claim against the negligent employer for contribution based on the proportionate fault of the parties. See, Skinner v. Reed–Prentice Division Package Machinery Co., 70 Ill.2d 1, 15 Ill.Dec. 829, 374 N.E.2d 437 (1977); Dole v. Dow Chemical Co., 30 N.Y.2d 143, 282 N.E.2d 288, 331 N.Y.S.2d 382 (1972). Unlimited contribution exposes an employer to damages that greatly exceed its liability under workers' compensation. Does the Dole–Skinner approach give appropriate weight to the employer's interest in limited liability reflected in the exclusive remedy doctrine?

Illinois subsequently adopted a rule akin to *Lambertson* under which the right of contribution against the employer is limited to the amount of compensation paid. Kotecki v. Cyclops Welding Corp., 146 Ill.2d 155, 166 Ill.Dec. 1, 585 N.E.2d 1023 (Ill. 1991). In 1995, the Illinois legislature adopted a system of direct reduction discussed in note 4 below. Under these rules, the plaintiff's tort recovery is reduced by the amount of compensation benefits and the employer's subrogation lien is reduced by the same amount. 740 Ill. Comp. Stat. Ann § 100/3.5, 820 Ill. Comp. Stat. Ann. § 305/5. For a history of the Illinois law see Michael A. Bilandic, Workers' Compensation, Strict Liability, and Contribution in Illinois: A Century of Progress?, 83 Ill. B.J. 292 (1995). In 1996, New York amended its statute to limit the *Dole* rule to cases involving "grave injuries" defined in terms of death, loss of certain extremities, and other specific conditions. N.Y. Work. Comp. Law § 11. For background on the New York legislation, see Martha T. McCluskey, the Illusion of Efficiency in Workers' Compensation "Reform," 50 Rutgers L. Rev. 657, 902–908 (1998).

4. Note that the combination of contribution and subrogation leads to money changing hands several times, and thus high transaction costs. Some jurisdictions address this inefficiency by directly reducing the tort recovery against the third party by the amount of compensation benefits paid by the negligent employer. E.g., Witt v. Jackson, 57 Cal.2d 57, 17 Cal.Rptr. 369, 366 P.2d 641 (1961); Barnett v. Eagle Helicopters, Inc., 123 Idaho 361, 848 P.2d 419 (Idaho, 1993); Runcorn v. Shearer Lumber Products, 107 Idaho 389, 690 P.2d 324 (1984); Hunsucker v. High Point Bending & Chair Co., 237 N.C. 559, 75 S.E.2d 768 (1953). Note that this approach still requires an adjudication of employer negligence. Some commentators have proposed a system that would reduce the plaintiff's tort recovery against the third party by the amount of the workers' compensation award in all cases, while at the same time eliminating the employer's right of subrogation. See 2 American Law

Institute, Reporters' Study on Enterprise Liability 197–98 (1991); Thomas A. Eaton, Revisiting the Intersection of Workers' Compensation and Product Liability: An Assessment of a Proposed Federal Solution to an Old Problem, 64 Tenn. L. Rev. 881, 908–911 (1997); Model Uniform Product Liability Act § 114, 44 Fed.Reg. 62,714 (1979). The direct reduction of the third party tort recovery would leave the worker fully compensated and reduce the transaction costs associated with contribution and subrogation. Is it fair to deny the non-negligent employer a right of subrogation? Is this fairness objection blunted by the no-fault nature of the employer's basic obligation under workers' compensation? What effect would such a system have on safety incentives for employers and third parties?

5. The manufacturer in *Lambertson* also sought indemnity from the employer. Indemnity, in contrast with contribution, shifts the entire loss to one party. A successful claim for indemnity by a third party would render the employer ultimately liable for both compensation benefits and tort damages. Also in contrast with contribution, a claim for indemnity is not based on the concept of a common liability. An indemnity claim against an employer is grounded on the employer's breach of some duty owed directly to the third party, rather than the employer's breach of duty owed to the injured worker. The exclusive remedy doctrine is less of a conceptual obstacle to indemnity since the third party's claim against the employer rests upon an independent duty. The employer's separate obligation to indemnify the third party may be express or implied. Virtually all courts allow third parties to enforce unambiguous express contractual rights of indemnity against employers. E.g., Goodyear Tire & Rubber Co. v. J.M. Tull Metals Co., 629 So.2d 633 (Ala.1993); General Tel. Co. of the Southeast v. Trimm, 252 Ga. 95, 311 S.E.2d 460 (1984); Union Pacific R.R. v. Kaiser Agricultural Chem. Co., 229 Neb. 160, 425 N.W.2d 872 (1988); Barsness v. General Diesel & Equip. Co., 422 N.W.2d 819 (N.D.1988); Redford v. City of Seattle, 94 Wash.2d 198, 615 P.2d 1285 (1980).

Claims for implied indemnity are generally less successful, however. Several opinions emphasize that one who is at fault is not entitled to indemnity for its own acts. E.g., Woodruff Constr. Co. v. Barrick Roofers, 406 N.W.2d 783 (Iowa 1987); Ramos v. Browning Ferris Indust., 103 N.J. 177, 510 A.2d 1152 (1986); Mulder v. Acme–Cleveland Corp., 95 Wis.2d 173, 290 N.W.2d 276 (1980). In other cases the relationship between the employer and the third party has not been deemed sufficiently "special" to give rise to an implied obligation of indemnity. In particular, courts have ruled that the purchaser-employer does not owe the manufacturer a duty of care in use of its products. E.g., Decker v. Black & Decker Mfg. Co., 389 Mass. 35, 449 N.E.2d 641 (1983) (refusing to imply a duty of care that "flows upstream from the purchaser [of a product] to the manufacturer"); Steinmetz v. Bradbury Co., Inc., 618 F.2d 21 (8th Cir.1980) (no implied obligation under Iowa law for purchaser-employer to indemnify the manufacturer for the purchaser's failure to instruct his employee in the safe operation of the machine). For a critique of this general approach, see Comment, Indemnity Under Workers' Compensation: Recognizing a Special Legal Relationship Between Manufacturer and Employer, 1987 Duke L.J. 1095. If the third party and the employer are found to stand in a special legal relationship, however, the third party may be entitled to implied indemnity from the employer. E.g., Tucson Elec. v. Swengel–Robbins Constr., 153 Ariz. 486, 737 P.2d 1385 (App.1987) (special relationship created by statute); Lunderberg v. Bierman, 241 Minn. 349, 63 N.W.2d 355 (1954) (owner of car who was liable for employee's injury under financial responsibility statute was entitled to implied indemnity from negligent employer; bailor-bailee relationship).

6. In recent years there have been several efforts to enact federal product liability legislation. One of these bills would bring about significant change in existing state practices. As discussed in note 2 above, in the vast majority of states workplace product manufacturers cannot recover contribution from negligent employers, but employers have a subrogation lien against employee's product liability recovery against the manufacturer. The combination of these rules channels money from the tort system in to the workers' compensation system. The proposed federal law would reverse this flow of money. It would reduce the product manufacturer's tort liability by the amount of compensation benefits paid to the worker in cases where there is clear and convincing evidence that the injury was caused by the fault of either the employer or a co-employee. It would also reduce the employer's subrogation lien by the same amount. Common Sense Product Liability Reform Act of 1996, H.R. 956, 104th Cong. § 111 (1996). The combination of these rules would result in compensation benefits reducing tort liability. Is a federal solution to the question of how to adjust the interests of product manufacturers, employers and employees appropriate? Is this proposed federal solution an improvement over the existing state practices? Why would the proposed federal solution differ from the one adopted by the vast majority of states? For commentary on this proposed legislation see Thomas A. Eaton, Revisiting The Intersection Of Workers' Compensation And Product Liability: An Assessment Of A Proposed Federal Solution To An Old Problem, 64 Tenn. L. Rev. 881 (1997).

7. Commentators have proposed a variety of solutions to the problems created by the intersection of the tort and workers' compensation systems. On the one extreme are proposals to eliminate third party actions entirely. Workers' compensation would become the employee's sole remedy. See, Don Dewees et. al., Exploring the Domain of Accident Law 432 (1996); Oliver, Once is Enough: A Proposed Bar of the Injured Employee's Cause of Action Against a Third Party, 58 Ford.L.Rev. 117 (1990); O'Connell, Supplementing Workers' Compensation Benefits in Return for an Assignment of Third–Party Tort Claims—Without an Enabling Statute, 56 Tex.L.Rev. 537 (1978); Berstein, Third Party Claims in Workers' Compensation: A Proposal To Do More With Less, 1977 Wash.U.L.Q. 543. On the other extreme are proposals to substantially eliminate the exclusive remedy doctrine thus subjecting the employer to tort claims by employees and third parties. Haas, On Reintegrating Workers' Compensation and Employers' Liability, 21 Ga.L.Rev. 843 (1987); Lynch, The Clash Between Products Liability and the Workers' Compensation Exclusivity Rule: The Negligent Employer and the Third–Party Manufacturer, 50 Ins.Couns.J. 35 (1983). Other commentators appear to accept the exclusive remedy doctrine and third party suit as givens and explore ways to reduce the friction at the intersection of the two systems. See, Larson, Third Party Action Over

Against Workers' Compensation Employer, 1982 Duke L.J. 483; Epstein, Coordination of Workers' Compensation Benefits With Tort Damages, 13 Forum 464 (1977); Davis, Third–Party Tortfeasors' Rights Where Compensation–Covered Employers Are Negligent—Where Do Dole and Suspan Lead?, 4 Hofstra L.Rev. 571 (1976). Having considered the interests of the various parties, what is your ideal allocation of workplace injury costs?

Chapter 12

CONFLICT OF LAWS

INTRODUCTION TO THIS CHAPTER

Prior to the advent of workers' compensation laws, personal injury claims by employees against employers typically "sounded" in tort, and courts using traditional choice of law conventions applied the law of the place of injury (lex loci delicti). Soon after the states began enacting workers' compensation laws, cases arose that presented questions as to whether the law of one state or that of another was to be applied. Such a case might involve an injury that occurred outside the state of the forum, the issue being whether to apply the statute of the forum or that of the state where the injury took place. It might involve an injury that occurred within the state of the forum, but for some reason the claim was made that the law of a state other than the forum should be applied.

The emergence of such questions was inevitable in view of the freedom with which American industry crosses state lines. Not infrequently an employee is hired in one state to perform work in one or more other states where he may suffer injury. There may be additional "foreign elements" in the case; e. g., the residence of the employee may be in a third state, the principal place of business of the employer in a fourth, or the parties may have agreed in the original contract of employment that the law of a specified state should be applied to a work injury.

An illustration is found in Carroll v. Industrial Commission of Illinois, 205 Ill.App.3d 885, 150 Ill.Dec. 763, 563 N.E.2d 890 (1990). Thomas Carrol was hired in 1966 as an over-the-road truck driver at the Chicago terminal of Consolidated Freightways. At the time of hiring, Carroll was a resident of Illinois. Carroll moved to Michigan in 1969 but continued to commute to work at the Chicago terminal. In 1970, petitioner was assigned to the North Platte, Nebraska terminal where he remained for seven years. In 1978, he was transferred to the Idaho terminal. On March 8, 1988, Carroll was injured in Kent, Washington while trying to unhook a dolly from a trailer. Consolidated began payments to Carroll pursuant to the terms of the Idaho workers' compensation law. Carroll then filed a claim under the more favorable terms of the Illinois Workers' Compensation Act claiming that Illinois jurisdiction was proper because his contract of hire was executed in Illinois. An arbitrator and the Industrial Commission determined that Illinois jurisdiction was proper and awarded benefits under that act. The Circuit Court reversed and the Appellate Court of Illinois affirmed and dismissed the claim holding that Illinois jurisdiction did not exist.

It is not difficult to envision some of the legal and practical possibilities created by such cases. In the early days of workers' compensation, one of the states involved might have a compensation act while the other state had an employer's liability act or was still dealing with work injuries on the basis of the common law of master and servant. Now that all states have adopted workers' compensation acts, there may be significant differences in the statutory provisions or case law governing types of employment covered, conditions of compensability, amount and character of benefits, requirements for notice, or periods of limitation. There is almost certain to be some difference in the procedure for enforcement of the obligation to pay compensation. As a result of these differences, the decision as to which law is to be applied in a given case may result in considerable advantage or disadvantage to one party or the other. If the law of more than one state is applied, the possibility of multiple recovery for the employee and multiple liability for the employer arises; such multiple recoveries and liabilities may be under two or more workers' compensation acts or may be a combination of compensation award and common law damages. If the law of *neither* state is applied, there is danger that the employee will receive no compensation at all for a work injury for which each of the states involved would normally provide compensation.

At the time workers' compensation acts came into existence, "choice of law" problems were not new to the jurisprudence of the United States. The federal system of separate states in this country had caused the American judiciary from the beginning to be confronted with cases involving this kind of question. Solutions had been found usually by resorting to that rather vague and flexible body of ideas that had evolved over the centuries on the Continent and in England, usually classified under the heading "conflict of laws." When workers' compensation cases involving similar questions came under consideration, it was natural for the courts to turn to conflicts doctrines with which they were familiar, and the early cases reflect this approach.

As time went on, however, difficulties appeared and substantial differences of opinion developed. One reason was that, in making the primary characterization, different courts made different assumptions as to the juridical nature of the liability created by the workers' compensation laws. Some regarded it as a species of tort liability and applied conflicts rules taken from torts cases. Others treated compensation liability as having its basis in contract and applied the conflicts rule normally used in contracts cases. Neither assumption was well founded and the results that followed application of orthodox conflicts rules were often unsatisfactory. Furthermore, it became apparent that more than the purely private rights of the parties had to be taken into account. In a workers' compensation case, the general interest of society in the well being of its members is, perhaps, more prominently involved than it is in most other types of controversy. Hence, established choice of law doctrines growing out of conventional private litigation might be quite unsuited to the workers' compensation situation.

These and other considerations prompted many legislatures to intervene with special statutory provisions to supersede court-made rules or to forestall court action and thus implement desired state policy in this area. As a result, in all but a few states the shape of the law on this issue is determined by a statute or by an intermixture of statutory provisions and judicial decisions. From a national viewpoint, the pattern that has emerged from these efforts over the last half century is far from harmonious. The theories and terms of the statutes differ substantially and the decisions applying them have not provided much uniformity. Certain categories may be set out as has been done in this chapter for purposes of study but they are only rough subdivisions. Each state's law has its own individual features.

It goes without saying that in order to apply the law of the forum it is essential that the employer be subject to service of process in that state so that personal jurisdiction can be acquired by the local court or administrative agency.

If it is concluded that the workers' compensation law of another state is applicable and that the law of the forum is not, the employee's claim is usually dismissed and jurisdiction will not be exercised by the local court or tribunal to enforce the rights that may have accrued under the workers' compensation law of another state. The reason for this policy is obvious: almost all workers' compensation laws provide special administrative machinery and procedure for enforcing rights of employees under the act. There may be no right at all until this administrative remedy has been pursued, but even if the right could be said to exist it is ordinarily considered impracticable for the courts or tribunals of one state to enforce the provisions of the workers' compensation law of another state. Logan v. Missouri Valley Bridge & Iron Co.,157 Ark. 528, 249 S.W. 21 (1923); Larson's Workers' Compensation Law, Matthew Bender, Vol. 9, Section 84.21 (1998). Also, pursuant to 28 U.S.C.A. Section 1445 (c), federal courts may not entertain removal of claims which arise under state workers' compensation laws. The result may be different if the foreign statute is designed to be administered by the courts. Texas Pipe Line Co. v. Ware, 15 F.2d 171 (8th Cir.1926); Watkins v. Jim Walter Homes, Inc., 666 F.Supp. 102 (S.D.Miss.1987), ("... where the workers' compensation law in question provides for its enforcement in the courts of that state, the liability created is enforceable in the courts of another state."). And see Ferguson v. Ram Enterprises, Inc., 900 S.W.2d 19 (Tenn.1995).

In a few states, however, the workers' compensation law provides that an employee who is hired outside the state may enforce rights acquired under the law of the state of hire before the forum state's commission or courts, provided that the rights are capable of being reasonably determined and dealt with by the local bodies. (Arizona Revised Stat. § 23–904B(1998); Hawaii Revised Stats. § 386–6 (1998); 21 Vermont Stat. Ann. § 620 (1998).)

Of course, if proceedings have been had under the workers' compensation law of one state and have resulted in an enforceable award in that state, such award may be sued upon in another state on much the same basis that applies in the case of a suit on a judgment of a foreign state. In re Phillips, 200 N.Y.S. 639, 206 A.D. 314 (1923); Chicago R. I. & P. Ry. Co. v. Schendel, 270 U.S. 611, 46 S.Ct. 420, 70 L.Ed. 757 (1926); Dennison v. Payne, 293 F. 333 (2d Cir.1923); Hagens v. United Fruit Co., 135 F.2d 842 (2d Cir. 1943). But cf. Kindle v. Cudd Pressure Control, 792 F.2d 507 (5th Cir.1986).

Another aspect of this general issue in workers' compensation cases in the United States is created by the provision that appears in Article IV, Section 1 of the Constitution of the United States stating that "Full faith and credit shall be given in each state to the public acts * * * of every other state." The statutes of a state, such as its workers' compensation statute, are "public acts" within the meaning of this provision. Consequently, in a specific case, a question may exist as to whether a particular choice of law rule, whether statutory or common law, is valid in the light of the Constitutional requirement.

With respect to maritime and waterfront employees, certain special issues exist because of federal jurisdiction of admiralty and maritime affairs. Also, employees of interstate rail carriers are covered by federal law. The relationship between state workers' compensation acts and federal statutes as they come together in these fields often raise difficult conflict issues.

SECTION 1. APPLICATION OF FORUM STATE'S LAW TO OUT–OF–STATE INJURIES

Claimant is employed by a State A employer to solicit orders in State B. While doing so claimant is killed in a street accident that meets all requirements of compensability. Are claimant's survivors entitled to an award of compensation under the law of State A?

JUDICIAL THEORIES

The early reaction of American courts confronted with this kind of problem was to invoke the "tort theory" which assumed that workers' compensation was merely a statutory substitute for the common law remedy of the employee for the employer's negligence. On this assumption, the conventional conflicts approach was that the law of the place of injury governed, and accordingly State A's workers' compensation law was deemed inapplicable to injuries occurring outside the boundaries of the state. In these early decisions, the courts were very concerned with the implications that the extraterritorial application of workers' compensation statutes would pose for federalism and for the sovereignty of the individual states.

Cases denying coverage for out-of-state injuries focused on geographical boundaries and the equal treatment of all who were within them. They also expressed great concern for the autonomy of individual states. In so doing, the courts discussed the ability of the states to govern affairs within their borders and to embody their chosen public policy within their statutes. See, e.g., In re Gould, 215 Mass. 480, 102 N.E. 693 (1913) ("If employees and employers from different states carry their domiciliary personal injury law with them into other jurisdictions, confusion would ensue in the administration of the law, and at least the appearance of inequality among those working under similar conditions."); North Alaska Salmon Co. v. Pillsbury, 174 Cal. 1, 162 P. 93 (1916) ("It will not be supposed that the legislature of this state undertook to pass a law which would trench upon the sovereign powers of any other jurisdiction. But the Workmen's Compensation Act would embody such attempt if it were construed in such manner as to create, to the exclusion of any other liability, a liability to pay for injuries received in another jurisdiction."); and Union Bridge and Construction Co. v. Industrial Commission, 287 Ill. 396, 122 N.E. 609 (1919), ("No law of this state has any effect as a law, by its own force, beyond the territorial limits of the state ... but a law effective in this state as such may create rights and liabilities arising from acts occurring outside of the state ... There have been decisions in other states that compensation is to be awarded for injuries occurring beyond the territorial limits of the state, but they have been based upon provisions of the acts showing such a legislative intention.").

The courts which found State A's workers' compensation statutes did apply to out-of-state accidents approached the questions of state sovereignty and control over internal public policy from the vantage point of the contract of employment. The courts employing this "contract theory" examined the expectations of the employer and the employee that were contained within that agreement. As in the "tort theory" cases which denied State A's workers' compensation coverage to out-of-state injuries, the courts in these "contract theory" decisions devoted considerable attention to the issue of predictability of results. Kennerson v. Thames Towboat Co., 89 Conn. 367, 94 A. 372 (1915); Marsdale v. Same, 89 Conn. 367, 94 A. 372 (1915)("The parties to each contract [of employment] had accepted the provisions of ... our Workmen's Compensation Act. As a consequence, the Act became a part of these contracts ... [Our Act] intended that the employee would know his liability in this regard ... If our Act intends its contracts of employment to include compensation for injuries occurring only within our jurisdiction, it manifestly defeats its own ends."); Industrial Commission of Colorado v. Aetna Life Insurance Co., 64 Colo. 480, 174 P. 589 (1918) ("... if we are to determine, in the absence of any provision of the statute to the contrary, that the doctrine of lex loci contractus does not govern, it will be to destroy the very spirit and purpose of the law as it affects the employer, the employee, and the public welfare.... Thus, the employer, the employee, his dependents and the public all have been deceived and cheated, because forsooth the accident occurred beyond the imaginary line that marks the boundary of the Commonwealth, though it happened within the line of employment.")

While this line of judicial reasoning achieves the desired result in most cases, it embodies a considerable element of fiction and does not stand careful analysis. The early workers' compensation law in many states was elective but in others compulsory. Today the reverse is true. Where the laws are compulsory it is unrealistic to say that the parties to the employment contract "agree" to come under it. Even when many laws were elective, the choice, as the Arizona court said, was comparable to the choice given to one who is told "your money or your life." Ocean Accident & Guarantee Corp. v. Industrial Comm., 32 Ariz. 275, 279, 257 P. 644 (1927).

Another judicial theory for dealing with this question is the "business localization test" enunciated in early Minnesota decisions. See, e.g., Chambers v. District Court of Hennepin County, 139 Minn. 205, 166 N.W. 185 (1918). In that case, the Supreme Court of Minnesota said:

> "A basic thought underlying the compensation act is that the business or industry shall in the first instance pay for accidental injuries as a business expense or a part of the cost of production. It may absorb it or it may put it partly or wholly on the consumer if it can. The economic tendency is to push it along just as it is to shift the burden of unrestrained personal injury litigation. When a business is localized in a state there is nothing inconsistent with the principle of the compensation act in requiring the employer to compensate for injuries in a service incident to its conduct sustained beyond the borders of the state. The question of policy is with the legislature. It may enact an elective compensation act bringing such result if it chooses. In the case before us the business of the employer was localized in the state. What the employee did, if done in Minnesota, was a contribution to the business involving an expense and presumably resulting in a profit. It was not different because done across the border in North Dakota. It was referable to the business centralized in Minnesota."

Under this test neither the place of contract nor the place of injury was controlling; the worker may have been hired in Iowa and injured in Wisconsin, but if the business was localized in Minnesota, the workers' compensation law of the latter was to be applied. Severson v. Hanford Tri–State Airlines, 105 F.2d 622 (8th Cir.1939). Conversely, if the business was localized in another state the Minnesota court would not have applied Minnesota law. See, e.g., De Rosier v. Craig, 217 Minn. 296, 14 N.W.2d 286 (1944), ("The business of constructing the airport was entirely localized in South Dakota. The contract of employment was made there, and the injury occurred in that state. Consequently, we have a typical situation for the application of this rule restated by the

American Law Institute: 'No recovery can be had under the Workmen's Compensation Act of a State if neither the harm occurred nor the contract of employment was made in the state.' Restatement, Conflict of Laws, Section 400.... We have, in some cases, treated one or the other element of the rule as not of controlling importance; but, never, so far as we can find, have we gone contrary to both elements combined.")

The common law test probably most suitable to the purpose of the workers' compensation system commonly goes under the name of the "place of employment" test. It relates the applicability of local law to the question whether the status of employer-employee existed within the state. Various factors are taken into account: the place of contract, the residence of the worker, any changes of residence made to accommodate work, whether there is a fixed or transitory location at which the work is performed, all play a part in the ultimate result. The approach was well stated by the New York Court of Appeals in Cameron v. Ellis Constr. Co., 252 N.Y. 394, 169 N.E. 622 (1930). The employer was a Massachusetts corporation engaged in building a highway in New York. For this purpose it operated a sand pit in Canada just across the border. The worker was a resident of Canada and was employed to work at the sand pit where he was injured in the course of his employment. The New York court said:

"Nothing in the statute suggests that the State of New York has attempted to stretch forth its arm to draw within the scope of its own regulations the relations of employer and employee in work conducted beyond its borders. Hazardous employment here is regulated by the Workmen's Compensation Law; hazardous employment elsewhere, though connected with a business conducted here, does not come within its scope. Even where the contract of employment is made within the State, we have said that the State 'does not attempt to regulate the duty of foreign employers in the conduct of their business within foreign jurisdictions.' * * *The principle is not, however, limited to foreign employers. The statute imposes upon every employer, foreign or domestic, the duty to secure to his workmen compensation for injuries, wherever sustained, arising out of and in the course of employment located here. Absence of a workman from the State in the course of such employment does not interrupt that duty where the duty has been imposed upon the employer under the statute. It has not been imposed upon the employer in connection with employment located outside the State. The test in all cases is the place where the employment is located.

"When the course of employment requires the workman to perform work beyond the borders of the State, a close question may at times be presented as to whether the employment itself is located here. Determination of that question may at times depend upon the relative weight to be given under all the circumstances to opposing considerations. The facts in each case, rather than juristic concepts, will govern such determination. Occasional transitory work beyond the State may reasonably be said to be work performed in the course of employment here; employment confined to work at a fixed place in another State is not employment within the State, for this State is concerned only remotely, if at all, with the conditions of such employment. Such illustrations may indicate the manner in which the test should be applied, we do not now attempt a more definite classification intended to cover all the varying circumstances that may enter into the question in other cases."

See also Ala. Code Section 25–5–35(b)(1992); Todacheene v. G & S Masonry, 116 N.M. 478, 863 P.2d 1099 (1993); and Conwood Corp. v. Guinn, 201 Ga.App. 43, 410 S.E.2d 315 (1991)(Corporation was located in Tennessee and claimant had office in his Georgia home. ". . . in addition to storing samples and damaged goods in his home office, claimant conducted company business from his home office. . . . [and] deducted the cost of his home office on his federal income tax return. . . . [Employer] shipped goods to claimant's home office [and] claimant began and ended each workday from his home office. . . . Claimant generally covered his entire 13–county area in a six-week period, spending approximately 14 to 15½ days in Tennessee stores and 13 to 14½ days in Georgia stores." Held, "we cannot conclude that the ALJ's determination that Georgia was the principal locality of the employment relationship was erroneous.").

The contract of employment may provide that the law of a particular state is to be applied to work injuries. In a number of states, the statutes expressly authorize this type of agreement. The Missouri Act was applied in Woodward v. J. J. Grier Co., 270 S.W.2d 155 (Mo.App.1954). (Compare to Alaska Packers, infra, where the U.S. Supreme Court found that California did not "exceed its constitutional power by prohibiting any stipulation exempting the employer from liability for the compensation prescribed by the California statute."). In the absence of a statute authorizing such a contract the courts have been inclined to disregard such provisions when it appears either that an existing jurisdiction was sought to be displaced, Gotkin v. Weinberg, 2 N.J. 305, 66 A.2d 438 (1949), ("Neither the implied intention of the parties respecting the law which was to govern their contract . . . nor any express intention . . . can vitiate the statute laws and declared public policy of this state."); Hartford Acc. & Indem. Co. v. Welker, 75 Ga.App. 594, 44 S.E.2d 160 (1947), or when the effect of the contract would have been to create a jurisdiction in a state where it did not otherwise exist. Daniels v. Trailer Transport Co., 327 Mich. 525, 42 N.W.2d 828 (1950), (". . . the legislature has established the boundary, and limits the jurisdiction, of the Commission for out-of-state injuries . . . the responsibilities and benefits provided under the act cannot be enlarged or diminished by agreement of the parties. It follows that the jurisdiction of the Commission cannot be extended by agreement.").

STATUTORY PROVISIONS

Most of the states have statutes that deal in one way or another with the question whether the workers' compensation law is to be applicable to out-of-state injuries. The provisions of these laws may differ widely, but a modicum of uniformity was achieved following the publication of the recommendations of the 1972 National Commission on State Workmen's Compensation Laws. See in this regard Larson's Workers' Compensation Law, Matthew Bender, Vol.9, Sections 87.11 and 87.12 (1998). The promulgation of the "model act" by the Council of State Governments (see Appendix B herein) further facilitated uniformity among the dozen or so states that adopted it wholly or in a modified form.

One type of statute does no more than state in general terms that the local law is applicable to out-of-state injuries, leaving it to the courts to work out any restrictions that may be necessary or advisable. See, e.g., 152 Mass. Gen. Laws Ann. 152 Section 26 (1998).

Most statutes, however, designate specifically the circumstances under which it is intended that the law will be applied to an out-of-state injury. An examination of these laws, reveals that in formulating them the legislatures have drawn heavily on the basic theories and tests that the courts originally worked out, although they frequently combine two or more theories or tests in a fashion that brings a result quite different from the original judge-made law in that state.

One type of state statute embodies the "contract theory." Under such a statute the single fact that the contract of employment was made in that state is enough to make the local law applicable to an out-of-state injury, sometimes with the limitation that the contract may provide otherwise. See, e.g., 85 Okla. Stats. Ann. Section 4 (1998).

The statutes of a number of states are oriented basically towards the place of contract approach, but some additional fact or facts must appear to warrant application of the local law to an out-of-state injury. Thus, in California it must also appear that the injured employee's residence was in California. See West's Ann. Cal. Labor Code, § 5305 (1998). See also, Janzen v. WCAB, 61 Cal.App.4th 109, 71 Cal.Rptr.2d 260 (1997), (Contract made over the telephone between employer located in Wyoming and employee located in California for work to be done exclusively in Wyoming; held, contract was formed where offeree, employee, was located; and because employee was a California resident at time contract was formed, California's workers' compensation law applied to industrial accident that occurred in Wyoming). A similar provision appears in the Michigan law, Mich.Comp.Laws Ann. § 418.845 (1998), but the Supreme Court of Michigan has construed the statute in such a way as to eliminate the requirement. Roberts v. I. X. L. Glass Corp., 259 Mich. 644, 244 N.W. 188 (1932); Wearner v. West Michigan Conference of Seventh Day Adventists, 260 Mich. 540, 245 N.W. 802 (1932); and Boyd v. W.G. Wade Shows, 443 Mich. 515, 505 N.W.2d 544 (1993).

In Georgia, O.C.G.A. Section 34–9–242 (1998) not only requires that the employment contract have been made within the state, but also that either the employer's place of business or the injured employee's residence be within the state and that the employment was for services not to be performed exclusively outside the state. See Guinn v. Conwood Corp., 185 Ga.App. 41, 363 S.E.2d 271 (1987), (The first inquiry is whether the employment was principally located in Georgia. If so, the worker is not employed "elsewhere than in this state" and the statutory section does not apply. Only if the employment is located primarily outside of Georgia does the issue of where the contract was signed arise.).

Some states have statutes which provide that if the employee has been hired within the state (or is regularly employed there), the local law shall apply to an out-of-state injury, provided that the accident occurs within six months after leaving the state, unless the employer has filed a notice electing to extend the coverage for a greater period of time. See, e.g., Colo.Rev.Stats., Section 8–41–204 (1993); see also Moorhead Machinery & Boiler Co. v. Del Valle, 934 P.2d 861(Colo.App.1996), (Time limit of six months is meant to limit the protection of the statute to those employees who are temporarily out of the state); and see Utah Code Ann. Section 34A–2–405 (1998).

Another type of statute makes the place of regular employment the basic element in determining the applicability of the local law to out-of-state injuries, sometimes as an alternative to the requirement concerning the place of the employment contract. See Ariz. Rev. Stats. § 23–904A(1998); and Minn. St. Ann.Section 176.041 Subds. 2 and 3 (1998).

Lastly, over a dozen states have patterned their statutes on the Workmen's Compensation and Rehabilitation Law as promulgated by the Council on State Governments ("Model Act"). See Appendix B, Sec. 7; and see, e.g., Alaska Stat. Section 23–30.011 (1998); and 77 Purdon's Pa. Stat. Ann. Section 411.2 (1998).

SECTION 2. APPLICATION OF FORUM STATE'S LAW TO INJURIES OCCURRING WITHIN THE FORUM STATE

Claimant is employed in State A by a State A employer to make freight deliveries throughout the United States. While passing through State B, in the course of employment, claimant was seriously injured in a traffic accident. May claimant recover under State B's workers' compensation law?

JUDICIAL THEORIES

The workers' compensation law of the state in which the injury occurred will be applicable to the vast majority of work injuries occurring within the boundaries of the state of the forum, but there may be cases from time to time in which a plausible argument is possible that the law of some other state ought to govern. If the state of the forum is one that has no statute expressly dealing with this question, its court is likely to resolve the issue in accordance with its earlier judge-made conflicts rule. Perhaps the state's statute dealing with out-of-state injuries may reflect a basic conflicts policy that will serve as a guide.

In a jurisdiction where the general approach was to resolve this issue by the "contract theory," the logical result would be that the law of the state of injury would not apply if the contract of employment was made outside that state. A number of early decisions have reached this conclusion. Hall v. Industrial Comm., 77 Colo. 338, 235 P. 1073 (1925); Hopkins v. Matchless Metal Polish Co., 99 Conn. 457, 121 A. 828 (1923); but see Cleveland v. U.S. Printing Ink, 218 Conn. 181, 588 A.2d 194 (1991), (Court noted that while early Connecticut cases followed the "contract theory," they would extend that theory when necessary to promote the interests of employers and employees. The court noted that Connecticut ultimately jettisoned this approach in favor of one suggested by the Restatement (Second) Conflict of Laws Section 181 and the 1972 recommendations of the National Commission on State Workmen's Compensation Laws.). The *Cleveland* case was effectively reversed by Conn. St. Ann. Section 31–275(9)(A)(i) (1997); and see Kluttz v. Howard, 228 Conn. 401, 636 A.2d 816 (1994) where the court discusses the effect of the legislative change upon cases such as *Cleveland*. See also Proper v. Polley, 259 N.Y. 516, 182 N.E. 161 (1932). If the basic approach of the jurisdiction had been the "tort theory," the logical result is that the local law, being the law of the place of injury, is applied. Bagnel v. Springfield Sand & Tile Co. 144 F.2d 65 (1st Cir. 1944) (Workers' Compensation Act of Massachusetts held applicable to injury occurring in that state even though contract of employment made in New York; court relied heavily on Gould's case 215 Mass. 480, 102 N.E. 693 (1913), generally regarded as the leading case for the "tort theory").

Most courts in reaching a decision on this issue (whether on the basis of a common law or statutory conflicts rule) take cognizance of the extraterritorial effect of the law of any other states having a significant interest in the case, and of the possibility or likelihood that by nonapplication of the law of the state of injury the worker may be denied any compensation, or may be seriously embarrassed in recovering the compensation due. If it appears that either of these consequences may ensue, courts feel free to apply the local law despite possible logical difficulties. Hopkins v. Matchless Metal Polish Co., 99 Conn. 457, 121 A. 828 (1923); Weaver v. Missouri Comp. Comm., 339 Mo. 150, 95 S.W.2d 641 (1936); and United States Cas. Co. v. Hoage, 77 F.2d 542 (D.C.Cir.1935). See also Cleveland v. U.S. Printing Ink, supra, and Larson's Workers' Compensation Law, Matthew Bender, Vol. 9, Section 87.24–87.25 (1998). A notable example to the contrary is found in House v. State Industrial Accident Commission, 167 Ore. 257, 117 P.2d 611 (1941). In that case, the employer had its main automobile dealership in southern Oregon just north of the California border. It had a branch business in California about six miles south of the Oregon border. Decedent, a resident of California, was employed for about four months as a used car salesman at the Oregon site and was then made manager of the California branch. He resided in California. Some time later while decedent was on his way to Portland to attend a salesman's meeting, he was killed in an accident that occurred in Oregon. The widow filed a claim first in California, but that state rejected jurisdiction because it required the place of contract to be in California. When she brought proceedings in Oregon that state's Supreme Court held that Oregon's statute did not apply to the accident because Oregon then required the place of regular employment to be in Oregon. Thus claimant was left without any remedy. The *House* case was unique in its apparent disregard of consequences for the sake of a somewhat slavish adherence to its own conflicts doctrines. The Oregon statute has been amended since the date of the House decision. See O.R.S. Section 656.126 (1997). Whether or not the amended statute would provide coverage under the facts of *House* is still unclear.

The court in Toebe v. Employers Mut. of Wausau, 114 N.J.Super. 39, 274 A.2d 820 (1971) resolved a difficult issue in a novel manner. Claimant was an employee of a Minnesota trucking concern injured in New Jersey. He claimed compensation in New Jersey and received an award, but the employer never paid it. Claimant then sued the employer's insurance carrier in New Jersey. The carrier defended on the ground that its policy limited its liability to awards arising under Minnesota law. The Minnesota statute of limitations had expired, and under its law the right ceased to exist. The Superior Court ordered the New Jersey compensation authorities to fashion an award which would reflect what the claimant would have recovered under Minnesota law for which the carrier would then be held liable. The Supreme Court of New Jersey ordered that under the doctrine of *forum non conveniens* "the amount of plaintiff's claim was to be determined under Minnesota law in a proceeding in the State of Minnesota under terms insuring a judgment on the merits in that state." When advised that the terms of the order had been carried out, the Supreme Court reversed the judgment of the Superior Court, 63 N.J. 198, 306 A.2d 66 (1973). Contrast, Philyaw v. Fulton, Inc., 569 So.2d 787 (Fla.App.1990) where the court found, "There is no provision in [Florida's workers' compensation statute] Chapter 440 in the nature of a *forum non conveniens* having jurisdiction to dismiss the claim in deference to the more substantial contact the claimant and the employer may have with another state."

STATUTORY PROVISIONS

The question whether the local workers' compensation law is to be applied to cases involving injuries occurring within the state is expressly answered in the affirmative in some states by the statute itself. The Missouri Act, for example, provides in material part as follows: "This chapter shall apply to all injuries received and occupational diseases contracted in this state, regardless of where the contract of employment was made...." 18 Vernon's Ann. Mo. Stat. Section 287.110 (1998). The Hawaii statute provides, "The provisions of this chapter shall be applicable to all work injuries sustained by employees within the territorial boundaries of this state." Hawaii Rev. Stat. Ann. Section 386–6 (1998). In some other states, coverage of an injury within the state is excluded if specified conditions exist. Montana has a rather elaborate provision for such an exclusion if it appears that the employee when injured was only temporarily in Montana doing work for a nonresident employer; that the employee and employer are bound by the workers' compensation act or similar act of the other state; that act applies to them when they are in Montana; and there is reciprocity of recognition of extraterritorial provisions and coverage between that state and Montana. Montana Code Ann. Sec. 39–71–402(2) (1997), and see West's Ann. Cal. Labor Code Section 3600.5 (b) (1997). The Ohio statute provides that if the employee is a non-resident and is protected by the workers' compensation law or similar law of another state, the law of that state shall cover him for injuries suffered while he is temporarily in Ohio and the Ohio law shall not be applicable. Baldwin's Ohio Rev. Code Ann. § 4123.54 (1998). States which have adopted the "Model Act" provisions regarding extraterritorial coverage often adopt that Act's terms regarding injuries which occur within the state in employment by an employee who is domiciled in another state. For example, Washington's statute begins as follows: "If a worker or beneficiary is entitled to compensation under this title by reason of an injury sustained in this state...." This language does not seem to mandate coverage of injuries simply because they occur within the state, but such an interpretation is plausible. See "Model Act," Appendix B, Section 7(c); and see, e.g., Idaho Code Section 72–219 (1998); 19 Del. Code Section 2303(c) (1998); and West's Rev. Code of Wash. Ann. Section 51.12.120 (1998).

RESTATEMENT OF THE LAW SECOND–CONFLICTS

§ 181. Permissible Range of Territorial Application

A State of the United States may consistently with the requirements of due process award relief to a person under its workmen's compensation statute, if

(a) the person is injured in the State, or

(b) the employment is principally located in the State, or

(c) the employer supervised the employee's activities from a place of business in the State, or

(d) the State is that of most significant relationship to the contract of employment with respect to the issue of workmen's compensation under the rule in §§ 187–188 and 196, or

(e) the parties have agreed in the contract of employment or otherwise that their rights would be determined under the workmen's compensation act of the State, or

(f) the State has some other reasonable relationship to the occurrence, the parties and the employment

SECTION 3. EFFECT OF FOREIGN WORKERS' COMPENSATION LAW ON LOCAL COMMON LAW ACTION

Today all states have workers' compensation laws. As Chapter 11 demonstrates, each of the state's acts contain exclusive remedy provisions granting the employer immunity from common law tort actions filed by injured employees. This immunity was a cornerstone of the original workers' compensation compromise as the U.S. Supreme Court recognized in its 1917 decision in *New York Central v. White*, supra Chapter 2. It remains a cornerstone today. It is, therefore, somewhat of a rarity to see employees suing their employers in common law tort actions.

There are, however, exceptions to the general immunity rule which are recognized to one degree or another in the various jurisdictions. These exceptions take different shape and form in the states sometimes because of variations in the statutory immunity provisions and sometimes because of judicial interpretations of them.

Areas where exceptions to the general immunity of the employer have developed are addressed in Chapter 11, supra. These include situations where the employer has intentionally harmed the employee or where, perhaps, statutory employers are accorded different immunity than immediate employers. Also, states may create tort remedies by statute despite the existence of workers' compensation coverage. See, e.g., West's Cal. Labor Code Section 4558 (1997). In the early days of workers' compensation when a significant number of state acts were elective, employers or employees could opt out of coverage of the workers' compensation system. When that occurred, the employer was subject to a common law tort action even though the compensation law of another state may have been applicable. See, e.g., Davis v. Morrison–Knudsen Co. Inc., 289 F.Supp. 835 (D.C.Or.1968), (To have decided otherwise would have been to contradict Oregon public policy which gives employers the choice whether or not to be bound by the workers' compensation act). *Davis* was cited with approval in Garcia v. American Airlines, 12 F.3d 308 (1st Cir.1993). Today, states in specific instances allow an employer or employee to elect exemption from coverage. See, e.g., O.C.G.A. 34–9–2.1 (1998)(corporate officers may exempt themselves from coverage).

These state to state variations create the possibility that conflict of laws issues will arise. This prospect is enhanced by virtue of employers conducting their businesses across state lines and across international boundaries. For example, in Spelar v. American Overseas Airlines, Inc., 80 F.Supp. 344 (S.D.N.Y. 1947) a flight engineer who was a resident of New York was killed in Newfoundland on an international flight in the crash of an airplane operated by a Delaware corporation that had its principal place of business in New York. It was held that the case was governed by the New York workers' compensation law rather than by the wrongful death statute of Newfoundland.

As a general rule, when employees sue employers in tort in one jurisdiction that jurisdiction will not override the workers' compensation exclusive remedy provisions of the laws of another state. See, e.g., Barnhart v. American Concrete Steel Co., 227 N.Y. 531, 125 N.E. 675 (1920), (Both employee and employer were residents of New Jersey and both had chosen to come under New Jersey's elective workers' compensation law. Employee's estate sued employer in New York. In denying the claim for wrongful death, the court focused on the voluntary selection made by the parties. "The plaintiff's intestate, having the right to accept or reject the statutory scheme of compensation, exercised the option to accept it and contracted accordingly with the defendant. Such contract became binding upon him and, like any other valid contract, enforceable in the State of New York, unless [contrary] to its public policy."); Mitchell v. J. A. Tobin Constr. Co., 236 Mo.App. 910, 159 S.W.2d 709 (1942); The Linseed King, 52 F.2d 129 (2d Cir.1931). See also Larson's Workers' Compensation Law, Matthew Bender, Vol. 9, Section 88.11 (1998).

A typical example of a case involving a conflict of laws issue in the context of the statutory employer setting is Busby v. Perini Corp., 110 R.I. 49, 290 A.2d 210 (R.I. 1972). That case also offers an example of a court following the general rule mentioned in the paragraph above. In Busby, the claimant, a resident of Massachusetts, was an employee of a subcontractor, a Massachusetts corporation, and was injured at work on a construction project in Rhode Island of which defendant was general contractor. The employment contract was made in Massachusetts. Massachusetts law barred tort actions against general contractors; Rhode Island law did not. Recognizing that it was not circumscribed by the Federal Full Faith and Credit Clause (see Section 4 below) the court affirmed summary judgment in defendant's favor. After pointing out that various courts have used different legal routes to the same result, the court expressed approval of the Restatement of the Law, Second, Conflict of Laws, Section 184 which is set forth below. For an article considering, inter alia, statutory employer immunity in the conflict of laws context see, Sedler, Interest Analysis, Party Expectations and Judicial Method in Conflict Torts Cases: Reflections on Cooney v. Osgood Machinery, 59 Brooklyn Law Review 1323 (1994).

§ 184. Abolition of Right of Action for Tort or Wrongful Death

Recovery for tort or wrongful death will not be permitted in any state if the defendant is declared immune from such liability by the workmen's compensation statute of a state under which the defendant is required to provide insurance against the particular risk and under which (a) the plaintiff has obtained an award for the injury, or (b) the plaintiff could obtain an award for the injury, if this is the state (1) where the injury occurred, or (2) where employment is principally located, or (3) where the employer supervised the employee's activities from a place of business in the state, or (4) whose local law governs the contract of employment under the rules of §§ 187–188 and 196.

While the principles set forth in the above-quoted section of the Second Restatement are quite consistently applied in cases in which the defendant is claimant's employer, or is a principal contractor in the position of a statutory employer, they will not be applied if the defendant's immunity is obnoxious to the public policy of the state of the forum. Thus, in Hutzell v. Boyer, 252 Md. 227, 249 A.2d 449 (1969), the injured worker sued his fellow employee in Maryland for an accident that occurred in that state while they were riding in an employer-owned truck in which they went to and from their Maryland homes to a paving job in Virginia. The employer was a Virginia corporation. The Maryland Workmen's Compensation Commission had denied a claim for want of jurisdiction. No claim was filed in Virginia, although it appears likely that a successful claim could have been made there. The Virginia compensation law extended immunity from tort liability to fellow-employees; the Maryland law did not. In affirming a judgment for plaintiff the Maryland court said it was unable to make a finding that the immunity was not obnoxious to that state's public policy. It disagreed with the decision in Stacy v. Greenberg, 9 N.J. 390, 88 A.2d 619 (1952), in which the opposite result was reached. See also, Powell v. Erb, 349 Md. 791, 709 A.2d 1294 (1998).

Where a third-party tortfeasor is subject to a common law suit in the forum state, State A, by an employee who has recovered workers' compensation from the employer in State B, the employer's subrogation rights under State B's workers' compensation act may be affected by State A's different treatment of the substantive and procedural aspects of the subrogation claim. Compare Hile v. Liberty Mutual Ins. Co., 281 Ala. 388, 203 So.2d 110 (1967), (holding workers' compensation insurance carrier was entitled to reimbursement under the terms of the Wisconsin act), with Middle Atlantic Transp. Co. v. New York, 206 Misc. 535, 133 N.Y.S.2d 901 (1954), (refusing to give extraterritorial effect to Michigan law). See also Larson's Workers' Compensation Law, Matthew Bender, Vol.9, Section 88.23 (1998).

Another problem area may be encountered when employees recover workers' compensation from their employers and then pursue a common law action against a third-party tortfeasor. In such a case, the third-party tortfeasor may seek to implead the employer to recover contribution or indemnity. The employer's immunity or lack thereof with respect to the contribution or indemnity claim may vary from one jurisdiction to another. See, e.g., Lamb v. McDonnell–Douglas, et. al., 712 F.2d 466 (11th Cir. 1983), where Lamb was an employee of Delta Airlines based in Chicago, Illinois. The flights on which she served originated from O'Hare Airport in Chicago. During Lamb's tenure with Delta, she underwent periodic training in Atlanta, Georgia. In one such training session, she was engaged in an emergency evacuation simulation using an evacuation slide manufactured by Sargent Industries, a California corporation. While using the slide, she suffered a fall leading to serious injuries. Even though she was eligible to receive workers' compensation benefits from Delta in either Illinois or Georgia, she chose to file her claim in Illinois. She later brought a product liability and negligence claim against Sargent in the U. S. District Court for the Northern District of Georgia based on diversity of citizenship. Sargent filed a third-party complaint against Delta alleging negligence and seeking contribution and indemnity. Under Georgia law, an employer who had paid workers' compensation benefits to an employee was immune from such a third-party claim. In Illinois, however, no immunity was recognized. Sargent argued that because Lamb had filed her workers' compensation claim in Illinois that state's law should control. The district court granted Delta's motion for summary judgment based on Georgia's conflict rule which looked to the law of the place of the injury. The Court of Appeals for the Eleventh Circuit affirmed.

SECTION 4. FULL FAITH AND CREDIT

The first serious attempt to determine the jurisdictional limitations on state workers' compensation laws imposed by the Full Faith and Credit Clause (Article 4, § 1, U.S. Constitution) was in Bradford Electric Co., Inc. v. Clapper, 286 U.S. 145, 52 S.Ct. 571, 76 L.Ed. 1026 (1932). Clapper, a resident of Vermont, entered into a contract of employment in that state with defendant, a Vermont corporation; he was a lineman for emergency service. He was sent on a temporary basis into New Hampshire to a substation to replace certain fuses. He was killed there while performing his job. Plaintiff, administratrix, was a citizen and resident of New Hampshire. She brought an action for damages under the New Hampshire Employers' Liability and Workmen's Compensation Act which then allowed an election of remedies. The Vermont Workmen's Compensation Law prohibited any action for damages for a work injury, whether it occurred within or outside of Vermont. Defendant moved to dismiss on the ground that the Federal District Court was bound to apply Vermont law under the Full Faith and Credit Clause. Ultimately, a divided Supreme Court concluded that the Full Faith and Credit Clause compelled dismissal of the action. Justice Stone in his concurring opinion would have placed the result on the basis of comity and thus avoided the full faith and credit issue. He wrote:

> * * * "The Full Faith and Credit Clause has not hitherto been thought to do more than compel recognition, outside the state, of the operation and effect of its laws upon persons and events within it." (Citations omitted.)

In four cases during the next 23 years, the Supreme Court revised the Clapper doctrine to the point of obliteration. Alaska Packers Ass'n. v. Industrial Acc. Comm., 294 U.S. 532, 55 S.Ct. 518, 79 L.Ed. 1044 (1935), involved a non-resident worker who entered into a contract of employment in San Francisco with an employer doing business in California. He agreed to work in Alaska during the salmon packing season and to be bound by Alaska's workers' compensation law. He was injured in Alaska and after his return to California he received an award of compensation under the workers' compensation law of California. The award was upheld, the Supreme Court centering its attention on the comparative interests of California and Alaska in the case. The interest of California involved consideration of the facts that claimant was an alien 2000 miles from his home in Mexico; that there was little chance of his returning to Alaska to pursue his remedy there; and he was, therefore, a potential public charge in California. That interest was deemed greater than the interest of Alaska where he "was never a resident and to which he may never return."

In Pacific Employers Ins. Co. v. Industrial Acc. Comm., 306 U.S. 493, 59 S.Ct. 629, 83 L.Ed. 940 (1939), the employer was a Massachusetts corporation that had a branch in California and its head office in Massachusetts. One of its employees was temporarily in California and was injured there. The California Commission awarded compensation and a petition was filed by the carrier to set aside the award. The state courts refused to do so and the United States Supreme Court affirmed. Recognizing that California's policy was to apply its own provisions for compensation to injuries occurring within its borders to the exclusion of all other remedies, Justice Stone quoted with approval the following statement from the opinion of the California Supreme Court: "It would be obnoxious to that policy to deny persons who have been injured in this state the right to apply for compensation when to do so might require physicians and hospitals to go to another state to collect charges for medical care and treatment given to such persons."

Another basis of interest or concern for the exercise of jurisdiction under the workers' compensation statute was recognized in Cardillo v. Liberty Mut. Ins. Co., 330 U.S. 469, 67 S.Ct. 801, 91 L.Ed. 1028 (1947). The employee lived in the District of Columbia, was hired there and the employer's business was headquartered there. The work was located in Virginia and the fatal injury occurred in Virginia while claimant was driving home at the end of the day. The claim for compensation was filed under the District of Columbia workers' compensation law and an award was entered. The employer and insurance carrier brought an action in federal court to set aside the award; the District Court dismissed the complaint but the Court of Appeals reversed. The United States Supreme Court granted certiorari and reversed the Court of Appeals. It held that in light of claimant's and decedent's residence in the District, the fact that he was hired in the District, that he was under orders from the District while working in Virginia, that he was subject to transfer at any time to a project in the District, that his pay was either carried to him from the District or given to him in the District, and that he commuted daily between his home and place of work in Virginia, the jurisdictional objection was without merit.

The demolition of *Clapper* to all intents and purposes was completed in Carroll v. Lanza, 349 U.S. 408, 75 S.Ct. 804, 99 L.Ed. 1183 (1955). Carroll was an employee of a subcontractor, both being residents of Missouri and the employment contract being entered into in that state. The work was to be done in Arkansas where the injury occurred. After receiving 34 weekly payments under the Missouri compensation law, Carroll sued Lanza, the general contractor, in Arkansas in a tort action. The Missouri compensation law provided that the rights and remedies granted by it "shall exclude all other rights and remedies" at common law or otherwise for injury or death. Arkansas law, however, did not extend such immunity to third parties which Lanza was considered to be. The Supreme Court held that the Full Faith and Credit Clause was not an obstacle to Carroll's action. Justice Douglas' opinion, after reviewing *Clapper* and the cases that came after it, concluded:

> "Missouri can make her Compensation Act exclusive, if she chooses, and enforce it as she pleases within her borders. Once that policy is extended into other states, different considerations come into play. Arkansas can adopt Missouri's policy if she likes. Or, as the Pacific Employers' Insurance Co. case teaches, she may supplement it or displace it with another, insofar as remedies for acts occurring within her boundaries are concerned. Were it otherwise, the State where the injury occurred would be powerless to provide any remedies or safeguards to nonresident employees working within its borders. We do not think the Full Faith and Credit Clause demands that subserviency from the State of the injury."

There was a dissent by Justices Burton, Frankfurter and Harlan which urged that the Court should continue to balance the competing interests of the states involved and not base the decisions simply on a recognition of one interest of the state of the forum. They seemed to suggest that *Clapper* was being overruled, saying:

> "and if Clapper is to be overruled, on which I and those who join me express no opinion, it should be done with reasons making manifest why Mr. Justice Brandeis' long-matured, weighty opinion in that case was ill-founded."

Thus it is clear so far as the Full Faith and Credit Clause is concerned, the Supreme Court recognizes a variety of bases for "legitimate interest" or "concern" on which local compensation acts may be applied, including the place of making the contract, the place of the injury, the residence of the injured person and the place where the employment activity is carried on. There may be others. It would seem also that the judicial function is not a matter of weighing or comparing the interests involved but only of identifying them. Thus, the exercise of state power in workers' compensation context is virtually untrammeled. See also, Dailey v. Dallas Carriers Corp., 43 Cal.App.4th 720, 51 Cal. Rptr.2d 48 (1996); Benoit v. Test Systems, Inc., 142 N.H. 47, 694 A.2d 992 (N.H. 1997); and Scoles and Hay, Conflict of Laws 2d Ed., Section 17.46, West Pub. Co. 1992.

SECTION 5. MULTIPLE AWARDS OF COMPENSATION

Prior to 1943, it was not uncommon for a state to entertain and grant an application for compensation even though a sister state had previously made an award growing out of the same accident provided that its law was properly applicable to the accident and that credit against its award would be given for any payments received under the first award. The decision of the United States Supreme Court in Magnolia Petroleum Co. v. Hunt, 320 U.S. 430, 64 S.Ct. 208, 88 L.Ed. 149 (1943), changed the situation at least for a time.

In the *Magnolia* case the worker was employed in Louisiana and went to Texas in the course of his employment to work on an oil well where he was injured. He was awarded compensation under the Texas statute. He then returned to Louisiana and brought an action in the Louisiana courts for compensation under the Louisiana law. Compensation was awarded. The Supreme Court granted certiorari and by a divided vote (5–4) reversed the Louisiana award. The Texas statute provided, inter alia, that employees subject to the act "shall have no right of action against their employer ... but shall look for compensation solely to the association" (the insurer). Relying to some extent on these terms of the statute the Supreme Court held that the compensation award had to be given the same effect in another state as in the state in which it was rendered, that the injured worker had only one claim which had been fully adjudicated in Texas and, hence, the Full Faith and Credit Clause barred the claim in Louisiana.

Four years later, Industrial Comm. of Wisconsin v. McCartin, 330 U.S. 622, 67 S.Ct. 886, 91 L.Ed. 1140 (1947) was decided. In that case the worker and employer were both Illinois residents. The job on which claimant was injured was in Wisconsin. Claimant sought and was awarded compensation under Illinois law paid in a lump sum, the settlement contract expressly reserving all rights under Wisconsin law. McCartin's claim for compensation under Wisconsin law was denied on the authority of *Magnolia*. The United States Supreme Court reversed. It distinguished *Magnolia* on the basis that the Texas award in that case purported to be "final" whereas as to the Illinois award "there is nothing in the statute or in the decisions to indicate that it is completely exclusive, that it is designed to preclude any recovery by proceedings brought in another state for injuries received there in the course of an Illinois employment." Only "some unmistakable language by a state legislature or judiciary would warrant" cutting off an employee's right to sue under other legislation passed for his benefit. Wisconsin was therefore free under the Full Faith and Credit Clause to grant an award of compensation in accord with its own laws.

In the years that have followed *McCartin* very few courts have held that a second award is prohibited by the Full Faith and Credit Clause. One that did so was the Arizona Court of Appeals in a case that it considered "squarely in point" with *Magnolia*. Claimant, a resident of Texas who was employed in Texas by a Texas employer, received an injury while working in Arizona. He accepted compensation, payments made to him in compliance with Texas law, for approximately 4 months. He then filed a claim for compensation in Arizona. The administrators held the claim non-compensable and the Court of Appeals affirmed, considering itself constrained by *Magnolia*, although it found that case to be "a questionable interpretation of the Texas statute." Cofer v. Industrial Comm., 24 Ariz.App. 357, 538 P.2d 1158 (1975). The District of Columbia Court of Appeals, applying what it conceived to be Maryland law, denied a second award in Gasch v. Britton, 92 U.S.App.D.C. 64, 202 F.2d 356 (1953), holding that award of compensation under the Maryland law barred recovery of additional benefits allowed under the District of Columbia law. But the Court of Appeals of Maryland reached the opposite result in Wood v. Aetna Cas. & Sur. Co., 260 Md. 651, 273 A.2d 125 (1971). See also, M & G Convoy, Inc. v. Mauk, 85 Md.App. 394, 584 A.2d 101 (1991) (court discussed and agreed with *Wood* holding that "the court [in Wood] held the right to recover [a supplemental award in another state] depends upon the workers' compensation act of the state where the claimant first elected.... That has been and remains the law of Maryland." The court in reaching this conclusion also considered the U.S. Supreme Court's opinion in Thomas v. Washington Gas Light Co., infra. Most cases since *McCartin* have reached a similar conclusion finding that the first award was not intended as final and hence the *Magnolia* rule was not applicable. Stanley v. Hinchliffe and Kenner, 395 Mich. 645, 238 N.W.2d 13 (1976); Houle v. Stearns–Rogers Mfg. Co., 279 Minn. 345, 157 N.W.2d 362 (1968); Chapman v. John St. John Drilling Co., 73 N.M. 261, 387 P.2d 462 (1963); Spietz v. Industrial Comm., 251 Wis. 168, 28 N.W.2d 354 (1947); Cook v. Minneapolis Bridge Constr. Co., 231 Minn. 433, 43 N.W.2d 792 (1950); and Lavoie's Case, 334 Mass. 403, 135 N.E.2d 750 (1956).

In 1980, the U.S. Supreme Court revisited the issues in Thomas v. Washington Gas Light Co., 448 U.S. 261, 100 S.Ct. 2647, 65 L.Ed.2d 757 (1980). There the employee was hired in the District of Columbia and was injured while working in Virginia. Although a workers' compensation claim could have been filed either in D.C. or Virginia, the employee first entered into a settlement and received an award therefrom for disability benefits in Virginia. He then filed a claim and received a subsequent supplemental award under the District of Columbia act. The employer argued that because the Virginia act precluded subsequent awards, the District of Columbia was compelled to give the Virginia act full faith and credit and thereby was prohibited from awarding supplemental benefits to the employee. The District of Columbia ALJ determined that the Virginia act did not preclude supplemental awards by other states. The Benefits Review Board upheld the ALJ's decision; but the U.S. Court of Appeals for the Fourth Circuit reversed. The U.S. Supreme Court reversed holding that the Virginia act did not by "unmistakable language" preclude a compensation award in another state. The plurality of four justices would have overruled *Magnolia* reasoning as follows:

> "... the Full Faith and Credit Clause does not require a state to subordinate its own compensation policies to those of another state," and that "it follows inescapably that the McCartin 'unmistakable language' rule represents an unwarranted delegation to the states of this Court's responsibility for the final arbitration of full faith and credit questions.... To vest the power of determining the extraterritorial effect of a state's own laws and judgments in the state itself risks the very kind of parochial entrenchment on the interests of other states that it was the purpose of the Full Faith and Credit Clause ... to prevent."

The opinion of the three concurring justices would not overrule either *Magnolia* or *McCartin*. The two dissenting justices concluded that the Full Faith and Credit Clause did not allot to the Supreme Court the task of balancing of interests. Thus, neither *Magnolia* nor *McCartin* was overruled. See Leflar, et. al., American Conflicts Law, 4th Ed., Section 162, The Michie Co. (1986); and Scoles and Hay, Conflicts of Laws, 2d Ed., Section 17.48, West Pub. Co. (1992).

In the *McCartin* opinion, the Illinois settlement approval was treated as a final award of compensation rather than as a voluntary payment. As to the effect of prior voluntary payments of compensation under the law of one state as a bar to a claim or ground for reduction of claim of compensation in another state, see Cline v. Byrne Doors, Inc., 324 Mich. 540, 37 N.W.2d 630 (1949), holding that voluntary compensation payments under the Florida statute did not bar a proceeding for compensation under the Michigan statute.

There are a few cases in which the employee recovers the entire second award without having to allow credit for payments received under the first award; in effect getting a double recovery. These are usually cases in which the employee appears to have been employed by two employers at the time of the accident and procures an award against one employer in the first state and the other employer in the second state. See, for example, Adams v. Emery Transp. Co., 15 Mich.App. 593, 167 N.W.2d 110 (1969), in which the court expresses great unhappiness that such a result could occur.

SECTION 6. LONGSHORE AND HARBOR WORKERS' COMPENSATION ACT

The Constitution of the United States vests jurisdiction over admiralty and maritime affairs in the Federal Government (Article III, Section 2; Article I, Section 8). In the exercise of this power Congress has made provision for the masters and members of the crew of vessels through an employer's liability statute, the "Jones Act", discussed in Section 7, infra. Waterfront workers who are not masters or members of crews of vessels may be covered by the Longshore and Harbor Workers' Compensation Act (33 U.S.C.A. Sec. 901 et seq.). The problem of compensating waterfront workers for injuries sustained in their employment has presented legal complications for more than 80 years. This section consists of a brief history of the difficulties and a summary of some aspects of the current situation. The record may be divided into 3 parts: the decade between 1917 and 1927; the 45–year period between 1927 and 1972; and the post–1972 era.

In Southern Pacific Co. v. Jensen, 244 U.S. 205, 37 S.Ct. 524, 61 L.Ed. 1086 (1917), the Supreme Court held that the New York workers' compensation law could not be applied to an injury sustained by a stevedore unloading a vessel on navigable waters, because to do so would impair the uniformity of the general maritime law. The decision deprived thousands of waterfront workers of a compensation remedy. Thereafter,

Congress twice attempted to deal with the situation by legislation expressly allowing state compensation statutes to operate. The U.S. Supreme Court, however, struck down both acts. Knickerbocker Ice Co. v. Stewart, 253 U.S. 149, 40 S.Ct. 438, 64 L.Ed. 834 (1920); and State of Washington v. W. C. Dawson & Co., 264 U.S. 219, 44 S.Ct. 302, 68 L.Ed. 646 (1924). Finally in 1927, Congress enacted the Longshoremen's and Harbor Workers' Compensation Act (33 U.S.C.A. § 901 et seq.). The 1984 amendment to the Act substituted "Longshore" for "Longshoremen's." See Sept. 28, 1984, Pub. L. 98–426, Section 27(d) (1), 98 Stat. 1654.

This 1927 enactment was a no-fault compensation statute applicable to disability or death of an employee "but only if the disability or death results from an injury occurring upon the navigable waters of the United States (including any dry dock) and if recovery for the disability or death through workmen's compensation proceedings may not validly be provided by State law." (33 U.S.C.A. Sec. 901).

It was apparent that the limiting language quoted above was an attempt by Congress to keep the Act within the constitutional limits theretofore identified by the Supreme Court. In the interim between *Jensen* and the 1927 enactment, however, the Supreme Court had expressed views and reached decisions that modified the effect of *Jensen*. The Court developed a concept of employment and employment activities that were "local in character though maritime in nature" in which state compensation laws could be applied if injury or death ensued. One kind of case held to be in this category was that of a worker engaged in the construction of a new vessel which, while uncompleted, was afloat in navigable waters. Grant Smith–Porter Ship Co. v. Rohde, 257 U.S. 469, 42 S.Ct. 157, 66 L.Ed. 321, 25 A.L.R. 1008 (1922); see also La Casse v. Great Lakes Engineering Works, 242 Mich. 454, 219 N ..W. 730 (1928), (carpenter working on a raft alongside a vessel in process of being "rebuilt" while floating in Detroit River, state act held applicable, good discussion of cases). The borderline was hazy, however, between those cases in which state law was applicable and those in which the Longshore Act was applicable. In an effort to solve the difficulty the Court developed the "twilight zone" concept in Davis v. Department of Labor and Industries, 317 U.S. 249, 63 S.Ct. 225, 87 L.Ed. 246 (1942). In that case, claimant was the widow of a worker drowned in a navigable river while dismantling a drawbridge. The Court noted that longshore and harbor workers were clearly protected by the Federal Act but that "employees such as decedent here, occupy that shadowy area within which, at some undefined and undefinable point, state laws can validly provide compensation;" and that both the Federal Act and the state compensation statute "show clearly that neither was intended to encroach on the field occupied by the other." Since this "jurisdictional, dilemma" made it difficult for an injured worker to determine on which side of the line his particular case fell, the result in some cases had been that the worker obtained no compensation at all. In this "twilight zone" where the facts of a given case might place an injured worker on either side of the line, the Court held that it would give great weight to the administrative findings in cases brought under the Federal Act, and to the presumption of constitutionality in cases arising under state statutes. Because of this presumption of constitutionality the claimant in *Davis* was allowed her state remedy.

The practical effect of the decision in *Davis* was that in "twilight zone" cases the claimant might claim under either law, depending on which might be most advantageous. The difficulty that it left in its wake was that of deciding which cases fell within the twilight zone and which were in the full light on either side. See Moores' Case, 323 Mass. 162, 80 N.E.2d 478 (1948) in which the state court called this a "most important question" and complained that no test had been suggested.

In 1962, the U.S. Supreme Court decided Calbeck v. Travelers Ins. Co., 370 U.S. 114, 82 S.Ct. 1196, 8 L.Ed.2d 368. In that case, claimants were workers injured while engaged in completing the construction of a vessel afloat on navigable waters. This was an established category of "maritime but local" cases in which state law could be applied validly. Awards were made under the Longshore Act over the carrier's objection that the act was not applicable by its terms since it covered injuries only if "occurring upon the navigable waters of the United States ... and if recovery ... through workmen's compensation proceedings may not validly be provided by State law." The Court upheld the awards. After reviewing the legislative history of the Longshore Act, Mr. Justice Brennan wrote:

> "There emerges from the complete legislative history a congressional desire for a statute which would provide federal compensation for all injuries to employees on navigable waters; in every case, that is, where Jensen might have seemed to preclude state-compensation. The statute's framers adopted this scheme in the Act because they meant to assure the existence of a compensation remedy for every such injury, without leaving employees at the mercy of the uncertainty, expense, and delay of fighting out in litigation whether their particular cases fell within or without state acts under the 'local concern' doctrine.

> * * *

> "We conclude that Congress used the phrase 'if recovery ... may not validly be provided by State law' in a sense consistent with the delineation of coverage as reaching injuries occurring on navigable waters. By that language Congress reiterated that the Act reached all those cases of injury to employees on navigable waters as to which Jensen, Knickerbocker and Dawson had rendered questionable the availability of a state compensation remedy. Congress brought under the coverage of the Act all such injuries whether or not a particular one was also within the constitutional reach of a state workmen's compensation law."

The dissenting opinion by Mr. Justice Stewart, in which Justice Harlan joined, pointed out that the effect of the majority's decision was to eliminate the language relating to permissible state compensation. Referring to the *Davis* case supra, the dissenters wrote:

"Whatever else may be said of the *Davis* decision, it thus clearly rested on a construction of the statute precisely opposite to that adopted by the Court today. Indeed, if today's decision is correct, then there was no reason for a 'twilight zone' doctrine worked out with such travail in Davis. For the Court now holds that the problem which led to the *Davis* decision never really existed. Yet as recently as 1959 the Court began a *per curiam* opinion with this topic sentence: 'By its terms, the Longshoremen's and Harbor Workers' Compensation Act does not apply if recovery for the disability or death through workmen's compensation proceedings *may validly be provided by State* law.' Hahn v. Ross Island Sand & Gravel Co., 358 U.S. 272. Today the Court simply removes these 'terms' from the Act."

There remained, of course, the requirement that in order for the Longshore Act to be operative the injury or death must occur on navigable waters of the United States. In Nacirema Operating Co., Inc. v. Johnson, 396 U.S. 212, 90 S.Ct. 347, 24 L.Ed.2d 371(1969), the Court held the Act inapplicable to employees who were "slingers" attaching cargo from railroad cars located on piers to ships' cranes for removal to the ships. One was killed and the other injured when the cargo swung unexpectedly. The majority held that the piers were land and not navigable waters, and that the language of the Act clearly limited it so that it did not apply to land injuries even though the injured person was a longshoreman. The three dissenters argued that the Act should apply to an injured person who was a longshoreman simply because of that status.

In the majority's opinion the following language appears:

"Congress might have extended coverage to all longshoremen by exercising its power over maritime contracts. But the language of the Act is to the contrary and the background of the statute leaves little doubt that Congress' concern in providing compensation was a narrower one." (396 U.S. 215–216, 90 S.Ct. 349).

Within three years Congress reacted to the constitutional implications of the *Calbeck* and *Nacirema* opinions. In the 1972 amendments to the Act (in which there were many amendments of the substantive provisions of the law) there was a substantial change in the language relating to coverage. Two sections of the Act are pertinent for this overview:

902. Definitions

(3) The term "employee" means any person engaged in maritime employment, including any longshoreman or other person engaged in longshoring operations, and any harborworker including a ship repairman, shipbuilder, and ship-breaker, but such term does

not include a master or member of a crew of any vessel or any person engaged by the master to load or unload or repair any small vessel under eighteen tons net (In 1984, the two exclusions were designated as subparagraphs "G" and "H" and six additional subparagraphs, "A" to "F," were added designating additional exclusions from the term "employee.")

903. Coverage

(a) Compensation shall be payable under this chapter in respect of disability or death of an employee, but only if the disability or death results from an injury occurring upon the navigable waters of the United States (including any adjoining pier, wharf, dry dock, terminal, building way, marine railway, or other adjoining area customarily used by an employer in loading, unloading, repairing, or building a vessel).

* * *

It is apparent as Judge Gibbons of the Third Circuit Court of Appeals observed that "the draftsmanship of the 1972 amendments leaves something to be desired." Sea–Land Service Inc. v. Director, 540 F.2d 629, 638 (3d Cir. 1976). Its deficiencies have bred litigation concerning coverage and led to sharp differences of opinion among the Federal Circuits.

There are two requirements that must be satisfied for the worker to come within the coverage of the Act. The worker must be working at a place within the statutory definition of "navigable waters," (Section 903) sometimes called the "situs" requirement, and must be "engaged in maritime employment," (Section 902) sometimes called the "status" requirement. Both requirements have divided the courts. The following references are intended only as illustrative.

As to the "situs" requirement, the 1972 amendment to Section 903 expanded coverage beyond navigable waters to "adjoining ... area[s]. ..." This language is, of course, susceptible to either broad or narrow judicial interpretation. Two examples of cases on opposite ends of the interpretation spectrum are *Sea-Land Services,* supra, and Jacksonville Shipyards, Inc. v. Perdue, 539 F.2d 533 (5th Cir. 1976). The Third Circuit in *Sea-Land Services* held the Act applicable to a worker injured in a public street in a "sprawling marine terminal area" in Port Elizabeth, New Jersey. The U.S. Supreme Court in Northeast Marine Terminal Co., Inc. v. Caputo, 432 U.S. 249, 97 S.Ct. 2348, 53 L.Ed.2d 320, fn. 40 (1977), observed that the 3rd Circuit in *Sea-Land Services* had essentially discarded the "situs" requirement. In contrast, the Fifth Circuit in *Jacksonville Shipyards* denied compensation to a shipfitter who left work on an aircraft carrier berthed at a naval station and was injured on his way to "punch out" at a time clock located on the station about a mile from the ship; the court rejected "the argument that the new Act covers every point in a large marine facility where a ship repairman might go at his employer's direction."

The "status" requirement of Section 902 has forced the courts to contend with its references to "maritime employment." In one case, for example, it was held by the Fourth Circuit that the concept of "maritime employment" did not extend beyond the "point of rest," which meant coverage was limited to workers who unload inbound cargo from the ship to the first point of rest at the terminal, or load outbound cargo on the ship from the last point of rest at the terminal. I. T. O. Corp. of Baltimore v. Benefits Review Bd., 529 F.2d 1080 (4th Cir.1975). On rehearing en banc the point of rest was moved out to the point where cargo is loaded for (or unloaded from) transshipment. 542 F.2d 903 (4th Cir.1976). The "point of rest" concept was rejected by the United States Supreme Court in *Northeast Marine Terminal Co.* supra. 432 U.S. 249, 275, 97 S.Ct. 2348, 2363, 53 L.Ed.2d 320, 340 (1977). Subsequently it vacated the *I.T.O. Corp.* judgment and remanded the case for further consideration. 433 U.S. 904, 97 S.Ct. 2967, 53 L.Ed.2d 1088 (1977).

The Third Circuit has adopted a test based on whether the worker's job bears a "functional relationship" to the activities mentioned in the statutory definition of "employee." Dravo Corp. v. Maxin, 545 F.2d 374 (3d Cir. 1976) held that the job of a worker in a steel structural shop "burning" steel plates that would ultimately become bottoms and decks of barges was an integral part of shipbuilding (as described in the 1967 Encyclopedia Britannica) and therefore satisfied the functional relationship test. In Alabama Dry Dock and Shipbuilding Co. v. Kininess, 554 F.2d 176 (5th Cir.1977), it was held that a worker who was injured while sandblasting a disassembled crane which would later be used for building ships was "directly involved" in shipbuilding and covered by the Act. The U.S. Supreme Court in Director, Office of Workers' Compensation Programs v. Perini North River Assocs., 459 U.S. 297, 103 S.Ct. 634, 74 L.Ed.2d 465 (1983), suggested that any worker who had been covered prior to 1972 would continue to be covered under the 1972 amendment despite the newly added "status" test in Section 902. For a discussion of the opinion and its somewhat ambiguous meaning see Larson's Workers' Compensation Law, Matthew Bender, Vol. 9, Section 89.27(c) (1998). Two years later the Court in Herb's Welding, Inc. v. Gray, 470 U.S. 414, 105 S.Ct. 1421, 84 L.Ed.2d 406 (1985), distinguished and explained the *Perini* case: "We point out that [Perini] was carefully limited to coverage of an employee 'injured while performing his job on actual navigable waters'.... [Perini] says nothing about the contours of the status requirement as applied to a worker like Gray, who was not injured on navigable waters." The Court further stated: "As we have said, the 'maritime' employment requirement is 'an occupational test that focuses on loading and unloading'" (citing case). The Court noted that the amendments were not meant "to cover employees who are not engaged in loading, unloading, repairing, or building a vessel, just because they are injured in an area adjoining navigable waters used for such activity."

The "twilight zone" continues to exist under the 1972 amendments. In Poche v. Avondale Shipyards, Inc., 339 So.2d 1212 (La.1976), decedents were engaged in new ship construction in a shipyard area located entirely over land when they were injured. The court held that the survivors could elect either a proceeding under the state workers' compensation act or under the Longshore Act. In Johnson v. Texas Employers Ins. Ass'n, 558 S.W.2d 47 (Tex.Civ.App.1977), plaintiff was an assistant crane operator in a fabrication shop at employer's shipyard about 75 to 100 feet from navigable water when he was injured. The court held that plaintiff was covered and eligible for benefits under the Longshore Act and also under the Texas compensation law and an award could be had under both statutes with appropriate credit. In Parfait v. Deroche, 356 So.2d 1051 (La.App.1977), claimant was working as a fitter's helper and sustained an injury when he slipped on a synchrolift (a submerged apparatus designed to lift a vessel from the water). The court found that claimant was within the twilight zone and could elect to seek compensation under the Longshore Act or under the Louisiana compensation act. The U.S. Supreme Court in Sun Ship, Inc. v. Pennsylvania, 447 U.S. 715, 100 S.Ct. 2432, 65 L.Ed.2d 458 (1980), confirmed these decisions holding: "Given that the pre–1972 Longshoremen's Act ran concurrently with state remedies in the 'maritime but local' zone, it follows that the post–1972 expansion of the Act landward would be concurrent as well. For state regulation of worker injuries is even more clearly appropriate ashore than it is upon navigable waters." See also, Bourgeois v. Puerto Rican Marine Management, Inc., 589 So.2d 1226 (La.App. 4th Cir.1991), (where stevedore's death occurred on land side of waterfront cargo facility, survivor's could choose between state workers' compensation coverage or Longshore Act.).

There are many more problems connected with the 1972 amendments than it is possible to cover in the limited space here. Excellent discussions are found in Larson, *The Conflicts Problem Between The Longshoremen's Act And State Workmen's Compensation Acts Under The 1972 Amendments,* 14 Houston L.Rev. 287 (1977); Note, *The Docking Of The Longshoremen's And Harbor Worker's Compensation Act: How Far Can It Come Ashore?,* 29 Fla.L.Rev. 681 (1977). See also annotation *"Maritime Employment" Coverage Under Longshoremen's And Harbor Workers' Compensation Act,* 41 A.L.R.Fed. 685 (1979); and see generally Larson's Workers' Compensation Law, Matthew Bender, Vol.9, Sections 89.00 through 89.74 (1998).

SECTION 7. JONES ACT

The Jones Act (Merchant Marine Act, 46 U.S.C.A. Section 688) provides, in part, as follows:

"(a) Application of railway employee statutes; jurisdiction

Any seaman who shall suffer personal injury in the course of his employment may maintain an action for damages at law, with the right of trial by jury, and in such action all statutes of the United States modifying or extending the common-law right or remedy in cases of personal injury to railway employees shall apply.... Jurisdiction in such actions shall be under the court of the district in which the defendant employer resides or in which his principal office is located."

* * *

The Act by its terms makes the Federal Employers' Liability Act (See Chapter 1, Section 3 and Appendix A) applicable to cases involving the personal injury or death of a seaman.

Cases often arise in which the issue is whether the claimant's remedy, if any, is under the Jones Act, a state workers' compensation act, or the Longshore Act. The crucial inquiry in many of these cases is whether or not the claimant is a "seaman" within the meaning of the Jones Act. For example, in Wilkes v. Mississippi River Sand & Gravel Co., 202 F.2d (6th Cir. 1953), the injured employee worked on dredges in the Mississippi River loading barges with gravel as it was pumped from the riverbed. The Federal District Court held that they were not "seamen" but were covered by the Longshore Act. A divided Court of Appeals reversed, holding that the employees who lived on board the dredge at their own option to take advantage of the free board and lodging, were sufficiently connected with the dangers of marine service to require a finding that they were seamen and could sue under the Jones Act. The *Wilkes* court also stated a three part test for determining "seaman" status developed in earlier cases: (1) the vessel must be in navigation; (2) the worker must be more or less permanently connected with the vessel; and (3) the worker must be aboard primarily to aid in navigation.

One of the most influential federal circuit court opinions defining "seaman" status was Offshore Company v. Robison, 266 F.2d 769 (5th Cir. 1959). *Robison* noted the three-part test as referenced in *Wilkes* and recast the definition of "seaman" as follows:

"... there is an evidentiary basis for a Jones Act case to go to the jury: (1) if there is evidence that the injured workman was assigned permanently to a vessel (including special purpose structures not usually employed as a means of transport by water but designed to float on water) or performed a substantial part of his work on the vessel; and (2) if the capacity in which he was employed or the duties which he performed contributed to the function of the vessel or the accomplishment of its mission, or to the operation or welfare of the vessel in terms of its maintenance during its movement or during anchorage for its future trips."

This opinion was followed in most federal courts over the next 32 years with the exception of the Seventh Circuit Court of Appeals. That court continued to apply the "aid in navigation" requirement. The U.S. Supreme Court in McDermott v. Wilander, 498 U.S. 337, 111 S.Ct. 807, 112 L.Ed.2d 866 (1991) agreed with the *Robison* approach holding that the "aid in navigation" test should be jettisoned.

Later Supreme Court decisions further refined the test of seaman status. See e.g. Chandris, Inc. v. Latsis, 515 U.S. 347, 115 S.Ct. 2172, 132

L.Ed.2d 314 (1995) (the test for seaman status has two essential elements: (1) the worker's duties must contribute to the function of the vessel or the accomplishment of its mission; and (2) the worker must have a connection to a vessel in navigation (or an identifiable group of vessels) that is substantial in both its duration and its nature.) See also, Harbor Tug and Barge Co. v. Papai, 520 U.S. 548, 117 S.Ct. 1535, 137 L.Ed.2d 800 (1997) (agreeing with and explaining the *Chandris* language "substantial connection to a vessel or fleet of vessels.).

Another requirement of the Jones Act is that the seaman must suffer personal injury or death while "in the course of his employment." Those who have seaman status do not automatically lose that status while on shore. They may recover under the Jones Act wherever they are injured in the course of their employment regardless of whether the injury occurs on or off the ship. See, e.g., O'Donnell v. Great Lakes Dredge & Dock Co., 318 U.S. 36, 63 S.Ct. 488, 87 L.Ed. 596 (1943); and Braen v. Pfeifer Oil Transp. Co., 361 U.S. 129, 80 S.Ct. 247, 4 L.Ed.2d 191 (1959) (if the seaman is performing a task "pursuant to his employer's orders" he is in the course of his employment and covered by the Jones Act).

This can work to the disadvantage of the seaman where there is little or no chance of showing negligence on the part of the employer, a requirement of the Jones Act. In Rudolph v. Industrial Marine Service, 187 Tenn. 119, 213 S.W.2d 30 (1948) decedent was a member of the crew of a vessel that was docked and his employer ordered him to go into the city to purchase a faucet for the boat. While so engaged, he was hit by a train and killed. It was held that the Tennessee workers' compensation law was not applicable and that the exclusive remedy of the widow was under the Jones Act.

A seaman on shore leave is often considered to be in the course of employment. See, e.g., Daughenbaugh v. Bethlehem Steel Corp., Great Lakes S.S. Div., 891 F.2d 1199 (6th Cir.1989) (intoxicated seaman returning from shore leave was in course of employment); but see Colon v. Apex Marine Corp., 832 F.Supp. 508 (D.R.I.1993) (seaman on shore leave injured while attempting to break up a fight in a bar between two shipmates; held seaman was pursuing his own private interests and was not injured in the course of his employment).

The seaman's commute from a shore-based home to work on the vessel is addressed under the going and coming concept and the results vary. See, e.g., Daughdrill v. Diamond M. Drilling Co., 447 F.2d 781 (5th Cir.1971) (seaman was not on shore leave nor within the course of employment when killed in automobile accident while traveling from home to work after several days off duty); but see Williamson v. Western Pacific Dredging Corp., 441 F.2d 65 (9th Cir.1971) (allowing recovery for death sustained while commuting from home to dredge).

Because the Jones Act preempts the field involving injury or death suffered by seamen, claims under state workers' compensation acts are almost always precluded. This typically presents no problem for seamen and their dependents. Even though under the Jones Act, the seamen or their dependents must prove employer negligence and the employer may assert the defense of pure comparative negligence, the more lucrative tort-type damages recoverable are preferable to the less generous benefits provided by state workers' compensation laws.

But, if there is no ability to prove employer negligence and thus no recovery available under the Jones Act (excluding the potential for the seaman to receive "maintenance and cure," a subject beyond the scope of this discussion) is it possible to apply state workers' compensation law to the claim? If not, the seaman and dependents may be left without remedy and those who provided medical, hospital and other care, services and subsistence may go unreimbursed.

In Maryland Casualty Co. v. Toups, 172 F.2d 542 (5th Cir.1949) all of this played a part in the court's decision. Decedent was a pilot of a boat that ferried pilots to seagoing vessels. On a day when his boat was undergoing repairs, he sat on the dock making fenders (cushions to soften the impact when docking the boat). While doing so, he fell into the water and drowned. Pointing out that there was no possibility of proving negligence under the Jones Act, the court held that the Texas workers' compensation law was applicable. (Citing Millers' Indemnity Underwriters v. Braud, 270 U.S. 59, 46 S.Ct. 194, 70 L.Ed. 470 (1926); Grant Smith–Porter Ship Co. v. Rohde, 257 U.S. 469, 42 S.Ct. 157, 66 L.Ed. 321 (1922); and Davis v. Dept. of Labor and Industries of Washington, 317 U.S. 249, 63 S.Ct. 225, 87 L.Ed. 246 (1942) (applying the "twilight zone" concept in context of Longshore and Harbor Workers Act; see Section 6, supra).

On the other hand, the Mississippi court, in a case in which the decedent was clearly a seaman and died of a heart attack while on the vessel, refused to apply the Mississippi Workers' Compensation Act, even though an action under the Jones Act held no promise for recovery. Valley Towing Co. v. Allen, 236 Miss. 51, 109 So.2d 538 (1959). See also, Indiana & Michigan Electric Co. v. Workers' Compensation Commissioner, 184 W. Va. 673, 403 S.E.2d 416 (1991) (Jones Act seaman injured while working on vessel in maritime waters precluded from filing claim under West Virginia's workers' compensation law; good discussion of "twilight zone" concept under Longshore Act as compared to Jones Act). Compare Cordova Fish & Cold Storage Co. v. Estes, 370 P.2d 180 (Alaska 1962) applying state workers' compensation act to fisherman injured while moving crab pots on deck of a boat tied to a dock and recognizing the "twilight zone" doctrine as applicable to Jones Act cases. See also, Anderson v. Alaska Packers Assn., 635 P.2d 1182 (Alaska 1981); Garrisey v. Westshore Marina Associates, 2 Wash. App. 718, 469 P.2d 590 (1970); and Larson's Workers' Compensation Law, Matthew Bender, Vol. 9, Sec. 90.41 (1998).

SECTION 8. FEDERAL EMPLOYERS' LIABILITY ACT

The Federal Employers' Liability Act (FELA), 45 U.S.C.A. sec. 51, et seq. (See chapter 1, Section 3, supra, and Appendix A) was first enacted by Congress in 1906, but declared unconstitutional by the United States Supreme Court as an invalid attempt to regulate intrastate commerce. See Employers Liability Cases, 207 U.S. 463, 28 S.Ct. 141, 52 L.Ed. 297 (1908). It was reenacted in 1908 in a form which carefully applied the Act only to interstate railroading activities. The 1908 enactment provided in part as follows: "every common carrier by railroad while engaging in commerce between any of the several states . . . shall be liable in damages to any person suffering injury while he is employed by such carrier in such commerce. . . ." The courts in applying this language used what was sometimes referred to as the "on the spot" or "pin-point" test. That test required a careful analysis to determine whether at the moment of the worker's injury, the worker was then and there engaged in interstate transportation or in work so closely related to it as to be practically a part of it . See, e.g., Shanks v. Delaware, L. & W.R. Co., 239 U.S. 556, 36 S.Ct. 188, 60 L.Ed. 436 (1916).

If the "on the spot" test did not bring the employee within coverage of the FELA, the worker would be left to pursue a state remedy. As the states began to enact workers' compensation legislation, the likelihood of conflict between the newly enacted workers' compensation acts and the FELA was significant because of the fact-sensitive nature of the "on the spot" test.

As commerce clause jurisprudence was evolving, Congress in 1939 amended the FELA substantially expanding its reach by covering "any employee of a[n] [interstate rail] carrier, any part of whose duties . . . shall be the furtherance of interstate or foreign commerce; or shall in any way directly or closely and substantially affect such commerce. . . ."

The U.S. Supreme Court interpreted this language expansively in Reed v. Pennsylvania Railroad Co., 351 U.S. 502, 76 S.Ct. 958, 100 L.Ed. 1366 (1956), holding that a clerical employee for the Pennsylvania Railroad was covered by the FELA. The Court reasoned that the 1939 amendment "... evinces a purpose to expand coverage substantially as well as to avoid narrow distinctions in deciding questions of coverage. Under the amendment, it is the 'duties' of the employee that must further or affect commerce, and it is enough if 'any part' of those duties has the requisite effect."

After *Reed*, it is plausible to argue that virtually every worker employed by an interstate rail carrier is covered by the FELA. See Larson's Workers' Compensation Law, Matthew Bender, Vol. 9 Section 91.60 (1998).

Because the FELA preempts the field involving injury or death of a covered railway worker, it will be much less likely, following the *Reed* case, that employees of interstate rail carriers will be able to maintain claims under state workers' compensation laws. Thus the likelihood of a conflict of laws issue arising is much reduced.

There is also a possibility of a conflict between the Longshore Act and the FELA. For a discussion of that issue, see Larson's Workers' Compensation Law, Matthew Bender, Vol. 9, Section 91.11, (1998).

*

Appendix A

FEDERAL EMPLOYERS' LIABILITY ACT

---

53 Stat. 1404 (1908) as amended, 45 U.S.C.A. § 51.

§ 51. Liability of common carriers by railroad, in interstate or foreign commerce, for injuries to employees from negligence; definition of employees

Every common carrier by railroad while engaging in commerce between any of the several States or Territories, or between any of the States and Territories, or between the District of Columbia and any of the States or Territories, or between the District of Columbia or any of the States or Territories and any foreign nation or nations, shall be liable in damages to any person suffering injury while he is employed by such carrier in such commerce, or, in case of the death of such employee, to his or her personal representative, for the benefit of the surviving widow or husband and children of such employee; and, if none, then of such employee's parents; and, if none, then of the next of kin dependent upon such employee, for such injury or death resulting in whole or in part from the negligence of any of the officers, agents, or employees of such carrier, or by reason of any defect or insufficiency, due to its negligence, in its cars, engines, appliances, machinery, track, roadbed, works, boats, wharves, or other equipment.

Any employee of a carrier, any part of whose duties as such employee shall be the furtherance of interstate or foreign commerce; or shall, in any way directly or closely and substantially affect such commerce as above set forth shall, for the purposes of this chapter, be considered as being employed by such carrier in such commerce and shall be considered as entitled to the benefits of this chapter.

§ 52. (Makes Act applicable to railroads in Territories and other Possessions of the United States.)

§ 53. Contributory negligence; diminution of damages

In all actions on and after April 22, 1908 brought against any such common carrier by railroad under or by virtue of any of the provisions of this chapter to recover damages for personal injuries to an employee, or where such injuries have resulted in his death, the fact that the employee may have been guilty of contributory negligence shall not bar a recovery, but the damages shall be diminished by the jury in proportion to the amount of negligence attributable to such employee: *Provided,* That no such employee who may be injured or killed shall be held to have been guilty of contributory negligence in any case where the violation by such common carrier of any statute enacted for the safety of employees contributed to the injury or death of such employee.

§ 54. Assumption of risks of employment

In any action brought against any common carrier under or by virtue of any of the provisions of this chapter to recover damages for injuries to, or the death of, any of its employees, such employee shall not be held to have assumed the risks of his employment in any case where such injury or death resulted in whole or in part from the negligence of any of the officers, agents, or employees of such carrier; and no employee shall be held to have assumed the risks of his employment in any case where the violation by such common carrier of any statute enacted for the safety of employees contributed to the injury or death of such employee.

* * *

§ 56. Actions; limitation; concurrent jurisdiction of courts

No action shall be maintained under this chapter unless commenced within three years from the date the cause of action accrued.

Under this chapter an action may be brought in a district court of the United States, in the district of the residence of the defendant, or in which the cause of action arose, or in which the defendant shall be doing business at the time of commencing such action. The jurisdiction of the courts of the United States under this chapter shall be concurrent with that of the courts of the several States.

Appendix B

WORKMEN'S COMPENSATION AND REHABILITATION LAW

(Revised)

THE COUNCIL OF STATE GOVERNMENTS

Lexington, Kentucky

Analysis

WORKMEN'S COMPENSATION
AND REHABILITATION LAW

Part I.   Coverage and Liability

Section

553

————

Suggested Legislation

(Title, enacting clause, etc.)

Part I

Coverage and Liability

Section 1. [*Liability for Compensation.*]

(a) Every employer subject to this act shall be liable for compensation for injury or death without regard to fault as a cause of the injury or death.

(b) A contractor who subcontracts all or any part of a contract and his carrier shall be liable for the payment of compensation to the employees of the subcontractor unless the subcontractor primarily liable for the payment of such compensation has secured the payment of compensation as provided for in this act. Any contractor or his carrier who shall become liable for such compensation may recover the amount of such compensation paid and necessary expenses from the subcontractor primarily liable therefor. A person who contracts with another (1) to have work performed consisting of (a) the removal, excavation or drilling of soil, rock or minerals, or (b) the cutting or removal of timber from land, or (2) to have work performed of a kind which is a regular or recurrent part of the work of the trade, business, occupation or profession of such person, shall for the purposes of this section be deemed a contractor, and such other person a subcontractor. This subsection shall not apply to the owner or lessee of land principally used for agriculture who contracts for removal of timber from such land.

(c) Liability for compensation shall not apply where injury to the employee was occasioned solely by his intoxication or by his willful intention to injure or kill himself or another.

Section 2. [*Definitions.*]

As used in this act unless the context otherwise requires:

(a) "Injury" means any harmful change in the human organism arising out of and in the course of employment, including damage to or loss of a prosthetic appliance, but does not include any communicable disease unless the risk of contracting such disease is increased by the nature of the employment.[1]

(b) "Death" means death resulting from an injury.

(c) "Carrier" means any insurer, or legal representative thereof, authorized to insure the liabilities of employers under this act and includes a self-insurer.

(d) "Self-insurer" is an employer who has been authorized under the provisions of this act to carry his own liability to his employees covered by this act.

(e) "Agency" means the [name of state administrative agency].

(f) "Director" means the director of the [name of state administrative agency].

(g) "Board" means the [Workmen's Compensation Appeals Board].

(h) "Disability" means, except for purposes of Section 16(c) relating to schedule losses, a decrease of wage-earning capacity due to injury. Wage-earning capacity prior to injury shall be the average weekly wage as calculated under Section 19. Wage-earning capacity after the injury shall be presumed to be actual earnings after the injury. This presumption may be overcome by showing that these earnings after injury do not fairly and reasonably represent wage-earning capacity, and in such cases, wage-earning capacity shall be determined in the light of all factors and circumstances in the case which may affect the injured worker's capacity to earn wages.

(i) "Income benefits" means payments made under the provisions of this act to the injured worker or his dependents in case of death, excluding medical and related benefits.

(j) "Medical and related benefits" means payments made for medical, hospital, burial and other services as provided in this act other than income benefits.

(k) "Compensation" means all payments made under the provisions of this act, representing the sum of income benefits and medical and related benefits.

---

1. Section 2(a) complies with the recommendations of the National Commission on State Workmen's Compensation Laws pertaining to coverage of work-related injuries and diseases. There is, however, a difference between the terminology used by the *Report* of the National Commission and the terminology used in Section 2(a), and the purpose of this note is to clarify the difference.

The *Report* defines "injury" as "damage to the body resulting from an acute trau-matic episode" and "disease" as "damage to the body resulting from a cause other than an injury." Section 2(a) defines "injury" broadly so that the term encompasses both "injury" and "disease" as those terms are defined in the *Report*. The consequence is that the coverage of injuries and diseases prescribed by the *Report* and the coverage prescribed by Section 2(a) are equivalent.

(*l*) ''Medical services'' means medical, surgical, dental, hospital, nursing and medical rehabilitation services.

(m) ''Person'' means any individual, partnership, firm, association, trust, corporation, [state compensation insurance fund], or legal representative thereof.

(n) ''Wages'' means, in addition to money payments for services rendered, the reasonable value of board, rent, housing, lodging, fuel or similar advantage received from the employer, and gratuities received in the course of employment from others than the employer.

(*o*) ''Agriculture'' means the operation of farm premises, including the planting, cultivating, producing, growing and harvesting of agricultural or horticultural commodities thereon, the raising of livestock and poultry thereon, and any work performed as an incident to or in conjunction with such farm operations. It shall not include the processing, packing, drying, storing, or canning of such commodities for market, or making cheese or butter or other dairy products for market.

(p) ''United States,'' when used in a geographic sense, means the several States, the District of Columbia, the Commonwealth of Puerto Rico, the Canal Zone and the Territories of the United States.

(q) ''Alien'' means a person who is not a citizen, a national or a resident of the United States or Canada. Any person not a citizen or national of the United States who relinquishes or is about to relinquish his residence in the United States shall be regarded as an alien.

(r) ''Beneficiary'' means any person who is entitled to income benefits or medical and related benefits under this act.

(s) ''Actually dependent'' means dependent in fact upon the employee, and refers only to a person who received more than half of his support from the employee and whose dependency is not the result of failure to make reasonable efforts to secure suitable employment. When used as a noun, the word ''dependent'' means any person entitled to death benefits under Section 18, or any person for whom added benefits for disability are provided under Section 16.

(t) As used in Sections 16 and 18:

(1) ''Wife'' or ''Widow'' means only the employee's wife living with or actually dependent upon him at the time of his injury or death, or living apart for justifiable cause or by reason of his desertion.

(2) ''Widower'' means only the deceased employee's husband living with and actually dependent upon her.

(3) ''Child'' means a child under 18 years of age; or a child 18 years of age or over and physically or mentally incapable of

self-support; or any child 18 years of age or over who is actually dependent; or any child between 18 and 25 years of age who is enrolled as a full-time student in any accredited educational institution. The term "child" includes a post-humous child, a child legally adopted or for whom adoption proceedings are pending at the time of death, an actually dependent child in relation to whom the deceased employee stood in the place of a parent for at least one year prior to the time of death, an actually dependent stepchild or an actually dependent acknowledged illegitimate child. "Child" does not include a married child unless receiving substantially entire support from the employee. "Grandchild" means a child, as above defined, of a child as above defined, except that as to the latter child, the limitations as to age in the above definition do not apply.

(4) "Brother" or "sister" means a brother or sister under 18 years of age, or 18 years of age or over and physically or mentally incapable of self-support, or 18 years of age or over and actually dependent. The terms "brother" and "sister" include stepbrothers and stepsisters, half brothers and half sisters, and brothers and sisters by adoption; but the terms do not include married brothers or married sisters unless receiving substantially entire support from the employee.

(5) "Parent" means a mother or father, a stepparent, a parent by adoption, a parent-in-law, and any person who for more than one year immediately prior to the death of the employee stood in the place of a parent to him, if actually dependent in each case.

(6) All questions of relationship and dependency shall initially be determined as of the time of injury for purposes of income benefits for injury, and as of the time of death for purposes of income benefits for death.

Section 3. [*Coverage of Employers.*]

The following shall constitute employers subject to the provisions of this act:

(a) Every person that has in the State one or more employees subject to this act.

(b) The State, any agency thereof, and each county, city, town, township, incorporated village, school district, sewer district, drainage district, public or quasi-public corporation, or any other political subdivision of the State that has one or more employees subject to this act.

Section 4. [*Coverage of Employees.*]

The following shall constitute employees subject to the provisions of this act, except as exempted under Section 5:

(a) Every person, including a minor, whether lawfully or unlawfully employed, in the service of an employer under any contract of hire or apprenticeship, express or implied, and all helpers and assistants of employees whether paid by the employer or employee, if employed with the knowledge, actual or constructive, of the employer.

(b) Every executive officer of a corporation.

(c) Every person in the service of the State or of any political subdivision or agency thereof, under any contract of hire, express or implied, and every official or officer thereof, whether elected or appointed, while performing his official duties. Every person who is a member of a volunteer fire or police department shall be deemed, for the purpose of this act, to be in the employment of the political subdivision of the State where the department is organized. Every person who is a regularly enrolled volunteer member or trainee of the civil defense corps of this State as established under the [State Civil Defense Act] shall be deemed, for the purpose of this act, to be in the employment of the State.

(d) Every person performing service in the course of the trade, business, profession or occupation of an employer at the time of the injury, provided such person in relation to this service does not maintain a separate business, does not hold himself out to and render service to the public, and is not himself an employer subject to this act.

(e) Subject to the proviso in subsection (d) of this section, every person regularly selling or distributing newspapers on the street or to customers at their homes or places of business. For the purposes of this act such a person shall be deemed an employee of any independent news agency for whom he is selling or distributing newspapers or, in the absence of such independent agency, of each publisher whose newspapers he sells or distributes.

Section 5. [*Exemptions.*]

The following employees are exempt from the coverage of this act:

(a) Any person employed in agriculture by an employer who has an annual payroll that in total is less than $1,000. This exemption shall terminate on July 1, 1975.

(b) Any person employed as a household worker in a private home or household who earns less than $50 in cash in any three-month period from a single private home or household and any person employed as a casual worker in a private home or household who earns less than $50 in cash in any three-month period from a single private home or household.

Section 6. [*Voluntary Coverage.*]

(a) An employer who has in his employment any employee exempted under Section 5 may elect to be subject to this act. Such election on the part of the employer shall be made by the employer's securing the payment of compensation to such exempted employees in accordance with Section 46. Any employee, otherwise exempted under Section 5, of such employer shall be deemed to have elected to come under this act if, at the time of the injury for which liability is claimed, such employer has in force an election to be subject to this act with respect to the employment in which such employee was injured and such employee has not, either upon entering into the employment or within five days after the filing of an election by the employer, given to such employer and to the Director notice in writing that he elects not to be subject to this act.

(b) Such employer, within five days after securing the payment of compensation in accordance with Section 46, shall give the Director written notice of his election to be subject to this act. Such employer shall post and keep posted on the premises, where any employee or employees otherwise exempted under Section 5 works, printed notices furnished by the Director stating his acceptance of this act. Failure to give the notices required by this paragraph shall not void or impair the employer's election to be subject to or relieve him of any liability under this act.

(c) Any employer who has complied with subsection (b) of this section may withdraw his acceptance of this act by filing written notice with the Director of the withdrawal of his acceptance. Such withdrawal shall become effective 60 days after the filing of such notice or on the date of the termination of the security for payment of compensation, whichever last occurs. The employer shall theretofore post notice of such withdrawal where the affected employee or employees work or shall otherwise notify such employees of such withdrawal.

Section 7. [*Extraterritorial Coverage.*]

(a) If an employee, while working outside the territorial limits of this State, suffers an injury on account of which he, or in the event of his death, his dependents, would have been entitled to the benefits provided by this act had such injury occurred within this State, such employee, or in the event of his death resulting from such injury, his dependents, shall be entitled to the benefits provided by this act, provided that at the time of such injury

(1) his employment is principally localized in this State, or

(2) he is working under a contract of hire made in this State in employment not principally localized in any State, or

(3) he is working under a contract of hire made in this State in employment principally localized in another State whose workmen's compensation law is not applicable to his employer, or

(4) he is working under a contract of hire made in this State for employment outside the United States and Canada.

(b) The payment or award of benefits under the workmen's compensation law of another State, territory, province, or foreign nation to an employee or his dependents otherwise entitled on account of such injury or death to the benefits of this act shall not be a bar to a claim for benefits under this act; provided that claim under this act is filed within the time limits set forth in Section 26. If compensation is paid or awarded under this act:

(1) The medical and related benefits furnished or paid for by the employer under such other workmen's compensation law on account of such injury or death shall be credited against the medical and related benefits to which the employee would have been entitled under this act had claim been made solely under this act;

(2) The total amount of all income benefits paid or awarded the employee under such other workmen's compensation law shall be credited against the total amount of income benefits which would have been due the employee under this act, had claim been made solely under this act;

(3) The total amount of death benefits paid or awarded under such other workmen's compensation law shall be credited against the total amount of death benefits due under this act.

(c) If an employee is entitled to the benefits of this act by reason of an injury sustained in this State in employment by an employer who is domiciled in another State and who has not secured the payment of compensation as required by this act, the employer or his carrier may file with the Director a certificate, issued by the commission or agency of such other State having jurisdiction over workmen's compensation claims, certifying that such employer has secured the payment of compensation under the workmen's compensation law of such other State and that with respect to said injury such employee is entitled to the benefits provided under such law. In such event:

(1) The filing of such certificate shall constitute an appointment by such employer or his carrier of the Director as his agent for acceptance of the service of process in any proceeding brought by such employee or his dependents to enforce his or their rights under this act on account of such injury;

(2) The Director shall send to such employer or carrier, by registered or certified mail to the address shown on such certificate, a true copy of any notice of claim or other process served on the Director by the employee or his dependents in any proceeding brought to enforce his or their rights under this act;

(3)(i) If such employer is a qualified self-insurer under the workmen's compensation law of such other State, such employer shall, upon submission of evidence, satisfactory to the Director, of his ability to meet his liability to such employee under this act, be deemed to be a qualified self-insurer under this act;

(ii) If such employer's liability under the workmen's compensation law of such other State is insured, such employer's carrier, as to such employee or his dependents only, shall be deemed to be an insurer authorized to write insurance under and be subject to this act; *provided,* however, that unless its contract with said employer requires it to pay an amount equivalent to the compensation benefits provided by this act, its liability for income benefits or medical and related benefits shall not exceed the amounts of such benefits for which such insurer would have been liable under the workmen's compensation law of such other State;

(4) If the total amount for which such employer's insurance is liable under (3) above is less than the total of the compensation benefits to which such employee is entitled under this act, the Director may, if he deems it necessary, require the employer to file security, satisfactory to the Director, to secure the payment of benefits due such employee or his dependents under this act; and

(5) Upon compliance with the preceding requirements of this subsection (c), such employer, as to such employee only, shall be deemed to have secured the payment of compensation under this act.

(d) As used in this section:

(1) "United States" includes only the States of the United States and the District of Columbia;

(2) "State" includes any State of the United States, the District of Columbia, or any Province of Canada;

(3) "Carrier" includes any insurance company licensed to write workmen's compensation insurance in any State of the United States or any State or provincial fund which insures employers against their liabilities under a workmen's compensation law;

(4) A person's employment is principally localized in this or another State when (1) his employer has a place of business in this or such other State and he regularly works at or from such place of business, or (2) if clause (1) foregoing is not applicable, he is domiciled and spends a substantial part of his working time in the service of his employer in this or such other State;

(5) An employee whose duties require him to travel regularly in the service of his employer in this and one or more other States may, by written agreement with his employer, provide that his employment is principally localized in this or another such State, and, unless such other State refuses jurisdiction, such agreement shall be given effect under this act;

(6) "Workmen's compensation law" includes "occupational disease law."

Section 8.   [*Inmates of Public Institutions.*] (omitted)

Section 9.   [*Presumption.*]

In any claim for compensation, where the employee has been killed, or is physically or mentally unable to testify, and where there is unrebutted prima facie evidence that indicates that the injury arose in the course of employment, it shall be presumed, in the absence of substantial evidence to the contrary, that the injury arose out of the employment, that sufficient notice of the injury has been given, and that the injury or death was not occasioned solely by the employee's intoxication or by his willful intention to injure or kill himself or another.

Section 10. [*Exclusiveness of Liability*]

(a) If an employer secures payment of compensation as required by this act, the liability of such employer under this act shall be exclusive and in place of all other liability of such employer to the employee, his legal representative, husband or wife, parents, dependents, next of kin, and anyone otherwise entitled to recover damages from such employer at law or in admiralty on account of such injury or death. For purposes of this section, the term "employer" shall include a "contractor" covered by Section 1(b), whether or not the subcontractor has, in fact, secured the payment of compensation. The liability of an employer to another person who may be liable for or who has paid damages on account of injury or death of an employee of such employer arising out of and in the course of employment and caused by a breach of any duty or obligation owed by such employer to such other shall be limited to the amount of compensation and other benefits for which such employer is liable under this act on account of such injury or death, unless such other and the employer by written contract have agreed to share liability in a different manner. The exemption from liability given an employer by this section shall also extend to such employer's carrier and to all employees, officers or directors of such employer or carrier, provided the exemption from liability given an employee, officer or director of an employer or carrier shall not apply in any case where the injury or death is proximately caused by the willful and unprovoked physical aggression of such employee, officer or director.

(b) If an employer fails to secure payment of compensation as required by this act, an injured employee, or his legal representative in case death results from the injury, may claim compensation under this act and in addition may maintain an action at law or in admiralty for damages on account of such injury or death, provided that the amount of compensation shall be credited against the amount received in such action, and provided that, if the amount of compensation is larger than the amount of damages received, the amount of damages less the employee's legal fees and expenses shall be credited against the amount of compensation. In such action the defendant may not plead as a defense that the injury was caused by the negligence of a fellow servant, that the employee assumed the risks of his employment, or that the injury was due to the contributory negligence of the employee.

Section 11. [*Third Party Liability.*]

(a) The right to income and other benefits under this act, whether for disability or death, shall not be affected by the fact that the injury or death is caused under circumstances creating a legal liability in some person (other than the employer or another personexempt from liability under Section 10 of this act) to pay damages therefor, such person so liable being hereinafter referred to as the third party. The respective rights and interests of the injured employee, or, in case of his death, his dependents and [any person entitled to sue therefor], and of the employer or person, association, corporation or carrier liable for the payment of compensation benefits under this act, hereinafter called "the carrier," in respect to the cause of action and the damages recovered shall be as provided by this section.

(b) The injured employee, or, in event of his death, his dependents, shall be entitled to receive the income and other benefits provided by this act and to enforce by appropriate proceedings his or their rights against the third party, provided that action against the third party must be commenced not later than [six months]² after the carrier accepts liability for the payment of compensation or makes such payment pursuant to an award under this act, except as hereinafter provided. In such case the carrier shall have a lien on the proceeds of any recovery from the third party whether by judgment, settlement or otherwise, after the deduction of reasonable and necessary expenditures, including attorneys' fees, incurred in effecting such recovery, to the extent of the total amount of compensation paid, and to such extent such recovery shall be deemed to be for the benefit of the carrier. Any balance remaining after payment of necessary expenses and satisfaction of the carrier's lien shall be applied as a credit against future compensation benefits for the same injury or death and shall be distributed as provided in subsection (g) of this section. Notice of the commencement of such action shall be given within 30 days thereafter to the Director, the employer and carrier upon a form prescribed by the Director.

(c) If, prior to the expiration of the six months period referred to in subsection (b), or within 90 days prior to the expiration of the time in which such action may be brought, whichever occurs first, the injured employee, or, in event of his death, [the person entitled to sue therefor] shall not have commenced action against or settled with the third party, the right of action of the injured employee, or, in event of his death, [the person entitled to sue therefor] shall pass by assignment to the carrier; *provided,* that such assignment shall not occur less than 20 days after the carrier has notified the injured employee or, in the event of his death, [the person entitled to sue therefor] in writing, by personal service or by registered or certified mail that failure to commence such action will operate as an assignment of the cause of action to the carrier. Prior to the expiration of 90 days after such assignment, the carrier shall give the Director, the injured employee, or, in event of his death, his dependents and [the person entitled to sue therefor] notice, upon a form

2. The language in this section should in each State be modified to fit (1) in reference to an action for injury, the state statute of limitations applicable thereto and (2) in reference to an action for death, the death statute, including limitations, of that State.

prescribed by the Director, that action has been or will be commenced against the third party. Failure to give such notice, or to commence such action at least 30 days prior to the expiration of the time within which such action may be brought, as fixed by [state statute of limitations], shall operate as a reassignment of such right of action to the injured employee or, in event of his death, [to the person entitled to sue therefor], and the rights and obligations of the parties shall be as provided by subsection (b) of this section.

If the carrier as such assignee recovers in an action (1) for injury, an amount in excess of the sum of the total of compensation paid or provided the injured employee and the reasonable expenses, including attorneys' fees, incurred in making such recovery, or (2) for death, an amount on behalf of the dependents of the employee in excess of the sum of the income benefits paid such dependents, and the reasonable expenses, including attorneys' fees, incurred in making such recovery, such excess shall be applied as a credit against future compensation benefits for the same injury or death and shall be distributed in accordance with subsection (g) of this section.

(d) If the persons entitled to share in the proceeds of an action brought under subsection (b) or (c) for death of the employee include any person who was not a dependent of the deceased employee, such person's share of any recovery made in such action, less a rateable share of the reasonable expenses incurred in making such recovery, shall be paid to such person or to the personal representative of the deceased.

(e) The injured employee, or, in event of his death, his dependents, and the carrier may, by agreement approved by the Director, or in event of a settlement made during actual trial of the action against the third party, approved by the judge presiding at such trial, provide for a distribution of the proceeds of any recovery in such action different from that prescribed by subsection (b) or (c) of this section.

(f) If the third party, with notice or knowledge of the carrier's lien, and the employee, or, in the event of his death, [the person entitled to sue therefor], make a compromise settlement without the written consent of the carrier for an amount less than the total of the compensation to which he or they are entitled under this act because of such injury or death, such settlement shall be invalid as against the carrier, which shall be entitled to maintain an action against the third party to recover the amount of compensation for which the carrier is liable under this act, less the amount actually inuring to the benefit of the carrier from the proceeds of such settlement.

At the trial of such action the fact of such settlement shall be prima facie evidence that the injury was proximately caused by a breach of duty owed to the employee or a warranty given by the third party.

The carrier shall not unreasonably refuse to approve a proposed compromise settlement with the third party. The injured employee or his dependents may make written application to the Director for a finding that a proposed compromise settlement with the third party is reasonable and fair to all parties. If the Director, after such inquiry as he deems necessary, and after hearing if demanded by either the carrier, the injured employee or his dependents, finds the proposed settlement reasonable and fair, it shall be deemed to have been approved by the carrier.

(g) When there remains a balance of $5,000 or more of the amount recovered from a third party by the beneficiary or carrier after payment of necessary expenses, and satisfaction of the carrier's lien and payment of the share of any person not a beneficiary under the act which is applicable as a credit against future compensation benefits for the same injury or death under either subsection (b) or subsection (c) of this section, the entire balance shall in the first instance be paid to the carrier by the third party. The present value of all amounts estimated by the Director to be thereafter payable as compensation, such present value to be computed in accordance with a schedule prepared by the Director, shall be held by the carrier as a fund to pay such future compensation as it becomes due, and to pay any sum finally remaining in excess thereof to the beneficiaries.

As soon as the Director has fixed the amount to be held by the carrier in such fund, or determined that no future compensation will be due, any excess of the third party recovery over the total amount necessary for payment of necessary expenses, satisfaction of the carrier's lien, and payment of the share of any person not a beneficiary under this act and creation of such fund, if any, shall be paid forthwith to the beneficiary, but shall continue to constitute a credit against future compensation benefits for the same injury or death as to any compensation liability that may exist after such fund has been exhausted.

(h) If death results from the injury and if the employee leaves no dependents entitled to benefits under this act, the carrier shall have a right of action against the third party for any amounts paid into the Special Fund established by Section 55, for reasonable funeral expenses and medical benefits actually paid by the carrier, and such cause of action shall be in addition to any cause of action of the legal representative of the deceased. Such right may be enforced in action at law brought against the third party within two years after the death of the employee.

Part II

Medical, Rehabilitation and Burial Services

Section 12.   [*Medical Services, Appliances and Supplies.*]

(a) For any injury covered by this act, the employee shall be entitled, without limitation as to time or dollar amount, to all medical services, appliances and supplies which are required by the nature of his injury and which will relieve pain and promote and hasten his restoration to health and employment. The employer shall furnish such services, appliances and supplies and necessary replacements or repairs of such appliances unless the need for such replacements or repairs is due to lack of proper care by the employee. In addition to the income benefits otherwise payable, the employee, who is entitled to income benefits, shall be paid an additional sum as for a medical benefit of not more than $50 weekly, as may be deemed necessary, when the service of an attendant is necessary constantly to be used by reason of the employee's being totally blind or having lost both hands or both feet or the use thereof or being paralyzed and unable to walk, or by reason of other disability resulting from the injury actually rendering him so helpless as to require constant attendance. The Director shall have authority to determine the necessity, character and sufficiency of any medical services furnished or to be furnished and shall have authority to order a change of physician, hospital or rehabilitation facility when in his judgment such change is desirable or necessary.

Alternative 1 for Section 12(b)

[(b)(1) Subject to the approval of the Director, the employer shall maintain a list of physicians (to be known as the Panel of Physicians) who are reasonably accessible to the employees. The employer shall post this list in a place or places easily accessible to his employees.

(2) The employee shall have the right to accept the services of a physician selected by his employer or to select a physician from the Panel of Physicians. The employee shall have the right to make an alternative choice of physician from such Panel if he is not satisfied with the physician first selected. If due to the nature of the injury or its occurrence away from the employer's place of business, the employer or the employee is unable to make a selection as outlined above, the selection requirements of this paragraph shall not apply as long as the inability to make a selection persists. The physician selected under this paragraph may arrange for any consultation, referral, extraordinary or other specialized medical services as the nature of the injury shall require. The employer shall not be responsible for the charges for medical services furnished or ordered by any physician or other person selected by the employee in disregard of the provisions of this paragraph or for compensation for any aggravation of the employee's injury attributable to improper treatment by such physician or other person.

(3) The Director may order necessary changes in a Panel of Physicians if he finds that it fails to contain a sufficient number of physicians who are conveniently available to or in the community in which the medical service is required and who are qualified to perform services necessary to meet the particular needs of employees of the employer. The Director may suspend or remove a physician from a Panel of Physicians under rules and regulations adopted by the Director.

(4) If the employer has knowledge of an injury to an employee and the necessity for treatment and shall fail to maintain the Panel of Physicians, or permit an employee to make choice of his physician from such Panel, the injured employee may select a physician to render service at the expense of the employer. No claim for such medical treatment shall be valid and enforceable against such employer, unless

within 10 days following the first treatment the physician giving such treatment furnish the employer and the Director a report of such injury and treatment on a form prescribed by the Director. The Director may, however, excuse the failure to furnish such report within 10 days when he finds it to be in the interest of justice to do so, and may, upon application by a party in interest, make an award for the reasonable value of such medical treatment so obtained by the employee.]

Alternative 2 for Section 12(b)

[(b)(1) The employee shall have the right to make the initial selection of his physician from a Panel of Physicians selected by the workmen's compensation agency.

(2) The Director shall select a list of physicians (to be known as the Panel of Physicians) who are reasonably accessible to the employees and shall furnish this list to the employer who shall post it in a place or places easily accessible to his employees.

(3) The employee shall have the right to make an alternative choice of physician from such Panel if he is not satisfied with the physician first selected. If due to the nature of the injury or its occurrence away from the employer's place of business, the employee is unable to make a selection as outlined above, the selection requirements of this paragraph shall not apply as long as the inability to make a selection persists. The physician selected under this paragraph may arrange for any consultation, referral, extraordinary or other specialized medical services as the nature of the injury shall require.

(4) The employer shall not be responsible for the charges for medical services furnished or ordered by any physician or other person selected by the employee in disregard of the provisions of this subsection or for compensation for any aggravation of the employee's injury attributable to improper treatment by such physician or other person.

(5) The Director may make necessary changes in a Panel of Physicians if he finds that it fails to contain a sufficient number of physicians who are conveniently available to or in the community in which the medical service is required and who are qualified to perform services necessary to meet the particular needs of employees of the employer. The Director may suspend or remove a physician from a Panel of Physicians under rules and regulations adopted by the Director.]

Alternative 3 for Section 12(b)

[(b)(1) The employee shall have the right to make the initial selection of his physician from among all licensed physicians in the State.

(2) The employee shall have the right to make an alternative choice of physician if he is not satisfied with the physician first selected. If due to the nature of the injury or its occurrence away from the employer's place of business the employee is unable to make a selection, the selection requirements of this paragraph shall not apply as long as the inability to make a selection persists. The physician selected under this paragraph may arrange for any consultation, referral, extraordinary or

other specialized medical services as the nature of the injury shall require.

(3) The employer shall not be responsible for the charges for medical services furnished or ordered by any physician or other person selected by the employee in disregard of the provisions of this subsection or for compensation for any aggravation of the employee's injury attributable to improper treatment by such physician or other person.]

Section 13. [Rehabilitation.]

(a) One of the primary purposes of this act shall be restoration of the injured employee to gainful employment. To this end there is hereby created a Rehabilitation Unit within the Agency which shall be composed of specialists in medical and vocational rehabilitation to be appointed by the Director.

(b) The Unit shall continuously study the problems of rehabilitation, both physical and vocational, and shall investigate and maintain a directory of all rehabilitation facilities, both private and public. The Director, in consultation with the Unit, shall approve as qualified such facilities, institutions and physicians as are capable of rendering competent rehabilitation service to seriously injured employees. No facility or institution shall be considered as qualified unless it is specifically equipped to provide rehabilitation services for persons suffering either from some specialized type of disability or general type of disability within the field of occupational injury and is staffed with trained and qualified personnel, and with respect to physical rehabilitation, unless it is supervised by a physician qualified to render such service. No physician shall be considered qualified unless he has had the experience and training specified by the Director.

(c) An employee who has suffered an injury covered by this act shall be entitled to prompt medical rehabilitation services. When as a result of the injury he is unable to perform work for which he has previous training or experience, he shall be entitled to such vocational rehabilitation services, including retraining and job placement, as may be reasonably necessary to restore him to suitable employment. If such services are not voluntarily offered and accepted, the Director on his own motion, or upon application of the employee or carrier, after affording the parties an opportunity to be heard, may refer the employee to a qualified physician or facility for evaluation of the practicability of, need for, and kind of service, treatment or training necessary and appropriate to render him fit for a remunerative occupation. Upon receipt of such report, and after affording the parties an opportunity to be heard, the Director, in consultation with the Unit, may order that the services and treatment recommended in the report, or such other rehabilitation treatment or service he may deem necessary, be provided at the expense of the employer.

(d) Where rehabilitation requires residence at or near the facility or institution away from the employee's customary residence, reasonable cost of his board, lodging or travel shall be paid for by the employer.

(e) Refusal to accept rehabilitation pursuant to an order of the Director shall result in loss of compensation for each week of the period of refusal.

(f) The Director and the Rehabilitation Unit shall cooperate on a reciprocal basis with the vocational rehabilitation section of the [Department of Education] and the employment service of the [Division of Employment Security].

Section 14.   [*Burial Expense.*]

If death results from the injury, the employer shall pay the cost of burying in an amount not to exceed [$] to any person who performed such service or incurred the liability for the service, whether or not the employee leaves dependents within the meaning of this act. Any such person is hereby authorized to file a petition with the Director for the fixing of the amount of the service and for an order requiring the employer to pay the cost of the service. If death occurs while the employee is away from his usual place of business or residence, the employer will be liable for the reasonable cost of transportation of the body to the employee's place of residence within the United States or Canada.

Part III

Income Benefits

Section 15.   [*Waiting Period.*]

No income benefits shall be allowed for the first three days of the disability; *provided,* however, that in case the injury results in disability of 14 or more days, income benefits shall be allowed from the date of the disability. The day on which the injury occurred shall be included in computing this waiting period unless the employee has been paid full wages for that day.

Section 16.   [*Income Benefits for Disability.*]

Income benefits for disability shall be paid to the employee as follows, subject to the maximum and minimum limits specified in Section 17.

(a) *Total Disability:* For total disability, 66⅔ percent of his average weekly wage during such disability.

(b) *Partial Disability:* For partial disability, 66⅔ percent of his decrease in wage-earning capacity during the continuance thereof.

(c) *Scheduled Income Benefits:* [7] For total permanent bodily loss or losses herein scheduled, after and in addition to the income benefits

----

7. The *Report of the National Commission on State Workmen's Compensation* Laws did not make a recommendation with respect to the 55 percent figure in this

payable during the period of recovery, scheduled income benefits in the amount of 55 percent of the average weekly wage as follows:

BODILY LOSS	*WEEKS OF DISABILITY* [8]
(1) Arm	[240–360]
(2) Leg	[160–240]
(3) Hand	[216–324]
(4) Foot	[112–168]
(5) Thumb	[86–130]
(6) Index Finger	[54– 81]
(7) Middle Finger	[43– 65]
(8) Ring Finger	[22– 32]
(9) Little Finger	[11– 16]
(10) Great Toe	[20– 30]
(11) Second Toe	[10– 20]
(12) Third Toe	[5– 15]
(13) Fourth Toe	[5– 8]
(14) Fifth Toe	[5]
(15) Total loss of binaural hearing	[156–208]
(16) Total loss of vision of one eye	[100–150]
(17) Total loss of bilateral vision	[520–750]
(18) Total loss, or total loss of use, of both hands, both arms, both feet or both legs	[520–750]

(19) Phalanges: For loss of distal phalanx, one half of the income benefits for loss of the entire digit. For loss of more than the distal phalanx of a digit, the same as loss of the entire digit.

(20) Amputated arm or leg: For an arm or leg amputated to a point no greater than one-third the distance from the wrist to the elbow joint or from the ankle to the knee joint scheduled income benefits shall be the same as those for the loss of the hand or foot.

(21) Two or more digits: For loss of two or more digits, or one or more phalanges of two or more digits, of a hand or foot, scheduled income benefits may be proportioned to the loss of use of the hand or foot occasioned thereby, but shall not exceed the scheduled income benefits for loss of a hand or foot.

(22) Total loss of use: Scheduled income benefits for permanent total loss of use of a member shall be the same as for loss of the member.

(23) Partial loss or partial loss of use: Scheduled income benefits for permanent partial loss of use of a member shall be for a period

subsection and, therefore, this Committee made no change in the suggested language. However, a State may wish to raise this figure to 66⅔ percent so as to be consistent with subsections (a) and (b).

8. The number of weeks in which scheduled income benefits are payable are based on 400 and 600 weeks respectively for the whole man and the American Medical Association's evaluation of the relationship of total loss or impairment of the particular member to the whole man. See the American Medical Association's *Guides to the Evaluation of Permanent Impairment.*

proportionate to the period benefits are payable for total loss or total loss of use of the member as such partial loss bears to total loss.

(24) Loss of hearing or partial loss of bilateral vision: Scheduled income benefits for partial loss of vision in one or both eyes, or total loss of hearing in one ear, or partial loss of hearing in one or both ears shall be for a period proportionate to the period benefits are payable for total bilateral loss of vision or total binaural loss of hearing as such partial loss bears to total loss. The provisions of paragraphs (4) through (8) inclusive of subsection (f) of this section shall apply to scheduled losses of hearing.

(25) In any case in which there shall be a loss or loss of use of more than one member or parts of more than one member set forth in paragraphs (1) to (24) of this subsection, scheduled income benefits shall be for the loss or loss of use of each such member or part thereof, with the periods of benefits to run consecutively, except that where the injury affects only two or more digits of the same hand or foot, paragraph (20) of this subsection shall apply.

(26) Other losses: Proper and equitable scheduled income benefits shall be paid for serious permanent disfigurement of face, head, neck or other area normally exposed and for loss or loss of function of a major member or organ when such disfigurement or loss is of a kind likely to handicap the employee in securing or holding employment, not to exceed 100 weeks, in addition to other scheduled income benefits payable under this section. However where scheduled income benefits are paid or payable for a particular member or organ, no additional benefits shall be made under this paragraph.

(27) In any case of total or partial loss of use of a member or organ, of hearing or vision, or in any case of disfigurement, determination of the period for which scheduled income benefits are payable shall not be made until the maximum of healing and of restoration of function has been attained.

(d) *Scheduled Income Benefits:* Scheduled income losses for bodily loss or losses, or loss of use, partial or total, shall be exclusive and in lieu of all income benefits payable after and in addition to the income benefits payable during the period of recovery except as otherwise provided in subsection (e) of this section.

(e) *Major Member Losses:* For total loss, or total and permanent loss of use, of an arm, hand, leg, both feet, or total loss of vision of both eyes, whether or not the injury also involves other impairments of the body, income benefits for such major member loss shall be for the period specified for such loss or loss of use in subsection (c), and with respect to any subsequent period of actual disability, income benefits shall be payable as provided in subsection (a) or (b) of this section, as long as the major member loss continues as a total loss and as long as actual disability as defined in Section 2(h) continues.

(f) *Scheduled Income Benefits for Occupational Deafness:* Occupational deafness means permanent partial or permanent total loss of hearing of one or both ears caused by prolonged exposure to harmful noise in employment. The following provisions shall apply exclusively to loss of hearing compensable under this subsection:

(1) No claim for scheduled income benefits shall be filed until the lapse of six full consecutive calendar months after the termination of exposure to harmful noise in employment. The time limitation for the filing of claims for occupational deafness shall not begin to run earlier than the day following the termination date of such six months' period. The time for filing claim as provided under this paragraph shall be applicable not only in respect of the last employer, but also in respect of any prior employer who may have liability to pay compensation for the occupational deafness.

(2) No employer shall be liable for the payment of scheduled income benefits for occupational deafness unless the employee claiming benefits shall have worked for such employer in employment exposing the employee to harmful noise for a total period of at least 90 days.

(3) An employer, otherwise liable under this subsection, whose employment has contributed to any extent to an employee's occupational deafness shall be liable for the full extent of the deafness of the employee, unless such employer shall establish by competent evidence (including the results of a professionally controlled hearing test) the extent of the employee's deafness as it existed prior to exposure to harmful noise in the employer's employment. Upon such showing the employer shall be liable to the employee only for the proportion of the deafness attributable to employment by him. An employer liable to the employee for the full extent of the employee's occupational deafness may implead, in a compensation proceeding on the employee's claim, any prior employer or employers in whose employment the employee had been exposed to harmful noise, and if it should be found that the impleaded employer would have been liable to the employee under this subsection, had the employee proceeded against him, under the claim being adjudicated, the employer held liable shall be entitled to an award against the impleaded employer. The impleading of an employer shall be accomplished by notice on a form prescribed by the Director. Such notice shall be sent to the impleaded employer and to the Director. An award may be made in favor of the employer liable to the employee, and against the impleaded employer or employers, which award may be enforced in the same manner as awards to employees. The impleaded employer or employers shall bear equal shares with the employer of the employer's liability to the employee, unless the evidence warrants a different apportionment.

(4) Losses of hearing due to industrial noise for compensation purposes shall be confined to the frequencies of 500, 1000, and 2000

cycles per second. Loss of hearing ability for frequency tones above 2000 cycles per second are not to be considered as constituting disability for hearing.

(5) The percent of hearing loss, for purposes of the determination of compensation claims for occupational deafness, shall be calculated as the average, in decibels, of the thresholds of hearing for the frequencies of 500, 1000, and 2000 cycles per second. Hearing threshold levels which average 25 decibels[9] or less in these frequencies involve no impairment and shall not constitute any compensable hearing disability. If the losses of hearing average 25 decibels or less in the three frequencies, such losses of hearing shall not then constitute any compensable hearing disability. If the losses of hearing average 92 decibels or more in the three frequencies, then the same shall constitute and be a total or 100 percent compensable hearing loss.

(6) In measuring hearing impairment, the lowest measured losses in each of the three frequencies shall be added together and divided by three to determine the average decibel loss. For every decibel of loss exceeding 25 decibels an allowance of 1½ percent shall be made up to the maximum of 100 percent which is reached at 92 decibels.

(7) In determining the binaural percentage of loss, the percentage of impairment in the better ear shall be multiplied by five. The resulting figure shall be added to the percentage of impairment in the poorer ear and the sum of the two divided by six. The final percentage shall represent the binaural hearing impairment.

(8) Before determining the percentage of hearing impairment, in order to allow for the average amount of hearing loss from nonoccupational causes found in the population at any given age, there shall be deducted from the total average decibel loss, one-half decibel for each year of the employee's age over 40 at the time of last exposure to industrial noise.

(9) No consideration shall be given to the question of whether or not the ability of an employee to understand speech is improved by the use of a hearing aid.

(g) The period of any scheduled income benefits payable under this section on account of any injury shall be reduced by the period of income benefits paid or payable under such schedule on account of a prior injury if scheduled income benefits in both cases are for disability of the same member or function, or different parts of the same member or function, and the scheduled income benefits payable on account of the subsequent

---

9. The hearing threshold (decibel) levels specified refer to readings on audiometers calibrated according to American National Standard Specifications for Audiometers, S3.6—1969, American National Standards Institute, Inc., 1430 Broadway, New York, New York 10018. To be equivalent, readings on audiometers calibrated according to American Standard Z24.5, previously applicable, should be increased by 10 decibels for each frequency.

disability in whole or in part would duplicate the scheduled income benefits payable on account of the pre-existing disability.

(h) When an employee, who has sustained disability compensable under subsection (c), and who has filed a valid claim in his lifetime, dies from causes other than the injury before the expiration of the compensable period specified, the income benefits specified and unpaid at the individual's death, whether or not accrued or due at his death, shall be paid, under an award made before or after such death, for the period specified in this subsection, to and for the benefit of the persons within the classes at the time of death and in the proportions and upon the conditions specified in this subsection and in the order named.

(1) To the widow or wholly actually dependent widower, if there is no child under the age of 18 or incapable of self-support; or

(2) If there are both such a widow or widower and such a child or children one-half to such widow or widower and the other half to such child or children; or

(3) If there is no such widow or widower but such a child or children, then to such child or children; or

(4) If there is no survivor in the above classes, then the parent or parents wholly or partly actually dependent for support upon the decedent, or to other wholly or partly actually dependent relatives listed in Section 18(a)(7) or to both, in such proportions as the Director may provide by regulation.

Section 17. [*Weekly Maximum and Minimum Income Benefits for Disability.*]

(a) The minimum weekly income benefits for total disability shall not be less than 20 percent (computed to the next higher multiple of $1.00) and the maximum weekly income benefit for disability shall be 66⅔ percent (computed to the next higher multiple of $1.00) of the average weekly wage of the State as defined herein; *provided,* that the maximum weekly benefit amount, rounded to the nearest dollar, shall be increased so that it shall be 100 percent as of July 1, 1975, 133⅓ percent as of July 1, 1977, 166⅔ percent as of July 1, 1979, and 200 percent as of July 1, 1981, of the State's average weekly wage as determined in subsection (b). In any event, income benefits shall not exceed the average weekly wage of the injured employee, except as provided in Section 21, nor shall the benefits be reduced by the amount of any payments from a welfare program or other program based upon need.

(b) For the purpose of this act the average weekly wage in the State shall be determined by the Director as follows: On or before October 1 of each year, the total wages reported on contribution reports to the [agency administering Employment Security Act or Unemployment Compensation Insurance Act] for the preceding calendar year shall be divided by the average monthly number of insured workers (determined by dividing the total insured workers reported for the preceding year by 12).

The average annual wage thus obtained shall be divided by 52 and the average weekly wage thus determined rounded to the nearest cent. The average weekly wage as so determined shall be applicable for the 12–month period commencing July 1 following the October 1 determination.

(c) The minimum and maximum income benefits as so determined in Section 17(a) that are in effect on the date of injury, or in effect on the date of disablement in the case of disease, shall be applicable for the full period during which income benefits for disability are payable, except as provided in Section 21.

(d) The minimum or the maximum weekly income benefits shall not be changed unless the computation herein provided results in an increase or decrease of $2.00 or more, raised to the next even dollar in the level of the minimum or the maximum weekly income benefits.

Section 18. [*Income Benefits for Death.*]

If the injury causes death, income benefits shall be payable in the amount and to or for the benefit of the persons following, subject to the maximum limits specified in Section 18(c):

(a) *Benefit Amounts for Particular Classes of Dependents.*

(1) If there is a widow or widower and no children of the deceased, as defined in Section 2, to such widow or widower 66⅔ percent of the average weekly wage of the deceased, during widowhood or widowerhood.

(2) To the widow or widower, if there is a child or children living with the widow or widower, 45 percent of the average weekly wage of the deceased, or 40 percent, if such child is not or all such children are not living with a widow or widower, and in addition thereto, benefits for the child or children which shall make the total benefits for the widow or widower and child or children 66⅔ percent of the average weekly wage of the deceased. When there are two or more children, the indemnity benefits payable on account of such children shall be divided among such children, share and share alike.

(3) Two years indemnity benefits in one lump sum shall be payable to a widow or widower upon remarriage.

(4) To the child or children if there is no widow or widower, 66⅔ percent of such wage divided among such children, share and share alike.

(5) The income benefits payable on account of any child under this section shall cease when he dies, marries, or reaches the age of 18, or when a child over such age ceases to be physically or mentally incapable of self-support, or if actually dependent ceases to be actually dependent, or, if enrolled as a full-time student in any accredited educational institution, ceases to be so enrolled or reaches the age of 25. A child who originally qualified as a dependent by virtue of being less than 18 years of age may, upon reaching age 18, continue to qualify if he satisfies the tests of being physically or

mentally incapable of self-support, actual dependency, or enrollment in an educational institution.

(6) To each parent, if actually dependent, 25 percent.

(7) To the brothers, sisters, grandparents, and grandchildren, if actually dependent, 25 percent to each such dependent. If there should be more than one of such dependents, the total income benefits payable on account of such dependents shall be divided, share and share alike.

(8) The income benefits of each beneficiary under paragraphs (6) and (7) above shall be paid until he, if a parent or grandparent, dies, marries, or ceases to be actually dependent, or, if a brother, sister, or grandchild, dies, marries, or reaches the age of 18 or if over that age ceases to be physically or mentally incapable of self-support, or ceases to be actually dependent.

(9) A person ceases to be actually dependent when his income from all sources exclusive of workmen's compensation income benefits is such that, if it had existed at the time as of which the original determination of actual dependency was made, it would not have supported a finding of dependency. In any event, if the present annual income of an actual dependent person including workmen's compensation income benefits at any time exceeds the total annual support received by the person from the deceased employee, the workmen's compensation benefits shall be reduced so that the total annual income is no greater than such amount of annual support received from the deceased employee. In all cases, a person found to be actually dependent shall be presumed to be no longer actually dependent three years after such time as of which the person was found to be actually dependent. This presumption may be overcome by proof of continued actual dependency as defined in this subsection and Section 2(s).

(b) *Change in Dependents.* Upon the cessation of income benefits under this section to or on account of any person, the income benefits of the remaining persons entitled to income benefits for the unexpired part of the period during which their income benefits are payable shall be that which such persons would have received if they had been the only persons entitled to income benefits at the time of the decedent's death.

(c) *Maximum and Minimum Total Payments.* The maximum weekly income benefits payable for all beneficiaries in case of death shall not exceed 66⅔ percent of the average weekly wage of the deceased as calculated under Section 19, subject to the maximum limits in Section 17, with a minimum of 50 percent (computed to the next higher multiple of $1.00) of the average weekly wage of the State as defined in Section 17(b). The maximum aggregate limitation shall not operate in case of payment of two years' income benefits to the widow or widower upon remarriage, as provided under subsection (a)(3) of this section, to prevent the immediate recalculation and payments of benefits to the remaining beneficiaries as provided under subsection (b) of this section.

The classes of beneficiaries specified in paragraphs (1) and (4) of subsection (a) shall have priority over all other beneficiaries in the apportionment of income benefits. If the provisions of this subsection should prevent payment to other beneficiaries of the income benefits to the full extent otherwise provided for by this section, the gross remaining amount of income benefits payable to such other beneficiaries shall be apportioned by class, proportionate to the interest of each class in the remaining amount. Parents shall be considered to be in one class and those specified in paragraph (7) in another class.

(d) *Social Security Offset.* The income benefits provided for in this section shall be reduced by the amount of survivor benefits paid under the Old Age Survivors Disability and Health Insurance Act.

(e) The minimum and maximum income benefits as so determined in Section 18(c) that are in effect on the date of injury shall be applicable for the full period during which income benefits for death are payable, except as provided in Section 21.

Section 19. [*Determination of Average Weekly Wage.*]

Except as otherwise provided in this act, the average weekly wage of the injured employee at the time of the injury shall be taken as the basis upon which to compute compensation and shall be determined as follows:

(a) If at the time of the injury the wages are fixed by the week, the amount so fixed shall be the average weekly wage;

(b) If at the time of the injury the wages are fixed by the month, the average weekly wage shall be the monthly wage so fixed multiplied by 12 and divided by 52;

(c) If at the time of the injury the wages are fixed by the year, the average weekly wage shall be the yearly wage so fixed divided by 52;

(d)(1) If at the time of the injury the wages are fixed by the day, hour, or by the output of the employee, the average weekly wage shall be the wage most favorable to the employee computed by dividing by 13 the wages (not including overtime or premium pay) of said employee earned in the employ of the employer in the first, second, third, or fourth period of 13 consecutive calendar weeks in the 52 weeks immediately preceding the injury.

(2) If the employee has been in the employ of the employer less than 13 calendar weeks immediately preceding the injury, his average weekly wage shall be computed under the foregoing paragraph, taking the wages (not including overtime or premium pay) for such purpose to be the amount he would have earned had he been so employed by the employer the full 13 calendar weeks immediately preceding the injury and had worked, when work was available to other employees in a similar occupation.

(e) If at the time of the injury the hourly wage has not been fixed or can not be ascertained, the wage for the purpose of calculating compensation shall be taken to be the usual wage for similar services where such services are rendered by paid employees.

(f) In occupations which are exclusively seasonal and therefore cannot be carried on throughout the year, the average weekly wage shall be taken to be one-fiftieth of the total wages which the employee has earned from all occupations during the 12 calendar months immediately preceding the injury.

(g) In the case of volunteer firemen, police, andcivil defense members or trainees, the income benefits shall be based on the average weekly wage in their regular employment.

(h) If the employee was a minor, apprentice or trainee when injured, and it is established that under normal conditions his wages should be expected to increase during the period of disability, that fact may be considered in computing his average weekly wage.

(i) When the employee is working under concurrent contracts with two or more employers and the defendant employer has knowledge of such employment prior to the injury, his wages from all such employers shall be considered as if earned from the employer liable for compensation.

Section 20.   [*Payment for Second Injuries From Special Fund.*] [10]

(a) If an employee who has a permanent impairment from any cause or origin incurs a subsequent impairment by injury arising out of and in the course of his employment resulting in compensation liability for disability that is substantially greater by reason of the combined effects of the preexisting impairment and subsequent injury or by reason of the aggravation of the preexisting impairment than that which would have resulted from the subsequent injury alone, the employer or his insurance carrier shall in the first instance pay all awards of compensation provided by this act, but such employer or his insurance carrier shall be reimbursed from the Special Fund created by Section 55 for all compensation payments subsequent to those payable for the first 104 weeks of disability.

(b) If the subsequent injury of such an employee shall result in the death of the employee and it shall be determined that the death would not have occurred except for such preexisting permanent impairment, the employer or his insurance carrier shall in the first instance pay the compensation prescribed by this act, but he or his insurance carrier shall be reimbursed from the Special Fund created by Section 55 for all compensation payable in excess of 104 weeks.

10. The Special Fund referred to here is the second or subsequent injury fund that   virtually all States have established.

(c) In order to qualify under this section for reimbursement from the Special Fund, the employer must establish by written records that the employer had knowledge of the permanent impairment at the time that the employee was hired, or at the time the employee was retained in employment after the employer acquired such knowledge.

(d) As used in this section, "permanent impairment" means any permanent condition, whether congenital or due to injury or disease, of such seriousness as to constitute a hindrance or obstacle to obtaining employment or to obtaining reemployment if the employee should become unemployed. No condition shall be considered a "permanent impairment" unless it is one of the following conditions:

(1) Epilepsy

(2) Diabetes

(3) Cardiac disease

(4) Arthritis

(5) Amputated foot, leg, arm or hand

(6) Loss of sight of one or both eyes or a partial loss of uncorrected vision of more than 75 percent bilaterally

(7) Residual disability from poliomyelitis

(8) Cerebral palsy

(9) Multiple sclerosis

(10) Parkinson's disease

(11) Cerebral vascular accident

(12) Tuberculosis

(13) Silicosis

(14) Psychoneurotic disability following treatment in a recognized medical or mental institution

(15) Hemophilia

(16) Chronic osteomyelitis

(17) Ankylosis of joints

(18) Hyperinsulism

(19) Muscular dystrophies

(20) Arteriosclerosis

(21) Thrombophlebitis

(22) Varicose veins

(23) Heavy metal poisoning

(24) Ionizing radiation injury

(25) Compressed air sequelae

(26) Ruptured intervertebral disk

or unless it would support a rating of disability of 200 weeks or more if evaluated according to standards applied in compensation claims.

(e) The Special Fund shall not be bound as to any question of law or fact by reason of an award or an adjudication to which it was not a party or in relation to which it was not notified at least three weeks prior to the award or adjudication, that it might be subject to liability for the injury or death.

(f) An employer or carrier shall notify the Director and the Director of the Special Fund of any possible claim against the Special Fund as soon as practicable, but in no event later than 100 weeks after the injury or death.

Section 21.   [*Benefit Adjustment.*]   (omitted)

Part IV

Procedures

Section 22.   [*Record of Injury or Death.*]

Every employer shall keep a record of each injury to any of his employees as reported to him or of which he otherwise has knowledge. Such record shall include a description of the injury, a statement of any time during which the injured person was unable to work because of the injury, a description of the manner in which the injury occurred, and such other information relating to the injury or its occurrence as the Director may by regulation require.   These records shall be available for inspection by the Director or by any governmental agency at such reasonable times and under such conditions as the Director may prescribe.   Upon willful failure or refusal of the employer to keep the record required under this section, the Director may assess against such employer a civil penalty not exceeding [$500], which penalty shall be paid into the Special Fund established under Section 55.

Section 23.   [*Report of Injury or Death.*]

(a) Within 15 days after the employer has notice or knowledge of the occurrence of a death or any injury which constitutes a permanent impairment, or which renders the injured person unable to perform a regularly established job at his place of employment during any portion of his regular shift on any calendar day subsequent to the day of injury, a report thereof shall be made in writing by the employer to the Director, upon a form approved by the Director for that purpose, setting forth (1) the name, address, and business of the employer; (2) the name, address, and occupation of the employee; (3) the nature of the injury and a description of the manner in which it occurred; (4) the year, month, day and hour when, and the particular locality where injury or death occurred; and (5) such other information as the Director may prescribe by regulation.   In addition, within the same period, except where claim has been filed under Section 26(e), if the case involves death or more than three days' disability, the employer shall notify the

Director in writing whether payment shall be made without an award or controverted. If the right to compensation is controverted, the grounds shall be stated, but the stating of such grounds shall not prevent the later assertion of other defenses. For other injuries not resulting in disability but which require medical treatment by a physician beyond ordinary first-aid, monthly summary reports may be required on a form prescribed by the Director. The form, as adopted by the Director to report an injury or death, shall include the information required by the Occupational Safety and Health Act of 1970, as amended.

(b) The mailing to the Director of any such written report as required in subsection (a) of this section within the time prescribed, shall be a compliance with this section.

(c) Whenever an employer willfully fails to file or refuses to file report of injury or death as required in subsection (a) of this section, the Director may assess a penalty not exceeding [$500], which penalty shall be paid into the Special Fund, established under Section 55.

(d) Where the employer has knowledge of any injury or death and willfully fails or refuses to file the report of injury as required in subsection (a) of this section, the limitations prescribed in Section 26 shall not begin to run against the claim of any person entitled to compensation until such report shall have been furnished as required by this section.

(e) All reports submitted to the Director under this section shall be confidential and not admissible in evidence in any administrative or judicial proceedings. Such reports may be made available to other state or federal agencies for study and informational purposes under such limitations as may be prescribed by the Director, but they shall not be used as evidence of any admission against interest for purposes of adjudication, litigation or determination of claims, whether administrative or judicial.

Section 24.   *[Method and Time of Payment of Compensation.]*

(a) Compensation under this act shall be paid promptly, and directly to the person entitled thereto, without an award, except where the right to compensation is controverted by the employer.

(b) The first installment of income benefits shall become due on the fifteenth day after the employer has notice or knowledge of the employee's disability or death due to injury, on which date all income benefits then due shall be paid. Thereafter, income benefits shall be paid in biweekly installments, except where the Director determines that payment in installments should be made at some other period.

(c) Upon making the first payment of income benefits, and upon stopping or changing of such benefits for any cause other than final payment under Section 27(c), the employer shall immediately notify the Director, in accordance with a form prescribed by the Director, that the payment of income benefits has begun or has been stopped or changed.

(d) If payments have been made without an award, and the employer then elects to controvert, the notice of controversy shall be filed with the Director within 15 days of the due date of the first omitted payment under this election.

(e) If, after the payment of compensation without an award, the employer elects to controvert the right to compensation, the payment of compensation shall not be considered a binding determination of the obligations of the employer as to future compensation payments. The acceptance of compensation by the employee or his dependents shall not be considered a binding determination of their rights under this act.

(f) The Director (1) may, upon his own initiative at any time in a case in which payments are being made without an award, and (2) shall, upon receipt of information from any person claiming to be entitled to compensation, from the employer, or otherwise that the right to compensation is controverted, or that payment of compensation has been opposed, stopped, or changed, whether or not claim has been filed, promptly make such inquiry as circumstances require, cause such medical examinations to be made, hold such hearings, make such determinations or awards, and take such further action as he considers will properly protect the rights of all parties.

Section 25. [*Notice of Injury or Death.*]

(a) Notice of injury or death shall be given to the employer within 30 days after the date of such injury or death, or within 30 days after the employee or his dependents know the nature of the injury and its relationship to the employment.

(b) Such notice shall be in writing, shall contain the name and address of the employee and a statement of the time, place, nature and cause of the injury or death, and shall be signed by the employee or by some person on his behalf, or, in case of death by any person claiming to be entitled to compensation for such death, or by a person on his behalf.

(c) Notice shall be given to the employer by delivering it to him or his representative or by sending it by mail addressed to him or such agent at the last known place of business of either. Such notice may be given to the employer, partner, superior, foreman, agent, or officer of the employer.

(d) Failure to give such notice shall not bar any claim under this act (1) if the employer (or his representative as identified in subsection (c) above) or the carrier had knowledge of the injury or death, or (2) if the Director excuses such failure on the ground that for some satisfactory reason such notice could not be given or that the employer or carrier has not been prejudiced by failure to receive such notice, or (3) unless objection to such failure is raised in the answer as filed with the Director in accordance with Section 26(e).

Section 26. [*Time Limitation for Filing of Claims.*]

(a) The right to compensation for disability shall be barred unless a claim therefor is filed within three years after the injury or last payment of compensation. The right to income benefits for death shall be barred unless a claim therefor is filed within three years after the death or within three years after the dependents know or by exercise of reasonable diligence should know the possible relationship of the death to the employment. However, in cases in which the nature of the injury or disease or its relationship to the employment is not known to the employee the time for filing claim shall not begin to run until (1) the employee knows or by exercise of reasonable diligence should know of the existence of the injury and its possible relationship to his employment and (2) sustains disability or incurs a scheduled physical loss under Section 16(c), (except paragraph (24)).

(b) Notwithstanding the provisions of subsection (a), failure to file a claim within the period prescribed in such subsection shall not be a bar to such right unless objection to such failure is raised in the answer to the claim filed under subsection (e) of this section.

(c) If a person who is entitled to compensation under this act is incompetent or a minor, the time for filing claim under subsection (a) shall not begin to run so long as such person has no guardian or other authorized representative, but shall run from the date of appointment of such guardian or other representative, or in the case of a minor, if no guardian is appointed before he becomes 21 years of age, from the date he becomes 21 years of age.

(d) Where recovery is denied to any person, in a suit brought at law or in admiralty to recover damages in respect of injury or death, on the ground that such person was an employee and that the defendant was an employer within the meaning of this act, the limitation of time prescribed in subsection (a) of this section shall not begin to run earlier than from the date of final termination of such action.

(e) Upon the filing with him of a claim, demand, or application of any kind by a person seeking determination of his rights under this act, the Director shall transmit a copy thereof to the other party with notice to respond thereto by answer. The Director shall prepare an appropriate form or forms by which to enable the other party to answer. The other party shall respond by answer (in duplicate) within 20 days after receiving such notices or within such extension of that time as the Director may allow. If answer is not filed, the Director or his hearing officer shall proceed to determine the rights following the procedure in Section 24(f).

Section 27. [*Payment of Compensation.*]

(a) If the right to compensation has not been controverted and any amount of compensation payable to the beneficiary without an award is not paid within 14 days after it becomes due, as provided in Section 24(b), there shall be added to such unpaid compensation an amount equal to [10] percent thereof, which shall be paid to the beneficiary at the same time as, but in addition to, such amount due, and without regard to any limitation otherwise applicable upon the amount of the compensation, unless such nonpayment is excused by the Director after a showing by the employer that owing to conditions over which he had no control such compensation could not be paid within the period prescribed for the payment.

(b) If any amount of compensation payable under the terms of an award is not paid within 30 days after it shall become payable under the terms of the award, there shall be added to such unpaid amount an amount equal to [20] percent thereof, which shall be paid to the beneficiary at the same time as, but in addition to, such compensation unless review of the order making such award he had, as provided in Section 34, or unless such nonpayment is excused by the Director after a showing by the employer that owing to conditions over which he had no control such compensation could not be paid within the period prescribed for the payment. If review is had, interest at the rate of [5] percent shall be added to the award from the date of the original award of the Director or hearing officer.

(c) Within 16 days after the final payment of income benefits has been made, the employer shall send to the Director a notice, in accordance with a form prescribed by the Director, stating that such final payment has been made, the total amount of income benefits paid, the name of the employee, and of any other person to whom income benefits have been paid, the date of the injury or death, the dates on which income benefits have been paid, and the period covered by the payment. If the employer fails to notify the Director within such time, the Director may assess against such employer a penalty in an amount not to exceed [$500] which shall be paid into the Special Fund, established under Section 55.

(d) Whenever the Director deems it advisable or necessary to protect a beneficiary, he may require an employer who has not secured the payment of compensation to his employees as required by this act to make a deposit of money with the [State Treasurer] to secure the prompt and convenient payment of compensation payable under an award or modified award. Payments therefrom upon any such award shall be made upon order of the Director.

(e) Whenever the Director determines after a hearing that it is in the interest of the rehabilitation of the injured worker in accordance with regulations established by the Director, and it is recommended by the Rehabilitation Unit, the liability for income benefits under this act, or any part thereof, may be discharged by the payment of a lump sum equal to the present value of future income benefits commuted, computed at [3] percent true discount compounded annually. The probability of the beneficiary's death before the expiration of the period during which he is entitled to income benefits shall be determined in accordance with the United States Life Table, and the probability of the remarriage of a widow shall be determined in accordance with the American Re–Marriage Table. The probability of the happening of any other contingency affecting the amount of duration of the income benefits shall be disregarded.

(f) Unless otherwise intended or agreed upon when the employer pays wages in whole or part during an injured employee's disability, he shall be entitled to a credit not to exceed the amount of income benefits due for the same period when such wages are paid except for scheduled benefits paid under Section 16(c) to which this subsection shall not apply.

Section 28. [*Minors or Incompetents.*] (omitted)

Section 29. [*Recording and Reporting of Payments.*]

Every carrier shall keep a record of all payments of compensation made under the provisions of this act, and of the time and manner of making such payments.

Section 30. [*Invalid Agreements.*]

(a) No agreement by an employee to pay any portion of premium paid by his employer or to contribute to a benefit fund or department maintained by such employer for the purpose of providing compensation as required by this act shall be valid, and any employer who makes a deduction for such purpose from the pay of any employee entitled to the benefits of this act shall be guilty of a [misdemeanor] and upon conviction thereof shall be punished by a fine of not more than [$1,000].

(b) No agreement by an employee to waive his right to compensation under this act shall be valid.

Section 31. [*Assignment and Exemption From Claims of Creditors.*]

No assignment, release, or commutation of income benefits due or payable under this act, except as provided by this act, shall be valid, and such income benefits shall be exempt from all claims of creditors, or other debts and from levy, execution, and attachment or other remedy for recovery or collection of a debt, which exemption may not be waived.

Section 32. [*Compensation a Lien Against Assets.*]

In case of insolvency or bankruptcy, every liability for compensation under this act shall constitute a first lien upon all the property of the employer liable therefor, paramount to all other claims or liens except for wages and taxes, and such liens shall be enforced by order of the court.

Section 33. [*Hearing Procedure.*]

(a) Upon application of a party in interest, or when ordered by the Director [or] his hearing officer, and when issues in a case cannot be resolved by pre-hearing conferences or otherwise, a hearing shall be held for determining the questions at issue. All parties in interest shall be given at least 10 days notice of the hearing and of the issues to be heard, served personally or by mail. Following the presentation of the evidence, the Director or his hearing officer shall determine the questions at issue and file the decision thereon in the office of the [appropriate state agency] within 30 days unless the time for filing the decision is extended by the Director. At the time of such filing, a certified copy of the decision shall be sent by certified mail to all interested parties at the last known address of each. The decision of the Director or his hearing officer shall be made in the form of a compensation order, appropriately titled to show its purpose and containing a report of the case, findings of fact, and conclusions of law, and other explanation of the action taken. A compensation order shall be final unless a timely appeal to the Workmen's Compensation Appeals Board is filed by a party in interest under Section 34.

(b) The Director must adopt rules and regulations of practice and procedure consistent with this act for the hearing, disposition and adjudication of cases, the text of which shall be published and readily available. Such rules shall include provision for procedures in the nature of conferences in order to dispose of cases informally, or to expedite claim adjudication, narrow issues, and simplify the methods of proof at hearings.

(c) In making an inquiry or conducting a hearing the Director or his hearing officer shall not be bound by common law or statutory rules of evidence or by technical or formal rules of procedures, except as provided by this act, but may make such inquiry or conduct such hearing in such manner as best to ascertain the rights of the parties.

(d) All hearings before the Director or his hearing officer shall be open to the public. The Director shall by regulation provide for the preparation of a record of each hearing.

(e) All powers, authority, and duties of the Director in respect to adjudications and hearings shall apply to a hearing officer.

(f) The authority of the Director or hearing officer or their duly authorized representatives to determine controverted claims for compensation shall include the right to enter premises at any reasonable time where an injury or death has occurred, and to make such examination of any tool, appliance, process, machinery, or environmental or other condition as may be relevant to a determination of the cause and circumstances of such injury or death.

Section 34. [*Appeals to the Board.*]

A party in interest may appeal a compensation order to the Workmen's Compensation Appeals Board within 20 days from the date of mailing of the compensation order. If the Board, after a request by any party, determines that a hearing is necessary, it shall schedule a hearing and give at least 10 days notice to all interested parties of the date of such hearing and the issues to be heard. The Board shall have power to review the findings of fact, conclusions of law and exercise of discretion by the Director or his hearing officer in hearing, determining or otherwise handling of any compensation case and may affirm, reverse or modify any compensation case upon review or remand such a case to the Director for further proceedings and action.

The proceedings before the Board shall be on the record made before the Director or his hearing officer and no new or additional evidence shall be received in respect of the appeal. If the Board determines that the case has been improperly, incompletely, or otherwise insufficiently developed on hearing by the Director or his hearing officer, the case may be remanded for proceedings and appropriate action with or without the Board's relinquishing jurisdiction of the case.

The Board shall make a decision disposing of the issues presented by the appeal and file a decision in its office within [60] days of completion of submission of the case to the Board. Upon such filing, the Board shall send a certified copy of the decision by certified mail to all interested parties at the last known address of each. The decision of the Board shall be made in the form of an order, supported by a written opinion or statement setting forth the reasons for the action taken and including necessary findings of fact and conclusions of law.

The decision of the Board shall be final and conclusive as to all matters adjudicated by the Board upon the expiration of the thirtieth day after copy of the decision has been mailed to the parties, unless prior to that day (1) the Board on its own motion or that of a party in interest, and after notice to all parties in interest, shall signify that it will reconsider the decision, or (2) a party in interest shall seek judicial review of the decision authorized under Section 37.

The decision of the Board upon reconsideration of the case shall become final as to all matters considered, upon expiration of the thirtieth day after copy of decision has been mailed to the interested parties unless prior to that day a party in interest shall seek judicial review authorized under Section 37.

Section 35. [*Application for Modification.*]

The Director may review any compensation case and make a determination upon his own initiative or upon application of any party in interest in accordance with the procedure in respect of hearings, which may terminate, continue, reinstate, increase, decrease, or otherwise properly affect the compensation benefits provided by this act, or in any other respect consistent with this act, modify any previous decision, award, or action including the making of an award of compensation if the claim had been rejected in whole or in part.

A review may be had upon application of a party in interest filed with the Director at any time but not later than within two years after the date of the last payment or furnishing of compensation upon the following grounds:

(1) Mistake in determination of fact or failure to make material findings of fact; (2) mistake of law; (3) clerical error or mistake in mathematical calculations; or (4) newly discovered evidence.

A review may be had upon application of a party in interest filed with the Director at any time but not later than within five years after the date of the last payment or furnishing of compensation upon the following grounds:

(1) Change in the nature or extent of the employee's injury, wage-earning capacity, or status of the claimant; or (2) fraud. The Director may review a case at any time in order to correct a manifest injustice. In unusual cases in which the nature of the injury, disease, or its relationship to the employment is not known to the employee, the time for filing an application for review shall not begin to run until (1) the employee knows, or by exercise of reasonable diligence should know, of the existence of the injury and its possible relationship to his employment; (2) the employee sustains disability or incurs a scheduled physical loss under Section 16(c) (except paragraph (24)).

Section 36. [*Authority of the Director and Board for Conducting Hearings.*]

(a) The hearings by the Director or his hearing officer and the hearings by the Board, unless otherwise provided by law, shall be held at such places as the Director and the Board may find most convenient for the parties and most appropriate for ascertaining the rights of the parties.

(b) The Director and any member of the Board shall have the power to preserve and enforce order during hearings; to issue subpoenas for, to administer oaths, and to compel the attendance and testimony of a witness, or the production of books, papers, documents, and other evidence, or the taking of depositions before any designated individual competent to administer oaths; to examine witnesses; and to do all things conformable to law which may be necessary to enable them effectively to discharge the duties of their office.

(c) If any person in proceedings before the Director or Board disobeys or resists any lawful order or process, or misbehaves during a hearing or so near the place thereof as to obstruct the same, neglects to produce, after having been ordered to do so, any pertinent book, paper, or document, or refuses to appear after having been subpoenaed, or upon appearing refuses to take the oath or affirmation as a witness, or after taking the oath or affirmation refuses to be examined according to law, the Director or Board shall certify the facts to the [_____ court] where the offense is committed and the court shall, if the evidence so warrants, punish such person in the same manner and to the same extent as for contempt committed before the court, or commit such person upon the same conditions as if the doing of the forbidden act had occurred with reference to the process of or in the presence of the court.

Section 37. [*Judicial Review of Decision by Board.*]

(a) Any party in interest may, within the time limit specified in Section 34, file application for judicial review of such decision with the [intermediate or final appellate court].

(b) The court shall have power and jurisdiction to review decisions filed by the Board under this act on matters of law only and to perform such other judicial functions and to hear such other matters as are provided for by this act. The court may affirm, suspend, remand, modify or set aside, in whole or in part, a decision of the Board or compel administrative action unlawfully withheld or denied. [Appeals from such court may be had as in other civil actions.]

(c) Proceedings to set aside a compensation order or decision shall not be instituted otherwise than as provided for by this act.

(d) Except as hereinafter provided in this subsection, the taking of an appeal shall operate as a *supersedeas* as to payment of compensation under the award. In proceedings brought to review administrative action in which an award by the hearing officer or Director has been affirmed by the Appeals Board the court may after at least three days' notice to all parties in interest hear an application by the employee for the payment of compensation required under a compensation order or decision pending the outcome of the appeal. If after summary hearing of the parties the court finds that failure to make payments may jeopardize the health or physical well being of the employee or his dependents, the court may in its discretion order payment in whole or in part. Such proceedings shall be given priority over all other cases and such orders shall not be reviewable.

Section 38. [*Enforcement of Payment in Default and Penalties.*] (omitted)

Section 39. [*Witnesses and Their Fees.*] (omitted)

Section 40. [*Costs in Taking Appeal.*] (omitted)

Section 41. [*Costs in Proceeding Brought Without Reasonable Ground.*]

If the hearing authority having jurisdiction of any proceeding under this act, administrative or judicial, determines that such proceeding has been instituted or continued without reasonable ground, the costs of such proceeding including a reasonable attorney's fee for necessary services rendered shall be assessed against the party who has so instituted or continued such proceeding.

Section 42. [*Payment by Employer of Fees for Claimant's Legal Services and Witnesses.*][12]

(a) If the employer or carrier declines to pay any compensation on or before the thirtieth day after receiving written notice of demand or

---

12. This section was drafted only with considerable difficulty and difference of opinion among the drafting group and the Committee on Suggested State Legislation.

claim for compensation, on the ground that there is no liability for compensation within the provisions of this act, and the person seeking benefits shall thereafter have utilized the services of an attorney at law in the successful prosecution of his right, claim, or demand before the Director or hearing officer, there shall be awarded, in addition to the award for compensation, a reasonable attorney's fee against the employer or carrier in an amount approved by the Director or hearing officer which shall be paid directly by the employer to the attorney for the claimant in a lump sum after final decision. If the employer or carrier pays or tenders payment of compensation, but controversy relates to the amount of compensation due, and if the award is greater than the amount paid or tendered by the employer or carrier, a reasonable attorney's fee based solely upon the difference between the amount awarded and the amount tendered or paid shall be awarded in addition to the amount of compensation; *provided,* however, that this sentence shall not apply if the controversy relates to degree or length of disability, and if the employer or carrier offers to submit the case for evaluation by impartial medical opinion as provided in Section 12(c)(3) and offers to tender an amount of compensation based upon the degree or length of disability found by the independent medical report at such time as an evaluation of disability can be made. If the claimant is successful in review proceedings before the Board or court in any such case an award may be made in favor of the claimant and against the employer or carrier for a reasonable attorney's fee for claimant's counsel in accord with the above provisions. In all cases, fees for attorneys representing the claimant shall be approved in the manner herein provided. If any proceedings are had before the Board or any court for review of any action, award, order or decision, the Board or court may approve an attorney's fee for the work done before it by the attorney for the claimant. An approved attorney's fee, in cases in which the obligation to pay the fee is upon the claimant, may be made a lien upon the compensation due under an award; and the Director, hearing officer, Board, or court shall fix in the award approving the fee, such lien and manner of payment. The amounts awarded against an employer or carrier as attorney's fee shall not in any respect affect or diminish the compensation payable under this act.

(b) In every case, any fees for attorneys representing the claimant, employer, or insurer shall be reported to the Agency. The Director shall

It is offered with some misgiving because it appears to fly in the face of the tradition that each party to an action is responsible for paying his own legal fees. The section, however, seeks to ensure that a claimant will receive in its entirety an award to which he is entitled by statute—a statute which requires that he give up his common law right to sue his employer for all injuries covered by its provisions. It is recognized that certain safeguards must be included to prevent the section's becoming an invitation to litigation. Fees are subject to approval. If only the amount of the award is controverted, the size of the fee awarded must be related to the difference between the amount of compensation and the amount awarded. Further protection is offered an employer or carrier by his being able to submit the case to impartial medical opinion. Of course, payment of a claimant's legal fees by an employer or carrier presupposes the successful prosecution of his claim by the claimant.

regulate the attorneys' fees for legal services provided prior to any review by any court. If any proceedings are had before any court for review of any action, award, order, or decision, the court shall regulate the attorneys' fees for the work done before the court.

(c) In cases where an attorney's fee is awarded against an employer or carrier there may be further assessed against such employer or carrier as costs, fees and mileages for necessary witnesses attending the hearing at the instance of claimant. Both the necessity for the witness and the reasonableness of the fees must be approved by the Director or hearing officer.

(d) Any person who receives any fees, other consideration, or any gratuity on account of services rendered as a representative of claimant, unless such consideration or gratuity is approved by the Director, hearing officer, Board, or court, or who makes it a business to solicit employment for a lawyer or for himself in respect of any claim or award for compensation, shall be guilty of a [misdemeanor], and upon conviction thereof, for each offense shall be punished by a fine of not more than [$1,000] or by imprisonment for not more than [one year], or by both such fine and imprisonment.

Section 43. *[Penalty for Misrepresentation.]*

Any person who willfully makes any false or misleading statement or representation for the purpose of obtaining or defeating any benefit, fee, or allowance under this act shall be guilty of a [misdemeanor] and on conviction thereof shall be punished by a fine of not to exceed [$1,000] or by imprisonment for not more than [one year], or by both such fine and imprisonment.

Section 44. *[Enforcement of Penalties, Deposits and Assessments.]* (omitted)

Section 45. *[Aliens.]* (omitted)

Part V

Insurance

Section 46. *[Security for Payment of Compensation.]* [14]

Every employer shall secure the payment of compensation under this act:

(a) By insuring and keeping insured the payment of such benefits with any organization authorized to insure workmen's compensation in this State, or

(b) By furnishing satisfactory proof to the Director of his financial and administrative ability to meet his obligations under this act

14. In States having a State Fund, appropriate provisions should be inserted at this point.

and by receiving an authorization from the Director to pay such compensation directly.

(1) The Director shall, as a condition to such authorization, require such employer to file with the [appropriate state agency] a bond of a surety company authorized to do business in this State or to deposit in a depository designated by the Director, negotiable securities, at the option of the employer, of a kind and in an amount determined by the Director, to secure the performance by the employer of all obligations imposed upon him under this act, for injuries occurring to his employees during the period of self-insurance and subject to such conditions as the Director may by regulation prescribe, provided that in no case shall the amount of bond or security required be less than [$100,000] for any one employer.

(2) Authorization of self-insurance shall be evidenced by a "Certificate of Authorization." Such authorization shall be granted for a period of not more than one year. The Director may, for good cause shown, including failure to provide adequate safety and loss prevention services, and after notice and opportunity of hearing, terminate the authorization of any self-insurer. Failure by a self-insurer to comply with any provision of this act, or of the lawful regulations issued by the Director, or with any lawful order of the Director or a hearing officer, or the failure or insolvency of the surety on his indemnity bond or impairment of financial responsibility of such self-insurer shall be considered good cause for such termination. No termination shall affect the liability of any self-insurer already incurred.

(3) The surety on a bond filed by a self-insurer pursuant to paragraph (1) of this subsection may terminate its liability thereon by giving the Director written notice stating when, not less than 30 days thereafter, such termination shall be effective. In case of such termination, the surety shall remain liable, in accordance with the terms of the bond, with respect to injuries to employees of the self-insurer prior to the termination of the surety's liability. If the bond is terminated for any reason other than the employer's terminating his status as a self-insurer, the employer shall, prior to the date of termination of the surety's liability, comply with the requirements of paragraph (1) of this subsection.

The liability of a surety on a bond filed pursuant to this section shall be released and extinguished and the bond returned to the employer or surety provided (a) such liability is secured by another bond filed or negotiable securities deposited as required by paragraph (1) of this subsection or (b) the employer files with the Director the policy of insurance specified in paragraph (4) of this subsection.

Securities deposited by an employer pursuant to paragraph (1) of this subsection shall be returned to him upon his written request provided the employer (a) files the bond required by paragraph (1) of this subsection or (b) files with the Director the policy of insurance specified in paragraph (4) of this subsection.

(4) Any employer may at any time terminate his status as a self-insurer by giving the Director written notice stating when not less than 30 days thereafter such termination shall be effective provided such termination shall not be effective until the employer shall have complied with the requirements of subsection (a) of this section.

If an employer who ceases to be a self-insurer files with the Director a policy of insurance in a form approved by the [Insurance Commissioner] and issued by an organization authorized to insure workmen's compensation in this State, and covering the entire liability of such employer for injuries to his employees which occurred during the period of self-insurance, the bond, bonds or securities securing such liability and filed or deposited by the employer pursuant to paragraph (1) of subsection (b) of this section shall forthwith be returned to him. The policy of insurance shall be non-cancellable for any cause during the continuance of the liability secured and so covered.

(5) The Director may in cases of default by the self-insurer after sending him notice by certified mail of his intention to do so, bring suit upon such bond or collect the interest and principal of any of the securities as they may become due or sell the securities or any of them as may be required to pay compensation and discharge the obligation of the self-insurer under this act and apply the proceeds to the payment of compensation under this act.

Section 47. [*Posting of Notices.*]

The Director may by regulation require that every employer subject to the provisions of this act shall post and keep posted in a conspicuous place or places in and about the place or places of business a typewritten or printed notice, in accordance with a form prescribed by the Director, stating that such employer has secured the payment of compensation in accordance with the provisions of this act. Such notice shall contain the name and address of the insurance organization, if any, with whom the employer has secured payment of compensation.

Section 48. [*Certificate of Compliance.*] (omitted)

Section 49. [*Insurance Policies.*]

(a) Every policy or contract for the insurance of compensation herein provided for shall be deemed to be made subject to the provisions of this act and provision thereof inconsistent with the act shall be deemed to be reformed to conform with the provisions of this act.

(b) An insurer insuring the liability of an employer under this act shall be deemed to be the insurer for all employees of the employer within the protection of this act. However, if specifically authorized by the Director, a separate insurance policy may be issued for a specified plant or work location if the liability of such employer under this act to all his other employees is otherwise secured.

Section 50. [*Claims Services and Medical Supervision.*] (omitted)

Section 51. [*Assigned Risk.*]

The [Insurance Commissioner], after consultation with carriers authorized to issue workmen's compensation policies in this State, shall put into effect areasonable system for the equitable apportionment among such carriers of applicants for such policies who are in good faith entitled to but are unable to procure such policies through ordinary methods. Such system shall be so drawn as to guarantee that such an applicant, if not in default on workmen's compensation premiums, shall, following his application to the assigned risk system and tender of required premium, be covered by workmen's compensation insurance. When any such system has been approved, all such carriers shall subscribe thereto and participate therein. Assignment shall be in such manner that, as far as practicable, no carrier shall be assigned a larger proportion of compensation premiums under assigned policies during any calendar year than that which the total of compensation premiums written in the State by such carrier during the preceding year bears to the total compensation premiums written in the State by all such carriers during the preceding calendar year.

Section 52. [*Performance of Insurance Organization.*] (omitted)

Section 53. [*Payment Pending Determination of Policy Coverage.*]

Whenever any claim is presented and the claimant's right to compensation is not in issue, but the issue of liability is raised as between an employer and a carrier or between two or more employers or carriers, the Director shall order payment of compensation to be made immediately by one or more of such employers or carriers. The Director may order any such employer or carrier to deposit the amount of the award or to give such security therefor as he may deem satisfactory. When the issue is finally resolved, an employer or carrier held not liable shall be reimbursed for any such payments by the employer or carrier held liable and any deposit or security so made shall be returned.

Section 54. [*Penalty for Failure to Secure Compensation.*]

(a) Any employer required to secure the payment of compensation under this act who willfully fails to secure the payment of such compensation shall be guilty of a [misdemeanor] and upon conviction thereof shall be punished by a fine of not more than [$1,000], or by imprisonment for not more than [one year], or by both such fine and imprisonment; and in any case where the employer is a corporation any officer or employee of the corporation who had authority to secure payment of compensation on behalf of the corporation and willfully failed to do so shall be individually liable to a similar fine and imprisonment; and such officer or employee shall be personally liable jointly and severally with such corporation for any compensation which may accrue under this act in respect to any injury which may occur to any employee of such corporation while it shall so fail to secure the payment of compensation as required by Section 46 of this act. [The fines shall be paid directly by the court to the Director for deposit in the Uninsured Employers' Fund provided in Section 56.]

(b) Any employer who knowingly transfers, sells, encumbers, assigns, or in any manner disposes of, conceals, secretes, or destroys any property or records belonging to such employer, after one of his employees has been injured within the purview of this act, and with intent to avoid the payment of compensation under this act to such employee or his dependents, shall be guilty of a [misdemeanor] and, upon conviction thereof, shall be punished by a fine of not more than [$1,000] or by imprisonment for not more than [one year], or by both such fine and imprisonment; and in any case where such employer is a corporation, any officer or employee thereof, if knowingly participating or acquiescing in the act, shall be also individually liable to such penalty of imprisonment as well as joint and severally liable with such corporation for such fine.

(c) An employer who has failed to secure payment of compensation for more than 20 days shall pay into the Uninsured Employers' Fund provided in Section 56 as a civil penalty for such failure an amount equal to 1 per centum of his payroll of employees covered by this act for the time during which such failure continued but for not more than three consecutive years. The assessment shall be made by the Director for the year or years immediately preceding the date on which such assessment is made against the employer. The assessment may be collected as a civil penalty in an action brought by the Director against the employer for and on behalf of the Uninsured Employers' Fund. All such assessments shall be deposited in the Uninsured Employers' Fund.

(d) This section shall not affect any other liability of the employer under this act.

Section 55. [*Special Fund.*]

(a) There is hereby established in the [State Treasury] a Special Fund for the sole purpose of making payments in accordance with the provisions of Section 20, Section 21 and this section. The Fund shall be administered by the Director. The [State Treasurer] shall be the custodian of the Fund and all moneys and securities in the Fund shall be held in trust by the [State Treasurer] and shall not be money or property of the State.

(b) The [State Treasurer] is authorized to disburse moneys from the Fund only upon written order of the Director. He shall be required to give bond in an amount to be fixed and with securities approved by the Director conditioned upon the faithful performance of his duty as custodian of the Fund. The premium of the bond shall be paid out of the Fund.

(c) Each carrier shall under regulations prescribed by the Director make payments to the Fund in an amount equal to that proportion of [175] percent of the total disbursement made from the Fund during the preceding calendar year less the amount of the net assets in the Fund as of December 31 of the preceding calendar year, which the total income benefits paid by such carrier bore to the total income benefits paid by all carriers during the fiscal year which ended within the preceding calendar year. An employer who has ceased to be a self-insurer shall continue to be liable for any assessments into the Fund on account of any income benefits paid by him during such fiscal year.

(d) Where there has been default in the payment of compensation due to the insolvency of an insured employer and his carrier or a self-insured employer, payment of any compensation remaining unpaid shall be made from the Special Fund.[16] Such employer and carrier, or self-insured employer and his surety, if any, shall be liable for payment into the Fund of the amounts paid therefrom by the Director under the authority of this subsection, and for the purposes of enforcing this liability, the Director, for the benefit of the Fund, shall be subrogated to all the rights of the person receiving such compensation.

(e) The Director shall be charged with the conservation of the assets of the Fund. In furtherance of this purpose, the Attorney General shall appoint a member of his staff to represent the Fund in all proceedings brought to enforce claims against the Fund.

Alternative (omitted)

Section 56. [*Uninsured Employers' Fund.*]

(a) There is hereby authorized in the [State Treasury] an Uninsured Employers' Fund for the purpose of making payments in accordance with the provisions of subsection (d) of this section. The Fund shall be administered by the Director. The [State Treasurer] shall be the custodian of the Fund and all moneys and securities in the Fund shall be held in trust by the [State Treasurer] and shall not be money or property of the State.

(b) The [State Treasurer] is authorized to disburse moneys from the Fund only upon written order of the Director. He shall be required to give bond in an amount to be fixed and with securities approved by the Director conditioned upon the faithful performance of his duty as custodian of the Fund. The premium of the bond shall be paid out of the Fund.

---

16. This provision would have to be modified in the many States which already have a security or guarantee fund for insurance companies. A separate security fund for self-insurers would have to be created in those States.

(c) All amounts collected as fines and penalties under this act except those collected under Section 42(a) and (b) shall be paid into the Uninsured Employers' Fund. The Fund shall become operative when the amount in the Fund reaches [$].

(d) Once the Uninsured Employers' Fund has become operative, compensation thereafter shall be paid from it when there has been default in the payment of compensation due to the failure of an employer to secure payment of compensation as provided by this act. Such employer shall be liable for payment into the Fund of the amounts authorized to be paid therefrom under the authority of this subsection and for the purposes of enforcing this liability the Director, for the benefit of the Fund, shall be subrogated to all the rights of the person receiving such compensation.

(e) The Director shall be charged with the conservation of the assets of the Fund. In furtherance of this purpose, the Attorney General shall appoint a member of his staff to represent the Fund in all proceedings brought to enforce claims against or on behalf of the Fund.

Part VI

Administration

Section 57. [*Agency to Administer the Act.*]

(a) This act shall be administered by the Director of the [state administrative agency] [18] who shall devote his entire time to the duties of his office. The Governor shall appoint the Director[, by and with the advice and consent of the Senate,] on the basis of administrative ability, education and training, and experience relevant to the duties of the Director under this act. Upon the expiration of his term the Director shall continue to serve until his successor shall have been appointed and qualified. [Before entering upon his duties the Director shall take and subscribe to an oath or affirmation to support the Constitution of the United States and of this State and to faithfully discharge the duties of his office.] Because cumulative experience and continuity in office are essential to the proper administration of a workmen's compensation and rehabilitation law, it is hereby declared to be in the public interest to continue the Director in office during good behavior and as long as efficiency is demonstrated. The Director may be removed by the Governor for cause, prior to the expiration of his term, but shall be furnished a written copy of the charges against him and shall be accorded a public hearing if he requests it. [He shall be paid a salary at the rate of [$] per year.] [19]

(b) The Director shall appoint such hearing officers and other employees, other than employees and assistants of the Workmen's Compensation Appeals Board, and may establish such branch offices, divi-

18. Provision is made for identifying the administration agency in Section 2. [*Definitions.*].

19. In States having a general pay act, the Director's salary should be fixed therein.

sions, sections and advisory committees as he deems necessary to administer the Workmen's Compensation and Rehabilitation Law, and such other offices and committees as are provided for by this act. All employees engaged in the administration of the act shall devote their entire time to their duties. [They shall take and subscribe to an oath or affirmation to support the Constitution of the United States and of this State, and to discharge faithfully the duties of office or employment.] All hearing officers and other employees shall be employed under the [state merit and classification system.]

(c) Hearing officers appointed after the effective date of this act must be lawyers licensed to practice in this State. They shall devote full time to their duties and shall not engage in the private practice of law.

Section 58.   [*Appeals Board.*] [20]

(a) There is hereby created a Workmen's Compensation Appeals Board composed of three [21] members appointed by the Governor [by and with the advice and consent of the Senate] for terms of nine years each, except that the terms of members first appointed shall be for three, six, and nine years respectively as designated by the Governor at the time of appointments. A member of the Board must be a lawyer licensed to practice in this State. The Governor shall designate the chairman of the Board. Each member shall hold office until his successor is appointed and qualified. Because cumulative experience and continuity in office are essential to the proper handling of appeals under a workmen's compensation and rehabilitation law, it is hereby declared to be in the public interest to continue Board members in office as long as efficiency is demonstrated. The members shall devote full time to their duties as members of the Board and shall not engage in the private practice of law. The Governor may at any time remove any member for cause after furnishing him with a written copy of the charges against him and giving him a public hearing if he requests it. Each member of the Board shall be paid a salary at the rate of not less than the minimum salary of [a judge of a state court of general jurisdiction].

(b) The Board shall have power to decide appeals from compensation orders of the Director or his hearing officers and it shall have authority to consider and decide all matters of fact and questions of law properly cognizable under this act.

(c) A decision concurred in by any two members shall constitute a decision of the Board.

(d) A vacancy in the Board, if there remain two members of it, shall not impair the authority of two members to act.

---

20. This full-time Board is recommended for States where the volume of cases is sufficient to justify it. In States where the workload would not warrant a full-time Board, it may be possible for members of the Board to be utilized by the State in similar capacities.

21. In larger States the Board should have five or more members with rotating terms, and other relevant subsections should be adjusted accordingly, including the use of panels where desired.

(e) The chairman of the Board shall employ such employees as may be required to carry out the Board's duties under this act, shall assign the work of the Board to the members thereof and its employees, and shall serve as administrative officer of the Board.

(f) The Board shall be within the [state administrative agency] for budgetary and administrative purposes only.

Section 59.   [*Authority to Adopt Rules and Regulations.*]

The Director and the Board each shall have authority to adopt reasonable rules and regulations within their respective areas of responsibility, after notice and public hearing, if requested, for effecting the purposes of this act.   All rules and regulations, upon adoption, shall be published and be made available to the public, and, if not inconsistent with law, shall be binding in the administration of this act.

Section 60.   [*Location of Office.*]   (omitted)

Section 61.   [*Seal.*]   (omitted)

Section 62.   [*Operating Expenses.*]   (omitted)

Section 63.   [*Administration Fund.*]   (omitted)

Section 64.   [*Reports.*]

(a) Each year the Director shall make a report to the Governor and through him to the [State Legislature] on the operation of this act, including suggestions and recommendations as to improvements in the law and administration thereof, a detailed statement of receipts and expenditures, and a statistical analysis of industrial injury experience and compensation costs.

(b) The Director shall prepare and publish such other statistical and informational reports and analyses based upon the reports and records available which, in his opinion, will be useful in increasing public understanding of the purposes, effectiveness, costs, coverage, and administrative procedures of workmen's compensation and rehabilitation in the State; and in providing basic information regarding the occurrence and sources of work injuries for the use of public and private agencies engaged in industrial injury prevention activities.

Section 65.   [*Cooperation With Other Agencies.*]   (omitted)

Section 66.   [*Severability.*]   (omitted)

Section 67.   [*Laws Repealed.*]   (omitted)

Section 68.   [*Effective Date.*]

[Insert effective date.]

Index

References are to Pages